# FAMILY THERAPIES

A Comprehensive Christian Appraisal

**SECOND EDITION**

Mark A. Yarhouse
and James N. Sells
Lily Amer

ISBN: 9798393622206 Paperback

# CONTENTS

**INTEGRATION OF FAMILY THEORY WITH CRITICAL ISSUES IN PSYCHOTHERAPY**

**CASTING A VISION**

# LIST OF FIGURES AND TABLES

**Figures**

**Tables**

# PREFACE

THIS IS THE SECOND EDITION of *Family Therapies: A Comprehensive Christian Appraisal.* We never imagined that marriage and family, both in regard to research content and social context, would expand and change as much as it has in the past eight years. While the first edition of this book has made a significant contribution in the education of family clinicians—particularly within the Christian faith community—this edition provides us opportunity for an update, a chance to think again of our understanding of marriages and families and how the mental health professions and the church become trained to conduct intervention. It also provides us opportunity to address how the church and the community of Christian counselors might respond to the rapid shifts in social attitudes and behaviors pertaining to marriage and family structures and perspectives.

We have taken what was and remains needed for the training of family counselors, psychologists, and other mental health professionals and added more of the twenty-first century to the text. While updating every chapter with relevant research findings, we have added two chapters—one addressing cohabitation and the other focusing on LGBT+ marriage and family formation. The tone and tenor in which Christian mental health professionals address the complexity of family relationships have a significant impact on how faith is understood within the culture, and how individuals, couples, and families seeking to understand their experience and create narratives to direct their lives can do so with integrity is the clinician's challenge.

We know so many people in our field who have expressed that there was a need for a resource for Christians engaged in family therapy/counseling/ ministry. Despite the many books on theories of family therapy, how to conduct family therapy, and so on, we could not find one that engaged the various models of family therapy from a Christian worldview. We came together to discuss this and both felt a desire to take on what is really a monumental task. We wrote this book in part to sort out how we think about family therapy as Christians and to provide a framework for Christians entering the field who might want some ideas for critical engagement and practical applications. Rather than creating a radically new model of family therapy, we draw attention to what theorists have gotten right and how their insights can be understood and acknowledged while relying more on a Christian view of the person and the family.

To do this, we took several steps. The first was to explore what we know about families from Scripture. Although we might think that families in the Bible would be exemplary in their functioning, we quickly learned that they are often a mess. What we found were not examples of ideal relationships but of ways in which God in his sovereignty uses all kinds of people and families to fulfill his purposes. We also learned that the Bible is not a family therapy sourcebook. Rather, we can find in Scripture broad principles that contribute to our understanding of family relationships. Our next step was to reflect on ways in which the church has historically approached family ministry and how this relates to the emergence of the profession of family therapy. An additional step involved reflecting on the most influential first-generation models of family therapy and engaging these models as Christians. We then wanted to look at the practical outworking of that engagement in key areas that affect families today.

The book is intended for a broad audience. We would like to see it help students and clinicians in the mental health fields (e.g., psychology, counseling, social work, marriage and family therapy), pastoral care staff and local pastors, and youth ministry leaders who work with families.

## OVERVIEW OF THE BOOK

The book is divided into four parts. In part one (chaps. 1–2) we set the stage for discussing the first-generation models of family therapy. Chapter one explores a distinctively Christian perspective on the family. Chapter two is a discussion of the field of family therapy, how it developed, and some key terms that will help the reader better understand the field.

Part two of the book (chaps. 3–12) devotes one chapter apiece to the major models of family therapy developed in what is sometimes referred to as the first generation of family therapists (e.g., structural family therapy). If each approach to family therapy is a "map" for getting families from a place of some kind of dysfunction to a place of better functioning, then each chapter in this section contains an explanation of the map, followed by a discussion of the theoretical and philosophical assumptions and practical implications. We then focus on Christian critique and engagement of the theoretical and philosophical underpinnings and the practical issues involved in using specific techniques associated with that theory. We also provide brief reflections that tie back to the three foundational themes introduced in chapter one: family identity, family functioning, and family relationships. In the closing chapter of this section of the book (chap. 12) we introduce a framework for integrative Christian family therapy.

Part three (chaps. 13–20) extends the discussion by taking topics that are commonly addressed in family therapy and inviting Christians to interact with the relevant materials. We introduce the reader to the issues (e.g., crisis and trauma, marital conflicts) and then review the literature in that area, followed by Christian engagement in light of what we see as particularly valuable from the first-generation models of family therapy and in light of what we propose for an integrative Christian family therapy. In the second edition we added a chapter on cohabitation and significantly revised the chapter on LGBT+ couples and families. We see cohabitation as an increasingly popular entryway into marriage and as a relationship status in and of itself. We want to help the reader grapple with that reality. An additional reality is the success of the marriage equality movement and the likelihood that Christian clinicians will work with LGBT+ couples and families in the years to come. We also want the reader to be familiar with those cultural shifts and to think deeply and well about some of the concerns that arise.

Part four (chap. 21) reflects our desire to cast a vision for integrative Christian family therapy/counseling/ministry. In particular, we see the need for local family therapy to be influenced by a shrinking, global world in which therapists will need to expand their understanding of family structure and relationships. Societal and cultural changes will have an impact on our work and the ways in which we think about and engage the families in ministry and service.

## ACKNOWLEDGMENTS

We feel very fortunate to have worked together on this project and to have seen our friendship develop and strengthen over the past year. We have been blessed by stimulating conversations with a number of people—probably far too many to acknowledge. Mark would like to thank those who taught him about models of family therapy, especially Fran White, Professor Emeritus at Wheaton College. He would also like to thank Patrice Penny and Victor Argo, his supervisors and colleagues in family therapy at the Outreach Community Center in Carol Stream, Illinois. It was through Patrice and Victor that Mark was able to see some of the theories in practice and begin to gain a sense of competence in the applied or practical dimensions of family therapy. He would also like to thank the students in the School of Psychology and Counseling at Regent University who took courses from him in family therapy as well as advanced marriage and family therapy over the past many years—especially those students who took these courses in the last couple of years, as they were asked to read, engage, and critique chapters in their various stages. Mark's former research assistant, Dr. Stephanie Nowacki, and his graduate assistant, Dr. Katie Maslowe, located numerous articles and books for review and provided critiques of various chapters, as did Justin Sides, a more recent graduate assistant, and former students on his research team, including Dr. Christine Gow, Dr. Trista Carr, Dr. Ward Davis, Dr. Veronica Johnson, Dr. Jill Kays, and Dr. Brooke Merino, who also provided him with valuable feedback.

Jim would like to thank those who have been most influential in forming his thinking on family, relationships, psychology, and Christian ministry. Terry and Sharon Hargrave actively contributed to the turning of his career path toward marriage and family therapy by demonstrating the power of reconciled relationship. Ken and Lee Phillips, Jim and Peggy Cassens, and colleagues at Alliance Clinical Associates provided the environment where sound family therapy and mature Christian faith could be wed. Fran Giordano and Laura Bokar provided seminal ideas for working with couples and for recognizing that which isn't readily seen. John Beckenbach and Shawn Patrick helped fill many whiteboards with ideas, statistics, and creativity. Their contributions reside in each chapter. Jim's graduate assistants Susan George, Leana Talbot, and Emily Hervey have been particularly helpful in researching, providing feedback, and editing ideas. The Regent Counselor Education faculty—

Mark Newmeyer, Jacquee Smith, and Lee Underwood—have created an environment where all ideas are worthy of consideration. In addition, colleagues in psychology—Rod Goodyear, Glen Moriarty, Jen Ripley, and Bill Hathaway—provided encouragement, ideas, criticism, and support. Current and former students also have contributed significantly, especially Dr. Justin Brogan, Dr. Joe Cook, Dr. John Kennedy, Dr. David Mikkelson, and Dr. Suzanne Mikkelson. Dr. Christine Pui-ting Lau and Dr. Rachel Heffield helped me think about marriage and family in contexts far from my own.

We would both like to acknowledge our formal reviewers who provided us with constructive feedback that helped us in the fine-tuning. We would also like to acknowledge Emily Hervey, Jill Kays, Ann Marie Hohman, Susan George, Shane Ferrell, and Katie Maslowe for their assistance in the creation of the indexes and visuals.

We dedicate this book to our families.

*Mark A. Yarhouse*
*James N. Sells*

# FOUNDATIONAL
# CONSIDERATIONS

# A CHRISTIAN
# UNDERSTANDING
# FOR FAMILY THERAPY

*Happy families are all alike;*
*every unhappy family is unhappy in their own way.*

**LEO TOLSTOY,** *ANNA KARENINA*

LEO TOLSTOY'S FAMOUS QUOTE indeed reflects the debauchery within marriage and family occurring within his culture. Pain, injury, tragedy, injustice, and sin left a unique scar on families in that era, as they do today. As with most who seek family therapy, Tolstoy experienced the despair of life within family and anguish within his marriage. Both of his parents died before he was ten. He witnessed the birth of thirteen children and the death of five. He experienced and expressed through his writings the joy of marital intimacy with his wife, Sonia, and the depths of despair in marital conflict and separation. It is in his great work *Anna Karenina* that he gives his treatise on marriage and family. It was written in 1875, a time when European aristocracy was seeing marriage as passé and even silly. The culture of his day had rejected the idea of sexual fidelity and the role of parents in nurturing children to adulthood. An existential malaise dominated the Russian nobility, and the idea of marriage was seen by many as idealistic, naive, and digressive. Yet he presented a view of human life that is made meaningful through the experience of marriage and family relationships. To Tolstoy, the DNA of civil society was a successful marriage that could provide illumination on life so as to prevent tragedy from creating despair, and bliss from creating naiveté.

Tolstoy lived and wrote during a time when a new idea was pervading Europe—that marital intimacy was based on "love" (where "love" meant a romantically idealized experience in which individuality is made whole by the attachment to the other). This concept had a profound effect on Western society, and it remains the dominating paradigm of marriage today. Aspects of this idea have a clear and definite Christian element. However, many components of love-based marriage refer to a different form of love. The romantic love of the nineteenth century was a sentimental love, and many hold that this idea of an emotionally-centered relationship is a primary reason for relatively high divorce rates in the twentieth and twenty-first centuries. With a touch of humor, Stephanie Coontz writes that in the nineteenth century the United States led the world in romantic marriage as well as divorce, when idealized romance was lost: "Between 1880 and 1890 it experienced a 70 percent increase in divorce. In 1891 a Cornell University professor made the preposterous prediction that if trends in the second half of the 19th century continued, by 1980 more marriages would end by divorce than by death. As it turned out, he was off by only 10 years!" (Coontz, 2005, p. 181).

We, like Tolstoy, have a high view of marriage and family, but not the romantic view that has been carried into the twenty-first century. Indeed, we carry a perspective that the Christian faith has a unique significance in understanding the potential of relational life. Furthermore, we believe that the effectiveness of the counselor, psychologist, therapist, and pastor who seeks to bring aid to families or couples in crisis is better equipped when he or she can utilize the central themes of the Christian tradition with the best practices drawn from mental health theory, research, and technique. In this first chapter we seek to articulate how the great themes of biblical Christianity—creation, fall, redemption, and glorification—interact with the essential challenges of marital and family existence: *family function*, *family identity*, and *family relationship*.

## FAMILY AS FIGURE AND GROUND: A METAPHOR TO UNDERSTAND FAMILY IN TWENTY-FIRST-CENTURY CULTURE

Marriage today is a topic that can raise sharp disagreements. An explanation as to how and why such divergent views exist can be understood through one of the great discoveries from psychological science: figure-ground perception. Most people recognize this concept by two popular images—one is an image of either a white vase or two facial cameos; the other is either an 1890s Victorian woman or a withered, wrinkled older woman. When you see one, you don't see the other. Much can be said about the similarity between figure-ground and the state of the family in the twenty-first century. We tend to see family in a way that does not permit us to see it any other way. Consider the following issues (listed alphabetically):

| | |
|---|---|
| Abortion rights | Infidelity |
| Cohabiting relationships | Pornography |
| Corporal punishment | Poverty |
| Divorce | Single-parent family structures |
| Family violence | Traditional family roles |
| Gay marriage | Transgender recognition |

When considering the issues on this list, are you seeing social change, advancement toward justice, and positive resolution emerging? Or are you seeing decline, disarray, and social degradation? How you see the social/political issues related to family will influence your perception about the unfolding of events. If we see the family in a state of decline, we will not likely perceive good emerging from any change. If we see the recent changes as good, we are likely vulnerable to a lack of discernment to some of the factors that affect spouses, parents, and children. Consider the basic supposition of notable authors.

Köstenberger states as his opening argument in his book *God, Marriage and Family* that "marriage and the family are institutions under siege in our world today, and that with marriage and family, our very civilization is in crisis. The current cultural crisis, however, is merely symptomatic of a deepseated *spiritual* crisis that continues to gnaw at the foundations of our once-shared societal values" (2010, p. 15). To Köstenberger, marriage and family are under siege and civilization is in crisis—powerful words that we don't seek to dispute. Rather, we seek to utilize a systemic mentality addressed throughout this book, which is, "If I see it this way, how will I not see it in other ways, even when those other ways might be accurate?"

Girgis, Anderson, and George wrote in the opening chapter of *What Is Marriage? Man and Woman: A Defense*, "In just a few years, the battle over marriage has engaged every branch and level of American government and the whole of our civil society . . . . It is hard to think of a more salient cultural conflict" (2012, pp. 4-5). Again, this is portrayed as a "cultural conflict" depicting warring parties in which the most powerful wins.

Sociologist Andrew Cherlin wrote in *The Marriage-Go-Round*,

> In the space of a half century, then, we have seen the widest pendulum swing in family life in American history. We have gone from a lockstep pattern of getting married young, then having children and for the most part staying married, to a bewildering set of alternatives which includes bearing children as a lone parent and perhaps marrying at some later point; living with someone and having children together without marrying; or following the conventional marriage-then-children script, perhaps later divorcing, then probably living with a new partner maybe remarrying. . . . Consequently we choose and choose again, starting and ending cohabiting relationships and marriage. (2009, p. 8)

Cherlin emphasizes a "bewildering set of alternatives," with Western civilization itself as literally dazed, befuddled, or confused. The wording is powerful.

Balswick and Balswick carry a different tone in assessing the landscape of family. They wrote in *A Model for Marriage*: "Though many family social scientists are concerned about these modern trends, some hold to a postmodern optimism that embraces alternative forms of marriage." According to them, the outdated, traditional, lifelong monogamous marriage needs to be revised. They advocate for alternative forms to better accommodate the diverse needs of a postmodern society, such as "same-sex marriage, cohabitation, remaining childless, serial marriage" (2006, p. 18). The nature of the cultural war emerges more clearly here; it becomes the battle between the "outdated" and the "updated."

Stephanie Coontz wrote in *Marriage, a History*:

> Many of the things people think are unprecedented in family life today are not actually new. Almost every marital and sexual arrangement we have seen in recent years, however startling it may appear, has been tried somewhere before. There have been societies and times when non-marital sex and out-of-wedlock births were more common and widely accepted than they are today. Step families were much more numerous in the past, the result of high death rates and frequent marriages. Even divorce rates have been higher in

some regions and periods than they are in Europe and North America today. And same-sex marriage, though rare, has been sanctioned in some cultures under certain conditions. (2005, p. 2)

This gives us reason to pause, to study—to think and then to act.

Finally, as Waite and Gallagher wrote in *The Case for Marriage*, the most basic becomes the most controversial:

In America over the last thirty years we've done something unprecedented. We have managed to transform marriage, the most basic and universal of human institutions, into something controversial. For perhaps the first time in human history, marriage as an ideal is under a sustained and surprisingly successful attack. Sometimes the attack is direct and ideological, made by "experts" who believe a lifelong vow of fidelity is unrealistic or oppressive, especially to women. (2000, p. 1)

Indeed, in regard to marriage, some see an impoverished old woman, some see an elegant youth in the prime of life. Figure-ground makes it impossible to see both at the same time. When addressing a contentious theme such as family, it is easy to see only what we want or only what is familiar and disregard everything else.

For us in writing this book, and for you in reading, great care must be exercised so that we don't end up confirming our bias in regards to marriage. How we see politics, theology, real experience, and desired experience emerge in how we think about marriage and family—both our own and those with whom we will sit, listen, understand, and provide care. The rules that govern what you will see and how you will act with families are influenced by starting points. In the statements above, Köstenberger begins as a theologian, but Coontz is a family studies historian, Waite is a sociologist, and the Balswicks are marriage and family professors. Some used a theological lens that explicitly influenced their thinking, some used worldviews that were less articulated. Each examined the content from a preconception and had postdestinations in mind. We all do.

Your freedom and restraint to advocate positions to the public classroom, the Christian college, the private counseling and consulting room, and the culture at large must be conducted with care. You may bear a license—extended to you by the state or country—with the expectation that you will exercise restraint in regard to your beliefs pertaining to a client's moral choices;

you also bear a conscience that renders you as a moral agent subject to God. This requires you to make decisions about how to act. Jesus acknowledged the moral tension that those in his day faced and that those in ours must still address: "Then Jesus said to them, 'Give back to Caesar what is Caesar's and to God what is God's.' And they were amazed at him" (Mk 12:17 NIV).

The natural inclination is to read ideas from authors and interact with others who already think as you think and believe as you believe. People who see the figure prefer to hang out together; people who see the ground sit at the other table. So we "retweet" those whose ideas on abortion, race relations, LGBTQ rights, or support for single-parent families in poverty we resonate with, and we delete ideas that are challenging or threatening. Our views of family are reinforced by others who see the same thing we see. And so learning becomes limited to reinforcement of what we already believe. A family therapist must be skilled to enter a relational community to bring peace, justice, hope, mercy, forgiveness, insight, acceptance, and countless additional virtues amid both people who see the figure and people who see the ground. This is not just a therapeutic skill. It is also a life skill, maybe even a calling.

## DEFINING THE RANGE AND REACH
## OF THE FAMILY RELATIONSHIP

There is much discussion today about the family—about what makes up a family, who counts as family, public policies to support the family, family values, and so on. It is humbling to think of writing about a Christian understanding of the family because there is so much discussion and debate associated with the topic. Any strong claims seem to leave some people today feeling like they do not belong or have any place, and yet not saying anything of substance about something as important as the family seems to be no viable alternative to us either.

We would like to begin by discussing a biblical view of the family. By this we mean to ask what we can know about the family based on a reading of Scripture. We must start with the essence of family that transcends culture, circumstances, and time. The examination of the family cannot be limited to North America, the twenty-first century, or upper-middle socioeconomic class. The initial examination and understanding of family must begin with a "transcendent family," the basic biological and sociological relationship that endures over time and across cultures.

When we look to the Old Testament for an initial understanding of the family, we find that the word used in Hebrew is *mishpachah*, a word that "blurs the distinctions between family and tribe and between family and nation" (Moynagh, 1995, p. 372). It includes what contemporary Western culture thinks of as family, at least with respect to a nuclear family or family of origin, but also includes "servants, resident aliens *(gerim)* and stateless persons, widows and orphans, who [lived] under the protection of the head of the family" (Kingdon, 1988, p. 251).

In the New Testament the words for family include *patria*, a word suggesting a "group similar to subtribe in the Old Testament," and *oikos*, or household (Williams, 1996, p. 245; see 1 Cor 16:19; 2 Tim 1:16). According to Williams, men in the New Testament were generally presumed by Paul to be the head of the household, although there are notable exceptions, such as Lydia and Nympha. Further, in the New Testament understanding, the kingdom of God corresponds to a family with God as Father (Gal 1:3-4), followers of Christ as children of God (1 Jn 3:1-2), and the idea that Gentiles are adopted into God's family (Rom 8:15) (Williams, 1996).

Family in the biblical narrative is a central organizing theme. The story line of the Old Testament develops around two types of family lineage. The first is through the lineage of Abraham in which Abraham and Sarah's heirs are the key actors in the depiction of God's sovereignty, God's judgment, mercy, and ultimately, faithfulness to the family with whom he made a covenant or promise.

The second family lineage is that of David and the subsequent kings of Israel and Judah. This "family story" describes the history of Israel and Judah through the lives of their leaders. The significance of this history is its culmination of God's promise to David that the Messiah would come through his descendants (2 Sam 7:10-13; 1 Chron 17:11-14; 2 Chron 6:16).

The story line of the New Testament does not follow a family lineage in the same manner as the Old Testament. First, marriage and family are frequent metaphors to describe God's relationship with his people, Jewish and Gentile. Second, family is also the organizing metaphor to define the nature of relationships between members of the church community in which the followers of Jesus are described as members of one family. Finally, family is written in through the experience of Jewish, Roman, and Greek influences. The authors and audience who first received the gospels and the letters were aware of the assumptions held about men, women, children, sexuality, roles, power, authority, change, social mobility, race, and commerce. While they understood the context, they were exposed to radical change in their perception of family. The Christian story served to rewrite the cultural understanding of family in ways that were threatening to the status quo.

As these references in the Old and New Testaments suggest, it is best to draw conclusions about a biblical view of the family by locating the family in the broader narrative of Scripture. It seems to us that the overwhelming evidence in the Holy Scriptures is that the importance of family is found in their function, not in their structure. That is to say, the emphasis is on how families are engaged to complete God's redemptive theme with his people rather than on what families are supposed to look like. Christians have historically recognized that there is a redemptive theme throughout Scripture, and we believe that it is this theme of redemption that must inform our discussion of the family. We also believe that such a redemptive focus provides us with a balanced view—one that neither overvalues nor undervalues the family. This balance is achieved when we locate the topic of redemption by thinking of the family with reference to the four "acts" of the biblical "drama": creation, fall, redemption, and glorification.

## CREATION

It is in the creation narrative in Genesis that we first read about humanity: "Then God said, 'Let us make humankind in our image, according to our likeness'" (Gen 1:26). The story of creation also tells us that human beings "have no independent existence" (Erickson, 2001, p. 168). We "came into being because God willed that [we] should exist, and acted to bring [us] into being" (p. 168). To be human is to be completely and utterly dependent on God, whether or not we recognize it.

Also implicit in the notion of being made by God is an understanding that not only are we created by and dependent on God but that *we are thus distinct from God*. As Jones and Butman put it, "if we were made by God out of nothing, then *we are different from and separate from God*, though we are continually dependent on him as the ultimate ground of our very being" (2011, p. 64). The two notions of being distinct from and dependent on God are important considerations:

> For Christians, separateness from God and others is real and good. We belong in relationship to God and others, but this relatedness is not meant to consume and destroy our separateness. Union with God is a theme of

Scripture, but nowhere are we taught that we cease being ourselves in the process of this union. (Jones & Butman, 2011, pp. 64-65)

The separateness we experience in our relationship with God is seen in even the most intimate of human relationships. In marriage, two persons become one but neither loses his or her personal identity. We will also see this in other family members as well: family members will participate in the life of the family and form a family identity, but each person will remain distinct and valuable in the eyes of God.

Not only is our existence distinct from and dependent on God, but our *purpose* and *value* are derived from him as well. We will want to explore the idea of purpose and value a little later, but we want to suggest that purpose is first found within the context of our family of origin.

Further, God's creational intent for human relations was to place human beings in a family by bringing man and woman together in monogamous union (Gen 2:21-24). As Kingdon (1988) puts it, "it is evident that the family unit is a basic part of the structure of creation. From the beginning it is God's purpose that mankind should increase by families, not as isolated individuals" (p. 251).

It should be noted that human beings also bear the image of God (*imago Dei*) and that while there are a number of proposed meanings for how human beings image God, one proposed understanding—a model espoused by Karl Barth and Emil Brunner—deals specifically with our capacity for relationships. It is actually that we are made male and female, and this gender difference, the diversification itself, was seen by Barth as a way in which we bear the image of God (Jones & Butman, 2011). That we are gendered selves also suggests we relate to one another as gendered beings, and in the context of heterosexual marriage, human beings become one with one another as gendered selves:

Yet the web of relatedness intended by God reaches . . . also out to our fellow believers in marriage by our capacity to become one with another who is separate and different from us. In this union we image God in having the capacity for procreation, a reflection of God's much more profound capacity for creativity and generativity. (p. 76)

It is commonly noted that two major themes emerge from the creation story: responsible dominion and loving relatedness (Jones & Butman, 2011, p. 75). Responsible dominion refers to our vocations and callings, and it is primarily through our relationships and work settings that we show ourselves to be stewards of what God has given us.

Loving relatedness refers to ways in which we image God in our capacity for meaningful relationships, as suggested above. The most intimate relationship is that of marriage, but other meaningful relationships have a great capacity for closeness and intimacy and also reflect this love and sharing in a relational context. In fact, the "relational view" of the image of God is not just that human beings have this capacity for relationships but that the image of God is the relationship itself: "We are said to be in the image or to display the image when we stand in a particular relationship. In fact, that relationship *is* the image" (Erickson, 2001, p. 173).

We have begun to suggest ways to think about the family in light of creation. And we want to extend this discussion by raising questions for our consideration. For example, What was God's creational intent in placing human beings in families? Certainly there is the obvious purpose of procreation—that families are the relationships through which human beings bear children and raise them as members of a culture or society. So families are a good of creation and are the means by which the human family is extended through generations.

Families are also the first relationships by which we image God. If we recognize the relational view of the image of God, then the relationships formed in our families of origin are based on our capacity for loving relatedness and image God as an aspect of the very relationships formed therein.

Jack and Judith Balswick (2007) discuss this idea of imaging God through our family relationships by referring to this as a trinitarian perspective on the family. They draw on the Christian concept of the Trinity—the relationship between Father, Son, and Holy Spirit—to argue for certain qualities and characteristics in family life. For example, they suggest that a husband and wife join and become one in marriage but also retain their individuality, in a way that is comparable to "God being one, yet composed of three distinct persons" (p. 18).

Anderson and Guernsey (1985) develop the theme of covenant to explain family relationships as both social and derived from divine love by God for his people. We will return to this in our discussion of redemption.

We also know that families have been affected by the fall. While families reflect God's creational intent, they also reflect the reality of our fallen condition. We turn now to a discussion of the fall and the implications for family relationships.

## THE FALL

We have seen the importance of loving relatedness and responsible dominion as understood from creation. But the created good is also tarnished by the fall. Christians recognize that sin entered into humanity through the fall. Human beings are now confronted with sin and guilt and depravity (Erickson, 2001).

Sin is evident in many ways. It is both a condition and the behaviors that express that condition. As a state or condition, it affects all of creation. There are no aspects of the created order that go untouched by the fall. Indeed, even the natural world labors under the weight of this fallen state (Rom 8:22). We will return to this momentarily, but sin certainly affects the family and the relationships therein.

At the level of the individual, we see evidence of sin in our own divided will. Paul talks about his own struggle with the part of him that wants to obey God and the part of him that is drawn toward disobedience. This disobedience, this "missing the mark," is a split will that is expressed in what we do and what we fail to do. Our sinfulness can be expressed through our actions and through the failure to act.

When we think about the effects of the fall on the family, we want to first recognize the unique place of the family in God's providence. As Kingdon (1988) suggests, the family is not only a part of God's creational intent but is the means by which God communicates his covenant (p. 251). Recall that the covenant God makes with Abraham is to bless all people through his lineage. The family becomes a "theological as well as a biological and social structure" (p. 251).

Not only is the family the intended social relationship for humanity and the means by which the covenant promises are fulfilled, but it is also a place of both great provision and great risk to the vulnerable. It is important to consider ways in which the family and our understanding of the family are affected by the fall. Distortions make it probable now to not only isolate and blame others but to make the family into an idol.

We can see the effects of sin on the family in many ways. There are the effects of others' sin on us. We see this within our own families. The incompleteness and sinfulness of others has an impact on us in our family relationships. Some people are raised in homes that have been damaging to them, in some cases through emotional, physical, or sexual abuse. Although such abuses are not common, there is a sense in which what makes families so powerful in shaping experiences for good is that they are also capable of contributing to such significant pain.

There are also the effects of our own sin in our family relationships. We contribute to the ways in which our family relationships are not all that they could be. We can become focused on our own interests in ways that further distort or take advantage of relationships.

It was mentioned above that sin affects the very structures of creation, including the family. We can ask whether a family is functioning properly because we recognize that a family as a structure and as part of God's initial creational intent can sometimes be kept from functioning as it was intended.

## REDEMPTION

Thankfully, the biblical drama does not end with the fall. God does not abandon us to our fallen condition. Rather, God set in motion a plan for the redemption of a chosen people. A Christian understanding of redemption extends beyond people, however, touching all of creation itself; all of the created order will be redeemed.

The plan of redemption can be traced to the period immediately after the fall, but it comes to a culmination with the birth, life, death, and resurrection of Jesus. It is in this sense that the victory over sin is complete, and we begin to see more clearly the effects of that victory in the lives of those who trust in Jesus for their salvation. At the same time, the victory is not yet complete. We live in the "in-between times" as one theologian put it. We are in the "now" and the "not yet" of a life that is redeemed and set apart for God's purposes.

How do we see the work of redemption in the family? Let us begin by acknowledging with Anderson and Guernsey (1985) that while the family is a social unit, it "finds its quintessential form in the particular quality of divine love that was expressed through redemptive history" (p. 36). It is both the first form of community and is held together by the very covenant agreement that lays the foundation for redemptive history.

At a more applied level, we see in Scripture some moments of reflection on the family that can be important for our consideration. Again, we want to be cautious here. Scripture does not outline the steps we need to take to ensure a better family life. It is not a manual for enhancing family life in contemporary society. However, in places we catch a glimpse of what families can be in the lives of believers.

We know that God's providence refers to his governing activity and fulfillment of his plan for various aspects of creation. God's providence extends throughout the universe and has been affirmed by Christians in relation to nature, animal creation, human history, the rise and fall of nations, and the events in the lives of individual persons (Erickson, 2001).

In some ways the family can be seen as a providential structure of creation. God's continuing work of providence is probably most readily experienced by most people through the family. The family, while incomplete and fallen, is still a structure that is part of God's provision to care for and provide a place for persons to grow into greater maturity and (ideally) to learn about the person and work of Jesus Christ.

The various models of family therapy discussed in part two of this book are theories for how to best understand family functioning by identifying what is dysfunctional in a family that is seeking counseling services. These models then offer a map to guide the family toward better functioning and cast a vision for how to improve relationships. We can recognize this as redemptive work, but we want to think carefully about what each theory is saying about family functioning, dysfunction, and ways to bring about change.

## GLORIFICATION

The story of creation, the fall, and redemption will come to a crescendo with Jesus' return. Christians refer to this as glorification, the fourth act of the biblical drama. As Erickson (2001) indicated, glorification can be considered for the individual, for the Christian community, and for all of creation.

It is interesting to consider the implications of glorification for the family. Perhaps an understanding of glorification will help to confirm why the church is "first family" and should not be idolized on this side of heaven.

Jesus was once asked about marriage in heaven. The purpose of the question was to trick Jesus by having him comment on a theological topic that had been a point of division among religious leaders of that day. But for our purposes what is particularly interesting is Jesus' claim that there would not be giving and taking of husbands and wives in heaven. Does this mean that there is no marriage in heaven? No. Rather, marriage will not exist between two human beings as we understand marriage today—marriage will be between the church, the bride of Christ, and Jesus, the bridegroom.

It is in this sense that we all will be married to Jesus in heaven. Such an understanding might inform how we approach our understanding of marriage today—that is, while family is important for a number of reasons, including procreative purposes, it is not our first identity. Our primary identity is that we are part of a body that is itself wed to Christ. Single or married, we are all part of the bride, and we are to find our primary identity in that standing.

## A REDEMPTIVE FOCUS

If we were to summarize the many characteristics of the Christian view of the family, we might want to examine and apply to families the Hebrew concept of *shalom*. To facilitate our understanding of the concept of shalom, we draw on the Christian philosopher Nicholas Wolterstorff, who, in his book *Until Justice and Peace Embrace* (1983), developed his understanding of shalom as a kind of undercurrent throughout his book.

Shalom as a kingdom principle has to do with living in proper relationship with God, with oneself, with others, and with nature or one's physical surroundings. For the family, we begin by living in right relationship with God, which means we take delight in him and come to have a heart for the things God has a heart for. According to Wolterstorff, shalom involves "right harmonious relationship to God and delight in his service" (1983, p. 70). Wolterstorff shares this image with the reader: the prophets in Scripture speak of a time when humanity "will no longer flee God down the corridors of time . . . when they will no longer turn in those corridors to defy their divine pursuer . . . when humanity acknowledges that in its service of God is true delight" (p. 70). What a helpful image—that humanity is running down this corridor and fleeing God. If we do anything, it is to turn to defy God. We do this in our families, too. In other words, families are not exempt from the effects of the fall. And we can live in our families in ways that essentially defy who God is and what his purposes are in our lives. The prophets, then, are speaking of a time when this will no longer happen. And God, in his mercy, lets us begin to delight in service to him today. So we want to begin thinking about families in terms of how we may be of service to God, how we might delight in such service in our families.

In addition to delight in relationships with God and with ourselves, shalom includes "right harmonious relationships to other *human beings* and delight in human community" (p. 70). According to Wolterstorff, shalom is not achieved when we act like "a collection of individuals all out to make [our] own way in the world" (p. 70). This speaks to the call on us to address injustices and oppression, to live in right relationship to others, and, beyond this, to enjoy and delight in one another (p. 70). So as you position yourself in the world, in your professional role, and in the way you continue to establish supports and meaningful relationships with others, ask yourself this: How will what I do and the way I do it reflect delight in relationships with others in my family?

In terms of nature or delight in our physical surroundings, we are talking about what happens when we "shape the world with our labor and find fulfillment in so doing and delight in its results" (Wolterstorff, 1983, p. 70). We see the family as a place for labor and investment of self and time and relationships, and we would want family members to be able to delight in their family life together, in the home they share. We would want the relationships formed in the home to reflect a kind of fulfillment that family members each experience as they come to a deeper and more meaningful understanding of God's call on their lives. So family members might ask themselves, How will what I do and the way I do it in my family lead to fulfillment and reflect delight in service of others in the name of Jesus?

To speak of redemption is to necessarily speak to the created good of human relationships as well as the fallen state in which we live and relate to one another and the future humanity moves toward. When we talk about helping families move in a better direction, we are recognizing that there was some creational intent to how we were to relate in families and that those ways of relating are incomplete and partial after the fall. But the ways we are to relate also point to something beyond our here-and-now relationships, to transcendent reality that is both now and soon to come.

## REFLECTING REDEMPTION: FAMILY FUNCTIONING, RELATIONSHIPS, AND IDENTITY

We will discuss a redemptive focus with reference to three important considerations to Christians and to the field of family therapy. These are *family functioning*, *family relationships*, and *family identity*. We want to express our appreciation for the work of Mark McMinn and Clark Campbell, whose book *Integrative Psychotherapy* was helpful to us insofar as they developed the themes of function, structure, and relationship as aspects of the *imago Dei*. We extend those meanings to incorporate our discussion of the family from a Christian perspective. We then use these reference points in our Christian critique and engagement of the various models of family therapy and specific family therapy concerns in parts two and three of this book, respectively.

*Family functioning.* When we consider family functioning, we are looking at how models of therapy suggest that families ought to function. While it is common within the Christian domain to discuss and debate family structure—such as the egalitarian versus complementarian view of marriage—our intent is to move beyond that limiting dialogue and discuss marriage and family function as it relates to the broader themes described earlier: creation, fall, redemption, and glorification. We want to come to a fuller and more complete understanding of what the various models suggest is the best way for a family to function in light of its kingdom mission. We believe that each model of family therapy makes either an explicit or implicit claim about how families ought to function and ways that functioning can be improved through participation in therapy.

Families that function under optimal circumstances are prone to fewer tensions and greater success, satisfaction, and opportunities. Likewise, families that function under duress are prone to conflict, violence, separation, divorce, and mental and physical health ailments. We would also be remiss if we failed to note the obvious: healthy, functional families are good for adults and children alike. The research is overwhelming that both men and women are more likely to thrive and prefer to be in families. In a seminal meta-analytic study of 130 empirical investigations of the effect of marital status on human well-being, Coombs (1991) found that marital status was a significant predictor of physical health and personal well-being. Both men and women, when connected to others in a secure, stable, trustworthy environment with those they love and are loved by are more likely to live longer, have fewer negative health problems, manage their health problems with stronger resources, and report a higher level of satisfaction in every stage of life (Waite & Gallagher, 2000). In other words, it is the function of love, trust, security, honestly, vulnerability, stability, and so on within family relationships that has an effect on both the psychological and physical well-being of its members.

It is also true that adults tied intimately to families report less sleep, less free time, less financial resources to spend on themselves, and more necessity to compromise in vital decisions. The summation of the data suggests that family remains, for most adults, a commitment that stretches and enriches them, that drains and renews them.

The data also indicate that successful marriages and thriving families are the result of relational skills demonstrated routinely in the small challenges of life and exhibited extraordinarily in the face of the severity of life challenge (see Blankenhorn, 2007). Furthermore, every marriage and every family, despite its heritage and pedigree of generations of success, is challenged, threatened, and taxed to the point of collapse. Coping with crises brought on by death, disease, economic calamity, childhood wounding, sexual infidelity, natural disaster, and so forth is reported by many to be the greatest challenge faced in life. Enter the marriage and family therapist. The pages of this book are aimed at assisting those gifted with the care of people who have injuries to the space between themselves and their most needed and cherished others.

How would a family functioning as God intends relate, and how might we help existing families more closely approximate functioning most closely associated with Christianity? The bulk of this book will explore, then, how well existing models of family theory reflect these assumptions as well as how well they direct families toward these kinds of qualities and characteristics. At the close of part two of the book, we will turn to whether there is a distinctively Christian approach to the therapy Christians provide to families.

The presence of family function within each theory can be ascertained by the expressed focus articulated by the theory—that is to say, the aspect of family functioning that the theory focuses on. Those theories that have as their immediate goal explicit functional characteristics will tend to emphasize the immediate containment of negative characteristics that are having an effect on family functioning and operation. In the same way, approaches that are oriented toward function will emphasize the presence of behavioral characteristics and values that are exhibited in the present that indicate healthy functioning. For example, a healthy functioning family will have effective communication as a characteristic. Therefore, a family theory that possesses a strong affinity for the function or impact of words would focus a noticeable amount of time toward developing positive communication skills and eliminating destructive communication patterns.

So we want to ask, what is valued in each particular model or theory of the family? How do we know when a family is not functioning as it should? What map should a family follow to function better?

*Family relationships.* When we consider family relationships, we are talking about how family members ought to relate to one another. What do these relationships look like? How is the "space between" members of a family defined? Each model of family therapy prescribes something about how family members ought to relate. Thinking relationally rather than individually brought about the "systems revolution" that led to the formation of the marriage and family profession. Each theory, to varying degrees, has defined itself through the manner in which it addresses issues that emerge relationally—that is, between people rather than intrapsychically.

Scripture does not offer a comprehensive view of family relationships. But we do see directives to parents to instruct their children in Deuteronomy and instructions to families in Leviticus. We see other glimpses of family life throughout Scripture. Of course, many examples are not held up as models for family functioning. One does not turn to the story of Cain and Abel or of Joseph and his brothers as models of sibling relationships. But when we read of Ruth and Naomi (Ruth 1:16-18), for example, we are moved by Ruth's commitment to the family of her deceased husband. Or when we read about Timothy's upbringing, we are reminded by Paul that he is indebted to his mother and his grandmother for his knowledge and character in Christ (2 Tim 1:5). We also read about mutual regard and love toward one another in marriage (Eph 5:21-33).

Tragically, our culture provides messages, themes, values, and expectations that run counter to efforts at relational resilience and success. The devotion of Ruth to Naomi in the Bible provides an example of this commitment:

> Where you go, I will go;
>> Where you lodge, I will lodge;
> your people shall be my people,
>> and your God my God.
> Where you die, I will die—
>> there will I be buried.
> May the LORD do thus and so to me,
>> and more as well,
> if even death parts me from you! (Ruth 1:16-18)

We need to be reminded that Ruth's commitment was not to marriage but to the family of her deceased husband. The tie between her and Naomi was a volitional one. She married the family, and to that family she would remain, even after the commitment of marriage was legally dissolved.

We enter into a discussion of family relationships cautiously. Just as we want to recognize diverse views as to what constitutes a Christian view of the family, we also want to recognize various understandings of distinctively Christian family relationships.

We agree with Roberts (1993) when he wrote:

> To love God with all one's heart and one's neighbor as oneself is what it *is* to be a fully functioning, fully formed, healthy person. This is what the Christian Word about persons tells us, and it is by this Word that Christians interpret themselves and so become formed as selves. (p. 12)

The questions in the present analysis include the following: How ought family members relate to one another to aid in the forming of us as "fully functioning, fully formed, healthy" persons who love God and neighbor and self? If a family were facilitating this formative process—and we believe families either do facilitate this kind of fully functioning personhood or they approximate it to one extent or another and in some cases fail altogether—how would family members be relating to one another?

Although not exhaustive, we believe family relationships would begin with acknowledging *dependence on God*. Family relationships—relating to one another in the context of daily family life—lead to vulnerability, and vulnerability can lead us to greater dependence on God (Roberts, 1993).

Christian family relationships also reflect a kind of dependence on God that brings the Christian to an understanding that they are to follow God's leadership through studying and implementing his revealed will. Further, God leads families and places parents in a position in this world to be the central figures in enacting that leadership in ways that are in keeping with God's will. Parents are to turn to God as a source for guidance, wisdom, and discernment.

This very act of following and relating to God models for family members how they are to think about their relationship to others in the family. Most family theories have neglected the role of the individual, perhaps to some extent in response to the focus on the individual found in the medical model and much of psychology. And in these contexts, mental health has often focused narrowly or exclusively on the self as the unit of concern and sought to actualize the potential of the self, often with respect to one's own interests and desires. A Christian view would begin by anchoring this sense of self in relation to God because the Christian claims that self-actualization is a word that is too "thin" to stand within the Christian tradition. To actualize one's self and one's potential means to take delight in one's standing as created in God's image and for his purposes, for his service.

A Christian view of the family also extends far beyond the interconnectedness so often underscored in systems theory. A Christian view recognizes that systems approaches simply describe the reality that family members are interrelated in such a way that changes to one person will affect the others in the system. Of course this is true, but it is also a "thin" view of our relatedness. A Christian understanding of interrelatedness speaks to the ontological reality of our family relationships. We can begin to see our true "self" only in relation to others, and the family provides a social context in which we are to come to know and relate to others and learn more about ourselves.

In one sense we do not have to be in a family to experience this. As Roberts (1993) reminds us, the apostle Paul writes of how the Christian suffers when others suffer, and rejoices when others rejoice (1 Cor 12:26). However, the family provides us with the earliest opportunities to experience this interconnectedness that is found in our relationships to others precisely because of a more fundamental relationship that we share together in relation to God as our creator.

A Christian view of family connectedness will also recognize the importance of *mutuality*, in which family members have obligations to one another made important because of the covenant made in relation to God. The valuing of mutuality has been mentioned by other authors, such as Jack and Judith Balswick (2007), who see it as necessarily tied to the trinitarian perspective mentioned earlier.

Perhaps it is in the context of valuing mutuality that we can say that we find ourselves valuing improved communication and problem solving in families—not in and of themselves but as expressions of mutuality. We want to see families know how to listen to and affirm one another. There is also a sense in which all families are made up of fallen and incomplete individuals, and conflicts will be an inevitable part of relationships in a family context.

But in addition to mutuality, the Christian also sees the value of *self-denial*, a concept not often discussed in contemporary models of family therapy. But the Christian sees within family life an opportunity to grow into maturity by seeing one's worth in relation to God and ultimately as part of the larger family of God. In this the Christian learns that what he or she wants is not ultimately the measuring stick of what he or she ought to have or has some claim to in this life. Rather, personal wants and desires are always subject to the larger purposes of God, and the Christian family can be a training ground for the kind of denial of one's personal wants that opens the door to greater maturity in Christ. It is precisely because I am in relationship with others and with God that I might say *no* to my own interests on behalf of another and out of obedience to God.

The family as seen through a Christian lens also models *perseverance* or *resilience*. Marriage and family life is difficult. While a competing view might look at familial ties as potential obstacles to personal satisfaction, a Christian view recognizes that it is precisely through these conflicts that family members both witness and model perseverance. Roberts (1993) reminds us, "Child rearing is an excellent school for learning virtues like patience and self-control" (p. 223). So is marriage, for that matter. A Christian understanding of the family recognizes that family relationships provide unique opportunities to grow in virtues that ought to characterize us as persons. Indeed, "Christian teaching emphasizes that living *through* one's trials with God's help makes one into a mature person, builds Christian character" (p. 37). But it takes a certain amount of perspective-taking to identify opportunities to grow in patience and self-control, among other virtues.

An understanding that we live "between the times" also helps us have realistic expectations for families. They exist in a fallen world, and they consist of individual members who are likewise fallen. So it should come as no surprise that Christian family therapists might find problems presenting both in the individual and as a result of patterns of relating among family members.

The only sure thing when it comes to something that can be trusted is the God who made us. Even the healthiest of families can offer only so much by way of security:

> Since Christianity regards human nature not just as relational but as God-related, we are freed to acknowledge that there is much in life to be anxious and distrustful about, even if our family members are as trustworthy as humans can be expected to be. Christian realism about the likelihood of finding security within the bounds of earthly relationships reveals the need for a trusting relationship with one who is trustworthy even when all else in life has fallen apart. (Roberts, 1993, p. 94)

Finally, we see Christian relationships as characterized by *integrity.* Family members are in this sense to be responsible to one another. This means, among other things, that family members make commitments and honor those commitments, taking seriously their family tasks, roles, and responsibilities (Jones & Butman, 2011). In this sense the family becomes a place in which early efforts to be honest, responsible, and faithful can be understood and enacted.

In our own cultural context we see value in encouraging the qualities mentioned above so that they come to characterize families in contemporary society. We are not saying that these family qualities are clearly derived from Scripture and hence applicable to all families at all times. Rather, they are principles that seem consistent with God's revealed will in Scripture and also relevant and applicable to our cultural context. This is not an exhaustive list, and it is certainly conceivable that other qualities might come to the foreground in other cultural contexts.

***Family identity.*** Identity refers to definition. It refers to how we are characterized and recognized by our distinction and uniqueness and also by our affiliation. When we consider family identity we are referring to the role a family plays in ordering the world. Families provide individuals with definition and identity—a sense for who they are and what ultimately matters in life. The "I" becomes part of the "us" of marriage, family, clan, and community. Whether they acknowledge it or not, each model of family therapy suggests ways to make sense of the world; each family shapes the way its individual members come to understand themselves and the world around them.

As Moynagh (1995) suggests, Jesus was brought up in a home that modeled what would have been expected of families throughout the Old Testament— that is, "his parents successfully pass on to him the faith" (p. 373). There is a real sense in which family identity will be founded on what it means to be a Christian. This is not merely intellectual assent to doctrines about the person and work of Christ, although it certainly can mean a deeper valuing of Christian doctrine, but it also means a life together in which family members relate to one another *as Christians* and by doing so create a larger, more encompassing family identity as followers of Christ.

As good as families are, we also want to recognize a perspective that is quite unique to a Christian worldview but one that is lost on many Christians today; that is, the people of God, the body of Christ, are to be considered our "first family," as Clapp (1993) put it. Clapp actually makes two declarations, one negative and the other positive. The negative declaration regarding the family is that

> the family is not God's most important institution on earth. The family is not the social agent that most significantly shapes and forms the character of Christians. The family is not the primary vehicle of God's grace and salvation for a waiting, desperate world. (p. 66)

The positive declaration is this:

> The church is God's most important institution on earth. The church is the social agent that most significantly shapes and forms the character of Christians. And the church is the primary vehicle of God's grace and salvation for a waiting, desperate world. (pp. 66-67)

While we agree with much of what Clapp is saying here, we might place our emphasis on how the family is to be valued by Christians—not for its own sake but in part because the Christian family is one part of the larger body of Christ and a part of the church. It is the part that provides stability and role modeling, love and nurturance, boundaries and consequences, and so much more. Lessons learned early in life in the family are then played out over and over again in the life of the believer in the context of the larger body of Christ.

In the end, the biological family, while so important in so many different ways, is not ultimately the most important institution in and of itself. It is *part* of the most important institution—that is, the church. God, through the covenant made with his people in the Old Testament, essentially establishes the primacy of those who follow him, and Jesus confirms that priority throughout the New Testament. The bride of Christ, the church, becomes "first family" to those who find salvation in Jesus.

This understanding of the family has tremendous implications—for those who are married and for those who are single. For example, for married persons it means that we may relate to one another in marriage and to children in the family but that those relationships all occur as a microcosm of the larger relationships we sustain in the body of Christ. We are not a family in isolation; rather, we are a family interconnected to others who are also part of the larger body of Christ.

This view of first family also has implications for those who are single. Although we will not be able to address this in great detail, it is important to affirm that Christian singles are "first-class" citizens of the most important institution established by God to further his purposes. The local church can fail to communicate this truth and live it out when singles are made to feel that they are "second-class" citizens because they do not exist in the family form that is idealized in many church contexts.

The question we want to ask about family identity is, what does it mean to form a family life together as Christians? How do we understand our family identity in relation to the larger community of believers?

## IN CLOSING: A LESSON FROM FATHER STANLEY

N-IV-16: it stands for North of the Cross, row 4, 16 graves in from the aisle. It is the burial site of Father Stanley Vesely at St. Procopius Abbey, in Lisle, Illinois. He was not famous—except that there is a baseball field named in his honor. There is really no reason for you to have ever heard of him. He was no authority on marriage, family, psychology, or counseling such that he should be noted in a marriage and family text. All but fourteen of his eighty-nine years were lived in a monastery. That hardly qualifies him for the opening chapter to a textbook on counseling families. But maybe, embedded somewhere in his life's story, there was evidence of the key principle for successful relationship. We suggest that Father Stanley's life represents a model for family and for the treatment of families that is fundamental to the purpose of this book, the purpose of our work with couples and families, and your purpose in studying how to assist them to thrive in relationship together.

In 1927 Stanley entered seminary with the intention to become a priest. Behind the church was a cemetery. Being the master of pun, he would say with a smile that at age fourteen, "I entered the cemetery . . . I mean seminary." In truth, he entered the service of God, and he made the decision to intentionally and purposefully join others in relationships that would shape his character and identity in significant ways. There, amid the trees and headstones, he declared to God that this place would be where he would live and serve and die and be buried. That decision, and the thousands of decisions to follow through on in fulfilling that initial commitment, would shape who he became in the context of the relationships to which he committed himself. In 2003, seventy-six years after making that promise, it was completed.

Father Stanley possessed a mental frame that was unusual in his day—and rare in ours. It was one in which the dedication of self toward an institution and toward others surpassed a love for self. It is this dedication of self toward institutions and toward others that we want to highlight as critical for our understanding of families today. We see successful married relationship as patterned after Father Stanley's triumphant life. "Here is where I will dedicate my life, and these people will be those to whom I serve, and allow to serve me." Marriage, in our frame, is most likely to thrive when the mentality of lifelong commitment is made toward each other. It is as if we are saying, "I will die here, with you holding me at age eighty-nine, after a life of service." This dedication, this frame, informs so many decisions in our day-to-day lives, and as a couple raises a family, the decision, the frame, continues to be a resource that informs decision making for the life of family relationships.

Such a life commitment, made at any age, will be difficult. One can only imagine the sadness that Father Stanley experienced with the comparison of his life path to those of his peers and extended family. He would know of others who made different choices than he made, whose lives were fulfilled by the choices they made and that perhaps part of him would have wanted to make but did not. The weights from our life choices are a heavy burden at times, sometimes because of the difficulties encountered because of those choices, other times simply because the choices also represent closing doors to other ways to live and other opportunities for growth. It is common to make comparisons. Singles compare their lives and dreams to those who are married. Married couples compare their lives to singles and to other couples. Family members make comparisons as they think about other couples and their children and the values and priorities and experiences of others. Who hasn't struggled when reading through an end-of-the-year Christmas letter from a family that seems to have made the best choices and have had the best experiences imaginable?

Couples also come to us, and will come to you, along with their families wanting assistance with their burdens that emerge with life commitments. The choice to join with another in forming a family is one that will bring pain that can be severe and frequent. In the same way that many must have aided Father Stanley in his commitment to keep his vows to God, so you and we aid families in maintaining theirs.

Such an understanding of the family brings us back to Father Stanley because the qualities and characteristics of the family will likely be reflected in the intentional, purposeful ways we are to relate to one another as believers. As Father Stanley made his vow to live intentionally with others and they with him, we can look at how we are to live with one another in the committed, purposeful relationships we refer to as family. So we come to the question, to what end are we seeking a redemptive focus in our work with families?

## CONCLUSION

Our intent in this opening chapter is to create an image of marriage and family that is not often articulated within most family therapy textbooks. In these opening pages we hope to cast a vision from a redemptive perspective as to what the family can be. We have a high confidence that all of us who are carefully committed to family well-being—the novice and the expert, the religious and the secular, the liberal and the conservative, the professional and the lay worker—must be extremely careful to see, read, hear, and respond to the family as our preconceptions permit us. We fully respect the restraint required of us as professional clinicians to not dictate or manipulate others who come to us for assistance toward directions that they wish not to go—such as refusing to work with a family because the adults see their relationship as being temporal while we see it as something that should be enduring. However, we are under no obligation to uncritically embrace the maps that guide us in assisting families, particularly when they do so based on the assumption that they are merely temporal. Our goal is to offer a text that critically engages the existing models of family therapy and begins to cast a vision for a distinctively Christian understanding of the family and of ways to support and sustain families in their many forms. We and you must engage our work with families with an eye on the figure and an eye on the ground.

We recognize that there is no one perspective on the family with which all Christians will agree. But we give general consideration that we believe many if not most Christians will agree and then ask for grace from those who might emphasize other considerations that we chose not to add to this present discussion.

We look at Scripture and see that God works in so many different forms of family toward his purposes. This is the redemptive focus of this book. God may have in mind a family form from creation, but he also recognizes our fallen condition and, because of the redemptive work of his Son, Jesus, he is at work in our lives, however broken they may be.

# REFERENCES

Anderson, R. S., & Guernsey, D. B. (1985). *On being family: A social theology of the family.* Grand Rapids: Eerdmans.

Balswick, J. O., & Balswick, J. K. (2006). *A model for marriage: Covenant, grace, empowerment and intimacy.* Downers Grove, IL: IVP Academic.

Balswick, J. O., & Balswick, J. K. (2007). *The family: A Christian perspective on the contemporary home* (3rd ed.). Grand Rapids: Baker.

Blankenhorn, D. (2007). *The future of marriage.* New York: Encounter Books.

Cherlin, A. J. (2009). *The marriage-go-round.* New York: Vintage Books.

Clapp, R. (1993). *Families at the crossroads: Beyond traditional and modern options.* Downers Grove, IL: InterVarsity Press.

Coombs, R. H. (1991). Marital status and personal well-being: A literature review. *Human Relations, 40,* 97-102.

Coontz, S. (2005). *Marriage, a history: How love conquered marriage.* New York: Penguin Books.

Erickson, M. J. (2001). *Introducing Christian doctrine* (2nd ed.). Grand Rapids: Baker.

Girgis, S., Anderson, R. T., & George, R. P. (2012). *What is marriage? Man and woman: A defense.* New York: Encounter Books.

Jones, S. L., & Butman, R. E. (2011). *Modern psychotherapies: A comprehensive Christian appraisal* (2nd ed.). Downers Grove, IL: InterVarsity Press.

Kingdon, D. P. (1988). Family. In S. B. Ferguson, D. F. Wright, & J. I. Packer (Eds.), *New dictionary of theology* (pp. 251-52). Downers Grove, IL: InterVarsity Press.

Köstenberger, A. J. (2010). *God, marriage and family: Rebuilding the biblical foundation* (2nd ed.). Wheaton, IL: Crossway Books.

Moynagh, M. (1995). Family. In D. J. Atkinson, D. F. Field, A. Holmes, & O. O'Donovan (Eds.), *New dictionary of Christian ethics and pastoral theology* (pp. 372-75). Downers Grove, IL: InterVarsity Press.

Roberts, R. C. (1993). *Taking the word to heart: Self and others in an age of therapies.* Grand Rapids: Eerdmans.

Waite, L., & Gallagher, M. (2000). *The case for marriage: Why married people are happier, healthier, and better off financially.* New York: Doubleday.

Williams, W. C. (1996). Family life and relations. In W. A. Elwell (Ed.), *Evangelical dictionary of biblical theology* (pp. 243-45). Grand Rapids: Baker.

Wolterstorff, N. (1983). *Until justice and peace embrace.* Grand Rapids: Eerdmans.

# HISTORICAL
# FOUNDATIONS OF
# FAMILY THERAPY

*It was hard for him who had lived with one
generation, to plead now before another.*

**PLUTARCH,** *LIVES*

THIS BOOK IS A GUIDE FOR CLINICIANS and pastoral
counselors who work with couples and families in the healing of
relational pain and injury. This guide is unique from most others
in that it is a fusion of the previous work of psychologists, counselors, and family therapists spanning over 130 years with the
Christian tradition of family care that has emerged from the biblical text and predominantly Protestant theology.

This chapter will lay the foundation for those that follow, which
will address specific marriage and family theories, therapies, and
interventions. Included in the discussion will be the philosophical
antecedents that have influenced its movement from primarily a
religious function through the emergence of a profession associated with the psychiatric treatment of schizophrenia and other
mental disorders to its current practice in a broad spectrum of
mental health, social service, religious ministry, and human development fields. In the process of presenting the history of the
family therapy movement, we will address the important philosophical antecedents and the salient constructs that transcend

individual schools of family therapy. These principles serve as a basic or common set of assumptions that separate the group of family interventions from psychology, counseling, and therapy targeted toward individual growth and development.

Therefore, in understanding the full depth and breadth of family therapy practice within the twenty-first century, one must have regard for two traditions. The first is the *theological/philosophical tradition* that established the practice of human caregiving as it pertains to family life and the well-being of individuals through the advance of the social institutions of marriage and family. The second is the *scientific/professional tradition* that established the empirical methodology of family therapy through the application of quantitative and qualitative science, psychology, and medicine. The expressed purpose of this text is to illuminate the latter through the respect and regard of the former. That is to say that the practice of family therapy, psychology, counseling, or social work are conducted and regulated through the respective professional regulations and licenses and are derived from a philosophy and a theology about human intra- and interrelationships. The authors, as Christian psychologists, are educated within the profession of psychological science, most succinctly defined by psychological functionalists as "the study of mental activity" (Marx & Cronan-Hillix, 1987, p. 129). Therefore, this chapter will explore the historical foundation of family counseling by paying regard to the science and the ministry of family care. While the subsequent chapters of the text will focus more specifically on theoretical approaches derived from the scientific/professional tradition, it is the theological/ministerial foundation that motivates us to conduct research, engage in practice, and instruct others in the methodology of family intervention.

To consider the history of family therapy is to examine how we have corrected ourselves within the context of real relationships. Therapy connotes the idea of repair, reconciliation, or remediation—commonly associated with a medical application that promotes healing. The profession of "psychotherapy"—literally the profession of "soul healing"—has historically constituted "temporary," "conditional," even "artificial" relationships, those based on an economic arrangement between a service consumer with an identified "self need" and a service provider with specialized training and credentials, to foster individual growth, maturation, and healing from the challenges and injuries of life and remediation of the targeted aspect of self.

Though we use the terms *temporary*, *conditional*, and *artificial* to describe the therapeutic relationship, we do not mean that the therapist pretends to care but rather that the care and concern are bound by the limits of the profession. Those limits are most fundamentally economic. The "soul healing" aspect of therapy between a professional clinician—therapist, psychologist, counselor, social worker, or religious/spiritual minister—and an individual imitates the real relationship of parent, sibling, extended family member, or friend but is limited to a specific focus of problem or issue that is experienced as intrapersonal pain.

Family psychotherapy is similar but integrates broader constructs. Its therapeutic focus is the healing of the family soul *and* the healing of individual souls communally within family relationships. That is to say, it focuses on (a) the repair or healing of the space between people in relationship and (b) people in relationship commonly attending to the healing within each member. We see family psychotherapy or family therapy to be the healing of families, the system or the "family soul," and the healing of individual souls that make up family constellations.

In the case of marriage and family therapy, the healing that occurs is within actual relationships—those that have a historical, a present, and a future set of experiences. Therapy within previously established and continuing real relationships is significantly different than those established between an individual clinician and client. The relationships of family—those established by marriage, offspring, extended relatives, legal contract, or personal volition—exist a priori to the presence of pathology, maladaptivity, or dysfunction, and they continue to exist post hoc. Family therapy is unique from all other psychotherapies in that it involves an outside person entering a closed relational system and helping to prompt change while never actually becoming part of the system. It is the task of the clinician to assist in the revitalization of a social organism such that the system creates its own perpetual motion. Perhaps Carl Whitaker articulated it best by likening the family therapist's relationship to the family as that of a coach who helps the team perform better but does not actually play in the game.

## A RATIONALE FOR FAMILY THERAPY

We see the developing of a "family therapy profession" emerging later in the twentieth century from three factors. The first is that humans are intrinsically help seekers. The second reason is that the complexity of culture has made help seeking within the traditional extended family structure insufficient. Finally, family therapy emerged when the economies of Western society could accommodate a helping profession funded by the discretionary income of families and of local communities.

For as long as there have been relationships, we suspect there have been persons appointed within the society to help others within the community to work out differences and solve problems together. Certainly within recorded Western history such roles were formally occupied by the philosophers of the Greek era; the rabbis of the Jewish tradition; and pastors/priests, lawyers, and physicians in Christian Europe and the Americas. The role of shaman, imam, spiritualist, or teacher in Native American, Islamic, and Asian cultures plays an equally important position in the counsel of families. In addition, there is the very important role of the family sage—that wise elder, be it an aunt, uncle, or grandparent—who could help the family understand and resolve challenges and threats to the family. That from this condition of nonformal intervention a profession of family therapy emerged should not be a surprise. We see this as an outcome of two important factors. First, it is within human capacity to seek assistance from others to resolve problems in living. Human nature has not changed, though the individual experiences as children, adolescents, and adults from one generation and one culture to another certainly have.

In North American culture, the image of "rugged individualism" has been a pervasive icon of life. However, in all likelihood, it is an exaggerated reality, a "sound bite mentality" that does not really reflect how we actually live in community. Even individualistic presses and values did not override the requirement to live interdependently with others and to seek advice and assistance when one encountered challenge. Benjamin Franklin, in the preface to *Poor Richard's Almanack*, said that "it is hard for an empty sack to stand upright." Just as much as people sought advice to live in the eighteenth century, they pursue it in the twenty-first. Advance the DVD of time 250 years and you have the equivalent form in Dr. Phil or the Supernanny dispensing advice to culture that is desperate for family insight, guidance, and direction—sprinkled with the same wit and amusement.

Second to the fact that we are prone to seek assistance from others within our community is the reality that life, to say the least, is knotty, thorny, and confusing. The rules that once applied, that defined family and gave direction for the maturation of the young, and the boundaries that define responsibilities and privileges for adults are in various levels of suspension. In the twenty-first century the family is, more than any other time in civilized history, a complicated blending of biological and sociological change. The "social instruction book"—the commandments of relationship passed from one generation to the next that instructed us where to live, how to live, and what to live for—has, for most people, been fractured. "The family as an institution perhaps suffers most from the fractionalization of relationships" (Gergen, 1991, p. 179). This is not stated to appeal for a return to the "good old days," for every day or historical period has problems of its own. This is meant to recognize the importance of understanding the pressures on family systems and to be an advocate for the institution of marriage and family and the individual marriages and families confused and perplexed in their formation of relational community.

Advances in biology have created a radically different life for us compared to our parents and the generation that preceded them. Because of knowledge from medical science, the life expectancy of billions of people has nearly doubled in just the last century. Changes in reproductive knowledge have altered family formation such that the timing of conception, the number of pregnancies, and even the sex of the child can be manipulated. The rapid advance of technology in communication, transportation, biology, and economics has created a pressure on the family system that is essential in maintaining social stability. Gergen refers to this phenomenon as *multiphrenia*. "Entering a relationship with a multiplicity of potentials, each a possible invalidation of the other, makes it enormously difficult to locate a steady form of relatedness. These difficulties are only intensified in the case of committed intimacy" (1991, p. 176). Multiphrenia is the loss associated with near-infinite opportunity regarding the expectation of personal freedoms and opportunities, limited by the realities of time and energy (Lyle & Gehart-Brooks, 1999).

Finally, significant economic gains have provided an independence from the subsequent generation like no other time in our history and with financial resources never before experienced. The North American economy in the twenty-first century allows for far more options for an individual's and family's discretionary income than in generations past. Americans have more money and can spend above and beyond the necessities of food and shelter. For example, the USDA statistics show that in 1929 nearly one-fourth of a family's income was required to pay for food. Today, that number is less than one-tenth.

In generations past, economic opportunities for most families provided for basic food, clothing, and shelter needs. Middle-class families might have a mule or a horse for transportation, but most often they walked. But now, it is impossible in today's economic climate to remain current with the array of products and services available to every economic class.

We can anticipate that social change will for the subsequent generation occur at a rate equally as fast if not faster than any previous generation. Within this era of greater wealth have emerged many services for the "wealthy middle class" that includes paid "personal/family advisers" to help them navigate the complexity of family life. In the past the need for support—brought on by the need for stability—was addressed by seeking counsel within one's family, clan, or religious community. The exception to this was the economically wealthy who could use their financial resources to pay for advice and counsel. Freud's work as an analyst was reserved for only the patrician class of Viennese society. Psychoanalysis was not available to the populace for sheer economic reasons. However, in the current social climate the need for support, which has always been present, is exacerbated by the intensity of change and embedded in the advantage of economic and social policy that has made individual, marital, and family therapy accessible to almost anyone within North American society.

## THE UNIQUE CONTRIBUTION OF MARRIAGE AND FAMILY THERAPY

Despite the radical social changes that have constructed, deconstructed, and reconstructed what it means for many to be in a family, some aspects have not changed. It was true in any age past and remains true today that the strongest of human bonds are those formed through the affection and dependence of family attachment (Bowlby, 1969). With economic and technological advancements, the individual's need for connection to family and the family's responsibility in nurturing its members has shown no evidence of change. Less academic, and possibly more meaningful, is A. A. Milne's explanation of attachment found in the dialogue between Piglet and Winnie the Pooh:

> Piglet sidled up to Pooh from behind.
>
> "Pooh!" he whispered.
>
> "Yes, Piglet?"
>
> "Nothing," said Piglet, taking Pooh's paw.
>
> "I just wanted to be sure of you." (*The House at Pooh Corner*, 1928)

Family psychotherapy has come to be the "healing of attached souls." Like Piglet, family members need to be sure of one another or to be confidently attached. When that security is destabilized or becomes detached by environment, circumstances, or behavior, the figurative glue that permits people to "keep their lives together" breaks down. People become "unglued." Theorists, described later in subsequent chapters, have argued over whether the therapeutic repair process—the "re-gluing" that occurs in marital or family counseling—is an individual's internal process with family as the tool (Whitaker & Keith, 1981) or is a repair process of the actual space between individuals (Boszormenyi-Nagy & Krasner, 1986). For now it must be sufficient to assume that healing involves both the individual soul as well as a mystical corporate "soul" of family—that is to say that family therapy is both an intrapsychic and an interpsychic intervention. Family therapy exists to evoke change, alleviate suffering, and promote growth for each of the identified patients with a system (intra) and for the family as a living organism (inter).

This tension between family and individual has transcended time and culture. While the laws of physics and biology are stable through time, the principles of family therapy are tied to how cultures embedded in time and place come to define the nature of individual existence and the individual's relationship to others. Rapid increases in biological science, economics, and technology during the twentieth century have accelerated the rate of change of family structures and definitions of individuality. In spite of changes such as the human migration away from ethnic geographies that have existed for centuries and economics that have changed the way individuals acquire the necessary resources for survival, certain facts regarding the stability and continuity of family remain. First, human beings are ill-equipped to survive in the earth's environment alone. Individuals must shelter themselves from the seasonal extremities of heat and cold and must protect themselves from micro- and macroscopic predators. These include everything from viruses and bacteria to lions, tigers, and bears ("Oh, my!") to scenarios where humans must compete for limited survival resources such as food and water. Therefore, humanity—in our view by God's design and in the view of others by evolutionary progression—must live with others. For the most part, these "others" are families.

Second, while society has come to provide much of the essential services previously provided by family (i.e., education, work, protection from predators, health care, and recreation), the empirical research is abundantly clear that offspring are most likely to thrive in the presence of stable, biologically based families. Biologically based parenthood and nurturance within a community of siblings, extended family, and communities provide the highest probability for later success in the exhibition of adult skills required to exist in the society (Stanton, 1997).

Third, end-of-life issues are best managed by those with whom the experiences of life were shared. We all know of the images of death: one with a spouse, children, and extended family at bedside to both embrace the life well lived and accept the death now visiting on the family, and another of the stark impression of death in one's eighth decade with no one present to share the significance of one's last breath. The research bears out the difference that the elderly adult who is engaged in life with extended family is more likely to live longer, in better health, and with fewer injuries and greater life satisfaction than those who are alone.

And finally, as much as pop culture places a value on the freedoms of the single life, the research presents a drastically different image. Married men and women are healthier physically and report lower frequency of missed work and lost wages; lower percentages of suicide, depression, and anxiety; and higher levels of life satisfaction (Stanton, 1997).

## A BRIEF HISTORY OF FAMILY THERAPY: HOW WE GOT WHERE WE ARE

Reading most mental health and family therapy texts, you would learn that "psychology" is a relatively new field of study compared to other scientific disciplines, having a beginning in Europe with Wilhelm Wundt and his laboratory at the University of Leipzig and in North America with the writings of William James, both occurring in the 1870s. Family therapy, one of the many specialties of the mental health profession emerging from psychological science, traces its origin as a profession from the era immediately following World War II. It is true that psychology as a scientific discipline defined as the empirical study of human behavior began then and there. And it is also true that family therapy as an academic discipline and as a profession is just over a half century in age. However, it is not true that psychology, as a term to describe the efforts to understand and alleviate mental anguish, began in a laboratory, clinic, or university. Likewise, family therapy—the process of

rendering aid to family groups to assist adults and children in the complications of life—can be traced through Eastern and Western societies for millennia, not decades.

We have divided the history of family therapy into three periods. The first
period is the family ministry period. The second is the family science period.
The third and current era is the social constructivist period. We will examine
the emergence of these three times, the first covering three hundred years,
primarily from the establishment of Western culture in North America in the
early 1700s continuing through the first generation of the twenty-first century,
but having a more diminished role in the larger society than it did up until the
rise of empirical science in the late 1800s. The second period, family science,
had its origin with the formation of the early adherents to structural, functional, and analytic psychology just prior to the dawn of the last century, continuing through the present. During this period the profession of family
therapy was established as something other than ministry and individual psychology. Its preeminence was the three decades between 1950 and 1980. This
period saw the establishment of a profession with a distinct theory, therapy,
and identity. The family science period continues as a powerful force but is
having to share the spotlight with social constructivists beginning in about
1980 up to the present. The third period, social constructivism, has a clear time
of emergence in the 1980s and has continued to grow in influence through the
first decade of the twenty-first century. Because it includes the present we do
not yet know its lasting imprint on the culture and the profession, nor where
it will lead in the future.

Conceptually, we liken these three periods to a trio of vocal musicians. For
about two hundred years religion's family counseling was a solo lead singer.
Then for much of the twentieth century religion's voice was a background
singer to the scientific approach. During this era the emphasis was on theory,
research, education, and licensure of clinicians who understood the practice
of family therapy to be a derivative of medical science. The religious approaches remained present but far less prominent. Then, most recently, a new
voice was introduced to the group; the social constructionist approach had a
new rhythm, a new lyric, and a new audience. This new musician did not
replace the previous two: it redefined the fundamental assumptions about the
music of therapy. Previously there was a struggle between these voices,
fighting for who would be heard. At other times they were discordant, singing

in competitive keys. And at other times, there has been a blending and a resonance of three different voices with a common purpose. We, the audience, have unique relationships with all three members of the band—we may prefer one and wish the others would retire or come down with an extended case of laryngitis. However, the fact remains that the religious, scientific, and relativistic influences remain and continue to have a place in the culture. So to understand family therapy, we must understand the unique contribution that all three of these traditions have made and continue to make to the practice of healing the attached souls of family.

## FAMILY THERAPY AS MINISTRY

We believe that Gladding was in error when he said that "Prior to the 1940s, family therapy in the United States was almost a nonentity" (2007, p. 56). As we have said earlier, it is true that the profession of family therapy had its genesis immediately following World War II. However, the historical evidence suggests that family counseling and therapy as a practice did not begin with Ackerman, Bell, Whitaker, or Bowen. Family intervention has a tradition lasting millennia within the realm of ministry and the church. University of Chicago sociologist Ernest Burgess addressed the emergence of formal study of the family in 1926. He wrote, "Nine years ago I gave for the first time a course on the family. *There was even then an enormous literature in this field.* But among all the volumes upon the family . . . [there was] not a single work that even pretended to study the modern family as behavior or as a social phenomenon" (1926, p. 4, italics added). Burgess found an abundance of writings on family processes and care from within the religious context because at that time churches were the ones doing the caring. His work was among the first to consider family processes with the emerging empirical sociopsychological paradigm.

Family therapy—that is, the healing, repair, education, and maturation of family units and of individuals within family units working with external caregivers—is a practice with a long-standing tradition. Rather than Gladding's short history of the secular profession of family therapy, we concur with McNeill that the care of families—that is, of soul care of the attached—is "a unique and sacred profession that spans the centuries" (1951, p. viii). In their classic work on the history of Christian ministry, Niebuhr and Williams (1956) cite cases of pastoral counseling ministry to families from the primitive church to the time of their writing in the mid-twentieth century. For example, they include Hudson's work on ministry in the Puritan era in which he cites the works of early American Puritan ministers who authored "family counseling manuals" available for pastors. "Even though many of the more prominent divines . . . busied themselves with the preparation of this type of literature, there was a continual demand for additional manuals or directories which would provide the clergy with guidance in dealing with 'cases of conscience' which they encountered in the course of their ministry" (Hudson, 1956, p. 196).

These manuals were the equivalent of pastoral case studies that provided family ministers with examples that served as templates for pastors to aid families with challenges to marriage, child development, employment, and economics. Hudson quotes Puritan pastor Richard Baxter: "We must have a special eye upon families to see that they be well ordered and the duties of each relation performed for if we suffer the neglect of this, we undo all. . . . You are likely to see no general reformation till you procure family reformation" (p. 194). Baxter goes on to state that one day a week was dedicated to visiting families in their homes within his parish so that by the end of a year's time he would have extended personal contact to each of the 800 families within his care (Hudson, 1956).

By far the most prominent tools used by the "family counselor" in this period of family ministry were the Sunday sermon delivered from the pulpit and the Sunday school for children. Learning of family life and thinking about resolving relational differences came from modeling conducted within one's own immediate and extended family and from the ministry received from the church. In our era, with the presence of a literate population, mass media, information technology, and professional services, the significance of a sermon as an educational tool and as the means by which a person received insight into repressed motives, realization of shortcomings, public and private declarations to change, and specific instruction toward effective living is not often perceived. The effect of the Christian pastor as a family counselor, mentor, model, teacher, and caregiver can be evidenced by the great British Baptist pastor Charles Haddon Spurgeon. In his book *Come Ye Children,* written to train parents and teachers to seek maturation in the children under their care, he writes,

> Next, get the children to love you, if you can. "Come, ye children, hearken unto me." You know how we used to be taught in the dame's school, how we stood up with our hands behind us to repeat our lessons. That was not David's

plan. "Come, ye children,—come here, and sit on my knee." "Oh!" thinks the child, "how nice to have such a teacher, a teacher who will let me come near him, a teacher who does not say, 'Go,' but 'Come!'" The fault of many teachers is that they do not get their children near them; but endeavor to foster in their scholars a kind of awful respect. Before you can teach children, you must get the silver key of kindness to unlock their hearts, and so secure their attention. Say, "Come, ye children." (1975, pp. 83-84)

The essence of family therapy in the prescientific era can be justifiably criticized for some of its methodologies, as is described by Kimball (2001). She points out that many "interventions" were based on guilt, manipulation, and coercion. She quotes John Wesley, cited in Moran and Vinovskis (1992), as saying, "It is this; never, on any account, give a child anything that it cries for. . . . If you give a child what he cries for, you pay him for crying: and then he will certainly cry again" (p. 349). In a similar fashion, Jonathan Edwards said, "The methods of disciplining most favored by evangelicals therefore had their most profound impact upon the moral conscience of evangelical children. For the rest of their lives, they would never be entirely freed from the pangs of guilt and the embarrassments of shame implanted within them during their earliest years" (p. 349).

While there was instruction and beliefs that maintained male dominance in social and political structures, the Christian counsel emerging from the Bible, theological systems, and the pragmatic Christian culture was that family members require mutual respect and support for survival. The predominating tone and instruction that emerges from the literature of early "pastoral family counseling" is the affection, care, and concern for every man, woman, and child. For example, McNeill (1951) writes of Ichabod G. Spencer, author of *A Pastor's Sketches or Conversations with Anxious Inquirers* (1850): "Mr. Spencer met his consultants with a gentle urgency that arose from confidence in his message and a genuine sympathy for mental suffering" (p. 262). Of Charles Spurgeon, who pastored in the 6,000-seat Southwark Tabernacle, London, McNeill writes that he was said to be a "counselor to many in person and letter" (p. 270).

To summarize the influence of the Christian tradition on forming family counseling skills, we can see that the cultural Zeitgeist spanning the centuries prior to the modern scientific era was for communities to encourage and at times coerce its members to adhere to a shared value. Individuals and adults responsible for nurturing, educating, and training their offspring to become mature adults were often encouraged to seek out the support, guidance, and wisdom of appointed or intrinsically gifted counselors.

## THE "GOLDEN ERA": FAMILY PSYCHOLOGY AS SCIENCE, 1950 TO 1980

The rise of science as a philosophy of life took a central place in the North American culture in the late 1800s and early 1900s. While beginning as a movement in science and technology, it encompassed all aspects of life, including theology, politics, education, art/literature, and economics.

As it pertains to formation of family therapy between 1900 and 1940 there was both a rise in the optimism of human potential and significant social change. Ernst Groves described these changes, including the alteration of gender roles, emancipation of women from single domestic duties, parenthood by choice, and the migration from rural to urban settings (Burgess, 1926). In addition, the modernist movement, which valued education, created an environment where lay and professional organizations were formed to help families adjust to the radical changes in the social structures. Education beyond grammar school became a middle-class value and expectation. Families shifted from rural agrarian to urban and suburban industrial and service economies. With this shift came the creation of new stressors—and new support systems to help families with the changes of modernity.

One of the early evidences of these changes occurred around 1905 with the Emmanuel Movement. Elwood Worchester, rector of the Emmanuel Church in Boston, was instrumental in the emerging science of therapy (Benner, 1998). By the influence of his personality he shaped an ecumenical movement that included adherents from most Christian denominations to seek to integrate the forming science of psychology to work with individuals, families, and groups (Gifford, 1998). Worchester sought to integrate the gentle work of a pastor with the science of human behavior emerging in Europe and North America:

> The two lines of thought from convergence of which this work sprang are the critical study of the New Testament and the study of physiological psychology. . . . I trust also that from the years devoted to the study of the life of Jesus some rays of His spirit, some feeling for the sorrows of men entered me. . . . From Fechner, Wundt and James, I learned how delicate and powerful an

instrument for the improvement of human life modern psychology places in our hands. (Worchester & McComb, 1909, pp. 10-11)

The influence of the Emmanuel Movement was directly linked to the development of Alcoholics Anonymous, and later group dynamic movement associations. Its importance in family therapy is that it served as a transitional link from the understanding of "therapy" as a ministerial duty toward the development of a profession of mental health clinicians that fifty years later would include marriage and family therapists.

There were many other early family therapy precursors. This list includes Hannah and Abraham Stone, a wife-husband physician team, who in 1929 established the first marriage clinic in New York City. Their book on marriage and family, *A Marriage Manual*, was first published in 1935 and went through twenty-two editions until it went out of print in 1952.

Emily Hartshorne Mudd formed the Marriage Council of Philadelphia in 1932, an organization targeted at providing counsel to families concerning marriage, sexuality, family formation, and child development. Her work led to the formation of a family studies program at the University of Pennsylvania and was influential in making Philadelphia an intellectual center of family therapy theory.

These and other individuals, such as Paul Popenoe in California, Ernest Groves in North Carolina, and Bela Mittleman in New York City, participated in forming organizations such as the National Council on Family Relations and the American Association of Marriage Counselors that preceded and helped seed current institutions that nurtured family therapy into a science and a profession. These organizations were designed to help families affected by the tumultuous years of the Great Depression and World War II.

Looking back, the years prior to World War II were characterized by the emergence of an important clinic here or an influential book there. Yet it was not a social movement or an emerging profession. However, immediately after the war new ideas were spawned about family intervention that led to the rapid coalescing of many theories and approaches to family intervention. Nichols and Schwartz's (2006) timeline of "Major Events in the History of Family Therapy" begins with Bertalanffy's presentation of general systems theory in 1945 (p. xi). The "Golden Age" is a term applied to a span of over three decades—from 1950 into the 1980s—in which family therapy theory was developed, institutions formed, and the profession established. The family therapy "giants"—Ackerman, Bateson, Bell, Bowen, Boszormenyi-Nagy, Haley, Jackson, Minuchin, Satir, Whitaker, and others—collaborated with one another to develop theory and technique. "These new-style of healers were pioneers, busily opening up new territory and staking their claim against unfriendly elements in the psychiatric establishment" (Nichols & Schwartz, 2006, p. 41).

The pioneering work accomplished by these early family therapists occurred in a context influenced by two important factors. First was the technology theory established through research and development stimulated by World War II. The second was the disease of schizophrenia.

World War II was fought in Europe, Africa, and the Asia-Pacific, but it was won in the laboratories and the factories of the United States. It could be said that the war was won by scientists—mathematicians, physicists, chemists, and engineers who designed machines, tools, and weaponry to defeat the Axis powers. The great minds of North American, European, and Asian technology were dedicated to winning the war effort—then in 1945 that energetic focus shifted from military to civilian applications. Bateson (1972, p. 474) describes it most succinctly in a quotation cited by Becvar and Becvar:

> Now I want to talk about the other significant historical event which has happened in my lifetime, approximately in 1946–1947. This was the growing together of a number of ideas which had developed in different places during World War II. We may call the aggregate of these ideas cybernetics, or communication theory, or systems theory. The ideas were generated in many places: In Vienna by Bertalanffy, in Harvard by Wiener, in Princeton by von Neumann, in Bell Telephone labs by Shannon, in Cambridge by Craik, and so on. All these separate developments in different intellectual centers dealt with different communication problems, especially with the problem of what sort of a thing is an organized system. (2006, p. 19)

The concept of systems thinking served as a transformational construct that continues to have a reverberating effect on technology. At that time, Norbert Weiner was developing at MIT the critical link between the perpetual feedback that could redirect machines and the internal psychological patterns of human thought developed by Freud and Jung (Becvar & Becvar, 2006, p. 18). Weiner referred to this feedback communication as cybernetics, in which a self-regulating system can "talk to itself." It can obtain information and feed that information back to other components of the system that prompt it to adjust. Machines can respond to data and implement alterations in order to maintain their designed or programmed function. Any machine that can turn itself on or off, such as a thermostat on a furnace, an electric eye on outdoor lighting, or the cruise control on our cars, utilizes cybernetic technology.

Weiner defined the information created by machines as either negative feedback or positive feedback. Negative feedback loops return a system to stability, positive feedback loops prompt a system to engage in change. Maybe because of the counterintuitive nature of negative and positive terminology, students often have difficulty distinguishing the two. Here is a story to illustrate the difference. The neighborhood boys are playing outside on a cold winter day. There is snow on the ground and sun in the sky. It's a great day for a snowball fight. Teams are chosen, boundaries marked, the snowballs start to fly. One boy realizes that he can throw ice chunks farther than snowballs, which allows his team to obtain an advantage. The other team has a shortage of ice in their territory, but they possess stones. One of the stones goes through a window, which prompts a parent to come out and deliver a scolding to the kids—"You know you are not supposed to do that . . ." After a brief cooling-off period the battle resumes but returns to the hurling of snowballs.

The positive feedback was the information that prompted the boys to escalate the "weapons of destruction" from snowballs to ice balls to rocks. These messages to the system are always change, change more, change again, increase speed, volume, mass, intensity, grow, expand, develop, *charge!!!*

On the other hand, negative feedback loops instruct the system to maintain and return to the limits of the range previously established. In this case, the parental intervention brought the boys back to the expected or the "normal." Systems that rely on positive feedback are in a perpetual expansion mode.

The idea of cybernetic systems crossed from the mechanical to the interpersonal when anthropologist Gregory Bateson, who was interested in human communication patterns, interacted with Weiner at a series of think tank conferences sponsored by the Macy family in New York beginning in 1946. "Attempting to understand how families in various cultures sustain stability, he introduced the notion that a family might be analogous to a cybernetic system in its use of self-regulating feedback mechanisms to maintain balance and constancy" (Goldenberg & Goldenberg, 2004, p. 15). A decade later, Bateson, having teamed with Don Jackson and Jay Haley, provided an important contribution to the theme of schizophrenia occurring in families by using these principles of feedback and communication.

## THE TREATMENT OF SCHIZOPHRENIA AND THE DEVELOPMENT OF FAMILY THERAPY

John Dillinger, the murderous bank robber and former "public enemy number one," was asked why he robbed banks. His response: "It's where the money is." When asking "How did family therapy come to be linked with schizophrenia?" the answer would the same. It was where the money was. World War II brought exposure to the disease of schizophrenia. The disorder commonly emerges in late adolescence and early adulthood—about the time that a generation of young men were being drafted and sent abroad. The number of new cases of schizophrenia occurring in young men while in the care of the US government prompted a significant amount of research dollars to be directed toward the development of medical and therapeutic interventions. Between 1940 and 1955 a number of large medical research grants were awarded. Many of the recipients of these projects were the founding thinkers of family theory—including Theodore Lidz, Lyman Wynne, Murray Bowen, Carl Whitaker, and Gregory Bateson, along with his associates Don Jackson, John Weakland, and Jay Haley. Becvar and Becvar state that "in an era of scientific prestige, schizophrenia loomed as mystery not amenable to solution by current therapeutic modalities. Thus, researchers were able to obtain grant money for the support of studies in this area, a factor whose importance must never be underestimated" (2006, p. 31).

Enter Freud. His writings were fundamental to the practice of psychiatry between 1900 and 1950; this remained true as the emerging discipline of psychology was developing its behavioral foundation. The deterministic perspective in psychoanalysis created an environmental implication for the cause of mental disorders: parents, especially mothers, did not fare very well. Any social scientist writing in that era seeking a "talking cause" and a "talking cure" would naturally be drawn to the influence of dysfunctional families—especially dysfunctional mothers. The frequently cited treatise espousing this concept was written by Frieda Fromm-Reichmann (1948). In this paper she used the term *schizophregenic mother*, laying responsibility for the formation of schizophrenia on mothers who displayed characteristics of domination, aloofness, detachment, and unpredictability. John Rosen (1962) theorized that it was just as likely that fathers were responsible for the formation of the disease. Haley, in summarizing the thinking at that time, wrote, "Typically the mother of the schizophrenic is described as dominating, overprotective, manipulative of the child and father, and also overtly rejecting. The father is usually described as weak and passive, holding aloof from the patient and occasionally overtly rejecting and cruel" (Haley, 1959, p. 357). To be fair, Fromm-Reichmann did not conclude that schizophrenia was caused by poor maternal parenting, only exacerbated by it.

The net result was that a number of emerging scholars launched a frenzy of empirical studies on the influence of family dynamics in the formation and management of schizophrenia. The effect was the formation of ideas pertaining to marriage and family interaction that served as new language in understanding conflicts occurring within families not addressing schizophrenia. These include *marital skew*, which was Theodore Lidz's discovery that dysfunction within a family was more likely related to conflict between adults than between adult and child; Murray Bowen introduced adult *differentiation* from the previous generation; Whitaker developed *conjoint marital therapy*; and the Palo Alto group brought the *therapeutic double bind* into the common vernacular. At the time that these ideas surfaced no one was intending to develop a new profession of family industry, but their combined research created a corpus of ideas that overflowed into the general population.

During the following decades the initial research was formalized into theories. Varying theories stirred debate that prompted the formation of formal organizations. The most prominent to emerge during this time was the American Association of Marriage and Family Therapists (AAMFT) in 1942. However, complementary organizations in psychology, counseling, and social work were also developed. The licensure in individual states and Canadian provinces began in 1970 and has continued to be a key factor in legitimizing marriage and family as a distinct mental health profession. "MFTs have sought legal recognition primarily because licensure has become synonymous with professionalism (Huber, 1994). And because reimbursements from health plans for providing clinical services are paid only to licensed providers" (Goldenberg & Goldenberg, 2004, p. 428).

## THE POSTMODERN, SOCIAL CONSTRUCTIVIST, AND CONSTRUCTIVIST MARRIAGE AND FAMILY THERAPY OF THE TWENTY-FIRST CENTURY

The current Zeitgeist of marriage and family therapies is a reflection of the contemporary practice of social science thinking. Theory in any scientific discipline is the product of its time. The theory does not emerge ex nihilo (that is, out of nothing). It is a result of the culture in which the thinkers think. That theory emerges within and is influenced by history and culture has been the motivation for the rethinking of many modernist, empirical assumptions. The "truth" of twentieth-century social science is in part a product of the twentieth-century history and culture.

Three related but slightly different terms have emerged that need definition: (1) postmodernism, (2) constructivism, and (3) social constructionism. *Postmodernism* refers to the broad social movement in the arts and sciences—including psychology, counseling, and marriage and family therapy—that challenges the previously held tenets of the "modern era." These challenges focus on the formation of "multiple realities" based on the experiences of the individual and the language used to describe those experiences (White, 1995). *Constructivism* emerged from the study of perception within cognitive biology. It is the belief that we hold perceptions or images about reality, never possessing the universal or absolute truth (Maturana, 1978). Finally, *social constructionism* is the view that reality is a product of communities or cultures. We build or construct a reality by putting words or language to our experiences and defining the experiences with meaning. The meaning is influenced but not controlled by our previous definitions and by the definitions that others have created to define similar experiences. Hoffman has created a humorous image of modern constructivist and social constructionist perspectives using the differing views of baseball's home plate umpires: "I call 'em as they are," says the modernist. "I call 'em as I see 'em," says the constructivist. And the social constructivist says, "There ain't nothin' till I call 'em" (Hoffman, 2002).

With this challenge to the assumptions of modernist truth the theories established in the past fifty years have been under reconsideration. The postmodern era has prompted us to reconsider our thinking of what family therapy is and how it is conducted. The theories that have driven the formation of the profession are seen to be cultural and historical creations that

are fluid and in transition. For example, in Western, economically advanta-
geous cultures, where individual autonomy and self-sufficiency are the principal cultural values, theories of individual and of marriage and family therapy
replicate the contours of the prevailing social mentality. Thus:

> The postmodern view of multiple realities is well suited to the concurrent
> acceptance of a widespread range of belief systems, the acknowledgment of
> the importance of cultural differences, and the growing awareness of the dif-
> fering experiences and perceptions encountered in growing up male or female.
> . . . That each person involved constructs his or her personalized views and
> interpretations of what they might be experiencing together—has a particu-
> larly significant impact on the field of family therapy. (Goldenberg & Gold-
> enberg, 2004, p. 321)

The scientific structure on which our "classic" family theories were constructed faced a significant challenge beginning in the final quarter of the
twentieth century—and will likely be a vociferous debate well into the twenty-
first century. Postmodern reflection sees the theories established and developed since the 1950s as encouraging a hierarchical family structure with
"dad at the peak, then mom, and the kids according to age and power." This
patriarchal structure of family was criticized as not just a cultural creation but
as restrictive to the development of human potential (Chodorow, 1978; Hare-
Mustin, 1978; Baber & Allen, 1992; Gilbert & Scher, 1999).

Furthermore, the nature of the therapeutic relationship established by the
modernist theories placed the therapist as the central point of power in the
family therapeutic process. The counselor assessed, diagnosed, and implemented a strategy or imposed a structure on the family to prompt change. This
created an impression of power held by the counselor that he or she did not
actually possess. Practitioners don't actually know why a family exhibits the
characteristics and behaviors of their unique system, nor do they have any
claim as to how it can be altered, or for that matter even whether it should be
changed. Because reality is seen as a construct developed by the participants,
any set of problems and solutions are not seen as preexistent but as created
entities (H. Anderson, 1994; T. Andersen, 1987; H. Anderson & Goolishian,
1988). A real problem exists when a family system creates an interpretation
of events as a "problem" or even a "crisis," then holds themselves imprisoned
by the circumstances and impotent toward any change. To counteract the

imbalance, therapeutic process was encouraged to be more collaborative and descriptive rather than authoritative and prescriptive (Hoffman, 1993).

To consider the origins of family therapy, from the perspective of the twenty-first century, we must look through nearly three hundred years of historical events, philosophy, and research. Gergen (2001) cites three themes emerging from the Enlightenment that formed the basis for science and the motivation for creating this new realm of thought—of psychology, or the study of the soul. These three themes were (1) the centrality of individual knowledge, (2) the objectivity of the material world, and (3) the stability and trustworthiness of language.

Regarding the importance of the *centrality of individual knowledge*, Enlightenment thinkers articulated a view that created the individual as a near "holy" institution and the mind as the ultimate in mystery and sovereignty— even greater than established political, religious, or social institutions. Descartes's "Cogito, ergo sum" exemplifies the idea that the human mind defines our existence. Moving from the Enlightenment to the age of modernity and science, Gergen states that "It is this 17th century construction of the individual mind . . . that served as the major rationalizing device for the nineteenth-century beginnings of systematic psychology. . . . The individual mind became the preeminent object of study" (2001, p. 804).

The second grand theme of the early twentieth century was the *objectivity of the material world*. Christian apologist and social critic Francis Schaeffer described this theme through the metaphor of a two-story house—with the bottom floor being "truth" based on science that is factual, measurable, stable, secure, reliable, valid, and discernable—real truth (Pearcey, 2005). The second floor, that of metaphysical truth, was subject to individual experience and opinion and was considered less reliable and with some sense of inferiority to the more important and reliable scientific truth. It is as if there is a real truth (science) and a nonreal or personal truth (metaphysics). This perspective on truth prompts the Western scientist to believe that the empirical investigation of truth (first-floor truth) is superior to all other methods in containing and understanding the causal relationships within our mental processes (Gergen, 2001).

The third theme regards the *stability and trustworthiness of language*. Mental health science from the modernistic era viewed language as the tool by which the human mind articulates its understanding of the objective world with other minds. To create a metaphor, if in the humanistic tradition each person is a god, then language is the priesthood that serves the gods. "We treat language as the chief means by which we inform our colleagues and our culture of the results of our observations and thought. In effect, we use language to report on the nature of the world as we see it" (Gergen, 2001, pp. 804-5).

Emerging in the scientific culture predominantly in the 1980s was a critique of these three themes and the presentation of alternative ways of understanding science, the profession, and the way that all psychotherapy, including family therapy, is conducted. Regarding how the theorists and practitioners saw themselves, the science that they created and the practice of family therapy was no longer considered a reflection of objective reality but a creation embedded in the time, condition, and culture of the creator. The individual mind was no longer viewed as the independent evaluator of knowledge. Rather, the individual is seen within a social, communal, and collective context.

Harlene Anderson (1997) advocated the premise that the individual was neither the creator of knowledge nor the one who can accurately determine the meaning of knowledge. The individual mind is second to the community mind. We are not individual thinkers but are individuals whose thought is influenced by the thoughts of others, particularly those who possess power and influence. This postmodern perspective on collectivism instead of individuality would appear to be a given within the systemic perspective. However, the modernist/empirical perspective of family theory and practice was that the theoretician and the therapist possessed an insight, skill, or competency that could assist the family in altering previous pathological patterns. In the postmodern era, there are no experts, authorities, or specialists. Family therapy is seen not as directed by the therapist but as an exploration conducted with the therapist (Gergen, 1985).

The clinician conducts a form of collaborative therapy because knowledge of a problem is not something that is objectively held; rather, it is seen as a characteristic that is socially constructed. "What one takes to be real, what one believes to be transparently true about human functioning, is a by-product of communal construction" (Gergen, 2001, p. 806). Most prominent in this collaborative effort of postmodern family therapy is the work of Norwegian Tom Andersen and his colleagues (1987, 1991). Andersen noted the supervision conversations post therapy to be an unusual therapeutic phenomenon. Noting two languages—the public talk, with the client, and the private talk, with colleagues—they sought to integrate the family within the conversation of the clinicians. This shift reveals an important emergence in the understanding and practice of therapy. Rather than the individual practitioner "helping" a family resolve a conflict or problem, the therapist participates in the search "for new descriptors, new understandings and new meanings" (Andersen, 1991, p. 65) with the family. The postmodern family therapist has turned from the clinician to the collaborator. Problems are not remediated or resolved, they are understood and redefined.

The understanding and re-creation of meaning occurs within the context of language. To postmodernists, all that is known is made possible only through language (Parry & Doan, 1994). This is particularly important for what is known about family—both in its motivation for seeking therapy and in the solutions that it implements. Gergen believes that languages will describe and explain and are always to occur within relationships (Gergen, 2001). These languages are not pervasive, like a therapeutic intervention; rather, they are created spontaneously by a family in the process of relationship. The counselor participates in the dialogue—becomes part of the family dialogue to assist it in understanding and accommodating the perspective needs of each member.

## POSTMODERNISM'S OFFSPRING IN MARRIAGE AND FAMILY THERAPY: FEMINISM AND MULTICULTURALISM

Postmodernism's effect on the profession of marriage and family therapy has encouraged two other crucial realms of thought: feminism and multiculturalism. In many ways, postmodernism and feminism emerged within the humanities and social sciences simultaneously. It was through the pathway established by postmodernism that feminist scholars questioned the formational structures of the field, and in true social constructionist fashion, feminist scholars were crucial in creating the perspectives that were defined as postmodern (Miller, 1976; Hare-Mustin, 1978).

Valued and highly regarded thought has been produced on this subject by scholars at the Stone Center for Developmental Services and Studies at Wellesley College; the work of Jean Baker Miller and her associates (1976, 1991) has provided challenging ideas to the meaning of feminine and masculine gender, the efforts that both men and women make for meaningful connection with family, and how family can both extend and impede an individual's dreams and aspirations for himself or herself.

Similarly, the multicultural emphasis within marriage and family counseling has found its voice along with the feminist perspective. McGoldrick, Pearce, and Giordano (1982) authored an important book in the early 1980s on which the emphasis of the profession has turned from a perspective of family "normalcy" that is North American, Caucasian, college-educated, and upper-middle class to a perspective that can transcend national, racial, generational, economic, and physical categories. "Multiculturalism has become a prevailing theme in family therapy, as reflected in conference agendas, journal articles, and graduate school curriculums. The attention to these issues represents a welcome sensitizing to the influence of ethnicity" (Nichols & Schwartz, 2006, p. 288).

## EMPIRICAL, POSTMODERN FAMILY THERAPY AND THE CHRISTIAN COUNSELOR: A TRIPARTITE UNION OF FAITH, PLURALISM, AND SCIENCE

We consider this era to be a unique, exciting, and pivotal period to be both a follower of Jesus and a counselor, psychologist, or therapist who conducts marriage and family interventions. In the spirit of thesis, antithesis, and synthesis, we have traced the movement of family intervention in this chapter from an exclusive activity of clergy, through the formation of a profession that held the therapeutic process to a near exclusivity against religious integration, to a postmodern era in which it becomes possible to be both Christian and explicitly professional simultaneously. We believe that it is no coincidence that the rise in masters and doctoral training programs in marriage and family therapy, counseling, and psychology has occurred at the same time that the profession was undergoing its postmodern, feminist, multicultural transformation. This is in no way to suggest that the postmodern movement is "Christian." However, there are components of postmodernism that have permitted Christian thinkers and practitioners to have a legitimate seat at the table of ideas.

The increase of institutions that seek to integrate Christian thought with the mental health profession has resulted in societies of scholars and volumes of quality scholarship that serve ministers and clinicians in their work with religiously committed families as well as provide a philosophical basis for the Christian engagement and participation in the broader professional culture. The scholarship emerging from Christian mental health has a powerful symbiotic relationship with Christian theology and with Christian ministry. The majority of academic Christian scholarship has emphasized the integration of psychology with Christian theology on a philosophical level. Scholarship such as that of Stanton Jones (1994) and Robert Roberts (1993) as well as many others provides thoughtful analysis, critique, and intervention in the pursuit of honoring the Christian tradition and respecting the complexity of the human condition. However, there are considerably fewer attempts to address the integration of family psychology with the Christian tradition. Balswick and Balswick (1989) and Garland (1999) are two exceptions. The former focus mainly on the sociological factors of family development, and the latter is a thorough guide to family ministry within the church context.

## CONCLUSION

Christian ministry has an important contribution to make to marriage and family therapy. It has been active in reconciling marriages and restoring families since the time of Jesus. The contribution to the process made by the profession of marriage and family has exponentially increased the knowledge available to the counselor, pastor, or therapist who is called to render assistance to family systems under strain.

The role that Christian pastors and counselors have played in the practice of family care extends beyond the relatively short existence of the mental health profession. However, the secular profession has overtaken counseling from a religious context because of the attention given by the broad culture toward professional interventions that have a scientific base. Christians are reclaiming some of their lost role by developing theory and demonstrating through empirical evidence the effectiveness of religious-based interventions for those families seeking assistance from that worldview. They are also demonstrating the effectiveness of religious-based intervention because of the key constructs introduced to the broader culture—such as fidelity, grace, forgiveness, reconciliation, justice—that have a positive effect on families apart from the family's adherence to any religious practice.

## REFERENCES

Andersen, T. (1987). The reflecting team: Dialogue and meta-dialogue in clinical work. *Family Process*, 26, 415-26.

Andersen, T. (1991). *The reflecting team: Dialogues and dialogues about dialogues.* New York: W. W. Norton.

Anderson, H. (1994). Rethinking family therapy: Delicate balance. *Journal of Marital and Family Therapy, 20*, 145-49.

Anderson, H. (1997). *Conversation, language and possibilities.* New York: Basic Books.

Anderson, H., & Goolishian, H. A. (1988). Human systems as linguistic systems: Preliminary and evolving ideas about the implications for clinical theory. *Family Process, 27*, 371-93.

Baber, K. M., & Allen, K. R. (1992). *Women & families: Feminist reconstructions.* New York: Guilford Press.

Balswick, J. O., & Balswick, J. K. (1989). *The family: A Christian perspective on the contemporary home.* Grand Rapids: Baker.

Bateson, G. (1972). *Steps to an ecology of mind.* New York: Dutton.

Becvar, D. S., & Becvar, R. J. (2006). *Family therapy: A systematic integration* (6th ed.). New York: Allyn & Bacon.

Benner, D. G. (1998). *The care of souls.* Grand Rapids: Baker.

Boszormenyi-Nagy, I., & Krasner, B. R. (1986). *Between give and take: A clinical guide to contextual therapy.* New York: Brunner/Mazel.

Bowlby, J. (1969). *Attachment and loss: Vol. 1. Attachment.* New York: Basic Books.

Burgess, E. W. (1926). The family as a unity of interacting personalities. *The Family, 7*, 3-9.

Chodorow, N. (1978). *The reproduction of mothering.* Berkeley: University of California Press.

Fromm-Reichmann, F. (1948). Notes on the development of treatment of schizophrenics by psychoanalytic psychotherapy. *Psychiatry, 11*, 263-73.

Garland, D. (1999). *Family ministry: A comprehensive guide.* Downers Grove, IL: InterVarsity Press.

Gergen, K. J. (1985). Social constructivist movement in psychology. *American Psychologist, 40*, 266-75.

Gergen, K. J. (1991). *The saturated self: Dilemmas of identity in contemporary life.* New York: Basic Books.

Gergen, K. J. (2001). *Social construction in context.* London: Sage.

Gifford, S. (1998). *The Emmanuel movement.* Boston: Harvard University Press.

Gilbert, L. A., & Scher, M. (1999). *Gender and sex in counseling and psychotherapy.* New York: Allyn & Bacon.

Gladding, S. T. (2007). *Family therapy: History, theory and practice.* Upper Saddle River, NJ: Pearson Prentice Hall.

Goldenberg, I., & Goldenberg, H. (2004). *Family therapy: An overview* (6th ed.). Pacific Grove, CA: Thomson Brooks/Cole.

Haley, J. (1959). The family of the schizophrenic: A model system. *The Journal of Nervous and Mental Disease, 129*, 357-74.

Hare-Mustin, R. T. (1978). A feminist approach to family therapy. *Family Process, 17*, 181-94.

Hoffman, L. (1993). *Exchanging voices: A collaborative approach to family therapy.* London: Karnac.

Hoffman, L. (2002). *Family therapy: An intimate history.* New York: W. W. Norton.

Huber, C. H. (1994). *Ethical, legal and professional issues in the practice of marriage and family therapy* (2nd ed.). New York: Macmillan.

Hudson, W. S. (1956). The ministry of the puritan age. In R. Niebuhr & D. Williams (Eds.), *The ministry in historical perspective.* New York: Harper & Brothers.

Jones, S. L. (1994). A constructive relationship for religion within the science and profession of psychology: Perhaps the boldest model yet. *American Psychologist, 49*, 184-99.

Kimball, C. N. (2001). Family brokenness: A developmental approach. In M. R. McMinn & T. R. Phillips (Eds.), *Care of the soul.* Downers Grove, IL: InterVarsity Press.

Lyle, R. R., & Gehart-Brooks, D. R. (1999). Postmodernism and divorce: Reflections on Gergen's notion of the saturation self in relation to modern divorce. *The Family Journal, 7*, 245-52.

Marx, M. H., & Cronan-Hillix, W. A. (1987). *Systems and theories in psychology* (4th. ed.). New York: McGraw-Hill.

Maturana, H. R. (1978). Biology and language: The epistemology of reality. In G. A. Miller & E. Lennenberg (Eds.), *Psychology and biology of language and thought.* New York: Academic Press.

McGoldrick, M., Pearce, J., & Giordano, J. (1982). *Ethnicity and family therapy.* New York: Guilford Press.

McNeill, J. T. (1951). *A history of the cure of souls.* New York: Harper & Row.

Miller, J. B. (1976). *Toward a new psychology of women.* Boston: Beacon.

Miller, J. B. (1991). Women and power. In J. V. Jordan, A. G. Kaplan, J. B. Miler, I. P. Stiver, & J. L. Surrey (Eds.), *Women's growth in connection: Writings from the Stone Center.* New York: Guilford Press.

Moran, G. F., & Vinovskis, M. A. (1992). *Religion, family and the life course.* Ann Arbor: University of Michigan Press.

Nichols, M. P., & Schwartz, R. C. (2006). *Family therapy: Concepts and methods* (7th ed.). Boston: Allyn & Bacon.

Niebuhr, R., & Williams, D. (Eds.). (1956). *The ministry in historical perspective.* New York: Harper & Brothers.

Parry, A., & Doan, R. E. (1994). *Story revisions: Narrative therapy in a post-modern world.* New York: Guilford Press.

Pearcey, N. (2005). *Total truth: Liberating Christianity from its cultural captivity.* Wheaton, IL: Crossway Books.

Roberts, R. R. (1993). *Taking the word to heart: Self and other in an age of therapies.* Grand Rapids: Eerdmans.

Rosen, J. (1962). *Direct psychoanalytic psychiatry.* New York: Grune & Stratton.

Spurgeon, C. H. (1975). *Come ye children.* Pasadena, TX: Pilgrim.

Stanton, G. T. (1997). *Why marriage matters.* Colorado Springs, CO: Piñon Press.

Whitaker, C. A., & Keith, D. V. (1981). Symbolic-experiential family therapy. In A. S. Gurman & D. P. Kniskern (Eds.), *Handbook of family therapy.* New York: Brunner/Mazel.

White, M. (1995). *Re-authoring lives: Interviews and essays.* Adelaide, Australia: Dulwich Centre Publications.

Worchester, E., & McComb, S. (1909). *The Christian religion as a healing power.* New York: Moffat, Yard.

# PART 2

# MODELS OF
# FAMILY THERAPY

# BOWENIAN
# FAMILY THERAPY

*But all that I could think of,*
*in the darkness and the cold,*
*Was just that I was leaving home*
*and my folks were growing old.*

**ROBERT LOUIS STEVENSON,**
**"CHRISTMAS AT SEA"**

IN THE SPORT OF BICYCLE RACING, the pack is your protection. The mechanical marathon is made grueling by isolation and individuality. All of the cyclists face the same hardship of hill and valley and distance. But when you break away from the pack, you must contend with the wind. It is the wind that saps the athlete of his or her stamina and speed. Cycling teams protect each other from the elements as they traverse the miles of roadway. Negotiating the terrain and strategizing against other teams, they try to place themselves in a position to launch one of their own ahead of the pack at the right instant to complete the race first, but not too prematurely so as to expose their designee to the restraining effects of wind and weather.

For Murray Bowen, Waverly, Tennessee—the small borough of a thousand people—was his team. Since the time of the American Revolution Bowen's forebears dwelled in Middle Tennessee. Multiple generations of Bowens lived in what is now Humphreys County. They worshiped at Bowen's Chapel, a Presbyterian church built on land donated by his family. His siblings and their descendants have remained in the area. But the eldest son of Jess Sewell Bowen and Maggie May Luff Bowen was launched by the team. After undergraduate and medical school training at the University of Tennessee, Bowen spent five years as an army surgeon in World War II. His experiences in the war prompted him to pursue a psychiatric specialization upon his return. He began to practice and conduct research at the Menninger Clinic in Topeka, Kansas, then as a researcher at the National Institute of Mental Health and at Georgetown University in Washington, DC.

## INTRODUCTION TO BOWENIAN FAMILY THERAPY

Bowenian family therapy is sometimes referred to as "transgenerational" family therapy because of its emphasis on spanning generations in its conceptualization of normal family functioning, family dysfunction, and methods of intervention. The theory is never far from the theorists. In the case of Bowen, the words that have emerged from his techniques are rooted in the bottomland of his family farm near the Tennessee River. Terms such as *triangles, differentiation of self, nuclear family emotional system, family projection process, multigenerational transmission process, emotional cutoff, sibling position,* and *societal emotional process* entered his awareness as a young man from a small country community, seeking to establish himself in the society of the university, within the tumults of a world at war, and finally as a medical scientist of the highest regard.

Bowen began his work as a psychiatrist with patients suffering from schizophrenia. Although he initially worked with individual patients, over time he began to include the mother and/or father in treatment, giving greater attention to the parent-child relationship and its influence on symptoms of mental illness. He shared how he began to observe a kind of emotional interdependence among family members evidenced in reciprocal relationships:

> A parent, for example, might feel and act "strong" in response to his or her schizophrenic child's acting "weak" and helpless. The schizophrenic child, in turn, would feel and act weak in response to the parent's acting strong. It was as if one person gained or "borrowed" strength in relationship to the other person having lost or given up strength. The functioning of one person, therefore, could not be adequately understood out of the context of the functioning of the people closely involved with him. (Kerr & Bowen, 1988, p. 7)

The reciprocity Bowen describes could be seen in overadequate/inadequate relationships in which one person did everything right while the other did everything wrong, as well as movement in cycles of distance and closeness in which family members would "move together, move apart, move together, move apart like an accordion" (Kerr & Bowen, 1988, p. 8).

This evolution led Bowen to see the family as the critical "emotional unit." In a paper presented in 1959 and later published in 1961, Bowen elaborated on "the family as the unit of treatment" (Bowen, 1961, p. 40). He began with the observation of "emotional oneness" between mother and psychotic patient. According to Bowen: "The oneness was so close that each could accurately know the other's feelings, thoughts and dreams. In a sense they could 'feel for each other,' or even 'be for each other'" (p. 40).

This idea of the family as emotional unit

> is the theoretical foundation from which family psychotherapy was developed as a logical orderly system. The terms "family as a unit" and "family unit" are used as short forms of "the family as the unit of illness." On one level this concept appears so simple and obvious that it hardly deserves second mention. On another level, the concept is subtle and complex, with far-reaching implications that involve a major shift in the way man thinks about himself and illness, and in the theory and practice of medicine. (Bowen, 1961, p. 40)

The shift from individual psychopathology to "family as a unit" represented a fundamental shift away from the individual that was and still is today so far-reaching in medicine: "The individual orientation in medicine is strict. It requires that the individual be called 'patient' and that individual pathology be defined with tests and labeled with a 'diagnosis.' Failure to focus on the individual can be regarded as medical irresponsibility" (Bowen, 1961, p. 40).

Although Bowen began to conceptualize "family as a unit" in the context of his work with patients suffering from schizophrenia, he eventually extended his theory beyond psychosis to various neuroses and to all families. The difference was one of degree. He developed a continuum called the "differentiation of self" scale, which conveyed this difference in degree:

> The scale was intended to convey the fact that not all families were the same in terms of their emotional functioning. Families that had serious clinical problems were *quantitatively* different but not *qualitatively* different from families that had less serious problems. (Kerr & Bowen, 1988, p. 12)

In keeping with this idea, Bowen would sometimes offer the quip that "there is a little schizophrenia in all of us" (Kerr & Bowen, 1988, p. 12). The person we identify as schizophrenic reflects a difference in degree of what we all reflect: "The schizophrenic person is more of a prisoner of his internal emotional reactions and of the emotional aspects of his environment than most people, but again, this is a quantitative difference from others and not a qualitative one" (p. 12).

Bowen's interest eventually extended beyond the limits of the family of origin. He included the role of the family over time. If the emotional unit of the family was to be understood properly, it would have to be understood across generations. After all, where does a person's ability to manage emotions such as anxiety come from? It is tied to what a person experiences in his or her family of origin—by the type of relationship with one's parents and how emotional relationships are resolved (or not) in early adulthood (Bowen, 1974). Hence, this approach to family therapy is sometimes referred to as "transgenerational" or "intergenerational" or just "Bowenian." The transgenerations of Bowenian therapy have emerged from a Bowenian family tradition. The theory is never far from the family.

## THEORETICAL AND PHILOSOPHICAL ASSUMPTIONS OF BOWENIAN FAMILY THERAPY

Recall from chapter two that general systems theory grew out of our understanding of physical systems created by human beings. These systems include the thermostat and computers, and the assumption is that various mathematical models are applicable to physical systems and to human systems. But Bowen disagreed with these assumptions. He understood the family to be a "naturally occurring system," believing that the family exists in nature without it having been created by human beings (Kerr & Bowen, 1988, p. 24). According to Bowen,

> The human family system sprung from the evolutionary process and not from the human brain. We did not create it. We did not design human relationships any more than the elephant or gibbon designed their family relationships. Family systems theory assumes that the principles that govern such things are there in nature for us to discover. (Kerr & Bowen, 1988, p. 24)

Bowen posits three systems that evolved in human beings: the emotional, feeling, and intellectual systems. The emotional system is closer to what most people today might refer to as animal instinct, and it is present in individuals and in families. Human beings are then higher-functioning animals with similarly emotionally determined behaviors. There is a distinction for Bowen, then, between emotions and feelings. Bowen would agree that lower-order animals do not have feelings, but he would say that they do have emotions:

> An example of emotionally determined behavior in a lower animal is the activity of a highly stimulated horde of soldier caste ants vigorously responding to intruders into their colony. The ants neither contemplate the meaning of their actions nor harbor strong nationalistic feelings; they simply *act*. (Kerr & Bowen, 1988, p. 30)

Bowen would see the development of the emotional system in human beings as more evolved than in lower animals, and it is experienced through generations:

> It must be understood that the emotional system is not just a happening, an accident. It has deep roots in the family tree and is passed down in changeable form through the generations. It is not uncommon to see a person involved in emotional systems that span three generations at the same time. The results of dysfunctional systems are emotional problems sprinkled throughout the family tree. Emotional problems represent the failure of the family to teach its members how to operate in emotional systems and maintain self-definition. (Fogarty, 1975, p. 83)

An emotional system is then passed down through generations—hence the focus on transgenerational family therapy. Our language today contains references to "enmeshment" and establishing healthy "boundaries" in relationships, and this language is tied in important ways to Bowenian theory about how emotional systems can be blurred in interpersonal relationships:

> Feelings . . . blur self boundaries because they have difficulty in discriminating between self and other in a close relationship. Because they blend into the other, they ordinarily see differences as liabilities, i.e., "Because I am this way, you should be this way too." In the process of diffusing into others, they seek certain reactions in response and cannot accept the other person the way he is. This sets up a struggle with the other and difficulties in direct proportion to the intensity and closeness of the relationship. (Fogarty, 1975, p. 85)

It was mentioned above that an emotional system exists for an individual and also for a family. Bowen referred to the emotional system in the family as the *nuclear family emotional system.*

Families can also raise children in an environment in which there is little differentiation of self; the child essentially experiences the enmeshment between the parents. This unhealthy family environment makes the child symptomatic, usually taking the form of dependency (Nichols & Schwartz, 2006). This is referred to as the *family projection process*, which we will discuss further below.

In addition to one's emotional system, people are also influenced by their intellectual system and their feeling system. The intellectual system reflects how people reason or process information and, thus, make changes, which we will discuss below. It is "that part of man's nervous system most recently acquired in evolution" (Kerr & Bowen, 1988, p. 31). The feeling system is considered the link between a person's emotional system and intellectual system (Jacobson & Gurman, 1995).

The ability to make decisions based on one's intellectual system—one's processing of information and reasoning—rather than one's emotional or feeling systems is called *differentiation of self* (Jacobson & Gurman, 1995). A person's failure to make decisions based on reasoning means that decisions will be made based on one's emotional system.

What about this idea of "differentiation of self"? Bowen posited that there is an

> instinctually rooted life force (differentiation or individuality) in every human being that propels the developing child to grow to be an emotionally separate person, an individual with the ability to think, feel, and act for himself. Also assumed is the existence of an instinctually rooted life force (togetherness) that propels child and family to remain emotionally connected and to operate in reaction to one another. The togetherness force propels child and family to think, feel, and act as one. The result of these counterbalancing life forces is that no one achieves complete emotional separation from his family. (Kerr & Bowen, 1988, p. 95)

As we have been suggesting, the critical issue for Bowen is the degree to which people are able to distinguish between feelings and reason so that they are free to choose to be guided by either feelings or reasoning (Kerr & Bowen, 1988).

The emotional systems we have been discussing are present in individuals but also in families. The emotional systems are thought to occur in families *in patterns*, so theorists like Bowen anticipated seeing sequences of fusion over years and eventually across generations in patterns that are played out time and time again. He referred to this as the *nuclear family emotional system*. These patterns might take the form of cut-offs and subsequent emotional fusion in relationships, or it could take the form of a less extreme form of general distance from others. Again, differences "in the severity of symptoms are quantitative and not qualitative" (Kerr & Bowen, 1988, p. 186). It is a matter of degree rather than kind. Bowen believed that these patterns could be evidenced in emotional problems in and among family members, where the patterns would be evidenced in marital conflict and in the impairment of children.

Let's elaborate briefly on the process that leads to children becoming impaired. When these nuclear family emotional systems are passed on to children over time—through a process mentioned above called *family projection*—the children risk becoming significantly affected. Such projection of the emotional system, according to Bowen, can lead to increased dependency by a child or greater behavioral problems that draw other family members in. Children can grow up in homes where it is unclear where they end emotionally and where their parents begin.

Eventually the family's emotion processes are passed from one generation to the next in a process referred to as *multigenerational transmission*. And children generally vary in how differentiated they are from their parents and other family members. Children caught up in enmeshed, emotionally fused relationships are less differentiated; those who are able to experience healthy boundaries between themselves and others in their family will be more differentiated. Bowen believed that people generally marry others at about the same level of differentiation of self, and recent research generally supports the idea that "family-of-origin processes are carried forward and transmitted to the next generation and suggest a means whereby this transmission occurs—differentiation of self" (Holman & Busby, 2011, p. 15).

The level and experience of differentiation of self, then, can be thought of as a result of relationships within one's family of origin. People become emotionally separated to the extent to which they are encouraged to demonstrate autonomy and individuality (Jacobson & Gurman, 1995). The ability to differentiate reflects the ability to manage the human tendency toward intimacy and meaningful relationships with the human tendency to maintain one's sense of self (Nichols & Schwartz, 2006).

The act of differentiation in current relationships involves separating out one's emotional and intellectual processes. The two ways to look at differentiation involve (1) an *interpersonal* dimension that entails differentiating oneself from others and (2) an *intrapersonal* dimension that involves regulating affect by differentiating one's feeling processes from intellectual processes (Holman & Busby, 2011; Jankowski & Hooper, 2012; Nichols & Schwartz, 2006). Regarding the former, differentiation of self involves having boundaries between oneself and those in one's family system. A person who is differentiated avoids emotional enmeshment or fusion; they are "flexible, adaptable, and more self-sufficient" (Becvar & Becvar, 2006, p. 147). Concerning the latter, differentiation of self also involves being aware of one's own feelings and the feelings of others, but in such a way that neither the person's feelings nor those of others dictate their behavior. Rather, the differentiated person's decision making is based on intellectual processes and a kind of emotional limit-setting that they can establish and maintain in relationships.

People create distance, then, in response to discomforting feelings in relationships. These distancing strategies can again be interpersonal or intrapersonal:

> Interpersonal distancing may be expressed behaviorally in geographic distance, lack of contact, and avoidance of personal conversation, eye contact, and touch. Intrapersonal distancing uses psychological mechanisms to manage the anxiety of close relationships. Some examples of intrapersonal distancing are denial of the importance of the relationships, lack of self- and/ or other-awareness, fantasy, repression, disassociation, distraction, blame, and lack of interest in self or the other. (Klever, 2015, pp. 339-40)

Bowen understood that two people relating to each other is a rather fragile arrangement and that these two people often bring a third person into the relationship to manage anxiety that exists in the relationship. For example, a husband and wife might deal with anxiety in their relationship by drawing in one of their children. This act of bringing in a third person to stabilize the couple is referred to as *triangulation*. It is essentially a way for two people to avoid resolving the conflict in their relationship as the focus often diverts to the third party that is brought into the exchange. Triangulation is a common experience in a lot of relationships; it becomes a problem to the extent that the two original persons need to resolve problems but are unable or unwilling to do so.

Research on Bowenian concepts has included measurement and operationalizing of the construct of differentiation of self. For example, while the Differentiation of Self Inventory had been previously developed, it was revised and recently validated (see Differentiation of Self Inventory-Revised; Skowron & Schmitt, 2003; Jankowski & Hooper, 2012). We have also seen applications of Bowenian concepts in research and applied contexts, such as with couples (e.g., Bartle-Haring & Lal, 2010; Holman & Busby, 2011). Bowenian concepts have also been studied with reference to diverse ethnic groups (e.g., Chan, 2013; Sauerheber, Nims, & Carter, 2014), attachment theory (e.g., Dallos & Vetere, 2012), spirituality (e.g., Heiden Rootes, Jankowski, & Sandage, 2010), and trauma services (e.g., MacKay, 2012).

## WHEN FAMILIES SEEK HELP

When family therapists consider what is happening when families seek help, they are often looking at what constitutes dysfunction. However, for Bowen, the primary focus was on differentiation, which is again related to the concept of an emotional unit.

The problems identified by the family are thought to be a reflection of the emotional systems in the family system. Family emotional systems are "vulnerable to dysfunction" (Fogarty, 1975, p. 87), and what happens is that family members will

> freeze automatically into a reactive, predetermined, triangular emotional system. Tension mounts, paralysis of thinking ensues, and freedom and self-determination are lost. In these frozen areas, people have a certain set of mind. Once triggered, the patterns are predictable, automatic, and self-sustaining. (p. 87)

The presenting problems are essentially symptoms of the anxiety discussed above, which is a reflection of emotional fusion: "The initial step in the development of a dysfunctional emotional system is the process of fusion. This starts as a tendency to fuse, attempts a fusion by one or more people, and finally the state of emotional fusion. This is a blending of one self into another" (Fogarty, 1975, p. 88).

Another way to discuss emotional fusion is to talk about a lack of differentiation of self. When families are dysfunctional, "Separation of self from the other becomes increasingly difficult. Inner balance and self-determination yield to behavior determined by reaction to others" (Fogarty, 1975, p. 87). Symptomatic behavior, then, reflects various degrees of differentiation of self.

From the perspective of the symptomatic family member, it can be helpful to remember that when a child grows up with very little differentiation of self, he or she is enmeshed—that is, he or she is essentially living out the emotional fusion that naturally results from not being able or given permission to make the transition from dependent child to independent young adult (Jacobson & Gurman, 1995). What that child is left with is a great deal of anxiety. According to Bowen (1961), anxiety is inevitable. The real question is what a person does with the felt anxiety:

> When anxiety increases, one has to decide whether to give in and retreat or carry on in spite of it. Anxiety does not harm people. It only makes them uncomfortable. It can cause you to shake, or lose sleep, or become confused, or develop physical symptoms, but it will not kill you and it will subside. People can even grow and become more mature by having to face and deal with anxiety situations. (Bowen, 1961, p. 56)

The anxiety felt at this point will be exacerbated in intimate relationships. To manage the conflict and anxiety, people who are not particularly differentiated will draw a third person to stabilize the relationship they have with their partner. The more differentiated the person is, the less the need to bring a child or other person into an emotional triangle (Jacobson & Gurman, 1995).

Family therapists can look for the tendency to pull a third person to stabilize a relationship (triangles) and other clinical indicators of this fusion and enmeshment. These include a kind of "emotional turmoil" that both reflects and can lead to "loss of individual self-definition" (Fogarty, 1975, p. 88). The individuals in the family are unable to maintain clear emotional boundaries in their relationships.

We already mentioned a common way to manage chronic anxiety: pull a third person in. In other words, a couple can manage anxiety in a marital system by projecting the problem onto a third party, usually a child. This is not a conscious act; rather, the parents may relate to their children or a specific child in a way that subtly reinforces the expression of pathology. It is also possible for a child to "act out" to bring parents who are not stable back together to provide a sense of stability to the marital dyad.

> Triangles stabilize by their structure of two against one, by avoiding confrontation between two people, by freezing the entire situation without a change in self, . . . by providing a third party to drain feelings onto, by defocusing

some of the real issues, by fostering one person focusing on the other, and by fostering the indirect and displaced expression of feelings away from the original object or person. (Fogarty, 1975, p. 91)

This act of triangulation stabilizes the relationship by allowing each person to focus on the third person.

In addition to creating triangles in relationships, less differentiated persons can create emotional distance (e.g., through silence, disinterest, and depression) or conflict (e.g., by magnifying the inadequacies of one's partner) (Jacobson & Gurman, 1995). In fact, it is this capacity to create emotional distance that accounts for the pursuer-distancer dynamic in marriage. Other dynamics may also be present. For example, one of the partners in a marriage may be symptomatic because of the accommodations negotiated in the marriage relationship. One partner may be passive with another who is assertive. In another marriage, one partner may be the caretaker while the other is needy and underfunctioning.

When thinking about family relationships from a Bowenian or transgenerational perspective, it can be tempting to think of a cut-off as boundary-setting in relationships—as a reflection of healthy differentiation of self. However, for Bowen, an emotional cut-off actually reflects an effort to protect oneself from a feeling of being lost or engulfed by either another person or by the system (Jacobson & Gurman, 1995). It is the result of and reflects extreme enmeshment.

## THE APPROACH TO FAMILY THERAPY

The theory underlying transgenerational family therapy provides a map for change in the family system. The family therapist wants to help individuals in the family increase their differentiation of self. This is in contrast to a number of other family therapy models in which the family therapist attempts to change the system to affect change in all of the individuals; rather, the transgenerational family therapist works with an individual—typically the most differentiated family member—to bring change in the family system (Nichols & Schwartz, 2006). As Fogarty (1975) puts it:

If one member really changes himself and refuses to play his part, the dysfunctional system cannot last. Others must pull out of the system and establish a new one or change. Therefore, real change can be accomplished by *one or more* members of the family who have the capacity and determination to carry it through. (p. 95)

Again, this comes directly from the theory that assumes that "If one member of a family has an *emotional* problem, others in the family do" (Fogarty, 1975, p. 96). In terms of family therapy, if one family member can have success in achieving greater differentiation of self, this will lead to changes in the family system, which will then aid in further differentiation of self in that family member.

Because of the role of the emotional process in leading to symptoms, the transgenerational family therapist wants to address both the level of anxiety and the level of differentiation of self among family members (Nichols & Schwartz, 2006). This involves asking questions that help to keep anxiety low and manageable, questions that help the person think about the challenges he or she is facing. Commonly, transgenerational family therapists ask *process questions*. For example, if a family therapist were meeting with a couple about the arguments they have about managing their finances, the therapist might ask questions like this:

THERAPIST: "What makes talking about finances so difficult?"

HUSBAND: "I get angry about how she overspends."

THERAPIST: "How do you express your anger?"

HUSBAND: "I blow my lid. Or I slam the door. I'm not subtle."

Process questions help people think through their concerns rather than have a strong emotional response in that moment. To the wife in this scenario, a family therapist might ask the following:

THERAPIST: "Can you tell me about how you think about the family finances?"

WIFE: "I know that I spend more than he wants me to, but I don't like being yelled at."

THERAPIST: "Do you have a sense for what makes him angry?"

WIFE: "Not really. We still have plenty of money. It's not like we can't pay the bills or anything."

THERAPIST: "If he could find a way to talk with you about it, would you be open to hearing him out?"

These are the kinds of questions that help an individual think about what is going on in an exchange that is often emotionally overwhelming. The questions themselves are intended to lower anxiety by focusing on the process both inside the person (e.g., *anger* about the spending behavior of his spouse) and also between people (e.g., *the way he expresses* his anger).

One goal in asking process questions is to help people think about the challenges they are facing. This is in stark contrast to the tendency among many clients to react to their conflicts.

Another goal of process questions is to enable a client to begin to see the "dance" that occurs in the relationship. The person can begin to understand and track the sequences or "steps" that are present that lead to the conflict. This helps the client recognize the emotional processes that are happening in relationships. This is partly didactic: the family therapist can educate family members on the functions of emotional systems for individuals and for the family (Jacobson & Gurman, 1995). Bowen would often liken the therapist's role to a "coach," with the idea of helping the client recognize the triangles and begin to identify ways to remove himself or herself from those triangles—that is, to stay de-triangulated in family relationships.

The family therapist also coaches the client on how to establish (or re-establish) person-to-person relationships with each member of his or her family so as to avoid relating (or not) to family members through others. Because other family members are not privy to all of the work the client is doing in Bowenian family therapy, the family therapist can help the client stay calm and rational in each exchange—with those he or she is initiating contact with as well as with those who may become emotionally "activated" by the fact that the client has established contact.

Another expression of differentiation of self is to use "I language" or to take an "I position" in all relationships. By establishing and maintaining person-to-person relationship, the client is now able to relate to others as a person rather than react to emotional dynamics in the family system. One way to consolidate these changes is to talk to others by speaking only for oneself—to speak of personal feelings and thoughts rather than parrot back the status quo or what has been given the "green light" by other family members. It can take several sessions to come to a place where a client is confident about his or her feelings on a subject. The family therapist is patient in working with a client who has never had to come to his or her own conclusions on a subject.

Another helpful clinical tool is the *genogram*. Bowenian family therapists often use genograms at the outset of therapy to aid in assessment of family information. Genograms provide a visual map of family relationships, and family therapists typically include three generations or more when they map out the family (see McGoldrick, Gerson, & Shellenberger, 1999). Common questions when gathering information for a genogram are factual: Who is in your family? When were they born? Where do they live? Where do they work? and so on. Major life events are also assessed, such as marriages, separations, divorces, deaths, geographic moves, and traumatic events. It is also common to ask about family strengths and resources, such as humor; expressions of affection and negative emotions, such as anger; and religious or spiritual beliefs, values, and rituals. The genogram allows family therapists to then illustrate the dynamics of closeness, enmeshment, emotional cut-offs, triangulation, and so on. Genograms can also be adapted to specifically address religious and spiritual themes and milestone events (see Frame, 2000).

When working with more than one person, the therapist continues to ask questions to help family members think about their present conflicts. The therapist is looking for topics or exchanges that reflect a kind of emotional sensitivity in which one or more persons is reactive or activated emotionally. A challenge rests in doing this in a way that resists the emotional pull toward triangulation between the family therapist and family members. Marriage therapy in particular assumes a kind of triangle from the outset, so the family therapist is to be aware of this dynamic and of the tendency on the part of both partners to pull the family therapist to their side in a conflict or to create an emotional reaction by the therapist that might draw the couple together (Nichols & Schwartz, 2006).

The family therapist at this point stays objective and neutral, not taking sides or allowing himself or herself to be drawn into the emotional triangle. By staying with the facts of the conflict—by discussing the issue itself and not becoming emotionally reactive to one another or the therapist, the couple may be able to hear one another, perhaps for the first time (Nichols & Schwartz, 2006). For the Bowenian family therapist, the content or subject matter is largely irrelevant—it can be thought of as the stage on which the drama in the family is acted out. What is most important is the emotional process between the couple, and the family therapist can begin to coach awareness of the process regardless of the content. This is the beginning of differentiation of self, and it is modeled by the family therapist and coached throughout the process.

## CASE ILLUSTRATION

Charlie, age twenty-seven, has been married for three years. When he first came in for therapy, he and his wife were expecting their first child. He initially requested help because of struggles with Internet pornography, finding himself conflicted about habits he had formed in college and frustrated with himself for what he saw as a "constant temptation." Charlie worked in therapy to learn the cycle of behavior that was distressing to him, and he was able to interrupt patterns of viewing and to manage his environment effectively in this regard.

As he was making significant progress in this area, Charlie shared some family struggles he was having. He shared that he grew up with a lot of verbal and emotional chaos in his home, with his father and mother constantly bickering. His parents divorced when he was twelve years old, and ever since that time he has genuinely struggled with each of them vying for his allegiance by trying to draw him in as a confidant against the other. When his father remarried a year and a half ago, Charlie felt especially conflicted, wanting to be happy for his father but feeling protective of his mother, who used the occasion to try to draw Charlie in to her and against his father and his new wife.

The renewed conflict between his father and mother led his father to appeal to Charlie to see that his mother and her side of the family were really against him and quite unfair and mean-spirited. He often strongly insisted that Charlie break off contact with his mother and that side of the family until they began to treat him better.

It was clear at this point that Charlie would benefit from some coaching of differentiation. This began with an explanation of what it means to be enmeshed or emotionally fused with others in one's family—the idea that it can be hard sometimes to know where Charlie ends and where his father or mother begins, at least emotionally. A genogram helped map some of the key people in the family, as well as Charlie's perceptions of emotional closeness, distance, conflict, and cut-offs. Just the act of completing a genogram provided an opportunity to think through what was happening in his family rather than experience at an affective level what was happening in the family. The genogram included a discussion of how strong emotions, such as anger and affection, were expressed in the family.

Completing the genogram also led to a discussion of qualities and characteristics Charlie sees in his father and mother that he sees in himself. As uncomfortable as this can be—many clients do not care to admit to similar-ities in personality, temperament, and so on when they are struggling with parent–adult child relationships—it can be helpful to identify these features as well as qualities that Charlie either does not see that he shares with either parent or qualities he would like not to see as much in his own life. This helps him complete a cognitive exercise by reflecting on each of his parents and distinguishing himself from them in meaningful ways rather than emotionally reacting to them and their way of drawing him in.

Charlie was also able to hear that geographical distance (his mother and father lived in two different states and approximately ten- to twelve-hours' drive away from him and his wife) did not represent a true boundary in rela-tionships. The boundary is an emotional one, and the boundary we were working on could be in place and exist whether they lived miles apart or in the same town.

At this point it was helpful to take existing exchanges between Charlie and each of his parents and practice distinguishing between his emotional re-action to them and ways in which he was able to process at a cognitive level what was happening in the exchanges. Charlie also clearly communicated to his father his intention to remain in relationship with his mother. The idea is that Charlie is forming person-to-person relationships with each member of the family and that he is not going to cut off from anyone because of the strained relationship his father and mother now have. Charlie also set and reinforced limits with both his father and his mother—limits as to what he would talk about—so that they could develop a relationship with Charlie that was not predicated on disdain for one another. He would not allow either of them to hook him emotionally or to form an emotional triangle.

Coaching differentiation is challenging work, and Charlie struggled at several points with guilt when he set limits or tried to reinforce them. It often meant drawing conversations to a close or giving one of his parents the choice to change the subject or have to wrap up a phone call. "You seem so cold," might be a comment he would hear as he took these new steps. Charlie was not interpersonally cold or aloof, of course. But these new boundaries were unfamiliar and uncomfortable for both of his parents (and for Charlie, for that matter), and it took time to really establish the expectation that he could be in relationship with each parent and do so without the relationship being at the expense of another.

## CHRISTIAN PERSPECTIVE ON BOWENIAN
## FAMILY THERAPY

*Theoretical and philosophical assumptions.* It was mentioned above that Bowen is committed to an evolutionary perspective that sees human beings as higher animals as compared to carpenter ants or dolphins. According to Bowen, we share similar systems with these animals, such as the emotional system, but we have more evolved intellectual and feeling systems.

The major concern we have with evolutionary theory as applied to human functioning and behavior or to family systems is that it is utterly reductive in its understanding of human relationships. We do not argue against the claim that humans have instincts that we might refer to as an emotional system, or even that emotion may contribute to how we relate to one another. But we see no need to embrace the view that this drive is as primary and fundamental as Bowen treats it.

From a Christian perspective, human behavior and relationships can be thought of with reference to our will and our reason as well as the role of feelings in our interactions with others. Bowen is committed to finding commonalities among all animals, and he sees this "instinct" as one way to communicate this. Christians may adopt a similar line of reasoning and see some models of evolutionary theory as attractive, but they are not obligated to make this connection and may reject it for various reasons. In the end, Christians will affirm not only reason and the will but also a motivation to live in response to transcendent reality and the claims of that reality on our lives.

In offering these comments, we acknowledge that Christians do not have to reject all of evolutionary thought. Christians may be drawn to versions of microevolutionary thought that provide testable hypotheses, theories that may explain subtle species adaptation without a worldview or philosophy or explanation for morality. This is similar to how Christians may draw on concepts from any number of first-generation theories in their clinical practice by utilizing empirically validated interventions while rejecting an utterly reductionistic and deterministic worldview found in some specific models.

Some students and many instructors are drawn to Bowen because of his appreciation for theory. Granted, Bowen's theory drew heavily on evolutionary theory. In some ways this allows Bowen to offer a much richer and more comprehensive understanding of the family. What we appreciate about Bowen's high regard for theory is that it contrasts sharply with other models of family therapy that are technique-driven, in that they focus pragmatically on what works, with much less regard (if any) for a comprehensive theory of the family. Other students, as we have mentioned, are drawn more to techniques than theory, especially early in their training, and so because Bowen is not technique-driven, these students often shy away from the model. This is unfortunate because there is a great richness in Bowenian family therapy due in large part to the theoretical comprehensiveness of the model itself.

Differentiation of self is an important mark of emotional maturity. If we were to take Bowen's assertions regarding emotional systems at face value, we do not believe it is God's intention to have his followers so emotionally reactive to each other that inevitable conflicts are the norm or that the believer is driven by his or her emotional reactions to people with whom he or she knows intimately. Differentiation of self is a valued emotional milestone that calls for proper exercise in relationships. Put differently, we might as Christians take issue with the evolutionary assumptions that tie differentiation of self to the emotional systems as human "instinct," but we can see tremendous value in exploring the ways in which human beings react to one another based on a blurring of emotional boundaries in family relationships.

The idea of losing ourselves in others through blurred emotional boundaries is an interesting one. To the Christian, we are taught to sacrifice ourselves in relationships. We are to lay down our lives for Christ and to relate to others in a spirit of humility. The ability to be self-differentiated, however, seems to us to provide opportunities to actually make meaningful sacrifices in relationships. We then have the freedom to obey God. If a person is never differentiated emotionally from others, that person loses himself or herself in others and is not truly offering a sacrifice or living sacrificially. The choice to do so is made for that person. In contrast, differentiation of self prepares the Christian for emotionally healthy relationships, not only by helping establish a sense of self but also because that very self can then make meaningful decisions about the nature of the sacrifices made on behalf of the Christian.

> A chief aim of Christian psychotherapy will be to foster an awareness of connection to others—in friendship, parenthood, filiality—so that the individual lives beyond the confines of his own psyche, as it were, ready to sacrifice his own interests, achievements, self-cultivation, and prominence for the sake of the other. For in such "loss of self"—in such love—is to be found, according to Christian teaching, the truest selfhood. (Roberts, 1993, p. 228)

Emotional fusion may result from blurred boundaries in relationships, such that a person has no sense of his or her own feelings but is always reacting to the emotional experiences of others. Emotional fusion reflects the lack of a strong, clearly identifiable, independent self. However, Christians may make choices that appear to reflect emotional fusion to the outside observer precisely because they have laid down their lives to give to others.

Differentiation of self is really meant to be an expression of mutual respect. It means living one's emotional life and allowing others to have their emotional life. There may be times when a Christian is also called to self-sacrifice that reflects a kind of emotional interdependency, and this may illustrate what Roberts refers to as "proper self-sacrifice, communal mutuality, proper caring, and helpfulness [that teaches] positively what it is to be a self so integrated that it can be genuinely for others" (1993, p. 231).

We should note, too, that to the Christian, maximized differentiation of self is not the pinnacle of human existence. While it is an important mark of emotional maturity, there is no identifiable line that is crossed that marks something essential to one's spiritual life. We see a difference in the developmental necessities of differentiation of self as a means for personal growth and genuine interpersonal relationships, and the psychological formations of differentiation as the definition and execution of life purpose.

In addition, Bowenian or transgenerational family therapy is truly systemic (Nichols & Schwartz, 2006). This may seem strange given that the therapy can be provided to an individual, but it is systemic in terms of who is taken into consideration in case conceptualization. Contrast Bowenian theory with narrative theory and therapy, which focuses not on patterns or systems but on deconstructing and co-constructing stories, and it is perhaps more readily apparent that Bowen's approach is concerned with *systems* that can be understood with reference to individual and family emotional units and how they relate over time. So while the treatment unit may not be systemic, the people represented by the presenting concern in an individual reflect a systemic emphasis.

Finally, we are drawn to the idea of raising others up. That is, we like the notion of being responsible for oneself to some extent but also of allowing changes in one's life to have an impact on those with whom we are interdependently related. If one member of the family grows toward greater differentiation of self, it has the potential to impact others in their differentiation of self.

*Model of family dysfunction and family functioning.* The continuum of functioning that Bowen espoused meant to Bowen that it is somewhat an arbitrary cut-off to claim that one family is "normal" and another family is "pathological" (Kerr & Bowen, 1988, p. 13). He saw the continuum reflecting gradations between families. Bowen is essentially locating normal family functioning on one end of a continuum and recognizing that we are more alike than we are different. He does not, then, have a specific view of the healthy family, although it would presumably be one in which emotionally differentiated selves relate with one another as governed by their intellectual systems.

In this sense Bowen may have been too suspicious of feelings. This makes some sense in light of the origins of Bowen's work with persons suffering from schizophrenia and the family therapy that followed as well as the ongoing research on emotionally charged exchanges and how they exacerbate already fragile and vulnerable relationships.

His concern with emotional reactivity stands in marked contrast to other models that tap into affect to promote healing and resolution of conflict (e.g., experiential family therapy). By identifying emotional reactions as reflecting enmeshment and a failure to differentiate, emotions in general can be viewed negatively. Positively stated, Bowenian family therapists help us remember the role of our thoughts in regulating emotions, and this can be a helpful corrective in many emotionally charged situations and relationships.

The potentially positive role of feelings is not well developed in Bowenian theory, however, and this has not been the case in the history of the Christian church. Rather, there is much throughout the history of pastoral care that has pointed to the importance of affections, a word that brings together both emotions and the will.[1] For example, in *The Religious Affections*, Jonathan Edwards (1746/1971) argued that what Christians ought to be concerned with are the objects of given emotions. For instance, love has God as its object, while hatred has sin as its object. We are to long for justice and express gratitude for God's blessings. Christians are concerned with the formation of some emotions and the eradication of others (Evans, 1992; Roberts, 1992). As Roberts suggests, certain emotions should characterize us as persons. For instance, we ought to be characterized by joy, gratitude, hope, and peace (which Roberts refers to as "emotions-as-character traits"). Likewise, hatred, envy, contempt,

---

[1]This section is adapted from Mark A. Yarhouse (2000), The vice of envy: Insights from the history of pastoral care, *Journal of Psychology and Christianity*, 19(1), 25-37.

and anger may be responses to various life circumstances or injustices and are only indirectly related to the Christian life; they are not meant to characterize us as persons.

## A REDEMPTIVE FOCUS ON FAMILY FUNCTIONING

We see reason as playing a positive role in regulating affect and in contributing positively to healthy family relationships. Recall that reason is often identified as a reflection of the *imago Dei*.

There is value in distinguishing between our feelings and our reasoning. We believe that many families function better for becoming increasingly aware of their feelings and their thinking. But there is a risk with Bowen that we will think of the fall as affecting only our feelings but not our capacity to reason. No, the Christian recognizes that the fall affects both our heart and our head.

Our minds can serve as a helpful resource both when our emotions are activated and when taking the lead in how we relate in specific situations and relationships, but we must be humble in our appraisal of our reasoning as well. We have found that classic spiritual disciplines of prayer, solitude and silence, and study of Scripture often help guide our minds and our hearts, and that gains made through these ancient practices can be brought into interpersonal and familial relationships.

*Think about it*: In what ways have you found it helpful to think through your emotional reactions to specific people? If you have been able to respond more out of your rational thought processes than emotional reactivity, what are some specific strategies you employ to guide your thought processes?

We can begin to see the potential value in understanding the positive role emotional reactions may play if we can assist people in understanding them to a greater degree. What Roberts, Evans, and others are suggesting is something more like character formation based on a deeper and richer understanding of our emotions. Put differently, our emotions signal ways in which our character is shaped over time, and therapy is a setting in which emotions, concerns, and passions overlap to shape and constitute our character (Roberts, 1988, 1992).

A family therapy that is truly Christian could recognize the potential value in distinguishing between emotional reactions and rational thought processes so that a person is not emotionally reactive to others and can draw on rational thought processes in determining how best to relate to others. At the same time, a Christian understanding of family therapy would not want to dismiss emotional reactions as unhelpful or as having little to say to us about our character as well as the nature and quality of our interpersonal relationships. Rather, Christians utilize insights gained from close attention to their emotional life so that they can begin to see how to shape the contours of their emotional life and eventually their character (as they become characterized by their emotions over time). As we have seen, certain emotions ought to characterize the Christian (e.g., hope), while other emotions (e.g., anger) may be experienced by Christians from time to time, but they do not characterize the Christian as such (Roberts, 1988). A family therapy that places higher value on the emotional life of persons will work with clients to identify and build on emotions that lay the foundation for relationships characterized by increased trust, mutuality, justice, and humility.

In these comments we are beginning to see what is perhaps the greatest criticism of Bowenian family therapy; that is, it does not recognize a real and meaningful relationship with a living God, and so the concepts developed by Bowen do not reference transcendent reality, an aspect of life that is fundamental and profound to the Christian. A secular theory like Bowen's can lead to a kind of life centered on oneself insofar as clients are attempting to take "I positions" in all of their relationships. While this is intended to avoid enmeshment, the pendulum may swing the other way, and a truly Christian understanding of these concepts unpacks them further so that the family therapist assesses the person's capacity to relate to God in a way that avoids relating *on one's own terms* but rather is an expression of the love God wants us to have toward him.

*Techniques in transgenerational family therapy.* We have mentioned throughout this chapter that Bowenian or transgenerational family therapy is more theory-driven than technique-driven. It is a strength of this model of family therapy. One result, however, is that there are not that many techniques to critique. The primary techniques of transgenerational family therapy are modeling and coaching the differentiation of self in family relationships.

But it may be helpful to reiterate that modeling and coaching the differentiation of self in family relationships is based on the premise that it is best to focus on the health and maturity of individual family members who are in relationship with one another. To explore the implications of this premise, it can be helpful to recognize that, from a transgenerational perspective, the essence of relationship is how multiple persons will occupy the same or adjacent space. Jacobson and Gurman (1995) offer a helpful analogy in which relationships can be thought of as adjoining plots of land that are separated by markers or boundaries. So from this point of view the land is separate, yet since it has shared boundary lines, there are also common interests. Further, these common interests, whatever they may be, will mean there exists the potential for conflict, particularly at the borders, where one plot adjoins another. But it is at these borders that we may also find resources for support and encouragement, as when landowners get together at the fence to talk, share, encourage, and visit. But these borders can also be where fighting will occur— "I just think I will throw my trash on the other side of the fence." Or "My neighbor (spouse, partner, child, parent, friend, employer) is not doing his or her responsibility, and it's having a negative effect on my space."

Bowenian family therapists, then, address at least to some extent both the borders between the plots of land (i.e., boundaries) and the plots of land themselves (i.e., the individuals). They do this, again, by modeling and coaching differentiation of self.

Therapists are to be aware of their own emotional reactions to specific family members and to monitor responses so as to model for an individual what it means to separate out thinking and feeling. Bowenian family therapists listen to individual family members, and they do so in a way that models the very differentiation they want the client to learn.

In addition to modeling differentiation of self, Bowenian family therapists also coach differentiation of self in relationships among various family members. Bowenian family therapists listen for emotional reactivity and sensitiveness and are prepared to assist individuals in exploring emotional responses with an eye for how to best separate out thinking and feeling.

We are drawn to theory-rich models of family health and functioning, and Bowenian family therapy is certainly more theory-rich and less technique-driven. However, one criticism of Bowenian family therapy is that it eschews other approaches to change in the family in favor of a differentiation of self.

While we value the insights into the emotional functioning of the individual and the family, we recognize that there may be limits to seeing all problems through the lens of these emotional units.

A related consideration has to do with the general approach to exploring emotional systems in relationships. Such explorations can be tremendously helpful to individuals and thus to family relationships. However, not all family members will express interest in exploring past relationships, and the Bowenian family therapist may have to find other ways to move toward greater relational wholeness.

## CONCLUSION

Bowenian family therapy is a theoretically rich contribution to the many models of family therapy. The focus is on emotional systems and the importance of differentiation of self, not only with respect to one's emotions and rational thought processes but also in establishing and maintaining emotional boundaries in one's relationships. Much attention is paid to the ways in which these emotional systems are passed down through generations and how people can become symptomatic in response to the extent to which people are differentiated. There is much that the Christian family therapist can utilize in transgenerational family therapy; indeed, it is an attractive theory that offers a great deal to case conceptualization and treatment planning. The emphasis on emotional reactivity is both a strength and a shortcoming from a Christian perspective because the Christian need not embrace all of the assumptions that lie behind a Bowenian understanding of the role of emotions and may instead seek guidance from classic Christian understanding of the role of emotions in reflecting and to some extent shaping our character.

## REFERENCES

Bartle-Haring, S., & Lal, A. (2010). Using Bowen theory to examine progress in couple therapy. *The Family Journal: Counseling and Therapy for Couples and Families, 18*(2), 106-15.

Becvar, D. S., & Becvar, R. J. (2006). *Family therapy: A systemic integration* (6th ed.). Boston: Allyn & Bacon.

Bowen, M. (1961). The family as the unit of study and treatment: I. Family Psychotherapy Workshop, 1959. *American Journal of Orthopsychiatry, 31*, 40-60.

Bowen, M. (1974). Alcoholism as viewed through family systems theory and family psychotherapy. *Annals of the New York Academy of Sciences, 233*, 115-22.

Chan, S. T. M. (2013). The manifestation of family triangulation in Asian-Chinese families and its relevance to father-son conflict. *Journal of Social Work Practice*, *27*(4), 393-406.

Dallos, R., & Vetere, A. (2012). Systems theory, family attachments and processes of triangulation: Does the concept of triangulation offer a useful bridge? *Journal of Family Therapy*, *34*, 117-37.

Edwards, J. (1971). *The religious affections*. Grand Rapids: Sovereign Grace. (Original work published 1746).

Evans, C. S. (1992). *Christian counseling as character formation*. Paper presented at the Second International Congress for Christian Counseling, Atlanta, GA.

Fogarty, T. F. (1975). The family emotional self system. *Family Therapy*, *2*(1), 79-97.

Frame, M. W. (2000). The spiritual genogram in family therapy. *Journal of Marital and Family Therapy*, *26*, 211-16.

Heiden Rootes, K. M., Jankowski, P. J., & Sandage, S. J. (2010). Bowen family systems theory and spirituality: Exploring the relationship between triangulation and religious questing. *Contemporary Family Therapy*, *32*, 89-101.

Holman, T. B., & Busby, D. M. (2011). Family-of-origin, differentiation of self and partner, and adult romantic relationship quality. *Journal of Couple & Relationship Therapy*, *10*(1), 3-19.

Jacobson, N. S., & Gurman, A. S. (1995). *Clinical handbook of couples therapy* (2nd ed.). New York: Guilford Press.

Jankowski, P. J., & Hooper, L. M. (2012). Differentiation of self: A validation study of the Bowen theory construct. *Couple and Family Psychology: Research and Practice*, *1*(3), 226.

Kerr, M. E., & Bowen, M. (1988). *Family evaluation: An approach based on Bowen theory*. New York: W. W. Norton.

Klever, P. (2015). Multigenerational relationships and nuclear family functioning. *The American Journal of Family Therapy*, *43*, 339-51.

MacKay, L. (2012). Trauma and Bowen family systems theory: Working with adults who were abused as children. *The Australian and New Zealand Journal of Family Therapy*, *33*(3), 232-41.

McGoldrick, M., Gerson, R., & Shellenberger, S. (1999). *Genograms: Assessment and intervention* (2nd ed.). New York: W. W. Norton.

Nichols, M. P., & Schwartz, R. C. (2006). *Family therapy: Concepts and methods* (7th ed.). Boston: Allyn & Bacon.

Roberts, R. C. (1988). What an emotion is: A sketch. *The Philosophical Review*, *57*(2), 183-209.

Roberts, R. C. (1992). Emotions among the virtues of the Christian life. *Journal of Religious Ethics*, *20*(1), 37-68.

Roberts, R. C. (1993). *Taking the word to heart: Self and other in an age of therapies.* Grand Rapids: Eerdmans.

Sauerheber, J. D., Nims, D., & Carter, D. J. (2014). Counseling Muslim couples from a Bowen family systems perspective. *The Family Journal: Counseling and Therapy for Couples and Families, 22*(2), 231-39.

Skowron, E. A., & Schmitt, T. A. (2003). Assessing interpersonal fusion: Reliability and validity of a new DSI fusion with others subscale. *Journal of Marital and Family Therapy, 29*(2), 209-22.

Yarhouse, M. A. (2000). The vice of envy: Insights from the history of pastoral care. *Journal of Psychology and Christianity, 19*(1), 25-37.

# STRATEGIC
# FAMILY THERAPY

*The paradoxes of conduct begin to twinkle into sight.*

**MONTAGUE**

M AKE HIM AN OFFER HE CAN'T REFUSE." Haven't we all heard and seen a friend or family member jut out their jaw and imitate Marlon Brando's chilling directive as godfather? The line makes us all squirm; because we know what it is like to be manipulated in small ways within our real families, we can identify with his manipulative threats of extortion, blackmail, and murder. Just as the real story of the mafia and the movie *The Godfather* create frequent images of family duplicity, real families exhibit similar messages—similar in kind but hopefully not similar in degree!

The paradoxical, double-bind messages form the genesis of family illness and are the center of intervention within the strategic system. The family of strategic theories holds that with every message or every interaction there are dimensions of communication that can be contradictory. An "offer that I can't refuse" is supposed to be so good that I would be foolish to turn it down. However, Brando's famous offer is backwards: it's so bad (i.e., my own murder if I don't comply) that I have no choice but to accept it and act as if it is good. Such is the power of a paradoxical message. In *The Godfather* it is used as family crime. In this chapter we will consider it as part of family counseling.

## INTRODUCTION TO STRATEGIC FAMILY THERAPY

The originators of strategic family therapy found that communication within families operates with similar mixed messages. To respect a family relationship by heeding one aspect of a message means that you will injure the relationship by disregarding another. Misunderstanding, conflict, and pathology are the result of messages that influence and manipulate covertly, while the overt message might suggest the contradiction. The cultural phrase, "Damned if I do, damned if I don't" applies here. So as you consider the strategic process in the subsequent pages, consider this illustration: "All competent clinicians are strategic clinicians."

## HISTORY

It is said that when the Spanish conquistador Coronado laid eyes on what would be known as the Grand Canyon, he wrote in his journal "Something happened here!" When we consider the history of family therapy as a whole and strategic therapy in particular, we could stand in front of the Mental Research Institute in Palo Alto, California, and say "Something happened here!" Indeed, the names of those associated with the origination of the strategic approach or of those who participated in its childhood or adolescent growth reads like a "Who's Who" of mental health originators. The list includes Erickson, Bateson, Weakland, Jackson, Haley, Satir, Watzlawick, Fisch, Bell, Minuchin, Selvini Palazzoli, Montalvo, and Madanes. The Mental Research Institute in Palo Alto was the geographical epicenter where their creative genius was synthesized.

Strategic family therapy can be understood in three phases. The first is the *theoretical stage* in Palo Alto, California, through the leadership of Gregory Bateson and Don Jackson and the stellar team of researchers and clinicians. The second phase, the *therapeutic stage*, is most closely associated with the clinical work and writings of Jay Haley and Cloé Madanes. The third phase is the *dissemination stage*, exemplified by the work of the Milan group and Mara Selvini Palazzoli as well as other centers of thought and therapy. Here the work of strategic therapy took divergent paths and became blended with other approaches.

During the early 1950s two new ways of thinking were having transforming effects in both the hard and human sciences. Cybernetic systems theory in mathematics/engineering and general systems theory in biology held in common the importance of a part affecting the whole. Cybernetics was a term developed by Norbert Wiener (1948), a mathematician who for nearly forty years was a professor at the Massachusetts Institute of Technology. During and after World War II, Wiener was involved in solving, through mathematics, the physics/engineering problems associated with automation. The challenge was to direct machines to be self-assessing and self-correcting instruments. His focus was in developing rockets and missiles that could make changes in flight toward the desired target. It was easy for humans to adjust the operation of a mechanical system like a watchmaker adjusting the time cadence of a watch, but could a mechanical system be designed to be self-adjusting? We take for granted today the common "feedback" machines such as a thermostat, an auto-focusing camera, a programmed drone, or a self-driving car.

For Wiener, the question of mechanical systems was solved with complex but predicable mathematical equations. A far greater challenge was to consider human systems—and how individuals and groups adjust or alter behavior.

> With this theory (cybernetics) it was possible for the first time to conceive of human beings not as separate individuals but as an ongoing group responding to one another in homeostatic ways, and so behavior had *present* causes. The family system was said to be stabilized by self-corrective governing processes which were activated in response to attempted change. (Haley, 1980, p. 15)

At about the same time, Austrian Ludwig Von Bertalanffy developed his General Systems Theory (GST) in biology (1949). His GST drew many similarities with cybernetic machines, but Bertalanffy believed that biological systems possessed a spontaneity that cybernetic mechanical systems could not. From him comes the famous phrase, "A system is greater than the sum of its parts." If individual parts influence other parts, which influence the whole organism, then the way that influence occurs must involve some form of communication—some sharing of information. Both cybernetics and general systems theory addressed how machines and nature transfer information.

## COMMUNICATION RESEARCH PHASE, 1952–1966

Enter now the cultural anthropologist Gregory Bateson. An established scientist and philosopher, he was involved in the formation of cybernetic thought in the years immediately following World War II (Broderick & Schrader, 1991). In the application of cybernetics to human behavior, he focused on messages of paradox. In particular, he blended a philosophical/

logical problem identified by Whitehead and Russell (1910/1913). Their logical conundrum can be contained in the phrase "I should not be trusted." This statement illustrates how all communication has multiple messages. These ideas underneath ideas—or metamessages—were the core problem in mechanical cybernetics, and Bateson believed that they served as important windows to observe problems in human communication. In 1952, Bateson received a Rockefeller grant to study this phenomenon through the Veterans Administration hospital in Palo Alto. He hired a social worker, Jay Haley, who was a young communication researcher, and John Weakland, a chemical engineer turned cultural anthropologist. Eventually, Haley would move to Philadelphia and Washington, DC, and develop his own following. However, Weakland remained at the Mental Research Institute (MRI) for decades and developed the brief therapy models that have had tremendous influence on current solution-focused models (Goldenberg & Goldenberg, 2004).

The Rockefeller grant was completed in 1954. Next the team looked for other sources of income to fund projects that examined human applications of cybernetics—particularly, context and paradox in communication. At that time there were research dollars available to study why so many soldiers went off to war "normal" and came home with schizophrenia—many without ever going to battle. The MRI team found funding through the Macy Foundation by focusing on the communication patterns associated with schizophrenia. Psychiatrist Don Jackson was invited to join the team because of his expertise with schizophrenia. In 1956, this team, led by Bateson and Jackson, produced the first of more than seventy collaborated articles. This article, "Towards a Theory of Schizophrenia," was important because it introduced the idea of "double-bind communication"; it suggested the cause of schizophrenia was influenced by contradictory messages given from parents to children. For instance, a parent screaming at a child, "Get over here right now, you little brat! Don't you run away from me! Come here!" The verbal content says "Approach me," but the behavioral context calls to the child "Run away, you're about to get a "whoppin'!" Children have to reconcile the mixed message of a parent being safe and threatening in the same person.

The significance of the Bateson et al. paper was to offer a challenge to the exclusive domain of intrapsychic conflict of psychoanalysis. "What the Bateson group did was focus on schizophrenia as an interpersonal, relational phenomenon rather than view it as an intrapsychic disorder of the individual that secondarily influences interpersonal relationships" (Becvar & Becvar, 2006, pp. 21-22). Without intending to do so, a paradigm shift was launched. Psychopathology was from this point forward required to consider a family system etiology.

The product of this first era of strategic family therapy was the realization that breakdowns in human psychological functioning are in part a product of miscommunication within family units. Furthermore, repair of problems initially assumed to be individually based can be addressed by a reorganization of the communication patterns within the system. Finally, strategic researchers from MRI advocated an active role for the therapist to initiate change by overcoming homeostatic resistance with creative circuitous paradox or by direct challenge and encouragement.

## THE THERAPEUTIC PHASE, 1966–1995

To many, the face of strategic family therapy was Jay Haley (Gladding, 2007). He was present in shaping the theory and technique from its beginning. He developed the term "strategic therapy" from observing the work of Milton Erickson. His nonconformist persona in many ways is a metaphor for the approach itself—edgy, clever, surprising, and provocative.

Haley grew into therapy, joining Bateson's team with expertise in communication theory. One of Haley's first assignments in his work with Bateson was to study the work of Erickson and the idea that hypnosis was a communication process. Haley formed a bond with him that remained until Erickson's death. He was instrumental in disseminating Erickson's ideas and techniques through the writing of his theory, case studies, and biography.

In 1967 Haley moved east and joined Salvador Minuchin at the Philadelphia Child Guidance Center. He altered the strategic approach developed at MRI. His tailoring of the original approach through the 1970s, 80s, and 90s included the integration of "ordeals" and later, influenced by and collaborating with Cloé Madanes, he used the term *strategic humanism* to describe his work. In every phase, there remained the intentional directive approach.

During the mid-1960s the focus of research at MRI took a turn toward the development of brief therapy models. The Brief Therapy Project at MRI, directed by Richard Fisch, included Haley as an original member. But Haley soon left for Philadelphia. He maintained his focus on strategic family interventions. MRI's change in focus influenced the formation of other approaches to individual and family intervention, including many brief and solution-focused models (Segal, 1991).

Haley continued to develop his ideas in Philadelphia and then at the Family Therapy Institute in Washington, DC, with Cloé Madanes. While the primary "face" of strategic therapy remained Haley's throughout the 1980s and 1990s, the image was significantly altered by the individual work of Madanes. She introduced the crucial issues of love and violence as the primary forces that create family health and dysfunction. Love and violence can be seen in polarized paired constructs of strategic conceptualization (Madanes, 1991).

***Involuntary vs. voluntary behavior.*** Families attend therapy with the mental frame that their problem is involuntary, but family therapists will assume that the core symptom has a voluntary root that is being misapplied to alleviate family pain:

> A strategic therapist generally prefers to think of all symptoms (except for organic illness) as voluntary and under the control of the patient. . . . Sometimes a first step in resolving the presenting problem is to redefine it as involving voluntary rather than involuntary behavior. This may be the only intervention that is necessary, as the client may solve the problem once the client accepts the idea that it is under his or her control. (Madanes, 1991, p. 398)

***Helplessness vs. power.*** Madanes describes a frequent strategic reframe regarding helplessness and power. In family therapy, both the identified patient and the other family members articulate an experience of helplessness but demonstrate a practice of power within the system. For example, in a marital dyad, Joan might feel depressed because she cannot get her husband, Mike, to be more attentive to her needs. Mike might feel angry because Joan has little energy and interest to "seize the day"—to go out and have adventure and fun. Joan appears to be in a position of despair, but she can control Mike by having little concern for his interests. While Mike appears to be the powerful one, his efforts are stymied by the expression of Joan's depression. To Madanes, the understanding of this helplessness and power dynamic is crucial for the therapeutic process. She writes, in italics, "*How a therapist thinks about power, and whether he or she thinks about power and helplessness at all, will determine how the therapist designs a strategy for change*" (Madanes, 1991, p. 399).

*Metaphorical vs. literal sequences.* Years ago a television commercial entered the popular psyche of American culture with the sales slogan "Is it live, or is it Memorex?" In all therapies, one must form a related opinion: "Is the symptom presented by a family the real problem, or is the symptom a facsimile or a substation for something else?" Therapies are built around answers to this essential question. The psychoanalytic and dynamic approaches tend to see the family symptoms as a recording of some other event; the brief, cognitive, and behavioral approaches tend to focus on the symptoms as the real problem. For strategic therapies, the focus is on metaphor.

The strategic approach articulated by Madanes and previously by Haley emphasizes the "Memorex" metaphor. The symptom presented is not the literal problem but a metaphor for multiple dimensions of the problem. However, a clear distinction needs to be made between the strategic understanding of the symptom and the historical analytic and dynamic approaches. Strategic approaches see the symptom as being interpersonal rather than intrapsychic. The symptom is a problem that exists between people rather than within people. The visible symptom is actually the family members trying to resolve a problem between them unsuccessfully. This intrapersonal theory of symptom directs the clinician to focus his or her interventions on the space between family members, not toward any one person. Furthermore, it is assumed that the interruption of the sequence of symptoms presented to the therapist will have a reverberating effect on other aspects of family relationship (Madanes, 1984).

*Hierarchy vs. equality.* The metaphoric communication experienced as symptoms alters the roles that family members assume. The influence of Minuchin, who gave Madanes her first employment upon her arrival in the United States from Argentina, and who worked closely with Haley in Philadelphia, can be seen in strategic theories' hierarchical view of family structure. It is theorized that families should have a structure in which parents attend to the needs of children and that this structure has a natural evolution progression as the needs of the family change.

Erickson believed that families have a natural progression and that they resist their own metamorphosis by shifting the healthy hierarchical power structure upside down. When children are showing symptoms, they are communicating through metaphor to the family that a problem exists and it needs to be attended to. In essence, children become the leaders of the family by declaring that an insufficiency exists. "There is a dual hierarchy in the family: In one, the child is in charge; in the other, the parents are in care of the child. The task of the therapist is to correct this hierarchy and reorganize the family so that the parents are in a superior position and help and support the child and the child does not take care of the parents in unfortunate ways" (Madanes, 1991, p. 400).

**Hostility vs. love.** A contribution that is uniquely Madanes's is her focus on the motivation of family functioning, usually by parents to children or between spouses. Actions within families can be motivated and/or interpreted to be anger-based or love-based. For example, a parent might discipline a child for misdeeds, with two conflicting motivations: punishment and instruction. Punishment is hostility-based and might be motivated by embarrassment or other parental focused concerns. ("How will I ever face my neighbors knowing that my son and his friends drove his car and mooned the children waiting for the school bus?") Alternatively, instruction is loved-based, motivated by the well-being of the child. ("Mature adolescents use cars for transportation, not for terrorizing children. You will walk to school for the next three months in order to learn this important lesson.")

The reality is that we have multiple motivations for our actions. This plurality of motives produces a plurality of messages that lend themselves to misunderstanding and family conflict. Madanes chooses to focus on the benevolent intent, the love component of an interaction that is behind even maladaptive behaviors (Nelson & Figley, 1990). She would encourage the love message that is intended to be prescribed more clearly.

## MILAN GROUP, 1967-1999

One of the great stories in the development of mental health theory is the work of Mara Selvini Palazzoli and her colleagues at the Milan Center for the Study of the Family. They represent excellence in scientific method, professional collaboration, and innovation. Their research and work was one of the first therapies that was developed outside the United States and then imported into the North American mental health culture. The group consisted of psychiatrists and psychoanalysts who met regularly to discuss the research emerging with the Palo Alto group. They chose to exclusively consider their ideas, inviting members of MRI to consult with them about the work in California and to provide feedback regarding their emerging approach in Italy. They published their first manuscript in 1974, years after they first began researching together. By that time they had a significant log of case studies, research data, and experience in their methodology.

The Milan group introduced many new dimensions to the theory and practice of family therapy. Their approach was thoroughly strategic.

*Team intervention.* Freud would have considered it incredulous for psychoanalytically trained clinicians to conduct therapy by co-therapy and by "committee." The associates within the Milan group would typically work with a family in male-female pairs. There would be a team of colleagues observing the family session through a windowed observing room. This observing group would make recommendations to the clinical dyad after the family story and circumstances were known and before an intervention was recommended: "The team facilitates the development of a system perspective as each member will contribute different emphases and viewpoints which guards against the danger of the solo therapist's accepting the family's view of reality and the losing of his or her curiosity" (Campbell, Draper, & Crutchley, 1991, p. 344).

*Circular questioning.* The tone of therapy between co-therapists and the family is quickly paced and is intended to create a syncopated rhythm that facilitates new thought within the family. "By neutrality, we mean the capacity of the therapist to conduct his investigation on the basis of feedback from the family in response to the information he solicits about relationships and, therefore about difference and change" (Palazzoli, Selvini, Boscolo, Cecchin, & Prata, 1980, p. 6).

If a team were working with a family, the therapist might ask a daughter, "How do you think your mother feels about your brother's attitude in the home?"

Then to the brother—not permitting him to take control and articulate defensiveness—the therapist could ask, "And what do you think your father would say about your older brother's traffic violations while he is away at college?"

Then to the wife, "Do you think that your husband's attitude toward his children and their driving would be different if his brother had not been killed in a car accident?"

Then to the husband, "How does your wife differ with you on how to raise your kids?"

The effect of circular questioning on the family is to promote community—to stimulate group-think about their current situation. The conversation moves quickly, and there is typically an avoidance of direct self-think but instead an emphasis on defining the dimensions of how the family thinks as a community.

Tomm (1987) introduced the idea of reflexive questions to the circular process. These inquiries have a future component that forces the family out of the status quo and creates imagination and problem solving. For example, "What would your father think about your mom's drinking if he could speak freely?" Around and around the conversation builds up from the opinions of all, collaborated and challenged by each other. The questions have an ultimate aim of intervention, created by the therapeutic pair and the observing team who caucus to establish a family assignment.

*Neutrality.* Within the strategic approach, the Milan clinicians maintained a directive stance of assertiveness, if not dominating the family within the session. While the therapist is authoritative, he or she is not to be preferential. Rather, the clinical and observing team view themselves being charged with organizing family data, forming a hypothesis, and implementing an intervention. In order to acquire the necessary information, a neutral perspective needs to be maintained. Circular questioning has its effect only when the attitude of neutrality is successfully conveyed. If the questioning is experienced as an inquisition seeking to identify guilty individuals, then the therapists would be blocked by the family's resistance in forming an accurate and comprehensive hypothesis of family behavior (Palazzoli et al., 1980).

*Positive connotations and rituals.* Central to the strategic approach is the sly and subtle act of the therapeutic reframe. The Milan group expanded this by seeing that all behavior—both that which individuals within the family define as problematic and that which by consensus is seen as positive—is indeed noble, but some behaviors are unsuccessful efforts to preserve the family and maintain its stability. Positive connotations permit therapeutic neutrality by seeking to reframe individual efforts to demonize or blame others in the family as efforts to bring health or prevent further calamity.

Positive connotations are more than just Rogerian unconditional positive regard. They are used as a means to challenge the family's resistance to change (Palazzoli, Selvini, Boscolo, Cecchin, & Prata, 1978). The Milan group hypothesized through the accumulation of many cases that families came to therapy with an established systemic paradox. The paradox might be something like, "We are a really good family [read: "we don't need to change anything"], but add name is struggling with add problem and it's causing us concern [read: "that somebody needs to change"]" (Tomm, 1984).

In creating a paradox to counter the paradox of the family, the clinician can apply the first intervention of the positive connotation. In essence it says, "Don't change anything at all. Because the original intent of add_name is to preserve and save the family, I think that the first step is to take no step at all lest the family fall headlong into chaos." The effect is to place the family in a therapeutic double bind that prompts them to cry out "But we must change!" (Palazzoli et al., 1978).

Rituals are the thoughtful, intentional interventions created by the team for the family to implement at home. Typically, rituals are targeted to maintain and reinforce the counterparadox. An example of a ritual for a family in which the responsibility of household tasks are assumed to be completed by the mother—to which the mother gets depressed—would be for the family to not take on any of the mother's "duties" but instead to gather each night and talk about all of the "important" tasks that each person was able to accomplish because they weren't sidetracked by cleaning their rooms, preparing meals, cleaning the kitchen, or washing clothes.

## THEORETICAL AND PHILOSOPHICAL ASSUMPTIONS OF STRATEGIC FAMILY THERAPY

The dominance of powerful personalities and the creative and humorous qualities of strategic family therapy can lend itself to a misunderstanding that this approach is therapy by personality or a therapy of the absurd—like Paris fashion designers developing a line of clothing that no one who actually cares about how they look would wear. Some paradoxical interventions might appear to be on the edge, ridiculous, or dishonest. But an absurd intervention is not a strategic one. If a family member were to threaten the system by saying, "I want to burn the house down," the therapist would not be implementing a strategic intervention by "prescribing the symptom" and encouraging him or her to do so. Established theory drives effective strategic psychotherapy. This approach, more so than most other family or individual therapies, is based on a rigorous scientific foundation of research. The formation of a therapeutic strategy is based on at least five theoretical assumptions.

Philosophically, strategic originators focused on pragmatic utilitarianism. Their primary concern was to direct attention to overt communication patterns that occurred in the present tense (Nichols, 1984). Little attention was paid to transgenerational determinism. More attention is directed toward *nonbeing* (that is, nonsymptomatic) than *being* (that is, family or relational maturity).

*Psychopathology as an interruption in the family life cycle.* Strategic theory includes a nonorganic view of family dysfunction. The emphasis differs from a psychopathological model that categorizes family dysfunction as a secondary issue for families since the problems are first experienced by individuals. Rather, family dysfunction or "stuckness" is the result of the system's inability to sustain continual adjustment to changing demands from the normal life cycle experienced by all families. The family problem emerges from "the way the family reacts, interacts and attempts to adapt to the crisis stage it has entered. The therapist would do well to talk to families in developmental terms rather than to try to define a family typology or a family symptomology" (Stanton, 1981, p. 365).

The life cycle is the nonformal stages or themes of family life around which there is constant change. Systems must be regularly attending to family feedback and instituting change and adjustment to external factors—such as marriage, economic advancement and decline, birth, sickness, death, changes in work or school tasks, extended family demands, and alterations in society (Haley, 1973).

*The power of the therapist to enact change.* The strategic therapist is seen as central in helping the family alter the symptoms/problems that bring them to therapy. Families are seen as stuck and lacking the knowledge or resources to get moving again. It's as though a family were sitting in their disabled car on the side of the road. They have a flat tire and are without a spare. They are stuck and must become reliant on the resources of another to assist them to get their car moving again. Nelson and Figley (1990), citing Fisch, Weakland, and Segal (1982), wrote, "the task of the therapist was to interrupt dysfunctional, homeostasis-maintaining behaviors and induce a 'requisite variety' or other alternatives into the family's system" (Nelson and Figley, p. 49). The therapist, by the use of an intentional intervention or strategy, guides and directs the family back toward the desired goal or to the next stage in family life (Haley, 1976; Madanes, 1991; Nichols, 1984).

"The roles of strategic therapists differ among their subschools. However, those who work within this methodology share a belief in being active and flexible with their family clients. Haley (1990) believes it is essential to make changes in people and families within the first three sessions" (Gladding, 2007,

p. 225). Furthermore, Haley (1976) believes that the therapist joins the family insofar as they become a part of the problem. Because family "stuckness" is seen as a communication problem, the solution is the insertion of an intentional, strategic directive that alters the established pattern of relationship. These are designed to

> subtly gain control over the presenting symptoms and force families to attempt different solutions: to the family these directives often appear to fly in the face of common sense. . . . The overall purpose of such paradoxical approaches is to jar or interrupt the family's established (if unsuccessful) pattern of interaction by powerful indirect means. . . . The therapist is attempting to circumvent family resistance to altering the interactive patterns that maintain the problematic behavior. (Goldenberg & Goldenberg, 2004, p. 246)

*Circular model.* Families will mistakenly think of their problems or concerns in simple cause-and-effect models. Returning to the flat tire metaphor, the cause is the nail. If the mom had not driven the car over the nail, then we wouldn't have become stuck. This linear process—A (driving over the nail) led to B (the puncture), which led to C (our motionless condition)—can simplify our attributions and will allow for a family to maintain a focus on a past event that can lead to becoming stuck. It is Oliver Hardy saying to his friend Stan Laurel, "This is another fine mess you've gotten us into." The cause of the mess is understood by looking at only a part of the equation.

Bateson believed that the linear causality was useful in predicting the physics of inanimate objects—like cars, tires, and nails. But it is less useful when addressing human behavior like responding to stress that is induced by change. Returning to the flat tire illustration, the cause of the family crisis was not the nail or the tire but the change in plans. That change provoked the father to speak through his stress to the mother, "If you wouldn't have driven so close to the shoulder, we'd have been on time." The multiple messages include statements (a) drive in the middle of the lane, (b) it's your fault, (c) you are incompetent to get the family to the designated destination, (d) I could have succeeded where you failed, and (e) I am competent, you are not. In response, all of the family members would receive the same message and selectively respond to some but not to all messages. Ultimately there is a complicated series of choices that are influenced by a cycle of previous choices and interpretations. The result is a cacophony of communications that cycle through the system and influence the expression of subsequent statements.

It should be noted that circular questioning—explained earlier as a component of the Milan approach—arose out of the principle of circularity. But they are not the same. The circular questioning is a technique developed by Palazzoli et al. to prompt the family to think outside of the linear progression and to see the social context of the family problem.

*Family stabilization.* King Solomon wrote that "as he thinks in his heart, so *is* he" (Prov 23:7 NKJV). If that passage were adapted to strategic therapy it would be "As people think about others within the system, they define themselves." For a therapist, a conceptual framework is the mental code that individuals and the family system create to define both the parts and the whole. For example, Walter says about his wife, Susan, "She's a nag." The therapist thinks about Walter and the system that he helped to create and how he encouraged a "nagging" existence environment for Susan to occupy. Another example would be "My oldest and middle children have never given us a problem, but our little one is a 'holy terror.'" The "angelic" children and "diabolical" children become conceptual frames by which the family defines itself and its members. They come to expect members to act in ways that they have acted in the past. It is similar to the idea of family scripts in other approaches. The self-fulfilling prophecy of a conceptual framework reveals how a system creates and maintains itself.

It is through this idea of a family framework that resistance to change traps the family into stagnation. Families don't see that their corporate attitudes toward each other encourage the very behaviors that frustrate, impede, and provoke.

*Logic and illogic of paradox.* G. K. Chesterton described paradox as "truth standing on her head to attract attention." Indeed, the contribution that strategic theory has made to the profession is to contain the power of paradox and channel it to circumvent obstacles that interfere with family progress. A good strategic paradoxical intervention is not a trick or a ploy that dupes a client or a family into "health." It is a reasoned intervention that challenges a "metalogic" operating within the system and maintaining the family in a fixed position. Strategic theorists believe that families form patterns and become stuck and stabilized around their immovable relational structures. At times, a direct cognitive appeal is sufficient to expose the unique family pattern to which the family can create their own solution (Becvar & Becvar, 2006). "Virtually all paradoxical strategies are designed to counteract stubbornly maladaptive responses by not actively contesting their existence. . . . By ironically joining forces with non-change, they may effect a fundamental shift in counselee attitude that clears the path for productive—and self-initiated change" (Seltzer, 1986, p. xii). Think of paradox as a means of interrupting a preestablished pattern of family behavior. If clients expect to be challenged around a behavioral pattern and they are not, and they are not challenged as they expect but are given an unexpected challenge, then they must think rather than merely act out of habit. A thinking family is one that can more easily change than a habituated family.

Strategic family therapy has evolved and taken on many forms, adaptations, and applications. The Brief Strategic Family Therapy (BSFT) model is perhaps most well-known today, as it has been developed for "youth with behavior problems such as drug use, sexual risk behaviors, and delinquent behaviors" (Szapocznik, Schwartz, Muir, & Brown, 2012, p. 134; cf. Robbins et al., 2011). It has been studied with favorable results for the treatment of social phobia (Rakowska, 2011) and, when compared to cognitive behavioral therapy, in the inpatient and outpatient treatment of Binge Eating Disorder (Castelnuovo, Manzoni, Villa, Cesa, & Molinari, 2011). Brief strategic therapy has also been extended as a model of collaborative partnerships to community settings (Szapocznik, Muir, Duff, Schwartz, & Brown, 2015), and it has been adapted for use with gang-affiliated Mexican American adolescents (Valdez, Cepeda, Parrish, Horowitz, & Kaplan, 2013). We have also seen several studies published on therapeutic alliance in BSFT and therapist adherence to the tenets of BSFT (e.g., Robbins et al., 2011; Sheehan & Friedlander, 2015).

## WHEN FAMILIES SEEK HELP

Families come to therapy with a hope that particular problems or symptoms will be removed. This level of change is recognized as *first-order change* (Watzlawick, Weakland, & Fisch, 1974). This level of change involves fixing felt needs or surface problems without addressing systemic changes. First-order change is like drying the carpet after a severe storm floods a home. *Second-order change* involves fixing the roof—that is, instigating solutions to the system that reduce the likelihood of problem recidivism. Strategic therapy places a value on addressing the underlying system and initiating change on one part of the system that promotes large-scale revision within the family.

## CASE EXAMPLE

The Atten family consists of married parents, Matt and Debbie, each of whom have been married before, and three children. Mike is Matt's son from a previous relationship. He is fourteen. Terry is Debbie's son from a previous relationship. He is twelve. And Erica, the daughter of Matt and Debbie, is nine. Mike lives half the time with Matt and Debbie and half the time with his biological mother and stepdad. Matt and Debbie have brought the family to counseling because the family members engage in shouting matches multiple times a day. It is particularly disturbing at dinnertime because the whole family becomes involved, and what was hoped to be a supportive family meal degenerates into a free-for-all.

The family therapist would establish himself or herself as the leader of the therapeutic process. Therapy would be contracted for a discrete period—usually about ten weeks. The family would define the problem along with some index for measuring change, such as "We want to reduce the number of arguments in the home, especially at dinnertime."

The focus of the sessions is maintained on the specific complaint of family arguments. At the end of the first session the therapist gives the following assignment: "For at least three nights over the next week every word spoken at the table must be delivered by yelling. If you want someone to pass the carrots, you have to yell it at the top of your lungs. The other nights of the week you can behave as a normal family, but for those three nights—scream your brains out!"

During the second session, the therapist asks about how the yelling went: who was best at taking the assignment seriously, who didn't seem to be able to do it, what things did you yell about. The therapist keeps the focus on the yelling assignment. Just as an aside, at the end of the session, the counselor asks, "By the way, what happened the other nights?" To which Matt said, "We only had one other night that we were all together as a family. That was last night, and it was OK."

The therapist proceeds to give a second assignment. The family is to eat in silence for three nights. They must all be present, and no words can be spoken. Dinner must take at least fifteen minutes—and you can't talk.

The discussion during the third session was heightened. No one liked the silence. Oddly, the yelling assignment was fun, but the silence made everyone uncomfortable. Again, the session was spent discussing the oddity of the dining experience. Then as an aside, the counselor asked Debbie about the fighting during dinner. She said, "I don't think we have fought at dinner this week. We have fought over homework and chores and late nights out past curfew, but those were not at dinner."

The therapist proceeds to give a third assignment: "In order to argue with someone the person initiating the argument must pay five dollars. In addition, the person to whom the argument is directed must pay five dollars. In other words, if you want to be involved in the fight, you have to pay your entrance fee. If you do not pay, then you can't speak to the topic of the conflict. The one who wants to fight can pay for you, and if another puts up the money then you cannot enter into the argument. However, if you don't want to fight then you don't have to do so. The fight money will be given to a homeless shelter to buy food. As long as you are going to spoil your meal, then others who would appreciate food should be given the opportunity to eat in peace."

In the next session the family was asked how it went. They said that they didn't fight at all during meal times. Mike said, "We are all pretty cheap. If you hit us in the wallet, then everyone behaves!"

The therapist then asks the family to assess how they have been able to go three weeks without fighting during meal time. Three more sessions were dedicated to mature ways to manage emotion, frustration, and failed expectations within the family. Erica suggested an "argument hour," which the family implemented as an alternative to the open season of fighting that had been previously employed. The family ended therapy at session ten.

In assessing the progress of therapy with the Atten family, the clinician created an offsetting experience—the dinner activity. Yelling, silence, or payment moved family meal time "off center" just a bit. Attention was redirected from anger expression to a type of communications game. In essence, one game, fighting, was replaced with another. Eventually, the family developed their own type of communication game that was neither absurd (silence) nor disruptive.

## CHRISTIAN PERSPECTIVE ON STRATEGIC FAMILY THERAPY

There is much to be said about the consideration of strategic interventions within a Christian worldview and within the practice of therapy within a biblical framework. There are two ways to consider the theological application of strategic therapy. The first way is to evaluate the theory, assumptions, and philosophy underneath the approach. The second way is to consider the technique of strategic therapy, particularly that of the paradoxical and metaphorical interventions in light of a Christian understanding of change.

***Strategic theory and a Christian worldview.*** Strategic theory is weighted by a significant paradox associated with human functioning and intervention. Fundamental to the approach is the belief that all families are "normal" within themselves—that is, families are not identified as dysfunctional unless the family self-selects as such. "As therapists, we do not regard any particular way of functioning, relating, or living as a problem if the client is not expressing discontent with it" (Fisch, 1978). Dysfunction is therefore understood as a frustration to adapt to change required of the family as it matures in a natural cycle of life and development.

## INTEGRATIVE FOCUS: *Family Functioning*

Strategic clinicians are "true systems thinkers" (Nichols, 1984). Translating this idea into family functioning, families are dynamic groups under constant adjustment and accommodation. When new information emerges through the process of negative and positive feedback loops, a healthy family is able to maintain or change course and recalibrate itself toward its intended target. In short, healthy families change.

*Think about it:* How did your family of origin alter its path as change occurred within the system? Consider inputs such as the maturation of children from childhood through adolescence to adulthood, and the shifts in power within the family as members changed roles.

***Nature of the human condition.*** In the writings of strategic theorists you frequently find the word *dysfunction* but find limited use of the term *pathology*. The use and nonuse of these terms is indicative of the principal views of strategic therapy. The theory emphasizes a nonmedical and amoral perspective on individual behavior. Because it sees individual and family dysfunction as the result of misunderstanding and confusion stemming from communication, there is not a judgment made or directed regarding goodness/badness. Rather, the emphasis is on the functionality of the system. Fisch (1978) advocates the belief that a dysfunction must always be identified and defined by the family through their discontentment. Furthermore, Stanton writes that "strategic family therapists see symptoms as the resultants or concomitants of misguided attempts at changing an existing difficulty. However, such symptoms usually succeed only in making things worse" (1981, p. 364).

## INTEGRATIVE FOCUS: *Family Relationships*

Strategic clinicians are resistant to defining healthy relationships—that is, normal family processes. John Weakland (1976) believed that there was no need for anyone to explain what is normal. Their emphasis has been on articulating the presence of abnormality within the system. The Milan group did define healthy relationships. Characteristics of relational health include acceptance of differences, emotional bonds or alliances, and healthy power struggles that result in family growth (Palazzoli et al., 1978). Their description is consistent with a family that is living under faith as a cover for fear. It parallels Paul's description of security and confidence in the midst of severe challenges (Phil 2:6-11).

*Think about it:* Reconsider conflicts that have occurred within your family. Identify how you could hold that conflict in a negative light, and reconsider it in a different frame. What positive changes are brought about by the presence of conflict within the family?

Here lies a significant insufficiency with family therapies in general and with strategic therapy in particular. If Jacques Ellul (1964) is correct that the most perplexing and significant question is to consider the nature and characteristics of the human being, then the strategic theorists sidestep a direct answer to the question by defining the individual as having existence within a system and therefore cannot be comprehended as an individual—or they fail to even consider the question.

Strategic theory, being influenced by Bateson's anthropological neutrality and Erickson's humanistic unconditional regard, has created a view of human nature that is consistent with Martin's (2003) assessment of the mental health profession's overall view of persons. He describes it as a minimalist view of human nature limited to a few cognitive structures through which cultures are created: "The variations we observe in human activity from culture to culture are said to be entirely learned, and none is to be preferred as more natural or normative than any other" (p. 126).

***Strategic and biblical uses of paradox.*** An easy error would be to consider the use of paradox within the strategic approach and immediately

connect it with the paradox of Christian theology and the biblical text—
particularly the parables of Jesus. Indeed, the paradox of Christ's atoning
work is central to our faith tradition. A few of the many theological paradoxes are these: to be first in God's kingdom you must be a servant; Jesus is
the wounded healer, and through his stripes we are healed; it is easier for a
camel to go through an eye of a needle than for a rich man to enter heaven;
and humanity is saved by grace, through faith alone and in accordance with
Scripture. The Christian faith exists around the paradox that the infinite
God became a finite and created being so that finite humans could experience eternity with their creator.

To us, it appears that the strategic use of paradox and the biblical/theo-
logical use of paradox share a common name and the feature of nonlinear
logic, but not much else. For the Christian, paradox is a central theological/
philosophical reality that defines one's faith as beyond logic and outside of
cognition. The Christian paradox boldly states that "this cannot be . . . but it
is!" Karl Barth included paradox in his theology as that which defines the
mystery of God and our faith in God (Barth, 1969). Paradox according to
Barth exposes the limitation of our finite mind, pointing to our need for infinite God. Similarly, both MacIntyre and Ricoeur (1969) and Stout (1981)
argue that paradox does not reveal inconsistency but rather indicates the
wonder and mystery of the work of God in human affairs.

The presence of paradox in the words of Jesus and the theology of Paul is
not a manipulative strategy to fool the Pharisees or to create cognitive dissonance. Paradoxes are declarations of reality that bring the hearer to faith. "For
him who has ears to hear" does not refer to the really smart people who can
figure this out but to the child in us who can respond faithfully to God's
message explicitly because he or she cannot figure this out. The purpose and
effect of theological paradox is a humble, submissive, and faith-driven response to God.

Paradox in strategic therapy is different. In therapy it is used as a tool to
coerce and manipulate—ethically, reasonably, and responsibly—but manipulate all the same. Haley (1986) reveals the depth and breadth of his paradoxical applications with the publication of the collection of essays titled *The
Power Tactics of Jesus Christ*. In the title essay, he reveals a thorough knowledge
of the New Testament text and the message of Jesus but an abysmal herme-
neutic in interpreting Scripture. The gist of the work is to describe the methods

used by Jesus to influence culture, "now that Christianity has declined as a force in the world of ideas" (Haley, 1986, p. 22). Theologically, he interprets the actions of Jesus through the paradigm of Albert Schweitzer (1948) and other theologians from the early twentieth century that denies his deity and regards his actions as brilliant but ultimately misguided (Capps, 2004).

---

**INTEGRATIVE FOCUS: *Family Identity***

Strategic therapy is functional and pragmatic, never ideal. That families would seek a higher purpose is largely outside the realm of the approach. However, there are values articulated within the strategic approach that does contribute to identity formation. Accommodation to new circumstances and to each other's growth is the key component to healthy families. This idea of accommodation can be seen in the biblical understanding of mutual submission. Family members adjusting, compensating, encouraging, and challenging in reciprocal relationship appears to be important in successful family functioning.

*Think about it:* How has accommodation toward others in your family been demonstrated over time and circumstance?

---

The writings of Haley in this essay are interesting, amusing, and challenging. In strategic therapy, Haley places responsibility on the clinician to be an active change agent within the dysfunctional family. Haley recognized that the therapist has no real authority to change a rigid system as an outsider. Furthermore, he understood that the family would resist any effort to change, lest individual members lose power. What Haley described as Jesus' "power tactics" is worthy to be emulated as a clinician who seeks to assert power over families for change. Haley writes, "A person has achieved power when he has established himself as one who can determine what is going to happen" (Haley, 1986, p. 37). He sees Jesus' unique power as a contrary power. We naturally think of the power of one who can command others to behave—like a caesar, emperor, or dictator. Haley reveals Jesus' tactic as appealing to an alternative control. "One man can order others to lift and carry him, while another might achieve the same end by collapsing. Both men are determining what is to happen in their social environment by the use of a power tactic" (p. 38).

Haley's interpretation of Jesus is not a theological work. It has usefulness as a tool to further understand the complexity of power and manipulation—

and the ethics of its use within a therapeutic setting. Haley is writing as an observer of social movement—to which Jesus occupies a central role and to which therapy functions as a microcosm. Haley's interpretation of Jesus is consistent with a theological system that views Jesus' work exclusively within the human realm. Other essays by Haley in this volume are clearly intended as satire. These chapters include "The Art of Being a Failure as a Therapist" and "How to Have an Awful Marriage." One difference is that the other chapters contain no references to other works but are solely his musings. By grounding "The Power Tactics of Jesus Christ" to the New Testament text and by asserting the theology of Schweitzer and others, he enters into a theological discourse in which he is clearly not prepared to debate. Therefore, we interpret Haley's views of Jesus to be informative as to his individual thought process but otherwise having little influence on the understanding or implementation of strategic therapy.

We believe that the paradox of Christianity has little to do with the paradox of strategic therapy beyond the commonality of the word *paradox*. The one exception is in the psychology of paradox—that is, the effect that paradoxical communication has on our process of thought and behavior. This does not make strategic paradox wrong or contrary to Christian thought, simply other. The only commonality between the two is that both produce a similar effect in standing against a rationalism and individual self-sufficiency. Paradox in both undermines our inflated and potentially arrogant assumptions about self and our perceived power and control over circumstances. Paradox achieves this aim by breaking established categories. This was Jesus' method in his confrontation of pharisaical religious structures, and it is the method of Haley et al. in the confrontation of pharisaical family structures.

The method of paradox was examined philosophically by Bertrand Russell (1901). He examined the rules around mathematical sets. He noted that exceptions to the rules of sets constituted a set in themselves—in essence a set of "non-sets," which was a logical impossibility. He and other philosophers and mathematicians have devised solutions to what has become known as Russell's paradox. His realization was that change in one's understanding of any situation can result through the realignment that comes when looking at its impossibility. Therefore, the use of paradox has a function in the promotion of learning and change. It was clearly an important tool used by Jesus and holds a substantial presence in Christian theology. That it is used also by strategic therapists does not make the approach Christian any more than it would make Aesop's fables Christian for his frequent use of the same learning tool.

*Outwit, outplay, outlast.* In the twenty-first century, reality television has become ubiquitous. Pick your favorite—*Survivor, The Bachelor/Bachelorette, The Biggest Loser, Dancing with the Stars, America's Got Talent, Top Chef, The Amazing Race* . . . (we apologize for omitting your favorite, but we can't name them all). The context is unique, but the process will follow a similar story line: participants are pitted against one another to see who can indeed endure or remain to the end. In this scenario, "honest people" will lie, control, and manipulate others within the context of the game. We see how people struggle toward success, overcome challenges, and relentlessly pursue the prize. Strategic family therapy, when done badly, can take the quality of reality entertainment, with therapist and family vying for control, for manipulation, for victory. Attend here to the important phrase "done badly." Indeed, therapy that relies on manipulation, covert persuasion, psychological games of mind control, or social experimentation may produce change—but they do so with the possibility of significant risk to the family's well-being. Rather, it was the originators' intent to teach therapy as a phenomenological experience between clinician and family. Strategic therapy is meant to bring balance to an aspect of empirically validated treatment protocols where you treat every circumstance and condition with a formulaic response. Haley (1976) reiterated that such interventions are done with a deep understanding of the individual family and are never used as "standard techniques" that can fit multiple families. So the intention of the strategic use of paradox and manipulation is to reinforce the central values that most clinicians carry as their primary motive for work with families—that of collaboration and engagement with families as they seek to be better at meeting individual and shared needs.

## CONCLUSION

Recall the double-bind message we made in the introduction to this chapter: "All competent clinicians are strategic clinicians." We believe that it is appropriate to end this elaboration of strategic therapy with a manipulative double bind that will require you to either comply with the tenets of strategic theory or wallow in the morass of therapeutic mediocrity! Such a statement forces one to adopt the tenets of strategic therapy in order to be competent. If one rejects the statement, then one risks being labeled as incompetent as it would be expected that only incompetent clinicians dare to object. Satire is the strategist's most effective tool.

Two metaphors remain with us from our experience of graduate training. The first was a one-sentence description of strategic therapy by a professor we both had who practiced from a behavioral perspective. With a look of incredulity he said, "All I can say is, strategic family therapy is *sneaky!*" Indeed, for one used to therapy restricted by the discipline of positive and negative reinforcements, strategic intervention would feel chaotic. One other metaphor used by a mentor was that strategic therapy was a sharp knife and must be used cautiously, carefully, and with watchful vigilance.

Strategic interventions are powerful techniques that have capacities to "outsmart" even the most belligerent family systems. Because of the power of the tool, clinicians must utilize caution in their application. We use these approaches and are grateful to the creative minds that have developed them, but we also recognize how much power becomes concentrated in the hands of the therapist with their use. The introductory metaphor of Don Vito Corleone regarding the offer that cannot be refused is appropriate in recognizing the power generated by the counselor who is using strategic interventions. However, at times the use of such powerful interventions is warranted, as indicated by another famous line by the same character in the movie *The Godfather*, "Never let anyone outside the family know what you're thinking."

## REFERENCES

Barth, K. (1969). *Church dogmatics.* (Vol. 2). Edinburgh: T&T Clark.

Becvar, D. S., & Becvar, R. J. (2006). *Family therapy: A systemic integration* (6th ed.). Boston: Allyn & Bacon.

Broderick, C. B., & Schrader, S. S. (1991). The history of professional marriage and family therapy. In A. S. Gurman & D. P. Kniskern (Eds.), *Handbook of family therapy* (Vol. 2). New York: Brunner/Mazel.

Campbell, D., Draper, R., & Crutchley, E. (1991). The Milan systemic approach to family therapy. In A. S. Gurman & D. P. Kniskern (Eds.), *Handbook of family therapy* (Vol. 2). New York: Brunner/Mazel.

Capps, D. (2004). Jesus as a power tactician. *Journal for the Study of the Historical Jesus, 2,* 158-89.

Castelnuovo, G., Manzoni, G. M., Villa, V., Cesa, G. L., & Molinari, E. (2011). Brief strategic vs. cognitive behavioral therapy for the inpatient and telephone-based outpatient treatment of Binge Eating Disorder: The STRATOB randomized controlled clinical trial. *Clinical Practice & Epidemiology in Mental Health, 7*, 29-37.

Ellul, J. (1964). *The technical society.* New York: Alfred A. Knopf.

Fisch, R. (1978). Review of *Problem-solving therapy,* by Jay Haley. *Family Process, 17*, 107-10.

Fisch, R., Weakland, J., & Segal, L. (1982). *The tactics of change.* San Francisco: Jossey-Bass.

Gladding, S. T. (2007). *Family therapy: History, theory and practice.* Upper Saddle River, NJ: Pearson Prentice Hall.

Goldenberg, I., & Goldenberg, H. (2004). *Family therapy: An overview* (6th ed.). Pacific Grove, CA: Thomson Brooks/Cole.

Haley, J. (1973). *Uncommon therapy.* New York: W. W. Norton.

Haley, J. (1976). *Problem-solving therapy.* New York: Jossey-Bass.

Haley, J. (1980). *Leaving home.* New York: McGraw-Hill.

Haley, J. (1986). *The power tactics of Jesus Christ, and other essays.* Rockville, MD: Triangle Press.

Haley, J. (1990). Interminable therapy. In J. Zeig and S. Gilligan (Eds.), *Brief therapy: Myths, methods and metaphors.* New York: Brunner/Mazel.

MacIntyre, A. C., & Ricoeur, P. (1969). *The religious significance of atheism.* New York: Columbia University Press.

Madanes, C. (1984). *Behind the one-way mirror.* San Francisco: Jossey-Bass.

Madanes, C. (1991). Strategic family therapy. In A. S. Gurman & D. P. Kniskern (Eds.), *Handbook of family therapy* (Vol. 2). New York: Brunner/Mazel.

Martin, J. E. (2003). Human nature vs. the hermeneutics of love. In R. C. Roberts & M. R. Talbot (Eds.), *Limning the psyche: Explorations in Christian psychology.* Eugene, OR: Wipf & Stock.

Nelson, T. S., & Figley, C. R. (1990). Basic family therapy skills, III: Brief and strategic schools of family therapy. *Journal of Family Psychology, 4*, 49-62.

Nichols, M. P. (1984). *Family therapy: Concepts and methods.* New York: Gardner Press.

Palazzoli, M., Selvini, Boscolo, L., Cecchin, G., & Prata, G. (1978). *Paradox and counterparadox.* New York: Jason Aronson.

Palazzoli, M. Selvini, Boscolo, L., Cecchin, G., & Prata, G. (1980). Hypothesizing—circularity—neutrality: Three guidelines for the conductor of the session. *Family Process, 19*, 3-12.

Rakowska, J. M. (2011). Brief strategic therapy in patients with social phobia with or without personality disorder. *Psychotherapy Research, 21*(4), 462-71.

Robbins, M. S., Feaster, D. J., Horigian, V. E., Puccinelli, M. J., Henderson, C., & Szapocznik, J. (2011). Therapist adherence in brief strategic family therapy for adolescent drug abusers. *Journal of Consulting and Clinical Psychology*, *79*(1), 43-53.

Robbins, M. S., Feaster, D. J., Horigian, V. E., Rohrbaugh, M., Shoham, V., Bachrach, K., Miller, M., et al. (2011). Brief strategic family therapy versus treatment as usual: Results of a multisite randomized trial for substance abusing adolescents. *Journal of Consulting and Clinical Psychology*, *79*(6), 713-27.

Russell, B. (1901). *Principles of mathematics.* Cambridge: Cambridge University Press.

Schweitzer, A. (1948). *The psychiatric study of Jesus: Exposition and criticism.* Gloucester, MA: Peter Smith.

Segal, L. (1991). Brief therapy: The M.R.I. approach. In A. S. Gurman and D. P. Kniskern (Eds.), *Handbook of family therapy* (Vol. 2). New York: Brunner/Mazel.

Seltzer, L. (1986). *Paradoxical strategies in psychotherapy: A comprehensive overview and guidebook.* Chichester, UK: John Wiley & Sons.

Sheehan, A. H., & Friedlander, M. L. (2015). Therapeutic alliance and retention in brief strategic family therapy: A mixed methods study. *Journal of Marital and Family Therapy*, *41*(4), 415-27.

Stanton, M. D. (1981). Strategic approaches to family therapy. In A. S. Gurman & D. P. Kniskern (Eds.), *Handbook of family therapy* (Vol. 1). New York: Brunner/Mazel.

Stout, J. (1981). *The flight from authority.* Notre Dame, IN: University of Notre Dame Press.

Szapocznik, J., Muir, J. A., Duff, J. H., Schwartz, S. J., & Brown, C. H. (2015). Brief strategic family therapy: Implementing evidence-based models in community settings. *Psychotherapy Research*, *25*(1), 121-33.

Szapocznik, J., Schwartz, S. J., Muir, J. A., & Brown, C. H. (2012). Brief strategic family therapy: An intervention to reduce adolescent risk behavior. *Couple and Family Psychology: Research and Practice*, *1*(2), 134-45.

Tomm, K. (1984). One perspective on the Milan systemic approach: Part I. Overview of development, theory and practice. *Journal of Marriage and Family Therapy*, *10*, 113-25.

Tomm, K. (1987). Interventive interviewing: Part II. Reflexive questioning as a means to enable self-healing. *Family Process*, *27*, 167-83.

Valdez, A., Cepeda, A., Parrish, D., Horowitz, R., & Kaplan, C. (2013). An adapted brief strategic family therapy for gang-affiliated Mexican American adolescents. *Research on Social Work Practice*, *23*(4), 383-96.

Watzlawick, P., Weakland, J., & Fisch, R. (1974). *Change: Principles of problem formation and problem resolution.* New York: W. W. Norton.

Weakland, J. (1976). Communication theory and clinical change. In P. J. Guerin (Ed.), *Family therapy: Theory and practice.* New York: Gardner Press.

Whitehead, A. N., & Russell, B. (1910/1913). *Principia mathematica*. Cambridge: Cambridge University Press.

Wiener, N. (1948). *Cybernetics, or control and communication in the animal and the machine*. New York: Wiley.

# STRUCTURAL FAMILY THERAPY

*To maintain a joyful family requires much
from both the parents and the children. Each
member of the family has to become, in a
special way, the servant of the others.*

**POPE JOHN PAUL II**

IN THE ENTRYWAY OF THEIR HOME IS the structure. It hangs on the wall in two languages—Spanish and English. Those that enter the home and pause in the foyer long enough to read it will learn something of the rules that Georgina and Javier have established to govern their lives and to influence the decisions that affect their family. It reads:

We will commit to seeking God's Kingdom first in all that we are and do. Our home will be a place where family, friends and guests find joy, comfort, peace and happiness. We will exercise wisdom in what we choose to eat, read and do in our home. We will learn to love another as we develop our own talents. We will exercise initiative in accomplishing our life's goals. We will act on situations as opportunities, rather than to be acted upon. We will always try to keep ourselves free from addictive and destructive habits. We will develop habits that free us from old labels and limits and expand our capabilities and choices. Our money will be our servant, not our master. Our wants will be subject to our needs and means. We will honor God and choose to obey him every day of our lives. (Javier and Gina Panting Sierra)

Structure is how organizations are made. It is the prevailing principle that influences behaviors. A government has a constitution that contributes to the order of a society. If the citizenry does not follow the rules laid out in the constitution there will be chaos and possibly anarchy. A corporation has a structure: there is a chief executive officer and a chief financial officer who follow the dictations of the board of directors and the law. The structure of a business includes job descriptions for all of its employees and typically a business plan that puts forth a strategy to fulfill the company's purpose. If the employees don't follow the rules, the organization suffers.

Families have structures too. When the structures are responsibly created— that is, they are not so restrictive that they prevent individuality, and not too impermeable that they inhibit guidance—and if the members of the family respect the structures that have been created, then the family probably works well.

Javier and Gina articulated part of their family structure. It is their core values and principles around which they structure their marriage. From these values flow the arrangements in living—the rules that govern decisions and influence actions. Not every aspect of a family structure can be put into words, because many of our structural realities are operating underneath our full awareness. But all families possess a set of rules, patterns, expectations, and values that permit individuals within to form purpose and pursue goals. For example, in their brief sentence "Our wants will be subject to our needs and means" is found an explicit structural guide for their economic decisions. That statement forms a boundary for making decisions about wealth, debt, and material goods. Also, embedded in the text are the words "us," "our," and "we." They are used twenty-three times. They appear to be setting the principle of power and decision making within the home—that the family is a plurality, and the commitment to uphold these values will be made by the community of "us." Georgina and Javier have put forth an intentional "structure," they have attempted to bring into conscious intention the values and principles that they would like to have pattern their lives. The structures that they articulate in this brief manifesto represent a few of the values and patterns that they want to direct their family. But there are hundreds of other structures that are at play in directing theirs and any marriage.

## HISTORY OF STRUCTURAL FAMILY THERAPY

Structural family therapy is a systemic approach to family interventions that focuses on identifying the underlying patterns or rules that regulate or dictate the space between people in relationship. Structural family therapy held a preeminent role in family theory and therapy during the 1970s and 1980s and continues to be a foundational approach currently. Its popularity is based on the simplicity of the theoretical constructs, the demonstrated effectiveness of the approach, and the dynamic persona of its primary developer, Salvador Minuchin.

Minuchin was born in 1921 in Argentina to European emigrant parents. He studied medicine in Buenos Aires and became a physician. He volunteered as a military doctor in the Israeli army during their struggle for statehood in the late 1940s. Afterward, he traveled to New York to obtain a psychiatric specialty and then returned to Israel in 1952, where he worked with Jewish families and orphans who were immigrating to Israel after the Holocaust.

In 1954 he returned to the United States and began psychoanalytic training at the William Alanson White Institute in Manhattan, becoming the psychiatrist for a juvenile delinquent residential program called the Wiltwyck School. Minuchin spent eight years there forming an important relationship with Braulio Montalvo, a clinical social worker whom Minuchin credits as being his most influential teacher (Goldenberg & Goldenberg, 2004). Montalvo was central to the development of structural theory and intervention and later would move to the Philadelphia Child Guidance Clinic with Minuchin.

Minuchin's primary responsibility at Wiltwyck was as an intake psychiatrist. However, with Montalvo and others, he sought to understand the problems faced by predominantly Puerto Rican and African American adolescents being admitted to the school. He considered the family structure of these youths—particularly how the factors of poverty have effects on family organization, which in turn prompts students to act out in ways that are harmful to them and to society.

Minuchin's search for a social etiology of adolescent pathology took him away from the medical and psychoanalytic paradigms of both his training and the current practice of his day. Minuchin developed theories and interventions that addressed the needs of the poor, urban, minority adolescents and their families. "Because the style of interaction in these families tended to be concrete and action-oriented, rather than abstract and verbal, the team looked into alternative, 'more doing than talking' therapies" (Colapinto, 1991, p. 418). A result to emerge from this initial focus was the widely acclaimed *Families of the Slums* (Minuchin, Montalvo, Guerney, Rosman, & Schumer, 1967).

Minuchin found that the work of the Mental Research Institute (MRI), in particular Don Jackson and Jay Haley, offered significant promise in addressing needs within urban families. He read their theory, consulted with them at MRI, and invited them to New York. While structural family therapy was separate and distinct from the strategic and brief models developed at Palo Alto, they shared many core principles, such as defining the family structure through the transactions between members, and equifinality—that is, the theory that systems may take alternative paths to obtain the final outcome. The relationship between structural and strategic theories was able to synthesize further when Minuchin moved to the Philadelphia Child Guidance Clinic in 1965 and recruited both Montalvo and Haley to join him. Goldenberg and Goldenberg (2004) report that the integration of ideas between these three innovators was encouraged by the daily carpool commute to the clinic in central Philadelphia from their suburban homes.

The Philadelphia Child Guidance Clinic thrived under Minuchin's leadership. When he started in 1965, the clinic had a staff of less than a dozen. When he left in 1981 there were more than three hundred employees, and the clinic was a major resource for families and a primary center for professional development. The clinic was able to continue its original commitment of providing mental health services and family education to the underserved populations of Philadelphia and to expand to be a primary source of family treatment research and training.

Though Minuchin continued to write and contribute to the profession, the torch was passed to the next generation of structural therapists. The approach continues to be an active force in family intervention and research. It has been adapted and applied to families coming from various cultures, structures, and socioeconomic backgrounds.

## THEORETICAL AND PHILOSOPHICAL ASSUMPTIONS OF STRUCTURAL FAMILY THERAPY

Structural family therapy focuses on identifying the underlying principles that govern a family's interactions; then reinforcing those rules, patterns, or values that support the achievement of family goals; and altering those that work in opposition to what the family desires. Structures exist on many levels within a family. They can be seen in the initial vows of marriage, the division of labor created by the members, the acceptable responses to events and emotions, the expectations for success, and the responses to failure. Family structures establish norms for the family groups. They are defined by the family and they in turn define the family.

**Definition of family structure.** Most people think of buildings when confronted by the word *structure*, and they often associate structural family therapy with the approach in which the counselor manipulates the physical distance between family members within the session. Structural family therapy is much more involved than merely "moving the deck chairs on the Titanic." And structure has far greater complexity than noting the placement and patterns of a family in the counselor's office. The term *structure* represents the pattern or style that a family utilizes to fulfill its goals. A structure is the rules, agreements, and assumptions that permit the organization to operate to successfully achieve its goals. "For Minuchin, structure refers to the invisible set of functional demands that organizes the way the family interacts, or the consistent, repetitive, organized, and predictable modes of family behavior that allow us to consider that the family has a structure in a functional sense" (Becvar & Becvar, 2006, p. 174).

Every family has a common structure—a *generic* set of patterns that transcend time and culture (Minuchin, 1974). These structures are the result of facts of human development and basic survival. Adults make decisions for children until the time when children have the capacity to make decisions for themselves. Adults must have a means to provide the necessities for life—food, shelter, a capacity to form community with others, and so on—and to teach children how they will eventually be responsible for their own survival. That parents have authority over their children is a near universal or generic phenomenon. Parents, in their unique ways, teach their children to become self-sufficient by gradually relinquishing their authority to the children to manage their own lives. Minuchin refers to this as the *idiosyncratic* structure of the family (Minuchin, 1974).

The generic and idiosyncratic characteristics of the family contain roles and responsibilities that are *complementary*. A complementary role might be something as simple as a family delineating the chores to be done on a Saturday morning. A parent may decide that the ten-year-old will vacuum, the eight-year-old will separate whites from colored laundry, and the six-year-old will help a parent dust the furniture. The complementary structures that are created by the family permit its members to coexist; if everyone wanted to clean the carpet and they fought over control of the vacuum cleaner (as inconceivable as that may sound), then the family would become stalemated in its effort to complete the most basic tasks.

The existence of complementary family structures implies the possibilities of alternative structures that run against the capacity for the family to accomplish its goals or to complete its operations (Aponte & Van Deusen, 1981). The essence of the therapeutic process is for the counselor, after joining with the family and witnessing the exhibition of the verbal and nonverbal transactions between family members, to identify the dimensions or components of the family structures that are "dysfunctional"; that is, those elements that fail in assisting the family to fulfill its intention.

**Family subsystems.** Within each family there are smaller groups that share unique responsibilities, characteristics, or roles. The husband/wife team has tasks that are distinct from the subsystem of children. The high school adolescents have expectations for behavior that are different from the elementary school children. Grandparents have special roles that are different than the roles they played when they were the parents. There are dozens of other subsystems. They can be defined according to gender, the extended family from each parent, even special interests—such as those that like to camp and hike and those that like to experience luxury and pampering. Subsystems can be formed around personality types such as the laid-back family members who can relate to the relative unimportance of having a clean room or doing homework as soon as you get home from school, compared to those whose lives are run with order and efficiency. Subsystems are a means by which children form complicated identities through the affiliation with family members with whom they share a special affinity.

The most powerful subsystem is the marital dyad because power to make decisions for the younger generation emanates from the husband/wife or adult team. While it is the case that therapy addresses the multiple subsystems occurring within a family, it almost always starts with the parental subsystem. The parental subsystem typically carries the most power and authority to instigate change within the system. Madden-Derdich, Estrada, and Updegraff (2002) refer to the importance of a healthy, vibrant, collaborative parental subsystem as a "universal tenet" for mature family functioning. It is often the case that the marital dyad is not composed of husband/wife but is concentrated within a single parent—usually with other extended family members playing ancillary but crucial support roles—or is split between divorced parents, often with two stepparents involved in family structure and strategy. By the fact that there are more people involved, the complexity of the parental subsystems creates greater vulnerability for misunderstanding between roles, traversing of boundaries and the formation of triangulations, and developing alliances that cross generations (Balswick & Balswick, 1989).

*Boundaries.* Probably no concept within family theory and therapy has transcended from academic and professional use to the level of the general public as has had the idea of boundaries. Bobes and Rothman (2002) state that "the concepts of boundaries and reframing, originally unique to Minuchin's structural therapy, are now universal concepts that are used by most therapists in the family therapy field" (p. 18).

Boundaries are the divisions that we create to form order—both internally within each individual's responsibilities to life, and externally between family members and others outside of the home. Minuchin (1974) sees boundaries as the "rules defining who participates and how" (p. 53). An individual boundary is evidenced by the ability to turn off the lights, shut the door, and drive away from work on Friday afternoon and not return—physically, mentally, or emotionally—until Monday morning, even though one acknowledges that there is much still to do in the office. Evidence of mature marital boundaries can be illustrated by the behavior of a couple that maintains the importance of daily time alone from children, and they do not break that commitment because of the children's acting out or attention-getting behavior. Boundaries are seen in the parental-adolescent subsystem when a parent purchases a diary or a journal for a young adolescent and writes in the front page, "This is your book to contain your private thoughts. I will respect this boundary by never seeking knowledge of its content, unless you volunteer it to me. If there are problems in your life, then I will trust you to communicate those problems to me in ways more direct than writing them in your sacred journal and secretly wishing that I will break our bond of trust to find out and bring you aid."

Boundaries are fluid dimensions of relationship. For instance, a closed bedroom door means "knock and ask permission to enter" in most homes—where children are conscious of sexuality and of privacy. But parents of infants and toddlers don't knock on the door of the nursery before checking to see if the naptime has produced the needed sleep for the two-year-old.

That boundaries change can be seen in a story frequently described by "empty nester" parents. They say, "When my son is away, I don't worry a minute at night, even though I know he might be out at a party, or driving late. However, when he comes home for Christmas or Easter break, I just can't sleep until I hear him come in the house." These examples demonstrate the strain on families because boundaries are in a constant state of movement. The expression of discomfort with the positioning of boundaries, the relinquishing of old controls, and the acceptance of new responsibilities represent strain on the family system.

*Alignments and coalitions.* Families are political entities. Decisions are made to accommodate ongoing changes in needs, interests, and desires by all of the family members simultaneously. Such decisions involve the negotiation between all of the members for the application of the family's resources of time, attention, energy, behavior, and emotion. In order to consolidate power— that is, to gain control of the decision making that suits individuals—the members will align themselves with others in order to accomplish their goals (Aponte, 1976). For example, the boys in a family may form a coalition against the girls over what the family will play on the radio or MP3 player when traveling in the car. Parents maintain a coalition against children to prevent eating pizza or chicken fingers for dinner—for the fourth straight night! Or children may split the parental coalition and persuade a parent to side with them— using a behavioral tantrum to reconfigure the alignments. "Within the boundaries of any family the members have patterns of working together or in mutual opposition about the many activities they must engage in as family members" (Aponte & Van Deusen, 1981, p. 313).

Alignment with others and the formation of coalitions carries all of the privileges and challenges of nations forming treaties with other nations. With the formation of coalitions, power is consolidated so that the less powered are inclined to possess the capacity to influence the system (there is strength in numbers). However, when family members are aligned with one another and coalitions are formed against other family entities, there is a loss of freedom and some sacrifice of trust and cooperation. For the same reason that George Washington warned the nation's leaders to be wary of the formation of treaties and alignments with other countries, so family members must be careful about the obligations that are created when members take sides.

*Triangulation.* Triangulation is a specific form of alignment and coalition building. Specifically, Minuchin refers to triangulations as "cross-generational coalitions." They occur when "each parent demands that the child side with him [*sic*] against the other parent. Whenever the child sides with one, he is automatically defined as attacking the other. In this highly dysfunctional structure, the child is paralyzed. Every movement he makes is defined by one parent as an attack" (Minuchin, 1974, p. 102).

Triangulation is employed in order to obtain power over the family or over individual members. There is a benefit and loss associated with triangulation. Typically the effect is successful acquisition of immediate goals but the loss of subsequent goals. In other words, a parent gets what he or she wants through the triangulation of a child, but ensuing interactions are met with similar or divergent manipulative acts by the other adult. The result is a self-sustaining dysfunction in the system.

*Power.* Power refers to who actually makes decisions for themselves or for the family group as well as who acts on them. Power is the exercise of control over others as well as the ability for self-determination. A parent has power to determine sleep schedules for the other family members. At 5:00 in the morning a mother or father can blow a whistle or beat a drum and get everyone awake. However, the parent becomes powerless to control the fatigue-related responses such as laying down in the middle of aisle 9 of the grocery store to take a nap. All of the previous concepts—boundaries, alignments, coalitions, and triangles—involve the negotiations within the system to make and manage power and control decisions. The maturity of the family system can be seen in the manner in which power is manipulated within the system. Gladding notes that "in dysfunctional families, power is vested in only a few members. The ability of family members to provide input in the decision-making process that governs the family is limited. Disenfranchised family members may cut themselves off from the family, become enmeshed with stronger members, or battle to gain some control in an overt or covert way" (2007, pp. 206-7).

*Family mapping.* The family strengths and dysfunctions—including the efforts to construct boundaries and form coalitions—can be visually represented through a "family map." Minuchin advocated the use of maps to indicate the family shape as well as to assess family development. Family shape uses the demographic details to obtain an image of the power structure managed by the system's leaders. Family shapes can be represented by the two-parent heterosexual family with no previous marriages or children from other relationships; divorced parents can be distinguished from single-parent homes; and extended family members can be depicted for their important family role.

Family development is a second component of the mapping of a family. Family development is a visual representation of the life stage of a family group that changes as the members advance through the phases of human growth. Imagine a parent saying that he or she regularly sleeps in the child's bedroom instead of with his or her spouse. Our "clinical judgment" would differ if the little girl were three years old and afraid of the dark and daddy would lay down in her bed to offer security, compared to our assessment if this were a seventeen-year-old boy and mommy was still "helping him" fall asleep. Both would be forms of enmeshment; the former is valued and seen as healthy within the general culture. The latter would be seen as odd by just about every group (especially the Freudians).

As in a genogram, the map reveals the "structural" components—such as the presence of family members and the condition of their relationship. Minuchin says that

> this family map indicates the position of the family members vis-à-vis one another. It reveals coalitions, affiliations, explicit and implicit conflicts, and the ways family members group themselves in conflict resolution. It identifies family members who operate as detours of conflict and family members who function as switchboards. The map charts the nurturers, healers, and scape-goaters. Its delineations of the boundaries between subsystems indicates what movement there is and suggests possible areas of strength or dysfunction. (Minuchin, 1974, p. 69)

Today structural family therapy is a popular, widely practiced approach to working with families, and it has been adapted and integrated with other approaches and applied to various clinical presentations. For example, ecosystemic structural family therapy is described as a "systemic, strengths-based, and trauma-informed family therapy model" that is based on structural family theory and integrated with a more ecosystemic or relational environment perspective, as well as recent work on attachment theory (Lindblad-Goldberg & Northey, 2013, p. 147). The five tenets of ecosystemic structural family therapy are family structure, family and individual emotional regulation, individual differences, affective proximity, and family development. Similar integrated theoretical models exist for general practice (e.g., James & MacKinnon, 2010) as well as for specific populations, such as low-income families from a structural community family approach (e.g., McNeil, Herschberger, & Nedela, 2013), pornography addiction (e.g., Ford, Durtschi, & Franklin, 2012), treatment of maternal depression (e.g., Weaver, Greeno, Marcus, Fusco, Zimmerman, & Anderson, 2013), and social networking sites and the family (e.g., Murphy, Lancy, & Hertlein, 2013).

## WHEN FAMILIES SEEK HELP

*Joining.* As the structuralist viewpoint of family is hierarchical, from parents, to older siblings, to younger siblings, likewise family therapy is hierarchical, with the therapist entering the relationship in a leadership role (Minuchin & Fishman, 1981). The family possesses knowledge of the idiosyncrasies of their system—they are aware of its history and of the players/participants within the extended boundary of the family clan, they have experience in conduct with each other, and they have a pattern of resolving differences. However, when current issues within the system have not been successfully resolved, they seek to join with a change agent who can assist them with an issue that has become a source of pain for individuals and a problem that the family has not been able to heal by themselves.

It is most common for the family to view the therapist as the expert on how problems such as theirs should best be resolved. They come to the counselor for help. However, there is usually an implicit expectation that the therapist will seek to make change within the system using methods similar to how the family has sought to address the problem previously. They commonly expect the counselor to understand the problem and develop a solution in ways that confirm their previous unsuccessful approaches.

Dr. James Cassens, a clinical psychologist and respected family therapy supervisor, would introduce the joining process in the following way:

> Imagine that I am an explorer/developer. I know rough terrain. I help others
> find and use their property. People hire me to survey their land and document
> its strengths and resources. You are a family that owns a very large piece of
> property—maybe even an island. It has been in your family for generations. It
> is so large that it has never been fully explored nor has anyone attempted to

make use of it—except right around the edges. So first of all I will learn what you as a family have—I will explore it with you, especially the places that are hard to get to, and maybe even dangerous to visit. I have been to many dangerous places so I help you all stay safe. Now once we know what is out there, you all will have to exercise some options regarding what you are going to do with it. I can help you here too because I have helped families develop their resources—but you know, sometimes families don't understand what potential richness they may already possess because they have lived for so long just utilizing the edges of their property. Throughout our relationship—the property remains yours, I can't tell you what to do with it, but I can say, because I have observed many other families utilize their resources, what some of the potentials for your land could be. Some of my suggestions might become upsetting to you. While my intention is not to disturb for the sake of disturbance, it happens anyway merely by considering the changes that might take place as a result of exploring all of the land. I will help you address the fears [or] threats that come from having these conversations. You will teach me options that I will share with others because of the creativity and courage that you demonstrate toward one another. (J. Cassens, 2000, personal communication)

In joining, the therapist is accepted into the family as an "honorary member," one who will be permitted to observe and participate in the family's established structure. Other approaches might refer to joining as forming a therapeutic alliance, establishing rapport, or building trust. Joining is also something that the therapist does continually. It "is an operation which functions in counterpoint to every therapeutic intervention. The therapist joins and joins again many times during a session and during the course of therapy" (Minuchin & Fishman, 1981, p. 49).

*Accommodating.* Minuchin extends the discussion of relationship formation by including an important "how to" in regards to joining. "Joining a family requires of the therapist a capacity to adapt. Such adaptation, which is here called accommodation, can be either unaware or deliberate. When it is used deliberately, it can speed the early phases of therapy and facilitate treatment" (Minuchin, 1974, p. 125).

As joining implies that the counselor has been invited into the family, accommodation suggests what a therapist must do to get there. The process of accommodation is unique to structural therapy as a component of the theory. Although the person-centered approach does emphasize the demonstration of empathy, unconditional positive regard, and congruence as the necessary pre-conditions to being accepted by the client or the family, these are generic re-sponses applicable to all families or individuals. The structural perspective is that therapists must accommodate—or change to become an acceptable member of the family. Minuchin (1974) draws a parallel to the work of anthropology:

> the family therapist joins the culture with which he [sic] is dealing. In the same oscillating rhythm, he engages then disengages. He experiences the pressures of the family system. At the same time, he observes the system, making deductions that enable him to transform his experience into a family map, for which he derives therapeutic goals. . . . Unlike the anthropologist, the therapist is bent on changing the culture he joins, and he has the skills to do so. But his goals, his tactics and his stratagems are all dependent on the processes of joining. (Minuchin, 1974, pp. 124-25)

*Assessment.* Many would consider assessment a pre-step to therapy. Within the structural tradition assessment is an essential component of the joining/accommodating phase (Colapinto, 1991). Assessment begins with the identi-fication of family demographics and initial description of the family, by which the clinician begins to form a mental image of the family shape.

In the first interview with the family the counselor learns the family lan-guage or the family dance. The counselor is looking to see who speaks, who withdraws, who humors, who disagrees, who forms alliances, who creates fear, sadness, hope, despair, rage, discouragement, collaboration, and so on. Ques-tions may be asked of the family or simply observed: Who's in charge in this family? How do the children or siblings interact with one another and with the parents? What are different people's theories about the problems? What would different people like to see changed? and How are conflicts responded to in the actual session? (Taibbi, 2015, pp. 215-16).

Assessment focuses on the behavioral manifestations of the relational problem occurring within the family. Behaviors of importance include the individual actions of each member, such as demonstrated attitude, breathing, facial expression, body position, and verbalizations, as well as the interactions, both verbal and behavioral, that occur within the system.

*Unbalancing.* To unbalance a family system, the therapist alters the hier-archical relationship that exists within the system. Minuchin and Fishman (1981) believe that under most conditions the entry into the family system by

the therapist at the "top of the relational food chain" occurs rather innocu-
ously. Families expect the counselor to enter as the authority—particularly
when the family is meeting in the counselor's office, sitting on the counselor's
chairs, and accommodating the counselor's schedule—as in the fifty-minute
appointment starting at the top of the hour. In addition, families are usually
accepting of lateral changes in the family structure. Moving the power from
one person to another, taking turns, and demonstrating mutual fairness
usually is received with acceptance. But changing the structural hierarchy
within the family is like demoting the "alpha dog" on the sled team. The alteration of the power structure changes everyone's relative position within
the group.

The therapist alters his or her position within the family by joining with a
person who has minimal power and aligning against others within the system
to alter the status quo. "To unbalance, the therapist uses her affiliation with
one family member to change his hierarchical position in the family system.
The focus on one family member changes the position of all family members"
(Minuchin & Fishman, 1981, p. 164). This unbalancing process is an aspect of
joining, assessment, and the intervention. Minuchin is changing the structure—
creating family disorganization, rebuilding new alignments, and forming new
patterns of cooperation.

*Tracking.* Tracking suggests Minuchin's somewhat paradoxical leadership
style of "leading by following." Again, it is a demonstration of the ongoing
joining and accommodating process. The process of tracking is like a news
reporter who chases down every lead—most might initially appear to have
little relevance, but each one supplies another component of a vast complicated family process. Tracking permits the family to reveal its idiosyncrasies.
It involves noting a comment or pattern and inviting the individuals to
comment and reveal it. For example, a counselor might learn of a family fight
that occurred while driving in the car. The youngest child was in the "wrong
spot." That evoked a power struggle with his or her older sibling. The counselor inquires, "What is a spot? How are spots wrong or right? Who determines spots? Do spots ever change?" The information reveals that "spots"
were seats designated by kids in the second row of the station wagon. The
eldest daughter sat behind the mom. The middle son sat behind the dad.
The youngest daughter sat in the middle without access to the windows and
with the big hump on the floor. This order was established when they were

preschoolers and continued to exist into their adolescence. The "third position" was clearly a less than optimal placement—like never getting the advantage of the window or aisle seat on an airplane. But the family, parents included, did not seek to accommodate the calls for change expressed by the youngest and least powerful. Tracking the story and following the lines of history and experience reveal the full richness of the family structures.

*Enactment.* As mentioned previously, assessment is an ongoing component of the therapeutic process. It occurs through direct but passive observation of the family dance. It also is observed by intentional manipulation of the family structures, as if the therapist is saying, "Let's see how the family dances after we cut holes in the floor." An enactment is a created challenge offered to the system or to subsystems that raises disequilibrium and forces the members to demonstrate their interaction patterns. Enactments emerge naturally through the tracking of individual stories. When a wife/mother says that she "gets no support from her husband, and no participation from the kids in running the home," the counselor can stop and say to the husband, "She finds you to be unsupportive. Could you two talk out the need and the offering of support?" The therapist then withdraws from the center of the conversation and watches the process, noting concession, blaming, avoidance, triangulation, acceptance, or other responses. Enactments, while they emerge naturally through listening and tracking exchanges, are deliberate assessment strategies and should not be confused with simply allowing a couple or other family members to argue with one another.

> In setting up an enactment, the therapist explains the purpose of the enactment, specifies the specific content and organizes the physical space so that the partners are sitting close together, able to maintain eye contact. The therapist sits back, avoids eye contact and stays out of the interaction until it seems useful or necessary to interrupt an evolving negative interaction. The therapist makes brief, specific and process oriented comments to help the couple stay on track, avoid interruptions and maintain the content focus. (James & MacKinnon, 2010, p. 6)

The process and outcome of an enactment provides you with potentially invaluable data about how the family itself and individual family members "dance" with one another in relationship (p. 6).

*Boundary realignment.* The intent and focus of structural therapy is to restructure the rules and the spacing that govern family relationships. Most often the enactments reveal structures of enmeshments and disengagements. This frequently occurs within the marital subsystem, in which conflict and life demands overwhelm the family leadership, and the members opt for a response pattern that includes the work, recreation, religious, hobby, or children's subsystem as an inappropriate or exacerbating factor. As a simple example, consider a couple that plans to have a conversation at the end of the day, after the kids are in bed. One of the children insists or demands that mommy or daddy sleep in her bed. When the child appears to be asleep the parent tries to leave, awakening the child and restarting the entire sequence. Eventually fatigue conquers both adults—one parent can't stay up any later, and the helping parent falls asleep in the single bed—until about 3:00 a.m. when she stumbles back to the master bedroom and crawls into bed. Clearly the parents have relinquished control of the marital subsystem and are permitting the child to interfere with the parental system to ease her "it's dark and I'm alone" fears.

As is the case in most circumstances similar to this, the kids are smarter than the parents. She knows how to get what she wants, but the parents don't. Boundary realignment is an exercise in returning to the intelligence of the parents to solve problems. Clearly, the child has attachment needs that are to be respected and addressed by concerned parents. Working with the parental subsystem, the counselor would identify creative alternatives that would permit a realignment of the boundaries. This could include using transitional objects; altering nap, sleep, and activity schedules to increase the level of exhaustion at bedtime (for the child, not the parents); offering incentives and rewards for being a big girl; and enforcing that essential lesson that all children must learn: "No! I will not lay down with you any longer. Good night." This will require accepting the use of manipulative strategies by the child to revert back to the secure homeostasis of having a parent in bed with them, but not yielding to them.

*Reframing.* One of the most common quips about seeing your children marry and begin their life under a new home ends with the punch line "You are not really losing a daughter; you are gaining a son-in-law." Depending on the quality of your adult daughter or son's judgment, that is either a consolation or a source of grief. To reframe is to consider the same experiential phenomenon under a different set of explanations and considerations.

A reframe is to consider the circumstances in alternative structures. Individuals come to be fused with their understanding of problems and their solutions. They repeat established, secure, but unproductive methods because they do not have the security to try alternative responses. "By 'reframing' the problem, and by talking to themselves with different words, the family discovers ways out of the psychological and emotional mental ruts in which they were constantly spinning" (Taibbi, 2015, pp. 9-10). Reframes can be introduced through a variety of means—a direct suggestion, a paradox, humor, education, reading assignment, or a direct challenge. The essence of reframing is to implement an alternative set of family rules that direct the family's behavior.

## THE APPROACH TO FAMILY THERAPY: THE NELSON FAMILY

The Nelson family offers a look into the family processes of structural conflict and the manner in which interventions were created, introduced, and implemented.

The Nelson family was a blended family that never quite blended. The family consisted of Joan, age forty-three, who was previously married and divorced. Her two children from that first marriage were Mike, age fifteen, and Natasha, who was thirteen. Marty was Joan's husband; he was forty-seven. He also had been married before, divorced twenty years ago. Marty had two adult children that were in their mid-twenties, living 1,500 miles away, and who rarely had contact with their father. Joan and Marty had been married for four years and had a three-year-old daughter, Tanya. Marty was a long-distance truck driver. He would be gone for ten to fifteen days, then home for a week, then on the road again.

The assessment process began when Joan called the therapist to say that she was "having problems with my husband getting along with my son" (figurative wording: the problem is my husband). She wanted to come in with him to get some help. The counselor asked for the initial session to meet with the full family of five members. There was initial resistance. "I don't see why I have to drag my three kids into this. I just need to get him to stop beating up on my son." Naturally, the implication of violence redirected the counselor's questioning. To track this idea, he asked about domestic aggression—what had transpired between son and stepdad. The mother described the situation as not being physical—no hitting, shoving, or other physical abuse. She said, "Marty will scream and yell at him to get him to do stuff like pick up his room or come to dinner. So I say, 'Don't you tell him what to do, I'll parent my own son, you just stay out of it.' But he doesn't listen to me; he just goes and does it again."

Joan's description affirmed the importance of seeing the whole family together. It appeared that her initial agenda was to strengthen the coalition between herself and her son by recruiting a psychologist to join the triangulation. While there would be no doubt that time would need to be directed toward the marital subsystem, not starting with the whole family would not present a realistic image of how the family actually worked, and would have lent support to the wife in what appeared to be a marital war between her and her husband, with the children as the battlefield. The situation might have been different if the husband had called and said, "I am having a difficult time with my wife regarding the raising of our child and her adolescent children." But because Joan described the problem systemically, assessing the system at the family level was important.

Later that week the family entered the counselor's office. Joan sat between Mike and Natasha, Tanya sat on Marty's lap directly facing Joan. The battle lines were clearly drawn. Introductions were made; Mike and Natasha showed the expected enthusiasm of adolescents. Having to breathe air in the same room as their parents seemed to be an affront. Tanya bubbled in cuteness—as if she was oblivious to the tension between the older siblings and her parents. More likely, "cute" was the three-year-old's solution to reduce family stress.

Joan described the situation—that Marty would be away for weeks at a time and the family operated very smoothly whenever he was gone. But as soon as he would walk into the house he would begin making demands, yelling at everyone, especially yelling at Mike. Everyone gets tense and can't wait for him to leave on his next trip.

Marty tried to interrupt Joan a few times during her explanation. She was quick to say, "Let me finish, Marty." When it was his turn, Marty said that he was gone a lot and could understand how the family gets used to him not being around. "But when I am at home, I am like an unwelcome relative in my own house. I sleep downstairs on the sofa. I make my own dinner. Do my own laundry. The one thing that I am permitted to do is pay the bills. I come back from being on the road for a week and my reward is to pay the bills. No one is glad that I am there. My truck is more comfortable than my home."

Tanya immediately disagreed, "I am glad you are at home, Daddy." Mike and Natasha rolled their eyes.

After hearing all of the kids tell their story, the remaining time was spent with the marital dyad, with the children in the waiting room. The counselor learned about their courtship and initial years of marriage. Their sexuality was expressed in a clandestine manner. Because the conflict between Joan and Marty was so open to the children, she did not want to convey to the adolescents that she was having sex with him. So, she demanded that he sleep on the sofa downstairs until all of the kids were asleep. Then he would quietly walk upstairs and sleep in his bed with Joan. They would have intercourse, but early in the morning, and before the children awoke he would return to the sofa.

Joan and Marty both agreed that this pattern was ridiculous—but for opposite reasons. Joan resented Marty for being so angry about sex. "If I don't let him come upstairs he's mean and grumpy until he gets something, . . . but there is no way that I am going to pretend to him or to my kids that everything is cool between him and me, because it's not!"

Marty said, "I feel humiliated. This is just stupid. I am treated like the family dog. She just throws me a bone once in a while. So I yell. I yell at Mike and Natasha—but I am really angry at Joan. I am angry at the kids too because they know that they don't have to do a thing that I say. Mike can say 'F-you,' and Joan would yell at me for making him mad."

The first session ended with bantering back and forth between the couple over who is the one most to blame for the frustrations in life experienced by both. Marty and Joan were in a defensive attack posture—angry and stubbornly entrenched.

The next session the family was asked to perform an enactment exercise. The counselor asked Marty to stand to the side of the room and asked the other four family members to stand in the middle of the room with their arms around each other tightly. Marty was then asked to enter the family. There was no instruction to the family to keep him out or to let him in; they were told to hug each other snugly. Marty looked a little sheepish as he approached this closed system, and no one accommodated his entrance. He walked around the group, and Joan would call out warnings—"Natasha, he's coming over to you, watch out." The adult and older kids would move the group hug to make it more difficult for Marty to find a spot where he could enter. All the while Tanya, who stood up to the waists of everyone else in the tightly held group, was saying, "Come over here, Daddy, I'll let you in. Come over here." But no one seemed to listen to Tanya's invitation. After about five minutes of jockeying and negotiations, Marty got a hold on Mike's arm and was able to pry it loose and gain access to the group.

In the discussion that ensued after the exercise, there were three observations made. First, there were never instructions given to keep Marty out of the system—the instruction was that Marty was to enter. The therapist asked how it was that Joan, Mike, and Natasha assumed that it was their task to keep him away. Second, he asked Marty how he went about determining how to enter the group, pointing out that he appeared to ponder options, discover resistance, and then use his strength to overpower others. He never said, "Excuse me, may I join the family?" Finally, the therapist noted that "Tanya seemed to have a different understanding of the game—she was trying to let Dad in, while the others tried to keep Dad out. And Marty, you could have entered the home through the open door created by your daughter. But you preferred to enter the home through a locked door with a sledgehammer."

This exercise revealed many key indicators of the family map. Joan and Marty showed an active relational conflict, with a cross-generational enmeshment and coalition between Joan, Mike, and Natasha. There was a rigid boundary with conflict between Marty and Mike, and to a lesser extent, Marty and Natasha. And there was evidence of a diffuse boundary between Marty and Tanya. The outside interest of Mike's work also served as an important consideration in the family's structure.

In the third session the family therapist addressed some of the rules or structures that seemed to be operational within the family. The therapist stood at the white board and wrote the "family rules." The family produced a comprehensive and condemning list of destructive regulations. Then, by comparison, they created a list of rules that would be expected in a family group that works well together.

The therapy was spread out over the next three months at a frequency of about every other week, due to Marty's driving schedule. The most frequent focus was the marital dyad in order to address the grievances and offenses experienced by both from the other. The couple worked at reconfiguring the boundaries—yes, Joan let Marty sleep in the bedroom. (We knew you would be wondering about that!) And Marty worked on developing other ways to relate to his stepchildren, particularly Mike, besides using his voice and his physical strength. Joan had to address an assumption that "she alone was responsible for the care of the family." Her dominating and controlling style was not surrendered easily, and it was not laid down the way surrendering soldiers lay down their weapons. More accurately, it was worn down; that is, the effort extended to maintain the control and domination seemed futile when Marty wasn't fighting with Mike and Natasha.

The turning point of therapy occurred with the realizations by Joan and Marty of their respective unspoken assumptions. First, Joan ran the family like a protective mother hen, with teeth! She was protective of her brood and saw Marty (and her previous husband) as threats that would harm her and harm her children. A core structure that Joan held was that men in general, and Marty specifically, were not to be trusted; therefore, she must guard her children and remove his ability to have influence.

Marty held an assumption that because it was his house and his money that he was entitled to privileges of respect and regard—without having to work at becoming respected in the eyes of his adolescent stepchildren. Both of these errant structures were causing the family to become stuck. The leaders were failing to provide an environment where relationships could thrive in a caring, responsible manner.

## CHRISTIAN PERSPECTIVE ON STRUCTURAL FAMILY THERAPY

*Theoretical and philosophical assumptions.* Structural family therapy operates under a set of theoretical assumptions that can fit appropriately with a Christian worldview or religious perspective. The most notable is the respect for an external structure of rules and a hierarchical organization through which human growth can be maximized. Students in our marriage and family classes frequently report that structural approaches makes intuitive sense and are easily translated into the language and culture of Christian psychotherapy settings.

The structural approach has not embedded itself in philosophies that run contrary to Christian worldviews such as determinism, collectivism, psychoanalysis, or humanism. The approach emphasizes the pragmatics of family functioning—particularly the rules of operation that can transcend culture. Furthermore, Minuchin emphasized the existence of fundamental core conditions of family functioning that every family must possess in order to be successful. "Family structure is shaped partly by universal and partly by idiosyncratic constraints. For example, all families have some kind of hierarchical structure, with adults and children having different amounts of authority. Family members also tend to have reciprocal and complementary functions"

(Nichols & Davis, 2017, p. 113). Though the structural theorist believes that the family constraints are "universal," they would not see the universality of family rules as something that emerges from a perspective of truth as might someone considering family from the Christian tradition. However, the similarity between universal family structures and that of biblically defined truth might permit the Christian clinician to utilize the approach without having to jettison major components of the theoretical underpinnings.

## INTEGRATIVE FOCUS: Family Functioning

Structural family theorists make important claims regarding the essence of family functioning by utilizing an architectural metaphor: "form creates function." In other words, the restraints and freedoms operating within a family system shape the external environment and influence the personhood of each individual. In this case, form means that the rules that both restrict and sanction behavior within the system have a central effect on the manner in which the system will then operate.

The biblical admonitions toward submission to structure are numerous. "Train children in the right way, and when old, they will not stray" (Prov 22:6). "Be subject to one another out of reverence for Christ" (Eph 5:21). "Therefore, since we are surrounded by so great a cloud of witnesses, . . . let us run with perseverance the race that is set before us" (Heb 12:1). These are examples of instruction as to how we are to live. In fact, the very word *instruction* implies that there is a structure in which we are to become well versed.

The essence of structure to the family structuralist is *boundary*. Seeking to apply this approach through a Christian paradigm, we find this essence to be a commendable first step—to which the second, third, and fourth steps, as well as the entire journey, are illuminated by an articulation of those boundaries. The structural approach declares that families function best in the presence of rules that define roles, rights, and responsibilities. The Christian tradition moves further by identifying the nature of the rules, rights, and responsibilities—found in the declaration of the Old Testament law, its completion in New Testament grace, and its application in Jesus' work of reconciliation.

*Think about it:* Is it possible to communicate family rules without creating family rigidity?

Christians vary significantly on their understanding of biblical hierar-chies—take note of the debate within theological and ecclesiastical groups regarding the complementary versus the egalitarian perspectives on family structures. While there has been tremendous intensity in the arguments around the "biblical family"—that is, the definition of a family structure or the family rules that God has ordained to be normative of human existence, growth, and development—the outcome of either structure is the same. Both the egalitarians and the complementarians encourage the same end goal; both view the existence of a family structure as a means to an end far more note-worthy than individual development. The protection that emerges through the exhibition of Christian hierarchy is to be a reflection of Christlikeness.

*Model of family dysfunction and family functioning.* In a structural model, families work when there is stability for individual growth. Power must be distributed across the spectrum of relationships so as to be appropriate for the individual's level of maturity. In addition, power must be held mutually so as to not stifle or suffocate the sense of freedom and responsibility for individuals operating in the system. Furthermore, families thrive when authority func-tions as a shield to cover and protect children who are not yet capable of self-determination, but can permit children to gradually increase their capacity to self-govern. Healthy families have the capacity to form boundaries—protecting the family from harm coming from outside the system and pro-tecting subsystems within the family structure. Boundaries suggest the exis-tence of standards, principles, and values that, if respected, offer family members the greatest chance for a successful interface with the complexities of life.

In addition to boundaries, successful families must exhibit flexibility or accommodation to new demands and circumstances facing the family. Family success requires adjustment to the changing developmental and cir-cumstantial needs of its members. Families that are newly formed, without children, burdened with college loans, and who have entry-level jobs but with the optimism of a bright future operate differently than families that have experienced tragedy and are weighted with hardships such as the care of children with special needs, economic problems, declining health, and death or divorce. In these extreme scenarios, it is the capacity to adjust that becomes the essence of successful family functioning, and it is those same characteristics that when present in a family lead to the individual maturity of its members.

It may sound paradoxical to think that families thrive when there are clear limitations, rules, and boundaries. The paradox lies in the fact that a structure defined by a "Thou shalt not" is the passage to relational freedom. Consider the words of Joy Davidman (1954) in the classic Christian work *Smoke on the Mountain*: "'Thou shalt not' is the beginning of wisdom. But the end of wisdom, the new law, is 'Thou shalt.' To be Christian is to be old? Not a bit of it. To be Christian is to be reborn, and free, and unafraid, and immortally young" (p. 20).

*Think about it:* What freedoms were created or lost as a result of boundaries formed within your family?

Minuchin does not extend the model of healthy family functioning much beyond the description of boundaries (not too high and not too low) and accommodation (not too rigid and not too flexible). Goldenberg and Goldenberg (2004) elaborate on these basic ideas and cite three characteristics of family well-being: clearly defined generational boundaries, alignments between parents on key family issues, and rules that regulate power and authority in decision making.

We can see no challenge to the basic premise of the structural understanding of systemic well-being. Shortcomings within the structural system are not found in problems with the content of the theory; rather, it is in the limited extent of the theory that we would recommend pause and consideration. To us the essence of family maturity espoused by Minuchin would be essential requirements for the prevention of family dysfunction but would fall short in the development of family success. To borrow from Rogerian language, these characteristics would be "necessary" but not "sufficient" for maturational formation and family success.

The Christian tradition extends the nature of structure to include a number of social, community, and familial characteristics essential for individual and systemic health. Rogerson (1996) developed a model from the Old Testament Scriptures that he refers to as the "Structure of Grace." Pertaining to family, such grace structures must include patterns of covenant, grace, empowering, and intimacy in order for individuals to thrive. Covenant structures offer stability and security; grace structures provide acceptance not based on performance or merit; empowering structures encourage growth and individuality; and intimacy structures offer safety, love, and trust. The biblical text provides ample evidence that structures, rules, and authorities are needed to protect all of us from harm. We are also in need of qualities of nurturance that can draw us into maturity as persons and as families. The family infrastructure permits essential qualities for growth to occur.

Furthermore, the Christian tradition includes a model structure that the family should strive to emulate—that of Jesus. The exhibition of Christlike qualities in one's personality, as the regulation of space between adults and as the image toward which we seek to nurture children into adulthood, is a structure not addressed within the formal theory of structural family therapy. But these structures provide patterns for parents to build family relationships and for clinicians to construct creative intervention.

Dangers exist for the Christian clinician espousing a "Christian structuralist" viewpoint in that it is easy to substitute *structure* for *law*, resulting in a therapeutic perspective that is paramount to religious legalism. Just as Minuchin was justifiably criticized by many in feminist theory for creating a potential for abusive male patriarchy, so too Christians are vulnerable to the same errors—even more vulnerable to them because of the ease by which *structure* can be substituted for *authoritarianism*.

Similarly, family dysfunction can be defined generally within the structural framework as absence or exaggerated imbalance of boundaries and accommodations. However, the Christian tradition offers much greater specificity as to the formation of family dysfunction as well. Family dysfunction can be attributed to failure of parents first, and children second, to recognize and respect the existence of human depravity, of our propensity toward self-centeredness, and of our capacity to measure the actions and intents of others with guarded suspicion that increases defensiveness, all the while masking over our own destructive contributions. Rather than attribute family dysfunction to the operations of dysfunctional structures (Rosenberg, 1983), Christian clinicians operating within a structural paradigm would see each individual operating in a family system as possessing an internal dysfunctional structure in the form of a sin nature. Using the visual language of C. S. Lewis in *Out of the Silent Planet*, humans are "bent ones." Therefore, if we engage in family construction using elements that are not straight, true, level, and balanced, it would stand to reason that every family and every individual—including the therapists who offer solutions and the professors who write books about how to conduct family restructuring—would be expected to have structural products vulnerable to decay and destruction.

## CONCLUSION

Structural family therapy emerged as one of the most functional and pragmatic approaches to family intervention during the "golden years" of the profession. The approach remains as a viable theory among the current cultures of therapy. The strengths of this approach include its foundation of empirical methodology, and its origin with the working poor and cultural diversity has made the approach transferable to different cultures and problems. Furthermore, its simple construction and use of common terminology (e.g., boundaries vs. undifferentiated ego mass) makes this approach easily grasped by novice and lay clinicians. Yet the artistic and spontaneous components of the theory make it attractive to experienced professionals. Finally, the structural approach can create flexible, short-term interventions suitable to current practices within the profession, and it is an approach that has been adapted and integrated with diverse theories (e.g., James & MacKinnon, 2010) and client and family populations (e.g., Lindblad-Goldberg & Northey, 2013; Weaver et al., 2013).

Counselors, pastors, and lay counselors would do well to study structural treatments, engage supervisors schooled and experienced in structural methodologies, and develop interventions that are consistent with structural theory and technique. Its pragmatic emphasis permits it to be integrated with other theories, techniques, and nonclinical philosophy and theology (e.g., James & MacKinnon, 2010; McNeil et al., 2013). It is a theory that can function compatibly within a Christian worldview and has a usefulness for the Christian clinician.

## REFERENCES

Aponte, H. J. (1976). Underorganization in the poor family. In P. J. Guerin (Ed.), *Family therapy: Theory and practice*. New York: Gardner Press.

Aponte, H. J., & Van Deusen, J. M. (1981). Structural family therapy. In A. S. Gurman & D. P. Kniskern (Eds.), *Handbook of family therapy* (Vol. 1). New York: Brunner/Mazel.

Balswick, J. O., & Balswick, J. K. (1989). *The family: A Christian perspective on the contemporary home*. Grand Rapids: Baker.

Becvar, D. S., & Becvar, R. J. (2006). *Family therapy: A systemic integration* (6th ed.). Boston: Allyn & Bacon.

Bobes, T., & Rothman, B. (2002). *Doing couple therapy: Integrating theory with practice.* New York: W. W. Norton.

Colapinto, J. (1991). Structural family therapy. In A. S. Gurman & D. P. Kniskern (Eds.), *Handbook of family therapy* (Vol. 2). New York: Brunner/Mazel.

Davidman, J. (1954). *Smoke on the mountain.* Philadelphia: Westminster Press.

Ford, J. J., Durtschi, J. A., & Franklin, D. L. (2012). Structural therapy with a couple battling pornography addiction. *The American Journal of Family Therapy, 40,* 336-48.

Gladding, S. T. (2007). *Family therapy: History, theory and practice.* Upper Saddle River, NJ: Pearson Prentice Hall.

Goldenberg, I., & Goldenberg, H. (2004). *Family therapy: An overview* (6th ed.). Pacific Grove, CA: Thomson Brooks/Cole.

James, K., & MacKinnon, L. (2010). Establishing the parental hierarchy: An integration of Milan systemic and structural family therapy. In P. Rhodes and A. Wallis (Eds.), *Working with families: A practical guide.* East Hawthorn, Victoria: IP Communication.

Lindblad-Goldberg, M., & Northey, Jr., W. F. (2013). Ecosystemic structural family therapy: Theoretical and clinical foundations. *Contemporary Family Therapy, 35,* 147-60.

Madden-Derdich, D. A., Estrada, A., & Updegraff, L. A. (2002). The boundary violations scale: An empirical measure of intergenerational boundary violations in families. *Journal of Marital and Family Therapy, 28,* 241-54.

McNeil, S. N., Herschberger, J. K., & Nedela, M. N. (2013). Low-income families with potential adolescent gang involvement: A structural community family therapy integration model. *The American Journal of Family Therapy, 41,* 110-20.

Minuchin, S. (1974). *Families and family therapy.* Cambridge, MA: Harvard University Press.

Minuchin, S., & Fishman, H. C. (1981). *Family therapy techniques.* Cambridge, MA: Harvard University Press.

Minuchin, S., Montalvo, B., Guerney, G. G., Rosman, B. L., & Schumer, F. (1967). *Families of the slums.* New York: Basic Books.

Murphy, L. S., Lancy, K., & Hertlein, K. M. (2013). Attending to social network usage in teen and family treatment: A structural-developmental approach. *Journal of Family Psychotherapy, 24,* 173-87.

Nichols, M. P., & Davis, S. D. (2017). *Family therapy: Concepts and methods* (11th ed.). Boston: Allyn & Bacon.

Rogerson, J. (1996). The family and structures of grace in the Old Testament. In S. Barton (Ed.), *The family in theological perspective.* Edinburgh: T&T Clark.

Rosenberg, J. B. (1983). Structural family therapy. In B. B. Wolman & G. Stricker (Eds.), *Handbook of family and marital therapy.* New York: Plenum.

Taibbi, R. (2015). *Doing family therapy: Craft and creativity in clinical practice* (3rd ed.). New York: Guilford Press.

Weaver, A., Greeno, C. G., Marcus, S. C., Fusco, R. A., Zimmerman, T., & Anderson, C. (2013). Effects of structural family therapy on child and maternal mental health symptomatology. *Research on Social Work Practice, 23*(3), 294-303.

# PSYCHODYNAMIC
# FAMILY THERAPY

*Hwæt! We Gardena in geardagum,*
*þeodcyninga, þrym gefrunon,*
*hu ða æþelingas ellen fremedon.*
*Oft Scyld Scefing sceaþena þreatum.*

**PROLOGUE TO BEOWULF**

PSYCHOANALYSIS NOW EXTENDS into its second century. Just as the opening words of Beowulf, the epic sixth-century poem and the oldest example of written English, exemplifies how drastically language changes over time, likewise, psychodynamic family therapy is so different from the original psychoanalysis that it's hardly recognizable. The family systems application of the original Freudian psychoanalytic and subsequent psychodynamic theories is an example of how theory changes over time yet still retains important aspects of the original idea.

## INTRODUCTION TO PSYCHODYNAMIC FAMILY THERAPY

Over the past hundred years, many approaches have splintered from the original analytic tradition. Psychodynamic family therapy is the application of a number of related therapeutic languages—both individual and systemic—that influence and inform each other. It is the product of crossfertilization with many theories, including object relations, ego, interpersonal, individual, attachment, contextual, and self. While each adds some unique characteristics—often including an originator, name, and constructs—they each come from and retain aspects of the genesis of ideas formulated by Freud.

The progression of psychoanalysis to the current practice of psychodynamic family therapy passes through the work of many noteworthy theorists and practitioners. But we must begin with the originator, Sigmund Freud. He did not practice family therapy. In fact, much of his work was dedicated to preventing the development and practice of interventions that involved participation of a plurality of family members. To Freud's way of thinking, family therapy destroyed the transference fantasy bond that is essential for the formation of insight. In other words, having one's mother literally in the room while a person spoke with an analyst would severely impede imagining and experiencing characteristics of one's mother in the person of the therapist. While actively fighting against the idea of family therapy, Freud inadvertently laid the foundation for it in two important ways: his theoretical formation of pathology and his process of intervention.

First, Freud saw the genesis or formation of individual pathology as embedded within the family relationship. While we are all familiar with the endless jokes blaming our mother, our father, or our repressed childhood for every personal problem, the fact remains that our childhood—particularly between birth and age six—is the crucial period from which our capacities for adult coping can be traced. Those capacities emerge in large part through the experiences of children living within a family system. We owe to Freud the idea that mental health and mental illness are associated with family health and family illness.

Second, Freud demonstrated the concept of systemic intervention, or working on a family level. While Bertalanffy and Bateson would not present their theories of biological and mechanical systems until the middle of the twentieth century, at the end of the nineteenth century, Freud understood and operated within a systems mentality through many of his treatments. He advocated the idea that a corrective system (analyst and patient) could overcome the limitation imposed by the malfunctioning internal psyche, social, or family system. Freud, on occasion, took steps that were closer still to the idea of "family intervention."

Through the famous case of "Little Hans" we see an example of a rudimentary systemic intervention (Freud, 2003). Hans was a five-year-old boy whose parents had been concerned about their son's behavior for two years. At age three-and-a-half his baby sister was born. During the pregnancy and since her birth he was startled by nightmares with giraffes and other animals. At that same time, Hans witnessed a terrible accident while on an outing in the streets of Vienna. A horse collapsed, died, and fell on a pedestrian, killing the bystander as well. Soon after both incidents, he exhibited agoraphobic patterns, fearful of venturing out in the street lest a horse bite him. Freud's explanation of the sexual root cause of the anxiety continues to stir active debate. (He claimed that Hans was demonstrating Oedipal tendencies of having a sexual desire for his mother and felt threatened by and in competition with his father who was symbolically represented by horses pulling carriages in the street.) However, what is not debated was the usefulness of Freud's treatment strategy. He chose to conduct his intervention through Hans's father, who was a former patient and family friend. He instructed Hans's father to permit the free association of fear to be expressed by his son and to permit the anxiety to be released naturally through transference. Eventually, Hans's fantasies ceased to contain the images of anxiety, his agoraphobia lifted, and he was declared cured. Freud believed that it was the intervention through the family system that permitted Hans to be freed from fear. Freud stated in his summary of the case, "I vanquished the most powerful resistance in Hans to conscious recognition of his unconscious thoughts, since it was his own father who was taking the role of the physician" (Eysenck, 1986, p. 101). "Unconsciously," Freud constructed a systemic intervention. In working with one component of a family system (the parents) he had an effect on the behavior of the child to relieve an obvious anxiety. It was as if Hans was asking, "Will I be hurt if I venture out of my home, and am I still loved now that I share my parents' attention with my baby sister?" To which Freud instructed Hans's parents to declare through their attention, "Yes, you are safe, and you are loved!"

It is important to note that while some of Freud's work is recognized as the initial structures of family therapy, Freud and the analytic tradition actively blocked the work of family intervention. Psychoanalytic theory held strict limitations on treatment with multiple members of the same family, believing that it would interfere with the essential transference process.

It wasn't until the 1950s—a half-century after Freud's treatment of Little Hans—that family therapy took a form that would be recognizable today.

There are dozens of esteemed clinicians who attempted to develop initial forays into systemic dynamic therapy. We will dedicate a description to just three groups or pioneering approaches to which psychodynamic family therapy owes its original ideas. These three groups are the "Middle School" of the British Psychoanalytic Association, Alfred Adler and the Society for Individual Psychology, and in the United States, the original work of the Interpersonal Psychoanalytic approach, articulated by Harry Stack Sullivan, among others.

*The British Psychoanalytic Association.* Included in this group were Anna Freud (Freud's youngest daughter), Melanie Klein, Ronald Fairbairn, and Donald Winnicott. These scholars, though never researching or writing collaboratively, influenced each other and the development of psychotherapy. Their collective work fused multiple themes with a grand idea. The themes included values of internalized unconscious processes, transference, countertransference, and the powerful influence of early child experiences. The grand idea was that relationships are central to human existence and maturation, as well as being foundational to any therapeutic intervention. In brief, relational attachment is fundamental to human maturation. That attachment is found first and most prominently in infancy and childhood. The transference process—that of substituting for real attachment figures such as parents who might have failed or caused pain—can be, in part, facilitated by the intermediating person of therapist, friend, pastor, or confessor. These scholars were the first to consider the family environment as a source of individual psychopathology and a means for reparation. Eventually the schools of object relations therapy, ego therapy, and attachment theory would become known as theories and techniques distinct from the psychoanalytic tradition.

*Adler and the Society for Individual Psychology.* The second important contributor to lay the foundation of psychodynamic family therapy was Alfred Adler. He joined Freud's Vienna Psychoanalytic Society in 1902 and was an active contributor to the association. He was a physician and peer of Freud, trained as an ophthalmologist. His work led toward neurology as he studied diseases affecting the optic nerve in children. The neurological link brought him in contact with Freud and other Viennese neurologists who were captivated with the idea of a talking cure. To Adler it was social dynamics—especially the dynamic of family relationships—that was most influential in human growth and development. Rather than emphasizing the biological drive theory espoused by Freud, Adler emphasized individual striving toward goal attainment. Individual goals emerged and were met through interactive social systems—of which the family was most fundamental. Adler emphasized the importance of family constellation, birth order, and sibling rivalry as essential components of goal attainment later in adult life. Adler and his associates formally broke with Freud and formed the Society for Individual Psychology in 1914. He was responsible for the establishment of child clinics in which he and his associates worked directly with families. His therapy emphasized empathic encouragement and education.

*Interpersonal psychoanalysis.* Finally, the pioneering work of Harry Stack Sullivan in the United States introduced a social psychology perspective to the treatment of individual need. Sullivan was the most prominent voice in the "interpersonal psychoanalysis" movement that also included Erich Fromm, Karen Horney, and Frieda Fromm-Reichmann. His influence covered the middle fifty years of the twentieth century, from the mid-1920s to well beyond his death in 1949. Sullivan studied psychoanalysis within Chicago's philosophical culture of pragmatism. He saw the emergence of human personality through the pragmatic reality of biology, individual psychology, and social influence. Obviously, there is no social structure with significance even remotely comparable to that of the family. Sullivan believed that familial factors such as love, conflict, relational patterns, and friendship are key to understanding pathology and its intervention (Sullivan, 1953).

These three sources did not initiate or even envision the concept of family therapy. Rather, they formulated significant essential ideas that produced the paradigm shift from individually based thinking to systemic thinking within the psychodynamic movement. Each of them offered unique explanations regarding the formation and treatment of psychopathology that included key elements of relationship and social influences. It was their ideas in the first half of the twentieth century that permitted others to develop family dynamic therapies in the second half.

To summarize, during the first fifty years of the twentieth century, at the very origins of the therapy movement initiated by Freud, there was germination of an alternative perspective of therapy that took root, blossomed, and reproduced during the second fifty years. At the origin of psychotherapy, in the home, office, and clinic of Sigmund Freud, we see the working presence of a formative family systems theory. As his successors and followers implemented their research and theory in specific practices, a culture and community of thought was formed that integrated family and couple interventions to address human suffering.

It is not accurate to attribute the origin of psychodynamic family therapy to any one person at a particular time. However, if a person does exist as the parent figure of psychodynamic family therapy, it would be Nathan Ackerman (Becvar & Becvar, 2006; Goldenberg & Goldenberg, 2004; Sholevar & Schwoeri, 2003). Beginning with "The Unity of the Family," an article published in 1937, Ackerman built over a period of more than three decades the application of Freudian analysis to family systems modality. Nichols and Schwartz state, "He was one of the first to envision whole family treatment and he had the inventiveness and energy to actually carry it out" (2006, p. 37).

Ackerman, an analyst by training, sought to understand and to intervene with clients regarding unresolved issues, conflicts, and losses. Ackerman held that it was these losses that produced an effect on the manner in which family members existed with one another. Ackerman introduced the idea of *complementarity*, which was the blending of personalities within a family along expected paths—much like a script learned for a play. As these roles become calcified or fixed within the family, they restrict individual growth. Or if there is insufficient structure, they fail to provide clarity and safety. These roles also function holistically—grooming a care "taker" to blend with care "giver," or a "talker" with a "listener," so that the family has persons capable of meeting the needs of the system.

Reflecting on the failure to effectively complement one another within a family led Ackerman to create a model of *interlocking pathology*. This idea blended his commitment to the analytic tradition that holds the etiology of individual psychopathology as related to internal unconscious drives with the social psychology and analytic psychiatry perspectives that consider social, environmental, and family factors. Interlocking pathology suggests that any individual psychopathology is influenced by internal psychodynamics and is also an image of the distorted social relationships occurring primarily within the home.

Ackerman is considered a brilliant Renaissance man—possessing authority in psychiatry, psychoanalysis, and social psychology. He assisted an emerging profession to enter into a family system and disturb the status quo, alter the structure, and create unorthodox interventions to break family maladaptive patterns—approaches later developed by other theorists. Ackerman's role in the history of family therapy is like a great director or producer in the film industry. He is not the name that therapists today associate with their professional identity. He does not have a following such as Bowen, Haley, or Minuchin. Yet he is considered the behind-the-scenes "master therapist" who directed the production of the profession in distinct and noticeable ways.

## THEORETICAL AND PHILOSOPHICAL ASSUMPTIONS OF PSYCHODYNAMIC FAMILY THERAPY

In the introduction to this chapter we put forth the idea that the language of psychodynamic family therapy has matured to be significantly different from its origins in the psychoanalytic tradition, such that to many it is not perceived even as the same language, much like Beowulf is not "real English." While the vocabulary has indeed evolved, there is a language syntax of the original theory that is still significant in the current practice of psychodynamic family therapy. While there are many dynamic approaches to family therapy, we chose to represent the approach by focusing on object relations therapy, as articulated by James Framo (1981) and David and Jill Scharff (1991) as well as numerous others who have preceded them.

*General overview of object relations family therapy.* Object relations family therapy takes its name from its Freudian origin. "Object" was the term used by Freud to describe an infant's initial experience relating to others. A baby cannot comprehend the complexity of personhood. He or she cannot gaze on mother or father's face immediately after birth and recognize them as the biological parent and think, *So, that's what Mom looks like; I pictured her as a little younger.* The child has no concept of otherness. Rather, the infant's understanding of mother, father, and others grows over the initial months of life. The first contact the infant has is with the mother's breast, receiving both nourishment and comfort. All of the safety and security needs of the infant are soothed by the presence of a breast. In Freudian analytical thinking, the breast becomes the first object that is experienced and relied on by the child for survival. That object expands over the subsequent months to include a voice, a hand, a whole body, then other voices, other bodies—all of which provide consistent care and protection to the infant and produce security and soothing. These initial objects expand in complexity and are transformed in the infant's mind. Eventually, they are understood not as things but as people.

Before we delve into the application of object relations therapy to families and couples, it is necessary to have a solid foundation of the components of the theory.

The fundamental concept is the construct of *object*. Do you remember the lessons from high school English? A subject acts toward or through an object. In the sentences "I like reading" and "Chris loves Terry," the subjects are "I" and "Chris." The objects of our interest and affection are "reading" and "Terry," respectively. I relate to the activity, and Chris relates to the person in unique, noteworthy, and important ways. There are two things that you can learn about both Chris and me—first, that both of us have an association or relationship with two other entities. The second thing is that our relationships are understood to be one of like and one of love.

To the object relations family therapist, the fundamental core idea is that all subjects—you, me, everyone—have associations, affiliations, or relationships with other objects. And those relationships have qualities and characteristics that vary because of factors that can be explained or realized.

The objects that we relate to are not always external things or people. We all have *internal objects*. Imagine being at a grand patriotic event on the Fourth of July with a very large band, a choir, and an extravagant fireworks spectacle. The choir and band begin "Battle Hymn of the Republic," growing in intensity of sound and sight, with the night sky alight with color. A friend turns to you and says, "I always get goose bumps every time I hear this song." Indeed, that music had become internalized in such a way that it had a special meaning. And that meaning was so strong that the body would react—without intention. In this case the occasion, the tradition, and the stimuli join together to form a unique object in our minds—part reality, part fantasy—and our body responds to the internal message associated with that mental object.

Melanie Klein (1975a, 1975b) and Ronald Fairbairn (1943/1954) believed that beginning in our infancy we create fantasy, or mental exaggerations. Like Freud, Klein saw these as primarily part of our biology. However, she didn't believe they were biological drives to manage sexual energy. She saw them as a drive to manage feelings toward the important caregivers. Fairbairn, who learned from Klein, went a step further by seeing these impulses not as biological drives at all. They are internal responses based on our need for meaningful human relationship. So those goose bumps were a physical response that was cued by the choir, the percussion, and the horns. We respond to ideas of truth, justice, righteousness, and protection—all of these were internal objects that would produce a euphoric experience whenever we might encounter this piece of music. These objects become part of ourselves—they influence our emotions, direct our behavior, and guide our thinking—often toward health but sometimes toward frustration.

The most important object is one that we can call the *primary object*. This is a euphemism for the maternal role. It is that first target of our affection. It is from our primary object that we derive our essential needs for safety, security, and, eventually, significance. These needs, met through relationship, are constant and demanding. In fact, it is impossible for any mother or father to meet the incessant needs of infants. Try as we might, we cannot remove the reality of pain, discomfort, and loss for our children.

To buffer and make sense of the reality of pain, infants employ a strategy known in object relations theory as *splitting*. Freud initially developed the idea as a defense mechanism to help resolve the conflict of living with coexisting contradictory forces. For instance, "My mother loves me, but my mother is not here for me. How can she not be here if she loves me? Well, she loves ME, but it is a different entity, one that I will name 'myself,' with whom she is not too keen." In splitting, the ego divides itself in order to contain messages that are in conflict. Later, Fairbairn developed the idea that these splits were a combination of part "us" (ego), part "object" (mother or father and eventually all relationships), and part "emotion" (affection, anger, longing, etc.). Maturity and immaturity are influenced by how a developing infant, toddler, child, and adolescent learns to manage these splits in ego, object, and emotion by integrating them into a single and workable pattern. The internal splits have to be coordinated with the external reality of actual relationships. Failure to have the internal splits synchronized with the external reality produces internal conflict that always "leaks" out into the way we relate to external objects—or people, hence the name *object relations*.

The fusion between our internal splitting and our external, real relationship is played out through a process called *introjection*. Introjects are the internal images that I have of my self and of my important objects. This is not how I or others are in reality, but it is how I have come to think of myself and of others. For example, I carry an image within my mind that influences much of my interaction with others. They are (1) be liked and (2) be self-sufficient. These two introjects define for me how I am to be in relationship with others. You could expect, if you were my neighbor, that I would go out of my way to be helpful and that I would rarely if ever ask to borrow your lawn tools.

I will seek to confirm the validity of my introjects through a relational interaction called *projective identification.* Cashdan states that "projective identifications are patterns of interpersonal behavior in which a person induces others to behave or respond in a circumscribed fashion" (1988, p. 54). In other words, object relations suggests that I will extend to others a form of my introjects. I will encourage you to act in a way that will confirm the internal image of a good person. If you comply, then I am my view of self, and the role that my self will play with you is confirmed and made more secure. However, if you don't comply with my projective identification, then tension will form between us that will be experienced as painful to me. It is painful because I need you to confirm and validate me, or my introjects. Without that validation I will need to be protective and defended from any and all possible threats.

In psychodynamic family systems theory, families consist of multiple individuals with unique but corresponding introjects. The family helps create the internal images of the children in a way that correspond with the preexisting introjects of the adults and the other members of the family. The phrase "the acorn never falls too far from the tree" suggests that the family, and especially the parents, are active in forming introjects that are a complementary match with how the family needs the new member to be and become. It is believed that children develop internal representations of self through numerous developmental stages as theorized by Erikson, Bowlby, Kohut, Bettelheim, and others. Children use their families to teach them how to attach, separate, individuate, identify, and eventually generate family reformation in the next generation.

The formation of capacity for intimacy and the selection of a marital partner are understood within the object relations theory as an extension of the introject/projective identification process. We select life partners as a result of the unique characteristics of our individual introjects. The musical ditty "I want a girl just like the girl that married dear old dad" is a truism within object relations theory. Indeed, whether our future spouse is more like mom or more like dad in personality type is determined by a complex set of internal relational drives that fulfill our basic need to be affirmed, to obtain security, and to experience significance through the process of introjection and projection.

The process of family therapy within object relations family therapy does not have a single integrated approach. Significant contributions have been

made by Framo (1981), Scharff and Scharff (1991), and Slipp (1984). Each theorist has variations and nuances that differ from the others. While there is
significant divergence, all of the approaches place an emphasis on the process
of transference and countertransference.

*Transference.* Transference, an essential component of the psychoanalytic
tradition, plays a crucial role in object relations family therapy. It is believed
that transference is an ongoing process within families; members are trans-
ferring—through the process of projection—internal wishes and needs to
others that are not articulated directly and therefore never accounted for by
the family. Failure for the individuals and family as a whole to understand this
process only creates more "emotional static" and greater individual frustration.
The family therapist joins the family and offers a protective *holding environment*, a term developed by Donald Winnicott from the British Middle
School tradition and utilized more emphatically by David and Jill Scharff. A
holding environment is similar to the Rogerian concept of unconditional
positive regard and the contextual idea of multidirectional partiality, explained later in this chapter. The holding environment permits the individual
family members to exhibit their patterns of behavior and emotional reactions
in the presence of the therapist.

*Countertransference.* The idea of countertransference in Freud's original
presentation referred to the fragments of immaturity within the clinician that
resonated with the unique psychopathologies of the clients he or she served.
In that regard, countertransference was a harmful pollutant to the therapeutic
process. However, in psychodynamic family therapy, particularly object relations family therapy, countertransference is a tool to be used. In fact, some
consider it the most significant and powerful therapeutic tool that clinicians
have available to them (Cashdan, 1988). Countertransference is the process by
which the dynamic family therapists are able to receive the transference projected by the family members but not react to them in the same manner.
Countertransference becomes the intentional reception of the family's projected transferences. The therapist catches the family's "stuff" projected in
terms of emotion and behaviors that reflect the internal underworkings of the
family system. Regarding this McConnaughy writes, "The therapist uses
herself or himself as a barometer of the disturbances in the system, and, by
virtue of this intimate connection with the system, the therapist can help restructure the faulty mechanisms" (McConnaughy, 1987).

***Process of therapy.*** The effectiveness of the therapeutic process is seen to rest largely on the therapist's ability to enter into the system (engagement), receive the family's accumulated projections (transference), interpret these transferred projections from the perspective of objectivity (countertransference), and implement an alternative set of responses that can be taught, practiced, and mastered by the family (intervention).

Engagement occurs through a unique form of validation. It is assumed that individual family members are projecting onto each other their undeclared and unmet emotional needs, and that is the source of the tension and conflict experienced in families. For instance, if a family member uses a defense of "bossiness" to protect himself/herself from injury—maybe injury as a result of childhood abandonment, etc.—and if in the same family other members project characteristics of avoidance, passivity, overt anger, sexualization, or ingratiation, then the family members would likely behave in such a way as to challenge the projected needs of individual family members. This behavior increases each person's need to project with greater earnestness. So the family yells "Get with it!" at the one who avoids, punishes the one who rebels for not being compliant, and tries to control the controller because "He always gets his way" or "She always gets what she wants." The family would likely be blaming the "identified patient" for the behavior defined as "acting out," all the while unknowingly reinforcing the behaviors that that family wishes to eradicate. Engagement occurs when the therapist connects with each family member as they exhibit their defenses, not with a demand that they must dismantle their protection as a precondition for a continued relationship.

***An example of engagement with the Compton family.*** Peter Compton was a fourteen-year-old boy who exhibited behaviors on the soccer field and in school that were a concern to his parents. Peter was an only child, a ninth grader, and a solid A student with exceptional abilities as a soccer goalie. There had been four or five recent occasions when he was "carded" by referees for unsportsmanlike conduct. He would lose his temper on the field when an opposing goal was scored, scream at the coach when he was taken out of the game, and yell at teammates when they failed to play their positions properly. He had exhibited similar behavior in school: outbursts of anger at teachers and students. He viewed the "problem" as "no big deal. I really can't explain what happened, I mean, I just get really mad sometimes."

His parents, Mike and Joan, were married, both professionals with graduate-level education. They lived a two-career-track system. Joan, his mother, viewed herself as the strict disciplinarian who "didn't really care very much about his soccer success. I care that he succeeds in school, and I care that he is a gentleman. Regarding his athletics, that is fine and I will support him and support my husband, but not at the expense of the essentials of life. When he received his first red card (an infraction that is considered a gross violation and results in expulsion from the game) for shoving that player, I just wanted to march right out there onto the field and grab him by the ear and say 'Get in the car. You are going home, and we will deal with this there!' I was just so embarrassed. Peter knows better."

His father, Mike, took on a less assertive, even compliant, role. He was calmly concerned about his son's acting out but was more invested and noticeably proud about his son's athletic success. Mike took a "strong" stance—right behind Joan—in regard to Peter's behavior. Mike preferred to talk about what an incredible goalie Peter was, his competitive spirit, perfectionistic work ethic, and how he needs to learn to control his emotions.

Engagement involves immediately identifying the affect used as protection and joining with it. For Peter, the affect apparent was a nonaffected cool and calmness. The therapist might give a statement such as "Peter, this issue is one that your parents are very concerned about. It is very important for me to attend to their concerns [this also is a message to the parents, particularly the mother], but it's equally important to me to respect the concerns that you have. And the anger issue doesn't appear to be at the top of your list."

To that Peter responds, "Well I wouldn't say that it's not a problem, but yeah, it's not a really huge deal." As a clinician, the little shift—his saying that he wouldn't say that it's not a problem—provided a chink in his armor. Taking a nonthreatening position during the engagement allows him to lower his adolescent defenses of denial and resistance.

Mom responds almost on cue to challenge the therapist and to reestablish her goals of the session. Joan says, "I want you to understand that we consider this a very big deal; we would not come to see you if it wasn't." Joan's assertiveness reestablishes herself as the "Alpha" personality with this issue and that she is not willing yet to relinquish that role to the therapist to help her son. Because this is the first session, it is important the counselor reassure her and soothe her concern that her son will "get help from me."

The family therapist says, "Joan, I want to absolutely affirm the seriousness of Peter's behavior and how concerned that you and Mike are that he learn all of the skills needed to be a mature adult, able to thrive in every area of his life." He goes on to address them both as to the nature of protective devices implemented by each person and validating them. At this point in the relationship with the family, the parents, particularly Joan, is thinking linearly—that there is a straight line between her and the therapist to her son and that the therapist is enlisted to create compliance toward the parents' wishes for Peter. The idea of multidirected partiality is that the therapist will figuratively move throughout the room, creating an emotional connection with each person. So, he reassures Joan and Mike, then goes right back to Peter and supports him.

The second phase of therapy involves defining the nature and utilization of the defenses projected through transference. These sessions include allowing the family to define itself to the therapist. Having joined in the family process through validation, the therapist then exercises an opportunity to remain in the family without seeking immediate and significant structural changes. By permitting the transference process to occur, the clinician can become clearer as to the complicated levels of need demonstrated by the full system. This ensures that the clinician does not obtain a premature understanding of the family's need. This second phase can continue by developing a thorough history of the parents and of the crucial developmental years in the Compton home.

The third phase is to interpret and confront the family projections. Typically, it occurs between sessions three and five. Through the countertransference process, the therapist possesses insight into the family's concerns in a form that encompasses its full dimension. In the confrontation phase, the family can develop alternative patterns of interacting with each other that emerge from the sources of security and significance of family stability rather than the individual's motivation to extract from the family because of his or her unarticulated psychological need.

To return to the example of Peter, Mike, and Joan, the confrontation would include a description of each person's actions and their failed meeting of the common goals of the family. The family therapist chose to start with the father. "Mike, what has emerged in your story is how much joy you receive when you see your son perform and succeed in every area of life, but especially soccer. And that you desire to be at every game and every practice, to encourage him in a way that you wished you were encouraged when you were playing baseball as a young man. You know what it is like to not have a father express his care on a daily basis—and maybe if you want one thing for your son it would be for him to know how much you love him whether he shuts out the opposing team or whether they score ten goals." The therapist sees from Mike's expression that he is absorbing every word. He continues, "I wonder if, in addition to showing your love in that way, there are other ways that your son needs you to show him that you love him, that you trust him and that you believe in him? And I'd like you to think about that question as I talk to the other members of your family."

The therapist then turns to Joan. "You have raised a gentleman. He is a kind young man who knows what is right and knows what is wrong. He is respectful of others; he is a man that your mother and father would be proud to know. As you consider the whole of Peter's life—how he treats you and others in your neighborhood, school, extended family, church, how he responds to strangers in the store, or how he responds to little stressors like long lines at the store or not getting elected for a school office—what is your overall assessment?"

Joan pauses a moment and says, "Peter is a good son, and we . . . I am very proud of him."

The family therapist continues, "Now with all that being true, with all of the evidence that you have about the maturity of your son, I can't help but feel an imbalance. Who he is or who you know him to be after watching him for fourteen years and how much you worry about who he is don't seem to match. Your worry and stress seem to be excessive compared to what you know."

Joan seeks psychological cover by responding, "Well, I think that every mother who loves her children worries about them."

Trying not to permit her from finding permanent shelter in that argument, the therapist says, "Sure, mothers are always concerned about their children's well-being. But we're not talking about hope-filled concern. I am referring to real worry that at times is very heavy to bear. And if your son doesn't succeed in the important category of personal maturity, that would be difficult for you to find forgiveness for allowing."

Peter tries to ease the tension by bringing humor into the room, "Mom, he's got you nailed . . ."

Lest it appear that the therapist is siding with the son against the parent, he is blocked. "Peter, no one is getting nailed here. In fact, we're all trying to get 'unnailed.'"

Joan is successful. She says, "It's really hard to always be afraid that something bad will happen. I worry about that constantly—and especially with Peter. And sometimes I feel alone . . ."

The family therapist is concerned that her statement was a slight dig toward her husband and doesn't want to open up that issue yet: "For now, we are working with Peter's behavior."

"Peter, there are two statements from your mother and father about weights that they carry. You have suggested earlier that the anger piece is some kind of problem but you are not able to go much further than that. My guess is that you are under some pretty intense stress."

With defenses down Peter says, "My mom and dad are terrific parents, and they never put out that expectation that I should succeed. But when I see how happy they get when I do pretty well, I just feel really angry with myself when I let them down."

The confrontation is focused not on confronting the "problematic behavior." The confrontation is directed to the defensiveness behind the projection. When that is acknowledged, not with the threat of eradication but with the concern that that manner in which he lives is hard, challenging, and impeding, then the family can rally around and bring aid and comfort.

The fourth phase, termination, permits opportunity for the family to develop an intervention with the clinician as an adviser, and quickly thereafter the therapist withdraws from direct input with the family. During the termination process the family is encouraged to pull together an alternative way of responding to one another because they are not acting out through their defenses. Instead they are acting in response to the newly formed insight regarding their actions and those of their loved ones.

With the Compton family, this phase was initiated by the following conversation: "You all have a new sense of what is driving you individually. So, what do you want to do now?"

Mike spoke first, "I have thought that being there for my son would be the best way that he would feel secure. But what he is saying is that being there too much makes him think that I really need him to succeed. So, I guess I need to stay at work once in a while. That will be really hard because I would much rather be watching him play soccer than spend more time in the office."

This closing phrase is marked by the exhibition of insight into their own processes. Mike was not saying that he intended to neglect his family through work, but he is showing that he understands how being "too proud" or "too supportive" conveyed a message to his son that he was supposed to "make dad proud of him." Mike's choice to stay at work was his way of saying to Peter that he is content and relaxed; therefore, Peter can be a little less driven as well.

The process of family therapy in the object relations psychodynamic paradigm is to call on the power of relationship both to understand the nature of our psychological wounds and their repair. In the case of the Comptons, the behavior of all three of them—Peter's anger, Joan's possessiveness, and Mike's cheerleading—were components of their needs for attachment and security. Once identified, the family could implement new ways of reassuring each other of emotional provision.

Psychodynamic therapy continues to be studied empirically, often in comparison to cognitive-behavioral therapy (e.g., Bögels, Wijts, Oort, & Sallaerts, 2014). When extended to family therapy, we continue to see psychodynamic theory applied to a range of presenting concerns, such as parenting (see Oren, 2011, on Psychodynamic Parenthood Therapy), treatment for the family when a family member suffers from psychosis (e.g., Martindale & Smith, 2011), and couples work (e.g., Cohen & Levite, 2012) as well as broader reflections on how a psychodynamic understanding can inform an agency's philosophy, as illustrated by one agency's approach to community mental health (see Sacco, Campbell, & Ledoux, 2014). As an extension of psychodynamic considerations, we see growth in attachment-based family therapy in general and in the care of depressive and suicidal adolescents (e.g., Shpigel, Diamond, & Diamond, 2012) and LGBT+ young adults and their families (e.g., Diamond & Shpigel, 2014).

## CHRISTIAN PERSPECTIVE ON
## PSYCHODYNAMIC FAMILY THERAPY

*Philosophical and theoretical assumptions.* The critique of the psychodynamic family therapies is a challenge. There is much within this approach that is useful for the Christian clinician and family minister. However, it is errant to see psychodynamic family therapies to be intrinsically Christian. In the opposite direction, anything Freudian has been historically viewed by many as intrinsically anti-Christian. Given this criticism of Freud and some analytical theorists, it is easy to understand the tone of rejection that many people of faith express. However, there is much within this domain that is useful and that we will embrace as insightful to the human condition. And there is some that must be held critically. The two components within object relations family therapy and contextual family therapy that are both most supportive, yet most conflictual with Christian ideals are the constructs of primary object and relational ethics.

*Primary object.* As Jones and Butman (1991) observed, the emphasis in object relations theory on the "centrality of relationship" is a touch point for Christian integration because it "provides a foundation for the integration of the relational model and Christian thought" (p. 105). They point out that there is some biblical precedent for the notion of internalizing relationships: the idea that our relationships "become part of us" in some meaningful way "corresponds with Christian belief in marital union (Eph 5), family relatedness in the body of Christ (1 Cor 12) and even the notion of God residing in our very being when we become his child" (p. 105).

In an oft-used quotation, Augustine said, "You stir men to take pleasure in praising you because you have made us for yourself, and our heart is restless until it rests in you" (Augustine, 1991, p. 3). Similar ideas have been attributed to Anselm and Pascal: that there is a God-shaped vacuum in each of us that can be filled only with the person of God. It is a small step from the spiritual realm of needing the possession and security of God to the psychological realm of needing the possession and security of some stabilizing figure—an object experienced as a protective parent. Many have pointed out the parallels between Freudian analytic thought and the subsequent object relations thought and our need for an ultimate source of power, protection, and purpose. While the association between the two is useful, it is inaccurate to say that they are the same. The object relations perspective of attachment to secure human caregivers is not merely a slightly misguided theology. Such attachments to human objects are essential for personality formation. Toward this end Roberts (2003, p. 208) states,

> We are made for attachments, made to live in terms of things that are not ourselves; it is not a fault in us to have our emotional life subject to the changing conditions of our fellow humans, or to the diverse attitudes and actions of God. Attachment is an essential structure of human personality that calls, not for mitigation or extirpation, but for proper development.

It is regarding that "proper development" that the Christian-biblical view of relationship to God and to others differs from the psychodynamic perspective. To Bowlby, attachments represent the essence of human existence. He says that from "intimate attachments a person draws strength and enjoyment of life and, through what he contributes, he gives strength and enjoyment to others" (Bowlby, 1980, p. 442). Along that same line of thought, Kohut, writing of self-psychology, a sibling of the object relations perspectives, considers appreciation as the fundamental longing and motivation (Kohut, 1971).

To the Christian, human attachments are not to be the pinnacle of human existence. While they are indeed essential to psychological development, they are a means to a greater and most fundamental end—that of communion with God, their creator. The biblical call to "seek first the kingdom of God" is in essence a call toward attachment. We see a difference in the developmental necessities of attachment as a means for growth, and the psychological formations of attachment as the definition and execution of life purpose.

Therefore, the object of our relations, from the biblical text and from the exercise of the historic Christian faith, extends beyond the definition and function of objects within the set of psychodynamic family theories. To the Christian, we attach to others as provision for our ultimate need for divine attachment. Human attachments are not psychological substitutes or temporary securities until the "real thing" can be manifested. Human attachments are a provision or gift that has resemblance to the nature of our divine attachment. They are related but not equal; separate, but not competing. We affirm Roberts's (2003) perspective that "good early attachments prepare us for mature personality, not only by enabling us to trust that other human beings will generally be there for us when we need them, but by readying us to trust God" (p. 228).

*Model of family dysfunction and family functioning.* The model of family dysfunction and family functioning in object relations family therapy is largely related to the health and maturity of individual family members: "The processes of introjection and identification ultimately determine the personality, the organization of mental processes, and the way individuals relate to each other" (Becvar & Becvar, 2006, p. 142). Put differently, "family health equals the ability of family members to relate fully to one another. And fully relating refers to the ability to express true understanding and compassion" (p. 142).

As Jones and Butman (1991) observe, it is difficult to be overly critical of a model that places so much emphasis on relationships, particularly if we approach a human need for relatedness as reflective of the *imago Dei* or one of the ways in which we image God. Put differently, if part of what it means to image God is that we have a "need for relatedness," then "our healthy development would depend largely on the adequate meeting of that need," particularly in our earliest and most influential relationships with our primary caregivers. Also, these early relationships may very well establish a foundation for how we relate to God (see Jones & Butman, 1991, p. 109; see also Moriarty, 2006).

---

**INTEGRATIVE FOCUS:** *Family Relationships*

The biblical text reveals the essential but insufficient relationship that we are to have with our families. We are to love and honor (i.e., be attached to) them by considering them to be more important than ourselves. Yet the Bible never sees our family as the focus of our primary relationship. Human attachment is to serve as a guide for a greater purpose, that of loving God. There is not a parallel within psychodynamic thought. Mature attachments within the dynamic theories increase life joy by reducing the anxiety associated with isolation, but they do not possess motivational force toward something greater than self.

*Think about it:* In some church traditions, marriage, and subsequently the family, is a sacrament (literally, "by the blood"). How then should the attachment relationship be viewed? Coming from the Christian tradition, how do marriage and family parallel some aspects of the dynamic tradition, then eclipse it?

---

Object relations family therapy also compensates for other models of family therapy that tend to either gloss over affect or view affect as problematic (e.g., Bowenian family therapy) (Nichols & Schwartz, 2006). By recognizing that highly charged negative affect (e.g., anger) can sometimes be a signal that there are unresolved concerns from an earlier stage of development, object relations family therapists help us take a second look at affect and the importance of attending to our responses in interpersonal relationships.

Perhaps the greatest criticism of a secular object relations family therapy approach is that it does not recognize a real and meaningful relationship with a living God. A secular object relations theory limits its focus to ways an individual comes to have internalized objects, including God objects, but it does not have room for a bidirectional relationship between a human being and a personal God (Jones & Butman, 1991).

Indeed, the broader concern with object relations family therapy is that it does not see relationships and actions between people as tied to transcendent reality. This is true for nearly every model of family therapy, so we do not mean to single out object relations family therapy; at the same time, with its emphasis on internalized relationships, it must be pointed out that these relationships are limited to the natural, observable world and do not include the sacred or divine.

***Techniques in family therapy.*** The primary techniques of object relations family therapy are listening, empathy, neutrality, and interpretation (Nichols & Schwartz, 2006). Object relations family therapists listen to individual family members, and they do so with a kind of neutrality (not taking sides or advocating for one perspective over another as such) that allows them to both demonstrate empathy and provide interpretations of potential meaning that lies behind affect and behavior. The interpretations are intended to bring unconscious motivations for behavior to conscious awareness so that family members can be more intentional about how they relate to one another.

As has been suggested, object relations family therapy is not a technique-driven approach to working with families. Indeed, the primary "technique" is forming a relationship with family members so that internalized objects can be identified and reworked with an eye toward greater health and wholeness. The therapeutic alliance is the critical component to object relations family therapy, as it "allows the manifestation of early ego functioning in order for therapist and clients both to understand the developmental process of the component parts and to grasp the logic of the ways in which the whole is functioning" (Becvar & Becvar, 2006, p. 142).

We are drawn to theory-rich models of family health and functioning, and object relations family therapy is certainly more theory-rich and less "technique-driven." However, one criticism of object relations family therapy is that it eschews other approaches to change in the family in favor of a therapeutic relationship. While we value the therapeutic relationship, we agree with Jones and Butman (1991), who point out that object relations approaches to therapy may be "criticized for their seeming lack of appreciation for methods for change *other than* having a curative relationship" (p. 113).

A related consideration has to do with the general approach to exploring past relationships. Such explorations of early relationships and their potential impact on present relationships can be tremendously helpful to individuals and thus to family relationships. However, not all family members will express interest in exploring past relationships, and the object relations family therapist may have to find other ways to move toward greater relational wholeness.

## CONCLUSION

Given these criticisms, we want to acknowledge that psychodynamic family theories and therapies do offer many perspectives that a Christian clinician may apply in ways that are consistent with biblical truth. We are encouraged by a model of family therapy that recognizes the central role of relationships in human health and development, and we see great value in a theory-rich approach as contrasted to more technique-driven family therapy approaches. Unfortunately, this has also led some psychodynamic family therapists to be suspicious of technique, and some family therapists may unnecessarily forgo the use of helpful techniques. We see ample room for integrative discussions between Christian family therapists and object psychodynamic theories, particularly in the exploration of how culture and religion influence early identification and introjection as well as relational ethics.

### INTEGRATIVE FOCUS: *Family Identity*

Countless country singers have crooned over hometowns, family, and childhood buddies that are all "back where I come from." Those songs have appeal because having a secure base is a core archetype of the life script. We all have to belong somewhere. A key component of psychodynamic attachments is the characteristics of a healthy bond. Such attachments must be stable, consistent, and secure, yet flexible, negotiable, and accommodating. The Christian tradition is guilty of mistaking our identity as being a church, a denomination, or even a family, whereas Galatians 3:28 clearly describes our identity to be "in Christ."

*Think about it:* Identity refers to definition and distinction. Identity separates "look alikes"—as when a victim identifies a criminal in a line up of innocents with similar appearance. What assets does the Christian possess that deepens the significance of identity?

## REFERENCES

Augustine (1991). *Confessions* (H. Chadwick, Trans.). Oxford: Oxford University Press.

Becvar, D. S., & Becvar, R. J. (2006). *Family therapy: A systemic integration* (6th ed.). Boston: Allyn & Bacon.

Bögels, S., Wijts, P., Oort, F. J., & Sallaerts, S. J. M. (2014). Psychodynamic psychotherapy versus cognitive behavior therapy for social anxiety disorder: An efficacy and partial effectiveness trial. *Depression and Anxiety, 31*, 363-73.

Bowlby, J. (1980). *Attachment and loss: Vol. 3. Sadness and depression.* New York: Basic Books.

Cashdan, S. (1988). *Object relations therapy.* New York: W. W. Norton.

Cohen, O., & Levite, Z. (2012). High-conflict divorced couples: Combining systemic and psychodynamic perspectives. *Journal of Family Therapy, 34*, 387-402.

Diamond, G. M., & Shpigel, M. S. (2014). Attachment-based family therapy for lesbian and gay young adults and their previously nonaccepting parents. *Professional Psychology: Research and Practice, 45*(4), 258-68.

Eysenck, H. (1986). *Decline and fall of the Freudian empire.* London: Pelican.

Fairbairn, R. (1954). Observations on the nature of hysterical states. *British Journal of Medical Psychology, 27*, 105-25.

Framo, J. L. (1981). *Family therapy: Major contributions.* New York: International Universities Press.

Freud, S. (2003). *The "wolfman" and other cases* (Louise Adey Huish, Trans.). New York: Penguin.

Goldenberg, I., & Goldenberg, H. (2004). *Family therapy: An overview* (5th ed.). Belmont, CA: Brooks/Cole.

Jones, S. L., & Butman, R. E. (1991). *Modern psychotherapies: A comprehensive Christian appraisal.* Downers Grove, IL: InterVarsity Press.

Klein, M. (1975a). *Narrative of a child analysis: The conduct of the psycho-analysis of children as seen in the treatment of a ten-year-old boy.* Oxford: Delacorte Press/Seymour Lawrence.

Klein, M. (1975b). *The psycho-analysis of children.* (A. Strachey, Trans.). Oxford: Delacorte Press/Seymour Lawrence.

Kohut, H. (1971). *The analysis of the self.* New York: International Universities Press.

Martindale, B., & Smith, J. (2011). Psychosis: Psychodynamic work with families. *Psychoanalytic Psychotherapy, 25*(1), 75-91.

McConnaughy, E. A. (1987). The person of the therapist in psychotherapeutic practice. *Psychotherapy, 24*, 303-11.

Moriarty, G. (2006). *Pastoral care of depression: Helping clients heal their relationship with God.* Binghampton, NY: Haworth.

Nichols, M. P., & Schwartz, R. C. (2006). *Family therapy: Concepts and methods* (7th ed.). Boston: Allyn & Bacon.

Oren, D. (2011). Psychodynamic parenthood therapy: A model for therapeutic work with parents and parenthood. *Clinical Child Psychology and Psychiatry, 17*(4), 553-70.

Roberts, R. (2003). Parameters of a Christian psychology. In R. C. Roberts & M. R. Talbot (Eds.), *Limning the psyche: Explorations in Christian psychology* (pp. 74-100). Eugene, OR: Wipf & Stock.

Sacco, F. C., Campbell, E., & Ledoux, M. (2014). Soul of an agency: Psychodynamic principles in action in the world of community mental health. *International Journal of Applied Psychoanalytic Studies, 11*(2), 101-13.

Scharff, D. E., & Scharff, J. S. (1991). *Object relations family therapy.* New York: Jason Aronson.

Sholevar, G. P., & Schwoeri, L. D. (Eds.). (2003). *Textbook of family and couples therapy: Clinical applications.* Washington, DC: American Psychiatric Publishing.

Shpigel, M. S., Diamond, G. M., & Diamond, G. S. (2012). Changes in parenting behaviors, attachment, depressive symptoms, and suicidal ideation in attachment-based family therapy for depressive and suicidal adolescents. *Journal of Marital & Family Therapy, 38*, 271-83.

Slipp, S. (1984). *Object relations: A dynamic bridge between individual and family treatments.* New York: Jason Aronson.

Sullivan, H. S. (1953). *The collected works of Harry Stack Sullivan.* New York: W. W. Norton.

# CONTEXTUAL
# FAMILY THERAPY

*I become in relation to the Thou; and
as I become the I, I say Thou.*

**MARTIN BUBER**

No Justice, No Peace!"—the slogan chanted by the masses to confront their sense of oppression. The 1960s marches on Washington for civil rights, the striving for ethnic equality for indigenous Mexican citizens in the province of Oaxaca, or the mistreatment of Muslim groups in Paris, France, are examples of great protests of injustice. They serve as a warning to civil authorities and declare, "Because of our historical mistreatment, we reserve the right to act out against the government, to disrupt order, peace, and calm, and will continue to act until there is fairness."

Peace has always been the product of justice—in all civilizations—including and especially the small, local civilization known as the family. However, protests for justice and peace, the kind you watch on the evening news that end with shielded police firing tear gas or a water cannon into the protesting crowds, are not the typical images associated with family injustice. Rather, the turmoil that is the product of family injustice is individual despair, hopelessness, fear, passive-aggressive actions, disengagement, falsehood, mistrust, cynicism, family violence, and relational destruction.

## INTRODUCTION TO CONTEXTUAL FAMILY THERAPY

We all are familiar with the phrase "That's not fair!" and we have no doubt experienced and expressed such sentiments toward our spouses and families. We identify with a child who sees privileges granted to older siblings, or spouses who argue over differences in household chores. Or a youth who is restricted from attending a party or from socializing with friends of his or her choosing. Or a spouse who learns of the most basic assault to marriage, sexual infidelity, and grieves over unmerited and undeserved treatment. In each case the offended party perceives the treatment received as being unjust, unfair, or unreasonable. And they act in response to that perception. And others within the family system respond to the responses. Their actions become a part of a complicated pattern of responses that are layered with time and amplified by repetition. Years of actions and reactions by the multiple members within a family system in which there have been chronic violations of fairness create a situation in which the abnormality of injustice becomes the standard and expectation of family relationships. Tragically, the commonality of consistent violations of love and trust make them "normal."

In another direction, we may also know of the richness of life when there is peace within families. In such cases love and trust within relationship are common. Couples and families who have successfully constructed relationships by the exhibition of negotiation, patience, sacrifice, acceptance, vulnerability, discipline, forgiveness, reconciliation, honesty, and truthfulness experience a stability, security, and significance in their lives. In contextual language, "Hargrave and Metcalf (2000) explain that humans come into the world with two spools that have no thread. As they experience love and trust or the lack of these two constructs—especially in childhood but also as adults—they formulate self-concepts for dealing with love and approaching future relationships with trust" (Hargrave & Pfitzer, 2003, p. 29).

Contextual family therapy can be associated with the leadership, research, and writing of a single individual: Ivan Boszormenyi-Nagy (pronounced Boz-er-men-yee-Naj; frequently professionals refer to him by his hyphenated name, calling him Nagy). He was a psychoanalytic psychiatrist who trained, researched, and practiced in Hungary before immigrating to the United States in 1950. In 1955 he participated in psychiatric residency at the Illinois Psychiatric Institute in Chicago. His instructor was Virginia Satir, who was influential in the development of contextual theory by introducing him to existential humanistic ideals that he integrated with the psychoanalytic tradition. Two years later, in 1957, he became the founding director of the Eastern Pennsylvania Psychiatric Institute (EPPI), where he developed his unique approach to family therapy. There he attracted a team of researchers and therapists who had a significant impact on the emerging profession of family therapy. Among them were James Framo, Gerald Zuk, John Rosen, and Geraldine Spark.

Boszormenyi-Nagy's approach is commonly associated with the psychodynamic tradition, in part due to his original training, and his emphasis on the importance of family-of-origin issues (Hargrave & Pfitzer, 2003). However, the theory and technique contains little of the original language from the analytic tradition, such that some are surprised that contextual family therapy is considered within the dynamic realm. To demonstrate its dynamic influence and its fusion with humanistic ideals, Boszormenyi-Nagy fused the object-relations ideas of Fairbairn with the humanistic values of Buber. From object-relations theory, he held that psychodynamics consisted of a dialogue between the ego (self) and the other. He saw similar language used by Buber to describe the interpersonal relationship of I-Thou (Boszormenyi-Nagy & Krasner, 1986, pp. 25-26).

Indeed the influence of the dynamic theorists such as Sullivan is evident by the emphasis on the social-familial elements of pathology. Boszormenyi-Nagy holds that conflict is experienced within a complicated context that transcends generations. The bonds, obligations, and loyalties that tie people together are possibly more powerful than the drives articulated by those in the original analytic perspective. Likewise, the humanistic influence of Satir is evident by the influence of the existential philosopher Martin Buber, who developed the social perspective of *I-Thou* (1958). I-Thou suggests mutual respect of other and respect for self—mutually held and reciprocally regarded. It is through the I-Thou perspective that the social influence of Sullivan's perspective can be applied. I-Thou demands an obligation to others by all who exist. These are not privileged obligations but are commitments that exist even before we develop obligations and duties.

To Boszormenyi-Nagy, the I-Thou manifests itself within a family through the building of trust. He contrasts a family as either moving toward the I-Thou and building trust or moving away from the I-Thou and destroying trust. The former he refers to as a *rejunctive* family, the latter he refers to as a *disjunctive* family. He believes that families have a moral obligation to move toward trustworthiness.

He further states that trustworthiness is the most important value or characteristic that parents are to display to their children, and that this characteristic is to be passed to each subsequent generation. In response, he holds that children possess a loyalty that emerges from the trust extended by parents to their offspring. Trust and loyalty are reciprocating values that permit families to mature and then replicate themselves to the next generation.

## THEORETICAL AND PHILOSOPHICAL ASSUMPTIONS OF CONTEXTUAL FAMILY THERAPY

*The four dimensions of contextual therapy.* Consider a simple phrase stating the obvious: context matters. Removed from context, the meaning is obscured. We know nothing by ourselves. Every aspect of our knowledge of self, of others, and of the physical and spiritual world is learned in relationship with and through others as we interact with our environment—both physical and circumstantial. While our bodies are individual, possessing unique combinations of genes, each of us are highly dependent on others, a social system, for survival. It is through the interaction of individuals with others that the formation of selves—the cognitive, emotional, physical, and spiritual development—occurs to enhance human existence. To Boszormenyi-Nagy, these relationships between individual and others exist in four dimensions, or four modes of expression, all of which make up context. The context is the realm of individual and family realities, and the interaction between individual and family realities. The four modes of contextual expression are *facts*, *individual psychologies*, *transactional or systemic interaction*, and *relational ethics*.

*Facts.* The coauthors of this text are both males of Caucasian race born in the latter half of the twentieth century. These are facts pertaining to their respective births. Facts include sex, race, physical characteristics and health, genetic makeup, timeframe, social values, language, personal history, and social history. Relationships form around the realities of history, geography, and economics. Grandparents whose childhood occurred in the Depression have a different perspective on life than the baby boomers who followed them because of the factual events occurring in their lives. The privilege of wealth, power, or position due to race, social class, or heritage afforded opportunity to some. Adults whose parents died of chronic heart disease in their early fifties have a different perspective on life when they reach the age of forty-nine than do adults whose parents are centenarians. These facts shape our very existence, and our existence influences how we interact with those with whom we have contact. Our relationships are altered by a parent who served in the military and was required to move frequently and be separated by distance. The parents who worked in the mines, the factories, or the executive penthouse each produced a unique effect on the relationships within their families.

Facts play an important role in the therapeutic process. First, they are the stuff from which diagnoses are made. As clinicians, we must first gather the facts. We conduct an intake assessment or personal history, administer a depression inventory, and develop a genogram. These data sets are factual. They permit the clinician to gain an image of how individuals and systems function. Likewise, facts are often the basis for client concerns. The divorce papers served, the arrest record, the poor grades and the yelling, and the history of previous anxiety or depression diagnoses are all factual events around which we seek therapeutic experiences.

*Individual psychologies.* The second dimension of relationships are individual psychologies. The individual structure of personhood begins with a context. The context is the set of factual realities that surround our circumstances. But immediately our context or factual environment must interact with a set of biological facts—that is, the genetically based personality of each individual. Facts must coexist with individual differences. Jim can remember the moment that each of his three children was born—the very first expression of their faces. Laura had a look that said, "Glad to meet you." Nathan had a look that said, "Let me think about this." Peter's expression was one that conveyed, "I am in charge now!" These looks were who they were from conception—the biological components of their personality. These individual psychologies, inward and internal components, interact with facts to shape the ego development of individual family members. The unique personality of each member within a family must be understood as important contributors to the family process.

Our individual psychology is distinct from facts mentioned previously. Facts are static, fixed realities of history. Individual psychology, though it can be described in factual terms, is a dynamic force, is spontaneous; it changes, grows, and exhibits self-determination. It is our individual psychology that interacts with our environment and our circumstances—our inside interfacing with our outside—that produces a complex, dynamic individual who then engages with other complex, dynamic individuals to form a family.

*Transactional or systemic interaction.* Where this interaction of fact and individual psychologies occurs on the interpersonal level Boszormenyi-Nagy refers to as the transactional or the systemic interaction dimension. In the 1970s there was a TV show called *The Brady Bunch.* It was about a single mother with three girls who married a single father with three boys. A line in the theme song said, "that this group would somehow form a family." In other words, when this configuration of persons is assembled underneath the same roof, a relational explosion and chain reaction occurs that makes a unique product—a family. The fictitious transactions among the Bradys became entertainment for others. The blending of multiple psychologies within a set of facts produces an entity that has phenomenal qualities; that is, it never existed before, and never again will it be repeated.

Change on the transactional level is the focus of most systemic approaches. Boszormenyi-Nagy writes, "family practitioners designed techniques to affect individual behavior through *changing transactional patterns*" (Boszormenyi-Nagy & Krasner, 1986, p. 31). Whether a clinician alters the boundaries between members, blocks the continuation of established communication patterns, or creates a paradox that demands that family members renegotiate models, the facts and the individual psychologies interact together on the transactional field. Therefore, it is on this field that change occurs.

*Relational ethics.* The final dimension is the most important consideration for family therapy and the most unique contribution to the profession. Boszormenyi-Nagy refers to it as relational ethics. Relational ethics is a set of rules or morals that transcend, guide, and direct the three previous dimensions. Boszormenyi-Nagy believes that mere change, without guidance from a regard for the family's intuitive sense of ethics, is a fruitless exercise. He wrote:

> A significant cautionary note was lodged against indiscriminate destruction of the old (patterns) in favor of anything new (Bateson, 1979). Yet it was especially rare to have anyone spell out the ways in which transactional changes were linked to genuinely favorable progress from everyone's vantage point. By and large, improvement was equated with the magic of changing people's invisible, here-and-now transactions with each other, often against their will. (Boszormenyi-Nagy & Krasner, 1986, p. 31)

A metaphor we created to explain his position is that change is like movement. It could be directed toward a goal or it could be directionless.

However, travel implies a destination. Those who are "on the move" have a target or a goal, and most importantly, are exhibiting an intention toward reaching their objective. To Boszormenyi-Nagy, the movement of family is toward the increased capacity for and exhibition of trustworthiness and loyalty. These, expressed in equilibrium between family members, create a sense of relational balance—or the sense of fairness. However, if in a family an adolescent is expected to be loyal but the mother and father are negligent in their roles as trustworthy leaders, there will be an imbalance in the relationship—or a violation of the ethic in their relationship.

Boszormenyi-Nagy theorizes the existence of psychological ledger sheets maintained within family systems that regulate the sense of fairness between members. This "ledger of merits" means that family members relate to one another through individual accountings of give-and-take, receptions and expenditures, or contributions offered and benefits received. Furthermore, he holds that when family members exhibit the fair execution of their responsibilities they are entitled to receive just and fair compensation. Even before that, children are entitled to receive the stability of parental trustworthiness just because they exist within families. It is on this entitlement that family security exists. He states, "In summary, the fairness of any ledger of give-and-take has to encompass the consideration of connectedness through consequences and inclusion of all those who are to be affected" (Boszormenyi-Nagy & Krasner, 1986, p. 89).

When there is violation of love and trust, or when family members fail to exhibit the loyalty to which others are entitled, an environment of *destructive entitlement* is created. Destructive entitlement occurs when individuals grant themselves the right to act in a way that is disjunctive; that is, it undermines or destroys trust within the family because the individual perceives that their entitled rights within the family have already been violated. "Destructive entitlement means destructive actions or emotions that result from an individual's claim to self-justifying compensation for an unjust and unbalanced relational ledger" (Hargrave & Pfitzer, 2003, p. 75).

## WHEN FAMILIES SEEK HELP

The exercise of mental health treatment begins with the therapist developing an understanding of the circumstances that bring a family into therapy. Unfortunately this assessment and diagnosis process can become depersonalized and separated from the humane relational process that is counseling. When families seek help by coming to a contextual family therapist, the assessment should occur on the four levels of interaction—*facts, individual psychology, systemic transactions*, and *relational ethics.* The overarching assumption of the approach is that all family challenges should be understood through the lenses of experiences of love and trust as well as violations of love and trust. Facts— the explicit events—are made meaningful by the manner in which a given event or circumstance is addressed by the family and its members with indicators of relational security and significance. In the same way, psychopathology, to the degree that it is a social/relational phenomenon (excluding biologically driven mental illness)—as well as other characteristics of family chaos such as anger, disengagement, hopelessness, disregard, manipulation, and control—is exacerbated when the qualities of love and trust are absent. Toward this end, two colleagues and collaborators of Boszormenyi-Nagy, Krasner and Joyce, write:

> The most common presenting problem of adults coming into therapy is their inability to say, "Here am I." In our experience, few people have cohesive ground under their feet. In general, people typically do not know what they want and do not want what they know. That basic stance tends to be reactive, implicitly blaming spouse, parents, children, employer, the "system" and friends. Anyone will do. Initially impelled by fear or pain, given or received, people actively opt, by omission and commission, for hurt withdrawal, imposition, and other well-entrenched barriers and dismissive defenses of *monologue.* (1995, p. 4)

The contextual approach assists families who do not have the capacity to speak with honesty in dialogue with one another. Philosophically, dialogic speech is based on the I-Thou ideals of Buber. A family that speaks in dialogue is respecting the existence of individual experience, honoring the legitimacy of rights held by every member, and insisting that all family members uphold their responsibility or obligation to the others in a mutually balanced manner. When families seek help, they have gone down the easy but wayward path toward self-centered and self-protected existence. Krasner and Joyce refer to this behavior as exhibiting the opposite of dialogue—that of *monologue.* Relational monologue is a manner of engagement based on self-protection. A family in monologue suggests a cacophony of one-way communication, a

Tower of Babel trying to exist as a home. Krasner and Joyce describe the condition of monologue through the metaphor of declarative self-acceptance, "Here am I."

> "Adam, where art thou?" is never a question for monologic humans. "Here am I" is never their response to life's call and demands. But a choice for trust is inevitably a choice of dialogue, dialogue as a method, process and way. . . . The fundamental premise of dialogue is that there is always some validity in every person's side. I may disagree with you. I may feel injured by you. But I cannot eclipse your reality. You may react to my stance. You may feel rejected by me. But you cannot use monologue to invalidate my reality. . . . Monologue is often the norm of family life. People talk at many levels, but deep loyalties typically silence family members from fairly raising hard questions with each other. The task of contextual therapy is to initiate dialogue. (Krasner & Joyce, 1995, p. 5)

When families seek help they are struggling to be honest, truthful, and accepting of the realities of their circumstances, the individual personalities that make up their family, and the mutual rights and obligations that exist from membership within the family. The families who see a contextual family therapist will experience therapy similarly to the experience of one who stands on the bank of a lake. The treatment that might be initially implemented may focus on understanding and accepting the factual reality, remaining in the shallows of the water. However, the family may choose to pursue experiences together that involve greater depth, more vulnerable communication, and an examination of the ethical obligations and entitlements that exist within the family.

When families seek help, they can benefit from what Hargrave and Pfitzer refer to as family salvage and family restoration. Families seeking help benefit from family salvage because they need help altering their patterns of violation of love and trust that have impeded basic family functioning. Family salvage means gaining "insight into how to keep the damage done in the past from continuing to affect one's life now and in the future" (Hargrave & Pfitzer, 2003, p. 140). Salvage should not be minimized as "less than" therapy. It is respectfully acknowledging the factual circumstances that exist with the unique personalities within the family and making a determination about the state of current skills and capacities to exhibit love and trust toward one another. Salvage can be understood by the humorous quip that the first step in getting out of a hole is to stop digging. Salvage may not mean that an issue is resolved or that historical damage to family security is restored. Rather, salvage implies that the family has learned to manage their interactions in such a way that the perpetuation of hurt and injury has ceased.

Families also benefit from restoration. Boszormenyi-Nagy uses the term "exoneration," which he defines as "a process of lifting the load of culpability off the shoulders of a given person whom heretofore we may have blamed" (Boszormenyi-Nagy & Krasner, 1986, p. 416).

Hargrave and Pfitzer have used the term "forgiveness" to describe the process of family restoration (Hargrave, 1994; Hargrave & Pfitzer, 2003; Hargrave & Sells, 1997). Hargrave's use of forgiveness refers to a deeper, more complicated process than the mere declaration of apology:

> Restoration means that the victim and the victimizer work together to restore love and trust and to make the relationship functional again. This work of forgiveness is accomplished by the victim allowing the victimizer to rebuild trustworthiness and love in a sequential fashion, called giving opportunity for forgiveness. (Hargrave & Pfitzer, 2003, p. 141)

Contextual family therapy remains more popular in European contexts than in North American contexts, but we do continue to see interest in theory, clinical practice, and empirical research among proponents of contextual family therapy worldwide. The concepts of relational ethics and justice continue to be creatively applied to a variety of topics, including care for the environment (e.g., Magistro, 2014), LGBT+ families (e.g., Roots, 2013), and ongoing reflection on theory (e.g., Gangamma, Bartle-Haring, & Glebova, 2012) and empirical research on treatment of depression in couples therapy (Gangamma, Bartle-Haring, Holowacz, Hartwell, & Glebova, 2015).

## THE APPROACH TO FAMILY THERAPY

*The process of therapy.* We have begun to suggest how contextual family therapists approach family therapy. Therapists approach individual families with a unique perspective that is aimed at developing dialogue. Multidirected partiality is the perspective articulated by Boszormenyi-Nagy that creates the therapeutic environment for give-and-take to occur within the family. "Toward the participants, the therapist does not adopt a stance of impartial contemplation of all competing interests. We hold that 'impartiality' or 'neutrality,' if it can be achieved, is an undesirable goal, and its pursuit can be deadening. The therapist is multidirectionally partial, i.e., directing empathy, endorsement, listening to one person, then in turn to that person's adversary" (Boszormenyi-Nagy & Ulrich, 1981, p. 178).

Hargrave and Pfitzer (2003) refer to multidirected partiality as both an attitude and a tool. It is an attitude in that it assumes that all participants are entitled to respect and possess legitimacy that must be actively demonstrated by the therapist. And it is a tool in that it is a specific technique that guides the nature of conversation occurring in treatment. It is manifested by the active, full engagement in the story of each participant while holding the other members passive. Listening to each story is not for the purpose of evaluating validity, pronouncing judgment, and exacting sentence. Rather, listening is essential for the rejunctive process of trust building. By holding family members passive during the storytelling of the other members, we don't want to imply that there is a gag order. However, the therapist must be active in protecting each member from disjunction—that is, the eroding of trust by the system that would result if a person's story is blocked, disregarded, overruled, or dismissed.

The ultimate effect of multidirected partiality is twofold. First, it is an active exhibition of trustworthiness on the part of the therapist toward each family member. Second, it is an active exhibition of boundaries and protection for each member. In essence it is the newly appointed sheriff humbly walking into the saloon and declaring, "There is a new law in town; I am here to protect everyone's rights." Such a statement permits the rebuilding of trust within the family because it promises they can take the risk necessary for family reconciliation without it being thwarted by the family.

***Case illustration.*** Marian is a thirty-eight-year-old married mother of two elementary-age children. She met her husband, Keith, in their senior year of college. They married a year after graduation and have been married for fifteen years. She has a master's degree in early childhood education and is the director of a preschool, which employs nine teachers and staff workers. She developed the preschool eleven years ago. It is part of a church ministry and is considered a vital aspect of the overall church ministry. Marian is introspective and soft-spoken in her demeanor. She is more cooperative than honest, caring for others above caring for herself.

Keith is employed as a regional sales manager with a technology company. He attended college on a basketball scholarship and earned a bachelor's degree.

He has held a number of positions in sales and sales administration. He travels about one week per month, usually single-night trips within a five-hundred-mile radius of their home. Keith is dynamic and forceful in his personality. He sells you stuff—while on the job and off. He is a persuasive individual.

Their children, Kelsey and Kevin, are in sixth and fifth grade, respectively. Kelsey is an athletic leader. She is independent and opinionated. Her interests lie in nonscholastic activity—soccer and basketball. Kevin likes machines and computers. He is less inclined toward athletics, unlike his sister and his father, and more inclined toward school.

Marian's initial motivation for therapy was the existence of a prevailing sense of despair and discouragement. Her work, family, and marriage were each "running smoothly," but she carried an overriding sense of dread about her life and her future. While not using the term *depression*, she complained of long-standing depressive symptoms—namely, a lack of creativity and joy from activities that bring pleasure, such as cooking, reading, exercise, and being with friends. Her life strengths were listed as her children and her work. She described her marriage and the relationships with her parents and adult siblings as a source of pain and discouragement.

The first session focused on developing an understanding of the concerns that Marian carried, her articulation of facts and circumstances, and developing a working relationship toward her goals. Marian spoke of a level of self-hate for choices that she had made, for not being able to stand up to her parents and to her husband. She felt stuck in her marriage. She entertained thoughts of leaving but immediately squelched that consideration as it would affect her children and her work.

During the two subsequent sessions Marian described her history. It proceeded from her present situation and worked backward to her family of origin and included the families of each of her parents. From this process a comprehensive genogram and narrative was developed. Crucial to her story was her description of pain associated with sexual behavior. Marian and Keith were sexually active as a dating couple in college. During her senior year Marian became pregnant. She told her parents, who insisted that she get an abortion. She stated, "Before I knew it, my mom had made an appointment for me at a women's clinic, my mom and dad drove me to the clinic. I met with the nurses and the doctor. And the next day, it was done. I told Keith a day later. He was stunned." He found it incredulous that her parents would insist on an abortion with such immediacy and that Marian would comply. She found even greater security in him as one who would stand up to her parents in the future. They were married four months after the abortion.

The sexual history contained another important fact that emerged from Marian's childhood. She acknowledged being sexually abused by an older brother when she was in elementary school. Her brother, Timothy, was five years older than she. When he entered the sixth grade he became the afternoon school sitter. Both parents worked, and there were two hours every day where they were both home unsupervised. Her brother would show her pornographic pictures and would tell her about sex in an explicit manner. Marian said that she told her mother, who reportedly told her father, who reportedly would "have talks" with their son. But the circumstances gradually worsened.

This situation culminated when Timothy, as an eighth grader, was accused of exposing himself to a younger child in the neighborhood. The parents changed their work, and from that point forward Marian's mother worked from their home. Marian stated that there was never actual sexual contact between her and her brother, but a constant sense of oppression. Furthermore, she felt the real pain as coming from her parents, who "did not take action to protect me, because I wasn't believed, but they sure jumped when the problem got out of the house and into the neighborhood."

As a married adult, she described her sexual intimacy with Keith as "loyal, but without much affection. He is a harsh man, an assertive man. He is much easier to live with when I just give him what he wants. There is less tension between us, and fewer conflicts with the kids when we have sex regularly. But I have ceased to enjoy it. In fact, I am not sure that I ever have enjoyed it."

The next ten sessions were conducted as couple therapy. This phase began with time with Keith, to learn of his story, and then evolved into couple therapy in which the couple focused on building dialogue around their respective pain.

Keith's story was in sharp contrast to Marian's. Keith grew up in a home in which, for all practical purposes, he was on his own by age thirteen. His father was a chronic substance abuser—"the town drunk," in Keith's words. When he was six his mother left his dad and raised him and his two sisters by herself with the help of an aunt and maternal grandparents. Keith's mom worked at night—which meant that she was at home sleeping during most of the day. Keith, equipped with a bicycle and residing in a small rural community, was free to roam and live as he wished.

The individual psychologies of Marian and Keith were developed individually and as a couple. For Keith, "No one will do it for you" emerged as a theme. Independent, resourceful, and strong were characteristics that both Marian and Keith used to describe his life patterns. With that came self-description of isolation and distance from others. Keith said, "I am not very good at being *with* people. I am good at competing against people—for getting the sale. And to do that you have to be friendly and engaging. But that is somewhat of an act. I am good at being with people when I want something, but not when I am just being." Marian, on the other hand, was the epitome of being with others—in a caretaking and serving manner. Her psychology leaned toward a capacity to see others in need, listen to those who hurt, comfort those with loss, and protect the children.

Together these personalities formed a systemic pattern that was consistent with their personalities and their families of origin. Keith functioned as the powerful decision maker—distant emotionally from the family but reliable, determined, and active in crisis. Marian was the caretaker. Her name, Marian, was a reflection of the Marianista role found in many Latin families; the role of Mary is the suffering servant who lives that others might have greater life—despite her sacrifice and suffering.

The dialogue between them grew in sessions eleven through twenty. The "here am I" could be characterized for Marian as a fearful child—trying to gain the courage to speak up and to insist on her wishes. For Keith it was the isolated rebel who earnestly sought a home—a place where he would be loved. They addressed the give-and-take that would be required of each of them to gain that which they both wished and feared. The ethics of this marriage required Keith to develop his skills of compassion and the capacity to sit with the pain of another. For Marian, it required the capacity to "name it"—to declare her wishes, even at the risk of creating misunderstanding.

The therapy reached a culmination with Marian's decision to discuss her childhood and the abortion with her parents. She requested that they be invited to attend a number of sessions around which Marian wanted to voice her experience. These past experiences continued to constrain her and restrict her view of self. It was Marian's wish to be able to speak to them in a way so as to release her parents and brother from the grip of resentment that she held. The family sessions went well, in a very limited sense. There was not the full acknowledgment of neglect by her parents. In fact, her parents believed that "the counselor was pushing Marian into thinking that her problems were our fault." That was what they told Marian after the second session. The success was that Marian was able to speak—not vindictively or seeking to pass blame. Rather, the exercise of declaring her experience and stating a desire to be in relationship even though great hurt had occurred was the therapeutic benefit.

At the close of therapy, the relationship between Marian and Keith accommodated Hargrave and Pfitzer's idea of relational forgiveness, and relational salvage between Marian and her family of origin. Everyone comes to the pain that the rest is between themselves and others who have varying capacities. Keith and Marian learned many things that permitted them to increase the quality of love and trust between them. Likewise, Marian and her parents were able to act in such a way that Marian could release them from her need to harbor dishonesty and untruthfulness as a protective defense to maintain relationship.

## CHRISTIAN PERSPECTIVE ON CONTEXTUAL FAMILY THERAPY

Giving a Christian and biblical appraisal of contextual family therapy likens this therapeutic journey to a wilderness adventurist who possesses a very good map but lacks a compass. This approach is commendable for the effort to embark into the wilderness possessed with a useful image of the terrain. However, with the absence of instruments that guide the use of the map in the actual terrain, the wanderers are vulnerable to becoming lost. Boszormenyi-Nagy's contribution of relational ethics is unique, substantial, and essential to the field. Strangely, it has been a lonely voice—for no other theoretician writing on family or individual theories, with the exception of William Doherty (1995) and, from a nonreligious perspective, Viktor Frankl (1963), has addressed the moral aspects of individual behavior as he has. Flowers (1997) states that Boszormenyi-Nagy was among the first to consider family therapy and morality as indivisible. Flowers believes that Boszormenyi-Nagy created an alignment between individual responsibility and social context through the use of a relational ethic.

While we encourage the development of a therapeutic structure, we find ourselves responding with the traditional feminist critique of a patriarchal social system by asking "Whose ethic?" Boszormenyi-Nagy's understanding of ethics, justice, and fairness is far from the biblical perspective. In fact, the contextual perspective of fairness and ethics is a relativistic construct that is subjectively defined. If left to individual interpretation the ethic would be vulnerable to power, and fairness controlled and defined by those with power. Indeed, Boszormenyi-Nagy states that "ethics carries no implication of a specific set of moral priorities or criteria of right vs. wrong. It is concerned with balance of equitable fairness between people" (Boszormenyi-Nagy & Ulrich, 1981, p. 160). His ethic becomes an ideal that likely would be guided and also misguided by the therapist's influence. While this ethic is grounded by facts, the factual reality is viewed as chance or, in the words of Boszormenyi-Nagy and Ulrich, "with what is provided by destiny" (1981, p. 159).

Finally, Boszormenyi-Nagy is tied theoretically to the work of Buber. The strength of that bond emerges from the intuitive power of the I-Thou. Mutual respect and regard is essential for the working of a family and essential in the process of therapy. However, Buber's position philosophically is criticized as being built on the circular reasoning of existential thought. The criticism is that it lacks a base of morality on which ethics can rest. In the same way, the motivation for moral or ethical actions within contextual family therapy becomes reliant on self-interest. If it is no longer within the self-interest of an individual to act fairly, then is there an ethical obligation? Obviously, from the Christian point of view, ethics is rooted within the judgment and grace of God articulated through the law and fulfilled in the gospel message of Jesus Christ.

*Model for family function and dysfunction.* For Boszormenyi-Nagy, fairness is healing. Contextual therapy, then, attempts to restore the "balanced reciprocity of fairness" among family members (Roberts, 1993, p. 87). In this model the family therapist tends to credit family members: an abusive father may be credited by acknowledging the injustice that someone suffered in the past (e.g., that the father himself was abused by one or both of his parents). But what restores justice is not this crediting so much as the family members' giving each other their due and acknowledging each other's merits. The central resource in contextual family therapy is the actual family relationships (not the therapist's transference) (Roberts, 1993, p. 90).

Boszormenyi-Nagy, then, tries to foster traits such as trust, mutuality, gratitude, generosity, and justice. Robert Roberts (1993), in his critique of contextual family therapy, offers several helpful contrasts between these concepts and Christian concepts. For example, in his discussion of trust, Roberts helps us see that a Nagyian view of trust is "seeing the other as a contributor, as a person of goodwill. It is the absence of anxiety—about being hurt, manipulated, used without credit, or let down" (p. 92). And Christian family therapists would affirm trust as something worth cultivating in a family. But the Christian does so with a deeper understanding of what trust is—that trust is related not to interpersonal or familial relationships, or at least not to these without reference to a relationship with God:

> Since Christianity regards human nature not just as relational but as God-related, we are freed to acknowledge that there is much in life to be anxious and distrustful about, even if our family members are as trustworthy as humans can be expected to be. Christian realism about the likelihood of finding security within

## INTEGRATIVE FOCUS: *Family Functioning*

Using the contextual paradigm, a family functions successfully when "fairness" is perceived by all members. Boszormenyi-Nagy used the metaphor of a ledger to illustrate the need for balanced "give and take" in relationships. Most of us have childhood memories of a mother, father, or other authority figure admonishing us to "play fair." Likewise as adults, we frequently hear our politicians referring to "the rule of law" when addressing the importance of civil order. Indeed, "playing by the rules," whether on the playground, in the broader society, or in the family, is essential for a system's success. For this contribution, contextual family theorists are to be commended.

But there is a vulnerability with the "fairness as family functioning" standard. As feminist therapy has appropriately articulated, the golden rule can easily be twisted to mean "the one with the gold makes the rules." Likewise, when fairness is permitted to float and not be moored to specific standards, it can be manipulated to mean whatever the persons with power permit it to mean. We believe that fairness must be further defined by some external ethical code by which individual behavior can be measured and appropriately restrained when necessary. We agree with Flowers (1997) in believing that this contribution is an invaluable first step, but it does not complete the need for helping families define that which is ultimately fair.

*Think about it:* What biblical/Christian constructs could assist a family in defining "fairness" within their system?

the bonds of earthly relationships reveals that need for a trusting relationship with one who is trustworthy even when all else in life has fallen apart. (p. 94)

Mutuality for Nagy is based on the idea that people are in relationships with one another and that these relationships are fundamental to their being (Roberts, 1993). We receive from others of past generations and we give to the next generation. We are placed in this context, and we have a fundamental and meaningful relationship with others in our family. The Christian family therapist might be drawn to this concept but will want to recognize that it needs to be further expanded to adequately reflect a truly Christian mutuality:

> The commandment "Love your neighbor as yourself" may be plausibly read as, "Love your neighbor because you and he are both members of the kingdom, children of the one Creator." Since the most momentous thing about you is that you are a member of that kingdom, ontologically related to your fellow children of God, loving your neighbor is in a strong sense loving yourself. Because persons are bound by kingdom ties, someone who does not love his neighbor is at odds with himself, just as, according to Nagy, a person who is unconcerned about the well-being of future generations is in friction with something fundamental about his own nature as an intergenerational being. (p. 98)

Contextual family therapy sees gratitude as a kind of complementary acknowledgment of what has been given to us by our parents, for example. We are indebted to them, and this is something that is quite refreshing for the Christian family therapist who might be looking for a more explicit acknowledgment of the gratitude that could exist among family members. At the same time, a Christian recognizes that our relationship with God is even more central to who we are than our family relationships, as important as they are.

With respect to gratitude, "Christian psychology disagrees with contextual therapy in affirming that it is more central to our nature to be God's children than to be children of our biological parents or primary caretakers" (Roberts, 1993, p. 102). Further, "Christian gratitude is simultaneously a state of well-being and a state of righteousness, since it is a happy and proper acknowledgement of our indebtedness to our Creator and Savior. It is an emotional adjustment to the way things are and thus a contemplative realization of our nature as dependent and gifted beings" (p. 102).

In a 1993 interview with the editors of *Psychology Today*, Boszormenyi-Nagy inferred that a large portion of failed relationships occur because of misconceptions regarding justice. The emerging marital therapist should not anticipate couples contemplating divorce coming into your office and stating the reason for the marital dissolution as "relational injustice."

However, when considering the idea of justice through a Christian paradigm, there are significant and powerful implications. In many Romance languages—Spanish, for example—the word used in the biblical text for "justice" is also used for "righteousness." The English-speaking mind tends to separate these words into different ideas, with *justice* being a legal term suggesting balance and equitability and *righteousness* being a religious term suggesting holiness and the absence of sin. For the Christian, seeking to do good to one's family and to permit the family to do good to each member, we suggest that righteousness as defined by the Christian tradition is indeed the just path for a family.

*Think about it:* What are the implications for understanding justice as righteousness?

The final major concept is justice, and contextual family therapy seeks to restore justice in the family context (Roberts, 1993). But a contextual approach is characterized by exoneration of an offending family member rather than forgiveness, and a Christian family therapist will recognize this as a shortcoming. A Christian family therapist will join the contextual family therapist in wanting to restore family offenders but will also recognize that exoneration (or freeing the offender from blame or responsibility) is a far cry from forgiveness (holding the person responsible for their behavior and its consequences while forgiving them for their offenses).

**Family therapy techniques.** The contextual family therapist essentially holds family members accountable to their relational commitments. The therapist does not use techniques as such, but instead positions himself or herself to facilitate awareness and sharing of one family member's perspective with another family member (Becvar & Becvar, 2006). Therapeutic "use of self" is important, as the therapist often begins with a gentle, curious posture that is largely "one down" but then, as Becvar and Becvar explain, moves to a place in which he or she is more confrontive.

## INTEGRATIVE FOCUS: Family Identity

The Old Testament prophet Zechariah wrote, "Administer true justice, show mercy and compassion to one another. Do not oppress the widow or the fatherless, the foreigner or the poor. Do not plot evil against each other" (Zech 7:9-10 NIV). We can think of no greater description of a successful family than one that is characterized by these words. In order to be just, each family member would be required to, as Philippians 2:4 states, "not looking to your own interests but each of you to the interests of others" (NIV). Families overrun with conflict are not able to operate on the dimension of justice. Open conflict suggests there is a lack of self-restraint. It would not be safe to attend to others, lest while exercising care one gets stabbed in the back. On the other hand, when a family takes small, careful, intentional, and disciplined risks trusting, with the mutual commitment to be trustworthy, the descriptive statement "this is a just home" can indeed be a family's address.

*Think about it:* In what way is justice an act of disciplined intention by those who hold power within a home?

## CONCLUSION

Contextual family therapy has much to offer the Christian clinician—the pastor or counselor—who seeks to reflect the values of Jesus and the biblical texts toward healing family relationships. The most important offering is that therapy can be an instructional experience that leads others toward realizing and accepting truth. The Christian and the trained contextual clinician exercise a faith that permits the reality to be addressed on its own terms.

## REFERENCES

Bateson, G. (1979). *Mind and nature: A necessary union.* New York: Bantam.

Becvar, D. S., & Becvar, R. J. (2006). *Family therapy: A systemic integration* (6th ed.). Boston: Allyn & Bacon.

Boszormenyi-Nagy, I., & Krasner, B. R. (1986). *Between give and take: A clinical guide to contextual therapy.* New York: Brunner/Mazel.

Boszormenyi-Nagy, I., & Ulrich, D. N. (1981). Contextual family therapy. In A. S. Gurman & D. P. Kniskern (Eds.), *Handbook of family therapy* (Vol. 1, pp. 159-86). New York: Brunner/Mazel.

Buber, M. (1958). *I and thou*. New York: Charles Scribner & Sons.

Doherty, W. J. (1995). *Soul searching: Why psychotherapy must promote moral responsibility*. New York: Basic Books.

Flowers, B. (1997). Are trustworthiness and fairness enough? Contextual family therapy and the good family. *Journal of Marital and Family Therapy, 23*(2), 153-69.

Framo, J. L. (1981). *Family therapy: Major contributions*. New York: International Universities Press.

Frankl, V. (1963). *Man's search for meaning*. New York: Pocket Books.

Gangamma, R., Bartle-Haring, S., & Glebova, T. (2012). A study of contextual therapy theory's relational ethics in couples in therapy. *Family Relations, 61*, 825-35.

Gangamma, R., Bartle-Haring, S., Holowacz, E., Hartwell, E. E., & Glebova, T. (2015). Relational ethics, depressive symptoms, and relationship satisfaction in couples in therapy. *Journal of Marital and Family Therapy, 41*(3), 354-66.

Hargrave, T. D. (1994). *Families and forgiveness: Healing the intergenerational wounds*. New York: Brunner/Mazel.

Hargrave, T. D., & Metcalf, L. (2000). Solution-focused family of origin therapy. In L. VandeCreek & T. L. Jackson (Eds.), *Innovations in clinical practice*. Sarasota, FL: Professional Resource Press.

Hargrave, T. D., & Pfitzer, F. (2003). *The new contextual therapy*. New York: Brunner Routledge.

Hargrave, T. D., & Sells, J. N. (1997). The development of a forgiveness scale. *Journal of Marital and Family Therapy, 23*, 41-62.

Krasner, B. R., & Joyce, A. J. (1995). *Truth, trust and relationship*. New York: Brunner/Mazel.

Magistro, C. A. (2014). Relational dimensions of environmental crisis: Insights from Boszormenyi-Nagy's contextual therapy. *Journal of Systemic Therapies, 33*(3), 17-28.

Roberts, R. (1993). *Taking the word to heart: Self and other in the age of therapies*. Grand Rapids: Eerdmans.

Roots, K. M. H. (2013). Wanted fathers: Understanding gay father families through contextual family therapy. *Journal of GLBT Family Studies, 9*(1), 43-64.

Sholevar, G. P. (Ed.), with Schwoeri, L. D. (2003). *Textbook of family and couples therapy: Clinical applications*. Washington, DC: American Psychiatric Publishing.

# EXPERIENTIAL
# FAMILY THERAPY

*Whenever a therapist steps off of
his throne, he is apt to grow.*

**CARL WHITAKER**

THE NORTH AMERICAN SLANG TERM *retro* is a Latin
prefix that has a French etymology from the word *retrospectif*, or
the English "retrospective." It means to revive or to draw from a
historical form or fashion. A revived relic might be a fair synonym.
In today's vernacular, something that is "retro" used to be in
vogue, then faded, but has reemerged. When considering experiential family therapy, it is possible to use the term *retro* as an
appropriate description. Experiential family therapy is rooted
and grounded deep in the 1960s values of humanistic, gestalt, and
existential perspectives of counseling. The experiential emphasis
of breaking free from family-initiated emotional suppression reminds us of a time when the breaking of restrictive social, civil,
religious, and familial controls was an essential and at times challenging part of our history.

Both individuals who are credited with this approach, Virginia
Satir and Carl Whitaker, were known for their innovation and
their nonformulaic approaches to counseling. Both were originators, and their approach reflected the cultural and historical
Zeitgeist of the era. However, one does not need to "turn on, tune
in, and drop out" or wear bell-bottoms, drive a flowered VW van,

and move to Big Sur, California, to benefit from this theory. Though experiential family therapy is rooted in the cultural forces of the 1960s, there is a significant resurgence of experiential family therapy that makes this original approach current to the work of family therapy in the twenty-first century. Emotionally focused therapy, most notably led by the work of Leslie Greenberg and Susan Johnson, contains humanistic-existential underpinnings of the experiential family approach but is linked with the current demands of the profession and the culture to be replicable and to demonstrate the validity and reliability of the interventions (Elliot & Greenberg, 1995). So, just as the Volkswagen Beetle and the Ford Mustang were icons of a previous era, but with modernization have become popular models today, so too experiential family therapy is a therapy of the past and a therapy of the present.

## HISTORICAL ORIGINS OF EXPERIENTIAL FAMILY THERAPY

Experiential family therapy emphasized the core elements drawn from the humanistic tradition. It valued the pursuit of self-actualization for all members of the family—adults and children. For example, Satir described the primary function of parents within families as being "people makers"; that is, they are to nurture children into their potential as adults to function with an awareness of self and a capacity to engage with others (Satir, 1972, 1988). To achieve this aim, therapy would be an encounter of immediacy and awareness of personal affect and experience. "Here and now" or "in the moment" were phrases used to describe the time-related focus for change.

Technically, Satir and Whitaker share a common historical era and a common set of values, but they did not collaborate in forming a single idea of psychotherapy. Therefore, it is more accurate to understand their individual contributions to experiential therapy as independent approaches that share the same traditions. More or less, they have been lumped together by these commonalities rather than having worked together to generate a common perspective on family intervention. Their writings represent autonomous views on counseling that utilize similar components and values. Surprisingly, given their many philosophical similarities, the look and feel of the counseling experience is drastically different. This suggests that the personality of the practitioner will play a significant role in *how* experiential family therapy is done, even though the *why* of family therapy (that is, the theoretical base) might be shared. The distinction between these two "masters" might serve as an encouragement to us as psychologists, counselors, or pastors who are given the freedom to develop our therapeutic selves by integrating the clinical knowledge of the profession with the God-given uniqueness of our personalities.

Satir's contribution focused on two powerful influences, that of communication and self-esteem. The former took shape through her work as an original researcher with Bateson, Jackson, and Haley at the Mental Research Institute (MRI). The latter, self-esteem, emerged after she left MRI and became the first clinical director of the Esalen Institute in Big Sur, California, in 1964. At the time Esalen was an emerging center for learning influenced significantly by the presence of Abraham Maslow and Fritz Perls. It served as a proving ground for the human potential and self-esteem movements popular during the 1960s.

Satir was born Virginia Pagenkopf in the rural Wisconsin farming town of Neillsville in 1916. She graduated from high school at the age of sixteen and trained to become an educator at the Milwaukee Teachers College, graduating in 1936. She began her graduate studies at Northwestern University in 1937, completing her degree in social work administration from the University of Chicago in 1943. During her young adult years she was married and divorced two times; the second was to Norman Satir, whom she divorced in 1957.

Satir began seeing families in a therapeutic context in 1951. In 1955 she helped establish a clinical psychiatric training program with Dr. Calmest Gyros at the Illinois Psychiatric Institute. Among her early supervisees was Ivan Boszormenyi-Nagy, who later developed contextual family therapy. Satir became one of the earliest voices for family intervention of psychiatric and relational dysfunction. Her pioneering work put her in relationship with Murray Bowen, who introduced her to Don Jackson. Jackson invited her to join the new Mental Research Institute as the clinical director in 1959. In 1966 she left the MRI and became the clinical director of Esalen. The move was more than a change in geography and employment. It also marked a theoretical expansion of Satir's views and professional attention. She was shifting away from being an exclusive systemic theorist and was becoming the "most celebrated humanist" (Nichols & Schwartz, 2006, p. 199). During the last two decades of her life, Satir wrote and presented her ideas of self-esteem as the key to human growth, and of rigid, repressive, or controlling families as being the lock that can suppress individual development or provide a sound, nurturing environment in which individuals can flourish. In the 1970s a professional conflict emerged between Satir and Salvador Minuchin regarding the direction of the profession of marriage and family therapy. Subsequently, Satir directed her career away from a family systems emphasis and toward one of human potential and growth.

In contrast to Satir's warmth, gentleness, and tenderness is Carl Whitaker. Both have been seen by their generation through live demonstrations and by scores of students through videotape and DVD. Satir creates the aura of a nursing mother, Whitaker the school bus driver! He is the gadfly of the profession, known for being spontaneous, unpredictable, funny, bold, confrontational, and direct. Maurizio Andolfi wrote soon after Whitaker's death that his legacy

> will be revalued even by those who kept their distance during his lifetime, labeling him "bizarre" and "irrational." Carl was a pioneer in family therapy, a giant, who did not allow himself to be seduced into creating a myth around his personality. . . . He had an iron-clad conviction that we all have a place in our own families, where we have deep historical roots. His faith in our capacity to rediscover these truths within the groups to which we belong guided him into the most secret and private reaches of the individual without ever losing his way back. This "adult" work of his was like child's play, where creativity, fantasy and play allow conscious thought to be more "crazy," more available for free association. (Andolfi, 1996)

Whitaker was born in 1912 and raised in upstate New York on a dairy farm. He has written extensively regarding how his life experiences influenced his formation of personhood—and his personhood on the development of his therapy, and his therapy on the formation of his theory (Whitaker, 1989; Whitaker & Keith, 1981). Key in his life story was his reference to friendship. He spoke of not being particularly outgoing, so early in adolescence he bonded with a few close friends who helped guide and navigate him through the throes of adolescence, college, medical school, and professional practice. Of central importance to him was the guiding relationship with his wife, Muriel, and the interaction between his role as a father of six children and a symbolic father of thousands.

The reliance on friends is seen in his value of cotherapy and, most importantly, as a check for his seemingly outlandish interventions. On numerous occasions in his writings and in his taped presentations, Whitaker reminds us that good therapy is dangerous; therefore, one should not attempt this alone:

The single therapist was all too prone to take sides, to become the covert agent of one family member or to avoid involvement altogether. The presence of two or more therapists provided both a safeguard and an opportunity for modeling of more desirable interpersonal behavior for the family. (Neill & Kniskern, 1982, p. 17)

Whitaker's approach to family therapy was rooted in the post–World War II era. After completing medical training at Syracuse, first as an ob-gyn, then as a psychiatrist, he joined the faculty at the University of Louisville. As a civilian physician during the war he went to the Oak Ridge research facility in eastern Tennessee, where the US government was secretly developing the atomic bomb. Whitaker writes with humor regarding his time at Oak Ridge in which everyone knew, by the mere size of the facility with 70,000 employees, that they were working on something very important, but no one knew what they were doing. It was indeed the largest family secret imaginable. Working with civilians and soldiers involved in the covert development of nuclear weapons, he along with his cotherapist, John Warkentin, stumbled into intense transference relationships with patients who in all likelihood were experiencing posttraumatic stress disorder. His patients were war victims at a time when there was little understanding of the psychological effects of war and violence. Whitaker writes of this time,

> I also discovered more about psychopathology and psychotherapy, albeit, rather serendipitously. Henry, a manic psychotic on the ward, was my next patient. I had just finished working with a five-year-old boy, whom I was treating with play therapy using a bottle with warm milk to help him regress. The bottle was left sitting on the desk. The manic came in, took one look at the bottle, and began a regressive sucking on it. Needless to say, I had another baby bottle with warm milk ready for him the next day. . . . It was only some time later that it dawned on me that it wasn't the patient who required the technique but the therapist. I was learning to mother, and once that awareness and skill were developed, I didn't need to use the technique. (Whitaker, 1989, p. 18)

Whitaker learned from that era to utilize the transference needs of families—to indeed become a symbolic mother and father through a combination of warmth, humor, personal revelation, confrontation, and absurdity. The effectiveness of the "bottle feeding," Whitaker believed, was not because clients had psychoanalytic wishes for oral gratification from infancy. It was in doing and being the ridiculous and incongruous that prompted creative resolution for families who were stuck in their pain. His discovery of symbolism, particularly his own figurative work as a symbolic mother and father, prompted his families to health. This metaphor became central to how he understood the change process. Later he said that the mature therapist is constantly parental (Neill & Kniskern, 1982). He wrote, "Perhaps the idea of a foster parent describes it best. . . . While he can care about them, it's generally clear that he's not really part of them. . . . I'm offering to get involved, but I retain the option of deciding I want out. It's not a lifetime commitment. Lastly, there's an exchange of money. This makes it clear that our arrangement is not one of unrestrained altruism" (Whitaker & Bumberry, 1988, p. 45).

After World War II, Whitaker established the department of psychiatry at Emory University in Atlanta, where he remained as the director from 1946 until 1955. This period was marked by significant advancement in the mental health field. He coauthored *The Roots of Psychotherapy* with Thomas Malone in 1953. An important premise of the book was to draw the distinction between his view of psychotherapy and psychiatry. His original thinking was that psychotherapy was a learning experience that is culturally derived and not a branch of medical science. He viewed therapy as a sacred relationship that should not be objectified into empirical quantification (Whitaker & Malone, 1953). Whitaker was pressured to leave Emory as superiors in the medical school desired a more psychoanalytic influence. Whitaker stayed in Atlanta and established a private practice clinic with valued colleagues, including John Warkentin and Thomas Malone. In 1965 he moved to the University of Wisconsin Medical School, where he retired in 1989. It was during this period at Wisconsin that his mentoring of students brought the proliferation of his ideas.

## CURRENT APPLICATIONS OF
## EXPERIENTIAL FAMILY THERAPY

The profession of marriage and family therapy has matured similarly to the growth and development of the United States frontier in the nineteenth century. First came the explorers who developed initial maps, then the pioneers who settled the land without the aid of preexisting structures—they cut roads into the land rather than just traveling on them. Finally came the settlements—towns and cities in which existence was regulated by codes, rules, and laws.

If Satir and Whitaker represent an initial "Wild West" creative force in humanistic family therapy, then licensure, managed care, and empirically validated interventions represent the regulated forces that come with civilization. The creative and spontaneous aspects of the original theorists were nearly lost in the codification and regulation of the profession. However, a resurgence of affect-oriented approach, Emotion-Focused Therapy (EFT) (sometimes referred to as Emotion-Focused Family Therapy) has established itself as being faithful to its philosophical originators and compatible with a twenty-first-century mental health civilization. It is an effort to maintain the experiential and phenomenal aspects with evidence of legitimacy required of current therapies. It is a fusion of the humanistic affective values of the originators with empirical evidence valued by third-party payers. Johnson and Greenberg write:

> EFT is a synthesis of experiential and systemic approaches to change; in both these schools, the ability to form strong alliance is seen as crucial to the therapy process. Systems theory refers to the therapists joining with each partner and the system *as it is* before beginning to create change (Minuchin, 1974). In experiential therapies, a therapist's empathy and respect for the client's experiences are essential and curative elements (Rogers, 1961), creating the safety that enables people to risk encountering threatening aspects of their experience in the interest of change. (Johnson & Greenberg, 1995, p. 130)

Johnson further states that EFT is one of the few approaches "to marital therapy that has been empirically validated and subjected to process research aimed at relating specific in-session changes to positive outcomes" (Johnson & Greenberg, 1995, p. 121). It is seen as an emerging marital and family therapy that is fundamentally an experiential approach but also an exception to the "nonscientific" and "nonempirical" tradition of the experiential founders (Nichols & Davis, 2017). Emotion-focused therapy has experienced phenomenal growth from the 1990s to the present. Gurman and Fraenkel (2002) identify it as one of the most cited and influential family therapies. Simon (2004) cites its unique strength as resonating with the current emphasis on integrative approaches and on empirical validity.

Emotion-focused theory is an intergenerational approach that draws from the humanistic systems and psychodynamic traditions. Its humanistic roots can be seen in a wide array of theorists, including Rogers, Perls, Satir, and

Whitaker. However, it is the view of many that Satir's approach is the most influential in sculpting the worldview and theoretical underpinnings of the approach (Gurman & Fraenkel, 2002; Nichols & Davis, 2017; Simon, 2004). The connection between Satir and EFT is through the priority of individual expression. The family is seen as the context through which personal affect is permitted to enter into individual awareness. Greenberg and Johnson (1988) use Bowlby's (1969) attachment theory as the link between communication and family relationships in that attachments are achieved through the direct and reciprocating expression of vulnerability within the family. Emotion-focused therapy as an experiential therapy is involved in helping couples and families in the lowering of defenses so as to permit honest dialogue between family members (Greenberg & Johnson, 1988; Nichols & Davis, 2017).

The approach utilizes the systemic idea of feedback loop to reinforce both the individual's definition of self and the individual's definition of the relationship. This definition or internal image influences the nature and depth of the family members' attachment to each other—which predicts a host of other variables related to relational quality, duration, resiliency, and so on. To Johnson and Greenberg, it is the emotional system that provides evidence and insight to the quality of attachments occurring in the family. "The emotional system is also a primary signaling system that allows for the prediction of individual behavior and regulates social interaction. Emotion and emotional communication are, there, key regulators of marital interaction" (Johnson & Greenberg, 1995, p. 125).

Emotion-focused therapy continues to be widely practiced and researched with couples (e.g., Hinkle, Radomski, & Decker, 2015) and families (e.g., Robinson, Dolhanty, & Greenberg, 2015) and has been creatively integrated with various family therapy protocols for treating eating disorders in children and adolescents (e.g., Robinson et al., 2015), attachment-based approaches to children and families (e.g., Stavrianopoulos, Faller, & Furrow, 2014), and other concerns.

## THEORETICAL AND PHILOSOPHICAL ASSUMPTIONS OF EXPERIENTIAL FAMILY THERAPY

Understanding the philosophical assumptions of experiential family therapy is a greater challenge than most other approaches. This is because experiential family therapy originates from an existential-humanistic perspective that, in its early years, defied rigid codification of theory and empirical evidence for its effectiveness. Its originators would not see their approach in terms of formal theory, which drives technique that students should imitate. Whitaker and Bumberry write, "The process of family therapy revolves around people and relationships, not intervention techniques or theoretical abstractions" (1988, p. 35). They saw the counseling process as a spontaneous phenomenal experience that operates under a few broad principles related to individual autonomy. Whitaker believed that theories "are bad except for the beginner's game playing, until he gets the courage to give up theories and just live, because it has been known for many generations that any addiction, any indoctrination, tends to be constrictive and constipating" (Neill & Kniskern, 1982, p. 318).

Indeed, as a theoretician, Whitaker devoted considerable energy at demythologizing himself by not creating a center of thought around his ideas. He created the paradox of being one whom others tried to copy, at the same time encouraging others to not copy him. Humorously, he stated, "How can one explode a self-myth? Partly by inducing laughter at the fact of it, and partly by a massive injection of some other counter myth (like, 'Isn't it wonderful that Freud wet his pants?'). One can learn to evolve a sense of the absurd, a capacity to laugh at the myth, to enjoy it for its fun rather than become a slave to it by taking it as a reality" (Whitaker, 1989, p. 41).

Likewise, Satir's career was fluid—moving between the formal academic areas of communication research, family therapy, and the nonacademic emphasis of the human potential movement. Understanding her theoretical perspective was made more complicated by her quiet withdrawal from the community of family therapy scholars in the early 1970s. This move occurred naturally by her emerging interest in the human potential movement, and unnaturally by a shift in the focus of the profession from "here and now" values of the humanistic tradition toward more structural and later strategic emphases (Nichols & Davis, 2017). The net effect was that there is not a "Whitakerian" or "Satirian" therapy (maybe because these approaches would be too difficult to pronounce!). Rather, family therapy approaches that adhere to their perspectives have developed through the modeling and demonstration of technique rather than through the development of schools of thought or practice.

A second reason the philosophical assumptions are difficult to define is that purposefully, Whitaker and Satir were inclined to not be theoretically driven.

The phenomenal nature of the humanistic approach is resistant to quantification and duplication. Whitaker, in one of his many quips on life and therapy said, "Nothing that is worth knowing can be taught. It has to be learned. It has to be discovered by each of us. The process of learning how you learn, of discovering your own epistemology—your method of handling discoveries, new thoughts, new ideas, new opinions is something you must struggle for in order to evolve more and more of who you are" (Whitaker, 1989, p. 50). Concurrently, Satir made a choice to move away from the theoretical model of family therapy—exemplified by her highly successful *Conjoint Family Therapy* (Satir, 1964, 1983) toward her equally successful *Peoplemaking* (1972). The difference in these two high-impact books was the audience to which they were written— the former toward the therapeutic audience, the latter toward the nonprofessional reader. Satir did not advance her theory of family therapy; rather, she changed her emphasis toward individual development.

Finally, the experiential family approach is understood not as a theory of family therapy but as a unique phenomenal expression of creative, inventive, and expressive personalities—of which replication is impossible. To some extent, experiential family therapy passed with the deaths of Satir in 1988 and of Whitaker in 1995. Referring specifically to Satir and Whitaker, Gladding writes that "both had a spontaneous theatrical style that was uniquely their own and made them difficult to emulate. Whitaker especially has been hard to model, partly because of his encouragement of intuitive action by a therapist and partly because of the need for a therapist to do an apprenticeship with him in order to really learn his approach" (Gladding, 2007, p. 172).

In spite of these challenges, there are core theoretical beliefs common to both Whitaker and Satir that separate experiential family therapy from other approaches. Specifically, both held to a phenomenal view of individuality and a belief in the environmental suppression of individual growth. Additionally, the therapeutic process is seen as an unshackling or a freeing of individuals and families for growth. The therapist plays an important coaching, modeling, nurturing, and provoking role in helping families free themselves of themselves.

*Self and family.* The first essential shared belief is an integration of the phenomenon of individual experience with the social relational context of systemic thought. The emphasis on phenomenology—that is, that individual behavior is determined by unique perceptions and understanding of outside events—stands in stark contrast to behavioral or psychodynamic determinism. Common to the phenomenological perspective is the importance of the self. Satir is vague regarding the definition of self, describing it as consisting of five parts: mind, body, spirituality, senses (the interaction between the mind and the body), and the interaction with others (social relationships) (Satir, 1983).

Satir and Whitaker applied the phenomenological perspectives originally expressed by Laing (1965), Binswanger (1967), and Boss (1963) to systemic contexts. A basic explanation of these existential views is that normal functioning is to assume "I" and "you" are separate but related. Essential within the separate but connected reality is the exercise of bilateral trust that our individual perceptions will be respected, protected, and encouraged to increase. Without this mutual regard our very existences become threatened. If this fundamental trust and responsibility within a family is disregarded or absent, then individuals must act in a self-focused manner. Laing refers to this as self-petrification—the depersonalization of the self before the family system has opportunity to engulf as a means to maintain autonomy: "One negates the other person's autonomy, ignores his feelings, regards him as a thing, kills the life in him. In this sense one may perhaps better say the one depersonalizes him or reifies him. One treats him not as a person, as a free agent, but as an it" (Laing, 1965, p. 46).

Satir and Whitaker stood as powerful voices for individual autonomy and for contextualizing that individual autonomy within families. At first glance there is an apparent contradiction between these humanistic and systemic views. However, this tension and paradox served as a restraint from the errors of self-absorption or egocentrism. All family theories must address the conflict between the systemic and cybernetic emphasis of Bertalanffy and Bateson and the existential-philosophical emphasis of individuality. The view of most systemic theorists is that the individual functions to support the system. However, the experiential view of Satir and Whitaker is that the family exists to provide growth, nurturance, and support for individual self-actualization.

*Self-esteem.* To Satir, self-esteem was the sine qua non of human existence. Toward this end, Satir wrote "My Declaration of Self-Esteem" in 1975. "I own my fantasies, my dreams, my hopes, my fears. I own all my triumphs and successes, all my failures and mistakes. Because I own all of me, I can become intimately acquainted with me. By so doing I can love me and be friendly with me in all my parts" (Satir, 1975).

She has noted that because communication is always to involve only two parties, a misalignment of relationships within families is always a likelihood. For example, she has described a typical family of five to comprise forty-five different relational configurations that are derived from thirty-three different triangular relationships, with ten pairs, not to mention the fundamental needs of the five individuals (Satir, 1988). Therapy within the family would involve an examination of how loving intention, the "relational oxygen" that is continually needed to reinforce our need for esteem, is blocked, miscommunicated, or neglected between family members, and how a family can be freed to resuscitate and revitalize our esteeming process and maximize individual potential through the supportive power of their relationships.

*The precipitation of growth.* Both Satir and Whitaker view growth as the primary function of psychotherapy. The counselor is a growth agent and the counseling is a growth process. However, the theoretical assumptions about how growth occurs and the interventions implemented to achieve growth could not appear more divergent. Whitaker uses anxiety created in the session to create confusion and cognitive dissonance. He states that he seeks to

> help the family get confused, and I frequently help them sense the fact that this is what they are there for, and I'm not trying to get them anyplace, I am trying to confuse them so they won't go on the way they have been going. We had a bunch of non-professionals who were running an alcoholic rehabilitation center. . . . What they ended up saying was, "we are just trying to screw it up so they can't enjoy their drinking anymore." I sometimes have the opinion that that's one of the important things to learn about family therapy. If you can screw it up so they can't enjoy the way it is going anymore, they'll work out ways of making a more adequate and effective methodology for living which will give them more enjoyment. (Neill & Kniskern, 1982, p. 221)

Whitaker's radical, brash, even dangerously reckless use of provocation to stimulate aversive responses by the family is based on his commitment that individuals have a natural inclination for growth—therefore, any release from the controlling structures of family rules will result in each family member realigning himself or herself toward maturity.

*Raising anxiety as a means of precipitating growth.* Experiential family therapists believe that the path to authenticity is through personal growth. Growth is achieved in the therapeutic encounter by raising the level of anxiety among family members. What Whitaker would do, for example, is raise the anxiety by being provocative with various family members. In one classic video segment in which he consults with a family after the death of the alcoholic and abusive father, he confronts the mother over her obesity. He frames it as a "suicide" and encourages the kids to find a suitable mate for their mother. As students observe this video and other exchanges by Whitaker, they are often stuck on his provocative (or, as they would put it, "offensive") manner, but they sometimes overlook his capacity to be supportive of individual family members and of the family as a whole.

A session might really vacillate between provocations and messages of empathy and support. But the purpose of it is to increase anxiety so that family members will take a chance on being genuine with one another. This family genuineness is first modeled by the experiential family therapist, and then family members themselves are to jump in, expressing themselves openly and honestly.

Aside from the evolution of experiential family therapy in the form of EFT for couples and families, the original experiential approach of Satir and Whitaker has not dominated family therapy circles in North America. Interestingly, experiential family therapy, specifically the Satir model, with its emphasis on transformational change, has grown in popularity in Thailand, South Korea, Singapore, and Hong Kong as well as China, the Czech Republic, and Slovakia (Banmen & Maki-Banmen, 2014). Experiential interventions continue to be used in family therapy (e.g., Thompson, Bender, Cardoso, & Flynn, 2011) and integrated with other approaches, such as motivational interviewing (e.g., Lloyd-Hazlett, Honderich, & Heyward, 2015), but as a school of family theory, the impact in North America has waned somewhat in recent years.

## WHEN FAMILIES SEEK HELP

*The approach to family therapy.* While it has been emphasized that experiential family therapy underplays the importance of formal or rigid steps to counseling, there are important broad principles in working with families that make this approach distinct from others. Roberto describes two overarching goals for counselors working with families within the experiential paradigm. First, there should be an increased bonding and belonging within the family so that the family identity is as a problem-solving unit. The second goal is for the family to be able to encourage family members' expression and individuation (Roberto, 1991).

Whitaker and Satir's approaches to helping families came from different starting points. Skynner (1981) identifies the variance of Satir's and Whitaker's approaches by using the Beels and Ferber (1969) paradigm describing three principal positions from which a counselor might enter and influence the family system. The three positions are "from above," "from the side," and "from below." Skynner regards Satir's approach as entering the family from above: She advocates "acting" as a "conductor," a "super-parent," or a grandparent figure, seeking to change the structure and function of the family by active intervention, giving advice, instruction, praise, and criticism, or educating by role-playing or deliberately "modeling" the new behavior considered more effective (Skynner, 1981, p. 56).

On the other hand, Skynner notes that Whitaker approached and engaged the family "from below." He does not "appear to involve any attempt at control. Rather, the therapist appears to submit to the control of the family, accepting exposure to and absorption of the family dynamics and so becoming affected by them . . . retaining the right to *describe* what is being experienced, thereby obliging the family to face the truth about their effect on each other" (Skynner, 1981, p. 56).

In essence experiential family therapy seeks to build families into "lean, mean fighting machines" where the fighting is not against one another but is a coordinated effort of the group to help individual members achieve their unique missions. The path taken by the therapist to accomplish that mission is likely more a determinant of the individual personality of the clinician rather than a dictum of the theory itself.

Given this freedom of approach, there are a number of essential experiences that counselors must create to encourage individual/family maturation and their capacity to move efficiently as a unit, to encourage and foster mutual growth and maturity, and to effectively communicate and exhibit attachment and intimacy.

*Joining.* While most therapies advocate an aspect of joining or therapeutic relation formation as the initial step in therapy, for experiential family therapists, joining can be seen as the therapy itself. Experiential family therapists—as modeled by Whitaker and Satir—join the family as a unique participant in the process. Their use of self in therapy is the hallmark of their approach. The manner in which a clinician would connect with the family is part of that self-presentation.

Satir joins by bonding with the individual members through the "here and now" identification of pain. "I would like to start with what goes on in me when I think about seeing myself as a helper to another person. In the first place, the person and his family—because I almost always think in the family context—would not be coming to me unless they had some kind of pain. . . . 'We've reached the end of our ability to cope, and we are searching for some way to cope better'" (Satir, 1983, p. 245). Her joining begins with an experience of deep compassion for the pain of others. Her compassion, unlike the work of most other clinicians, becomes active through the use of touch, drama, movement, and positioning. She writes,

> Suppose you are someone that I am just meeting. . . . You are with members of your family. I stand in front of you and reach out my hand to you at arm level. As I reach for your hand and you give it to me, I feel a connection. At that moment in time, I am looking at you; I am in touch with your skin feelings and my skin feelings and for that moment there is no one else in the world except you and me. You are the receiver of my full attention at that moment. You can feel that what I am connecting with is your personhood, and I feel that I am giving mine to you. . . . This is why I do not start out my treatment session with a discussion of the problem, but rather make the basic connection with everyone. (Satir, 1983, p. 247)

For Whitaker, joining is equally important but markedly different. Whitaker did not seek the emotional connection through compassionate understanding as did Satir. He joined through his humor and his absolute commitment to be transparent to the family with his feelings. Joining meant to gradually bond with the group as a parent figure. Indeed, he believed that the therapist was to occupy the role of a mythical mother and father figure for each family member, to parent them in a way that would free them to express anger, aggression, play, fear, and hope without recrimination or threat. He wrote,

> The basic idea of joining merits a closer look in working with families. While it's a relatively straightforward issue to be able to emphasize support to an individual in distress, it's much more complicated with a family. Any comment you make is heard and filtered through a number of ears. A move to be empathic with a wife is heard by the husband as you being duped into believing her side of the story. . . . The solution is to let them know that . . . you are pushing the entire family to grow. . . . One of the basic things we're hired for

as therapists is to be honest. No one really needs phony support. Being a psychological prostitute may offer some level of tainted comfort, but it's not the real thing. . . . When you confront the family, you do it out of a sense of your own honesty, not with the intent of getting them to acquiesce to it. (Whitaker & Bumberry, 1988, p. 46)

***Individual growth and maturation.*** No concept is as strong for Satir and nearly as strong for Whitaker as the concept of individual growth. Whitaker viewed individual maturation as an integration between the in-tuitive aspects of personality—what he saw as our unconscious—and the realm of our cognitive awareness. Similarly, family maturity is viewed as a dialectical struggle.

> The most significant dialectic is that found in the opposition/synthesis of be-longing and individuating. I have pointed out how individuation, when carried to its extended and evolved limit, was thought to produce a kind of wholeness in the person, which then made for maturity. This brand of ma-turity, however, turns into a kind of isolationism brought on by the denial of any need for belonging. At the other end of the continuum is a way of trying to escape the threat of belonging, called enmeshment by Salvador Minuchin. The individual who lives at home with his family into adulthood is enslaved by this belongingness and is sacrificing all of his individuation. (Whitaker, 1989, pp. 105-6)

In a similar voice, Satir wrote, "The most important concept in therapy, because it is a touchstone for all the rest, is that of maturation" (Satir, 1983, p. 117). She went on to describe growth and maturation as social and com-munication skills. Maturity as communication and maturity as social com-petence are central and foundational to her counseling theory. As a result of her work at MRI in communication processing, she came to view ma-turity as communication as far greater than being able to speak your mind. It includes the ability to manifest oneself to others, to be connected with the internal self so that one is aware of one's thoughts and feelings, and to accept responsibility for thinking and feeling rather than to turn crucial aspects of one's self over to others. Along similar thought lines, social ma-turity becomes the reason that Satir, as a humanist who values individual growth, places such a central emphasis on family therapy. Individual ma-turity is present in relationship with others. Therefore, her maturation as a social skill involves the capacity to be differentiated from that which is outside the self, to behave toward others with respect for mutual separateness, to learn through separateness rather than be threatened by it, and to address situations with others as they are instead of how it should be or we wish them to be (Satir, 1983).

As mentioned earlier, the manner in which the counselor fosters maturity and growth is a product of his or her individual dynamics. Satir advocates the nurturing of growth through compassion, touch, identification, and the instillation of hope and courage.

Whitaker, on the other hand, is more likely to "provoke" maturity than foster it. He attempted to instill maturity by raising the anxiety and tension within the family—forcing the family to cope with this new challenge to their stability by adaptation and reorganization. The case study cited below is considered "classic Whitaker." The tape and transcript are used frequently to demonstrate the loving and affectionate nature he possessed to relate to each family member.

His approach utilizes humor, confrontation, surprise, even shock to raise the anxiety. It is important to emphasize that Whitaker was not a "shock doctor"—creating turmoil within a family in a sadistic manner and calling it therapeutic. But his work with this family consisting of husband, wife, and three adult daughters could be described as fearless. He is not timid or afraid of asking questions that may produce discomfort because of the strength of his relationship with each member (Whitaker, 1981).

CARL: The real problem is, with most men, that they give up hope of really getting anything out of life when they're very young. They're trained to fall in love with things. With machines and animals and work.

MOM: Yes! Yes! That's exactly it! He's in love with his tractor. When it was out of kilter and didn't work he moaned, "Oh! I've got to have that tractor. You know I need that tractor!" So Mike had to fix it.

CARL: With a passion.

MOM: Yes! With a passion! That's his passion!

CARL: Do you have any sense of when it was that you gave up on trying to humanize him? How long after the marriage before you decided it was hopeless?

| MOM: | Oh, not right away. |
|---|---|
| CARL: | Well, it usually isn't right away because usually the woman confuses sex with love. She doesn't realize that the man isn't really loving, he's just sexual. |
| MOM: | Right. Well, it must have been at least a couple of years. Maybe five years. |
| CARL: | . . . ever since then, you have been depressed? |
| MOM: | I don't know. I know since I've had rheumatoid arthritis I've been depressed. For fourteen years now. |
| CARL: | Is it getting worse? |
| MOM: | I don't know. |
| CARL: | Let me ask you a crazy question that just popped into my head. Do you think Gail's sickness has kept your arthritis from getting worse? |
| MOM: | Maybe a little bit, I don't know. |
| CARL: | That's how I think about families. |
| MOM: | I don't have time to think about myself because of her. |
| VANESSA: | You also yell at Gail a lot. You get a lot of anger out at her. |
| CARL: | So you're really having an affair with Gail while he's having an affair with the tractor. |
| MOM: | Maybe. |
| CARL: | Where else is there passion in the family? I had a feeling when Dad made a crack about . . . Is it Marla? Is that your name? . . . Crazy: My grandmother was named Marla. That's why I wasn't sure. When Dad made a crack about Marla's drinking yesterday, I had the feeling there was a real passion fight between them. Is that true? That Dad's worried about your future? He thinks you're going to end up being a bad girl and he's trying to beat you into submission, so you'll be a good housewife for some farmer? |
| MOM: | I think that's right. |
| MARLA: | I never thought about it before. I suppose it could be. |
| MOM: | Yes, he's worried. |
| CARL: | Can you fight him? Can you stand up to the old man? |
| MARLA: | Not really. |

You can see in this example that Whitaker is able to be highly confrontational, but the family does not run away, melt, or become defensive. They remain engaged. It is the quality of the therapeutic relationship, specifically the trust between Whitaker and the family, that permits him to conduct questions that might otherwise feel aggressive.

*The practice of emotionally focused therapy.* In contrast, the more recent emotionally focused couple's therapy would intervene using nine steps (Johnson, 1998). As was suggested above, the entire approach is premised on genuineness on the part of the family therapist. The first step is assessment, and it focuses on information that matters to the couple. The second step involves defining the problem cycle between the couple that reflects marital distress (and is tied to "attachment insecurity" [p. 454]). This is achieved by carefully identifying emotions, recognizing that "softer" feelings, such as disappointment, may provide an entryway into more significant affect. Therapists can also validate emotions here. The third step involves identifying feelings that lie beneath the surface of these exchanges. Step four involves clarifying the unarticulated emotion so that the problem can be reframed "in terms of the [destructive interaction] cycle and unmet attachment needs" (p. 454). The family therapist can then move to step five, which involves the "owning of needs and of new, expanded aspects of self and experience" (p. 454).

Therapists then move to step six, which involves fostering a therapeutic atmosphere in which each partner can accept these newly discovered and articulated "aspects of the self" (Johnson, 1998, p. 454). This involves tapping into emotions that may have been difficult to accept as part of one's experience and sharing these in the relationship as it becomes a safer place to do so. The next step is to encourage acceptance of the spouse's self-discovery. It can be helpful for the therapist to support the risks associated with self-disclosure. This is followed by step eight: encouraging the expression of needs alternatively from the problematic patterns. Some of the problems that brought them in for therapy may now be more accessible to the couple because the emotions associated with them have been "neutralized." The final step involves facilitating new solutions and consolidating the gains made in therapy in light of improved communication of honest emotions.

In the end, emotion-focused couples and family therapy is not about the expression of emotion for the purposes of catharsis or emotional expressiveness for its own sake. Nor is it concerned, obviously, with a rational, "detached" way of talking about what one feels (Johnson, 1998, p. 468). Rather, according to Johnson, tapping into emotions provides an inroad into new ways of relating that in turn open a way to more emotional experiences.

## CHRISTIAN PERSPECTIVE ON EXPERIENTIAL FAMILY THERAPY

No theory derived through secular paradigms will be consistent on all levels with a biblical worldview or faithful to the Christian tradition. And there is no single biblical/Christian counseling theory by which to compare this or any other approach, just as there is no single theology within the Christian tradition. With that as a given, there are elements of theory that can be broadly seen as consistent with the general process of Christian thought. Likewise, theories contain ideas that are, to varying degrees, contrary to the traditions linked to New Testament faith. Therefore, with experiential family therapy we seek to identify and describe components of the approach that are consistent with mental health care that is compatible with Christian thought, value, and practice.

*Theoretical and philosophical assumptions.* Experiential family therapy is an integrative tradition that merges important philosophical and therapeutic elements from the humanistic, systemic, and, to a lesser degree, psychodynamic traditions. A number of Christian thinkers have expressed the view that the humanistic perspective is essentially Christian, even though its originators have not intended it to be such. Indeed, aspects of the humanistic tradition, as well as the systemic and psychodynamic perspective, incorporate ideas that are compatible with Christian thought. However, as C. S. Lewis suggests in *The Allegory of Love*, though truth and falsehood are in opposition, truth remains the standard to measure falsehood (Lewis, 1958). Applied to our context, ideas that are contrary to central and foundational biblical theology can still be shaped and molded from a truthful model. Therefore, we have observed components of experiential family therapy that we find to be consistent with the broadest interpretation of Christian thinking, and other components that are incompatible, no matter how broad the theological lens being used. Let's begin first with the aspects that are compatible with Christian thought.

*The intrinsic worth and dignity of every individual.* The value and worth of persons is the central concept of the humanistic tradition. Christians are challenged by the importance that adherents to this perspective place on understanding and demonstrating compassion for both mighty and weak, healthy and infirmed, young and old, male and female.

We believe that Christian theology permits a rationale for the valuing of individual dignity that is missed in the humanistic tradition. The *imago Dei* that distinguished human creation from all other created goodness is a critical starting point for the Christian. Individual family members bear the image of God, and they are valued precisely because they are created in God's image.

## INTEGRATIVE FOCUS: *Family Functioning*

To the humanistically oriented experiential family therapist, the function of a family is to reciprocally enhance individuality and for individuals to return the family's investment toward the self-actualization of each member. Family functioning is seen as the degree to which the system permits each member to be freed from the restraints of socially construed expectations. Psychopathological symptoms held by individuals and tensions between family members are indicators that the family system has not created an environment where individuality is permitted to flourish. In its original form, families functioned as the "runway" where members launched to find fulfillment in their individual creative endeavors and "landed" to be refueled, repaired, and restored for future excursions. When families failed to function there would be a "failure to launch" or an "avoidance/resistance to return" behavior exhibited by individual family members.

Criticism of the historic humanistic tradition by Christians has been that it is "all about *me*." The individual fulfillment, or self-actualization, is held as the highest priority and value, and little regard is paid to other concerns. We believe that the insertion of the systemic/family element does bring some correction to the humanistic emphasis on individuality. This adjustment is taken a step further with the utilization of attachment theory in emotionally focused therapy.

We believe that the Christian family therapist may be drawn to this approach because it provides avenues for the exhibition of grace and love to be generated and applied as a healing agent to the wounds of the families. It is easy to observe in the work of Satir or Whitaker a beautiful exhibition of Christian *charis* (grace) and *agape* (love). The family therapist who seeks to bridge the isolated, estranged, and wounded family members, much as Jesus did through his healing touch and restoring words, might indeed resonate with this approach.

*Think about it:* What can be understood about the power of relationship and the freedom to speak truthfully by examining the life of Jesus?

*Individual choice and freedom.* Christians have argued for centuries regarding the nature of free versus determined will. Arminian Christian and Reformed Christian traditions do not agree on the level of divine involvement in human affairs. However, the followers of both Wesley and Calvin would likely have a level of comfort with the experiential position. The fusion of existential individuality and the systemic indicates a "yes, but" perspective on free will and determinism.

*The spiritual aspect within the dynamic of life and therapy (Satir).* Toward the end of her career, Satir integrated the term spirituality as one of the key elements of growth and maturity. Consistent with her relativistic stance, it remained undefined as a philosophy or a theology. However, consistent with other values, it would best be defined as an Eastern transcendent pantheism. While far from a Christian theology, it does acknowledge a reality beyond materialism or scientific naturalism.

*Humans are in need of security and significance through attachment with something greater than themselves (family, God).* The tradition across most therapies is to value the individual to such an extent that humanity is deified. (However, the terminology would not include reference to deity.) Roberts (2003) notes that there are some exceptions to this tendency, citing Bowlby, Vygotsky, and Boszormenyi-Nagy as three examples of theories that adhere to a good that is greater than our individuality. Tentatively, we place the experiential theorists within this group. Satir, Whitaker, and the experientialists offer a potential for balance between the tendency to elevate humanity to the pinnacle of existence, thus denying the greater existence of truth, and the supernatural reality of the triune God. Our tacit endorsement is due to the fact that their integration of humanistic-existential-gestalt orientation with their systemic values brings them close to what could be considered the Christian ideal of humanity as the pinnacle of creation, but not the pinnacle of existence.

*Turmoil as a tool for learning and change.* Christians recognize that God often works through and is present to us in our personal turmoil, whether it is of our making, if you will, or something that appears quite distinct from the choices we have made. The famous French writer Paul Claudel is quoted as saying, "Jesus Christ did not come to take away suffering from the world. He did not even come to explain it. He came to fill suffering with his nearness" (Depoortere, 1995, p. 109). The Christian recognizes God's presence in suffering and sometimes God's purposes in suffering and can recognize that we often learn a great deal through our personal hardships as we grow dependent on God for all of our needs.

So those are the areas of particular agreement, or at least areas for potential connection, between experiential family therapy and a Christian understanding. But what of the potential points of conflict? We recognize several, including an exaggerated view of human worth and dignity, identifying emotional suppression as the root of all human/family problems, and identifying God as our unconscious.

*An exaggerated view of human worth and dignity.* The experientialists have adopted the traditional position of humanistic thinkers—upholding a high view of humanity. At first take, Christians also place a central value on the worth and dignity of the person. But with a second examination, there are clear differences between the position of humanistic psychology and Christian theology on the value and condition of humanity. Christianity does not have a lower view of the human condition than do theoreticians emerging from the experientialist/humanistic tradition. It is a difference in exclusivity rather than degree. The experiential approach has an exclusive value of human worth, decontextualized from the existence of evil. To the experientialist, individualized humanity is just good. Their goodness is an intrinsic quality, a reflection of their soul. Evil is an externalized force that impedes and disrupts individual potential. Evil comes from the outside onto a person and can interfere with one's innate goodness.

The Christian may resonate with the experientialist regarding the inherent goodness of humankind. But the discussion cannot rest with innate decency. Christianity demands that we address our indecency as an internal rather than an external quality. Interpreters of biblical texts do not encourage the lessening of human worth; rather, they encourage the placement of human value in a proper relationship with other characteristics of our existence. C. S. Lewis described the Christian view of humanity in the classic children's tale *Prince Caspian*: "'You come of the Lord Adam and the Lady Eve,' said Aslan. 'And that is both honor enough to erect the head of the poorest beggar, and shame enough to bow the shoulders of the greatest emperor in earth. Be content'" (Lewis, 1951, p. 218).

*The root of all human/family problems is emotional suppression.* The experientialists have adopted the traditional position of humanistic thinkers—upholding a high view of humanity. At first take, Christians also place a central view on the worth and dignity of the person. But with a second examination, there are clear differences between the position of humanistic psychology and Christian theology on the value and condition of humanity. Christian thinkers and interpreters of biblical texts do not encourage the lessening of human worth; rather, they encourage the placement of human value in proper relationship with other values. Humanistic thinkers value humanity as of great worth and recognize nothing greater. But the Christian à la C. S. Lewis recognizes the comparative value of humanity: that the comparison is God and humanity rather than just humanity. Our worth pales in comparison to who God is, and our worth—what there actually is of it—is tied directly to the God who created us and gives us that worth.

***God as our unconscious.*** Perhaps it is because of his medical background and his identity as a scientist that Whitaker does not speak of spirituality in the same way that Satir, a social scientist, does. He makes frequent reference to Christian imagery and Christian theology. It clearly has had an influence on his thinking, most likely because of his religious upbringing. However, as a theorist the references to Christian thought are placed within metaphoric language or are seen within the context of human personality and conscious and unconscious awareness as synonyms for theological concepts. For example, he wrote,

> The body is the temple of God; the bodily sensations are probably the closest to God, the unconscious, than any part of our experience, closer than the interpersonal experience, probably closer than the fantasy experience, since they are more direct. Therefore, the child's competitive athletic work is at work with his hands; his experiencing of his body sensations, whether it is with masturbation or physical illness probably informs him best about potentials and the possibilities of his own unconscious self, his own God. (Whitaker, quoted in Neill & Kniskern, 1982, p. 365)

Whitaker viewed God as cultural creations that ultimately caused imposition on individual and family growth and development. His therapy did not have a place for theology or the supernatural, let alone the transforming work of Jesus. He saw religious values as an inert aspect of life, at best, and a serious imposition to individual growth at worst. With such a perspective, it is good that he also emphasized the separation and individuation of his approach to therapy from his persona as a therapist. This permits us as Christian clinicians to accept the creative contribution that he has made to the field without needing to accept his personal views of formal religion in general and the Christian tradition in particular.

We would also take issue with the view that growth is a natural process, as espoused by experiential family therapists, rather than a discipline, as is more reflected in a Christian worldview.

***Model of family dysfunction and family functioning.*** Family problems really reflect the denial and suppression of feelings and impulses (Nichols & Davis, 2017). When people in a family deny and suppress feelings and impulses, they experience a lack of genuineness—a lack of real intimacy or authenticity. But what does this mean practically?

Whitaker and Keith (1981) described several characteristics of a healthy or "well-functioning" marriage or family that seem consistent with a Christian understanding of the family. These include being able to "handle constructive input . . . with power and comfort" (p. 190), and they see this as something that also occurs for individual members within the family—that they have the family as a safe "security blanket" but also can be stretched within the safety of the family itself.

The healthy family is also one in which three or four generations are integrated, by which Whitaker and Keith (1981) mean "the family and the subgroups and the individual members related to an intrapsychic family of three plus generations. Interaction within the extended family is related to this sense of historical ethos" (p. 190). There are also boundaries to these generations so that parents can be parents and children can be children. Again, the Christian family therapist would find much to agree with here, as Christians recognize the value of seeing family across generations and recognizing generational boundaries and roles.

Whitaker and Keith (1981) go on to say that there is a "flexibility" to the "power distribution," "with a casualness evolved through the freedom to express individual difference and to renegotiate role structure and role expectations and to reevaluate past experience" (p. 190). Christian family therapists, too, can acknowledge the benefits of flexibility within the family system based on circumstances, individual gifts, and so on.

Many of these qualities reflect what might be seen in structural family theory and, to some extent, Bowenian or transgenerational family theory. But Whitaker and Keith (1981) also add that the "healthy family is one that continues to grow in spite of whatever troubles come its way" (p. 190). By facing crises, the family itself can change and grow because "frustration is a useful enzyme for accelerating change" (p. 192). According to experiential family theory, a healthy family or one that is well functioning is also one that is able to relate honestly, a family moving toward growth. This is a family that is in touch with and expressive of their emotions so that real, honest selves are in relationship with one another.

Again, the Christian recognizes the value of growth through hardship, but these experiences are all with reference to God who is seen as sovereign over our individual and family circumstances and the difficulties we face. What growth we experience is not due to our own resilience as such but must be understood with reference to God's mercy and grace and to larger purposes that are often beyond our understanding this side of eternity.

Also, it should be noted that honesty and awareness are insufficient and can be brutalizing to individual family members. From a Christian perspective, awareness should lead to repentance and, eventually, reconciliation.

***Techniques in family therapy.*** Whitaker and Satir fused into one amalgamation the combination of "tough" and "love" that is so frequent in the contemporary Christian tradition. Whitaker was particularly provocative, but he could be alternately supportive and empathic. Satir was quite supportive but could also be provocative. It is the combination of these two positions (provocation and support) that characterize experiential family therapy techniques (Nichols & Davis, 2017).

Many of the techniques, though, can heighten intensity, and the experiential family therapist must be mindful not to create intensity for the sake of intensity. Students in training may see this in group therapy from time to time. Group therapy itself is an intense format that can be powerful for change, but it can also be powerful in ways that must be carefully monitored by group therapists so that we do not achieve levels of intensity simply because we are able to but because doing so is tied to a theoretical road map that helps the person move from where they are with their presenting concern to where they would be functioning better in terms of what they had hoped to achieve in therapy.

It should be noted, however, that experiential family therapy is not a technique-driven model of family therapy. There are specific techniques identified, but recall that the most powerful "technique" is the openness and honesty of the family therapist, not whether a particular technique can be implemented in the session.

But some of the techniques are worth considering. For example, experiential family therapists sometimes make use of family drawings. This is when family members are asked to draw their family and comment on the thoughts and feelings of the people they have drawn.

## INTEGRATIVE FOCUS: *Family Relationships*

To the integrative family therapist, it is the relationship that functions as the lifeblood for survival of the individual. It is the family relationship that functions as the "home" that affords protection and nourishment for the individual. The family relationship is an essential tool used by individuals through which the rich experiences of life can be manifested.

In humanistic theory, self-actualization was held as the highest good. In experiential family theory, self-actualization is placed in the family relationship and cannot be accessed except through the experience of human intimacy. The relationship does not supersede the importance of individuality. It serves as the essential context for self-actualization to emerge.

To the Christian family therapist, the insertion of the relational component into the humanistic tradition is a movement toward addressing the ultimate tension—that of one's individuality within vital relationship with the creator. Frequent use of biblical metaphors of marriage and family to describe and understand the duality of being both a "self" and a "self attached to a system" is an obvious parallel to the tension of self and other identified within this approach.

The experiential family therapist attends directly to the tension between individual and system in ways similar to how the Christian must address the paradox of being awarded by God the gifts of individual will and human dependence. Self-actualization becomes an oxymoron. It is recognized as both the highest value and the most impossible of pursuits apart from relationship with others, therefore the contradiction of the original claim of independence. Similarly, the Christian paradox of being gifted with both independence and the need for submissive protection simultaneously is a challenge of all Christians.

*Think about it:* In what ways do you live with the balance of personal independence and dependence in relationships? How does this conflict with the ubiquitous emphasis on self-actualization in our culture?

Virginia Satir was known for valuing touch in family therapy. This would include facilitating touch among family members, gently touching family members as they talk to one another, allowing children to touch her face, and so on. The reason for Satir was to keep family members in the "here and now" of their actual relationship, and touch could often accomplish this. The use of touch today would likely be rare, as it is an important boundary that many professionals would say is not the norm for what typically occurs in therapy and may leave a clinician open to liability. In some ways this is an understandable but unfortunate development, as watching Satir's use of touch gives clinicians a glimpse into what touch can provide in human encounters.

## INTEGRATIVE FOCUS: *Family Identity*

We see the truths of Christian theology bringing completion to the ideas formulated by the experiential family therapists and their humanistic family of origin. Experiential theory has revealed the importance of human individuality and the legitimacy of each family member. The approach has brought integrity to every person on the basis of existence, not merit. The theory and its subsequent techniques have declared, "I am here, I am present, and I have value!" and that existence and value are intrinsic and immutable. However, the humanistic approaches could not articulate a reason why a person has value, other than because the person exists.

The Christian tradition, we believe, gives justification to the value of individual existence based on the *imago Dei*. The individual within family is understood through the fact that every person is endowed by God as an example of love and grace. The experiential approach that has been criticized for being very loving and compassionate but not very intelligent or rational can be seen as moving toward completion when Christian theology is placed under it as the theoretical foundation. Love has reason beyond a soft emotion. Individuality has purpose beyond narcissistic self-fulfillment. And family has identity in the full story within the narrative of the creative Father and his redemptive work of creation.

*Think about it:* How is the maintenance of both an individual identity and corporate identity essential to healthy family functioning?

Another technique is family sculpture, in which family members are actually "sculpted" by one family member to express how they experience family relationships. This is a good example of an emotionally powerful technique that ought to be wielded by a therapist who has an understanding of what is to be achieved in session and what the possible benefits and risks might be. But, again, the technique itself is a helpful one for bringing up feelings among family members that might not be as readily accessible using verbal exchanges.

## CONCLUSION

Experiential family therapy is unique in many ways. The focus and valuing of emotions stand in rather stark contrast to some of the other models of family therapy. But the failure to offer a well-developed theory of the family and a map for assisting a family leaves the model open to a number of interpretations and seems at least initially to have been a model based on the personalities who gave it life (e.g., Whitaker, Satir). But as the newer approaches that emerged out of experiential family therapy take hold (e.g., emotionally focused family therapy), we are interested to see new developments and new possibilities for the field of family therapy.

## REFERENCES

Andolfi, M. (1996). Let it flow: Carl Whitaker's philosophy of becoming. *Journal of Marital and Family Therapy, 22,* 317-20.

Banmen, J., & Maki-Banmen, K. (2014). What has become of Virginia Satir's therapy model since she left us in 1988? *Journal of Family Psychotherapy, 25,* 117-31.

Beels, C. C., & Ferber, A. (1969). Family therapy: A view. *Family Process, 9,* 230-318.

Binswanger, L. (1967). Being in the world. In J. Needleman (Ed.), *Selected papers of Ludwig Binswanger.* New York: Harper Torchbooks.

Boss, M. (1963). *Psychoanalysis and daseinsanalysis* (L. B. Lefebre, Trans.). New York: Basic Books.

Bowlby, J. (1969). *Attachment and loss: Vol. 1. Attachment.* London: Hogarth Press; New York: Basic Books.

Depoortere, Kristiann. (1995). *A different God: A Christian view of suffering.* Dudley, MA: Peeters Publishing.

Elliot, R., & Greenberg, L. S. (1995). Experiential therapy in practice. The process-experiential approach. In B. Bongar & L. E. Beutler (Eds.), *Comprehensive textbook of psychotherapy.* New York: Oxford University Press.

Gladding, S. T. (2007). *Family therapy: History, theory and practice.* Upper Saddle River, NJ: Pearson Prentice Hall.

Greenberg, L. S., & Johnson, S. M. (1988). *Emotionally focused therapy for couples.* New York: Guilford Press.

Gurman, A. S., & Fraenkel, P. (2002). The history of couple therapy: A millennial review. *Family Process, 41,* 199-260.

Hinkle, M. S., Radomski, J. G., & Decker, K. M. (2015). Creative experiential interventions to heighten emotion and process in emotionally focused couples therapy. *The Family Journal, 23*(3), 239-46.

Johnson, S. M. (1998). Emotionally focused couples therapy. In F. M. Dattilio (Ed.), *Case studies in couple and family therapy* (pp. 450-72). New York: Guilford Press.

Johnson, S. M., & Greenberg, L. S. (1995). The emotionally focused approach. In N. S. Jacobson & A. S. Gurman (Eds.), *The clinical handbook of couples therapy* (2nd ed.). New York: Guilford Press.

Laing, R. O. (1965). *The divided self.* New York: Penguin.

Lewis, C. S. (1951). *Prince Caspian.* New York: HarperCollins.

Lewis, C. S. (1958). *The allegory of love.* New York: Oxford University Press.

Lloyd-Hazlett, J., Honderich, E. M., & Heyward, K. J. (2015). Fa-MI-ly: Experiential techniques to integrate motivational interviewing and family counseling. *The Family Journal, 24*(1), 31-37.

Minuchin, S. (1974). *Families and family change.* Cambridge, MA: Harvard University Press.

Neill, A. S., & Kniskern, D. P. (1982). *From psyche to system: The evolving therapy of Carl Whitaker.* New York: Guilford Press.

Nichols, M. P., & Davis, S. D. (2017). *Family therapy: Concepts and methods* (11th ed.). New York: Allyn & Bacon.

Nichols, M. P., & Schwartz, R. C. (2006). *Family therapy: Concepts and methods* (7th ed.). New York: Allyn & Bacon.

Roberto, L. G. (1991). Symbolic-experiential family therapy. In A. G. Gurman & D. P. Knikein (Eds.), *Handbook of family therapy* (Vol. 2). New York: Brunner/Mazel.

Roberts, R. C. (2003). Parameters of Christian psychology. In R. C. Roberts & M. R. Talbot (Eds.), *Limning the psyche: Explorations in Christian psychology.* Eugene, OR: Wipf & Stock.

Robinson, A. L., Dolhanty, J., & Greenberg, L. (2015). Emotion-focused family therapy for eating disorders in children and adolescents. *Clinical Psychology and Psychotherapy, 22,* 75-82.

Rogers, C. R. (1961). *On becoming a person.* Boston: Houghton-Mifflin.

Satir, V. M. (1964). *Conjoint family therapy: A guide to theory and technique.* Palo Alto, CA: Science and Behavior Books.

Satir, V. M. (1972). *Peoplemaking.* Palo Alto, CA: Science and Behavior Books.

Satir, V. M. (1975). *Self esteem* (Poem). Millbrae, CA: Celestial Arts.

Satir, V. M. (1983). *Conjoint family therapy: A guide to theory and technique* (3rd ed.). Palo Alto, CA: Science and Behavior Books.

Satir, V. M. (1988). *The new peoplemaking.* New York: Science and Behavior Books.

Simon, G. M. (2004). An examination of the integrative nature of emotional focused therapy. *The Family Journal, 12,* 254-62.

Skynner, A. C. R. (1981). An open systems, group-analytic approach to family therapy. In A. S. Gurman & D. P. Kniskern (Eds.), *Handbook of family therapy* (Vol. 1). New York: Brunner/Mazel.

Stavrianopoulos, K., Faller, G., & Furrow, J. L. (2014). Emotionally focused family therapy: Facilitating change within a family system. *Journal of Couple & Relationship Therapy, 13,* 24-45.

Thompson, S. J., Bender, K., Cardoso, J. B., & Flynn, P. M. (2011). Experiential activities in family therapy: Perceptions of caregivers and youth. *Journal of Child & Family Studies, 20,* 560-68.

Whitaker, C. A. (1981). *Experiential family therapy* (Video). Kansas City, MO: Golden Triad Films.

Whitaker, C. A. (1989). *The midnight musings of a family therapist.* New York: W. W. Norton.

Whitaker, C. A., & Bumberry, W. M. (1988). *Dancing with the family.* New York: Brunner/Mazel.

Whitaker, C. A., & Keith, D. V. (1981). Symbolic-experiential family therapy. In A. S. Gurman and D. P. Kniskern (Eds.), *Handbook of family therapy* (Vol. 1, pp. 187-225). New York: Brunner/Mazel.

Whitaker, C. A., & Malone, T. (1953). *The roots of psychotherapy.* New York: Blakiston.

# SOLUTION-FOCUSED
# FAMILY THERAPY

*We all do "do, re, mi," but you have*
*to find the other notes yourself.*

**LOUIS ARMSTRONG**

IF THE COUCH IS A SYMBOL for Freudian psychoanalysis, and the Skinner box a symbol for behavioral therapy, then the symbol for solution-focused family therapy is the saxophone. Before Steve de Shazer—the originator of solution-focused family therapy—was a therapist, he was a musician. He played the saxophone in the jazz clubs of Milwaukee and Chicago. He received formal musical training at the University of Wisconsin, Milwaukee, obtaining a bachelor's degree in fine art. His love was the spontaneity of jazz. Just as Louis Armstrong said "Never play the same thing twice," so also is the language of solution-focused family therapy. De Shazer once said, "Make up your own explanation; it is as good or better than mine" (de Shazer, 1991, p. xviii). In a sense, solution-focused family therapy is not rooted in Palo Alto, Philadelphia, Washington, DC, or New York, even though the other centers of family theory are extremely important, and it has allegiance to many core ideas. We should not even look to the behavioral sciences to understand the origin of solution-focused family therapy. Rather, consider music, and specifically focus on understanding jazz.

## INTRODUCTION TO SOLUTION-FOCUSED FAMILY THERAPY

As we discussed in the chapter on strategic family therapy, the Mental Research Institute (MRI) method emphasized brief approaches to treatment that did not regard the family from a pathology-based perspective. Solution-focused family therapy is a descendent of the MRI approach, with many leading figures and proponents, such as Insoo Kim Berg, having been influenced by Watzlawick, Weakland, and Fisch and the Brief Therapy model at MRI in Palo Alto, California.

From a student perspective, perhaps the hallmarks of solution-focused family therapy are the easily recognizable techniques, such as the miracle question. We will discuss these in greater detail below, but techniques like the miracle question, scaling questions, and the exception question often stand out in the mind of the student just learning about the solution-focused approach to family therapy. For the student or novice therapist, they are techniques that are easy to learn and use right away; in the hands of a seasoned family therapist, they can be useful tools that facilitate at least some changes quite quickly.

As we will see in our discussion below, the use of these techniques points to a kind of pragmatic minimalism or commitment to what "works" with a family, beginning with minimal interventions that target what the family reports matters to them (Nichols & Schwartz, 2006). In other words, the work of the solution-focused family therapist is going to focus on the presenting concern and not on something that may or may not lie "beneath the surface."

Solution-focused family therapy itself tends to be organized around clearly articulated goals and direct and helpful strategies. The therapist identifies what works in the family and has them do more of *that*. But how do solution-focused family therapists identify what works? One way is by focusing on the untapped resources within the family itself. Put differently, solution-focused family therapists focus on family strengths. In contrast to other models and theoretical orientations, solution-focused family therapy is not a pathology-focused approach to the family.

Another way to identify what works is to identify how the family thinks about the problem so that another way of thinking about the problem may be introduced. Taken together, changes can occur in perspective or in behavior. As O'Hanlon and Weiner-Davis (1989) put it, "therapy involves deliberate attempts to produce a change in viewpoint and/or action leading to solution" (p. 10).

## THEORETICAL AND PHILOSOPHICAL ASSUMPTIONS
## OF SOLUTION-FOCUSED FAMILY THERAPY

The philosophical assumptions underlying solution-focused family therapy can be difficult to identify. There is no explicitly identified model of normal family development. Indeed, proponents of solution-focused family therapy emphasize making no assumptions about what is "normal" for a family, nor does it concern itself with a model of abnormal family functioning:

> The theory has nothing whatsoever to say about "problems, complaints, difficulties," etc. In fact, the theory explicitly neither includes nor excludes the various ideas about problem maintenance: it only deals with doing therapy. (de Shazer, 1988, p. xix)

In this respect solution-focused family therapy is uniquely atheoretical. In their discussion of theories of psychotherapy, O'Hanlon and Weiner-Davis (1989) help the reader move away from theory ("explanations") to practice ("solutions"). They point out that different theorists can have quite different viewpoints; in fact, "diametrically opposed views about crucial elements and techniques involved in successful therapy" (p. 11). In response, they write, "Some might think this is bad news, but we think it is good. There is no one right theory of psychotherapy. Many different theories and many different techniques and approaches seem to produce change and positive results" (p. 11).

Of course, in any effort to change what the family is doing—in any effort to identify a "solution"—one is implicitly making some assertion about the problem, even if all the while denying any explicit model of normality or abnormality. The same is true for solution-focused family therapists. They believe that problems exist primarily because of how families construe events taking place around them.

Ludwig Wittgenstein is one philosopher cited by some solution-focused family therapists, particularly de Shazer. Wittgenstein favored observing "how language is used in everyday life" and held that "the meaning of words is not inherent, but resides in the context of their everyday use" (Chang & Nylund, 2013, p. 78).

Solution-focused family therapists also cite George Kelly's (1955) work as particularly influential, particularly to the extent that he came to value how people construe difficulties.

The essential postulate in Kelly's theory is that situations are made sense of through the application of a variety of "constructs," which make up the unique way each of us draws distinctions and categorizes our experiences, thus affecting the ways in which we anticipate future events. (Cade & O'Hanlon, 1993, p. 23)

So in order to work out this understanding of how people construe difficulties, Cade and O'Hanlon (1993) discuss two levels of reality: the "things and events" that are related to "sensory-based observations and descriptions of what we perceive, or remember perceiving, through our various senses; what is happening, or has happened" (p. 32). The other level of reality is essentially an explanatory framework or all of the "interpretations, conclusions, beliefs, and attributions that are derived from, imposed upon, or related to these perceived things and events" (p. 32). So there is a distinction made between these two levels: on the one hand those things "that can reasonably be taken as being 'out there,'" and on the other hand, the explanatory frameworks "through which these are perceived and interpreted" (p. 41).

These explanatory frameworks are considered by some solution-focused family therapists to be nothing more than metaphors: "All explanatory frameworks are metaphors, though they are metaphors that can have very real consequences. . . . Problems often occur . . . when these frameworks become confused with 'reality' and reified" (Cade & O'Hanlon, 1993, p. 49).

The philosophical perspective that lies beneath the discussion of explanatory frameworks and metaphor is *social constructionism*, with its emphasis on how language aids in creating and negotiating the future (DeJong & Berg, 1998). Solution-focused therapies, along with narrative therapy, reject a modernist view of language in which "language represents internal mental constructs"; rather, both approaches favor a postmodern understanding of language "in which language constitutes social reality" (Chang & Nylund, 2013, p. 73). Solution-focused family therapy, then, draws on assumptions found in *constructivism* or the understanding that perceptions and descriptions of the family's experience leads to the construction of not only our understanding of that experience but also of the reality about that experience (Becvar & Becvar, 2006). This commitment to constructivism may vary somewhat among solution-focused family theorists, as at least some (e.g., O'Hanlon) speak of a real world that exists "out there," but it is not a distinction that is grappled with sufficiently by these theorists in our view.

We can see in solution-focused family therapy assumptions reflecting the related social constructionist perspective—that is, that how perceptions are constructed and communicated within the family and between the therapist and the family has a significant impact on identifying and constructing resources (solutions) for change.

The very act of looking for exceptions is, according to de Shazer (1988), an act of deconstruction that is tied to social constructionism:

> Developing some doubt about global frames involves a process that can best be called *deconstructing the frame*. During the interview, first as the therapist helps the client search for exceptions, and then as the therapist helps the client imagine a future without the complaint, the therapist is implicitly breaking down the frame into smaller and smaller pieces. (pp. 101-2)

But the solution is not limited to what might be constructed linguistically, at least not in the same way seen in narrative family therapy (see chap. 11). Rather, solution-focused family therapy assumes "that the client constructs his or her own solution based on his or her own resources and successes" (de Shazer, 1988, p. 50). Narrative therapists identify and deconstruct discourses and stories that ultimately problematize the family; solution-focused family therapists "would not shut down conversations about larger cultural constructs," but they "would not go there by default" (Chang & Nylund, 2013, p. 73).

In addition to solutions being tied to construals, it should be noted that there is a *pragmatic minimalism* associated with this approach to therapy. What we mean by this is that the focus is on what changes work—and these changes will be the most accessible without going into great depth or history of family difficulties. In part because different perspectives may be equally valid, solution-focused family therapists consider whether the family "view" is keeping people "stuck"—meaning that the view is not useful to the family. Usefulness is defined pragmatically and subjectively.

There is, then, also a link between pragmatism and a commitment to therapeutic neutrality. Cade and O'Hanlon (1993) discuss therapeutic neutrality as a pragmatic consideration: "The therapist's position of neutrality is, in our view, necessitated by the *pragmatic* requirements for being therapeutic when working at the interface of relationships" (p. 66). This is not to be confused with a nonemotional presence or with a detached posture as such, but with a pragmatic neutrality in relation to the outcome of therapy.

Also, solution-focused family therapy has at times been accused of ignoring emotions. Proponents argue that the questions solution-focused family therapists ask "are used to elicit external signifiers of internal experiences—usually descriptions of what the client wants, or when solutions are occurring" (Chang & Nylund, 2013, p. 79). In other words, emotions are not a focus insofar as it is assumed that emotions drive behavior; rather, emotions can be "clarified by discussing external signifiers" (p. 79).

Finally, solution-focused family therapists draw on philosophical humanism in their emphasis on clients having within themselves the resources and ability to improve their circumstances if they make the choice to do so. The family therapist's responsibility is to essentially tap into these untapped resources and to use language and perspective-taking to assist in identifying and moving toward solutions.

As O'Hanlon and Weiner-Davis (1989) put it, "each person already has skills and resources which can be used to resolve complaints. It is the task of the therapist to access these abilities and put them to use" (p. 34). Or, as de Shazer (1988) puts it, "The greater majority of the time, the tasks that are given are already within the clients' experience and repertoire. . . . Thus, in a great many cases, designing tasks is simplified to telling clients to do more of something they are already doing" (p. xviii).

## WHEN FAMILIES SEEK HELP

According to solution-focused family therapists, most family therapists assess help-seeking families by looking for the problem; they are essentially assessing what constitutes dysfunction. Solution-focused family therapists view this as a natural consequence of a pathology-based medical model and problem-focused approaches to therapy. In contrast, solution-focused family therapists deliberately "position themselves outside of dominant pathologizing mental health" conceptualizations (Chang & Nylund, 2013, p. 74); they assess an intervention so that the family begins to identify strengths and solutions. Assessment for solution-focused family therapists *is* an intervention. "We view the process of interviewing as an intervention; that is, through the use of various solution-oriented interviewing techniques, clients can experience significant shifts in their thinking about their situations during the course of the session" (O'Hanlon & Weiner-Davis, 1989, p. 78).

How does assessment shift the way families think? Distinctively solution-focused assessment questions include *future-oriented* questions that get family members to think about change as well as *reflexive* questions that help families reframe their circumstances (O'Hanlon & Weiner-Davis, 1989, p. 78). O'Hanlon and Weiner-Davis describe three things they try to do in solution-focused family therapy. The first is to change "*the 'doing' of the situation that is perceived as problematic*" (p. 126). A change in how people respond and relate to one another can change how people come to see their circumstances.

The second is to change "*the 'viewing' of the situation that is perceived as problematic*" (p. 126). This is essentially helping families change how they "frame" the situation. Their frame is seeing it as a problem, and the frame is itself a problem. But this can be changed.

The third thing O'Hanlon and Weiner-Davis do is evoke "*resources, solutions, and strengths to bring to the situation that is perceived as problematic*" (p. 126).

The goals of solution-focused family therapy are directly related to the presenting problem. The presenting concern is not seen as signaling difficulties elsewhere, as might be the case with other family therapy approaches, such as psychoanalytic family therapy or strategic family therapy.

The solution-focused family therapist considers family strengths in assessment and intervention. One way they do this is by looking for exceptions to problems. For example, if the parents are concerned about their "out-of-control" ten-year-old son, the solution-focused family therapist is going to begin to ask about times when their son demonstrates appropriate behavior as well as times when they as parents are able to manage their son's behavior effectively.

As we mentioned above, solution-focused theory has no explicit model of healthy family development. Rather, the presenting concern is taken for granted, and the solution-focused family therapist works pragmatically toward solutions based on family strengths and resources. What becomes important is that the family clearly identifies what has to change and what would constitute change.

The solution-focused family therapist need not know much about the presenting problem to address it successfully. Recall that the focus is on what is working well rather than what is causing the problem. If the family can identify what they are doing when the presenting problem is not a problem, then they can work on doing those things again and again in order to resolve the presenting concern.

As a theory or map, solution-focused theorists have explicitly stated that the approach to the family is not prescriptive: "The map is '*de*-scriptive' rather than '*pre*-scriptive.' It describes what solution-focused therapists *do* rather than what they should do" (de Shazer, 1988, p. 82).

But what solution-focused family therapists do is help family members predict behavior to set that behavior into motion. These are referred to as "prediction tasks" (de Shazer, 1988, p. 184). "Prediction tasks are based on the idea that what you expect to happen is more likely to happen once the process leading up to it is in motion. In pragmatic terms, this means that the prediction, made the night before, can sometimes be seen as setting in motion the processes involved in having a better day" (p. 184). It is essentially a "self-fulfilling prophesy" (p. 184).

Recent theoretical and empirical contributions have also explored the meaning of positive emotions—particularly hope—in solution-focused family therapy (Blundo, Bolton, & Hall, 2014; Kim & Franklin, 2015). It is widely thought that "the therapist will observe not what the clients are doing wrong, but rather what they are doing well, which can help create positive emotions for them" (Kim & Franklin, 2015, pp. 32-33). This emphasis on positive emotions connects solution-focused family therapy to the broader emphasis on positive psychology and the "broaden-and-build" theory of positive emotion in which a family can broaden awareness and behavioral options and build skills and resources to find solutions (Kim & Franklin, 2015, p. 37).

Research on solution-focused therapy has also expanded to address group therapy formats as well as work with persons with intellectual disabilities (Roeden, Maaskant, Bannink, & Curfs, 2011), depression, and suicidality (e.g., Javanmiri, Kimiaee, & Abadi, 2013). Outcome studies and meta-analyses have also been conducted showing solution-focused approaches to be as effective as other interventions (for a summary, see Chang & Nylund, 2013, pp. 79-80).

## THE APPROACH TO FAMILY THERAPY

A solution-focused approach to family therapy is often faster-paced than other models of family therapy. The solution-focused family therapist is present with the family, identifying ways in which the family is construing the problem, because it is these construals that may be access points to a solution. The assumption in this approach is that the construals or ways of seeing things in the family contribute to the family being stuck.

So when we talk about construals we are talking about how families "frame" behavior. Solution-focused family therapists are in this sense referring to ways in which individuals in the family understand how people relate to one another. As de Shazer (1982, p. 23) puts it, "The family thinks and operates as though it has a certain set of rules or overlapping sets of individual rules plus 'unit rules,' which are used to define its situation."

De Shazer adds that solution-focused family therapy

> can be described as an attempt to help people change the frames that cause them trouble and give them reason to complain. In general, the therapy is designed to change the definitions that make up a family's frame and to do this in a gradual fashion. (de Shazer, 1982, p. 25)

It is not that the "facts" change. No, it is that the understanding and meanings associated with the facts change:

> Although the "facts" of the situation are not changed, the context in which they lie is described by the therapist from a different angle, and therefore the intervention (or reframing) is in positive terms rather than in the negative terms used by the family. The effects of reframing are confirmed by the appearance of a new set of beliefs, or perceptions, *and* behavioral modifications that can be described as a logical consequence of the shift in perception. . . . The result is that the family can look at things from a different angle. Once they "see" things differently," they can behave differently. (de Shazer, 1982, p. 25)

For example, a common solution-focused family therapy technique is the *formula first session task*. In this task the solution-focused family therapist is helping the family focus on what is working: "Between now and next time we meet, we would like you to observe, so that you can describe to us next time, what happens in your family that you want to continue to have happen" (de Shazer, 1985, p. 137).

The idea behind the formula first session task is to have a set assignment at the close of the first session that gets the family to think about what is happening in the family that they would like to see continue to happen. It is a simple refocusing exercise that gets the family away from focusing on the problems and on what will essentially become the "solutions" insofar as what is good will continue and be expanded in the next week and beyond.

Part of what is thought to be helpful both for assessment and as intervention is to ask questions that help family members "see" what is happening differently.

Any number of questions can help elicit how the family is currently viewing the problem. Matthew Selekman (1997, p. 39) offers several such questions:

If there was one question that you were dying to ask me about your problem situation, what would that question be?

In what ways can I be most helpful to you?

What's your theory about why this problem exists?

If there was one question that you were hoping I would ask you while we are working together, what would that question be?

In addition to the formula first session task and questions that help the therapist determine how the family "sees" the problem, there are three well-known techniques that are viewed as rather central to solution-focused family therapy: *the miracle question, exception questions*, and *scaling questions*.

According to Insoo Kim Berg, solution-focused theorists first discovered "exception" questions as they came across times when families were not having difficulties. This was followed by the development of "the miracle question" in 1984, based on the assumption that families actually have some sense for how they would like family relationships to be. Solution-focused theorists then developed scaling questions, which have been understood as essentially self-assessment tools in which family members can assess their circumstances and progress over time.

**The miracle question.** There are many variations on the miracle question, but Selekman (1997) frames it this way:

Suppose you go home tonight and you go to bed, and while you are sound asleep a miracle happens and all of your problems are solved. When you wake up the next day, how will each of you be able to tell that the miracle really happened? (p. 58)

Elsewhere de Shazer (1988), referring to the miracle question, writes, "We have found this way of quickly looking into the future to be a most effective frame for helping clients set goals and thus describe how they will know when the problem is solved" (pp. 5-6).

These questions can be followed by additional questions focusing on what will be different and what differences those changes will make as well as the effects of these changes on others. If these changes suggested by the miracle question lead to lessening of conflict, then follow-up questions will explore how relationships will be worked out with less conflict.

*The exception question.* Another solution-focused question that attempts to get the family to step outside of their current, problem-focused approach is the exception question. Essentially, the solution-focused family therapist is saying, "Tell me about the most recent time when you were able to negotiate [your finances]." What the clinician is looking for are those times when the family is not stuck, when they have actually been able to work through one of the concerns that have brought them into therapy. This is followed by a series of questions that explore what was different about those times of successful negotiation—anything to identify aspects of their successful exchanges that might increase the likelihood of future "exceptions"—so that the exceptions eventually become the norm. This question also serves as an intervention that disarms family members who might be focusing exclusively on the ubiquitous nature of the problem.

In his explanation of exceptions de Shazer (1988) writes that exceptions are "whatever is happening when the complaint is not" (p. 53). As O'Hanlon and Weiner-Davis (1989) put it,

> Bed-wetters have dry nights, combative couples have peaceful days, teenagers sometimes comply with the rules without an argument, and so on. . . . The exceptions to the problem offer a tremendous amount of information about what is needed to solve the problem. Solutions can be unearthed by examining the differences between times when the problem has occurred and times when it has not. (p. 82)

Further, "If people want to experience more success, more happiness and less stress in their lives, help them assess what is different about the times when they are already successful, happy, and stress-free. Therein lies the solution—increasing those activities which have a track record of having achieved . . . the desired goal" (O'Hanlon & Weiner-Davis, 1989, p. 83).

*Scaling questions.* Another common solution-focused family therapy technique is scaling questions. The family therapist might ask, "How much conflict is there between the two of you right now? On a scale of 0 to 10, with 0 reflecting no conflict whatsoever and 10 being the worst your conflict has ever been, how would you rate your level of conflict today?" This question can be used to help family members identify specific steps they can take to make improvements in their relationship. For example, Selekman adds that clinicians can ask, "Let's say we get together in one week's time and you proceed to tell me that you took some steps and got to a 6 [the family was at 7], what will you tell me that you did?" (1997, p. 64).

*Additional techniques.* Other techniques associated with solution-focused family therapy include compliments intended to highlight what family members are already doing that they are essentially encouraged to keep doing. Coping questions, such as "How have you managed to keep things from spiraling out of control?" can highlight family resilience and resourcefulness. Summary messages are also a common technique in solution-focused family therapy. This might be a verbal or written message from the solution-focused family therapist or from an observing team that highlights a key theme from their work in the session. The message could offer another way of construing the ways the family is relating, or it might simply encourage more of the same behavior, particularly if successful strategies have been identified.

Still other solution-focused family therapists utilize various anecdotes, parables, and stories to help families think about the patterns of interaction that have become problematic for them (Cade & O'Hanlon, 1993).

*Case example.* Alex, age forty-nine, and his wife Andrea, age forty-eight, present in therapy with their two sons, Keith, age fifteen, and Kelvin, age seventeen. The concern they have has to do with recent arguments between Kelvin and his mother and father. The arguments center on Kelvin's homework and other household responsibilities as well as time he would like to spend with friends from school and in the neighborhood. The therapist meets with the family and in the context of the interviews asks the following questions:

THERAPIST: I'd like each of you to give me an idea of how things are for you at home. On a scale of 0 to 10, with 0 being very good and 10 representing the worst it has been in terms of conflict, what number represents how things are going right now?

FATHER: I would have to say that we are at about an 8.

MOTHER: Yes. I agree with Alex. I think a 7 or 8 is about right. It's been difficult recently.

THERAPIST: How about for you, Kelvin? What number represents the level of conflict you see?

KELVIN: I don't know. I guess a 7. I'm not sure it's that big of a deal, I have to say.

**THERAPIST:** OK. So you would say that a 7 represents the level of conflict for you, but you are also not sure why it is such a big deal either.

**KELVIN:** Yeah.

**THERAPIST:** How about for you, Keith?

**KEITH:** I am going to agree with my mom and dad. About a 7 or so. I don't know.

**THERAPIST:** OK. That's helpful. Let me ask you this: What number represents where you would like things to be when we wrap up our time together? Keep in mind that few families really are at a 0 or even a 1. Families have conflict from time to time, so we are not looking for perfection—for no conflict whatsoever. What we are looking for is improvement—something we could all live with. So on that same scale from 0 to 10, given that the family is at about a 7 or 8 today, what number represents improvements that we could all live with?

**FATHER:** That's an interesting question. Maybe a 3 or 4.

**MOTHER:** I'd probably have to agree. I know we won't be perfect, but if we could be at a 4 that would be good.

**THERAPIST:** OK, a 3 or 4 for you both. How about for you, Kelvin?

**KELVIN:** I guess that would be fine. If that's what they want.

**THERAPIST:** And how about for you, Keith?

**KEITH:** I'd be OK with that. A 4 or so. Maybe even better.

**THERAPIST:** Let's just take a minute to clarify what a 3 or 4 means to you. How would I know that your family had reached a 3 or 4 on this scale? What would be different, do you think? Let's put it this way: what would you be doing that you are not doing right now? Dad?

**FATHER:** Well, I guess the biggest thing is that we would be more patient with one another. We would spend time in the same room and be OK with each other. Kelvin would be able to be around more and would work on his homework before going out. Things like that.

**THERAPIST:** OK. So Kelvin would get his homework done. He'd still be able to go out with his friends, but he would do that after he finished his work. You also said that you would be more patient with each other—that you could be in the same room and that would feel OK. How about for you, mom?

MOTHER:   Yes, I agree that homework is important. I guess it isn't as critical right now, since he did get into college. But we don't want him to just ignore his school work because he has been accepted into college. I'd like him to complete the school year on a positive note. And I'd like to be able to have him around a little more—to see him and be able to ask him about picking up his room or setting the table without worrying that I'm going to make him angry.

THERAPIST:   So homework isn't as critical as it was, say, in the fall when he was applying to colleges and when his GPA was being scrutinized by half a dozen admissions officers. But you would like him to finish the race and to leave high school on a good note. OK. You'd also like to see him a little more. He's about to head off to college, and as a mother you'd like some time with him before he goes. That makes sense. You also want him to do his part. Pick up this. Pick up that. Maybe set the table. Sort of pull his weight around the home without getting ticked off if you ask him to help out, right? OK. How about for you Kelvin? What does a 4 mean to you? When would you know that things are better for your family?

The interview would continue like this, with the family therapist checking in on the meaning of the numbers for both Kelvin and his brother, Keith. The anchoring of behavior in scaling questions is quite flexible, and it allows family members to identify what it is they would actually like to see change, and it gives the therapist a way to look for solutions to the presenting concerns.

## CHRISTIAN PERSPECTIVE ON SOLUTION-FOCUSED FAMILY THERAPY

*Theoretical and philosophical assumptions.* We are drawn to the idea of how language and perspective-taking can influence a family to identify and create solutions. In many respects this is a helpful corrective to other models that may keep the therapist in a "one-up" position as expert on what is happening in the family. The solution-focused family therapist does not run the risk of being undervalued in the way we see this potential with narrative family therapy (see chap. 11); instead, the solution-focused family therapist is an important figure in identifying exceptions to problems and assisting the family as they tap into existing resources.

At the same time, we recognize that Christians will rightly be concerned with an uncritical acceptance of postmodern assumptions that lie behind solution-focused family therapy. Christians can recognize the role of language in producing certain habits of thought that influence not just thinking about oneself and one's family but also behavior and interactions within the family.

But the Christian would want to resist the pull toward social constructivism if it means affirming that reality is simply linguistic constructs and beliefs shared by a group of people. The Christian need not endorse the view that various groups "construct" reality.

But what of the claims of social constructionism? What is the Christian to make of the claim that problems and solutions are constituted in language? We believe the Christian can acknowledge the role of language in "framing" both problems and solutions. The Christian need not commit him- or herself to the view that makes more of such a claim than is warranted; rather, language is an important consideration both in how families may get "stuck" and in how they may get "unstuck."

We see value in understanding language and experience and giving the family experience through techniques that expand their understanding. A willingness to do so does not require a commitment to constructivism, social constructionism, or even great sympathy for postmodernism. Rather, the Christian family therapist can recognize and value different perspectives, realizing that there is always going to be more than one perspective on a matter being addressed in family therapy.

It is important to consider the role of pragmatic minimalism in solution-focused family theory as well. One criticism of this minimalist aspect of pragmatic minimalism has been asked more in the form of a question: Can solution-focused family therapists sit with people in their pain (Nichols & Schwartz, 2006)? In other words, does the emphasis on what "works" run the risk of a shortcut through the lived, painful experience that clients present with in a clinical setting?

Further, and having more to do with the pragmatic aspect of solution-focused family therapy, the emphasis on what "works" raises interesting considerations for the Christian. Solution-focused clinical pragmatism does not evaluate beliefs or behaviors in a family in relation to an explicit model of family development or family functioning. What is a problem for a family is that which impedes or hinders the family from relating in ways that they would like.

Let's extend this discussion of pragmatism further. Christians training to become family therapists face the challenge of having religious beliefs and formed judgments about behaviors that are right and wrong. In training, Christians learn early in supervision and case consultation that they are expected to "contain" or "bracket" their religious beliefs and values in therapy and work with families to achieve goals they themselves do not believe in. This can be especially difficult when first training because Christians more often than not may view their training as a family therapist as a calling to minister in this unique way. Although this is true for training in most if not all of professional therapy today, it seems especially poignant when Christians are exposed to a model of family therapy—solution-focused family therapy—that trades on the idea of therapy in which the consumer is paying for (and expecting) results.

Some Christian family therapists might view this as a necessary lesson in learning how to "play the game" of providing services within the existing framework. But others might discuss it as "role integration" in which the Christian who is a family therapist, by virtue of being licensed by the state, is functioning in a fiduciary relationship in which power is entrusted to them for the betterment of others (see Hathaway & Yarhouse, forthcoming).

Still others might make the distinction Tjeltveit (1999) between being an ethicist and being a moralist. An ethicist is someone who reflects on ethical issues and is capable of assisting others in sorting out the complexities that exist in difficult ethical decisions. A moralist attempts to impose moral beliefs on family members. From a Tjeltveitian perspective, family therapists function as ethicists by being adept at careful reflection on ethical issues, exercising good judgment, and modeling this for clients. They also function as ethicists to the extent that they are able to create a therapeutic space in which family members learn how to think well about complicated ethical decisions and make decisions that they have been able to weigh and for which they are ultimately able to take responsibility.

In any case, another dimension related to pragmatism is that—as with other secular understandings of the family—the family dynamics are unrelated to transcendent reality. Spiritual and religious considerations have no place in solution-focused family theory because the theory is not comprehensive and offers no real understanding of either personality or the family.

As we have suggested, solution-focused family therapy might be criticized from a Christian perspective as being superficial in its understanding of family dysfunction and healthy family functioning. It is ahistorical in its understanding of families. Although there is some interest in identifying times in the past when families have had success in negotiating a conflict, what is most important is what is happening at present.

We want to raise an additional point that is different from that of pragmatism and superficiality. Solution-focused approaches to families are not just pragmatic; they also reflect a strength-based wellness approach, as we mentioned above. The more recent theoretical and empirical contributions on the role of positive emotions, and especially hope, are promising in explaining emotional and behavioral change. As with the positive psychology movement (Seligman, 2000), solution-focused family therapists view diagnostic labels and pathologizing language as part of the problem. The Christian family therapist must wrestle with the role he or she plays in potentially being a part of the problem insofar as there is merit to this critique of the mental health establishment as it is currently being practiced. The Christian can find much to affirm about a strength-based approach. This is a challenge, though, as Christians will quickly recognize that the strength-based approach of most secular solution-focused family therapists draws on the "plausibility structure" of secular humanism (Moreland, 2007), by which we mean that assumptions about human worth and value are not argued for by solution-focused family therapists or located within a broader theory as such, but simply asserted as factual knowledge.

This brings us to the implicit theoretical assumption of humanism. The question is, do families have within themselves the resources and ability to make changes? In a sense we want to say "yes" and "no." We hold to a high view of families, and we see families as having many resources that can be tapped and applied to presenting concerns. So in this sense we would say "yes." At the same time, we do not affirm humanistic assumptions about the individuals in the family; that is, we do not claim that if given the right environment, people will flourish and that they have within themselves a kind of natural process that unfolds toward the "good." No, individuals in the family are fallen, and the family, like every other institution, is tainted by the fall.

But solution-focused family therapists also emphasize making changes when changes are possible to be made, while accepting the "givens" in one's life. The parts of the client's concern that are intractable should not be focused on; rather, family therapists are to focus on what can be changed. We like that there is an approach that emphasizes not dwelling on the problem and that the use of compliments (in terms of identifying strengths and reflections of resilience) is in some ways a very biblical pronouncement to build each other up, to encourage one another in Christ.

Solution-focused family therapists make no claims about proper or healthy family functioning. They tend to take presenting concerns at face value but then consider the way the problem is "framed" by the family and how another way of constructing reality might lead to a solution. Can you see how a problem might be "framed" in helpful rather than unhelpful ways? It has to do with how people use words to communicate their chief concerns, and in that sense problems are thought to be constituted in language.

Solution-focused family therapy is an approach that is quite pragmatic. No deeper meaning is sought; rather, solutions are developed to address the concern that is keeping the family from functioning as members would like. Christian family therapists may be drawn to the pragmatism in solution-focused family therapy. We see the potential benefits, too, but we want to also think about improving family functioning in ways that "work" pragmatically but also reflect how God would want family members to relate to one another. Simply reducing symptoms may be of some benefit, particularly in the short run, but there is more to family functioning than keeping symptoms of problems at bay.

*Think about it:* What are the potential integrative benefits to the pragmatism associated with solution-focused family therapy? In other words, why might a Christian be drawn to an approach that is more pragmatic and less philosophical? What are the potential risks? Also, in what ways are you drawn to the strengths-based aspect of focusing on solutions?

The Christian family therapist would also like to see families identify solutions within but also in their relationship with God. Christians look to God for "solutions" to their problems and do not always look "within" for those solutions. True, often God provides solutions through existing strengths and resources in the family. But the Christian can also affirm that it is the very relationship with God that provides solutions to many potential conflicts among family members.

*Model of family dysfunction and family functioning.* It was mentioned above that solution-focused family therapy has no explicit model of healthy family functioning and so no model of family dysfunction, at least according to the adherents of this approach. Put differently, solution-focused family therapy is not a comprehensive therapy in that there is no theory of personality and no substantive theory of the family in terms of family development and healthy functioning (Nichols & Schwartz, 2006).

This pragmatic agnosticism, if you will, is an outgrowth of the view that there is no correct way to construe family dynamics. It is a question of being "stuck"; if a family is stuck because of how they see things and relate to one another, then that way of "seeing" and relating is not useful to the family. Usefulness is the pragmatic element and yardstick. The agnosticism can be seen in the commitment to there not being any one way that is the right way to construe things. Any number of different construals or ways of seeing things may be just as valid and "fit the facts" just as well.

## INTEGRATIVE FOCUS: *Family Identity*

What identity is thought to emerge from a solution-focused understanding of the family? A potential positive that comes out of solution-focused family therapy is the emphasis on family strengths. Solution-focused family therapists assume that families have the resources to make meaningful changes and that they are often functioning quite well. Therapists can tap into the "exceptions" to find solutions to the presenting problem.

Christians can also join solution-focused family therapists in being hesitant about assigning diagnostic labels to family members that run the risk of reducing their personhood to what constitutes pathology. Indeed, a resilient family identity can emerge from solution-focused approaches because they assume family strengths and abilities that are currently being overlooked because of the focus on the "problem."

*Think about it:* Think about your own family for a moment. Rather than focus on your family shortcomings, think for a few minutes about what your family does well. What are some of the things you appreciate about your family? How would you characterize your family identity in a word or short phrase?

So who defines useful family functioning? And who decides which view is privileged? Not the therapist. The family as the client determines the utility of any way of seeing and relating. And what the family identifies as a useful way of seeing things is what will then be privileged.

What the therapist does, again, is help the family reconsider how they have been seeing things. The evidence that the status quo is not working is that the family is stuck. So the solution-focused family therapist refocuses the family not on the problem (of being stuck) but on the solution of what can be changed—this is a kind of appeal to what is most accessible in terms of likelihood of being changed. Such a move is meant to be empowering and to essentially provide family members with a newfound sense of hope.

*Techniques in family therapy.* The easily learned techniques are attractive to students who are first exposed to the various models of family therapy. We see this time and time again in graduate-level training. Students are drawn to techniques that they can understand and apply to the session they have scheduled later that week!

However, as Nichols and Schwartz (2006) observed, solution-focused family therapy can come across as an overreaction to managed care and the influence of third-party payers on the practice of family therapy, especially the current value placed on briefer forms of therapy. Certainly, with solution-focused family therapy, the nature of the interventions lends itself to relatively fast changes and resolution of concerns. Critics will say, however, that solution-focused family therapists overlook other reasons for the family's concerns other than those the family states are the cause of their concerns.

The techniques themselves tend to facilitate positive thoughts and experiences about their present struggles. It is assumed that these positive thoughts and experiences will lead the family to make changes, and that is certainly an empirical question that can be examined through the course of research on treatment process. Also, some critics point out that solution-focused family therapy may ignore people's pain (Nichols & Schwartz, 2006).

The amorality of solution-focused family therapy is again a concern. By not tying interventions to a more comprehensive theory of the family, the solution-focused family therapist allows the family to determine the course of therapy.

Of course, by not tying techniques to normative claims about healthy family functioning, the Christian family therapist is free to utilize interventions that do not necessarily take family members in a direction that is fundamentally in conflict with a Christian worldview.

Despite these concerns about solution-focused family therapy techniques, it should be noted that many family members have tremendous difficulty identifying a time when they handled a problem well, and they fail to see themselves as having strengths. We see great potential benefit in focusing on exceptions, on times when family interactions are "working." It is a *potential* benefit because some families will come into therapy with multiple constraints and may have limited resources to draw on, and a model that focuses on inherent resources may have to adapt for some of the most challenging family presentations.

## CONCLUSION

Solution-focused family therapy is an exciting, focused approach to identifying untapped resources within the family itself. The focus is on identifying and utilizing indigenous family strengths to help the family move from feeling "stuck" to feeling "unstuck." Much attention is paid to the ways in which the family "frames" their concerns, and this focus on framing is based on assumptions about

### INTEGRATIVE FOCUS: Family Relationships

How ought family relationships to be characterized in a solution-focused approach? There really is not an explicit discussion of how to characterize family relationships. Remember that solution-focused family theorists do not explicitly describe how people in families *ought* to relate, so they attempt to avoid a discussion of family characteristics as such. The emphasis on how family members frame concerns can aid family relationships, and Christians can see integrative connections insofar as we value how we view others in our families. We realize that we can see people through a lens of our own self-interest and mischaracterize them to fit our interests, or we can see people through a lens that captures how God views them and intends for us to relate to one another in families.

*Think about it:* Try to think of an example of someone framing a concern. What are your thoughts about how different people frame the same concern? Can you think of helpful ways to frame concerns? What about unhelpful ways to frame concerns? Is there in your view a distinctively Christian approach to framing issues associated with family conflicts? Why or why not?

the nature of reality and the role of language in construing behavior in family relationships. There is much that Christian family therapy can utilize in solution-focused family therapy; indeed, it is a pragmatic approach, placing great emphasis on what "works." This is both a shortcoming and an access point from a Christian perspective, because the Christian need not embrace all of the assumptions that lie behind solution-focused family therapy and may instead make choices about specific techniques and strategies that assist in identifying and harnessing untapped resources in the family.

## REFERENCES

Becvar, D. S., & Becvar, R. J. (2006). *Family therapy: A systemic integration* (6th ed.). Boston: Allyn & Bacon.

Berg, I. K. (n.d.). *Students' corner*. Retrieved from www.sfbta.org/bftc/Steve&Insoo_PDFs/insoo_students_corner.pdf.

Blundo, R. G., Bolton, K. W., & Hall, J. C. (2014). Hope: Research and theory in relation to solution-focused practice and training. *International Journal of Solution-Focused Practices, 2*(2), 52-62.

Cade, B., & O'Hanlon, W. H. (1993). *A brief guide to brief therapy*. New York: W. W. Norton.

Chang, J., & Nylund, D. (2013). Narrative and solution-focused therapies: A twenty-year retrospective. *Journal of Systemic Therapies, 32*(2), 73-88.

DeJong, P., & Berg, I. K. (1998). *Interviewing for solutions*. Pacific Grove, CA: Brooks/Cole.

de Shazer, S. (1982). *Patterns of brief family therapy: An ecosystemic approach*. New York: Guilford Press.

de Shazer, S. (1985). *Keys to solution in brief therapy*. New York: W. W. Norton.

de Shazer, S. (1988). *Clues: Investigating solutions in brief therapy*. New York: W. W. Norton.

de Shazer, S. (1991). *Putting differences to work*. New York: Norton.

Hathaway, W. L., & Yarhouse, M. A. (forthcoming). *Integration of psychology and Christianity*. Downers Grove, IL: IVP Academic.

Javanmiri, L., Kimiaee, S. A., & Abadi, B. A. G. H. (2013). The study of solution-focused group counseling in decreasing depression among teenage girls. *International Journal of Psychological Studies, 5*(1), 105-11.

Kelly, G. (1955). *The psychology of personal constructs*. New York: Norton.

Kim, J. S., & Franklin, C. (2015). Understanding emotional change in solution-focused brief therapy: Facilitating positive emotions. *Best Practices in Mental Health, 11*(1), 25-41.

Moreland, J. P. (2007). *Kingdom triangle*. Grand Rapids: Zondervan.

Nichols, M. P., & Schwartz, R. C. (2006). *Family therapy: Concepts and methods* (7th ed.). Boston: Allyn & Bacon.

O'Hanlon, W. H., & Weiner-Davis, M. (1989). *In search of solutions: A new direction in psychotherapy*. New York: W. W. Norton.

Roeden, J. M., Maaskant, M. A., Bannink, F. P., & Curfs, L. M. G. (2011). Solution-focused brief therapy with people with mild intellectual disabilities: A case series. *Journal of Policy and Practice in Intellectual Disabilities, 8*(4), 247-55.

Selekman, M. D. (1997). *Solution-focused therapy with children: Harnessing family strengths for systemic change*. New York: Guilford Press.

Seligman, M. E. P. (2000). Positive psychology: An introduction. *American Psychologist, 55*(1), 5-14.

Tjeltveit, A. (1999). *Ethics and values in psychotherapy*. New York: Routledge.

# COGNITIVE-BEHAVIORAL
# FAMILY THERAPY

*What reinforcement we may gain from hope,*

*If not, what resolution from despair.*

**JOHN MILTON**

YOU'VE COME A LONG WAY, BABY!" That was the key phrase
used to launch the Virginia Slims brand of cigarettes, with an
attractive model smoking a cigarette juxtaposed with a picture of
a woman folding laundry or otherwise preoccupied with the
"mundane" aspects of family life. The ad was essentially saying
that women are in a remarkably better place today as a result of
the feminist movement. Look! They too can smoke!

## INTRODUCTION TO COGNITIVE-BEHAVIORAL
## FAMILY THERAPY

"You've come a long way, baby!" is the phrase that comes to mind
when thinking about the present state of behavioral family
therapy. In their earliest and purest forms, behavioral models followed John Broadus Watson (1913, 1930) and his emphasis on
reducing behaviors to stimuli and response. These models did not
take into consideration what happens in the mind (sometimes
referred to as the "black box" by some radical behaviorists, including Burrhus Frederic Skinner, 1938, 1969), but what occurs in
terms of behavior. Also, early models essentially worked with

individuals even in the context of working with families, so they did not appear to fit as well with systems concepts.

Albert Bandura (1986) would expand behaviorism by recognizing that while environment shapes behavior, the reverse is also true: behavior can influence a person's environment. These insights led to a discussion of the role of modeling in social learning. Many theorists today incorporate cognitive aspects of human experience so that therapists are able to look at ways in which thoughts affect feelings and subsequent behavior.

## THEORETICAL AND PHILOSOPHICAL ASSUMPTIONS OF COGNITIVE-BEHAVIORAL FAMILY THERAPY

*Behavioral family therapy.* The primary theoretical assumption of cognitive and behavioral family therapy is that of social learning theory (Patterson, 2014). Bandura (1976, 1986) was a leading figure in advancing social learning theory and its emphasis on observational learning (modeling). Horne (1991) provides a helpful explanation of social learning:

> Social learning is a result of the process of people teaching people how to relate interpersonally. It refers to learning that takes place within a social environment as one person observes, reacts to, and interacts with other people; in short, social learning is an education in human relations. People do not develop in isolation, but rather they are born into a social system. . . . No one is exempt from the learning experience. Within such a social matrix, children learn ways of behaving—behavior patterns—by receiving support for some actions and punishment for others, by imitating behavior they see supported and avoiding activities they see discouraged. The result of this selective social reinforcement is the behavior that we characteristically exhibit: our personality. (Horne, 1991, p. 464)

Social learning theory has much to say about ways in which people learn and how best to intervene to make positive changes in family relationships. One such consideration is the *theory of behavioral exchange*, which "explains relationship behavior in terms of costs and benefits" (Piercy, Sprenkle, Wetchler, & associates, 1996, p. 112). Family members try to increase "benefits" and decrease "costs" in their relationships. A family that is functioning well would be seen as one in which family members experience more "benefits" than "costs" in the relationships. A troubled marriage, in contrast, would be one in which there is a decrease in rewarding exchanges and an increase in unpleasant exchanges (see Gottman, 1999a, 1999b).

Based on social learning theory and behavioral exchange, behavioral family therapy draws on extensive research in the areas of classical (or respondent) conditioning and operant conditioning. *Classical* or *respondent* conditioning was initially demonstrated by Ivan Pavlov, who students will recall was able to pair an unconditioned stimulus (in this case, food), which itself led to an unconditioned response (salivation of the dogs), with a conditional stimulus (a bell). Over time, the conditioned stimulus—the bell—began to evoke salivation in the dogs. The salivation was a conditioned response to the bell.

On the surface, Pavlov's dogs may seem a little removed from family therapy, but the principles associated with classical conditioning have been used in the treatment of individual psychopathology, such as anxiety disorders, and, more specific to family therapy, classical conditioning has been used with couples struggling with particular sexual dysfunctions. For example, a widely used intervention for the treatment of some forms of genito-pelvic pain/penetration disorder is systematic desensitization. Genito-pelvic pain/penetration disorder is a condition in which a woman experiences pain in anticipation of or during intercourse, and it may involve the involuntary spasms of the outer third of the musculature of the vagina. Treatment may include systematic desensitization (Leiblum, 2000), an approach developed by Joseph Wolpe (1958) in which anxiety is conceptualized as an autonomic nervous system response that is itself acquired through classical conditioning (Nichols & Schwartz, 2006). Systematic desensitization uses reciprocal inhibition in which a response such as muscle relaxation is paired with behaviors that cause the anxiety.

We can see, then, that classical conditioning can be used in the behavioral treatment of specific sexual dysfunctions in couples counseling. But what about operant conditioning? What is it and where might a family therapist see it used in behavioral family therapy? *Operant conditioning* refers to reinforcing certain voluntary behaviors (Patterson, 2014). A reinforcer is anything that increases the frequency of the desired behavior, while punishment is just the opposite. Behavioral family therapists distinguish between positive and negative reinforcement. If a family member is praised or otherwise rewarded for a specific behavior, they are likely to repeat that behavior. The introduction of praise in this case increases the behavior that the family wants to see increase. This is *positive reinforcement. Negative reinforcement* refers to the removal of something, and the removal of that event increases the targeted behavior.

Many behavioral family therapy interventions involve identifying and targeting specific behaviors that are positively reinforced.

For example, Timmy is a ten-year-old boy who is learning to do chores around the house. His parents reward (positively reinforce) his completion of chores by using a token economy in which their son gains credits for completing certain tasks in the home. He can then turn those credits in for things he would like to have, such as extended time to watch television or play games.

Or consider Jon and Alexandra, a couple being seen for marital therapy. The family therapist might use contingency contracting with the couple to help them make positive changes. Contingency contracting is based on operant conditioning, as both Jon and Alexandra contract to engage in voluntary behaviors valued by the other. Not engaging in the specified behavior would also lead to specific consequences. There are two main types of contingency contracts: good faith contracts and quid pro quo. *Good faith* contracts specify behaviors Jon and Alexandra will engage in regardless of what their partner chooses to do. *Quid pro quo* contracts specify behaviors that Jon will engage in provided Alexandra engages in specified behaviors.

If reinforcement does not occur, that behavior might decrease over time. Behavior family therapists refer to this as *extinction*. If behavior is being changed through smaller steps, behavioral family therapists refer to this as *shaping*. A good example of shaping would be when behavioral family therapists help a child with a pervasive developmental disorder learn to feed or clothe herself. The therapist would break down all of the components involved in feeding oneself and then assist the parents in reinforcing each small step in a chain of behaviors that—taken together—constitute feeding.

We discussed how antecedents and direct consequences affect behavior in family relationships. We should also note that while reinforcement can occur directly, it can also be learned by observing consequences for behavior. This is what behavioral family therapists refer to as *modeling*. In social learning theory (Bandura, 1986), with its concern for reinforcement, modeling refers to "acquiring new behavior or strengthening-weakening previously learned responses on the basis of noticing rewarding or punishing consequences for observed behavior" (Piercy et al., 1996, p. 113). If a young girl observes that her older brother's complaints and disruptive behavior get him out of doing chores, his sister will be more likely to use complaining and disruptive behavior over time.

*Cognitive-behavioral family therapy.* A cognitive-behavioral approach to family therapy essentially emerged as an extension of work being done with couples in conflict in the 1980s (Dattilio, 2001; Patterson, 2014). This work with couples was then extended to patterns of interaction among various family members. According to Dattilio, an increasingly comprehensive approach to family therapy was then developed (e.g., G. R. Patterson, 1971).

Cognitive-behavioral family therapy relies on many of the assumptions of behavioral family therapy, but there is significant awareness and exploration of how thoughts influence behavior. One particular expression of cognitive-behavioral family therapy reflects the work of Albert Ellis (Ellis, 1991; Ellis & Harper, 1997), whose rational-emotive approach to family therapy "places emphasis on each individual's perception and interpretation of the events that occur in the family environment" (Dattilio, 2001, p. 6). From this perspective, the family therapist would then work with individuals in the family to increase awareness of how "illogical beliefs and distortions serve as the foundation for their emotional distress" (p. 7). The family therapist could, for example, then work with family members by walking them through the A-B-C approach in which activating events (A) in family relationships precede irrational beliefs (B) that can lead to consequent emotions (C) that can be discussed in the context of other family members (Dattilio, 2001; Ellis, 1991).

According to Dattilio (2001), other cognitive-behavioral approaches are perhaps more compatible with a broader systems perspective insofar as they explore in greater depth family patterns of interaction. Generally speaking, such approaches consider the many ways in which family members are interacting with one another and how such interactions influence cognitions, behaviors, and emotions across the various relationships. Such approaches seem to recognize the many layers of complexity that exist and so appear much more compatible with systems theory in general.

These other approaches to cognitive-behavioral family therapy might be thought of as extensions of Aaron Beck's work in cognitive theory (rather than Albert Ellis's rational emotive approach) with its focus on both automatic thoughts and schemas. *Automatic thoughts* are thoughts that come to mind spontaneously in response to one's circumstances, and they are considered a subset of a person's schemas (Becvar & Becvar, 2006). *Schemas* refer to "fundamental assumptions an individual has about the world that tend to be resistant to change and all-encompassing" (p. 239). Schemas or core beliefs among family members reflect a way of making sense of one's circumstances, including family relationships, and so they have a significant impact on how members relate.

In terms of philosophical assumptions, behavioral family therapy is essentially the extension of behavior therapy to couples and families. As Jones and Butman (1991) point out, behavior therapy is the practical application of behaviorism, which is tied to naturalism and empiricism.

*Naturalism* is the dominant worldview in contemporary psychology. It is the position that the natural world is the sole reality, and every event, change, or occurrence is a manifestation of its activity. Naturalism denies the supernatural. The mind or consciousness, if it is recognized at all, is considered devoid of meaning, purpose, and intentionality (Yarhouse & Jones, 1997). It is presumed to function by the same physical laws that explain all behavior. To be human, then, is not to be in any way distinct or special in terms of transcending natural laws of the universe through the will or volition.

It is because human beings are material beings and hence subject to the same laws as the rest of the observable world that behaviorism could emerge as a strong and compelling voice in science (and specifically in psychology). The view of science that influenced behaviorism and subsequently behavior therapy is *empiricism* (an approach to knowledge that emphasizes experience over innate ideas); hence we see an emphasis on the scientific method in testing hypotheses by what can be observed in the natural world (Jones & Butman, 1991).

In terms of theoretical assumptions, cognitive and behavioral family theory posits that "family interactions are maintained and changed by environmental events preceding and following each family member's behavior" (Piercy et al., 1996, p. 107). These philosophical assumptions provide a foundational justification for the study of human behavior or experience (empiricism) based on rigorous assessment, manipulation, and measurement (scientific method) of interactions that are reinforcing.

Patterson (2014) describes the current thinking on the complementarity between cognitive behavioral therapy (CBT) and family systems concepts, making the case for integration today. The key "interlocking concepts" for Patterson include (1) *structure and organization* in which CBT offers a more structured approach to recognizing and modifying unhelpful thoughts and connecting those thoughts to behaviors, (2) *contextuality* or the idea that individuals and families do not exist in isolation but rather "affect the environment and are in turn influenced by it," (3) *communication* and other behaviors that contribute to various feedback loops, and (4) *homeostasis* in which energy is expended to maintain homeostasis and the use of both therapy sessions and homework to change existing patterns with an eye for greater functionality (p. 138).

Patterson goes on to describe the application in clinical practice:

> Applied in conjunction with systems concepts, then, CBT relies heavily on organization and wholeness, placing emphasis on the structural elements of client behaviors (antecedents and consequences), and views clients in the entire context of their environment. Therapeutically, CBT adheres to a fluid structure involving assessment, treatment formulation, and ongoing evaluation. (p. 139)

Looking at the complimentary aspects of CBT and systems theory, Patterson observes: "CBT approaches add structure and techniques to the systems approach, while systems concepts broaden basic CBT methods" (2014, p. 142). Conversely, "CBT in isolation can result in rigid, formulaic methods, while systems models can ignore situations where clear cause and effect sequences exist, temporary equilibrium may rapidly lead to family breakdown, and urgent situations may not be addressed in a timely manner" (p. 142).

As we have been suggesting, recent theoretical contributions have centered on a cognitive behavioral systems approach by clarifying ways in which systemic considerations and cognitive-behavioral therapy can be brought together in a comprehensive, integrated manner to assist families (Patterson, 2014). Empirical contributions extend principles from behavioral couples therapy and cognitive behavioral therapy to child- and family-focused care for pediatric bipolar disorder (West et al., 2009), obsessive compulsive disorder (Storch et al., 2010), and anxiety disorders (Podell & Kendall, 2011) as well as family reconciliation (Dattilio & Nichols, 2011) and a range of other concerns (see Patterson, 2014).

## WHEN FAMILIES SEEK HELP

From a classic behavioral family therapy perspective, when families seek help it is because a certain problematic behavior is being maintained in some way by its consequences (Nichols & Schwartz, 2006). The family's concerns reflect patterns that have been learned and reinforced in ways that make change difficult. Generally speaking, there is no attempt to find out what is "really going on," as no underlying meaning of the behavior would be sought. This has changed somewhat with more recent trends in cognitive-behavioral family therapy, and some family therapists may consider meaning, particularly as attributions influence both affect and subsequent responses in family interactions.

For example, Ricky, age five, is brought in to therapy by his parents. The presenting concern is Ricky's behavior, which the parents report to be "unmanageable." His parents do not know what to do when he has temper tantrums at home and in public. But when Ricky is with his mother in the grocery store, she often resorts to buying him something he wants to quiet him down. She reasons that she cannot simply leave the store every time he has a tantrum: "I would never get any shopping done!" A behavioral family therapist will assume that Ricky's behavior is maintained by its consequences. The therapist would take the presenting concern at face value, meaning no underlying meaning is typically sought for the temper tantrums. The "out of control" behaviors would reflect learned responses.

A cognitive-behavioral family therapist working from a rational-emotive perspective would add some exploration of ways in which beliefs about behavior contribute to consequences that can be explored and disputed (Ellis, 1991). Other cognitive-behavioral family therapists might alternatively explore automatic thoughts and delve into family schemas that reflect assumptions about family, childrearing and so on, as well as attributions about intervening with Ricky in the process of conducting family therapy. The main point is that adding a cognitive component to family therapy is based on the assumption that the symptoms may be directly related to learned behavior but that learned behavior may also interact with cognitions in ways sometimes overlooked by behavioral theory alone.

## THE APPROACH TO FAMILY THERAPY

The general "map" for behavior family therapy is illustrated in figure 10.1. Therapy usually begins with a formal assessment referred to as *functional analysis*, which includes "(1) systematic observation of the problem behaviors; (2) systematic observation of environmental antecedents and consequences to those behaviors; (3) therapeutic manipulation of a condition that is functionally related to the problem behaviors; and (4) further observation to record change in the behaviors in response to the manipulations" (Jacobson & Margolin, 1979, p. 68). Essentially, this is a time when the family therapist is able to establish a baseline of targeted behavior or changes family members would like to see over time. A *baseline* refers to identifying the frequency of a behavior that is targeted to be changed in the course of treatment.

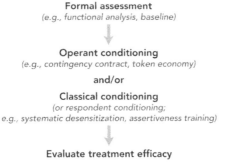

**Formal assessment**
*(e.g., functional analysis, baseline)*

**Operant conditioning**
*(e.g., contingency contract, token economy)*

**and/or**

**Classical conditioning**
*(or respondent conditioning;*
*e.g., systematic desensitization, assertiveness training)*

**Evaluate treatment efficacy**

**Figure 10.1.** Behavioral family therapy

Once a baseline is recorded, behavioral family therapists introduce interventions based on operant or classical conditioning. As was mentioned above, operant conditioning might include shaping, contingency contracting, or the use of a token economy. Classical conditioning might include techniques such as systematic desensitization or assertiveness training (Nichols & Skowron, 2006).

Throughout the course of treatment and especially at the end, therapy is evaluated to determine the efficacy of the intervention. This is done by looking at changes in the targeted behavior and related symptoms following the intervention as compared to what had been established at the baseline.

Behavioral family therapists will typically emphasize increasing positive interactions while decreasing negative interactions. This might involve homework assignments in which family members create a family game night with plenty of rewarding interactions while placing limits on exchanges that have been experienced as troublesome (Nichols & Schwartz, 2006).

The behavioral family therapist typically takes more of an "expert" role in therapy, often taking time to teach concepts associated with communication and problem solving. This might be contrasted with models of family therapy that are intentionally more collaborative, such as narrative family therapy.

The addition of cognitive components (e.g., irrational thoughts, automatic thoughts, exploration of schemas) to cognitive-behavioral family therapy is illustrated in figure 10.2. Cognitive techniques would be added to a typical behavioral family therapy approach in which formal assessment, operant and/or classical conditioning, and, at the end of treatment, some kind of treatment evaluation is conducted to determine efficacy.

**Formal assessment**
*(e.g., functional analysis, baseline)*

↓

**Operant conditioning**
*(e.g., contingency contract, token economy)*

**and/or**

**Classical conditioning**
*(or respondent conditioning;*
*e.g., systematic desensitization, assertiveness training)*

**and/or**

**Cognitive techniques**
*(A-B-C model, exploration of family schemas)*

↓

**Evaluate treatment efficacy**

Figure 10.2. Cognitive-behavioral family therapy

The cognitive components might take different forms. As was mentioned above, a cognitive-behavioral family therapist who is operating from a rational-emotive perspective might teach the A-B-C approach and focus on identifying and challenging irrational thoughts that have been unhelpful to the individual family member.

Other cognitive-behavioral family therapy approaches might focus on automatic thoughts and family schemas associated with the presenting problem. This can include an exploration of attributions about why specific events are occurring in the family as well as what assumptions are held about what ought to be occurring in the life of the family.

*Case illustration.* Trish, age twenty-four, and Kenny, age twenty-eight, are a Caucasian couple who have been married for one year. Trish is a substitute teacher in an elementary school; Kenny is an electrical engineer. They were referred to therapy by Trish's gynecologist. Trish reports symptoms of recurrent spasms of the musculature of the outer third of the vagina that interferes with sexual intercourse. These spasms cause her marked distress and interpersonal difficulty. Her symptoms meet the diagnostic criteria for genito-pelvic pain/penetration disorder.

The pain can be traced to a clumsy gynecological exam and an insensitive gynecologist who was checking on sensitive tissue from a previous surgery when Trish was younger. Trish's dating history includes having dated only one or two people (that involved light kissing only) prior to Kenny and having no previous history of sexual behavior. Kenny reported a similar dating history and indicated that he had no prior history of sexual behavior apart from occasional masturbation. Trish and Kenny were friends for five years and dated for approximately four months before they were engaged. Trish shared that she and Kenny both felt a lot of "sexual tension" on their wedding night, seeing sex as a potentially "huge release" after all the time they spent together when they were dating. Trish reported feeling "nervous" and "excited" about her wedding night, giving no thought to the pain she had felt years earlier.

Trish reports that she had no sex education from her parents, peers, or from her school. She says she was "really naive" when she was married. Kenny says he was more experienced than Trish, having dated several more women before Trish, but he also indicated having little sex education, and most of it was from friends and "locker room" discussions.

Sex therapy is a good example of when cognitive-behavioral family therapy can be particularly useful in targeting a specific symptom presentation. Assessment began with a sex history, which asked for specific and detailed information in a wide range of areas related to sex that complemented the standard diagnostic interview. Assessment also involved getting a baseline of anxiety associated with a range of imagined sexual encounters, including penetration.

From a cognitive-behavioral perspective, genito-pelvic pain/penetration disorder is a conditioned fear reaction (Leiblum, 2000; cf. Penner & Penner, 1990; Rosenau, 2002). It is a learned phobia that for Trish is reinforced by the belief that sexual intercourse can be completed only through significant pain. From a cognitive-behavioral theoretical orientation, the clinical consideration is how to address both the cognitive and phobic aspects of genito-pelvic pain/penetration disorder.

Therapy involved several components. For example, psychoeducation was provided to improve Trish and Kenny's understanding of sexual anatomy, functioning, and the cycle of sexual arousal. Also, homework assignments were common. These included assigning self-exploration to improve Trish's awareness of her own body and the practice of relaxation therapy to lay a foundation for systematic desensitization. In addition, prior to self-directed dilation, it was also helpful to assign nondemand sensual touch exercises (i.e., sensate focus) to facilitate self-awareness of what both Trish and Kenny found arousing and to facilitate feedback-rich communication about what each experienced as pleasurable.

Concerning the phobic response, what was particularly helpful was systematic desensitization, with a hierarchy of situations involving imaginal vaginal insertion. This was followed by in vivo systematic desensitization using Hegar dilators in graduated sizes. The use of dilators allowed Trish to facilitate penetration using an object that is initially much smaller and eventually much larger than a penis. This self-directed dilation program provided Trish with greater control over her own body. The successful use of dilators was facilitated by progressive muscle relaxation and other anxiety-reducing techniques.

The cognitive dimensions also needed to be addressed. Trish shared that she and Kenny wanted to start a family, and some of her worries and fears about being unable to have children seemed to intensify the anxiety she felt as they previously initiated sex, and this anxiety only led to increased muscle contractions. Therapy focused on addressing Trish's fears and worries as well as identifying and challenging irrational beliefs about the size of her husband's penis, the size of her vagina, and the likelihood of pain.

The end of therapy involved evaluating the treatment's efficacy. This meant reviewing anxiety-rating scales and comparing them to assessments of anxiety at the baseline. Also, Trish and Kenny's self-report of their frequency of and satisfaction with sexual intercourse was another measure of treatment efficacy.

## CHRISTIAN PERSPECTIVE ON COGNITIVE-BEHAVIORAL FAMILY THERAPY

*Theoretical and philosophical assumptions.* The philosophical underpinnings of behavioral family therapy—that is, the commitment to naturalism in particular—is obviously at odds with a Christian worldview. Christians affirm that God exists and created the natural world and that there is a supernatural order of which we are a part.

We encourage Christian family therapists to recognize that we are part of the natural world and have an embodied existence that can be overlooked in terms of how our "embodied existence conditions, shapes and even determines some aspects of our experience" (Jones & Butman, 1991, p. 155; Jones & Butman, 2011). But Christian family therapists can keep this understanding in tension with the affirmation of key dimensions "of human nature, [including] the interplay of body and soul-spirit and the distinctively transcendent aspects of our natures" (p. 155).

As Christians we can also value and affirm the scientific method as we establish baseline behavior and manipulate variables through interventions that can then be assessed to determine efficacy. Indeed, such a practice might reflect well on stewardship of limited mental health resources and the potential worth of establishing "best practice" based on what actually works with specific presenting concerns.

At the same time, we recognize that there is a risk that pride in science, empiricism, and the scientific method limits our understanding of human experience to that which can be observed, manipulated, and measured, and that it elevates the science above the person. We want to balance an appreciation for science and what can be known through general revelation with a high view of Scripture and what is revealed through special revelation.

We are especially encouraged by the developments in cognitive-behavioral family therapy. Recognizing the role our thoughts play in subsequent experiences of affect and in behavior is a significant development that can be affirmed by the Christian family therapist.

However, at a theoretical and philosophical level, most cognitive-behavioral family approaches rely on the assumptive framework of behaviorism: "The general approach to the mind-brain problem in cognitive-behavioral therapy is consistent with that of behaviorism in . . . viewing thought as a naturalistic process rooted in our neurology and governed by causal laws" (Jones & Butman, 1991, p. 209).

In addition to naturalism, some expressions of cognitive-behavioral family therapy are grounded more explicitly in humanism. For example, Albert Ellis described how rational-emotive family therapy is humanistic and existential in its basic assumption that "family members largely create their own world by the phenomenological view they take of what happens to them" (1991, p. 413). What this is translated into for Ellis is "full acceptance of oneself and others," which is tied to our concrete activities, and it is the occasional rating and evaluation of these activities that can "strengthen . . . our . . . self-esteem . . . in order to *be* ourselves and *enjoy* ourselves" (p. 413).

What family identity is thought to emerge from a cognitive-behavioral understanding? The cognitive-behavioral family theorists did not cast a vision for family identity, so in some ways the integrative Christian family therapist might readily utilize the various approaches and techniques while leaving open the possibility of a range of family identity considerations. However, the theoretical assumptions that lead to a cost-benefit analysis can also contribute to a family identity that can be individualistic and reductionistic, and this should at least be kept in mind by the Christian family therapist who is interested in casting a vision for family identity that is more communal and rich in its recognition of mutuality and family interdependence.

*Think about it:* In what ways have you relied on a cost-benefit approach to relationships? Why do you think people tend to think about relationships in this way? In what ways might it have an impact on relationships? In what ways might it shape family identity?

So in the end we can say that Christians interested in behavioral and cognitive-behavioral family therapy can practice what might be referred to as methodological naturalism in which they draw on theory-based interventions that were developed through natural explanations and methods. They would do so without rejecting Christian claims regarding the supernatural. The humanism espoused by some expressions of cognitive-behavioral family therapy (e.g., Ellis, 1991) is contrary to a Christian understanding of personhood, as it fails to recognize the person and the family as oriented in relation to God in a substantive and meaningful way. It also fails to recognize with humility that while people are made in the image of God they also exist and relate to one another in the context of a shared fallen state.

We would also raise a concern about reducing interactions between family members to a cost-benefit analysis. We recognize that this is to a great extent a reflection of what it means to live in a therapeutically oriented market culture. Family members may not think this way when their relationships are rewarding; however, when relationships are strained or deteriorating, family members often fall back on cost-benefit analysis. In other words, a couple may come into a marriage talking about their love and commitment to one another "for better or for worse," but they can start talking and thinking like aggravated consumers if something in their marriage goes wrong or if their partner does not meet their expectations.

The cost-benefit model fails to adequately reflect an understanding of sin, and it too quickly jumps to an individualistic assumption of what one person wants rather than what might be best for the system or community. While we see value in supporting family members in the decision to increase positive exchanges and decrease negative or aversive interactions, we are concerned that conceptualizing family relationships through economic constructs is reductionistic and could lead to a preoccupation with what is "due" to a person rather than what they might contribute to other family members.

*Model of family dysfunction and family functioning.* As with behavioral therapy focusing on individual mental health concerns, behavioral and cognitive-behavioral family therapy offers little by way of a model for proper *individual* functioning, let alone proper *family* functioning. There is no explicit vision for how a family *ought* to function apart from an awareness of the ways in which behaviors result from various antecedents and patterns of reinforcement.

For example, Jacobson (1981), in his discussion of behavioral marital therapy, admits that

> it is inconsistent with the principles of social learning theory to define *a* successful marriage. This is because it is believed that each partner brings into a relationship his/her own unique reinforcement history, and his/her own goals for a long-term relationship. The social learning model adopts a largely idiographic stance toward each couple's attempt to form and maintain a mutually satisfying relationship. Just as there are many routes to marital distress, similarly there are many paths to marital satisfaction, and any general attempt to describe *the* successful marriage must take into account the wide divergence of standards and goals on which couples may base their union. (p. 557)

Broadly understood, behavioral approaches are really interested in describing behavior and patterns of reinforcement, and cognitive-behavioral approaches also consider ways in which the cognitive processes may contribute to behavior.

When a family presents with concerns, they are then, by definition, dysfunctional in ways that matter to at least some of the family members. This leaves behavioral and cognitive-behavioral therapy open to the charge of subjectivism in its account of dysfunction and family functioning, as it is left with what amounts to symptom identification, exploration, and amelioration. This is not so significant a departure from other models of family therapy, and there are many models today that do not commit themselves to an explicit model of health for the family for a wide range of reasons.

## INTEGRATIVE FOCUS: *Family Functioning*

A cognitive-behavioral perspective is going to consider the presenting concerns as a predictable result of behavior that is being reinforced in the system. This would be particularly true of the more *behavioral* cognitive-behavioral professionals, while those who are more cognitive will likely see the presenting symptoms as reflecting irrational or unhelpful cognitions that reflect a maladaptive schema. We see cognitive-behavioral family therapy as bringing many helpful resources to the work of the Christian family therapist. A caution around family functioning is that such an approach with its emphasis on cognitions and reinforcement schedules can be enhanced by an understanding of ways in which affect and its regulation can impact the individual and the system. These kinds of concerns might be overlooked or understood through the specific lens afforded the family therapist by a cognitive or behavioral emphasis.

*Think about it:* What do you see as the unique benefits in a *cognitive* approach to the family that enhance what has been valuable in a *behavioral* approach to the family? In what ways might a Christian perspective inform rational responses to difficult circumstances? Are there any cognitive distortions that you see as unique to Christians or at least particularly difficult for Christians to avoid when they go through difficult times?

The potential benefit to the amorality (not making normative moral claims) of cognitive-behavioral family therapy is that by not casting a normative vision for family relationships, therapists are able to explore this with the family and perhaps develop ways of relating that more intentionally reflect a Christian view of familial relationships or otherwise work toward congruence with the family's interests and values.

*Techniques in family therapy.* There is great potential for integrating cognitive-behavioral family therapy with other models of family therapy:

In a general sense, because most approaches to family therapy involve human communication, many therapies may be said to be "cognitive." For similar reasons, most modalities may be said to be "behavioral" as well because communication is behavior and all behavior is communicative. And because the human condition involves emotion, most modalities address emotion to a significant degree. Consequently, any given therapy can be viewed through a variety of lenses—as cognitive, behavioral, emotional, and so on. (Dattilio, 2001, p. 13)

Can the same be said for integrating cognitive-behavioral family therapy techniques with a Christian worldview? We think so. As Dattilio (2001) suggests, much of what Christians are concerned about when they meet with families can be conceptualized in terms of thought processes (cognitions), behavior, and emotions. The techniques are certainly then compatible with a Christian perspective, but the Christian would want to anchor the techniques in a broader vision of both individual personhood (with consideration given to human agency and volition, for example) and the family (with greater attention to the qualities that ought to characterize family relationships; see also chap. 18). A Christian family therapist could hold a broader vision of the individual and the family by talking openly and intentionally about the free choices people make in a relationship, the virtues one wishes to cultivate in oneself and for the betterment of the family as a whole, and the family identity that might be formed over time.

What of specific techniques? What about contingency contracting, token economies, systematic desensitization, and so on? None seem problematic in and of themselves. However, we would encourage the Christian to reflect on some of them, at least in terms of how they are conveyed and what goals are being accomplished.

For example, we tend to prefer "good faith" contracts over quid pro quo contracts. Why? We like the idea of couples taking steps toward each other regardless of what their partner does. But other Christian clinicians might have experienced greater benefit in a quid pro quo exchange. We want to recognize that possibility while creating a forum for discussion of what may occur in the marital relationship if a kind of cost-benefit analysis were to characterize attempts to improve the marriage.

Another technique that sometimes raises questions among Christian clinicians is the use of assertiveness training. There seem to be perceptions about humility in relationships among some Christians that seem at odds with a technique to learn how to be assertive in interpersonal relationships. But we see assertiveness training as intended for those who are either *passive* in their exchanges (take their own feelings out of the equation) or are *aggressive* in their exchanges (take other people's feelings out of the equation). Assertiveness training is intended to take both the client's and other people's feelings into account, and we see this as a helpful technique when done correctly, not as a technique that is fundamentally at odds with a Christian worldview.

---

**INTEGRATIVE FOCUS:** *Family Relationships*

How ought family relationships be characterized in a cognitive-behavioral approach? The theoretical assumptions behind cognitive-behavioral approaches have historically lent themselves to more of a cost-benefit analysis of relationships. This is an area of concern for some Christians who would see relationships as more bound by covenantal approaches. Although a therapist can choose between a quid pro quo contract and a good faith contract, the theoretical underpinnings of a cognitive-behavioral approach have supported more of a "this for that" exchange in family relationships that we see as important to question from a Christian worldview.

*Think about it:* What do you think contributes to a "this for that" approach to relationships? How might that be a benefit to families? In what ways might it be detrimental? Can you identify a presenting concern that might be an issue for which "this for that" is especially appropriate?

---

The identification and exploration of automatic thoughts, as well as the recognition and appreciation of family schemas, is also something we value. Helping people understand their immediate thoughts and core beliefs, how they were formed, and the ways in which they contribute to current attributions and exchanges in family relationships is an important goal (McMinn & Campbell, 2007). The Christian family therapist would recognize that some core beliefs and not others might characterize the Christian, but the promotion of self-monitoring and thought-stopping as well as careful limning of family schemas can be especially helpful.

## CONCLUSION

Behavioral and cognitive-behavioral family therapy is a valuable addition to
the models of family therapy. Early approaches might seem somewhat removed from the systemic consideration that characterized most early family
therapy models. However, more contemporary expressions of cognitive-
behavioral family therapy seem to appreciate the interrelatedness of family
members and the many layers that must be taken into consideration when
working with families to make sustainable changes. The approach has developed language and theoretical handholds to work with the family, and it is
an important resource with which Christians providing family therapy will
want to be familiar.

## REFERENCES

Bandura, A. (1976). *Social learning theory.* Englewood Cliffs, NJ: Prentice-Hall.
Bandura, A. (1986). *Social foundations of thought and action.* Englewood Cliffs, NJ:
    Prentice-Hall.
Becvar, D. S., & Becvar, R. J. (2006). *Family therapy: A systemic integration* (6th
    ed.). Boston: Allyn & Bacon.
Dattilio, F. M. (2001). Cognitive-behavioral family therapy: Contemporary myths
    and misconceptions. *Contemporary Family Therapy, 23*(1), 2-18.
Dattilio, F. M., & Nichols, M. P. (2011). Reuniting estranged family members: A
    cognitive-behavioral-systemic perspective. *The American Journal of Family
    Therapy, 39,* 88-99.
Ellis, A. (1991). Rational-emotive family therapy. In A. M. Horne & J. L. Passmore
    (Eds.), *Family counseling and therapy* (2nd ed., pp. 403-34). Itasca, IL: F. E. Peacock.
Ellis, A., & Harper, R. A. (1997). *A guide to rational living* (3rd ed.). North Holly-
    wood, CA: Wilshire.
Gottman, J. M. (1999a). *The marriage clinic: A scientifically based marital therapy.*
    New York: W. W. Norton.
Gottman, J. M. (1999b). *The seven principles for making marriage work.* New York:
    Three Rivers Press.
Horne, A. M. (1991). Social learning family therapy. In A. M. Horne & J. L.
    Passmore (Eds.), *Family counseling and therapy* (2nd ed., pp. 463-96). Itasca,
    IL: F. E. Peacock.
Jacobson, N. S. (1981). Behavioral marital therapy. In A. S. Gurman & D. P.
    Kniskern (Eds.), *Handbook of family therapy.* New York: Brunner/Mazel.

Jacobson, N. S., & Margolin, G. (1979). *Marital therapy: Strategies based on social learning and behavior exchange principles.* New York: Brunner/Mazel.

Jones, S. L., & Butman, R. E. (1991). *Modern psychotherapies: A comprehensive Christian appraisal.* Downers Grove, IL: InterVarsity Press.

Jones, S. L., & Butman, R. E. (2011). *Modern psychotherapies: A comprehensive Christian appraisal* (2nd ed.). Downers Grove, IL: InterVarsity Press.

Leiblum, S. R. (2000). Vaginismus: A most perplexing problem. In S. R. Leiblum & R. C. Rosen (Eds.), *Principles and practice of sex therapy* (3rd ed., pp. 181-204). New York: Guilford Press.

McMinn, M. R., & Campbell, C. D. (2007). *Integrative psychotherapy.* Downers Grove, IL: IVP Academic.

Nichols, M. P., & Schwartz, R. C. (2006). *Family therapy: Concepts and methods* (7th ed.). Boston: Allyn & Bacon.

Nichols, M. P., & Skowron, E. (2006). *Instructor's manual and test bank, Family therapy: Concepts and methods* (7th ed.). Boston: Allyn & Bacon.

Patterson, G. R. (1971). *Families: Applications of social learning to life.* Champaign, IL: Research Press.

Patterson, T. (2014). A cognitive behavioral systems approach to family therapy. *Journal of Family Psychotherapy, 25,* 132-44.

Penner, J. J., & Penner, C. L. (1990). *Counseling for sexual disorders.* Dallas: Word.

Piercy, F. P., Sprenkle, D. H., Wetchler, J. L., & associates. (1996). *Family therapy sourcebook* (2nd ed.). New York: Guilford Press.

Podell, J. L., & Kendall, P. C. (2011). Mothers and fathers in family cognitive-behavioral therapy for anxious youth. *Journal of Child and Family Studies, 20,* 182-95.

Rosenau, D. E. (2002). *A celebration of sex* (2nd ed.). Nashville: Thomas Nelson.

Skinner, B. F. (1938). *The behavior of organisms.* New York: Appleton-Century-Crofts.

Skinner, B. F. (1969). *Contingencies of reinforcement.* New York Appleton-Century-Crofts.

Storch, E. A., Lehmkuhl, H. D., Ricketts, E., Geffken, G. R., Marien, W., & Murphy, T. K. (2010). An open trial of intensive family based cognitive-behavioral therapy in youth with obsessive-compulsive disorder who are medication partial responders or nonresponders. *Journal of Clinical Child & Adolescent Psychology, 39*(2), 260-68.

Watson, J. B. (1913). Psychology as the behaviorist views it. *Psychological Review, 20,* 158-277.

Watson, J. B. (1930). *Behaviorism.* Chicago: University of Chicago Press.

West, A. E., Jacobs, R. H., Westerholm, R., Lee, A., Carbray, J., Heidenreich, J., & Pavuluri, M. N. (2009). Child and family-focused cognitive-behavioral therapy for pediatric bipolar disorder: Pilot study of group treatment format. *Journal of the Academy for Canadian Child and Adolescent Psychiatry, 18*(3), 239-58.

Wolpe, J. (1958). *Psychotherapy by reciprocal inhibition.* Stanford, CA: Stanford University Press.

Yarhouse, M. A., & Jones, S. L. (1997). A critique of materialist assumptions in interpretations of research on homosexuality. *Christian Scholar's Review, 26*(40), 478-95.

# NARRATIVE
# FAMILY THERAPY

*Heirlooms we don't have in our family.*
*But stories we've got.*

**ROSE CHERIN**

Every family has a story. The photographs lining the hallways of our homes are visual biographies of our families. They not only describe the major events in our lives—marriages, the birth of children, and the vacation at the cottage where the children caught their first fish—they also tell a story bigger than the story, a metastory. That narrative says that this home is a happy place. Those stories convey emotional nutrition and restoration.

The stories represented by the pictures on the wall tell only a part of a family story, usually the nostalgic part. Other story lines—losses and disappointments, violence and failure—are not usually represented in the gallery of memory. These are the suppressed stories, the ones that the family would prefer to forget, for they remind us of our failures, negligence, and abuse of each other. It is around these stories that families can feel stuck. Narrative family therapy will suggest that the family is not stuck; for indeed the story, even the tragic story, is not set but is in constant motion. The events are not static histories but are understood in light of later events. For example, the great tragedy of the failure of the family potato farm and the forced relocation of many family members from Ireland to the United States was a tragic story that later included chapters of the building of a new community, of both success and failure, great and small.

## INTRODUCTION TO NARRATIVE FAMILY THERAPY

The effect of stories—the good stories and the bad stories—is the focus of narrative family therapy. The intervention is an examination into the family stories: the literal events and the interpretations that are held uniquely by each member. Narrative is a story. A story is a recollection of experience to which we attach meaning. We interpret ourselves, our families, and our cultures through our narratives.

Narrative family therapy approaches families from a rather unique perspective. It assumes that the people in the family can find their own solutions or rewrite their own stories. Furthermore, it assumes that the people in the family rather than the professionals outside of the family are the real experts. It is an approach that is interested in history and context, and it involves hearing the stories of people's lives and considers a collaborative relationship that facilitates reauthoring people's stories. This approach considers how families have come to see themselves, asserting that people (and therefore, families) are constituted in language. Families live the stories they are told or come to tell about themselves.

Narrative family therapy believes that families can learn how they write themselves (as individuals) and the family into a story line. Furthermore, it is held that families can learn to make changes to the story line and so alter the way that they create story together. A narrative family therapist assists a family by helping them articulate their story and identify the meaning that they have attached to it. So what becomes critical is recognizing and giving voice to the family reality as it is locally defined. By locally defined, narrative family therapists are thinking of the subjective view of the family members themselves as contrasted with how others view, label, and relate to the family.

This understanding of local reality ties into the presenting "problems" families bring into therapy. Narrative family therapists are concerned that other family approaches can fail to adequately distinguish between the problems and the people in the family or the family itself. Pathological persons or dysfunctional families as understood in other models of family therapy are indebted to machine models that require repairs, organic models that require healing of pathology, or strategic game models (e.g., chess) that require counterstrategies (Barry, 1997).

So in narrative family therapy, problems are thought of as different from people, and a number of techniques underscore this difference, setting it in contrast to the many other models of family therapy. A common technique we will discuss further below is to punctuate this difference in language that places the problem behavior outside of the person. To "punctuate" is to treat something as especially significant, in some cases to treat it as that which is the cause of concern itself (rather than the result). For example, violent behavior becomes a story of *trouble* that is outside of the person. In this particular story, trouble can sometimes get the upper hand. We will return to this technique as well as others that are most characteristic of narrative family therapy.

Michael White is the founder of the narrative therapy movement. Beginning in the late 1980s and until his untimely death at age fifty-nine in 2008, White articulated this emerging approach through his writings and his work at the Dulwich Centre, Adelaide, Australia. The significance of the approach has grown, in part, because of its compatibility with current cultural values of postmodernism and deconstructionism. White was influenced by the writings of French postmodern philosophers Michel Foucault and Jacques Derrida and by the clinical work of Gregory Bateson. Foucault, writing in the 1960s and 1970s, addressed the use of language as a tool of the powerful. He believed that the powerful possessed control of the language of the culture. If you controlled the language you controlled how reality and truth were defined for the powerless. He came to reject the systems approach to family therapy, however, and came to appreciate the importance of how people construe the world around them.

David Epston, working in Auckland, New Zealand, is another influential leader and narrative family therapist. He has been particularly influential in developing narrative as a metaphor, and he introduced the concept to Michael White. He is known for developing community resources and support networks for people struggling with similar concerns, so that they can share and become mutual supports and resources. Epston also developed the technique of letter writing so that the client can reread letters by the family therapist that highlight and consolidate the gains made in therapy.

## THEORETICAL AND PHILOSOPHICAL ASSUMPTIONS OF NARRATIVE FAMILY THERAPY

*Postmodern influence.* The philosophical assumptions underlying narrative family therapy can be traced to the emergence of postmodernism in the early twentieth century. Postmodernism grew out of a critique of modernist assumptions, particularly those that were related to rationalism, foundationalism, and a confidence in the pursuit of objective knowledge through science. The influence of postmodernism as a philosophical movement has touched literature, politics, the physical science, architecture, and the arts (Dickerson, 2014). Postmodernism and poststructuralism are often used interchangeably. Dickerson prefers poststructuralism as a critique of any structure deemed normative (e.g., a theoretical model or family/couple composition).

Related to these specific postmodern and poststructural assumptions, narrative family therapy is indebted to existentialism, literary criticism (e.g., Derrida), and French philosophy (e.g., Foucault). Existentialists came to value individual experience and decisions as the essential source of knowledge and morality. Jacques Derrida argued against "onto-theology," or the "ontological descriptions of reality," and the "metaphysics of presence," or "the idea that something transcendent is present in reality" (Grenz, 1996, p. 6). Michel Foucault critiqued social institutions and underscored the relationship between power and knowledge, holding that "every interpretation of reality is an assertion of power" (Grenz, 1996, p. 6).

These postmodern assumptions stand in contrast to a modernist confidence in objective knowledge and absolute truth (Becvar & Becvar, 2006). What is claimed to be real or true is merely a subjective construction based on one's perspective. So we can see that "postmodern truth is relative to the community in which a person participates," suggesting that the "postmodern consciousness . . . entails a radical kind of relativism and pluralism" (Grenz, 1996, p. 14). And, as Grenz observes, the relativism and pluralism of postmodernism are different from those found in some expressions of modernism:

> The relativistic pluralism of late modernity was highly individualistic; it elevated personal taste and personal choice as the be-all and end-all. . . .
>
> The postmodern consciousness, in contrast, focuses on the group. Postmoderns live in self-contained social groups, each of which has its own language, beliefs, and values. As a result, postmodern relativistic pluralism seeks to give place to the "local" nature of truth. Beliefs are held to be true within the context of the communities that espouse them. (Grenz, 1996, p. 15)

This has implications for sources of knowledge and for sources of authority. The modernist was confident that absolute truth exists and is attainable in this sense: the world "out there" can be known to those of us who observe it; the world "out there" presents itself to us objectively (Becvar & Becvar, 2006). The postmodern underpinnings of narrative approaches to therapy reject any claims to universal, timeless truth. In the absence of absolute truth, postmodernism regards personal experience and individual belief as the dictum for behavior. Thus, the language of postmodernism will include statements such as "My personal truth is . . ." or "My experience tells me . . ."

With the shift from modernist to postmodernist assumptions, from Truth with a capital "T" to truths with a lowercase "t" (or multiple perspectives), we now emphasize narrative, discourse, and language, recognizing that the distinction between therapist and client is somewhat arbitrary, at least if we were to work from the assumption that the therapist has expertise or should be privileged in some way over and above what the family brings to the session. Indeed, the family's perspective is of equal validity and is to be given voice in a narrative family therapy approach.

> In general, by bringing forth multiple points of view, as opposed to a normative or expert view, clients can decide how and where they would like to situate their lives, based on their preferred values and intentions. (Zimmerman & Dickerson, 1994, pp. 235-36)

It was mentioned above that a narrative approach has philosophical underpinnings that can be traced to the writings of Foucault, who emphasized power-laden relationships and categories. From a narrative therapy perspective, these can be created when people are labeled with a diagnosis and the individual or family construe themselves in keeping with that diagnosis: "Instead of 'making the problem the problem,' persons experiencing problems are problematized. Once in this position, a sense of helplessness and loss of personal agency can arise, making self-initiated change quite difficult" (Barry, 1997, p. 33).

*Constructivist influence.* Constructivism refers to a number of related philosophical perspectives that trace back to Giambattista Vico (eighteenth century) and Immanuel Kant (late eighteenth and early nineteenth century) and the belief that individual learning is based on a person's perception. It holds that through the act of perceiving and describing our personal experience we construct our own understanding of that experience as well as the reality about that experience itself (Becvar & Becvar, 2006). In terms of epistemology, or how we know things, our perception of the way things are is a function of our beliefs.

A related term with a different twist is *social constructionism*. If truth is based on personal experience, then truth or reality can be built, created, or constructed. People living in social relationships can make "a reality" together.

From a social constructionist perspective, individuals within families make meaning out of their circumstances, which is communicated in error as absolute reality rather than human-created reality. In family therapy, we focus on how these constructions are communicated to individuals within the family as well as how family therapy can be a resource in exploring these constructions.

So what are the implications of the view that knowing or knowledge is actually socially constructed through language and communication and is therefore situationally or context dependent? One implication is that what families take to be "real" in terms of how they are functioning, what their strengths and weaknesses are, and so on, can be related to dominant beliefs within the family and within the society (Piercy, Sprenkle, Wetchler, & associates, 1996). Social constructionism places a premium on communal meaning, including what we take to be true about human functioning:

> In this sense, what one takes to be the real, what one believes to be transparently true about human functioning, is a by-product of communal construction. This is not to offer a form of linguistic solipsism or reductionism; it is not to say that nothing exists outside linguistic constructions. Whatever exists simply exists, irrespective of linguistic practices. However, once one begins to describe or explain what exists, one inevitably proceeds from a forestructure of shared intelligibility. (Gergen, 2001, p. 806)

The client in the family or the family itself cannot be approached as though it were isolated from its context. Indeed, "a social constructivist would say that we cannot accurately observe a family because what we see is colored by our previous beliefs and interactions with the family" (Piercy et al., 1996, p. 130).

Each of us is born into and assimilates preexisting forms of language in a culturally created linguistic system. In the process of socialization, we learn to speak in accepted ways and simultaneously to adopt the shared values and ideology of our language system. Thus, our words are a critical consideration. Our words express the conventions, the symbols, the metaphors of our particular group. And we cannot speak in a language separate from that of our community (Becvar & Becvar, 2006, p. 93).

*Assumptions about healthy family functioning, healthy behavior.* Narrative family therapy has historically resisted the urge to develop a model of healthy family functioning, at least not a model that is comprised of universally accepted principles that can be applied to all families across time. Narrative family therapists avoid making judgments about what is normal and abnormal family functioning. They tend to be skeptical about diagnostic labels because they fear the oppressive use of "expert" language. What is viewed as oppressive is the assumption of the expert that he or she "knows best" how to understand the family experience and that the diagnostic label is reductionistic insofar as it limits our understanding of the person or family to psychopathology. The language of "pathology" or "disorder" or even "dysfunction" is a reflection of what White (2007) refers to as *internal* state understandings—the outcome of distortions of elements or essences, such as unconscious motivations, needs, drives, and personality traits. In contrast, narrative theorists discuss *intentional* state understandings steeped in personal agency in which people and families are seen as "originators of many of the preferred developments of their own lives" (p. 103). For White there is not a wholesale rejection of internal state understanding, but he favored placing greater emphasis on helping people live out their lives "according to the intentions that they embrace in the pursuit of what they give value to in life" (p. 103).

Narrative family therapists also tend to be somewhat dismissive of some of the other systems concepts, arguing that the shift from individual to the family achieved in most models of family therapy simply shifts the focus on pathology from the individual to the family. Narrative therapists do not focus on systems and patterns, which they see as betraying structural assumptions, but prefer to focus on narratives "produced by cultural meaning systems and having real effects on how persons make meaning of (story) their lives" (Dickerson, 2014, p. 403). Perhaps one of the greatest challenges from a narrative family therapy perspective is the challenge to the view that problems are functional for families.

Let the Ortiz family serve as an example. Manuel and Lucia are third-generation Americans whose families migrated to the United States during World War II. Their grandparents and parents were farm and factory workers. Manuel and Lucia are both very proud of the fact that they own a small business—a stationary store franchise. Their marriage and family is traditionally structured. They have three children: Ramon is seventeen, Miguel is thirteen, and Estella is nine. The expectations of parents toward children are high regarding behavior and school performance. Both parents work in the store, along with the children. Manuel is there full time; Lucia and the children work in between other responsibilities of school and home.

> THERAPIST: Welcome all, it's a pleasure to know you as a family. You all have an advantage over me because I don't know you individually or as a family like you know yourselves. Could you all tell me what's important to you, and what brings you here to see me?
>
> LUCIA: Well, being a family is important to us all. We are a close family and we want to stay that way. We are becoming worried that our children are not respecting my authority as their mother. And that Miguel is making choices about school and friends that really concern my husband and me.
>
> THERAPIST: Really. Tell me of the things that are a concern for you.
>
> MANUEL: Well, my son is not taking school seriously. He is a smart boy, but he's getting Cs and Ds in his classes. He is supposed to come home after school and work in the store, but he doesn't come home—instead he's hanging around with friends. We can't leave the store to go chasing after him. We're stuck there until he comes to do his job.

Family therapies operating in a modernist perspective would understand that the family has identified the individual patient as Miguel, "the kid with the problem." Furthermore, the therapist would seek to shift the conceptualization of the problem from Miguel to the full system—labeling the family structure or the relational dynamics or patterns between members as dysfunctional. Narrative theorists would critique the assumption that there is an essential family structure or a "structure below the level of meaning, and that this structure constitutes the reality of . . . ," in this case, this family (Madigan, 2011, p. 171). Narrative family therapy would see the family through multiple story lines, all of which have legitimacy and must be reconciled with the other family story lines. In this case, we have parts of three stories: Manuel's story is of hard work, overcoming cultural challenges, pride in success, orderly family functioning, and expectation of compliance. Lucia's story includes strain from managing home and business and providing for the family's emotional needs. Miguel's story includes breaking the expectations of others and asserting independence regarding school and schedule.

The goal for the narrative therapist is not to get Miguel to comply nor to encourage his father to "go easier" on his son. To a narrative therapist, that's not the counselor's business. Rather, it is to encourage the voicing of each narrative and to help the family blend all of the story lines together. Narrative family therapists are urged to honor individuals within the family and the family itself in terms of the unique story or narrative that is brought to the clinical experience. This includes but is not limited to the individual and family cultural heritage.

Recent work in narrative theory and therapy has been a feminist-relational critique of language and approaches to care. Narrative therapy has also been extended to specific populations and concerns in theory and in some cases in empirical study, such as gender issues, relationship concerns, LGBT+ populations, people seeking help for eating disorders, anxiety disorders, ADHD, domestic violence, and trauma (see Chang & Nylund, 2013, pp. 74-77). There is a general tension in narrative theory with valuing story over existing methodologies cited to show effectiveness, but that discussion is ongoing because many proponents recognize the potential benefits to demonstrating efficacy.

## WHEN FAMILIES SEEK HELP

When family therapists consider what is happening when families seek help, they are often looking at what constitutes dysfunction. In contrast to several other models of family therapy, narrative family therapists are skeptical of naming dysfunction as such. What they are concerned with is how families are influenced by their family story, how the family story came to make sense to them over time. This is what might be referred to as looking for "sense-making stories" (Barry, 1997, p. 32), and they are told over and over again and become part of the individual's identity and the identity of the family as a whole.

So families seek help for any number of reasons, but those reasons are often assumed to be tied to individual and family identity as understood by "sense-making stories" and dominant narratives. "Dominant story" is a phrase from White and Epston (1990) that describes an individual's or a family's principal view of themselves and the world. A dominant story can be helpful or unhelpful, and this distinction is essentially based on whether the family is able to resolve the concerns that bring them in for therapy. Help-seeking families often have a dominant story that is unhelpful to them. Gergen refers to this dominant story as the "regressive narrative" (Gergen, 1999, p. 72). It is the story that we hold from our experience that maintains the family in its current state. The family will maintain the story because to describe it as "truth," the narrative family counselor will see the story as that which maintains the family's current state.

In the case of the Ortiz family, the dominant story included a story line with the following themes:

Life is hard; you have to work even harder.
We're supposed to work together.
Don't fail; have dignity.
It's not fair.
I am angry.

An assumption in narrative family therapy is that interpretation has a powerful influence on one's life, and the problems families have are viewed as resulting from internalizing dominant discourses from the broader culture (see fig. 11.1). This is essentially the practice of hermeneutics, which, in a narrative family therapy approach, refers to the activity of understanding achieved through the interpretation of stories (Nichols & Schwartz, 2006). According to Nichols and Skowron (2006), the dominant culture influences individuals and families to see themselves in particular ways. These ways of seeing become stories individuals and families tell themselves to "construe their experience in unhelpful ways." These construals lead to "problem-saturated stories" that leave individuals and families powerless and contribute to their relating to others in ways that "fit their problem-saturated story" (Nichols & Skowron, 2006, p. 175).

The dominant culture influences individuals and families
to see themselves in particular ways.

These ways of seeing are stories individuals and families
tell themselves to construe their experience in unhelpful ways.

These construals lead to problem-saturated stories.

This leaves individuals and families powerless and contributes to their
relating to others in ways that fit their "problem-saturated story."

Figure 11.1. The influence of dominant discourse on families

Families vary as to how much they are influenced by culturally dominant narratives. But individuals born into families are born into preexisting dominant narratives that are more local expression of cultural narratives.

Taken further, families not only "story" their lives, they "act out" those stories because they live based on the script from which they find themselves reading:

> Not only do we, as humans, give meaning to our experiences by "storying" our lives, we are empowered to "perform" our stories through our knowledge of them. . . . Some of these stories promote competence and wellness. Others serve to constrain, trivialize, disqualify, or otherwise pathologize ourselves, others, and our relationships. Still other stories can be reassuring, uplifting, liberating, revitalizing, or healing. The particular story that prevails or dominates in giving meaning to the event of our lives, to a large extent determines the nature of our lived experience and our patterns of actions. When a problem-saturated story predominates, we are repeatedly invited into disappointment and misery. (White & Epston, 1989, p. 7)

The goal in narrative family therapy, then, is to deconstruct the presenting "facts" about an individual in the family or the family as a whole. This is done by "delineating the assumptions, values, and ideologies on which [the 'facts'] rest" (Becvar & Becvar, 2006, p. 93). This brings us to a discussion of the approach that narrative therapists take when they work with families.

The Ortiz family could identify the "facts" or the cultural discourse that encourages the articulation of a problem-laden story within their family.

LUCIA:    Miguel, we are concerned for you because you don't know what we have had to face just to get where we are. I don't want you throwing that away or ruin your life.

MIGUEL:   Mom, do you think that I don't know that? I work, but what do I get for it? Nothing! What's the point? You work, for what? No matter how much I do, or you do, it doesn't matter.

MANUEL:   But Miguel, flunking out of school is no way for anyone to respect you.

THERAPIST: I wonder if all of you have feelings about not being respected by the society—and all have your own reactions as well.

A common story with which all members of the family identified was the longing for respect. Each had unique ways to achieve it. Manuel worked for his respect through business efforts. When he encountered overt and covert racism he internalized the pain and determined within himself to work harder. But his children didn't hear that story—they just read the lines of "Work, work, work!" and "Be respected."

Miguel's story was one of frustration—his work did not produce respect. If he worked hard at school or if he gave up, he felt that he was treated the same by the majority culture in his school. The deconstruction of the facts led to the family identifying with the therapist the problem-saturated story and supporting one another in the rewriting of the family's role with each individual.

*The approach to family therapy.* The essential task of narrative family therapy is to deconstruct oppressive, problem-saturated stories and by "wondering," "exploring," and "opening" together so that it is possible to co-construct empowering and more helpful stories (Dickerson, 2014, p. 411). The narrative family therapist does not move the family from their experiences of dysfunction to healthier functioning. Rather, the narrative family therapist joins the family in a collaborative relationship in which the family's story may be told. This means it is essential that the narrative family therapist avoid an "expert" stance when meeting with the family—the focus is really on understanding and giving voice to the family's lived experience.

The narrative family therapist is to take a more active and collaborative posture, listening to the family and identifying times in the family history when individuals were resilient. The questions asked are respectful, and narrative family therapists avoid labeling individuals or the family as a whole and treat people with respect. The essential purpose of the narrative approach to family therapy is to assist family members in separating themselves from the dominant cultural discourses that have been shaping the contours of the family identity. This process itself creates opportunities for new family stories or narratives.

Specific methods for helping families in the process of change include mapping the influence of the presenting concern, externalizing the problem, identifying unique outcomes, and therapeutic audiencing (Barry, 1997). Again, all of these methods may be utilized, and their utilization is in service of "deproblematizing" the family.

A narrative family therapist begins assessment by listening to the family's story. This means hearing about their problems and listening for presuppositions with respect to their stated problems (Nichols & Schwartz, 2006). White (2007, p. 78) distinguished between the "landscape of action" and the "landscape of identity." The landscape of action "is the 'material' of the story and is composed of the sequence of events that make up the plot" (p. 78). It refers to the events and circumstances the family discusses, those experiences that mark their family story line. The landscape of identity refers to the meaning given to those events:

> People give meaning to their experiences of the events of life by taking them into frames of intelligibility, and on the conclusion that it is the structure of the narrative that provides the principal frame of intelligibility for acts of meaning-making in everyday life. (p. 80)

The assumption is that the stated problems will be situated in a context that must be understood in more of a collaborative relationship with the therapist. "'Getting the family's story' is not just information gathering. It is a reconstructive inquiry, designed to move clients from passivity and defeatism toward a sense that they already have at least some power over the problems that plague them" (p. 344).

A narrative family therapist might then move toward *mapping the presenting concern*. This involves first unpacking ways in which the symptom has influenced the individual or family. For example, with a family presenting a child who has temper tantrums, a narrative family therapist might talk about ways in which the tantrums have affected the family. Note that by doing so the therapist first *externalizes the problem* of temper tantrums. The temper tantrums are given a name and then they are treated as if they were a character in the family story. They are "out there" and part of the drama itself rather than "inside" the child. That way the tantrums can be discussed, questioned, interviewed, and so on.

Because problems tend to dominate a family's life, the narrative family therapist also maps the concern by talking about ways in which the child or family has had an influence on the temper tantrums. This brings to the foreground other individual and family events and experiences that may have receded into the background. Another way to put this is that the family is aided in identifying *unique outcomes* or ways in which the child or the family got the upper hand on the tantrums themselves. The more these stories are told and retold, the more the family is able to "thicken the plot" of their lives (White & Epston, 1990). Toward the end of his life, White was drawn to the concept of what is "absent but implicit" and the idea of "difference" (Dickerson,

2013, p. 108). For example, when a person is suffering or in despair, what may be absent but implicit is hope. Suffering or despair is understood in part by contrast.

White would later write about the "zone of proximal development" as the "difference between what a learner can do without help and what he or she can do with help," which can often help with mapping (Chang & Nylund, 2013, p. 76). These lead to scaffolding conversations. If you think of a scaffold as a temporary structure on which work can be done to build or restore a building, you begin to get a picture of how therapeutic conversations lead to new ways of responding to the concerns (Chang & Nylund, 2013).

A specific technique that might help contrast the story of the person with the story of the problem is to take a sheet of paper and draw a line down the center. In the one column the family therapist can write down the story of the problem, whether that is anger, temper tantrums, encopresis, or being a "difficult teen" or a "problem child." In the other column the family therapist can write down the story of the person with reference to their interests and qualities as well as perhaps how they wish to be known by others, what story they wish to write about themselves and have read and known by others.

In addition to mapping the influence of the presenting concern, externalizing the problem, and identifying unique outcomes or what is absent but implicit, narrative family therapists also participate in *therapeutic audiencing*. The narrative family therapist "acts as an enthusiastic audience, applauding client efforts to author and enact a preferred story" (Barry, 1997, p. 35). The "applause," if you will, occurs in session and through a number of creative ways of demonstrating support. For example, a narrative family therapist might write a letter to the family that brings home the point of the work they have been doing together in therapy. The letters themselves may be varied and dramatic, and they may include invitations sent to family members who are not participating in therapy, letters that cast a vision or in some way predict a certain outcome for the family, and letters of reference that support and endorse specific family members or the family as a whole (Barry, 1997).

Again, the letters are a way to discuss and confirm the family's preferred story. But whether it is through letters or through conversations in the context of therapy itself, the narrative family therapist becomes the audience to the story the family is enacting. As the family plays out the drama, reading from the preferred script, the narrative family therapist applauds the family's efforts by recognizing gains, highlighting strengths and resilience, and underscoring efforts.

Through all of these interventions we can begin to see that there is a discourse that occurs. The discourse or reading from the script is really about who has the authority to write and edit existing scripts from which the family reads. Again, because problems tend to dominate the life of the family presenting for therapy, the work of the narrative family therapist is to draw attention to the problem narrative or problem discourse and to help the family see other dimensions of themselves besides those apparent from the problem narrative. From a narrative family therapy perspective, the problem narrative often comes from messages taken in by the family from the dominant culture, and these messages are simply taken for granted; they are ways of knowing that are in a sense global, taking on an "everybody knows" quality. The narrative family therapist looks instead for local knowledge about what is happening in the family.

## CHRISTIAN PERSPECTIVE ON NARRATIVE FAMILY THERAPY

***Philosophical and theoretical assumptions.*** It is important to recognize that American evangelical Christianity has a special relationship with modernism, one that may play a role in an evangelical critique of postmodernism:

> Historically, the modern sciences relied on empiricism, and American Evangelicalism came into its own in the context of these historical developments. Evangelicals came to have "faith" in this method, in part because the method involved observation and analysis of data derived from immediate observation of God's world. (Yarhouse & Russell, 2006, p. 115)

By offering a critique of postmodernism, we are not suggesting that Christians uncritically embrace modernism. But it may be helpful to recall that there is a certain familiarity with modernism that many evangelicals share, and that there has not been the same historical familiarity with postmodernism. Indeed, it is an area for potential integration from a Christian worldview, but it is one that may involve some risks (Grenz, 1996).

Christians can recognize, for example, that the relativism and pluralism that emerged in late modernity was individualistic (Grenz, 1996) and that the unique expression of relativistic pluralism that has been associated with postmodernism is related to local communities. For the Christian, however, this expression of relativism falls short of a Christian understanding of a world created and cared for by God. Christians can stand against postmodern philosophical assumptions that call into question whether truth exists and can be known, as well as the call to replace the authority of science (found in modernism) with the authority of personal narrative. The Christian can value a critical examination of how personal bias can influence science, and such a critique can lead to humility with respect to the scientific endeavor while at the same time affirming that God made this world and that he acts in this world. Furthermore, God created human beings and gave them the faculties to experience this world and to come to some level of knowledge and understanding of his creation.

So while we recognize problems with positions that uncritically embrace postmodernism and the attending philosophical assumptions, we see the potential value in some of the therapeutic models and approaches to interacting with individuals in a family context and with families themselves.

We appreciate the concern raised by narrative family therapists that therapists may misuse their position and power in the therapeutic relationship. We value the move toward collaborative partnerships in identifying the presenting concern and mapping out a treatment plan to address the many issues that arise. We are also drawn to the idea of multiple accounts, perspective-taking, and the many meanings that come out of telling and retelling one's story. Again, this can be a helpful corrective to approaches that treat the therapist as the "expert" and exclusive holder of "truth" on the family's presenting concerns. At the same time, we do want to value the training, education, and clinical experience that therapists bring to their work with families.

Also, we see value in organizing experience and giving it meaning. Overall, we prefer a more collaborative approach to therapy and the intrinsic respect shown to families. However, the model itself can come across as politically correct and can run the risk of being clinically neglectful of the need for the therapist's expertise and leadership (Nichols & Schwartz, 2006).

There are additional implications to endorsing a model or theory that is more political. By positioning itself in an advocacy position, the question comes up, why are some approaches "preferred"? Why prefer a specific form of feminism, for example, over other understandings of feminism or other ways of understanding male-female relationships? In terms of clinical applications, How would a narrative family therapist work with a conservative

Christian family who preferred and gave voice to a complementarian narrative that the family viewed as derived from Scripture?

Although they are not always explicit in their philosophical and theoretical commitments, narrative family therapists privilege individual and family stories over dominant cultural narratives or family therapist expertise because of their devotion to Foucault's view of language and power. They then draw on postmodernism to undercut any claims to universal or metanarrative truth. What they do not see is that they then assert that postmodernism is itself the "true" metanarrative that reduces all other claims to mere perspective, and they are free to privilege (but not argue for) particular discourses that fit their own political frame, such as marginalization.

This brings up our last concern with narrative family therapy. Narrative approaches, as an outgrowth of postmodernism, reduce Christianity to *mere* narrative, as though it were one of many voices clamoring to be heard in an open forum. From this understanding, Christianity has no actual claim to truth. Although Christians may value perspective-taking, and we may recognize the past abuses and power plays made by those in hierarchical positions of influence, we may frame the concerns quite differently.

For example, in our understanding of integrating science and religion, we take the position that there is a real world out there, one that can be known (see Jones & Yarhouse, 2000). Postmodernism makes meaningful dialogue between science and religion difficult because the authority of science (not to mention religion) has been challenged, and the emphasis today is put on personal narratives, stories that can be true for one person and not for another. The position we endorse is critical realism, the view that there is a real world out there and that it is possible to know and study it (*realism*). But we recognize that the theories we hold, including our religious beliefs and values, color our capacity to know the world we study (*critical* realism). So we may have to be humble in our assumptions and declarations, showing our need to rely on God's direction, including what we can learn about God and this world through natural revelation (e.g., science) and special revelation (Scripture).

***Model of family dysfunction and family functioning.*** The model of family dysfunction is located in dominant narratives that become problematic for the family. However, the narrative family therapist is to avoid judgments about what constitutes normal family functioning (Dickerson, 2013, 2014; Nichols & Schwartz, 2006).

What is interesting about narrative family therapy is that there is no explicit model of family functioning. As with judgments about what constitutes normal family functioning, the narrative family therapist is to avoid judgments about what is abnormal family functioning. Recall that narrative family therapists disapprove of both diagnostic labels and many systemic concepts, preferring to discuss narrative rather than systems or patterns, which, in their way of thinking, reflects a commitment to structuralism that they reject.

A Christian critique of this understanding of family dysfunction and family function must call into question an approach that has so little to say about what is normal and abnormal. While there is much to be gained from hearing family members and honoring local knowledge and unique stories, much is lost by failing to cast a vision of the kind of family and family relationship that might be gained through the course of therapy. And this has to be intentional, at least to some extent.

Robert Roberts (1997), in his chapter on the "parameters of a Christian psychology," discusses several basic structures related to human nature that are relevant to narrative family therapy. Roberts argues that there is no such thing as basic human edification but only Rogerian edification, Jungian edification, rational-emotive edification, Freudian edification, varieties of family systems

## INTEGRATIVE FOCUS: Family Functioning

Although there is not an emphasis on the rules that govern family functioning à la structural family theory, narrative therapists would focus on dominant stories that may influence how people in the family relate to one another.

How is family functioning improved by a narrative understanding of the family? As with solution-focused family therapy, a positive we see with narrative is an emphasis on family strengths. Identifying unique outcomes by considering when a family has been successful or shows resilience brings what might be in the background of the family to the foreground.

*Think about it:* Can you think about ways in which you have seen either your family or another family deal with challenges effectively? When you have seen this, what would you say are the family strengths that were evident at that time? If that family were to go through another crisis, what would you see as the potential benefits of that unique family memory of resilience?

edification, and Christian edification. Each edification is structurally similar in some ways, but they contain discontinuities and mutual inconsistencies.

According to Roberts (1997), psychologies edify by saying something about personhood that explains why we are the way we are, as well as provide us with a call to shape our personality so that it is different from or even better than what we are at present. Most provide some methods for moving from "here" to "there" that we call "techniques." We will discuss narrative therapy techniques below, but what Roberts says of human nature is that human beings have basic structures, and one of these is "verbiverousness." Human beings are verbivores: we eat and digest words about ourselves. We come to know who we are by virtue of the stories, the categories, the metaphors, and explanations we use to construe ourselves (to see ourselves in a certain sort of way). It is because we are verbivores, according to Roberts, that the psychologies have an "edifying" effect on us. "They provide diagnostic schemata, metaphors, and ideals for us to feed upon in our hearts, in terms of which our personalities may be shaped into one kind of maturity or another" (1997, p. 81).

So we might ask, what are the "words" a narrative therapy approach is using to feed the hunger of clients? In a very real sense the words have to do with the family finding within itself what is needed to function properly. But while it serves to deconstruct dominant narratives, it does so with little by way of vision for what the individual in the family or the family itself is to move toward.

There is nothing specifically valued in narrative approaches to the family, save the act of identifying and giving voice to local knowledges. What we appreciate about this emphasis on local knowledges in narrative family therapy is how this can cultivate a kind of cultural humility that is necessary in clinical practice (see Kim, Prouty, & Roberson, 2012). It seems to lend itself to serving underserved populations in a way that is respectful and collaborative. We see this as sorely needed. But questions do arise in the assumptions behind postmodernism and poststructuralism: Does a family have any guarantee that accessing local knowledges will be a more reliable guide to living than the dominant narratives that currently inform their individual and family identities? By questioning these assumptions, we are concerned with the "standpoint epistemology" that is evidenced in narrative family theory. That is, by virtue of one's standpoint as oppressed or victimized or marginalized, one has ways of knowing that are more accurate or are superior to existing ways of knowing. But for the Christian, both the oppressed and the oppressor, both the victim and the victimizer, need to look outside of themselves for meaning and direction.

In this sense narratives do not exist to be deconstructed when they are unhelpful, reflecting a kind of subjective pragmatism. Rather, narratives ought to be evaluated against those words, stories, scripts, and narratives that are more fundamental to what it means to be human and to be in relationship to one another and to God.

But Christianity, too, sees the individual in the family and the family as a whole as inseparable from narrative, as it were. But the narrative is not one of many influencing forces; rather, the narrative is the Christian grand narrative—that is, the kingdom of heaven. There is a whole literature on the idea of a Christian grand narrative. For example, Olson has provided a historical overview of Christian theology in narrative perspective (Olson, 1999). Other scholars include George Lindbeck, Stanley Hauerwas (1981), L. Gregory Jones (Hauerwas & Jones, 1997), Michael Goldberg (2001), Kevin Vanhoozer (2005), William Willimon, and Charles Gerkin (1984, 1986, 1997), who has written extensively on pastoral care, often from a narrative perspective.

The scholarship of C. S. Lewis can offer important insight into how a Christian therapist or Christian thinker might understand the idea of story and narrative as it relates to the therapeutic process. In the *Voyage of the* Dawn Treader, Lewis describes Lucy as she reads the magician's book; she becomes captivated by the "spell that refreshes the soul." To her, "it reads more like a story than a spell," and she discovers that it is the great story through which all other stories are judged (Lewis, 1952, p. 157). Lewis, through the character of Lucy, is communicating his views, articulated elsewhere in his essays "On Stories" (1982) and "The Weight of Glory" (1980), on the power of narrative. To Lewis, we are always using story to "get in"—that is, to find ourselves and find relationship with the great story: the myth that is true. Lewis, whose passion was the study of literary myths, believed that myths held their place because they contained transcendent truths, especially truths about good and evil and human redemption.

There was one great story—the biblical narrative that was not just mythically true but historically true. It is the human metastory through which all other narratives have meaning. From Lewis we learn that all narrative has significance because they draw us to the great story. Likewise, the great story has relevance in the unfolding of our personal and family narratives. All

Christian counseling and therapy can be seen as narrative in that the counselor will be helping the family integrate the intertwined stories of individual members with the great story of redemption.

What identity is thought to emerge from a narrative understanding of the family? Christians can share the reservations narrative family therapists have about diagnostic labels, especially if they reduce an individual or truncate his or her personhood by framing the person as pathology. Christians might be drawn to writing a resilient family identity based on previously overlooked family strengths.

*Think about it:* Think about your own family. What narrative threads would you say characterize your family? What are some things that reflect positively on your family? How have members of your family been born into an existing narrative based on culture, religion, or national origin? How would you characterize your family identity in a word or short phrase?

*Techniques in family therapy.* In terms of practical considerations or the outworking of the philosophical and theoretical assumptions, as well as the model of dysfunction and family functioning, a number of critiques of narrative family therapy have emerged in the literature (e.g., Minuchin, 1998). They tend to address some of the implications of postmodern assumptions and perspective-taking. Most of the critiques are not from a distinctively Christian perspective, but they raise concerns that many Christians might share. For example, to what extent does externalizing the problem detract from a client taking responsibility for his or her part in it? We would want to distinguish between a technique that enables an individual or family to have success in dealing with a concern, such as anger, and an approach that, by virtue of making anger into a something that is "out there," one is no longer responsible for what one does with one's anger or for what we can contribute to the cultivation of qualities and character traits in our lives that either express or curb our anger.

An additional concern raised by Minuchin (1998) has to do with whether the family is lost in narrative family therapy. Put differently, in narrative family therapy the focus is on the language and narrative of each family member to the exclusion of the patterns of relationship between family members. A related concern is that the family itself is somewhat suspect, as "family" is a linguistic construct fashioned by society and carries with it implications that are imposed from a dominant societal narrative.

We like the emphasis here on the individual—family system approaches can simply shift the discussion away from the individual and relocate it on the family instead. In a sense, an approach that can address individual concerns and perspective-taking can be a valuable resource in therapy. However, our reservation is that this may be done so rigidly, with blind acceptance of the view that there is nothing to be gained by examining family relationships and patterns. Similarly, we view "family" not as merely a linguistic construct used in power plays by those who write and live the dominant narrative; rather, the family, while it comes in many forms and is itself fallen, still reflects something intended by God and is good for human relationships.

An additional concern is that as narrative family therapy deconstructs dominant narratives, the ultimate end is to help a family become the narrator of its own story. We can certainly support the family in questioning dominant narratives that essentially constrain the family from more meaningful and health-promoting ways. At the same time, there is a point of diminishing returns if individuals in the family or the family as a whole turns to its own experiences to narrate their own story. Listening for a person's voice can take a person only so far. It reminds us of the way C. S. Lewis critiqued the assumption within humanism that people do well to listen to their instincts to determine what is right or wrong: "Telling us to obey instinct is like telling us to obey 'people.' People say different things: so do instincts. Our instincts are at war" (Lewis, 1962, p. 48).

From a Christian perspective, individuals within the family and families themselves can look outside of themselves for information on the way they are supposed to be and relate. Of course, this too can be abused, as when more dependent persons rely too much on external authorities who abuse their position of influence. But the point we are making is that creating one's own sense of right and wrong can be equally misguided.

## CONCLUSION

We are intrigued by the idea of helping people and families seek congruence. This is often thought of in terms of *organismic* congruence, which is based

again on the assumption that the organism and its impulses function as a reliable guide for how one ought to live (American Psychological Association,
2009). This is a common assumption in the mental health fields. But Christians have historically valued *telic* congruence, which refers to one's values and
strivings and connecting one's decisions about how one lives to transcendent
reality and purposes. While narrative theory might well reject a Christian
grand narrative as a reference point for telic congruence, narrative therapists
would, in theory, support beliefs and values and an underlying personal
agency to help a Christian move toward "what they give value to in life" (White,
2007, p. 103).

What family identity is thought to emerge from a narrative understanding
of the family? Narrative family therapy, much like solution-focused
family therapy, is going to focus on family resilience and strength. By
identifying "unique outcomes," the narrative family therapist begins to
identify moments that reflect a possible counternarrative that eventually contrasts significantly with the dominant-problem narrative. Family
relationships, then, can be enhanced by intentionally moving away
from problem stories of family members or of the family as a whole.

Narrative family therapists remind Christian family therapists of the
potential abuses associated with reductionistic approaches to using
diagnostic labels. The person is not pathology, and narrative therapists challenge us to expand our view of the family to see beyond any
specific diagnoses.

*Think about it:* Take some time to think about your own family. Can
you identify ways in which people relate to one another in reference
to a larger narrative that you share together? What would you say is
the story of your family so far? Can you divide the story into chapters?
What names would you give each chapter? What do these chapter ti-
tles say to you about your family identity?

It was mentioned above that one of the central critiques of postmodernism
is to call into question any claims to knowledge that are situated external to
the individual. When it comes to the practice of family therapy, we assert that
truth about the family exists and is accessible to us, at least to some extent. We

believe this to be true in part because God made this world and created us with the capacity to know it. What we do here is related in meaningful ways to transcendent reality. We also recognize and affirm the importance of perspective-taking and the idea that one person's understanding of the concerns that bring the family in for therapy may not be the same as the concerns articulated by others in the family.

Furthermore, because of the historical prominence of Christianity, narrative therapy approaches have tended to see it as a dominant narrative that has been unhelpful to people by virtue of being a major religion with prescriptive and proscriptive dimensions that affect people's lives. Christianity, as an authority, can be deconstructed by those who see it as suspect so that the unhelpful scripts that are written in the name of that particular religion can be rewritten.

But we also believe that Christianity can be a narrative in a helpful sense of that word. It can be a story that is true and one that has significant implications in people's lives. More than that, we affirm that Christianity is not merely a narrative but the grand narrative and source of ultimate truth, even if we only come to approximate that truth in our understanding and outworking of our faith.

## REFERENCES

American Psychological Association (2009). *Report of the Task Force on Appropriate Therapeutic Responses to Sexual Orientation.* Retrieved from http://www.apa.org/pi/lgbt/resources/therapeutic-response.pdf.

Barry, D. (1997). Telling changes: From narrative family therapy to organizational change and development. *Journal of Organizational Change Management, 10*(1), 30-46.

Becvar, D. S., & Becvar, R. J. (2006). *Family therapy: A systemic integration* (6th ed.). Boston: Allyn & Bacon.

Chang, J., & Nylund, D. (2013). Narrative and solution-focused therapies: A twenty-year retrospective. *Journal of Systemic Therapies, 32*(2), 73-88.

Dickerson, V. (2013). Patriarchy, power, and privilege: A narrative/poststructural view of work with couples. *Family Process, 52*(1), 102-14.

Dickerson, V. (2014). The advance of poststructuralism and its influence on family therapy. *Family Process, 53*(3), 401-14.

Gergen K. J. (1999). *An invitation to social construction.* Thousand Oaks, CA: Sage Publications.

Gergen, K. J. (2001). Psychological science in a postmodern context. *American Psychologist*, 56(10), 803-13.

Gerkin, C. (1984). *Living human document: Revisioning pastoral counseling in a hermeneutical mode*. Nashville: Abingdon.

Gerkin, C. (1986). Faith and praxis: Pastoral counseling's hermeneutical problem. *Pastoral Psychology*, 35, 3-15.

Gerkin, C. (1997). *An introduction to pastoral care*. Nashville: Abingdon.

Goldberg, M. (2001). *Theology and narrative: A critical introduction*. Eugene, OR: Wipf & Stock.

Grenz, S. (1996). *A primer on postmodernism*. Grand Rapids: Eerdmans.

Hauerwas, S. (1981). *A community of character*. Notre Dame, IN: University of Notre Dame Press.

Hauerwas, S., & Jones, L. G. (1997). *Why narrative? Readings in narrative theology*. Eugene, OR: Wipf & Stock.

Jones, S. L., & Yarhouse, M. A. (2000). *Homosexuality: The use of scientific research in the church's moral debate*. Downers Grove, IL: InterVarsity Press.

Kim, H., Prouty, A. M., & Roberson, P. N. E. (2012). Narrative therapy with inter-cultural couples: A case study. *Journal of Family Psychotherapy*, 23, 27-86.

Lewis, C. S. (1952). *Voyage of the Dawn Treader*. New York: HarperCollins.

Lewis, C. S. (1962). *The abolition of man*. New York: Scribner.

Lewis, C. S. (1980). *The weight of glory*. New York: HarperCollins.

Lewis, C. S. (1982). *On stories, and other essays on literature*. New York: Harcourt.

Madigan, S. (2011). *Narrative therapy*. Washington, DC: American Psychological Association.

Minuchin, S. (1998). Where is the family in narrative family therapy? *Journal of Marital and Family Therapy*, 24, 397-403.

Nichols, M. P., & Schwartz, R. C. (2006). *Family therapy: Concepts and methods* (7th ed.). Boston: Allyn & Bacon.

Nichols, M. P., & Skowron, E. (2006). *Instructor's manual and test bank, Family therapy: Concepts and methods* (7th ed.). Boston: Allyn & Bacon.

Olson, R. E. (1999). *The story of Christian theology: Twenty centuries of tradition and reform*. Downers Grove, IL: IVP Academic.

Piercy, F. P., Sprenkle, D. H., Wetchler, J. L., & associates. (1996). *Family therapy sourcebook* (2nd ed.). New York: Guilford Press.

Roberts, R. (1997). Parameters of a Christian psychology. In R. C. Roberts & M. R. Talbot (Eds.), *Limning the psyche* (pp. 74-101). Grand Rapids: Eerdmans.

Vanhoozer, K. J. (2005). *The drama of doctrine: A canonical-linguistic approach to theology*. Louisville, KY: Westminster John Knox.

White, M. (2007). *Maps of narrative practice.* New York: W. W. Norton.

White, M., & Epston, D. (1989). *Literate means to therapeutic ends.* Adelaide, Australia: Dulwich Centre Publications.

White, M., & Epston, D. (1990). *Narrative means to therapeutic ends.* New York: W. W. Norton.

Yarhouse, M. A., & Russell, S. R. (2006). Evangelicalism. In E. T. Dowd & S. L. Nielsen (Eds.), *Exploration of the psychologies in religion* (pp. 111-26). New York: Springer.

Zimmerman, J. L., & Dickerson, V. L. (1994). Using a narrative metaphor: Implications for theory and clinical practice. *Family Process, 33*(3), 233-45.

# TOWARD AN
# INTEGRATIVE CHRISTIAN
# FAMILY THERAPY

*If you read history you will find that the Christians
who did most for the world were precisely those who
thought most of the next. It is since Christians have
largely ceased to think of the other world that
they have become so ineffective in this.*

**C. S. LEWIS**

IN THIS CLOSING CHAPTER of part two, we consider the
ways in which we might begin to develop an integrative Christian
family therapy. Several theorists have attempted to bring together
the best of what has been offered by first-generation models of
family therapy. This is essentially an extension of the discussions
we had in most of the previous chapters about how early first-
generation models are being either practiced today or folded into
more contemporary manifestations in the clinical service delivery.

In addition to the various contemporary manifestations discussed in each specific chapter, one approach we see among
second-generation family therapists is the blending of important
theoretical contributions of first-generation models of family
therapy. For example, William Pinsof developed *Integrative
Problem-Centered Therapy*, which draws on object relations and

self psychology as well as an appreciation for the role of biology in setting the stage for individuals.

Another example of a blending approach is *Narrative Solutions Therapy* by Joseph Eron and Thomas Lund. This approach draws on the theoretical assumptions found in narrative approaches (see chap. 11) as well as some of the practical interventions that anchor solutions approaches to family therapy.

*Integrative Couple Therapy* by Neil Jacobson and Andrew Christensen draws on even more first-generation approaches, such as transgenerational, object relations, strategic, and experiential models, and these are brought together with Jacobson's classic behavioral couples therapy with its emphasis on communication training and problem solving.

In addition to the blending of first-generation models, we have also seen some innovative models that have explored often-neglected areas of inquiry among family therapists. For example, a particularly interesting approach is *Internal Family Systems Therapy* developed by Richard Schwartz. It is particularly innovative because it applies systems theory to the internal processes of the mind.

We have also seen second-generation models of family therapy that try to organize several themes from first-generation models into broader, more manageable categories for conceptualization and intervention. For example, Patterson, Williams, Grauf-Grounds, and Chamow (1998) help new therapists organize the many first-generation models of family therapy into four major approaches: *historical, process, structural,* and *experiential.* Examples of historical approaches include Bowenian and psychoanalytic, while process approaches include cognitive-behavioral and strategic approaches. Similarly, structural approaches refer to structural family therapy, while experiential approaches include experiential and narrative approaches to family therapy.

Another attempt to organize themes from first-generation models into a coherent approach is *Metaframeworks* by Breunlin, Schwartz, and Kune-Karrer (1997). Breunlin and colleagues assess and intervene with reference to six overarching frameworks: *sequences, organization, culture, gender, development,* and *internal family systems.* The six frameworks are *meta*-frameworks because they are considered overarching systems concepts that capture the essentials of the first generation of systems theories.

So the idea of pulling various aspects of first-generation approaches together into a more complex model is nothing new. But rather than follow attempts to do so, we are interested in whether a Christian integrative family therapy can reflect dimensions of the first-generation approaches that are consistent with a Christian understanding of family.

## CASTING A VISION: CAN THERE BE A
## DISTINCTIVE CHRISTIAN FAMILY THERAPY?

Readers may question whether there is such a thing as Christian family therapy or, if it exists, what makes a family therapy distinctively Christian. Is it the therapist? Is a family therapy Christian when it is conducted by a Christian? There will be some who would say so, keeping in mind comparable examples, such as how feminist family therapy is feminist by virtue of the therapist who conducts the therapy. The clients need not be feminist for the therapist to be a feminist and to practice a therapy that values, for example, egalitarianism rather than complementarian marital relationships.

Others may view family therapy as Christian when the therapist and the family identify themselves as Christians. Whether they ever talk explicitly about their faith may be less relevant to the presenting concern, but they both recognize that they share a common Christian faith that could be referenced if appropriate.

Still others might look not to the family but to the therapy. They might want to know what happens in therapy to determine if the process and values by which therapy is guided is Christian in some meaningful way.

We can recognize the potential value in identifying as Christian a family therapy that is facilitated by a Christian or with Christians or with reference to Christian themes and commitments. In this section we will explore some of what it might mean to practice intentionally as a Christian with reference to Christian commitments, recognizing that there are certainly other viable ways of thinking about Christian family therapy. Also, these themes and commitments are tentative and preliminary—not the final word on the subject but part of an opening dialogue we hope others in the field will pick up and expound on.

## FIRST-GENERATION APPROACHES REVISITED

We mentioned earlier that many second-generation approaches to family therapy have creatively brought together insights from a number of first-generation approaches. Now we want to consider how a Christian might enter into the discussions that are occurring about family theory to identify points of intersection for the Christian interested in integration of the various family theories with a Christian worldview.

In order to talk about a Christian view of family therapy, it may be helpful to first recognize the defining assumptions found in first-generation models of family therapy (table 12.1). We do this to illustrate that the first-generation theorists and therapists often identified important elements of family functioning and dysfunction that the Christian need not reinvent. Rather, the Christian is free to recognize insights wherever they are found and to consider ways in which they might be useful in developing a Christian approach to families in therapy.

Table 12.1. Defining assumptions and road maps in selected models of family therapy

| Model | Family Dysfunction | Family Functioning | Suggested Road Map |
|---|---|---|---|
| Bowenian | Emotional fusion | Differentiation of self | Process questions |
| Strategic | Communication patterns | Alternative patterns | Improved communication |
| Structural | Enmeshment/ faulty structure | Proper structure, leadership, clear boundaries | Enactments, boundaries |
| Psychodynamic/ Object Relations | Projective identification | Insight | Interpretation |
| Contextual | Destructive entitlement | Give and take | I-Thou |
| Experiential | Suppressed emotions | Authenticity, self-actualization | Authentic relationships |
| Solution-Focused | Talking about problems | Talking about solutions, doing more of what is working | Exceptions |
| Cognitive-Behavioral | Learned and reinforced thoughts and behaviors | Selected reinforcement and rational thoughts | Replace automatic thoughts, address schema, change behaviors |
| Narrative | Dominant narratives | Counternarratives, shared stories of identity | Unique outcomes, counternarrative |

We will then turn our attention to the potential value found in eclecticism in family therapy in particular. This discussion will lead us to a review of family dysfunction and family functioning and a discussion of techniques that might be used in family therapy.

Rather than commit themselves to any one specific model of family dysfunction and family functioning, many second- and third-generation family therapists are drawing on many different models, recognizing that each has tapped into something important and useful for some clinical presentations. What we recommend is that Christian family therapists treat the first-generation approaches as essentially ways of relating to a family that may be helpful to employ in a given clinical situation rather than a template that is simply applied to each and every family, as if faulty structure or suppressed emotions or dominant narratives could alone explain and be practically useful to each and every family presenting in therapy.

A metaphor for this recommendation is drawn from the telecommunications industry. The analogue technology used in establishing the telephone industry during the twentieth century remains one of the great human achievements. However, changes in economics, human need, and new technology have created a decline in landline communication technology. The knowledge from analogue communication remains fundamental to the field, but the demand for communication has so drastically changed the world of communication that the industry must adjust with new technologies to apply to the emerging market.

So also the corpus of knowledge that drives family therapy is under new demands from the changing of North American society and the emergence of family cultures worldwide. What must emerge for a Christian counselor dedicated to applying biblical truth to the social context of marriage and family is a revised eclecticism that holds the core tradition of Christianity as a constant and then intelligently considers the emerging theology contributions from scholarship and integrates it with the advancement of the mental health profession.

## APPROACHES TO ECLECTICISM

This brings us to the topic of responsible eclecticism. In one of the closing chapters of their book *Modern Psychotherapies*, Jones and Butman (1991) introduce the reader to the concept of "responsible eclecticism." They first contrast it with other approaches to eclecticism, and we would like to summarize that reading before discussing the idea of responsible eclecticism.

One approach to eclecticism is *chaotic eclecticism*. This is perhaps the approach that is often thought of when critics want to dismiss the idea of eclecticism altogether. It is "unsystematically throwing together a hodgepodge, 'syncretistic' approach to counseling" (Jones & Butman, 1991, p. 384). Thankfully, few clinicians in general appear to use this approach, and presumably this is true among family therapists as well, although we know of no systematic evaluation of this question in the empirical literature.

Another approach is that of *pragmatic eclecticism*. The pragmatism here rests in what works best for a specific client:

> It centers on the commitment to operate not out of theoretical preference, but out of what seems best for the client. Specifically, it means to use the methods that comparative outcome research has shown to work best with the problems manifested by the clients. (Jones & Butman, 1991, p. 384)

This approach is favored by many in the broader secular field of psychotherapy. It raises the question, however, of how effective psychotherapy is, and the research here has been mixed, with some approaches "within the major traditions [having] demonstrated a wide range of usefulness in treating a variety of psychopathologies" (pp. 384-85). This is even more so (or less so) the case in family therapy, where there are far fewer studies of what works best with whom.

A third approach discussed by Jones and Butman is that of *metatheoretical* or *transtheoretical eclecticism*. This approach "looks for a theory or practice behind or beyond the theory" (1991, p. 390). This might be the case among those who examine the capacity of a family therapist to connect well with a family or to build a working therapeutic alliance. Perhaps it is this and not a structural or strategic approach that makes the difference in working with a family. This is an attractive approach to eclecticism, to be sure, but it often fails to provide substantial evidence that the metatheory is itself real and the defining element in what makes family therapy successful.

A fourth approach is that of *theoretical integrationism*. In this approach a family therapist would have one model serve as the main road map while "reaching out beyond that theory to one or two other models which can, by assimilation of parts of the new approaches, help to expand and enrich the foundational approach" (Jones & Butman, 1991, p. 393).

Jones and Butman conclude that their preference at this time in terms of general approaches to psychotherapy is for *theoretical integrationism*. At the time of their writing, they recognized that there appear to be fewer obvious tensions for the Christian counselor with contemporary psychodynamic and cognitive-behavioral approaches to psychotherapy. We can certainly appreciate that decision as well as the complexities involved in deciding among approaches to various theories and even approaches to eclecticism.

We face a similar concern when we think about the various models of family therapy. But we also see some important differences in our discussion of responsible eclecticism. When we look at the models that inform family therapy, it is not as clear that these approaches are the best primary road maps for family therapy or that theoretical integrationism is the best approach to eclecticism in family therapy as such. We would certainly support the Christian family therapist who could identify with a first-generation approach as their primary road map and then draw in one or two other approaches in a meaningful way that would enhance and enrich the services they were providing through that primary map. However, the first-generation approaches to family therapy have evolved and matured into second-generation approaches in ways that were not accounted for at the time *Modern Psychotherapies* was first written. And the changes in the field of family therapy do not mirror the changes in the broader field of psychotherapy.

In addition, family therapy has not historically relied on a broad theory of personality but competing views of the family and interesting techniques and strategies for making families function better. So the family therapies cast a vision for how family members are to relate, but rather than think of one model as capturing an exclusive vision for the family, we see the first generation as providing insights into facets of family life, such as communication, patterns of interaction, emotional expressiveness, and boundaries. They leave a vacuum of sorts for a broader vision for the family, which is why we see specific, value-laden models of the family, such as feminist family therapy. Feminist family therapists cast a vision for how family members are to relate. They reference an overarching valuing of certain ideological commitments. This vacuum leaves room for the Christian to cast a vision for family functioning and relationships that reflect the commitments Christians might hold with respect to the family.

## TOWARD AN INTEGRATIVE CHRISTIAN FAMILY THERAPY

We appreciate efforts to identify common themes among first-generation family therapy models. We encourage Christian family therapists to move in a similar direction but to do so with reference to the three major extensions of how individuals come to image God: functioning, relationships, and identity (see chap. 1).[1]

We have seen throughout the last several chapters of part two that each model of family therapy suggests how families ought to function. This prescription can be either implicit or explicit, but each model suggests a map for how to get from how the family presently functions to how it ought to function through involvement in family therapy.

In our experience, family functioning is typically the first thing that is assessed when meeting with a family. The family is in some way not functioning as it could, and this failure is evidenced in the symptoms often discussed at intake. The first question often asked in family therapy—What brings you in to see me today?—is likely to elicit a response focused on symptoms that reflect a problem with proper functioning.

As we begin to explore the possibility of an integrative Christian family therapy, we want the reader to be aware of what each model has to say about family functioning and to begin to identify resources from each model that might be brought to bear on any particular case in which family functioning is a primary concern.

In addition to family functioning, we also considered what each model of family therapy has to say about family relationships. Some models emphasize improving family relationships, while others see these improvements as a by-product of improved functioning. As a reminder, when we discuss family relationships, we are talking about how family members relate to one another, and each model of family therapy posits how family members ought to relate. Again, this can be implicit or explicit.

Before we turn to a discussion of family identity, we want to first highlight ways in which family functioning and family relationships are emphasized in the various models of family therapy discussed in part one of this book.

---

[1]As we mentioned in chapter 1, we would like to acknowledge the work of Mark McMinn and Clark Campbell, whose book *Integrative Psychotherapy* (Downers Grove, IL: IVP Academic, 2007) helped us to organize our thinking around the three themes of function, identity, and relationship as an extension of the themes they developed of function, structure, and relationship as aspects of the *imago Dei*.

Table 12.2 organizes some of the ways in which the models of family therapy emphasize function and relationships by suggesting which is the primary emphasis and which is the secondary emphasis. We can see that most of the early models of family therapy tended to emphasize family relationships and ways of relating or rules that covered relating—truly systemic considerations—and saw family functioning, with its emphasis on symptom reduction, as secondary. It was not that functioning was less important but that it was a byproduct of improved family relationships.

Each model addressed family relationships with different points of emphasis. For example, structural therapists focused on the rules that govern family relationships, organization, leadership, and boundaries among subsystems. These emphases addressed family relationships, and family functioning was thought to improve as a result. Contextual family therapists also focused on relationships, but they looked at relationships through a lens of mutuality, justice, and gratitude. Functioning was believed to improve if the relationships could be characterized by these qualities.

We see strategic family therapy as equally emphasizing as primary both family functioning and family relationships, and perhaps each of the various schools and theorists that constitute strategic family therapy will have their own particular emphasis.

Later models, such as narrative family therapy, tend to focus less on functioning or relationships and more on a broader narrative out of which symptoms would then be reduced and relationships improved. This is why we see narrative theory as treating both functioning and relationships as secondary—they both appear to be deemphasized in favor of locating the family within a plot or narrative that provides meaning. Both family functioning and family relationships are believed to improve once a counternarrative emerges from the work in family therapy.

We also discussed throughout part two of the book that the family provides individuals with definition and identity. The family provides individuals with a sense for who they are and what matters in this world.

As we turn to a discussion of an integrative Christian family therapy, we want to begin with the notion that this idea of ordering the world and providing a sense of definition and identity is fundamental to any type of therapy. This has been discussed extensively in critiques of various models of psychotherapy (e.g., Roberts, 1993; Jones & Butman, 1991). The same is true in the models of family therapy.

Table 12.2. Emphases placed on functioning and relationships within models
of family therapy

| Model of Family Therapy | Family Functioning | Family Relationships |
|---|---|---|
| Bowenian | Secondary emphasis, functioning as a byproduct of differentiation of self | Primary emphasis, differentiation of self as both interpersonal and intrapersonal experience |
| Strategic | Primary emphasis, focus on patterns and sequences of relating which directly affect functioning | Primary emphasis, focus on patterns and sequences in family relationships |
| Structural | Secondary emphasis, functioning as a byproduct of effective leadership/ organization, boundaries, subsystems | Primary emphasis, leadership/organization, clear boundaries among subsystems |
| Psychodynamic | Secondary emphasis, functioning as a byproduct of healthy attachment | Primary emphasis, intrapersonal focus, intimacy in relationships |
| Contextual | Secondary emphasis, functioning as a byproduct of justice/fairness | Primary emphasis, mutuality, justice, fairness in relationships |
| Experiential | Secondary emphasis, functioning as a byproduct of authentic relationships | Primary emphasis, authenticity in interpersonal relationships |
| Solution-Focused | Primary emphasis, focus on exceptions to identify family strengths | Secondary emphasis, improved relationships as a byproduct of improved functioning |
| Cognitive-Behavioral | Primary emphasis, reinforcement of behavior, symptom reduction, improved functioning | Secondary emphasis, improved relationships as a byproduct of improved functioning |
| Narrative | Secondary emphasis, functioning as a byproduct of a developed counternarrative | Secondary emphasis, relationships as a byproduct of a developed counternarrative |

## CASTING A VISION: THE CHRISTIAN FAMILY THERAPY IMAGE FOR FAMILY AND FAMILY THERAPY

Can you recall Harold Hill enticing the good townsfolk of River City, Iowa, in the musical *The Music Man*? In order to separate them from their money, he needed both a crisis and a solution. The crisis was that their children were being led into moral decadence by such seedy influences as a pool hall and drug store novels. He sang, "You got Trouble with a capital T, that rhymes with P, and that stands for Pool." His "solution" was to cast a vision for the family that the River City community could embrace. He persuaded the naturally suspicious Iowans that a boys' band would protect their young ones from the lure of debauchery. In the twenty-first century there is little need to persuade parents of the dangers that could harm their children. Today's parents have greater sophistication in identifying solutions and protections; few would be tricked into the "seventy-six trombones" remedy. Many parents today rely on the mental health profession to research, theorize, and educate the public as to the best means to guard families from calamity and harm. To accomplish this comprehensively, we believe that counselors, secular and Christian, must embrace a vision for the role that the institution of marriage and family is to play within the culture. Bettelheim (1987) and Elkind (1994, 2001) are examples, among many, of family researchers who have illuminated the path for parents and professionals to travel by recommending a vision of experiences that shape relational quality.

Therapists are not limited to the clinician's office; they also serve as active change agents through researching, teaching, preaching, modeling, and administrating social and institutional policy that shape the form and function of family life. Clinicians have a professional, moral, and ethical obligation to not only understand the repair process for couples and families but to have an internalized vision as to what is possible in regard to family relationships. Just as a physician carries the obligation to guide a patient toward individual health, so the family therapist should have a conceptual model for healthy relational functioning within marriage and family structures. Toward this end the Christian tradition can make an explicit contribution to the profession because, like many other faith traditions, it is possible to build a model of purpose and function for marriage and for the family from the corpus of Scripture and theology that would be widely accepted by Christendom as a whole.

We see Christian family counseling as being influential in three areas of family life because of the message and themes of the Christian tradition. They correspond with the three integrative themes we have been emphasizing so far of *functioning, relationship,* and *identity.* These are (1) to help devise strategies that curtail destructive behaviors to individuals or the system (functioning), (2) to assist the system by facilitating restoration or reconciliation when destructive actions have caused a breach in the relational space between its members (relationship), and (3) to support the system in prompting the growth or development of its members (identity). Each of these three purposes contains specific components that are explicitly Christian, and each should be considered individually.

**Purpose one: Marriage and family development and the Christian family therapist.** Garland (1999) defines family as "the organization of relationships that endure over time and contexts through which persons attempt to meet their needs for belonging and attachment and to share life purposes, help and resources" (p. 39). There is little argument that families develop in their capacity to meet one another's needs to belong, attach, and to share life purpose. These are not innate skills. Rather, they grow, develop, and mature through plan and intention.

Family therapists knowledgeable in human growth and development play an important role in transmitting knowledge regarding how children develop into capable, interdependent adults who can assume needed roles in the society. Within the therapeutic process, they assist parents with the challenge of helping children acquire the necessary life skills. Skills such as managing emotions, directing cognition, and problem solving are part of the routine of the family therapist. But there is more.

While Christian family therapists carry the same moral obligation as other professionals trained to assist families in maximizing their potential within the society, they also carry an obligation to assist parents in becoming models and training their children to both know themselves and to know God. Knowledge of self and knowledge of God are core components of Christian theology. In his treatise of Christian doctrine, *Institutes of the Christian Religion,* Calvin asserts in chapter one the bidirectional reality that without knowledge of self, there can be no knowledge of God; and without knowledge of God, there can be no knowledge of self. Then in chapter two Calvin states that the result of knowing both God and self is *piety.* He argues that knowing

God and knowing self leads one toward reverence and love of God because we grasp the benefit of relationship.

The Christian family therapist is in a unique position to interface the body of knowledge regarding individual human growth and development with the Christian objective of maturity or piety. Balswick and Balswick (1999) state,

> The typical nuclear family in the United States is a partial community at best. It is plundered on one side by demands and intrusions of mass society and on the other by an individualism which has become increasingly narcissistic. What is needed most is a recapturing of the biblical tradition of what it means to be a family. (p. 352)

The statement "what it means to be a family" has little to do with family structure—that is, married parents with a working father and a stay-at-home mother, or a single-parent home, or grandparents as parents—and more to do with what the internal characteristics of a healthy home are. These characteristics are the biblical pictures of God's character exhibited through human relationship—grace, justice, integrity, truthfulness, fidelity, reliability, mercy, discipline, devotion, love, and so forth. Here the Christian family counselor can represent and advocate a model of being for families that the culture has limited. Toward this end, Fincham, Stanley, and Beach (2007, p. 281) write, "Religion has the apparent potential to help couples build marital intimacy, stimulate companionship, and perhaps offer unique cognitive and behavioral resources for couples dealing with marital stressors. Indeed, religion provides one domain in which the concept of transformation is fundamental and meaningful."

*Purpose two: The Christian counselor assists families in curtailing destructive behaviors.* Ask almost any person about what they think counselors do, and the most likely answer is "They help people with problems." Indeed, the "with problems" has been the primary focus of the mental health profession. Pathology, symptoms, dysfunction, and disorder are the terms of the trade. The construct of problem has evolved within each therapeutic tradition. For example, in the dynamic therapies, the problem is intrapsychic; in strategic therapies, the problem is communication; and in the narrative approaches, the problem is the problem—circumstances existing outside of any individual.

For the Christian family therapist, the understandings from each tradition are useful in building effective interventions. However, there is another dimension of pathology that is not fully understood and therefore not utilized by the mainstream therapeutic traditions. Menninger's (1973) classic and controversial work *Whatever Became of Sin?* remains a crucial question for the Christian clinician working in family mental health. With dry humor he notes that American society apparently stopped sinning sometime after 1953. That was the last year that a US president mentioned the word *sin* as part of their proclamation on the National Day of Prayer. Instead, we have "shortcomings." Menninger argued then that there are components of human behavior that cannot be explained by intrapsychic conflict, affective repression, behavioral conditioning, or social modeling. Some behavior is attributed to intentional disregard for others in the pursuit of self-interest.

A central therapeutic role of Christian therapists is to address the effects of sin on the system and on individual development. Toward this end, Christian family counselors can address two common errors frequently made by families in regard to sin. The first error is to disregard the existence of sin as a factor in the family process. This mistake is common to the majority culture that may consider sin a social construct, a remnant from a previous era. The failure to recognize the existence of sin altogether is an important part of Menninger's argument, as well as Plantinga's (1997). Likewise, Howsepian writes, "In human beings sin is an impulse toward self-destruction. . . . It is an impulse that cuts us off from the very source of reality, from Him who is most real" (1997, p. 278).

A second mistake is to see sin as limited to a list of behaviors or activities—do's and don'ts. While we affirm that sin can be identified as discrete behaviors, family counselors can help families recognize that their goal as a healthy family is not just the removal of bad behaviors as a means of becoming a healthy, functional relational system. Seeing sin as a list of behaviors to eliminate, prevent, or be ashamed of lends itself to a legalistic Pelagian perspective that suggests we can and should try to raise perfect kids who don't sin if we just work hard enough at doing "everything right."

A contrary example—one that illustrates a mature understanding of sin and family functioning—is given by Niel Nielson, formerly the president of Covenant College, Lookout Mountain, Georgia. He has shared the experience of being nurtured into adulthood by the influence of his parents. He recalled his father saying to him and his brother, "I will never be surprised at anything you do . . . and I will never be ashamed." Dr. Nielson goes on to explain that his father

> understood the human condition well enough to realize what we are all capable of, but for the grace of God and the abiding presence of the Holy Spirit. He said that he had witnessed many parents who seemed embarrassed by their children's behavior, took it very personally and tried to make excuses for it. He believed instead that, while he could certainly be disappointed by our behavior, he should never be surprised or embarrassed by it—and he would therefore be able with God's help to walk alongside us through the most difficult situations. He would be our father and hold his head up high no matter what. (Niel Nielson, personal communication, May 14, 2007)

The Christian counselor working with families seeks to create an environment in which both our behavior and our character can be addressed within the community of family. Sin is caused by feeding on words or ideas that destroy the beauty of our personhood and corrode the bonds of trust and security with our kin. The Christian faith applied in a Christian family counseling setting pays regard to the seriousness of the family's capacity for self-destruction.

***Purpose three: To facilitate the restoration or reconciliation of family in relationship.*** The space between people becomes polluted by both accidental circumstances, deliberate acts of injustice, inconsideration, and sin. The Christian faith has as its central theme the act of forgiveness and reconciliation. If relationships are maintained over time, they are maintained because of their capacity to forgive, to let go of the right to retaliate, and their ability to reconcile, to rebuild a relationship after injury. Worthington states that "the central day-to-day skill of marital survival and growth is reconciliation" (Worthington, 1999, p. 128).

The mental health profession's affiliation with the ideas of forgiveness and reconciliation have historically been inconsistent, at times hostile, and then at other times, friendly (Sells & Hargrave, 1998). During the 1990s and through the first decade of the new millennium, forgiveness and reconciliation research and interventions have advanced dramatically (McCullough, Pargament, & Thoresen, 2000). Numerous theories have been advanced and interventions created to restore families from injury that have demonstrated themselves to be effective in family or relational intervention (Ferch, 1998; Finkel, Rusbult, Kumashiro, & Hannon, 2002; Freedman & Enright, 1996).

The Christian or religious influence of forgiveness research and intervention on family therapy permits the formation of a new depth, a new responsibility, and a new vulnerability to others in family (McCullough & Worthington, 1999; Pingleton, 1997; Worthington, 1999). The Christian tradition brings a unique dimension to the discussion and practice of family forgiveness and reconciliation. Forgiveness drawn from the Christian tradition has a distinctiveness that creates openness for restructuring relationships. In most contexts, forgiveness is applied to end something. It ends the fight. It provides closure to the injury. Yet within the Christian faith, forgiveness serves as a beginning. The forgiveness of sin through the work of Jesus introduces humanity to a new covenant, a new relationship with God. Likewise, forgiveness in its full dimension within families creates opportunities for new forms of family relationships to emerge.

The criticism of forgiveness is that it empowers the powerful to hurt and injure again, and again, and again. Such conduct has nothing to do with Christian forgiveness but is relational manipulation. Paul addresses this theme theologically in Romans 5. Just as one cannot sin with the intention of meriting more grace from God, in the same way one cannot seek forgiveness with the intention of continuing to cause harm. Forgiveness is a relational, bidirectional aspect of family and marriage restoration. It is to be conducted within the Christian tradition as a normal component of existence within community—as all of us are sinners who need to speak the truth in love, confess and receive confession, forgive and be forgiven, reconcile and be reconciled.

## INTEGRATIVE CHRISTIAN FAMILY THERAPY IN PRACTICE

The questions asked about identity have to do with what it means for that family to form a life together. We recommend that the Christian family therapist approach family therapy with an understanding that it is hard to discuss identity apart from functioning and relationships in therapy. What we do to address functioning and how we do that work with the family will contribute directly or indirectly to family identity. Similarly, what we do to address family relationships and how we do that work with the family will contribute directly or indirectly to family identity. So we will talk more about family identity considerations as foundational to any work being done with families in the areas of functioning and relationships.

We illustrate the relationship by showing that family identity considerations exist and are part of all of our clinical work, even if implicitly. In fact, family identity considerations are often implicit, with the primary focus of our work being family functioning, which tends to place more of an emphasis on symptom reduction, and family relationships, which can be a longer process of working out intrapersonal and interpersonal dynamics. So we locate family identity considerations as foundational in figure 12.1 by locating them "underneath" the family entering therapy. They include culture, gender, socioeconomic status, and other identity considerations, including a Christian identity and related worldview assumptions.

**Family Functioning**
→ Individual and systemic
→ Rules by which family members relate to one another
→ Patterns or sequences that reflect functioning

**Family Relationships**
→ Intrapersonal, interpersonal, and generational relationships
→ Developmental considerations (individual, relational, familial)

**Family Identity**
→ Culture, gender, religion, socioeconomic status, and so on
→ Definition, locating self in the world, worldview
→ Meaning, significance

Figure 12.1. Family functioning, relationships, and identity

It is unclear at this stage of our understanding of family therapy which issues are best addressed by which models. We are not prepared to say that divorce and remarriage should always be addressed first from a Bowenian perspective, or that trauma and grief are best approached from an experiential perspective. Rather, we look at the issue (e.g., trauma) and what has happened to the family, how various family members have responded and are affected, and what each model of family therapy brings to the clinical encounter.

In the case of trauma, identity considerations will be foundational insofar as a family considers over time how to make meaning out of a traumatic event and how to locate that experience within a broader framework that gives their family meaning and purpose. Family functioning may be an important starting point because it taps into symptom presentation and where a family may feel stuck in how they are responding to the event and in their exchanges

with one another. Over time, family relationships may become especially salient, and models that emphasize delving into the dynamics of those relationships may come to the foreground.

*Case example of a blended family.* Kevin and Karla Jefferson request family
therapy because of problems they are having in their family. They have been
married for the past five years. It is the second marriage for Karla. She had
been married previously and has a child, Jon, from that first marriage. Jon has
lived with his biological father for four years prior to his recent move to live
with his mother and her second husband. Jon had been having trouble relating
to his biological father and his new spouse. The conflicts they had concerned
his mother, who offered to take him in. Jon has now lived with his mother and
Kevin for the past year. Although they state that the first month or two were
reasonably calm, the past several months have been quite difficult. They are
coming to therapy because they view Jon as "rebellious" and "disrespectful,"
particularly to Kevin, who often takes a lead in setting limits and meting out
consequences. This gets Karla involved, because she experiences Kevin as
"domineering" and she feels quite "protective" of Jon when Kevin gets angry
about Jon's disrespectful and rebellious language and behavior.

The integrative Christian family therapist can begin by organizing what he
or she knows about this case by thinking about family functioning, relationships, and identity. The initial concerns having to do with family *functioning*
are present both in the rules and expectations for family functioning and in the
patterns of relating. For example, the family therapist could discuss how expectations for family chores are communicated, how compliance and non-
compliance are addressed, and so on. Also, the therapist could explore the sequence of interaction between Jon, Kevin, and Karla that leads to the kinds of
concerns that bring them in for therapy. Are there any times when the pattern is
interrupted? Are there times when Kevin or Karla relate to Jon more effectively?

The sequences also suggest some triangulation, which would be consistent
with a Bowenian understanding and reflects a concern for family *relationships*,
and this could be explored further. The family therapist could also explore the
quality of relationship between Kevin and Jon especially, as efforts to implement rules before establishing a foundational relationship may contribute
to the problem.

Family *identity* might focus on issues facing a blended family in which
members come together to form a new system, one that may struggle to realize

a coherent identity with a clear sense of how different members are located both within the family and within a broader community.

The integrative Christian family therapist would be free to intervene in a number of ways, drawing on techniques from a number of models of family therapy. But the decision to do so can be organized around the three aspects of functioning, relationships, and identity as well as what is most salient both in the family presentation and with respect to any of the specific models of family therapy.

*What does therapy look like?* We agree with Breunlin et al. (1997) that there is a general blueprint for actual family therapy practice. It involves the four stages of *hypothesizing* based on one's model, *planning* (relating, staging, creating events), *conversing* (statements, questions, directives), and *reading feedback* (recognizing how the family responds to the therapy conversation, what is working, what could be approached differently, and so on).

*Hypothesizing.* At the outset the family therapist seeks to understand the family or individual and identify possible constraints through the lens of integrative Christian family therapy. This means reflecting on family functioning and family relationships while keeping in mind the fundamental questions of family identity. These initial considerations are hypotheses, and so in a family therapy blueprint this stage is the hypothesizing stage (Breunlin et al., 1997). Family therapists will want to be open to seeing any specific hypothesis refuted, as these are initial considerations noted at the time of the intake and developed for consideration in a case staffing meeting or in consultation or supervision.

Hypothesizing from an integrative Christian family therapy perspective begins with a preliminary assessment based on the facts of the case at intake and in the first few sessions. This is followed by examination, through observation and questions, of family functioning around the presenting problem. The focus is typically on both the content (what is actually said) and the process of these sequences (who says what, when, what happens next—actions have meaning), which gives you more questions for assessment. Family therapists are then encouraged to ask questions that test the assessment so far and to ask open-ended questions that encourage the client/family to provide any additional information. In this sense assessment is generally not separate from therapy, and the family therapist continues to hypothesize throughout the course of therapy.

In the vast majority of cases, the issues addressed first in family therapy will reflect family functioning. Family functioning is often illustrated in patterns of how family members interact with one another. Solution-focused, strategic, and structural considerations each contribute something to tracking these exchanges. There are ways in which the family is not functioning properly, and these dysfunctions bring the family in to see the therapist. We illustrate this in figure 12.2 by showing it as the first main focal point. It is what is addressed early in session with the question, what is it that brings you in to see me today? Many early models offer resources for responding to problems in family functioning. We find that experienced family therapists often identify with one major model of family therapy (e.g., psychodynamic, strategic, Bowenian), but they feel they can draw on other models as needed, and this is determined often by the presenting concern, the length of time they have with the family, and what is most salient in the family presentation.

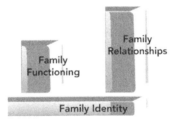

Figure 12.2. Functioning, relationships, and identity in clinical practice

*Planning.* Planning is what happens when the family therapist prepares for the session by considering what will actually happen in the fifty-minute hour. It involves but is not limited to simply relating to the family—having a real relationship with the family and taking an intentional posture with them (e.g., collaborative). It also involves constant mindfulness as to where the family therapist is in the course of therapy (early stages, mid-stage, or toward the end stage of therapy). Planning also refers to a plan to use specific interventions or techniques. The family therapist might be thinking of setting up a family sculpture or incorporating structural techniques such as unbalancing or role reversal.

*Conversing.* The third stage involves what actually happens in the session, at least in terms of what is said to the family or asked of specific individuals. This is called the *conversing* stage, in which the actual questions, directives, or statements communicate the planned actions from the previous stage (Breunlin et al., 1997).

*Reading feedback.* The conversing stage is followed by reading feedback, the last stage of the four-stage blueprint for family therapy. As the statements are made, questions asked, and planned interventions occur, the family therapist essentially "reads" the family's response to what is occurring in the session. This reading of individuals and of the family is data for holding up as either support for the hypotheses or as a challenge to the hypotheses. This data set is then taken back for additional hypotheses to be formed (or existing ones to be further adapted) and for planning purposes, and so the stages are played out again and again throughout the course of family therapy.

We agree with many second-generation family therapists and theorists that family therapists should be informed by a variety of approaches, not constrained by a priori commitments to only one particular model. Family therapists are then encouraged to utilize methods, interventions, and techniques drawn from a variety of models or schools of family therapy, as long as they are consistent with the presuppositions on which the larger integrative Christian family therapy perspective rests. By reflecting intentionally on family functioning, relationships, and identity, Christian family therapists can explore presenting problems both flexibly and systematically, which is what seasoned therapists do when they work with families.

**Techniques in integrative Christian family therapy.** There are no established techniques in an integrative Christian family therapy per se. Family therapists can draw on a range of techniques for relating to clients in much the same way more experienced family therapists relate to families. As far as specific techniques, such as use of genograms or enactments or scaling questions, the Christian family therapist is free to draw on various techniques, but the reliance on any technique ought to correspond to the way the case has been conceptualized through the lens of identity, function, and relationship in keeping with the general framework for understanding families.

The reader may appreciate the flexibility seen in integrative Christian family therapy. It allows family therapists to be quite eclectic in choosing among a range of techniques in family therapy. We appreciate not being too limited by one theoretical orientation, as it can be helpful to draw on a number of techniques throughout the course of therapy. However, the benefit to following a model, particularly for students of family therapy and new family therapists, is that the techniques that are tied to that particular model can function as an extension of sorts of the theory. The student is able to get some sense of where to go and how to get there when drawing on a single model. But most family therapists today do not appear to be committed to one first-generation model of family therapy. Rather, family therapists often view the first-generation models of family therapy as techniques themselves, as expressions of ways to interact with families but not as comprehensive, in-depth maps of how best to work with complicated issues often facing families.

Part three of this book addresses specific concerns that often face family therapists. Although not exhaustive, we offer a fairly comprehensive overview of some of the key areas that can be quite challenging in family therapy. It is in these chapters that we want to begin the task of applied integration by thinking about these topics from a distinctively Christian perspective while also recognizing what the broader field is often thinking about these topics and recommending for family intervention.

In this chapter we hoped to accomplish two purposes. The first was to assess where we are as a result of having cast a vision for family therapy in chapter one, having established the major contributions and current themes within the profession. We hoped to reformulate and focus the vision cast in chapter one based on the information you have examined in this volume.

The second task was to help family therapists move in a specific direction. We wanted to cast a vision for a distinctively Christian integrative family therapy (see McMinn & Campbell, 2007) based on a Christian understanding of family dysfunction and family functioning as well as provide suggestions for how a family might use a map based on Christian claims to get them from a place of dysfunction to a place of proper functioning.

## REFERENCES

Balswick, J. O., & Balswick, J. K. (1999). *The family: A Christian perspective on the contemporary home*. Grand Rapids: Baker Academic.

Bettelheim, B. (1987). *A good enough parent: A book on child rearing*. New York: Alfred A. Knopf.

Breunlin, D. C., Schwartz, R. C., & Kune-Karrer, B. M. (1997). *Metaframeworks: Transcending the models of family therapy* (Rev. ed.). San Francisco: Jossey-Bass.

Elkind, D. (1994). *The ties that stress: The new family imbalance*. Cambridge, MA: Harvard University Press.

Elkind, D. (2001). *The hurried child: Growing up too fast too soon.* Cambridge, MA: Da Capo Press.

Ferch, S. R. (1998). Intentional forgiving as a counseling intervention. *Journal of Counseling and Development, 76,* 261-70.

Fincham, F. D., Stanley, S., & Beach, S. R. H. (2007). Transformative processes in marriage & analysis of emerging trends. *Journal of Marriage and the Family, 69,* 275-92.

Finkel, E. J., Rusbult, C. E., Kumashiro, M., & Hannon, P. A. (2002). Dealing with betrayal in close relationships: Does commitment promote forgiveness? *Journal of Personality and Social Psychology, 82,* 956-74.

Freedman, S. R., & Enright, R. D. (1996). Forgiveness as an intervention goal with incest survivors. *Journal of Consulting and Clinical Psychology, 64,* 983-92.

Garland, D. R. (1999). *Family ministry.* Downers Grove, IL: InterVarsity Press.

Howsepian, A. A. (1997). Sin and psychosis. In R. C. Roberts & M. R. Talbot, *Limning the Psyche* (pp. 264-81). Grand Rapids: Eerdmans.

Jones, S. L., & Butman, R. E. (1991). *Modern psychotherapies: A comprehensive Christian appraisal.* Downers Grove, IL: InterVarsity Press.

McCullough, M. C., Pargament, K. I., & Thoresen, C. E. (Eds.). (2000). *Forgiveness: Theory, research, and practice.* New York: Guilford Press.

McCullough, M. E., & Worthington, E. L. (1999). Religion and the forgiving personality. *Journal of Personality, 67,* 1141-64.

McMinn, M. R., & Campbell, C. D. (2007). *Integrative psychotherapy.* Downers Grove, IL: IVP Academic.

Menninger, K. A. (1973). *Whatever became of sin?* New York: Hawthorn Books.

Patterson, J., Williams, L., Grauf-Grounds, C., & Chamow, L. (1998). *Essential skills in family therapy: From the first interview to termination.* New York: Guilford Press.

Pingleton, J. P. (1997). Why we don't forgive: A biblical and object relations theoretical model for understanding failures in the forgiveness process. *Journal of Psychology and Theology, 25,* 403-13.

Plantinga, C., Jr. (1997). Sin and addiction. In R. C. Roberts & M. R. Talbot (Eds.), *Limning the psyche* (pp. 245-63). Grand Rapids: Eerdmans.

Roberts, R. C. (1993). *Taking the Word to heart.* Grand Rapids: Eerdmans.

Sells, J. N., & Hargrave, T. D. (1998). Forgiveness: A review of the theoretical and empirical literature. *Journal of Family Therapy, 20,* 21-36.

Worthington, E. L. (1999). *Hope-focused marriage counseling: A guide to brief therapy.* Downers Grove, IL: InterVarsity Press.

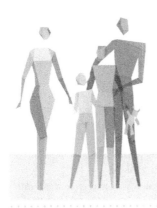

# INTEGRATION OF FAMILY THEORY WITH CRITICAL ISSUES IN PSYCHOTHERAPY

# CRISIS AND TRAUMA

*A parcel of their fortunes, and things outward*
*Do draw the inward quality after them*
*To suffer all alike.*

**WILLIAM SHAKESPEARE,**
*ANTONY AND CLEOPATRA*, **ACT 3**

Sunday evening at 8:00 p.m. is not a normal time for a family therapy session. But for the Chang family, these were not normal times. Just six days earlier John and Toni and their young adult daughters, Megan and Erin, watched in hopeful desperation as emergency room doctors and poison control specialists tried to save the life of their seventeen-year-old son and brother, Peter. They failed. Peter died of an intentional overdose from recreational drugs he got from friends. The family had no reason to suspect that Peter was suffering. His grades were good. He had social position in his school, elected as the senior class vice president. Just the week prior he traveled with his parents to visit two universities out east that he had selected for consideration. There was no conversation to raise concern, there was no note, no recognizable evidence that Peter was in trouble. Nothing . . . Nothing . . . Nothing. There was only a corpse and a need to have answers to questions. The most fundamental was, why? Why is this happening to us? Why did my son die? Why didn't he seek us out for help? Why didn't I see warning signs?

## ATTENDING TO FAMILIES IN CRISIS
## SUBSEQUENT TO TRAUMA OR LOSS

That Sunday evening was one like many other sessions when therapists enter into the sacred space of family grief. We are invited with no notice, often by complete strangers, to become an "adopted" member of a family and to take a leadership role to guide, nurture, protect, and serve others at their most vulnerable moment. The duration of the adoption may be just one visit, or it may extend over decades. Counselors may work with whole family groups, in subsystems, or with individuals as they learn to cope, realign, and alter their life course subsequent to some significant event.

My work with the Chang family etched in my mind the power of suicide on a family. My mind marks the date on a mental calendar—January 2, Peter's birthday, August 13, Peter's death. I have not had a January or August in which Peter has not come to mind, even though it has been years since I last saw the family. Attending to grief and crisis with a family places the family therapist inside his or her personal grief as well. We hug our children longer, are more careful to say goodbye as we separate from our spouses at the beginning of our work day, and are acutely sensitive to our environment, such as the phone that rings at 10:30 p.m.—though it was a wrong number, our mind races ahead to the family member who has succumbed to illness or accident.

Good grief work gets on you, like soil settling on the skin of a farmer, or splinters in the hands of a carpenter. The practice of good family crisis and grief work will include professional self-care that permits the professional counselor to be touched but not overwhelmed, involved but not enmeshed. Family counselors in grief and crisis must be affected in order to be effective, but simultaneously they must be able to maintain objectivity and strength to guide and direct others who are in crisis. We must touch their waters but not be pulled in and swept away by the currents of their tragedy.

Crisis, trauma, and grief family counseling is systemic like no other set of problems. We all have heard it said, "It's too bad that it takes a funeral to bring this family together." Indeed, in times of crisis, trauma, and grief we turn to those with whom we are bonded and connected. Whether it is in the loss of the life of a loved one, the abandonment of a spouse, the ending of a career or other economic downturn, or a house fire that turns a bucolic tree-filled cul-de-sac dream home into a heap of blackened earth with only a chimney standing above the ruins, hard times cause families to rally around one another.

But family members who rush in to rescue those who are suffering can easily find themselves caught in the undertow of the crisis. The burden of the trauma can easily reduce our resilience, provoking additional injury rather than bringing healing. Families are often destroyed not by the trauma itself but by the trauma's aftermath.

It is into this environment that the Christian family counselor can offer a realistic hope, a gracious ointment to others. But it's not an easy gift; family counselors must be prepared to walk hip deep in the ashes of a family home to find keepsakes around which a new home can be reconstructed. If it doesn't affect you, then you're probably not doing it very well. Likewise, if it leaves you emotionally decimated, you will not be able to walk with the family through this difficult experience.

## CRISIS AND TRAUMA: MANY CIRCUMSTANCES LEAD TO COMMON SUFFERING

Hard times come to all families; they vary in frequency, nature, and duration. And they differ in how they are managed. Difficulty visits through death, disease, violence, natural disaster, economic downturns, criminal victimization, legal quagmire, work demands, and many other situations. Sometimes it stays for just a short duration, at others it marks a permanent residency within the family.

Crisis involves change. It could be rapid onset change such as a bullet that strikes a police officer while on duty—ending a life and altering the lives of many others, on both sides of the gun. Or it could be gradual onset change such as the slow differences in the behavior of an adolescent or elderly parent that eventually becomes diagnosed as schizophrenia or early onset Alzheimer's disease. In all cases, families are required to adjust to a set of circumstances that are not of their choosing and that force multiple adjustments and accommodations of life's goals and plans.

Change creates psychological disequilibrium and disrupts systemic homeostasis. Two conflicting realities are evident in crisis counseling. First, change is everywhere. Second, humans are poorly equipped to manage it. Recall the importance of the term *homeostasis* in both individual organism and communal systemic functioning. People and families need balance, stability, security, and predictability in order to exist. "A healthy homeostatic balance requires stable psychological functioning with a minimum of dysphoric affect and the maintenance of reasonable cognitive perspective on experience and the retention of problem-solving skills" (Baldwin, 1979, p. 44).

Families respond to crisis in ways that suggest intentional or subliminal accommodation. In crisis, everyone hurts—but surprisingly we seem to manifest our despair in shifts. It is as though family members take turns in allowing the pain of their circumstances to affect them. Punamäki, Qouta, El Sarraj, and Montgomery (2006) found that families showed a complementary pattern between family members. When one was emotionally distraught, others were resilient and vice versa. This mutual adjustment to pain and suffering through the temporary demonstration of hope and resilience by some members appeared to be the primary source of recovery for families. To think of family adjustment within a structural paradigm, families face a problem when there is a failure for parents and children to permit the "passing of the tissue"—that is, when the adults must maintain a perpetual image of strength for their children, or when children need to present an artificial image of strength so as to not burden mom or dad. If family members are not permitted to adjust or alter their roles in accommodation to the change in life situations provoked by the crisis, or if the manner of adjustment to the disequilibrium brought on by the crisis or trauma is allowed to incite defensive reactions from other members of the family, then the family will turn against itself and work in a way that is destructive to the system because it will destroy individual members' essential coping styles.

The disequilibrium from change brought on by the crisis and the imbalances and role shifts required by the family to accommodate the changes make the system vulnerable to decomposition. In the confusion, family members are more likely to respond to the events with negative emotion, aggression, or defense mechanisms in order to manage the pain provoked by the loss and change. Anger can be directed toward others, toward God, and toward oneself. Family members become vulnerable to resentment for the perceived unfairness of the events and for the "odd" reactions from others. The reduced accommodation toward others as they address their pain incites others to reciprocate with their own anger, creating a self-sustaining pattern within the family.

## PROCESSES

*Trauma reception.* The immediate reaction to traumatic or crisis experiences varies between individuals but collectively includes responses such as numbness, shock, anxiety, disorganization, physical agitation, fainting, nausea, and with-drawal (Thompson, 2004). Family members report being stunned, sickened, or disoriented when they witness or become informed of tragedy. Those who witness trauma and tragedy such as a house fire or a traffic accident are more likely to experience greater physiological effects than those family members who learn of events after the fact. Whether trauma is observed or learned, there are commonly reported intense emotions of fear, shame, panic, guilt, grief, depression, anger, desperation, impatience, irritability, denial, and profound disruption in cognitive, social, and affective functioning (Juhnke & Shoffner, 1999). The cognitive and emotional reactions to the crisis are followed by al-terations in behavioral patterns, disrupted daily routines, anhedonia, alcohol and/or drug use, sleep disturbance, appetite change, hypervigilance, and reac-tivity to normal everyday events. The weight of trauma has a significant effect on each individual reaction. The trauma sets in place a chain reaction in which each family member is responding to both their trauma reception and to everyone else's response to the stressor simultaneously.

*Pain displacement.* Soon after the experience of trauma, usually within a few days, there is a settling of the group's heightened functioning. Our brains cannot exist in a hyperalert mode for an extended period. It is usual for ev-eryone to become exhausted. Sleep is slow in coming and seldom reported as restful. The pain from the crisis, exacerbated by increasing fatigue levels, prompts the members to convert or displace the painful adjustments and un-certainties onto the family. It is common for a set of inter- and intrapersonal reactions to emerge as the immediate shock of an event settles within and between family members as the pain from loss and the confusion from the unknown emerge. Individuals are often observed making unusual or poor decisions; being hypervigilant or negligent of common details; having diffi-culty maintaining focus, solving problems, or thinking abstractly; and expe-riencing nightmares, daydreams, intrusive thoughts or images, and a sense of despair or depression.

Between family members there is often reported impatience, anger, irrita-bility, and agitation. Members may cling, control, withdraw, or isolate from one another. The pain from the crisis or trauma must be managed or controlled. Because most crises are uncontrollable—hence the development of a crisis state—the pain is displaced into relationships within the family. In essence a second military front is formed. The first is the crisis itself where individual family members are conducting a psychological battle with a threat to well-being. The second front is the family relational battle lines. As each member reacts to stress, the stress accommodation and adjustment are placed between self and those in close relational proximity. It is as if individuals within a family find solace by screaming loudly and constantly in response to the pain from crisis. Every family member screaming produces a cacophony of noise in the home that increases the overall level of frustration and pain. Family members receive hurt from the external crisis, and they receive hurt from their family as it tries to attend to the pain separate from each other yet in the presence of everyone else.

*Family accommodation.* It can be said of families in crisis, "What goes up, must come down." The crisis will settle, even though during the stage of shock or painful readjustment it may feel as if the period of despair will last forever. It is also true that though the family will come down from its state of alarm, it will not land in the same place. The family will be forever different as a result of the crisis. The experience of death, severe illness, economic collapse, violence, natural disaster, or accident permanently changes the psyche of a family structure.

One can anticipate that crisis and trauma opens a family to vulnerability that often is not manifested until weeks, months, or years later. Crisis and trauma become like the computer worm that insidiously introduces destruction into the system, works underneath the level of awareness, and emerges later through the manifestation of relational injury.

John Chang, father of Peter, said, "He destroyed our family just like he packed the garage full of dynamite. What else could he have done to hurt us so much?" These despairing remarks by John later were inflammatory and infuriating to others in the family. His response characterized by despair was matched by the daughters' variation of denial and disengagement, and by Toni's effort to "bring everyone tighter, and to hold them tightly." In family crisis, though the music is common, the dances are all individual.

While it is true that crisis events place a permanent stamp on a family's history, John's view of crisis is not true. The evidence suggests that pairing family debriefing immediately after crisis or trauma with extended counseling involvement improves the likelihood of controlling painful psychological symptoms and destructive behaviors (Stallard & Salter, 2003). The effect of the trauma/crisis on the family is partially mitigated by the way that it manages its pain in the immediate aftermath of the events and in the subsequent months and years of recovery.

## CRITICAL INCIDENT STRESS MANAGEMENT FOR FAMILIES

The most frequented mental health intervention for crisis situations is Critical Incident Stress Management (CISM), developed by Jeffery Mitchell (1983). Central to CISM is the experience of Critical Incident Stress Debriefing (CISD), a single-session intervention for emergency medical technicians and ambulance drivers to cope with the effects of secondary trauma. The intervention has grown to include military, disaster victims, rescue personnel, trauma patients, and psychological service providers (Dyregrov, 1989; Stallard & Salter, 2003) as well as prevention and follow-up services to individuals, families, and organizations beyond the debriefing intervention applied immediately after trauma.

The essence of CISM is to develop a single-session intervention as soon as possible after the experience of the trauma—typically within seventy-two hours of the event. The debriefing, when led by a crisis counseling team, is more likely to be conducted as a structured group exercise. The progressive experience leads groups through the facts of the event, the thoughts occurring during the experience, the reactions that arose, an articulation of symptoms or variations of behavior, a teaching/learning experience, and the reentry into typical work and family cadence (Thompson, 2004).

Juhnke and Shoffner (1999) made a valuable contribution to professional practice by developing a CISM Family Debriefing Model. Their focus was on families addressing suicide, but the model is flexible so as to easily accommodate other areas of grief and crisis intervention. Their adaptation of CISM was a four-session family therapy expansion of the single-event crisis debriefing experience.

The first session of the Family Debriefing Model (FDM) may last for two or three hours and includes each of the CISM steps that are adapted for the family. It is appropriate for either a single family therapist or cotherapists to work with the family. The first session follows closely after the CISM structure (Mitchell & Everly, 2001). They then advocate short-term solution-focused family therapy sessions to consolidate family strengths and render support.

*Joining/introduction.* No therapeutic joining is more critical than the first moments of connection with a family that has been traumatized. Families in crisis usually begin therapy in a condition of individual and group shock. It is recommended that this stunned family immediately address their experience after an introduction in which the counselor joins the family on an emotional level. Frequently it is the case that this joining period permits the counselor to establish a leadership role in the family crisis. Because of the duress on the entire system, individuals often make poor personal or group choices. Guidance on how the family navigates itself for the immediate future of weeks is often beneficial for the family. Included in this guidance is the establishment of ground rules that will dictate behavior within the home during this special circumstance.

One of the most important rules for the family to respect is the double commitments to respect and flexibility. The respect commitment is a pledge to not provoke secondary crisis through acts and attitudes that are known to cause additional pain for other family members. For example, family members might soothe their pain by stopping at a sports bar after work and watching a NASCAR race and drinking a beer, or walking alone in the woods before coming home. Both activities might take two hours—and the race fan or nature lover fails to inform others of their whereabouts and their plans. Or an adolescent might choose to spend $400 of his or her money saved for college on clothes or stereo equipment—impulsively, without consultation with a parent. The respect commitment says that for the time being each member will respect others by not engaging in actions that are within your "individual right" but are also known to be potentially incendiary.

The flexibility commitment asks that individual family members give each other sufficient space to act unusual, out of the realm of the common, or even odd or strange. For example, one family was upset by a father who, in his week of grieving over the loss of a daughter to cancer, decided to start a building project and turn the unfinished basement into a guest bedroom. He said, "My wife has been asking for this for years. Now that I am home for this week, I thought that I should just do it." But the wife's response was, "I don't want you to do this now! Now is the time when you are supposed to be grieving." Indeed, the husband was grieving. And a component of his grief was the compulsion to divert his attention, to stay busy and to create something constructive. The commitment to honoring each other's unique manifestations in the grief response will be essential for the counselor to value and convey to the grieving family.

The relationship between the two commitments of respect and commitment can become a source of conflict for the family. In the illustration above, should the husband demonstrate respect for the wife by not starting a substantial building project in the home, or should the wife demonstrate flexibility by allowing him to grieve according to his personality and need? We suggest the contextual emphasis of fairness and give-and-take. If the husband builds, he must do so with accommodation for others whose grief process might be obstructed by the sounds of hammers and electric saws. Likewise, if the wife objects to the project she must concede him sufficient room to grieve in a way that provides relief from his pain and permits reorganization of his identity.

**Establishing facts related to the crisis.** The second step in FDM, occurring in the first session with the family, is to establish the facts of the crisis or traumatic event. The facts include where everyone was at the time of the event or at the time when each became aware of the event, the details of the event from eyewitnesses, or information learned secondhand from police, emergency workers, nurses, or doctors. The establishment of a factual base permits the counselor to become informed as to the details of the event and forms an oral encyclopedia of the individual experiences related to the event. For example, in working with a family who experienced a house fire during the previous night, each member was asked to share the sequence of events that allowed them to escape the structure, how they discovered the well-being of everyone else in the family, and what they learned from firefighters, neighbors, and police about their home and their experience.

The factual reporting is important for the counselor since the experience of the event becomes skewed as emotions bend memory of the events like light through a prism. In addition, secondhand stories about the experiences of other members in the family can become convoluted over time. The documentation of experience provides a fixed record of the sequence of events. Also, the formation of a factual base will allow family members to separate facts from perception as they attribute and create meaning of events later.

For example, the Todd family experienced the trauma of a criminal act of burglary that evolved into a hostage incident resulting in the husband/father being killed by the criminal. Months after the event, Mrs. Todd was berating herself for not stopping her husband from confronting the attackers who subsequently killed him. Having established the facts during the first session regarding what family members said and did while under the duress of being held hostage, the counselor was able to remind Mrs. Todd that she indeed reminded her husband to not engage in confrontation, as did other members of the family. Her husband made a mistake, but she was not responsible.

***Thoughts and cognitions.*** The third step recommended by Juhnke and Shoffner (1999) in their FDM approach during the extended first session is to address the process of thoughts regarding the experience of trauma or crisis subsequent to the events. They advise that the focus remain on the immediacy of the event: What was your first thought when you learned of your father's death? The purpose is to identify initial and subsequent meaning making to events.

The emphasis on the expression of initial thoughts serves as a link between the reality of the experience and the natural tendency to deny, dilute, or diffuse the events. For example, during the initial conversation with the Chang family introduced at the beginning of the chapter, Megan, age twenty-three, said, "I remember thinking that this just can't be happening to us." Her sister Erin, age twenty, joined in and said, "I had the same thought, these last few days are like what you read about in some magazine, you know, 'Happy, contented teenager kills himself while the family watches from behind the glass.' I always thought 'Right, what are they hiding?' But now . . . here we are. I am in the nightmare, living it out."

A second function is that it permits children and adults to put voice to some of their initial fears—to which others in the family can respond with messages of security. Jonathan, age thirteen, was with his mother and siblings in a family session discussing the death of his father who had a heart attack at work and died. He recalled the thought, "I remember asking myself, *Are we going to have to move?*" Because the recollection was in the past tense it became easier for him to articulate the ongoing worry about the future of his family and the changes that might occur because of his father's death. This permitted his mother to reassure him and the rest of the family about their finances and about her commitment to not uproot the children and move.

***Expression of emotional reactions to the event.*** Thompson (2004) states, "This is usually the longest stage in psychological debriefing. The earlier questions concerning thoughts and impressions lead to answers that reflect emotions" (p. 203). The purpose of this stage is to permit the family to identify the nature of trauma experienced by its members so as to permit the expression of emotional responses (Mitchell & Everly, 2001). This period can be one of great intensity for all and requires the greatest sensitivity from the counselor.

Successful expression of emotional reactions is not likely to occur through the unmitigated voicing of affective catharsis by family members.

Such "emotional dumping" on members who themselves are not likely capable of carrying the load of other's expressions can easily turn into family chaos as members attempt to control the emotional expression of others and protect themselves from being blamed. The counselor takes an active role in directing the expression of emotion for each person. For instance, with the Chang family I asked, "What emotional reactions occurred while you were each waiting in the hospital?"

*Assessment of individual symptoms.* The experience of emotional responses to trauma should be conducted in small doses. The counselor should control the amount and degree of affect recollection by visiting the pain for a short while, then returning to a more cognitive-focused recollection of the experience (Juhnke & Shoffner, 1999). One way to accomplish that is to elicit the self-report of behavioral symptoms among the family members. Families then also have an opportunity to identify and support one another in their responses to trauma.

The articulation of symptoms in the presence of the family permits the reframing of the symptoms and permits the family to shift from the victims of individual family members' emotional outbursts to "family healers." Merscham (2000) encourages families to identify and relabel their symptoms with verbal imagery to diffuse the symptoms when present in common family interaction. In this reframing of symptoms, anger can become "the Hulk," depression can be "Mr. Poe" (as in Edgar Allen Poe, hardly the "pick you up and feel good about yourself writer"). Labels can provide a language to declare and to observe each other's symptoms and to introduce a humorous diffusion in the effort to create dialogue.

*Teaching the family about crisis/trauma response patterns.* Teaching the family what to expect and anticipate in the coming weeks and months is crucial for family and individual well-being. If trauma or crisis is like radical surgery, this facet of the therapeutic process can be like the physician's aftercare instruction. Families rely on counselors to inform them of what to expect as the crisis stabilizes.

The instruction does not control or eradicate the intense responses that occur within the grief process. It would be an error to seek to manipulate the responses to grief by suppressing unique eccentricity or emotional expression. Rather, teaching prepares the family to anticipate the unique articulation of pain uttered through articulation, action, and attitude. Fritz Perls popularized the expression "Awareness is everything." In this case awareness permits a family to anticipate the response patterns by the family members and not create reactions to grief processing that exacerbate family pain.

*Family reentry into a normal life pattern.* "Life must go on" is a cliché attached to the process of trauma and crisis recovery. You may recall in the classic Dickens novel *Great Expectations* that Pip encounters the bizarre world of the elder Miss Havisham who, having been jilted on her wedding day decades before, has remained in her wedding dress, with a rat-infested wedding cake still resting on the dining room table. This would be failure to reenter to an extreme degree. Reentry is a reengagement of life, a plan for the formation of new life goals beyond the loss experienced. The Changs returned to life. Prior to children their hobby was to restore old homes. Together they would purchase a small cottage and spend their evenings renovating structures. Not long after Peter's death they made the decision to return to this activity as a marital team.

*Subsequent family sessions.* Trauma recovery is never wrapped up in one, three, or five sessions. It may seem to the family that it will never be wrapped up at all and that life will continue to exist with the emotional pain from loss or the trauma. I use the metaphor of a tsunami for families who are stabilizing after their crisis experience. The first wave is a horrendous experience with rampant destruction. In the immediate days and weeks after the flood the evidence of tragedy is everywhere. However, the sea recedes and the repair of the community occurs. Trees are planted, homes are rebuilt, tourists return. The incessant rhythm of ocean waves serves as a constant reminder of the trauma, and at times of seasonal storms anxiety will return as the sea appears that it will convulse again with crisis. In the same way families adjust, but there will be reminders in everyday life that will constantly provoke angst regarding the return of the suffering.

The task of the family counselor during this stage, using a solution-focused model, is to instigate thought and conversation about the positive change that is occurring in the family. The sense of dread might be a prevailing mood within the family, like a heavy covering of a blanket of snow. But pushing through the family dismay is often evidence of healing—like spring flowers pushing through the cold coverings. Juhnke and Shoffner suggest that counselors make inquiries into the evidence of growth with questions such as, what little things have you noticed since our last session which suggest to you that your family is beginning the healing and recovery process? (1999, p. 345).

Grief counseling during these subsequent sessions has a focus on pre-vention of relational destruction by building and maintaining channels of communication and care. However, not all grief is the same, because the nature of the traumas that families face vary in the drain on resources and the degree and depth of change. Counselors must consider with families the unique effects the nature, depth, and degree of this trauma will have on them and formulate a strategy to manage it over their lifetime.

## UNIQUE MANIFESTATIONS OF CRISIS AND TRAUMA

*Health-related trauma crisis and family therapy.* Not every family experiences a natural disaster in which their home is destroyed or life is lost from an earth-quake, flood, or storm. Likewise, many go through all of their years without the burden of victimization from violent crime. But every family knows sickness and death. While there is variation in the amount and nature of disease and the timing of death, every family must face it. Two variations in the experience of a health crisis are the burdens placed on families from progressive health issues and those created by the sudden onset of an emergency health issue. An example of the former is the birth of a child with a physical or mental disability, the latter the losses from death or injury in a traffic accident. Some families must face both, as when an emergency health crisis leaves a permanent effect—such as a closed head injury of an adult who requires life-long extended care.

*Progressive health crisis.* Crises are commonly understood as an "unset-tling event." However, some events are not limited to a single point in time but are perpetual and progressive. Families attending to ongoing challenges such as caring for family members who have progressive health needs or members with physical, mental, or developmental disorders experience crisis on a dif-ferent scale than those who are overwhelmed by single events.

We recommend to counselors attending to families who are engaged in progressive health crises to familiarize themselves with the "compassion fa-tigue" literature (Figley, 2002), which will track the family's experience more closely than will the crisis/trauma counseling literature. The difference in the two bodies of information is that the compassion fatigue literature focuses on the psychological effects experienced by human service workers in long-term caregiving—the crisis that is created by a continual demand on individuals within the system. It is crucial for this population to integrate components of family-member care in the presence of ongoing strain from family care.

Thompson and Doll (1982) found that families involved in long-term care experience an extended crisis that produces four common responses among its members: (1) The sense of being overloaded. Family members would identify with feelings such as exasperated, frustrated, and drained. (2) The sense of being trapped. Family members saw no exit to the demands of being a focused caregiver. Also present was a sense that they were left helpless to attend to the responsibilities of their family member alone. (3) The sense of resentment. Family members held sympathy and anger toward the needy person simultaneously. Their anger was from the interruption of life and the lack of reinforcers that would otherwise prompt and motivate involvement. (4) The sense of exclusion. Family members reported being removed and withdrawn from the circles of relationships, and at other times numbed and apathetic about social involvement.

The Peters family provides an example of these types of strain and the therapy required with this trauma. Marilyn Peters was a very sick eleven-year-old girl. But you wouldn't know it by looking at her or by watching her at school. Her autistic spectrum disorder left her with mild social dysfunction that was successfully addressed within the school. However, it took all that Marilyn had to manage her behavior at school. At home she had minimal resilience to manage even the slightest life challenge. She would show regular tantrums—throwing objects, kicking, screaming, and hitting anyone who was close to her. At calmer moments she would become remorseful to the point of self-injury because she was so "bad." She had come to take the family hostage through her behavior and through the manifestation of her disease. Her mother, Petera, provided her constant care, not because she was seeking to be enmeshed but because Marilyn required constant supervision and no one was capable of managing the complexities of her care. After years of constant attention to the needs of her daughter at the expense of her son, her husband, and herself, she was depleted. Gary, Marilyn's father, was equally exhausted. When he started family therapy his work was under threat because of the frequent demands of home interruption, where it required two adults to manage Marilyn.

The therapy focused on the marital dyad—squeezed over Gary's lunch hour and before Petera had to be home to meet Marilyn after school. Their therapy focused on three things: (1) Pain/defense management. Because both spouses were run down, depleted, exhausted, and bitter as they carried a unique burden, it was crucial for them to discuss openly the ways that they would remain a team that carried their stresses together. (2) Affective expression. In order to share their burdens with one another they had to develop skills at emotion identification and communication. Both parents were "cerebral"—Gary was trained as a mathematician and Petera was educated to be an accountant; hence, their abilities to express themselves on an emotional level were not a natural component of their personality. (3) Cathartic expression. They needed a place to vent—sometimes alone with me, sometimes together. Few understood their predicament. Many would offer trite advice, such as "Have you seen *Supernanny*? That show has really helped me be strong enough to control my child. It will really help you too." They had learned to calmly nod their head and thank them for the suggestion, then weep with me and with each other for the challenging strains that they carried daily.

Crisis counseling with Petera and Gary provided time to weep, plan, contemplate, and understand. They needed a place to process the consistent disappointment from state social service programs, the threats from insurance programs, and the "help" of the well-intentioned neighbor or congregant. This crisis counseling paralleled the work of a chaplain working with soldiers in an ongoing threatening circumstance. Families in this type of circumstance understand that they are under siege, that they are each other's primary resource for survival, and that the relationship is under direct threat of destruction unless they are perpetually attending to their respective needs.

*Emergency health crisis.* The chief concern with families addressing an emergency health crisis is the question of life or death, and the second is life adjustment. Frequently, psychologists, counselors, and pastoral counselors are called to intervene with families who are facing the possibility of death or disability due to accident or illness. A highway catastrophe might leave a loved one's life in the balance, with a parent needing to meet the needs of small children, make health and well-being decisions, and attend to his or her own emotional needs. In other situations, families may not be overwhelmed with the threat of death but might be having to process their futures in the face of permanent disability such as paralysis or other physical impairment. The family may be facing the elimination or reduction of income-earning capacity. Their future may be in doubt economically. Changes in physical capabilities may have far-reaching effects on children's sense of security.

Similarly, a family that is facing a cancer diagnosis or other extended illness for a parent or child faces many important, confusing, and threatening decisions and challenges. Medical advances provide far more optimism for patient survival—but still with significant economic costs. Weighing the effects of chemotherapy and multiple surgeries on a family can be devastating to the psychological well-being of both adults and children.

The Keyes family was a "Brady Bunch" clone. Jim and Loretta had known hardship in their previous marriages. They met at a Cancer Spouses Survival Group at their local hospital. They had lost their respective life mates, and both were facing raising their elementary-age children without a mother or a father. They went slowly, attending to the needs of three children (Loretta had a four-year-old daughter, and Jim had an eleven-year-old son and a nine-year-old daughter when they married).

Five years after their marriage Loretta was diagnosed with breast cancer. Everyone knew the process—having walked through it to the end with a spouse or parent but a few years before. In this crisis counseling there were two major challenges for the family and counselor. The first was to attend to the adjustment to the disease and its treatment. The second challenge was to attend to reminiscent experiences of the sickness and death of a parent or spouse. Loretta underwent a mastectomy and chemotherapy and is a cancer survivor.

At the time of the diagnosis, the ages of the children were nine, fourteen, and sixteen. The important functions of family therapy were to learn to speak about the unspeakable—the possibility of death and the hope of life on earth and of heaven. They had to return to the feelings they had when their respective mother, father, husband, or wife became sick, and the importance of separating the feelings they had at that time from the events occurring now. The crucial component of this crisis was the unknown and the tendency to fear the worst—as drawn from previous experience.

***Terrorist violence–related crisis and family counseling.*** Two events in recent North American history—the bombing of the Federal Building in Oklahoma City and the 9/11 attacks on the World Trade Center and the Pentagon—have brought terrorist violence to the forefront of family crisis and trauma work. Those events brought the nation to feel the effects of trauma. Other events have been very important as well in bringing terrorist-like violence to the forefront of family treatment. School shootings and office violence are most notable.

Much of our knowledge of terrorist-related family therapy is extrapolated from data derived in family-therapy homicide intervention (Miller, 2003). Spungen (1998) has described the counseling process for families addressing terrorism victimization to include rage, guilt, and grief responses to the events.

Forgiveness is a more salient issue for the family to address at the appropriate time when responding to terrorist violence because there is a discrete individual responsible for the loss, trauma, and injury (Enright & North, 1998; Sells & Hargrave, 1998). One reason that forgiveness might be particularly salient in this context is that in terrorism violence the victim typically has no past or future with the perpetrator. Victimization has occurred randomly. Direct interaction with the one who causes injury is usually not possible; however, the rage directed at a "faceless" person responsible for death and destruction often is best addressed through forgiveness rituals. Many tools exist to help counselors attend to forgiveness themes with families (Hargrave, 1994; Hargrave & Sells, 1997; Worthington, 2001). The randomness of terrorism leaves families vulnerable to unique aspects of posttraumatic stress disorder. Counselors who can facilitate the releasing of self-destructive psychological vengeance promote a more comprehensive recovery (McCullough & Root, 2005).

***Family violence.*** Family therapy addressing family violence brings up the essential developmental issue of trust. Children are taught to be wary of strangers: Never get into a car with a person you don't know. Trust your family. "Home, sweet home." Violence from a loved one is such an insidious disease to families because it undermines the core essentials of security and safety that home is to provide for both children and adults. Home is the sanctuary and shelter, not the theater of war.

Two essential themes emerge in all family-violence crisis counseling sessions. First is the reestablishment of the essential physical security and safety for adults and children. The children might be placed in the grandparents' or an aunt or uncle's home. They might be with a mother, living in a protective shelter. They might not have directly witnessed the violence and not understand why mommy or daddy isn't living with them. All of these and other drastic changes in circumstances as an aftereffect of the trauma exacerbate the threat to safety and security of children. Family and pastoral counselors play a key role in helping parents understand the importance of domestic stability, the return to family routines and rituals, and the need to talk about the changes that are going on in their family.

The second task is to restore psychological safety to those affected by the trauma. Amanda was a mother of two boys, ages five and seven. She had come to consult with me regarding how to heal and help her children. Amanda thought her nightmare of family violence ended with her divorce from Fred. He was a mean man—crazy mean. He would lose control of himself and become a raging carnivore. Fearing for her life, Amanda found protection in a women's shelter; with support from her family, she filed for divorce, winning full custody of their children, and she got a job as a waitress and saved enough for an apartment. She was starting anew. While at work she met Allen. They dated for a while, and then Allen moved in with Amanda and the two boys. Six months later Amanda awoke to the sound of a shotgun blast. Standing at the foot of the bed was Fred. Allen was dead, lying at her side. The boys were in the other bedroom awakened by the sound. They were calling for their mommy. Amanda presumed that she was to be murdered next. She has trouble remembering what she said and what he said. Only she remembers the boys knocking on the door that had been locked by Fred when he broke into the apartment. Fred then took out a handgun and killed himself.

The whole event was over in less than ten minutes. But to Amanda, it will never be over. The boys were spared the visual exposure to the violence, but not the sounds. They were traumatized by what they heard and by the knowledge of the murders that occurred in the bedroom. Likewise, there was a secondary trauma—they were affected by their mother's trauma. She could not deny her own grief and mother them as though nothing had happened.

Counseling with the family was separated into three components. First, there was attention dedicated to the individual trauma experienced by Amanda. Second, there was the family therapy—primarily conducted for the children's healing. The goal of working with the family unit was to reinforce the mother in the eyes of her children as one capable of protecting them. Finally, Amanda chose to utilize her extended family support in this tragedy by inviting her sister and parents to additional sessions. All were part of the process—they were present at the divorce, encouraging of the changes in the time prior to the violence. Amanda believed that they needed to be part of this healing. She needed their presence and support to grieve, develop courage, and to heal.

## FAMILY CRISIS AND CHRISTIAN MINISTRY—
## THE MOST NATURAL OF RELATIONSHIPS

> I am convinced that neither death nor life . . . nor anything else in all creation,
> will be able to separate us from the love of God that is in Christ Jesus our Lord.
> (Rom 8:38-39 NIV)

A central message of the Christian faith is how one copes with the weighty
existential issues of life. Life and death, health and sickness, wealth and
poverty, plenty and want, power and powerlessness, joy and pain are common
themes in the pages of Scripture. The message of the Christian faith for counselors working with families in crisis is hope, faith, and purpose in the
presence of suffering.

### INTEGRATIVE FOCUS: *Family Functioning*

Functioning is reconfigured when a family endures hardship. Members describe the time as surreal. The extended vigils at hospital
bedside, the decisions made at a mortuary for services and burial, or
the conversation at an attorney's office over immediate options
when entering the justice system cause the family to express itself in
crisis mode. The norm of routine and pattern is altered as each member moves back and forth between the stages of shock, confusion,
and grief. Counselors play a crucial role as a stabilizing influence for
the system.

Counselors should be careful to not overstep their boundaries during
initial days of a crisis or trauma. There is often a pull toward directing
the family in its decision making rather than helping the family proceed
through the emotions and circumstances of their predicament. The goal
must always be to foster interdependence on one another rather than
reliance on the counselor. The emergent health of family function is
seen by the family's realization of their need for one another, not the
realization of their need for a mental health professional.

*Think about it:* The power of crisis work can easily pull the family
therapist too deep into the family's grief or trauma. What preventa-
tive steps can be taken to maintain therapeutic closeness without
sacrificing objectivity?

## UTILIZING A FAMILY'S CHRISTIAN COMMITMENT TO
## PROMOTE HEALING FROM CRISIS AND TRAUMA

There are two fundamental questions that any counselor should be asking of family members who face the disorganization and chaos of crisis. The first asks, is your faith system sufficient to carry you and your family during this time of crisis? The second question is, how faithful and consistent are you at living the principles of your faith so that it guides, soothes, and provides meaning during the time of crisis?

Crisis is a time when many people reconsider the issues of faith. It is a common characteristic of humanity to be underprepared emotionally and psychologically for trauma and crisis. Investments in life values may have been toward the material, sensual, or pleasurable rather than a disciplined focus on and commitment to the eternal. Therefore, when a family is faced with a life-changing crisis there is a frequent return to core "meaning of life" questions and a change in priorities. As we have all heard, "There are no atheists in foxholes." Crisis time creates circumstances where counselors can facilitate these considerations with families. The counselor can and should openly discuss with the family their utilization of their Christian, religious, or spiritual tradition and whether their answers to *why?* and other considerations of purpose and meaning are sufficiently addressed.

Pastoral counselors and professional counselors who have established a Christian orientation as the basis for counseling are more free to discuss the shared perspective of life and death, sickness and health, suffering and joy, than are counselors to whom clients are coming without a shared Christian worldview. The Christian counselor working in a secular setting or working with families of divergent faith perspectives than his or hers should still pursue such discussions but respect the boundary of expertise and be prepared to make referral to pastors, rabbis, teachers, priests, or other religious authorities within the client's faith tradition as they so wish.

The second question essential for the Christian counselor to address with a family in crisis is the degree to which the family is faithful to the disciplines and beliefs that they hold. In other words, are you practicing what you preach? The family may hold a well-developed theology but fail to maintain the Christian discipline from which flows the stability and security for the family during a time of crisis. This "we know it, but we don't live it" family may be interested in reclaiming some of the spiritual distinctives and disciplines but not know how or where to begin.

Counselors may be instrumental in connecting families to spiritual resources and encouraging them to develop rituals and practices that can unite family members and provide support, security, and significance to the process of family healing. We encourage the formation of an extensive network of church communities and pastors to aid professional counselors facilitating Christian discipleship and growth. When clients have selected the counselor because the counselor has an explicit Christian foundation, the two have greater freedom to address their need through a common language.

The Chang family provides an example of answers to these two questions. To the first question, there was wide divergence within the family. The family came from a Catholic tradition. The parents were committed to the heritage of the church but were not practicing Catholics. John had not attended his local parish church for many years and was cynical about rather than grateful for the church's involvement. Toni also had not been active, but Peter's death stirred in her a desire to return to something—she could not articulate what it was early in the counseling sessions. The daughters were more like their father in terms of interest in spirituality, but they were more willing to cooperate with their mother—for the sake of her recovery.

When Peter's death brought about numerous interfaces with the church— the funeral, burial, home visitation, Mass on the anniversary of Peter's death— the family reacted with various responses. Toni was compliant and welcoming. John was passive-aggressive—attending the church function but expressing anger and resentment for the duration. Erin and Megan were unmoved but not resistant.

In asking the initial question of whether their Christian commitments were able to sustain them during this time, the family responded with significant differences. Toni wanted to respond to an internal call or yearning toward spiritual renewal. John, Megan, and Erin were not so motivated. The daughters expressed skepticism toward religious issues but did not harbor animosity. However, John was angry at the church because of differences in theological and social issues. Peter's death provided an avenue to direct a portion of his resentment back toward the religious structures of his childhood. The variation of desire and intent among the family members prompted conversation about how they could support one another and how they must be careful to avoid inadvertent injury due to the differences in needs and desires for Christian renewal.

The second question, does the family live in accordance with their beliefs, prompted movement along three paths. On the first path, the daughters spoke of apathy toward the Christian life—they were neither antagonistic nor friendly toward it. Their perspective, shared commonly between them, was that it was fine for their mother and they wanted to assist her in securing peace, but for them there was no real motivation or perceived need. We were able to discuss "spiritual numbness" as a protection and defense with them and to provide for them the freedom to seek or to avoid the considerations of their faith.

**INTEGRATIVE FOCUS:** *Family Relationships*

The emergence of interdependent relationships is a primary objective of a family counselor working with families in crisis. The initial tendency when a family is placed in crisis is toward fragmentation. However, as mental health professionals understand their role as "paraclete"—the Greek word for one who comes alongside and ministers—families increase their capacity to sustain themselves through this trauma. Foremost in our minds must be the importance of encouraging—literally to instill courage—rather than directing or even leading. The utilization of systemic interventions—realignment of boundaries, paradoxical intervention, family mapping, narrative story telling, reframing, and so on—are all to be directed toward the reconfiguration of relationships within the system.

*Think about it:* Some family therapists, especially those from the humanistic traditions, would say that "instilling courage" is the essence of their work. What do you think?

The second path, traveled by John, was one of understanding the anger he felt toward the church. John was able to develop insight around the concentration of anger for the loss of his son. "We live within the sound of the church bells. I never really liked that, now I hate it. I hear the bells all the time. I heard them at the funeral. I hear them in the night. Every hour I am reminded that my son is dead, courtesy of St. Mark's." It appeared that he needed someone or something to become responsible for this tragedy, as a channel for his grief. The church was a target toward which he could alter his sorrow into rage and cast blame. The family was able to accept his anger but also to challenge him to take responsibility for what it really was—a displacement of suffering.

Toni's path was one that pursued greater consistency between what she believed and how she lived. She felt responsible for Peter's death: "I am his mother. Every mother is supposed to be aware of their children. While I can say that I thought I was doing a pretty good job, obviously I wasn't and I am condemned to carry that burden." Toni, more than the others, was aware of a burden of guilt and responsibility. Counseling, both individually and with her

---

## INTEGRATIVE FOCUS: *Family Identity*

Grandma Smith was the family glue. She was loved, adored, and at times feared by her adult siblings. Well into her 90s, she had a power and influence on the extended family such that Thanksgiving and Christmas were always spent with her on the farm. No Smith would ever dream of missing the Smith tradition. Then the family faced a real crisis: Grandma Smith died. And so did the adhesive agent. The Smith family never gathered again as a full family. The extended families pursued other options for holidays. They went to the homes of in-laws or just stayed at home and celebrated as individual nuclear families.

The "emergency" of Grandma Smith's death brought on an "emergence" of new family identities. It is not true that the family split, splintered, or disintegrated. The monolithic Smith family reconstituted itself into smaller "Sub-Smith" families. In essence, they multiplied rather than dissolved. They moved outward, taking some of what was good and some of what was bad, and recreated themselves in new relationships.

The result of trauma or crisis will always be change. Events of significance have a permanent effect on the identity of the family. Its permanence is the continual reformation of identity in relationship. Loss can engulf a person and a family. And identity can form from that loss either for good or for ill. Loss can lead to redemption, and family identity can be forged and emerge on the other side of loss, having gone deeper and further on toward greater meaning and more clarity.

*Think about it:* What do you see as the important tasks for the family therapist to address as the family realizes that they are in the process of change? What role does a family therapist play in relation to a redemptive understanding of loss?

husband and daughters, was able to focus on specific tasks to challenge that sense of culpability for Peter's death. The conversations revealed previous guilt for not providing care for her mother prior to her death from Alzheimer's complications. Even though Toni visited her mother three or four times a week, she carried the weight of insufficiency and blame. "I am not good enough, and it's my fault" became the phrase that she identified as a life theme—to which Peter's death could cause an emotional crippling unless it was challenged and contained. The family's work became to help each member in the respective paths, acknowledging that the ways chosen were motivated by both their courage prompting pursuit and their fear prompting escape.

## CONCLUSION

Grief is part of every family's existence. Counseling sessions with families during times of grief are likely to be the most powerful and provocative. Families will seek answers to questions that you as a counselor will not be able to answer—without sounding vapid, insensitive, or simplistic. Yet they are coming to counseling to reattach to life, hope, and meaning. C. S. Lewis asked the same questions in his *A Grief Observed* (1961), and he found that

> when I lay these questions before God I get no answer. But a rather special sort of "No answer." It is not the locked door. It is more like a silent, certainly not uncompassionate, gaze. As though He shook His head not in refusal but waiving the question. Like, "Peace, child; you don't understand." Can a mortal ask questions which God finds unanswerable? Quite easily, I should think. All nonsense questions are unanswerable. How many hours are there in a mile? Is yellow square or round? Probably half the questions we ask—half our great theological and metaphysical problems—are like that.

Years after concluding the therapeutic experience with the Chang family, I find that they are still not far from my mind and I am not far from theirs. A letter received four years after the death of their son reveals the constancy of grief and the struggle that some families endure for the length of their existence:

> Dear Jim,
>
> These are still such sad days for us. I had just said to John last week how much I missed you and how much you meant to our family.
>
> I want you to know that so many of the words that you said to us come back over and over again as we finally realize some of the things you were

trying to tell us. I cannot help but remember the family that you saw on that first morning four years ago and wonder what exactly did you see? I wondered what went through your mind as you prepared to meet with us on your way over to the office. How do you prepare to meet with people who are totally clueless as to what had just happened to them? People who four years later, are still emerging from their tragedy.

We have changed greatly in these four years . . . some changes for the good and some not. We continue to struggle with our own individual ways of handling our loss of Peter. John still prefers to just get through these days and every day, Megan and Tim (spouse) try hard to ignore the reality of it, and Erin struggles somewhere in between. I continue to want the natural coming together of my family to remember and cherish the blessing of Peter in our lives. Sadly at this point, we can only remember the details of our nightmare, not the memories of our son and brother. I know you would probably say that will still come. I pray for that. I do not push anything any more. I have learned that much.

What continues to amaze me is how much depth there is to grief. Rather than feeling less grief four years later, I think I am feeling a deeper sense of my loss. Our hearts are forever broken. But, true to form, we have not stopped putting the proverbial carrot in front of our noses to keep moving forward. Six months ago, John wanted to retire and sell real estate (YIKES!).

When I start to think about what a difference you made in our lives and especially mine, I get overwhelmed with gratitude. I will miss you always.

Thank you for remembering us and our Peter,
Toni, John and Family

## REFERENCES

Baldwin, B. A. (1979). Crisis intervention: An overview of theory and practice. *The Counseling Psychologist, 8*, 43-52.

Dyregrov, A. (1989). Caring for helpers in disaster situations: Psychological debriefing. *Disaster Management, 2*, 25-30.

Enright, R., & North, J. (1998). *Exploring forgiveness*. Madison: University of Wisconsin Press.

Figley, C. R. (2002). Introduction. In C. R. Figley (Ed.), *Treating compassion fatigue*. New York: Brunner/Routledge.

Hargrave, T. D. (1994). *Families and forgiveness*. New York: Routledge.

Hargrave, T. D., & Sells, J. N. (1997). Development of a forgiveness scale. *Journal of Marriage and Family, 23*, 41-62.

Juhnke, G. A., & Shoffner, M. F. (1999). The family debriefing model: An adapted critical incident stress debriefing for parents and older sibling suicide survivors. *The Family Journal, 7*, 342-48.

Lewis, C. S. (1961). *A grief observed.* New York: HarperCollins.

McCullough, M. E., & Root, L. M. (2005). Forgiveness as change. In E. L. Worthington Jr. (Ed.), *Handbook of forgiveness* (pp. 91-107). New York: Routledge.

Merscham, C. (2000). Restorying trauma with narrative therapy: Using the phantom family. *The Family Journal, 8*, 282-86.

Miller, L. (2003). Family therapy of terroristic trauma: Psychological syndromes and treatment strategies. *The American Journal of Family Therapy, 31*, 257-80.

Mitchell, J. I. (1983). When disaster strikes . . . The critical incident stress debriefing process. *Journal of Emergency Medical Services, 8*, 36-38.

Mitchell, J. T., & Everly, G. S. (2001). *The basic critical incident stress management course: Basic group crisis intervention* (3rd ed.). Ellicott City, MD: International Critical Incident Stress Foundation.

Punamäki, R. L., Qouta, S., El Sarraj, E., & Montgomery, E. (2006). Psychological distress and resources among siblings and parents exposed to traumatic events. *International Journal of Behavioral Development, 30*(5), 385-97.

Sells, J. N., & Hargrave, T. G. (1998). Forgiveness: A review and critique of the clinical forgiveness literature. *Journal of Family Therapy, 20*, 21-36.

Spungen, D. (1998). *Homicide: The hidden victims; A guide for professionals.* Thousand Oaks, CA: Sage.

Stallard, P., & Salter, E. (2003). Psychological debriefing with children and young people following traumatic events. *Clinical Child Psychology and Psychiatry, 8*, 445-57.

Thompson, E. H., & Doll, W. (1982). The burden of families coping with the mentally ill: An invisible crisis. *Family Relations, 31*, 379-88.

Thompson, R. (2004). *Crisis intervention and crisis management: Strategies that work in schools and communities.* New York: Brunner-Routledge.

Worthington, E. L. (2001). *Five steps to forgiveness: The art and science of forgiving.* New York: Crown House.

# ATTENDING TO
# MARITAL CONFLICT

*Love consists of this, that two solitudes protect
and touch and greet each other.*

**RAINER MARIA RILKE**

A CRUCIAL COMPONENT OF FAMILY THEORY and practice is to focus on the family core, the adult couple that through marriage, conception, and adoption forms and directs families. Within the context of systems theory, it is the couple, working as a team, that successfully integrates health and maturity in the family life. Kids don't typically make mature and healthy families happen, parents do. Toward this idea, Weeks (1989) states, "It is the quality of the marital relationship that greatly influences, and may in fact determine the quality of the total nuclear family" (p. vii).

## THE IMPORTANCE OF MARITAL
## CONFLICT TO FAMILY THERAPY

Given the importance of marriage on the health of the family, it should not be a surprise that focusing on conflict between spouses is a frequent reason for therapy. Donavan (1995) found that marital conflict accounts for 40 percent of all mental health referrals. The major motive for couples to utilize mental health services and professional therapists is relief from relational conflicts (Todd, 1985; Worthington & DiBlasio, 1990).

But what is a surprise is how often professional therapists and pastoral counselors dislike working with couples, particularly conflicted couples. Worthington (1999) offers the opinion that "most counselors dread dealing with troubled marriages even though troubled marriages often form the majority of their caseload" (p. 20). Counselors meeting with conflicted partners can easily be pushed or pulled into the role of judge or referee—adjudicating marital violations, sending each "fighter" to his or her respective corner. It is easy to be blindsided with the intensity of anger displayed by one or both partners because we lack the historical antecedents in the relationship. Furthermore, it is possible for counselors to become an artifact used in the conflict by either partner as a triangulating attempt for power and control.

The dread of couple therapy can also be explained by its frequent lack of effectiveness. While marital interventions are important in systems thinking and are frequently utilized by couples, sadly, they are often unsuccessful. A *Consumer Reports* survey indicated that marital therapy and addictions counseling have the least favorable outcomes in the mental health field (1995). About two-thirds of the couples who come to therapy to address a conflict can expect to experience significant improvement in their relationship—but one-third of those who improve report falling back to previous patterns within two years of the treatment (Jacobson & Addis, 1993).

In spite of the challenges the research also suggests powerful indicators that predict success in marital therapy. Jacobson and Christensen (1996) consolidated research findings and found five couple factors that predicted success and failure.

The first predictor of success was couple *commitment*. Couples who had dedication to remaining in the marriage regardless of the outcome of therapy were more likely to improve than those who used marital change as the factor in the decision to divorce. Couples who are in the marriage "for the long haul" are more likely to be open to facing the difficult challenges of therapy than couples who are actively maintaining the option of divorce.

The *age* of the couple was the second predictor for couple success. Younger couples were more successful than older couples in changing patterns in their relationship. Jacobson and Christensen do not believe that this is a case of "can't teach an old dog new tricks"; rather, the data imply that the severity of the problem is linked to the age of the couple and the number of years that they have been married. This suggests that when couples attend to problems earlier in their relationship there is a greater likelihood that they will develop a more satisfying pattern of relationship.

The third factor was *emotional engagement*. This refers to the bonds or connections that that couple has outside of the conflict issue. Couples who had strong positive connections were more likely to successfully address conflict. Positive connections include assets such as common interests and activities. Couples who have other positive interactions that they can draw on and escape to as a team were more capable at resolving conflicts in therapy.

The fourth factor was *marital traditionality*. It was found that couples who had greater egalitarian perspectives to marriage were more likely to improve as a result of therapy. This suggests that couples who maintained some openness to change of roles, responsibilities, duties, and power are more likely to benefit from an inquiry into the fairness of the marital process than couples whose idea of marriage was fixed or rigid. If therapy is about change and adjustment, then couples who are more flexible in altering their established duties in the family are more likely to benefit from therapy.

Finally, the fifth factor was *convergent goals*. Couples who had similar values and aims in life were more likely to work together to achieve those aims through therapy. It is in this realm that a common faith is such an important factor for marital counseling.

Other researchers (Giblin & Chan, 1995; Gottman, 1993a, 1993b, 1994a, 1994b; Notarius & Markman, 1993) indicate that the successful management of emotional pain is a significant predictor of marital success and family health. Couples who are able to manage their emotional pain well are able to bounce back from relational injury and successfully manage conflicts. Furthermore, some family theorists (e.g., Framo, 1976; Hargrave & Anderson, 1992; Madanes, 1991) advocate models of relationship restoration as a "viable and necessary intervention to move a couple past unresolved hurt and anger emerging from current or past family injustices" (Hargrave, 1994b, p. 339). Models of relationship restoration seem to hold the key to teaching couples the emotional and conflict-management skills necessary to heal from relational injury and prevent additional cycles of injury and destructive conflicts.

## MARITAL CONFLICT PATTERNS

The examination of relational conflict, particularly conflict occurring in marriage, has been a primary focus of social science research for decades because of its long-established strong relation to marital satisfaction (Heavey, Christensen, & Malamuth, 1995; Roberts, 2000; Shi, 2003). Data from this research indicate that the manner in which a couple engages in conflict is the best predictor of long-term relational success (Gottman, 1994a; Notarius & Markman, 1993). An additional conclusion from research is that couples fight in patterns, and that these patterns are cyclical; that is, couples appear to follow a systemic blueprint that makes components of relational conflict predictable (Bradbury, Fincham, & Beach, 2000; Gottman, 1994b; Murray, Bellavia, Rose, & Griffin, 2003; Rusbult, Verette, Whitney, Slovik, & Lipkus, 1991; Shi, 2003). The effect of these patterns is that "couples often selectively interpret each other's behavior and responses in ways that perpetuate their distress" (Johnson, Makinen, & Millikin, 2001, p. 148).

It stands to reason that couples who can successfully resolve differences in mutually beneficial ways have a strong motivation for maintaining relationship. Conversely, couples who become mired with argument evidence a cyclical nature of conflict with a reciprocal or spiraling experience (Fishbane, 2001; Gottman, 1999). In such circumstances, couples report being stuck or stymied in conflict that is both disturbing and characterized by excessive negative emotion and familiarity. Negative emotion includes anger, hurt, vulnerability, anxiety, fear, withdrawal, and aggression. Familiarity includes the experience of repetition, the sense that we have been down this road before. Bergman and Surrey (1994), citing Stiver, state that "the partners become less and less able to keep from going down the same path. There is a feeling of being trapped or taken over by this habitual, stereotypical movement, less sense of freedom, . . . a feeling of being locked into a power struggle" (p. 5).

While the process of repetitive conflict is well documented in the literature, explanation and intervention into this process is lacking: "A wife's negativity appears to promote her husband's withdrawal, . . . and the husband's withdrawal promotes his wife's increased negativity. . . . *This dysfunctional cycle without clear cause and effect must be disrupted*" (Giblin & Combs, 2003, p. 548, italics added). Toward that same end, Murray et al. (2003) express the opinion that there is little empirical investigation into the process of marital relational conflict cycles, even though it is central to understanding relational distress.

## COUPLES COUNSELING THEORIES
## AND CONFLICT PATTERNS

Research-based theory into conflict in general and marriage and family conflict specifically is plentiful and useful for the therapist in understanding the complicated factors of family quarrels. The original research on conflict by Dollard (1938) offers insight and observation that remains current:

> It does not seem unreasonable to assume that aggressive behavior of the usually recognized varieties is always traceable to and produced by some form of frustration. . . . It must be kept in mind, however, that one of the earliest lessons human beings learn as a result of social living is to suppress and restrain their overtly aggressive reactions. This does not mean, however, that such reaction tendencies are thereby annihilated; rather it has been found that, although these reactions may be temporarily compressed, delayed, disguised, displaced, or otherwise deflected from their immediate and logical goal, they are not destroyed. (pp. 1-2)

While all theories about conflict espouse a component of frustration, not all agree as to whether this frustration symptom is substituted, as Dollard suggests, into other conflict-related actions. Likewise, there is divergence among theories as to how counselors might address conflict resolution with couples. Some of the more common approaches to marital conflict intervention include Solution-Focused Brief Therapy (SFBT), behavior therapy, emotionally focused couples therapy, and contextual therapy.

**Solution-Focused Brief Therapy.** SFBT offers many useful ideas concerning the origination and alteration of marital conflict patterns. This approach owes it originating ideas to Fisch, Watzlawick, and Weakland, who developed "Brief Problem-Focused Therapy" during the 1960s and 70s. During the 1980s, Steve de Shazer and his colleagues extended the original ideas and developed the current solution-focused approaches. Michele Weiner-Davis (1992) is also a frequently heard voice for this approach to conflict resolution.

The key difference between SFBT and other models of marital conflict intervention is that it emphasizes the exceptions to the conflict pattern rather than the examination of the conflict pattern. The exceptions offer insight into how a couple has intuitively or intentionally created solutions for their conflicted patterns but has yet to apply those solutions in specific circumstances. De Shazer (1991) states,

> Problems are seen to maintain themselves simply because they maintain themselves and because clients depict the problem as *always happening*. . . . For the clients, the problem is seen as primary (and the exceptions, if seen at all, are seen as secondary), while for therapists the exceptions are seen as primary; interventions are meant to help clients make a similar inversion, which will lead to the development of a solution. (p. 58)

Solution-focused approaches affirm the presence of a circular pattern. Weiner-Davis states that "each person's behavior is a response to an action or event which preceded it, while at the same time a trigger for that which follows it" (1992, p. 69).

Rather than seek understanding in the pattern, SFBT will seek the "anti-pattern" as the source for change within the couple. Couples who have come to counseling because of conflict issues tend to perceive their situation as worse than it really is. The negative interactions are more readily brought to awareness than their positive engagements. They are implementing an "expectation bias" in which they anticipate the next conversation to be antagonistic because they are retaining an antagonistic impression from a previous interaction. They come with a sense that the conflict exists "all the time," when indeed it occurs often, maybe frequently, but not continuously or perpetually. By examining how the couple integrates exception to the conflict, the solution-focused marital counselor is attempting to invert the expectations. The emphasis is to break the negative anticipation and to utilize the effective strategies that are already implemented by the couple in isolated situations for areas that are currently producing conflict.

***Behavioral couple theory.*** The prolific work of John Gottman over the past three decades has resulted in extensive data on couples' conflict processes and in treatments. During the 1970s Gottman's research influenced the profession toward understanding marital conflict through communications-based behavior (Gottman, Notarius, Gonso, & Markman, 1976). At the time, his research revealed that conflict between spouses was largely the result of communication inadequacies. The influence of his communication research permitted Heyman (2001) to state that "communication is the common pathway to relationship dysfunction because it is the common pathway for getting what you want in relationships. Nearly all relationship-relevant conflicts, emotions and neuroses are played out via observable communication" (p. 6). More recently, Gottman's work has focused on the link between marital behaviors and marital conflict and satisfaction. We have learned that couples who resolve conflicts with agreement, compromise, and humor are more likely to exhibit stability of satisfaction over time (Gottman, 1999).

*Integrative marital therapy.* Since the mid-1990s, behavioral marital therapy has undergone a radical shift in emphasis. Jacobson and Christensen, collaborators with Gottman in previous studies, led the "behavioral revolt." For twenty years they developed behavioral interventions that focused on altering communication patterns and creating positive exchange ratios. Positive exchange involves increasing the number of positive, encouraging, and relationship-building behaviors and reducing the number of negative, antagonistic, and destructive behaviors. If buying flowers, attending NFL football games, and dedicating time for conversation were seen as positive actions, then therapy involved helping couples increase them. And if golfing five times a week, going on unilateral shopping trips to Rodeo Drive, and yelling at one another were seen as negative, then therapy involved helping couples eliminate these. The problem was that Jacobson and Christensen found that these interventions were immediately helpful but would not maintain the benefit over time. During the late 1990s they developed Integrative Marital Therapy that utilized the tradition of behavioral components, including an emphasis on assessment and measured change with the emotional and transgenerational therapies described below (Jacobson & Christensen, 1996).

*Emotionally focused marital therapy.* An important contribution made by the originators of emotionally focused marital therapy was to see marital conflict related to childhood attachments (Johnson & Talitman, 1997). Bartholomew and Horowitz (1991) and Shi (2003) have developed interventions using variations of classical attachment theory articulated by Bowlby (1969). The central tenet of this approach is to see conflicted relationships as emerging from threat or experience of insecure attachments that create volatility in the space between the couple—thereby exacerbating the problem with greater insecurity (Johnson & Talitman, 1997). Conflict within intimate relationship is understood through attachment theory as an underlying threat to an individual's internal model of self/others in relationship. This relational model, derived through the stabilizing effect of love/attachment bonds, produces a homeostatic effect essential for secure perception of one's environment.

Individuals conduct life through these complicated models of relationship in which the world is seen through a variation of safe and trustworthy images and dangerous and uncertain images (Shi, 2003). When these models are threatened by any factor that brings vulnerability and potential harm to the attachment bond, a protective response is created to defend the sheltering characteristics of the relationship.

> From the attachment perspective, negative working models of self as undeserving of love and of the other as undependable guide interpretations of the partner's behavior. Small disappointment may then, for an insecure spouse, echo back to major hurts and injuries and disproportionately reinforce relationship distress. Unhappy couples develop a generally negative schema about the entire relationship history and tend to remember particular relationship events in ways that are consistent with such schema. They then perceive current interactions in the light of past negative events, and the more significant these events are, the more the preset relationship becomes hostage to them. (Johnson et al., 2001, p. 148)

To summarize, attachments are essential for an individual's security. Any injury or threat of injury to the attachment raises a self-protective process that, in the name of self-survival, places the relationship and the attachment in further jeopardy.

*Contextual family therapy.* The contribution of contextual therapy is important to our understanding of conflict because of the priority placed on injury or violation of love and trust. The theory was developed by Boszormenyi-Nagy based on the philosophical theory of Martin Buber. A current articulation of contextual theory is seen in Hargrave and Pfister (2003).

Buber's (1970) I-Thou relationship establishes a theoretical foundation of the understanding for emotional management occurring in marital relationship. According to Buber, healthy human relationships, labeled I-Thou, are characterized by a balanced exchange of mutual respect.

Boszormenyi-Nagy (Boszormenyi-Nagy, 1987; Boszormenyi-Nagy & Krasner, 1986; Boszormenyi-Nagy & Spark, 1984; Hargrave & Pfister, 2003) describes contextual family therapy through this I-Thou concept. The capacity to appropriately manage emotions is influenced by the subjective perception of fairness and trustworthiness within a relationship brought about by the presence of I-Thou. Boszormenyi-Nagy referred to this balance as relational justice. Relationships can maintain healthy existence only when there is equity between giving and receiving. Relationships grow in depth and stability when they exhibit altruistic acts such as mercy and grace. Acts of entitlement create emotional obligations that require reciprocating responses to maintain balance and fairness. Always giving or always receiving are not indicators of maturity of relational skills but speak more to an individual's dependence or narcissism. (Contextual therapy is described in greater detail in chap. 7.)

To summarize, the unique contribution of contextual therapy to intervention in marital conflict is the construct of relational ethic. Relational ethic is the balance of obligations and entitlements—giving and taking—that produce an environment of safety in relationship. Failure to meet relational obligations, or conversely to demand entitlement in a destructive manner, are violations to the balance of love and trust, resulting in conflict.

## MODEL FOR MARITAL CONFLICT RESOLUTION

Regarding the use of conflict interventions, Heyman states:

> All couples intervention involves, at the very least, an implicit model of what is important in relationships. Every clinician, with every client, must decide to intervene in some things and not others. This decision-making process typically is called *case formulation or case conceptualization* and is defined as a general model . . . to understand problems and generate solutions to them. (2001, p. 5)

The following model of marital conflict resolution is drawn from the theories articulated above. This model is intended to provide counselors with a road map to address couples' conflicts in a therapeutic setting. In addition, this model can be used with couples to guide forming insight into their own individual and systemic patterns that draw them into cyclical and repetitive conflicts.

*Introduction: The conflict is usually about the conflict . . . and more.* Often the first problem that counselors contend with in addressing conflicted couples is the failure to maintain focus on one problem. It is common for couples and counselors to fail to realize the subtle changes in communication evoked by the partners. The result is that fights are moving targets. As soon as counselors obtain a sense of the functional focus of the conflict, there is a twist and the couple is off addressing a different theme, leaving the counselor to try to figure out the change and its meaning. If a counselor is frustrated within the session, the cause is often the failure of the three to recognize this communication factor.

The example of Jerry and Marcia Martin can illustrate what easily happens. The Martins have been married for nineteen years. Marcia comes from a divorced home where her father was an alcohol abuser who eventually abandoned the family. Jerry is a recovering addict but has been clean and sober for twelve years.

> **MARCIA:** Jerry, when you didn't call last week I was really worried. You said you would call, and I sat waiting by the phone completely powerless, not having any way to reach you.
>
> **JERRY:** Look, I am sorry that I didn't call. I said I was sorry. There was nothing I could have done at the time. Besides, it was only a few hours and you are making a bigger deal out of this than it really was.
>
> **MARCIA:** Making a big deal out of this? I can't believe that you said that. Look, I know now that it was something innocent and couldn't be helped. OK, I accept that. But you are forgetting the number of nights that I waited for you at night—when you were drinking . . .
>
> **JERRY:** I can't believe you'd bring that up. I have been sober for twelve years—twelve years! You are blaming me for this—but I think that it's more to do with you and how terrified you become whenever I am late because of your family—and thinking that I am neglecting you and the kids like your father did. But I am not your father and I wish you would stop treating me like I am.
>
> **MARCIA:** I think that is really cheap that you would bring my father into this . . .
>
> **JERRY:** No cheaper than bringing my actions a dozen years ago. Besides, he is involved here, not directly, but his leaving has made you much more sensitive to me walking out. You know that, we've already talked about that.

This dialogue reveals not one but three conflicts or three origins of injury. Both Jerry and Marcia are seeking to exercise control over the other with their accusations and defenses. As soon as the defenses become penetrated with the facts of irresponsibility, Jerry or Marcia will shift the focus of the conflict to another dimension. Each is actively thwarting or sabotaging the relational process.

The fight begins with Marcia making a legitimate accusation toward Jerry that he is responsible for her pain—anxiety and worry over his safety and her threat of loss. This is the first fight, the *present conflict*. Jerry does not stay on that topic but shifts the focus of responsibility to Marcia. He accuses her of being overreactive.

When Marcia realizes that she is not going to obtain her desired goal, which is probably reassurance or security, she changes the topic from the present focus to a problem/injury that occurred between the two of them in the past. This is the second fight, the *historical conflict*. She raises Jerry's past actions as justification for her current reaction.

Finally, Jerry pulls the trump card of all fights—he states that this fight is really not about him at all but about Marcia's residual injury from childhood. This is the third level of disagreement: our *family-of-origin conflicts*.

The three concurrent conflicts are depicted in figure 14.1. The diagram indicates that in any conflict there are three dimensions occurring simultaneously: the present conflict, the historical conflict, and the family-of-origin conflict that is triggered by both the present and historical quarrels. The present conflict is contextualized within the historical conflict. A couple that has not addressed, forgiven, and reconciled from previous injury and has not chosen to not return to that historical conflict when the opportunity presents itself will find that they pull each other back into previous conflicts when frustration from the present conflict occurs. Furthermore, each partner has the residual effect of injury from the painful realities of childhood and adolescence. These exist outside of the direct interaction of the couple but can easily be brought into the present and historical conflict by intention or by accident.

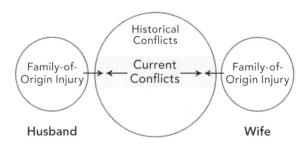

**Figure 14.1.** Three concurrent conflicts

### Pain and vulnerability.

> It is not true that suffering ennobles the character; happiness
> does that sometimes, but suffering, for the most part makes us
> petty and vindictive.

W. Somerset Maugham, *The Moon and Sixpence*

The starting point of this marital-relational conflict cycle is *pain* (Hargrave &
Sells, 1997). According to contextual theory, pain, hurt, vulnerability, or threat
is the felt experience of perceived or real imbalance in relationship. Pain is
experienced by any assault or injury or psychological violation resulting in
humiliation, shame, guilt, exhibition, or perception of injustice. Pain refers to
adverse emotional reactions to perceived unfairness. It includes the wide range
of unpleasant emotions that Thorndike originally labeled "annoyers." It is any
aversive stimuli from which one actively seeks to escape when it is present and
to avoid if it can be anticipated. The marital conflict cycle focuses on relational
pain rather than sensory pain such as literal physical infliction of pain.

Figure 14.2 depicts pain and vulnerability experienced simultaneously by
spouses. Of particular importance is that pain emerges from the three conflicts:
(1) the pain emerging from the actual incident provoking the disagreement (the
current conflict), (2) residual pain from previous injuries occurring in the marriage (the historical conflict), and (3) the pain experienced outside of relationship with one's spouse, particularly those injuries that occurred in
childhood within one's family of origin (the family-of-origin injury).

Figure 14.2. Pain/vulnerability and the sources of injury

In regards to the complicated set of behaviors employed by individuals in
intimate relationship as a response to aversion or pain, Krasner and Joyce
(1995) state that individuals are "impelled by fear of pain, given or received,

people actively opt, by omission or commission, for hurt withdrawal, imposition, and other well-entrenched barriers and dismissive defenses of monologue" (p. 4). "Defenses of monologue" is their revealing description of the effect of defenses—they create protective isolation. Monologue is distinct from dialogue in that it is a conversation of one. It is safe. It does not need to exercise the effort of understanding another, but neither can it experience support and strength from others. Defenses misapplied create monologue.

The role of pain in relational conflict is described in contextual, emotion-focused, and behavioral theories using different terminology but portraying a common construct. Pain becomes the trigger that propels an individual into a pattern of coping behaviors that can pull the intimate partner into a cycle of conflict. Numerous researchers have attempted to categorize the painful provocations that produce the subsequent set of conflict reactions (Buss, 1989; Snell, McDonald, & Koch, 2002). The behaviors include condescension, abuse, inconsideration, possessiveness, neglect, aggression, self-centeredness, and substance abuse. Notarius, Lashley, and Sullivan (1997) state any list of potential pain-producing provocateurs will be incomplete. "However, we believe that underlying these discrete behaviors is a much smaller list of threats to self" (p. 226). Threats to self are any potential or real cause of harm, pain, or discomfort.

The presence of pain suggests a distortion in the relational ethic, defined as "an innate sense of justice that demands balance between what they are entitled to receive from a relationship and what they are obligated to give in order to maintain relational existence" (Hargrave & Sells, 1997, p. 42).

Similarly, within the emotion-focused paradigm, Johnson, Makinen, and Millikin (2001) created the term "attachment injuries" to describe the unique aspects of psychological pain resulting from interdependent relational injury. Pain and injury occurring between individuals where there is no family, marital, or relational tie that produces an obligation or commitment are more easily resolved by individuals.

Finally, in the behavioral paradigm, exchange theory (Adams, 1963, 1965; Bagarozzi & Wodarski, 1977) is described as a motivation to maintain relationships based on expected and perceived benefits compared to losses. Exchange theory demands a mutually beneficial economy; that is, the relationship must seem "worth it" to both parties. If not, the aversive effect of inequitable exchange is experienced by either or both individuals. In other words, people can tolerate pain when there is an identifiable benefit. If pain is not offset by hope, it is seen as intolerable.

## Defensiveness.

*A man in armor is his armor's slave.*

Robert Browning, "Herakles"

The term "defense" is commonly held synonymous with the terms "ego-defense" and "defense mechanism" within the psychoanalytic tradition. Valiant's (1992) seminal work on defense mechanisms revealed that when one encounters a stress, annoyer, or some form of pain that a protective response to that stress is an essential reaction. Furthermore, he posited that quality of life and quality of relationship could be determined by the quality of the stress-reaction response (Vines, 1979).

Defensiveness is commonly labeled as an obstructive reaction in marital conflict. It is our natural and necessary reaction to emotional pain or injury. Within classical conditioning theory, it is the unconditioned escape response to an aversive stimulus. One does not teach another to seek to reduce discomfort.

Vangelisti and Crumley (1998) studied responses of hurt through communication research. They suggested that the ways cognitions and expressions of feelings occur are related with one's evaluations of the hurtful episode and, most likely, one's feelings about the relationship. Their exploration of different responses to pain and hurt identified ten behavioral/communication responses. Their findings included silence, crying, attacking, defending, sarcasm, inquiry, ignoring, conceding, laughing, and apologizing. Of these, their research found that silence, attacking, defending, and conceding were the most common.

Similarly, Wile (1993) identified forty-four types of defenses used when the threat of pain necessitates self-protection. He placed these defenses into six categories: denying, excuse making, counterattacking, self-accusing, fixing, and withdrawing.

Defenses are self-protective, yet their use has a deleterious effect on the relationship. The implementation of defenses can easily provoke a chain reaction of pain-defense-pain-defense between spouses, resulting in an escalation of conflict.

**Destructive defenses.** Beyond the existence of common defenses that emerge in the presence of pain, the literature identifies a certain kind of defense that is particularly corrosive, even destructive to relationships. We have just described defenses as a common, even essential response to pain that has a negative secondary effect that is harmful to relationships. However, when a painful experience is anticipated, the spouse can employ a destructive, proactive, offensive pattern; as one anticipates a painful experience, he/she can reduce its threat by hurting the other before hurt comes to oneself. The idea of destructive defensiveness is drawn from Boszormenyi-Nagy and Krasner's (1986) construct of destructive entitlement. They stress that an injured person may be justified in seeking reparation, but such reparation is not constrained within ethical limits: "The destructively entitled person is often blocked from experiencing remorse as a consequence of his/her unjust treatment of an innocent party" (p. 63). It is as if the pain from previous violations, both recent and historical, distorts one's sense of relational fairness. It is a perversion of the Mosaic law, "an eye for an eye." Instead it states that since in the past the other has shown the potential to injure my eye, I am justified in injuring their eye first.

The effect of defenses on the relationship is negative. It prompts the other spouse to act protectively, even aggressively, exacerbating the state of conflict. Destructive defenses are significantly more harmful to the relationship in that they not only provoke pain, they are more likely to undermine trust within the relationship. If I accidentally bruise your shin with a chair as I move it across the kitchen, it hurts. In the future you will likely be more wary of me when I move furniture around the house. But if I, in anger, throw the chair and your shin is bruised, you are likely to see me as not merely clumsy, but dangerous. While the defensive reaction tends to produce collateral damage, the destructive defenses produce targeted damage. The effect is almost the same—they both hurt. Defensiveness provokes painful emotions that prompt a reciprocating defensive management, completing the conflict cycle and initiating a new round. The relationship between common defenses and destructive defenses is illustrated in figure 14.3.

## BUILDING RELATIONAL INTIMACY IN
## PLACE OF RELATIONAL CONFLICT

Understanding the reciprocating patterns of conflict is important in that it helps therapists understand the chaos that is often present when couples voice their frustrating experiences with one another. It gives definition to the hole into which couples have fallen. Now we have to help them climb out. Pastoral counselors and Christian therapists are in a unique position to intervene in the relational pattern with the central elements of the Christian faith.

Building on the diagram of relational conflict, we propose that there is another cycle that couples may employ in place of the pain-defense pattern

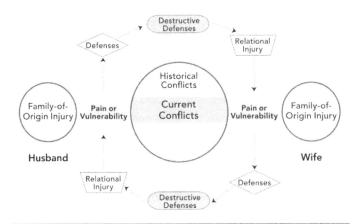

**Figure 14.3.** Relational conflict cycle

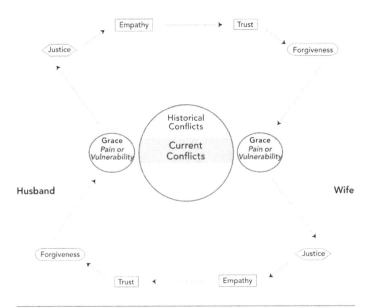

**Figure 14.4.** Relational intimacy cycle

that provides an alternative to relational conflict. The relational intimacy cycle (fig. 14.4) consists of five constructs common in the Christian tradition that the therapist can help couples understand, practice, and demonstrate to each other. The components that make up the cycle are grace, justice, empathy, trust, and forgiveness.

We believe that the emotion-defense conflict cycle can be altered through a targeted learning experience in which couples implement components of relational repair as espoused by Hargrave (1994a), Hargrave and Sells (1997), and McCullough, Worthington, and Rachal (1997). The central task is to learn and implement relational skills and values that incorporate grace, justice, empathy, trust, and forgiveness in order to displace painful experiences and the use of defensive protective reactions.

In the diagram, grace surrounds pain. It insulates it. It holds and provides comfort. Grace is the essential healing agent that counselors can assist couples to employ toward each other to redirect the initial impulse of defensiveness. People in pain, particularly the pain that emerges from conflict, are more inclined to not pursue or receive grace; they are inclined to pursue defensiveness. Grace invites them to pursue a different path.

## INTEGRATIVE FOCUS: Family Functioning

In the context of military operations, the first step required to establish peace is for both sides to stop shooting at one another. Marital and family conflict is similar. This means that initially, the family therapist must occupy a very large presence. Just as a United Nations peace-keeping force is an army that exists to keep other armies from fighting, and does so with the use of force, so also the marital therapist functions with the force and power of his or her authority as a counselor to demand compliance that is civil and constructive while under therapy. Without this strength, the therapist can be pulled into the fight and find oneself undermatched by the firepower that both parties might direct at each other.

*Think about it:* Most often we think of a therapist as possessing qualities such as empathy, compassion, patience, and warmth. Yet here we are suggesting that a marital therapist involved in conflict resolution must be authoritative and forceful. Reconcile this role with the more common and typical roles of therapy.

We believe that the message of grace, applied to couples in a healing process, is best modeled by the therapist simultaneously to both spouses in the presence of the other. Returning to the example of Jerry and Marcia, the counselor has the capacity to redirect the pattern of conflict:

COUNSELOR: Marcia, I hear in your words, and see in your face the pain and sorrow that you feel and know, and I would guess that it's only a fraction of the degree of hurt you felt last week when you couldn't contact Jerry.

MARCIA: Yes, it was awful. I just didn't know what to do.

COUNSELOR: And from what I could piece together, these were familiar pains—hurt from long ago, both with Jerry, who has been successful at change, and with your family as a child.

MARCIA: Jerry has been great over the years, I am very proud of what he has done. But I am easily reminded of what that hurt feels like . . .

COUNSELOR: And you just can't get it out of your mind . . .

MARCIA: Right.

COUNSELOR: When you feel that fear and remember that terror—what do you do?

MARCIA: I worry. I get scared. And I guess that I try to find out what's going on.

COUNSELOR: You want to know if this fear is a real problem or a feared problem.

COUNSELOR: Jerry, you're one of the few men who have success over drug abuse. That says a lot about you.

JERRY: Well, I live one day at a time.

COUNSELOR: I know, but you have lived one day at a time for a pretty long string of days. That means that you have consistently made good decisions. I wonder, as you sit here and hear of Marcia's fear, if you knew right now that she was full of anxiety and fear, what would you want to do about it? She is not angry, she is not blaming you, she is just afraid. What would you want to do about it?

JERRY: Well that's easy, I would want to make her feel safe.

COUNSELOR: Good, I believe that you would. Now, Marcia, you too have had to overcome a great deal in order to sit where you are today.

You have had to see Jerry struggle to face his addictions when probably many people counseled you to leave and start a new life with someone else.

MARCIA:      That was a really hard time . . .

COUNSELOR: What did you tell yourself when it was hard and when it looked hopeless?

MARCIA:      I prayed, I called my friends who would help me and come over when I needed them . . . and I think about where my hope was, and just stay on track.

COUNSELOR: You gave him a gift—"I believe in you and I will stay with you."

MARCIA:      That's right, I did.

COUNSELOR: Now to both of you, I am asking that you think about a gift for each other. It's not deserved. It hasn't been earned. It's just a gift. For you Jerry, it is "I will give Marcia the gift of security." For you Marcia, it's "I will give Jerry the gift of trust." These gifts are not the long-term solution to your conflict. They are meant to give immediate relief to pain that you both are saying that you feel, and that you both are saying that you would wish to relieve from each other.

In this example the counselor is utilizing the contextual therapy technique of multidirected partiality. It is "a technique of understanding and crediting all relational parties for the different concerns, efforts, and impacts of what people have done in relationship and what has been done to them" (Hargrave & Pfister, 2003, p. 100). The counselor offers a calming gift of validation of each person in the presence of the other.

The function of grace is to disarm, to alter the natural response toward defensiveness and self-protection that inevitably leads to an exacerbation of the conflict pattern. Grace is accepting of pain and position. It moves close to people in their state of emotional suffering. Grace is 1 Corinthians 13 applied to life. It is offering patience when the impulse is to demand action. It is kindness when there has not been kindness extended first.

Unlike theological saving grace, this relational grace cannot be self-sustaining. When Luther articulated "Grace alone" he was referring to how God's gift of salvation is without merit from beginning to end and is never exhausted. However, human grace extended to loved ones does not have the same perseverance as God's grace does. Grace must be supported or it will not be sustained.

*Justice.* Our use of justice is adapted from Hargrave (1994a). He focused on the contextual therapy dimension of relational ethics, which is the subjective balance of justice, trustworthiness, and entitlement between family members. The give-and-take process is the basis for family and marital interactions.

Justice requires that a couple attend to problem solving, weighing alternatives and charting a course that is just, balanced, and mutual. It is the assumption of responsibility, the declaration of mutual violations, and the pursuit of mutual fairness. Because of grace, couples can pursue justice. Without grace, justice is lost in competition for power.

Marital justice is possible in the context of grace. One can courageously confront issues that will harm our "us," and look at one's lover with compassion and a willingness to assist him or her in the effort of holiness. Justice exists in the form of boundaries. Boundaries set limits of obligations and privileges. Boundaries declare how we must be in order to fully enhance our "us." The demonstration of justice between Marcia and Jerry is seen in a conversation regarding the jumping from present, historical, and family-of-origin fights.

JERRY:   I knew that when I brought up your father, that that was out of line. I guess I did it because I wanted to . . . well to get you to stop. But I see how it's not fair and only makes things worse.

MARCIA: I know. And really, I did the same thing when I brought up your drinking and your drugs. While I do sometimes fear that you will go back to the old way—that's not coming from you. That's my fear inside of me.

Marcia and Jerry's understanding and practice of justice is a commitment to disciplined fighting. It is placing a boundary around the types of communication that are spoken and the forms of behavior that are exhibited. The conflict remains, but it is a conflict that is controlled by discipline and self-restraint. The fight will appear more like a boxing match—legislated by rules strictly respected by both—rather than a street fight that has no restraint. The latter is violence, the former is sport.

*Empathy.* Empathy is a relatively new word in the lexicon of human relationships. Its closest biblical synonym is compassion. While counselors who are schooled in basic counseling skills understand empathy in the clinical sense, the professional empathy pales in comparison to the empathy potential that emerges from real relationships. Empathy involves the capacity to perceive, understand, and accept another. Empathy is an intimacy that opposes the suffering of isolation (Jordan, 1991).

Within marriages, McCullough, Worthington, and Rachal (1997) found that empathy plays a mediating role between offense and forgiveness, or between conflict and resolution. Empathy requires a lowering of defenses. It gives legitimacy to the position of the other. Toward this end, Framo states, "One of the things which seems to help marriages, as I stated previously, is that the partners have a more empathic understanding of each other. Having been given the opportunity to hear each other's life history and now knowing what the spouse had to struggle with, partners find each other's behavior more understandable" (Framo, 1981, pp. 153-54).

Empathy is far more challenging than occupying a kind and supportive posture. It involves an intense, sustained, and personal understanding of another. It includes the laying aside of one's interests in order to maintain the interests of another. Finally, it involves a grasping or an acceptance of another (Bohart & Greenberg, 1999).

Teaching the exercise of empathy to couples is essential in maintaining a redirection of relational conflict. Empathy is identification; it is drawing near to another's circumstance with full appreciation for its causes. Empathy is to become with the sufferer as if he or she were suffering themselves. It has a transformational quality because it challenges the internal belief that I am indeed all alone. Empathy turns companionship into a rich intimacy.

In the case of Marcia and Jerry empathy was caught by the couple after it was demonstrated by the counselor. Recall previously that it was the counselor who exhibited the empathic position of validating the pain that both individuals had experienced. This was not directed at blaming someone for acting in an injurious manner. Rather, it was focused on validating the real experience of suffering.

COUNSELOR: *(to both Jerry and Marcia)* You each observed me earlier ask questions and give responses that seemed to have changed your mood. Can you recall what you felt?

MARCIA: Well, I sure can. You listened to me, and you acknowledged that I wasn't nuts or selfish. I was hurt and afraid.

COUNSELOR: Now, you both are smart people and are perfectly capable of exercising such basic kindness as listening. What happens that you don't do that with one another?

JERRY: I think that we both are so caught up in being angry and mad that we won't give in and let down.

COUNSELOR: Do you remember the conflict cycle part that addressed your defenses? What you are saying is that when you are protected and guarded there is not much room to be kind, close, and to listen with care.

MARCIA: It seems that when we are really angry, we can't listen to each other.

COUNSELOR: OK, right now you are not angry. So we can work on this skill together. Marcia, I'd like you to be mad. Jerry, I'd like you to be empathic—to listen without getting riled up.

JERRY: You mean you want us to fight in here?

COUNSELOR: No, I mean that I want you to practice calming each other rather than getting into a tit-for-tat argument that just continues to escalate.

MARCIA: OK, here goes . . . Jerry, I came home today and the kitchen was a mess. You said that you would clean it up before you left for work. This just shows that I can't count on you for anything . . .

COUNSELOR: Marcia, stop. Now if you want Jerry to be able to respond empathically, then you will have to fight justly—saying "I can't count on you for anything" is probably an exaggeration that only serves to be provocative.

MARCIA: Yeah, I see that. So, OK . . . you promised to do the dishes!

COUNSELOR: Good!

JERRY: You are angry at me because I broke my promise.

COUNSELOR: Well said.

Empathy, preceded by both grace and justice, allows the couple to listen. The selfless gift of grace and the stabilizing presence of justice must be present for empathy to exist without shifting toward self-protection. When empathy or compassion is present the conflict dissipates.

*Trust.*

> *You can fly. All it takes is faith and trust. . . . [And] a little bit of Pixie dust.*

Peter Pan

> *Love anything and your heart will be wrung and possibly broken. If you want to make sure of keeping it intact you must give it to no one, not even an animal.*

C. S. Lewis

Empathy leads to trusting and trustworthiness. The two are not the same. In fact, I often find that individuals are good at one but not the other. To trust is to place yourself in a position of vulnerability with your partner. I will risk myself with you because I trust you. That is, I believe that you have my well-being at the top of your priorities and place my interests above your own when necessary. Being trustworthy is to model a quality of commitment and security such that trusting can occur.

Often in marriages one person has dedicated himself or herself to being the trustworthy person so that the other can exercise trust. Unless trusting and trustworthiness—both characteristics of trust—exist, there will be a limitation on the couple's growth.

Trust and trustworthiness skills often fall along gender lines. Women are more often better at trusting, and men more often better at exhibiting trustworthiness. This imbalance can be a source of problem. With Marcia and Jerry, a pattern became apparent. When they would talk at night, Marcia would detail her day and Jerry would listen. Then Jerry would summarize his day—in about five words. Their challenge of trust/trustworthiness was that Marcia would be the trusting "talker" revealing her thoughts and emotions, and Jerry the faithful "listener." Jerry would not take the risk of revealing himself, and Marcia would make his nontrusting easier. She would tend to more frequently offer opinion or become impatient with the amount of time it took for him to formulate his feelings. The effect was that it shifted the focus back to Marcia and the status quo.

*Forgiveness.* Forgiveness is a complicated and multifaceted construct involving three forms: the healing of self, or self-forgiveness; assuming responsibility for one's injurious acts toward another, or seeking forgiveness; and receiving from another restorative gestures because of injury experienced, or granting or receiving forgiveness (Enright & the Human Development Study Group, 1991). While some work has focused on self-forgiveness and seeking forgiveness (Bauer et al., 1992; Enright & the Human Development Study Group, 1991; Snow, 1993), the majority of the literature is directed toward granting/receiving forgiveness subsequent to injury or violation (Gassin, 1996).

Forgiveness is also a transtheoretical theme. The most common and basic understanding of forgiveness involves some aspect of release or letting go over time. The release may focus on anger (Davenport, 1991; Fitzgibbons, 1986), revenge (Cloke, 1993), shame (Halling, 1994), record of wrongs (DiBlasio, 1992), and resentment (Enright & the Human Development Study Group, 1991; North, 1987). The literature includes efforts to utilize some aspect of forgiveness in virtually all of the major theoretical paradigms.

## INTEGRATIVE FOCUS: *Family Relationships*

The vast majority of attention paid to forgiveness and restoration within families addresses the question, how do I forgive a family member who has hurt or wronged me? But Jesus' words in the Gospels define two aspects of forgiveness. He says, "Forgive us our sins, for we also forgive everyone who sins against us" (Lk 11:4 NIV). The implication is that families consist of members who are both perpetrators of sin and affected by the sins of others.

*Think about it:* Consider your behavior within your family. Is there a balance between feeling wronged by the actions of others and realizing the wrong of your actions toward others?

Trust allows for the process of forgiveness to occur. Forgiveness is such a deep and heavy word that unfortunately it is frequently trivialized. Forgiveness is not anything like saying "I'm sorry" or accepting an apology. Forgiveness is the letting go of the continual punishment from being offended and being an offender. It is to restore full relationship between parties where there has been friction, tension, and injury. Hargrave (1994a, 1994b) views it as the growing restoration of love and trust.

There are variations of depth to forgiveness. It is not an all-or-nothing construct. An initial form of forgiveness is when an individual or couple is able to stop the conflict, preventing more injury from occurring. This type of forgiveness should not be confused with manipulative withdrawing from the other—declared to stop injury but in effect it is to exercise control. This type of forgiveness can be seen in the actions of a husband or wife who says, "No, I will not go to the party with you. For some reason, when I am in that context with you, you have said things that have been hurtful. That combination of people evokes something in you that I don't understand, and it usually results in our conflicts increasing. I want to be with you, but not there. I will stop it before it starts."

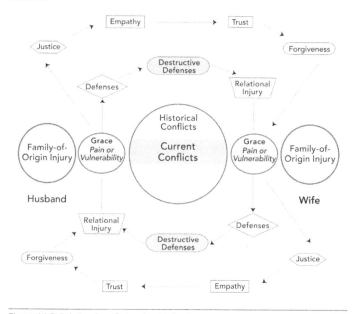

**Figure 14.5.** Relational conflict cycle with forgiveness

Ultimately, forgiveness leads us back to grace—it refuels our capacity to act graciously with the pain of "us," that is both my pain and my spouse's. Grace is not very enduring. It cannot sustain itself for endless periods. Forgiveness becomes the recharging source that allows us to continue the ongoing confrontation of our pain.

*Christian engagement.* To the Christian, conflict resolution is not a peripheral issue. The central theme of the Christian story line is the resolution of a conflict between God and humanity. Forgiveness, reconciliation, trust, empathy/compassion, justice, and grace are the great theses of the biblical narrative. Therefore, the idea of relational conflict resolution is not a technique to be implemented as much as it is a lifestyle for the Christian to embody and exhibit with all, particularly within the family and the household of faith.

However, it is easy to errantly make harmony the goal of relationship. The dangerous effect is that we can substitute conflict with compliance, and intimacy with an artificial image of closeness. In truth, mature families should have conflict. Couples should disagree with one another, and those disagreements should produce emotional intensity. Research indicates that it is not the frequency or the intensity of the marital conflict that measures relational maturity. It is the time required for a couple to resolve their differences, attend to each other's needs, and return to a state of equilibrium (Gottman, 1994a).

## CONCLUSION

We believe that pastoral counselors and family therapists are in a unique position not just to help couples resolve problems but to help them become transformed toward greater maturity. Couples who understand and experience the reconciliation of God through grace, justice, faith, and reconciliation are able to feed one

### INTEGRATIVE FOCUS: Family Identity

Over time families create internal rules and patterns. There is an expectation of how we do things. These patterns function as identification markers—like a family fingerprint. One such marker is conflict. Families form identity around how conflict will be conducted among members. In some ways this creates security because the family knows what to expect. But tragically, the security might be destructive, as in we expect to lose our temper and say hurtful words or throw small appliances! As Christians we are called to form an identity through Jesus that is to shape and form the nature and quality of our patterns with others. The family identity established around conflict is to be reformed into a reflection of Christlike qualities and attributes.

*Think about it:* What are the characteristics of conflict that are a reflection of Jesus? Can we become angry? Can we raise our voices? Can a couple or family fight and be a reflection of Jesus at the same time?

another with the same relational nutrition. The blessing of reconciliation has an effect not just on the immediate marriage: multiple generations become the beneficiaries of a couple's capacity to exhibit relational maturity and instruct children in the path of forgiveness and reconciliation (Hargrave, 1994a, 1994b).

## REFERENCES

Adams, J. S. (1963). Towards an understanding of inequality. *Journal of Abnormal and Normal Social Psychology, 67,* 422-36.

Adams, J. S. (1965). Inequity in social exchange. *Advanced Experimental Psychology, 62,* 335-43.

Bagarozzi, D. A., & Wodarski, J. S. (1977). A social exchange typology of conjugal relationships and conflict development. *Journal of Marriage and Family Counseling, 3,* 53-60.

Bartholomew, K., & Horowitz, L. M. (1991). Attachment styles among young adults: A test of a four-category model. *Journal of Personality and Social Psychology, 61,* 226-44.

Bauer, L., Duffy, J., Fountain, E., Halling, S., Holzer, M., Jones, E., Leifer, M., & Row, J. (1992). Exploring self-forgiveness. *Journal of Religion and Health, 31,* 149-60.

Bergman, S. J., & Surrey, J. L. (1994). *Couples therapy: A relational approach.* Wellesley, MA: Stone Center Work in Progress.

Bohart, A., & Greenberg, L. (1999). *Empathy reconsidered: New directions in psychotherapy.* Washington, DC: American Psychological Association.

Boszormenyi-Nagy, I. (1987). *Foundations of contextual therapy: Collected papers.* New York: Brunner/Mazel.

Boszormenyi-Nagy, I., & Krasner, B. (1986). *Between give and take: A clinical guide to contextual therapy.* New York: Brunner/Mazel.

Boszormenyi-Nagy, I., & Spark, G. M. (1984). *Invisible loyalties: Reciprocity in intergenerational family therapy.* New York: Brunner/Mazel.

Bowlby, J. (1969). *Attachment and loss: Vol. 1. Attachment.* London: Hogarth Press; New York: Basic Books.

Bradbury, T. N., Fincham, F. D., & Beach, S. R. H. (2000). Research on the nature and determinants of marital satisfaction: A decade in review. *Journal of Marriage and the Family, 62,* 964-80.

Buber, M. (1970). *I and thou.* New York: Charles Scribner's Sons.

Buss, D. M. (1989). Conflict between the sexes: Strategic interference and the evocation of anger and upset. *Journal of Personality and Social Psychology, 56,* 735-47.

Cloke, K. (1993). Revenge, forgiveness and the magic of mediations. Special issue: Beyond technique: The soul of family mediation. *Mediation Quarterly, 11,* 67-78.

Consumer Reports. (1995, November). Mental health: Does therapy work? 734-39.

Davenport, D. S. (1991). The functions of anger and forgiveness: Guidelines for psychotherapy with victims. *Psychotherapy: Theory, Research, Practice, Training, 28*(1), 140-44.

de Shazer, S. (1991). *Putting differences to work.* New York: W. W. Norton.

DiBlasio, F. A. (1992). Forgiveness in psychotherapy: A comparison of younger and older therapists. *Journal of Psychology and Christianity, 11,* 181-87.

Dollard, J. (1938). *Frustration and aggression.* New Haven: Yale University Press.

Donavan, J. M. (1995). Short-term couples group psychotherapy: A take of four fights. *Psychotherapy: Theory, Research, Practice, Training, 32*(4), 608-17.

Enright, R. D., & the Human Development Study Group. (1991). The moral development of forgiveness. In W. Kurtines & J. Gewirtz (Eds.), *Moral behavior and development* (Vol. 1, pp. 123-52). Hillsdale, NJ: Erlbaum.

Fishbane, M. D. (2001). Relational narratives of the self. *Family Process, 40,* 41-58.

Fitzgibbons, R. P. (1986). The cognitive and emotive use of forgiveness in the treatment of anger. *Psychotherapy, 23,* 629-33.

Framo, J. L. (1976). Family of origin as a therapeutic resource for adults in marital and family therapy: You can and should go home again. *Family Process, 2,* 193-210.

Framo, J. L. (1981). *Family therapy: Major contributions.* New York: International Universities Press.

Gassin, E. A. (1996). *Receiving forgiveness from others.* Paper presented at the American Psychological Association Mid-Winter Conference. Scottsdale, AZ.

Giblin, P., & Chan, J. (1995). Predicting divorce. *The Family Journal: Counseling and Therapy for Couples and Families, 2,* 134-38.

Giblin, P., & Combs, M. P. (2003). Marital enrichment in clinical practice. In G. P. Sholevar (Ed.) with L. D. Schwoeri, *Textbook of family and couples therapy: Clinical applications* (pp. 434-65). Washington, DC: American Psychiatric Publishing.

Gottman, J. (1993a). The roles of conflict engagement, escalation, and avoidance in marital interaction: A longitudinal view of five types of couples. *Journal of Consulting and Clinical Psychology, 61,* 6-15.

Gottman, J. (1993b). A theory of marital dissolution and stability. *Journal of Family Psychology, 7,* 57-75.

Gottman, J. (1994a). *What predicts divorce? The relationship between marital process and marital outcomes.* Hillsdale, NJ: Erlbaum.

Gottman, J. (1994b). *Why marriages succeed or fail.* New York: Simon & Schuster.

Gottman, J. (1999). *The seven principles for making marriage work.* New York: Crown Publishers.

Gottman, J., Notarius, C., Gonso, J., & Markman, H. (1976). *A couple's guide to communication.* Champaign, IL: Research Press.

Halling, S. (1994). Shame and forgiveness. *Humanistic Psychologist, 22,* 75-87.

Hargrave, T. D. (1994a). *Families and forgiveness: Healing wounds in the intergenerational family.* New York: Brunner/Mazel.

Hargrave, T. D. (1994b). Families and forgiveness: A theoretical and therapeutic framework. *The Family Journal: Counseling and Therapy for Couples and Families, 2,* 339-48.

Hargrave, T. D., & Anderson, W. T. (1992). *Finishing well: Aging and reparation in the intergenerational family.* New York: Brunner/Mazel.

Hargrave, T. D., & Pfister, F. (2003). *The new contextual therapy.* New York: Brunner-Routledge.

Hargrave, T. D., & Sells, J. N. (1997). The development of a forgiveness scale. *Journal of Marital and Family Therapy, 23,* 41-62.

Heavey, C. L., Christensen, A., & Malamuth, N. M. (1995). The longitudinal impact of demand and withdrawal during marital conflict. *Journal of Consulting and Clinical Psychology, 63,* 797-801.

Heyman, R. E. (2001). Observation of couple conflicts: Clinical assessment applications, stubborn truths, and shaky foundations. *Psychological Assessment, 13,* 5-35.

Jacobson, N. S., & Addis, M. E. (1993). Research on couples and couple therapy: What do we know? Where are we going? *Journal of Consulting and Clinical Psychology, 61,* 85-93.

Jacobson, N. S., & Christensen, A. (1996). *Acceptance and change in couple therapy: A therapist's guide to transforming relationships.* New York: W. W. Norton.

Johnson, S. M., Makinen, J. A., & Millikin, J. W. (2001). Attachment injuries in couple relationships: A new perspective on impasses in couples therapy. *Journal of Marital and Family Therapy, 27,* 145-55.

Johnson, S. M., & Talitman, E. (1997). Predictors of success in emotionally focused marital therapy. *Journal of Marital and Family Therapy, 23,* 135-53.

Jordan, J. V. (1991). The meaning of mutuality. In J. V. Jordan, A. G. Kaplan, J. B. Miller, I. P. Stiver, & J. L. Surrey (Eds.), *Women's growth in connection: Writings for the Stone Center.* New York: Guilford Press.

Krasner, B. R., & Joyce, A. J. (1995). *Trust, truth and relationships.* New York: Brunner/Mazel.

Madanes, C. (1991). *Sex, love and violence.* New York: W. W. Norton.

McCullough, M. E., Worthington, E. L., Jr., & Rachal, K. C. (1997). Interpersonal forgiving in close relationships. *Journal of Personality and Social Psychology, 2*(73), 321-36.

Murray, S. L., Bellavia, G. M., Rose, P., & Griffin, D. W. (2003). Once hurt, twice hurtful: How perceived regard regulates daily marital interaction. *Journal of Personality and Social Psychology, 84*, 126-47.

North, J. (1987). Wrongdoing and forgiveness. *Philosophy, 62*, 499-508.

Notarius, C., Lashley, S. L., & Sullivan, D. J. (1997). Angry at your partner: Think again. In R. J. Sternberg & M. Hojjat (Eds.), *Satisfaction in close relationships* (pp. 219-48). New York: Guilford Press.

Notarius, C., & Markman, H. (1993). *We can work it out: Making sense in marital conflict.* New York: Putman.

Roberts, R. C. (2000). A Christian psychology view. In E. L. Johnson & S. L. Jones (Eds.), *Psychology and Christianity: Four views* (pp. 148-77). Downers Grove, IL: InterVarsity Press.

Rusbult, C. E., Verette, J., Whitney, G. A., Slovik, L. F., & Lipkus, I. (1991). Accommodation process in close relationships: Theory and preliminary empirical evidence. *Journal of Personality and Social Psychology, 60*, 53-78.

Shi, L. (2003). The association between adult attachment styles and conflict resolution in romantic relationships. *The American Journal of Family Therapy, 31*, 143-57.

Snell, W. E., McDonald K., & Koch, W. R. (2002). Anger provoking experiences: A multidimensional scaling analysis. In W. E. Snell (Ed.), *Progress in the study of physical and psychological health.* Cape Girardeau, MO: Snell Publications.

Snow, N. E. (1993). Self-forgiveness. *Journal of Value Inquiry, 22*, 75-80.

Todd, E. (1985). The value of confession and forgiveness according to Jung. *Journal of Religion and Health, 24*, 29-48.

Valiant, G. E. (1992). *Ego mechanisms of defense: A guide for clinicians and researchers.* Washington, DC: American Psychiatric Press.

Vangelisti, A. L., & Crumley, L. P. (1998). Reactions to messages that hurt: The influence of relational contexts. *Communication Monographs, 65*, 173-96.

Vines, N. R. (1979). Adult unfolding and marital conflict, *Journal of Marital and Family Therapy, 5*(2), 5-14.

Weeks, G. R. (1989). *Treating couples: The intersystem model of the marriage council of Philadelphia.* New York: Brunner/Mazel.

Weiner-Davis, M. (1992). *Divorce busting.* New York: Summit.

Wile, D. B. (1993). *After the fight: A night in the life of a couple.* New York: Guilford Press.

Worthington, E. L. (1999). *Hope-focused marriage counseling: A guide to brief therapy.* Downers Grove, IL: InterVarsity Press.

Worthington, E. L., Jr., & DiBlasio, F. A. (1990). Promoting mutual forgiveness within the fractured relationship. *Psychotherapy, 27*, 219-23.

# SEPARATION, DIVORCE,
# AND REMARRIAGE

*Being divorced is like being hit by a Mack truck.*
*If you live through it, you start looking very*
*carefully to the right and to the left.*

**JEAN KERR**

EDDIE CAME INTO THERAPY ASKING for help for his
daughter, Elizabeth, age five. She was "argumentative" and "disrespectful" and "not very nice" to him and to his girlfriend. As
the story unfolded, Eddie shared that he had been married for
eleven years. He was currently separated from his wife, Elisa, the
mother of Elizabeth. They were going through a messy divorce
that resulted from many things, including an ongoing affair with
the woman he is with now—the woman he introduces as his girlfriend. Eddie was asking for help in making his daughter accept
his new relationship, to "get over" the breakup of her parents'
marriage and to accept the girlfriend into her life. It became clear
in the course of the consultation that Elizabeth may have been
the healthiest person in the family, because she was at least quite
forthright in expressing her feelings of disapproval of the current
arrangement—it was not what she signed up for when she was
born into her family.

This chapter focuses on the challenges faced by families experiencing separation, divorce, and remarriage. Such experiences,
while increasingly common, bring about rapid change and real or

potential losses of essential structures for family members. We discuss the effects of separation, divorce, and remarriage on family functioning, and the key elements of family therapy. We provide a Christian engagement of some of the most critical issues.

## DIVORCE AND REMARRIAGE: A BRIEF OVERVIEW

What do we know about divorce? In terms of rates of divorce, young married couples in their first marriage have about a 40 percent divorce rate (Ahrons, 2016; Raley & Bumpass, 2003). This rate increases significantly for those in subsequent marriages. Also, education has some bearing on risk of divorce, as the divorce rate for those with college education is about 30 percent compared to about a 60 percent divorce rate for those who do not complete high school (Raley & Bumpass, 2003). A number of other factors appear to be associated with an increased risk of divorce, including neuroticism, premarital cohabitation, religious differences, being young at the time of marriage, and having one's parents divorce (Ripley, 2007).

About 75 percent of spouses who divorce will remarry, and the vast majority of these remarriages occur within five years of the end of the first marriage (McGoldrick & Carter, 2016). People enter into these subsequent marriages believing that the problems they had in their first marriage will be solved or that they will not make the same mistake the next time. Sadly, about 65 percent of those second marriages will also end in divorce. What people often fail to realize is that, among other things, they carry with them ways of relating that will not be fixed by divorce.

What is increasingly clear is that divorce is not something that happens and then ends quickly, but is an important and emotionally draining and consuming process. As Overbeek and his colleagues (2006) put it, "getting divorced does not represent a discrete event, but rather is part of an ongoing process" (p. 284). It is a lived reality that extends far beyond the divorce itself and affects the lives of all involved for years to come (Wallerstein & Blakeslee, 1989).

For example, divorce has significant implications for mental health and well-being. Divorced individuals, when compared to those who are married, report lower levels of self-esteem and happiness and report elevations on measures of psychological distress (Amato, 2000). Some recent research (e.g., Overbeek et al., 2006) suggests that it is not divorce but the marital discord and perceptions of marital quality prior to the divorce that leads to mental health difficulties (with the exception of substance disorders, which divorced individuals appear to be at risk for regardless of marital quality prior to divorce). Other longitudinal studies suggest that negative emotions, such as anger, are reported by as many as half of women and a third of men ten years following divorce (Wallerstein & Blakeslee, 1989).

The effects of divorce are also felt by the children. Over one million children each year experience the divorce of their parents (U.S. Bureau of the Census, 1999). These children tend to struggle in various areas of adjustment in many ways compared to children whose parents do not divorce. These struggles with adjustment are more marked among children whose parents divorce when they are in preschool compared to children who are older (Zill, Morrison, & Coiro, 1993); similar differences exist between boys and girls, with boys showing more negative affects of divorce, particularly in the area of conduct problems (Amato, 2001).

Some of the initial adjustment problems among children may lessen somewhat over time, although the long-term effects of divorce on children should not be underestimated and appear to even impact the capacity to form trust-filled, intimate relationships (Wallerstein & Blakeslee, 1989). We turn now to the developmental context for best understanding divorce and ways to work with families navigating the emotional challenges therein.

## THE FAMILY LIFE CYCLE: UNDERSTANDING DIVORCE IN DEVELOPMENTAL CONTEXT

It can be helpful to provide a developmental context for understanding the risk of divorce. The family life cycle (McGoldrick, Preto, and Carter, 2016) provides that context.[1] This cycle refers to recognizable stages of family development that begin with separation from one's parents in young adulthood and extend from there to the decision to marry and to have children that are raised through childhood and adolescence and eventually launched into young adulthood. The family life cycle actually continues through growing older together, retirement, and, ultimately, death.

Many people, of course, do not follow this cycle as we are about to describe, nor should we see following this cycle as a sign of maturity or a preferred

---

[1] The following section is adapted from JoEllen Patterson, Lee Williams, Todd M. Edwards, Larry Chamow, and Claudia Grauf-Grounds, *Essential Skills in Family Therapy*, 2nd ed. (New York and London: Guilford Press, 2009), 134-51; and Monica McGoldrick and Tazuko Shibusawa, "The Family Life Cycle," in Froma Walsh (ed.), *Normal Family Processes*, 4th ed. (New York and London: Guilford Press, 2012), 384-94.

pathway for the individual. This is particularly true as we consider relationships from a Christian perspective, as we see opportunities to serve the culture, to enrich broad kinship networks, and, ultimately, to respond to unique ways in which God equips all of us to serve the kingdom, which is different for single and married people. We do not place a premium on one path over any other, as we will discuss as the close of this chapter. Although we might say it differently and with reference to a Christian worldview, we agree with McGoldrick and Shibusawa (2012) on their observation about maturity, marriage, and childrearing:

> [We do not] view healthy maturation as requiring a single sequential pathway through marriage and childrearing. In contrast to the traditional view that not marrying is an "immature" choice, or that women who do not have children are unfulfilled, we hold a pluralistic view, recognizing many valid, healthy options and relationships over the life course. (p. 385)

What the family life cycle does provide us with is a scaffold we can climb to get a closer look at potential relational and systemic vulnerabilities that may place a marriage at risk for divorce.

## STAGE-RELATED VULNERABILITIES

The question we are asking is this: If we look at each of the stages of the family life cycle, what can we learn about the unique vulnerabilities at each stage? For example, we can look at the opening stage in which each person—who may eventually make up a new family—leaves the family they grew up in. Traditionally, the new family begins if a couple decides to marry, but in terms of the family life cycle, there is both the leaving (one's family of origin) and the cleaving (to one another) (Mk 10:7-8). Leaving one's family or being launched into emerging and/or early adulthood entails taking responsibility for oneself, which may be seen in greater financial independence, emotional maturity, and self-sufficiency.

When two single adults commit themselves to the establishment of a new system—a marital system—and negotiate relationships with family and friends to reflect that new system, they are seen as a new couple, which marks the next stage of *couple formation* (McGoldrick et al., 2016). There are typically a lot of explicit and implicit negotiations going on when single adults form a new couple, but it is also a time in family life in which the marriage may be buoyed up above water by the initial stage of a new life together and related hopes and expectations for the future.

During new *couple formation*, how might navigating emotional "leaving" lead to problems with "cleaving" that could put a couple at risk for divorce? There are many possible considerations, but imagine a young man or woman who physically leaves home but does not emotionally leave home. Perhaps the person has great difficulty navigating intimate relationships and emotional vulnerability. Or perhaps the person turns to his or her parents for emotional support rather than to that person's spouse: "At times the inability to formalize a marriage indicates that the partners are still too enmeshed in their own families to define a new system and accept the implications of this realignment" (McGoldrick & Shibusawa, 2012, p. 387). As a result, the new marriage could be quite vulnerable compared to a marriage in which both partners were able to successfully leave home. In any case, for single young adults to successfully navigate this stage of development, they must differentiate themselves from their family of origin and develop their own intimate relationships and meaningful peer group connections and social networks. We discuss in chapter twenty that this can be a particularly challenging stage for LGBT+ couples who may also be navigating lack of acceptance of the relationship from one or both families of origin.

The couple may then enter into the next stage: *families with young children.* This stage can be complicated by decisions about whether and when to start a family, how many children to have, and concerns about infertility, among other things. A couple who is unable to have biological children will face a unique set of challenges and may pursue options ranging from in vitro fertilization, an egg donor, or adoption, but navigating the myriad of decisions while reconciling themselves to the reality of infertility can place a strain on their marriage. Different cultural backgrounds may also have expectations about whether a couple ought to stay together if one or the other spouse is unable to have biological children. One couple we saw for marital therapy was from a mixed cultural background in which the paternal grandparents were highly invested in the question of fertility and placed great pressure on the couple to have children, which they were struggling with due to questions about infertility. Sometimes these discussions across generations (messages from grandparents) and cultures can be difficult.

For couples who have children (either biological or via adoption or another means), the couple is now incorporating new members into what has been a marital dyad. How does the system change to include children? As Patterson, Williams, Edwards, Chamow, and Grauf-Grounds (2009) observe, the key marital issues at this stage have to do with taking the time and energy to develop an emotional attachment to a new baby; a family may range from a closed boundary ("not noticing") to an open boundary ("everything revolves around the child") that places the child above all else, including the couple.

Any time a couple makes adjustments, they may be at some risk if they are unable to do so or if the necessary adjustments place too great a strain on an already fragile relationship (fragile, perhaps, from the failure to successfully navigate any preceding stage) (Patterson et al., 2009). This stage—*families with young children*—is considered the stage of family life when the couple is at greatest risk for divorce. In this stage it is not uncommon for a couple to argue and need to problem-solve about childrearing and other household tasks as well as the financial issues associated with an expanding family. The ability to successfully problem-solve around these difficult topics is often predicated on successful transition from the previous stage—that is, forming a new system and joining together two families (Patterson et al., 2009).

Economic challenges may also play a role in added strain that ties into gender roles and expectations that may or may not have been discussed up until now. McGoldrick and Shibusawa (2012) observe that with an increase in both parents working outside of the home, more focus is placed on finding reliable child care, and there are many gender roles and expectations that couples navigate in terms of often having two careers and involving fathers in child-rearing and other household tasks. These gender roles may also be tied to cultural and religious expectations for male-female differences that many couples find themselves negotiating.

As children grow and become school-age, the family has increased contact with school and other social systems. A child who may (or may not) have been compared to siblings is now going to be compared to his or her peers. The family typically wants to be like other families and to "fit in" (Patterson et al., 2009, p. 141). If a child has difficulty with attention, anxiety, learning, or hyperactivity, it is likely to be noted at this stage. Families that come in for therapy tend to be referred by teachers or school counselors (Patterson et al., 2009).

*Families with adolescents* make up the next stage in the family life cycle. What had been a parent-child relationship develops into a parent-adolescent relationship that allows the adolescent to move into and out of the family system (McGoldrick et al., 2016). At the same time, there is a shift in focus for the parents to midlife career and marital issues as well as the needs of their aging parents. Successful navigation of this stage requires increased flexibility, particularly with family emotional boundaries, so that the family allows for the adolescent's independence.

We mentioned that the couple may also be caring for their own parents. Women, in particular, are much more likely to carry added responsibilities:

> Women today at midlife have been termed "the sandwich generation." Most are in the workforce, still attending to the responsibilities for emerging young adults, as they take on primary caregiver roles for aging parents. (McGoldrick & Shibusawa, 2012, p. 392)

This stage is also a time when couples are especially at risk for divorce. Raising adolescents is uniquely challenging, and many parents struggle with their role *as parents* and may try to be "friends" with their teens in ways that present new challenges that may threaten the capacity to set and enforce limits and consequences.

Also, the child who is now an adolescent has more to say about moving in and out of the system. The teen typically comes to spend more time with and value friendships and other relationships that are outside of the family system (Patterson et al., 2009). This can be a source of anxiety or conflict for parents, who have to navigate these boundaries and the valuing of relationships outside of the family to relationships inside the system. Teenagers are also navigating a challenging sociocultural context characterized by sexualization, or finding one's worth or value in one's appearance or sexual appeal, as well as a dramatic increase in and access to pornography and images that objectify the person. Teens are also navigating various social media platforms that increase access to both resources (for example, one's peer group) and threats (such as pornography), and parents are often struggling to keep up with advances in technology. Families that come in for therapy at this stage often bring in an adolescent as the "identified patient" or the person they would like to see "fixed." A focus on what the adolescent needs from the family this next year may set the concerns in developmental context and create a context for change.

The stage that follows is called *launching children and moving on at midlife*. The successful launching of children (who are now young adults) is tied to how well a system can accept the many exits from and entries into the family (McGoldrick et al., 2016). This stage also requires the couple to revisit their relationship as the marital dyad—an identity that has been in the background over the childrearing years. Families that successfully negotiate this transition are able to reestablish cohesion as a couple (a sense of "us"), develop adult-to-adult relationships with grown children, and are able to deal with the health concerns of parents/grandparents.

This stage can be challenging for the couple as they now return to the primary identity as a couple or dyad. As with all of the other stages, success at this stage is predicated on successful navigation of the previous stage. As a family "let's go" of a young adult they are building on the success they have had with allowing greater permeability in the boundaries in and out of the family system throughout adolescence.

The role of the family therapist at this stage is primarily to serve as a consultant—to offer brief sessions and to problem-solve specific concerns (Patterson et al., 2009). This affords the family access to information and suggestions without the concern that they are signing up for a long-term course of therapy.

We have also both worked with couples in which one partner really struggled in their marriage in light of the many sacrifices they made in their career or with respect to lost dreams or other considerations. They may have mentally committed themselves to raise their children and launch them into young adulthood. Once that goal has been met, that spouse may give serious consideration to divorce. They may see this new chapter of life as an opportunity for a "fresh start."

*Families in later life* represent the last stage of the family life cycle. A key challenge identified by McGoldrick et al. (2016) is the acceptance of the shift in attention away from the family that had raised and launched children to the new family (their children's) that is currently raising children and has become the central generation.

In addition, Worthington (2003) observed the medical fact that couples are now living longer, and this has some bearing on divorce: "Over 25 to 50 years, a huge threat to marriage will probably be the lengthening of the life span. Longer lives will mean that happy marriages must last longer than they now last. Simply because there will be more time spent in marriage, more problems are likely to occur" (p. 232).

## SEPARATION, DIVORCE, AND REMARRIAGE

When a family goes through separation and divorce (and in many cases re-marriage), there are additional stages and challenges faced in the context of the "normal" family life cycle.

> In our experience as clinicians and teachers, we have found it useful to con-ceptualize divorce and its aftermath as an interruption or dislocation of the traditional family life cycle, which produces the kind of profound disequi-librium that is associated throughout the entire family life cycle with shifts, gains and losses in family relationships. (Carter & McGoldrick, 1999, p. 373)

Families that do not go through divorce sometimes struggle with the devel-opmental challenges faced with going through these predictable stages, so it is no wonder that families facing divorce and changing family dynamics and compositions are at greater risk for emotional triangles and cutoffs as well as other dynamics that may hinder a successful transition.

Carter and McGoldrick (1999) offer this helpful analogy:

> If we visualize a family traveling the road of life, moving from stage to stage in their developmental unfolding, we can see divorce as an interruption that puts the family on a "detour"—an additional family life cycle stage—in which the physical and emotional losses and changes of divorce are put into effect and absorbed by the three-generation system. The family (now in two house-holds) then rejoins the "main road" and continues its forward developmental progress, though in a more complex form. If either spouse remarries, a second detour occurs—a second additional family life cycle stage—in which the family must handle the stress of absorbing two or three generations of new members into the system and struggle to define their roles and relation-ships to existing family members. When this task of merging in mid-journey with another three-generation system has been completed, the new, highly complex system rejoins the "main road," and individual and family devel-opment continues. (p. 374)

*Separation and divorce.* There are a number of special issues to keep in mind when working with families going through separation and divorce. A helpful place to begin is to understand what McGoldrick and Carter (2016) identify as the developmental tasks associated with divorce: *the decision to divorce, planning the breakup of the system, separation,* and *divorce.* The first task is *the decision to divorce*, which itself can be very difficult. Ahrons (2016) describes the "individual cognition" that is the decision to divorce:

> Although divorce often ends up being a mutual decision, at the early stages there is one person (the initiator or leaver) who harbors the secret desire to leave and one person who is initially unaware of that desire (the opposer or the left). In some cases, both partners may have had similar fantasies, but one person usually takes the first step and begins the process. (p. 382)

At some point each partner comes to terms with their own part in the decision to divorce, and the decision involves at some level an acceptance that the couple is unable to repair the damage or resolve the conflicts that are part of the marital system (McGoldrick et al., 2016). Ahrons (2016) indicates that in the United States between 60 and 75 percent of divorces are initiated by women, and he attributes this to increased options and independence from an economic standpoint. It is suggested that many women have stayed in marriages (and many may continue to stay in marriages) due to economic dependence.

About half of all divorces involve families that have children (Greene, Anderson, Forgatch, DeGarmo, & Hetherington, 2012). The decision to divorce is at some point communicated to children and to other members of the extended family. This is referred to as "family metacognition" (Ahrons, 2016, p. 382). It essentially involves making the announcement—communicating the decision to divorce to the rest of the family, which can come as a shock or feel abrupt, and it may involve division of emotions and allegiances that further complicate an already difficult situation.

There are a number of helpful resources for parents trying to find a way to talk to their children about divorce. For example, Sara Bonkowski's (1987) book *Children Are Nondivorceable* provides a few guiding principles. The first is to tell each child what that child can understand based on his or her age and maturity. This will be different for a four-year-old than for a six- or seven-year-old, and older children still will have a different understanding of issues like visitation and custody. Another principle is to tell the truth, answering questions honestly with an awareness of what a child can take in. A third principle is to take the initiative rather than wait for children to come to the parents. As Bonkowski observes, children often take cues from their parents, so if the parents wait for the children to initiate a discussion or ask questions about divorce, they may not take the initiative. Finally, it is important that parents not use children as emotional confidants. There is some information that children need to be protected from, and much of that is related to what the parents are processing at an emotional level, which is experienced by many children as a significant emotional burden.

*Planning the breakup of the system* involves "supporting viable arrangements for all parts of the system" (McGoldrick & Carter, 2016, p. 413). This involves making plans for cooperative, working arrangements regarding custody, visitation, and finances. It may also involve emotional challenges in dealing with extended family and how they are affected by the decision to divorce. Family members may deal with a range of responses to this announcement, especially if there is a sense of betrayal and/or blame, which is not uncommon in divorce situations. Nor are feelings of loss, especially current losses and loss associated with the idea of an "ideal" family or of an anticipated future that is not going to come to pass (Ahrons, 2016).

While communicating the decision to divorce is a major event in the process of divorce and is often a memory that stands out to family members, *separation* is perhaps the most significant memory and emotional marker. As Ahrons (2016) indicates,

> Most people remember the day they separated—not the day their divorce was legally awarded—as the day their divorce began. Separation day is one of those marker events that divorced people never forget. For children, this is when they realize the enormity of what is going on, even though they may have suspected or feared the prospect for some time. (p. 384)

In terms of clinical issues facing family therapists, the couple is dealing with who is to move out and how often and under what circumstances they see each other during the separation as well as how and when to inform friends and family members of the decision (Ahrons, 2016).

Indeed, separation begins to test the cooperative arrangement negotiated in the previous phase. The separation begins to demonstrate whether in fact the couple can continue to cooperate in a coparenting arrangement and share financial and emotional support of the children (McGoldrick & Carter, 2016). It has been estimated that only about half of divorcing families have cooperative arrangements for coparenting (Patterson et al., 2009). The others continue in a more conflicted and adversarial relationship with their former husband or wife or otherwise fail to successfully attend to their parenting role.

Emotionally, this phase can require a number of adaptations to the separation, including grieving the loss of the previously familiar marital dyad and family system (McGoldrick & Carter, 2016).

The *divorce* itself requires additional work on the emotional aspects of the end of the marriage, such as resolving anger, hurt, and resentment as well as guilt and shame (Ahrons, 2016; McGoldrick & Carter, 2016). What is grieved is the loss of an intact family and the dreams that that initial family represented to each spouse. Children and teens grieve this loss, too, although they may express their experience of loss in remarkably different ways. Some may externalize their negative emotions through disruptive behavior, non-compliance, and so on, while others may internalize their negative emotions and experience depression, anxiety, guilt, or shame.

It has been suggested that it can take two to three years to proceed through these stages of divorce (Patterson et al., 2009). But the effects of divorce last much longer, and a family therapist cannot overlook the economic impact of divorce on people, particularly women with young children (Greene et al., 2012).

As we have suggested, successful navigation of these stages among post-divorce families is complex and multilayered, but it leads to the single parent maintaining contact with the ex-spouse for the purposes of the parental role and responsibilities while also developing their own meaningful relationships and social support system. Ahrons (2016) describes this as "family redefinition" (p. 388). It often involves remarriage, and we turn our attention to this common next "chapter" in the stories of families going through divorce.

***Repartnering and remarriage.*** Bev and Anthony called for therapy for Bev's son, Brian, age fourteen. They said they were having trouble with him because he was "rebellious" and "argumentative," particularly toward his step-father, Anthony. Anthony came into therapy steamed. He said he expected Brian to do what he told him to do when he told him to do it. He shared an example of taking out the garbage—or, more to the point, *failing* to take out the garbage when told to do so. Anthony shared that he had no trouble what-soever getting his daughters to do what he tells them to do.

Anthony and Bev have two girls from their marriage, ages three and five. Bev agreed with Anthony that Brian is not doing everything he should do in the home, but she feels protective of Brian and does not want Anthony to get so domineering about chores and household responsibilities. Brian appreciates his mom sticking up for him, but he would like to see more of that, and he is angry with Anthony for being "a jerk." The family is asking for help figuring out how to relate better to one another.

Now that we understand the developmental considerations in how a family system is initially established and what is required for successful transition to various stages in the life cycle, it should come as no surprise that repartnered and remarried families face unique challenges as they determine what it means to be a "family."

About half of those who go through divorce are in a serious dating relationship within a year of filing for divorce, and about one-third of mothers and fathers reported "having dated three or four more partners by 1-year after filing for divorce" (Greene et al., 2012, p. 104). Some of these repartnering relationships will lead to cohabiting or remarriage and represent a number of "adaptive challenges that confront parents and children" (p. 104).

Patterson et al. (2009) discuss stepfamily formation, which begins with entering into a new relationship while (often) simultaneously coping with the emotional losses from the dissolution of the first marriage.

Patience is needed as the new marriage and family requires time to adjust to what might seem ambiguous or complex rules, expectations, and emotional commitments.

> The emotional issues of remarriage go back at least to the disintegration of the first marriage. The intensity of emotion unleashed by the life cycle disruption of divorce must be dealt with over and over again before the dislocated systems are restabilized. (McGoldrick & Carter, 2016, p. 415)

Entering into a new relationship also raises anxiety "about investment in a new marriage and a new family" (p. 415), which is only complicated further if there are gaps in life cycle experiences between the new partners. As McGoldrick and Carter (2016) observe, "the wider the discrepancy in family life cycle experience between the new spouses, the greater the difficulty of transition will be and the longer it will take to integrate a workable new family" (p. 419). It is challenging enough for two people with young children to remarry, but the challenges increase when one person has older adolescents who are soon to be launched into young adulthood, while the partner has young children and only has experience with the developmental themes associated with only that stage of the family life cycle.

Fears can often come to the surface, as can questions about loyalty as the former spouses are working out how they will relate to one another and whether or how they will cooperate in their coparenting responsibilities (Patterson et al., 2009).

This is also a time for grief. Former spouses may grieve the loss of the intact family that had at one time been "ideal." They are now faced with something less than ideal and they may struggle with guilt about decisions that led to the separation and divorce.

The family therapist will want to be mindful of the many competing allegiances and fears and do all they can to keep from aligning with one family member over another, especially if doing so would cut the person off from much-needed emotional support (Patterson et al., 2009).

It can be helpful if the family therapist understands that some noncustodial parents are cut off from their children because they experience the relationship itself as becoming fragmented (Bonkowski, 1987). As Bonkowski suggests, it should be communicated that, while painful for the noncustodial parent, it is important to the development of the child that they see both parents regularly and often. It is also important for custodial parents to recognize what they can and cannot control, especially in the area of visitation and the noncustodial parent-child relationship.

The pain that people go through having been in a "failed" relationship is often brought into the new relationship. This pain and other emotional responses, such as fears about new intimacy and trust, may be exacerbated by the circumstances that led to the divorce (e.g., infidelity). People are often unaware of how they bring themselves and their unique emotional experiences and concerns into subsequent relationships.

Patterson et al. (2009) also remind family therapists to keep in mind that supportive and often influential extended family members and broader kinship networks, such as grandparents, aunts/uncles, or cousins as well as family friends and one's religious faith community, may have been cut off from an ongoing relationship with children. This can lead to another layer of loss that can be overlooked by the new family therapist.

McGoldrick and Carter (2016) discuss practical goals and guidelines family therapists can keep in mind when working with remarried families. One such goal is to work through the "emotional divorce" of each former spouse. Entering into a new relationship and, particularly, remarriage, is difficult enough, but trying to lay a foundation for a new family while not having resolved the feelings of loss and grief associated with the first marriage only complicates the process further. Another goal would be to have a firm enough boundary between parents and children so that children do not have the power to veto the decision to remarry or other major decisions, such as custody or visitation.

Guidelines for family therapy would also include helping each family member tolerate emotional ambiguity associated with divorce and remarriage. A place to begin is to recognize that new families do not just "come together" into a trusting, safe, and nurturing system by a sheer act of the will. New systems require time and patience as well as shared activities and healthy communication.

## INTEGRATIVE FOCUS: *Family Functioning*

The issue of divorce once figured prominently in what have at times been referred to as the "culture wars" in the United States. On the one side were those who wanted easier access to divorce and to remove the stigma often associated with it. On the other side were those who viewed easily accessible divorce as a symptom of a society emphasizing individualism and personal preferences rather than covenantal ties. We see marriage as valuable to society, and we recognize that two-parent homes provide a level of stability for children that should be valued by the broader culture. The church and broader society should do all that they can do to provide support to families and to prevent separation or divorce if at all possible. At the same time, we recognize that when that is not possible or when a person has gone through a divorce, it is important to provide support to single-parent families as they seek ways to function effectively, providing the kind of structure and family functioning in which children respond favorably.

This is an area where the church could certainly make itself known. Rather than abandon certain family forms that do not reflect the ideal, the church can stand with families in the many forms they take to identify and remove the constraints that keep them from functioning properly. Depending on the family and the expressed needs, we want to be careful, of course, not to create more stress for those with limited resources. The church would do well to reflect on when to intervene and when not to intervene, and to always have its doors open—to always be prepared to be a resource to those in need in very practical and tangible ways.

*Think about it:* Think about ways in which the local church could be more supportive to families in the local community. What suggestions would you offer to those who make decisions in these areas?

It can also be helpful to encourage the biological parent to take the lead in communicating expectations and establishing patterns of discipline of the child while allowing time for the spouse to establish more of a relationship out of which expectations and discipline are more likely to be communicated successfully.

Repartnering via cohabitation rather than remarriage is even more challenging, perhaps due to more open boundaries or lack of security, and family therapists may need to adapt services accordingly (Greene et al., 2012).

## CHRISTIAN CRITIQUE AND ENGAGEMENT

There are a number of important threads of engagement for Christian family therapists. It may be helpful to have a better understanding of ways society tends to devalue marriage, the causes of divorce, and the current efforts to prevent divorce. We will then turn our attention to the need to cast a vision for the family that extends beyond the family itself.

***Devaluing marriage as a society.*** In a special issue of the *Journal of Psychology and Theology*, Jennifer Ripley (2003) brought together leading Christian mental health professionals who shared their understanding of many issues pertaining to marriage, separation, and divorce. We summarize some of what they shared throughout that special issue on ways in which society itself seems to devalue the institution of marriage.

The rise of cohabitation within society is perhaps one of the most important developments and messages about the institution of marriage. Michael and Harriet McManus (2003; citing Popenoe & Whitehead, 2002) discussed how there is less social expectation that people, particularly men, marry, and how men in particular gain a number of benefits that used to be tied to marriage, such as sex, without the financial risks associated with divorce.

Keith Edwards (2003) discusses research on casual attitudes toward intimate relationship commitment among younger people. He observes that decreased commitment is likely multidetermined but may include a focus on self-interest rather than relationship interest. In other words, a cultural shift has occurred so that individuals are orienting themselves toward marriage with reference to their self-interest. Scott Stanley (2003) discusses it this way:

> We live in a culture that thrives on messages dominated by individual needs and concerns. As part of this, people no longer see their vow to their mate as part of a commitment to the community, but as more of the nature of an agreement between two consenting parties. (p. 225)

Divorce represents a profound loss of family relationship. Some people cope with that loss by insisting it will not happen to them—that they will maintain the same relationship throughout the coming changes. Others deny that the changes are of great significance; they might say that they are not hurt by the changes. In some cases changes may mean greater safety and security, while for others it places the single-parent family at great risk for lost resources and financial instability.

As Christians we want to recognize the reality of the loss, even if it is a change away from something that has not been healthy. The shift is a movement away from marriage and family life that could have been. In some respects it is the loss of potential—of what was possible. We do not want to idealize marriage and family, but we also refuse to devalue the potential in marriage that many people aspire to when they first say their vows—when they anticipate in their own minds how their family will relate and come to care for one another over time.

Family relationships form a foundation for one's sense of self-worth. When they are broken we cannot underestimate how cracks in the foundation can impact a person throughout their lives. The Christian recognizes that the foundational aspect of family life is part of God's intention and that the brokenness occurs for all of us to a degree, as no family relationship is ever what it could have been prior to the fall. And we can anticipate a time when all relationships will be restored under the family tree in which Christ and the church, the bride of Christ, are brought together into a fuller and more complete relationship.

*Think about it:* What are some of the challenges family members face when they go through a divorce? What might it mean to a family member to know that the loss felt through divorce may one day be redeemed? Is this a small comfort in light of the magnitude of loss, or is it a compelling and comforting insight? How so?

Stanley (2003) shares his understanding of how apathy and fear place marriage as an institution at some risk. Summarizing the data, he says:

> People have begun to shy away from marriage—not because they do not desire it or seek it, but because they fear that it is not really possible to have a lasting, healthy, and satisfying marriage. Those currently studying the

youngest generation say that they have an interesting combination of conservatism about marriage and family, but with a loss of confidence about the ability of any couple to make marriage work as a life-long union. (p. 224)

*Causes of divorce.* Of course, changes in societal expectations and attitudes about the institution of marriage are also tied to reasons why people decide to divorce, as was suggested above with respect to casual attitudes about intimate relationship commitment and the primacy of self-interest (Edwards, 2003), as well as apathy and fears about whether "any couple can make marriage work as a life-long union" (Stanley, 2003, p. 224).

In addition, Les and Leslie Parrott (2003) mention a number of factors that may contribute to divorce, including cohabitation, the appeal of "serial monogamy," less access to premarital counseling, the stigma of counseling that still exists, and easy divorce laws.

Regarding cohabitation, McManus and McManus (2003; citing Popenoe & Whitehead, 2002) discuss ways in which cohabitation is a threat to marriage and places people who later marry at greater risk for divorce (a 50 percent increased risk). We noted above that there is less social expectation that people marry.

Still other scholars (Browning et al., 2000) have indicated that women initiate most divorces in the United States today. This suggests to them that economic viability is a significant consideration for many women, and it may contribute to divorce in instances in which divorce would not have been economically viable in the past.

There are undoubtedly many causes of divorce in the United States today, and many of these contributing factors are not isolated to the non-Christian community but are factors that place Christian marriages at risk also. We turn our attention now to prevention of divorce and how to make that a priority in our culture.

*Prevention of divorce.* A number of experts on marriage have offered their perspective on the best ways to prevent divorce. We offer an overview of several of the strategies in place today (see Ripley, 2003).

*Clinical training and church-based education and skills training.* There is a general appreciation for the role of educating and training couples in skills that are thought to be essential to a successful marriage. Many leaders (e.g., Clinton, 2003; Edwards, 2003; Schumm, 2003) share how they are involved in teaching or training family therapists to work with couples as well as how they facilitate marital retreats to strengthen marriages. There have also been a number of resources developed through professional Christian organizations, such as the American Association of Christian Counselors (Clinton, 2003).

*A reinvestment in the concepts of hope and forgiveness.* Everett Worthington (2003) at Virginia Commonwealth University is a leading Christian scholar who conducted a six-year longitudinal study funded by the Templeton Foundation that involved ways to intervene in early marriage. This has led to enrichment interventions developed around the theme of facilitating a hope-focused approach in marriage and ties into communication training and conflict resolution that has recently been updated (Ripley & Worthington, 2014). Worthington has also developed another intervention centering on forgiveness called FREE (Forgiveness and Reconciliation through Experiencing Empathy).

*The development of "community marriage policies."* Michael and Harriet McManus (2003) discuss the use of mentor couples to prevent bad marriages based on an understanding of relational variables that predict divorce. Mentor couples follow a step-by-step manual (M. J. McManus, 2003) that addresses enriching existing marriages through retreats, reconciling separated couples, and facilitating successful "blended families" by identifying and working through the key issues these families face. Marriage Savers, the not-for-profit organization founded by the McManuses, has seen divorce rates lower within entire metro areas (as compared to comparable cities) by the implementation of the community marriage policies.

*Premarriage and early marriage education.* Les and Leslie Parrott (2003) are codirectors of the Center for Relationship Development at Seattle Pacific University, and the focus of their work is premarital and early marriage education. They essentially target marriages in their earliest stages when they are most vulnerable to divorce. The marriage preparation weekend they have developed, called SYMBIS ("Saving Your Marriage Before It Starts"), involves matching newly married couples with couples who have been married longer.

*The development of state marriage initiatives.* Scott Stanley (2003) is one of two senior consultants to the Oklahoma Marriage Initiative, which encompasses a broad, statewide strategy to support marriages and prevent divorce. It involves collaboration on a massive scale between the public and private domains. It takes the Christian beyond the local church and even beyond the various faith communities throughout one's state and into a more collaborative stance within the broader culture. The Oklahoma Marriage Initiative involves translating concerns that are often discussed in

Christian circles into language and policies that can be supported by the public and secular government.

*The purpose of the family.* Diane Richmond-Garland and David Garland (2003) wrote a book titled *Beyond Companionship*, with the thesis that mar-

Family identity quickly becomes a concern for many people who go through divorce. For example, a Christian woman whom Mark recently saw was grieving her separation and pending divorce, saying that she did not want to become a statistic. She struggled with her self-worth and what it means to her and her children to be a family when they anticipate little if any support from her family and from her church.

Rediscovering family identity or, perhaps more accurately, intentionally living out a new family identity takes time, and it is important to extend one another grace as identity is challenged by a range of feelings from separation through divorce and possibly remarriage with the issues facing blended families and family identity in that context.

The Christian family therapist recognizes that ultimately family identity is not found in intake family forms or in the context of improved blended family relationships but in who we are as members of God's family, who have an identity founded on that far-reaching experience of salvation and restoration of right relationship with God the Father.

*Think about it:* What are some practical strategies families can take to explore their identity as part of God's family? What are some of the challenges and opportunities in exploring this aspect of family identity?

riage has been reduced to the feelings of romance that are meant today to hold relationships together. Historically, marriages had several additional threads that gave them multiple purposes. For example, at different times throughout history, parents educated their children at home and children provided much-needed labor, particularly in agrarian communities. The reduction of marriage ties to mere feelings of romance is a remarkable historical departure and leaves marriages today vulnerable both in the perception that marriage is unnecessary as an institution and that it is dependent on emotions that are quite subjective and susceptible to the ebb and flow of stressors and strains on any intimate relationship.

This leaves the Christian family therapist in the position to explore the meaning and theology of the family so that it is understood properly and in light of a Christian worldview. For example, a Christian worldview would not conceptualize marriage and the family as having the fundamental purpose of making individuals satisfied with their lives. Rodney Clapp discussed some of these themes in his book *Families at the Crossroads*:

> Kingdom mission and Christian hospitality and community are not instrumental. They are not undertaken *in order to* strengthen and make families happy. The strength and happiness of families is an important thing. But it is a byproduct of service to a kingdom larger than the family, not the object of the service to that kingdom. To be healthy, the family needs a mission or purpose beyond itself. (Clapp, 1993, p. 163)

Clapp suggests that the family is not a refuge for the Christian, or, if it is that, it is not only a refuge. A refuge mentality keeps a "family fixated on itself. . . . We need a cause large and exciting enough that many people, not just a spouse and two or three children, can devote their lives to it" (p. 164). So we join Clapp in saying that the family is a mission base in the world today. But if the family is a mission base, what constitutes a family mission or purpose? In the final analysis, the Christian has one and many missions. The one mission is a *kingdom* mission. That is, our families are to live based on kingdom principles and serve others to establish a greater awareness and appreciation for the kingdom of heaven.

But the single kingdom mission may take many different forms for different families. Some families commit their lives as a family to long-term missions; others participate regularly and often in short-term missions. Still others support children in Third World cultures. We know of families who have adopted hard-to-place children as a part of their family mission, while others provide a foster home for children of all ages. Some families approach home schooling as a ministry to their children first but also as a way to set the stage and create a context for family vision and mission in outreach and in expressing care and regard to those in need, such as when they adopt an older adult at a local nursing home.

## CONCLUSION

This is an area that can be developed further and unpacked in an intentional way so that families have a greater sense for what other families are doing when they reflect on the vision and mission of the family. In each of these cases, however, we want to stress the importance of the family having a purpose beyond itself. If the family is a haven, it is only temporary; the family is ultimately the mission base for a range of strategies for living intentionally and radically in the world today.

## REFERENCES

Ahrons, C. R. (1999). Divorce: An unscheduled family transition. In B. Carter & M. McGoldrick (Eds.), *The expanded life cycle: Individual, family, and social perspectives* (3rd ed., pp. 381-98). Needham Heights, MA: Allyn & Bacon.

Ahrons, C. R. (2016). Divorce: An unscheduled family transition. In M. McGoldrick, N. G. Preto, & B. Carter (Eds.), *The expanding family life cycle: Individual, family, and social perspectives* (5th ed., pp. 376-93). Needham Heights, MA: Allyn & Bacon.

Amato, P. R. (2000). The consequences of divorce for adults and children. *Journal of Marriage and the Family, 62,* 1269-87.

Amato, P. R. (2001). Children of divorce in the 1990s: An update of the Amato and Keith (1991) meta-analysis. *Journal of Family Psychology, 15,* 355-70.

Bonkowski, S. (1987). *Children are nondivorceable.* Skokie, IL: ACTA Publications.

Browning, D. S., Miller-McLemore, B. J., Couture, P. D., Lyon, K. B., & Franklin, R. M. (2000). *From culture wars to common ground* (2nd ed.). Louisville, KY: Westminster John Knox.

Carter, B., & McGoldrick, M. (1999). The divorce cycle: A major variation in the American family life cycle. In B. Carter & M. McGoldrick (Eds.), *The expanded life cycle: Individual, family, and social perspectives* (3rd ed., pp. 373-80). Needham Heights, MA: Allyn & Bacon.

Clapp, R. (1993). *Families at the crossroads: Beyond traditional and modern options.* Downers Grove, IL: InterVarsity Press.

Clinton, T. (2003). The state of Christian marriage. *Journal of Psychology and Theology, 31,* 179-87.

Edwards, K. (2003). It takes a village to save a marriage. *Journal of Psychology and Theology, 31,* 188-95.

Greene, S. M., Anderson, E. R., Forgatch, M. S., DeGarmo, D. S., & Hetherington, E. M. (2012). Risk and resilience after divorce. In F. Walsh (Ed.), *Normal family processes* (4th ed., pp. 102-27). New York and London: Guilford Press.

McGoldrick, M., & Carter, B. (1999). Remarried families. In B. Carter & M. McGoldrick (Eds.), *The expanded life cycle: Individual, family, and social perspectives* (3rd ed., pp. 417-35). Needham Heights, MA: Allyn & Bacon.

McGoldrick, M., & Carter, B. (2016). The remarriage cycle: Multi-nuclear and recoupled families. In M. McGoldrick, N. G. Preto, & B. Carter (Eds.), *The expanded life cycle: Individual, family, and social perspectives* (5th ed., pp. 408-29). Needham Heights, MA: Allyn & Bacon.

McGoldrick, M., Preto, N. G., & Carter, B. (2016). *The expanding family life cycle: Individual, family, and social perspectives* (5th ed.). Needham Heights, MA: Allyn & Bacon.

McGoldrick, M., & Shibusawa, T. (2012). The family life cycle. In F. Walsh (Ed.), *Normal family processes* (4th ed., pp. 375-98). New York and London: Guilford Press.

McManus, M. J. (2003). *How to create a marriage savers congregation.* Potomac, MD: Marriage Savers.

McManus, M. J., & McManus, H. (2003). How to create an America that saves marriages. *Journal of Psychology and Theology, 31,* 196-207.

Overbeek, G., Vollebergh, W., de Graaf, R., Scholte, R., de Kemp, R., & Engels, R. (2006). Longitudinal associations of marital quality and marital dissolution with the incidence of *DSM-III-R* disorders. *Journal of Family Psychology, 20,* 284-91.

Parrott, L., III, & Parrot, L. (2003). The SYMBIS approach to marriage education. *Journal of Psychology and Theology, 31,* 208-12.

Patterson, J., Williams, L., Edwards, T., Chamow, L., & Grauf-Grounds, C. (2009). *Essential skills in family therapy: From the first interview to termination* (2nd ed.). New York: Guilford Press.

Popenoe, D., & Whitehead, B. D. (2002). *The state of our unions: The social health of marriage in America, 2002.* Retrieved from the National Marriage Project website: www.stateofourunions.org/pdfs/SOOU2002.pdf.

Raley, K., & Bumpass, L. L. (2003). The topography of the divorce plateau. *Demographic Research, 8*(8), 245-60.

Richmond-Garland, D. S., & Garland, D. E. (2003). *Beyond companionship: Christians in marriage.* Portland, OR: Wipf & Stock.

Ripley, J. S. (Ed.). (2003). Introduction: Reflections on the current status and future of Christian marriages. *Journal of Psychology and Theology, 31,* 175-78.

Ripley, J. S. (2007). Couples counseling: Beloved by research geeks and relationship freaks. Plenary session presented at the Christian Association for Psychological Studies Annual Conference, March 22, 2007.

Ripley, J. S., & Worthington, E. L., Jr. (2014). *Couple therapy: A new hope-focused approach.* Downers Grove, IL: IVP Academic.

Schumm, W. R. (2003). Comments on marriage in contemporary culture: Five models that might help families. *Journal of Psychology and Theology, 31,* 213-23.

Stanley, S. (2003). Strengthening marriages in a skeptical culture: Issues and opportunities. *Journal of Psychology and Theology, 31*, 224-30.

U.S. Bureau of the Census. (1999). *Statistical abstract of the United States 1999* (119th ed.). Washington, DC: U.S. Government Printing Office.

Wallerstein, J. S., & Blakeslee, S. (1989). *Second chances: Men, women, and children a decade after divorce.* New York: Tichnor & Fields.

Worthington, E. L., Jr. (2003). Hope-focused marriage: Recommendations for researchers, clinicians, and church workers. *Journal of Psychology and Theology, 31*, 231-39.

Zill, N., Morrison, D. R., & Coiro, M. J. (1993). Long-term effects of parental divorce on parent-child relationships, adjustment, and achievement in young adulthood. *Journal of Family Psychology, 7*, 91-103.

# INDIVIDUAL
# PSYCHOPATHOLOGY

*The family is the school of duties . . . founded on love.*

**FELIX ADLER**

THIS CHAPTER FOCUSES ON theoretically driven interventions designed to address families who are confronting individual psychopathology. When depression, anxiety, schizophrenia, ADHD, and so on are exhibited in a family member, the system and structure of the family is altered. We discuss the effects of pathology on family functioning and the key elements of intervention drawn from the theoretical models presented in the previous chapters. We provide a Christian integrative critique of the philosophical assumptions, concepts, and techniques.

## INDIVIDUAL PSYCHOPATHOLOGY: A BRIEF OVERVIEW

The current diagnostic nomenclature (i.e., DSM-5) comes out of the medical model and as a result focuses on individual psychopathology. The diagnoses themselves are limited to individual expressions of pathology. The only mention of relationships is really in the V-Codes, such as "Spouse or Partner Neglect" or "Spouse or Partner Violence, Physical," which are meant to communicate additional concerns that might be a focus of professional attention but are not in and of themselves the pathology.

Much of this book, in contrast, examines family concerns and primarily family-oriented approaches to addressing the concerns. For example, we talk about conflict in marriage (chap. 12); challenges faced in separation, divorce, and remarriage (chap. 14); and ways in which families respond to sexual identity concerns (chap. 18). We also examine models of conducting family therapy (for example, structural, strategic, and solution-focused) that are often unique in their treatment of the family as the "client," something that frequently occurs even in the face of an "identified patient," as when a family comes in for therapy to help the parents deal with a "rebellious" teen. In other words, the primary unit considered in assessment, case conceptualization, and intervention is often the family and not any one individual.

But we do not want to make the mistake at the other extreme of the DSM. That is, we do not want to suggest that all mental health concerns are necessarily systemic concerns or that all presenting problems, especially those that appear to reflect individual psychopathology, are really systemic issues best assessed, conceptualized, and intervened with reference to the entire family system.

A balanced view takes into consideration how to best utilize family therapy when dealing with individual psychopathology. Family therapists tend to use DSM diagnostic labels for the purposes of third-party reimbursement, but they might focus more systemically on broader and more far-reaching considerations when they provide clinical services. We have seen an emerging literature on this very topic, and we want to summarize that in this chapter and further explore the benefits found in bringing family considerations to the work clinicians do with individuals struggling with mental health concerns.

## MODELS OF PSYCHOPATHOLOGY: BIOLOGICAL, PSYCHOLOGICAL, AND SOCIOCULTURAL

According to McRay, Yarhouse, and Butman (2016), there are three broad models of abnormality in the field of psychopathology: biological, psychological, and sociocultural. The biological and sociocultural are of particular interest in the field today. McRay, Yarhouse, and Butman argue for a "responsible eclecticism" (Jones & Butman, 2011, chap. 11), a perspective that adopts a "biopsychosocial" and integrative mindset.

A family therapy approach can complement this form of responsible eclecticism, particularly as it often reflects a broader and more holistic approach— one that tries to avoid the extremes of psychological reductionism so often witnessed in the mental health field (what McRay, Yarhouse, & Butman, 2016, call the sin of "nothing-but-ism"). It is exceedingly rare to see a case of individual psychopathology that does not seem to reflect a complex combination of biological, psychological, and sociocultural factors.

**Biological considerations.** The past three decades of mental health research have witnessed an explosion of biologically oriented research that is premised on the assumption that mental disorders are best explained as malfunctions within the individual. These malfunctions are usually centered in the brain or nervous system. Research from this perspective has led to substantive advances in the development of psychotropic medications for the most serious mental illnesses, such as schizophrenia, bipolar disorder, and unipolar depression. Even beyond these major advances, we see that nearly every cluster of disorders has been linked with deficits or vulnerabilities in neuroanatomy, brain chemistry, genetic abnormalities, or viral infections. The model has gained considerable respect in the field and has been enormously fruitful in generating new and often effective treatment strategies.

Still, the model is far from being as complete or conclusive as proponents would have us believe (or we would wish). And many Christians are profoundly ambivalent about the widespread availability of psychotropic medications, wondering whether or not their utilization will interfere with "character development" or contribute to the avoidance of "legitimate suffering" (Stapert, 1994). As this criticism suggests, the major risk that comes with these advances is the tendency toward biological reductionism among both mental health providers and consumers of services. By this we mean that both clinicians and clients can see people in fragmented (less than holistic or integrated) ways that center on symptom reduction.

**Psychological considerations.** The most influential psychological models for explaining abnormality are psychodynamic, cognitive-behavioral, and person-centered approaches, with a remarkable number of variations on often similar themes. Contemporary models of psychodynamic psychotherapy were initially influenced by classic psychoanalytic theory but have evolved beyond the "deterministic and mechanistic assumptions of the Freudian system" (Jones & Butman, 2011, p. 135). The three contemporary expressions of psychodynamic psychotherapy are ego psychology, object relations theory, and self psychology. Ego psychology places greater emphasis than had Freud on ego and "the ego strivings for adaptability, competency and mastery" (p. 137). Object relations theory emphasizes how personality is developed in response to internalized images (objects) derived from early, formative relationships with primary caregivers. Self psychology emphasizes the importance of healthy, nurturing early relationships that lead to a "true" self that is capable of healthy and mature relationships (Jones & Butman, 2011).

Cognitive-behavioral theory is a descendent of behavioral theory and rational emotive therapy. There are many expressions of contemporary cognitive-behavioral theory, but the chief departure from traditional behavioral theory is the belief that "some human behavior is caused by internal or mental events," and that these internal mental events (cognitions) are "real, powerful in their own right, and not *ultimately reducible* to environmental events" (Jones & Butman, 2011, p. 202). In understanding psychopathology, cognitive-behavioral theory targets maladaptive thoughts and broader schemas for understanding oneself and the world and attempts to modify them so that they facilitate adaptive emotional responses.

Person-centered theory emerged in contrast to determinism and reductionism and emphasizes a holistic view of the individual person as a unique human being. This model assumes that people are motivated to achieve self-actualization, "to develop their capacities to the fullest, in ways that will either maintain or enhance their own well-being" (Jones & Butman, 2011, p. 264).

*Sociocultural considerations.* This model of abnormality focuses first and foremost on social and cultural forces that influence individuals, families, and communities. Emphasis is placed on ways in which age, gender, race/ethnicity, socioeconomic status, and so on contribute to our understanding of contemporary expressions of psychopathology. Further, social norms are also considered and critiqued. More so than any other model of abnormality, this tradition has sensitized us to the broad *context* in which psychopathology is expressed or observed (McRay, Yarhouse, & Butman, 2016). It is not surprising, then, that growing numbers of academicians, clinicians, and researchers are adopting a community or systemic mindset reflective of their desire to always be sensitive to how external forces potentially impact the ways in which we think, feel, and act. The sociocultural perspective has also sparked interest in the possible prevention of psychopathology.

As we reflect on the biological, psychological, and sociocultural considerations, we are reminded of the emphasis today on the "stress-diathesis" understanding of many contemporary psychopathologies. Briefly, it is assumed that people have inherited vulnerabilities that may be tied more to biological factors (diathesis). These can become strained under stress, which can be tied to a number of psychological and sociocultural considerations. So some expressions of psychopathology may develop when inherited weaknesses or vulnerabilities become strained by internal and/or external factors—that is, stress (McRay, Yarhouse, & Butman, 2011). Given sufficient stress over time, an individual may develop certain mental disorders. The challenges that we face include the inability to know what those diatheses might be or how the stressors might be experienced through the individual's interpretive framework.

We turn now to common presenting concerns. Although we are unable to review even most of the individually orientated diagnoses in the DSM, we cover some of the more common concerns, under the headings of the various problem clusters, as delineated by McRay, Yarhouse, and Butman (2011) and following the review by Patterson, Williams, Grauf-Grounds, and Chamow (1998, chap. 9). We discuss family-based approaches to a range of concerns that are often treated by individual psychotherapy.

## COMMON PRESENTING CONCERNS

*Problems of mood.* The problems of mood refer principally to major depression, bipolar I and II disorders, cyclothymia, and dysthymia. From a systemic perspective, the family's response to the person struggling with a problem of mood can influence the course of the mood disorder itself. There is some research showing that it is particularly helpful to provide marital therapy in response to a married woman's experience of depression (Patterson et al., 1998; see Keyes & Goodman, 2006). As Patterson et al. (1998) observe, if the woman's depression is treated in isolation, there is reason to believe that the most important relationship in her life—that is, her marriage—will not improve or change in a way to support the improvements she is making to alleviate depression.

When responding as a family therapist to an individual family member's reports or symptoms of depression, family therapists often provide education about the nature and contributing factors that might lead to or exacerbate symptoms of depression (Patterson et al., 1998). What a family therapist brings to the family sessions is an awareness of how the individual person's depression affects family relationships as well as how family interactions affect the symptoms of depression.

Patterson et al. (1998) recommend that family therapists assess for a family history of depression and be open to a referral for antidepressants as one possible resource in alleviating symptoms of depression. A family therapist can also assess how a marital relationship, for instance, influences symptoms of depression. This can be part of the diagnostic interview itself or reflect an ongoing awareness of this dynamic throughout the initial assessment phase of therapy. Along these lines, it can be helpful to ask how other family members have responded to the depressed family member. For example, who has distanced themselves? Who has been most empathic? Has anyone become over-involved with the family member, or has anyone become hostile or critical of the depressed family member? Again, if it is a spouse, it will be helpful to ask how the other spouse has responded to the symptoms of depression. If it is a parent who is depressed, it can be important to assess the impact of the depression on the children (Patterson et al., 1998).

Being familiar with depression is also important as it can sometimes mask as other symptoms, such as irritability, agitation, or anger, and this is especially likely when seen in children or adolescents. This may facilitate psycho-education about the causes of depression, what depression looks like in childhood and adolescence as well as throughout the lifespan, and ways to prevent or reduce the impact of depression on other family members.

*Problems of anxiety.* The general consensus is that there is less research on family therapy and the treatment of problems of anxiety, such as generalized anxiety disorder, panic disorder, agoraphobia, and social phobia. But it is not surprising when evidence suggests that poor family relationships predict poorer outcomes when treating anxiety disorders, including panic disorder and agoraphobia. These findings support the role of involving spouses in the treatment of anxiety disorders, so that if a husband is suffering from agoraphobia or a wife is suffering from generalized anxiety disorder, it may be helpful to incorporate the nonsymptomatic partner in treatment planning and intervention. Also, meeting with the nonsymptomatic spouse provides an opportunity to provide much-needed education about the etiology and course of an anxiety disorder as well as the best ways to intervene.

In addition to working with spouses, it can be important to work with the family as a whole when a child is suffering from symptoms of an anxiety disorder. Certain responses are learned by observation, and it can be helpful to work with parents as they want to support their child in reducing symptoms of problems of anxiety.

The general suggestions by Patterson et al. (1998) for problems of anxiety are similar to those for problems of mood. One consideration is to assess for the role of marital or family concerns on symptoms of anxiety and to consider how the problem of anxiety is affecting other family members. It can also be helpful to consider any secondary gains that might come from being symptomatic in this family. Do the symptoms serve a function for the person who is struggling with them? If family therapists are working with children struggling with anxiety, consider evaluating the parents in terms of how they deal with stress and anxiety and what coping activities they may have exposed their children to as they have been trying to bring order out of emotional chaos.

*Problems involving addiction.* The Ackerson family asked for help because their son, Aaron, age seventeen, came out to them as gay. Actually, they were told by a family friend about Aaron's webpage on a popular social network, and the page had a number of suggestive pictures on it. When confronted by his parents, Aaron "confessed" his gay identity. Aaron's father, Ted, shared at the end of the first session the fact that he was an alcoholic: "Doc, I just want to be clear with you that I am an alcoholic. Have been for years. I am looking into it, but I didn't want to hide anything from you. It's something that I know is important. So . . . just so you know." This was an unusual opening statement in the course of family therapy. Often families hide their struggle with alcohol. In the course of therapy it became clear to Ted that his credibility was seriously compromised by his struggle with alcohol. If he wanted his son to be able to hear his concerns—if he wanted to be able to speak into his son's life, he would need to make changes and take care of himself in ways that would begin to establish credibility.

Problems involving addiction include alcoholism and drug abuse as well as a range of addictive behaviors. As Patterson et al. (1998) observe, alcoholism, drug abuse, and addictive patterns of behavior are rarely identified as the presenting problem when families initially seek professional services. What is much more likely to happen is that the family will come in for services because a child or adolescent is having difficulty in school. A couple might also present for marital therapy but not mention that alcoholism or drug abuse has been an ongoing concern for the couple for the past decade or more.

What has been interesting from studying these families is that they can organize themselves around a family member's experience of drug or alcohol in such a way that the family does not recognize it as the problem. Or there may be a fear that grips family members so that they do not share with others outside of the family.

Family therapists are advised to assess for alcoholism or substance abuse in their initial assessment and to come back to it as a consideration when they are having difficulty making sense of explanations or descriptions shared by family members (Patterson et al., 1998).

Family therapists will want to keep in mind that an "alcoholic family," as they are often called, is dealing with an active drug and that the misuse of that drug is chronic and cyclical in nature, producing responses that can be predicted by an outsider trained to work with these families.

Family therapy itself can be quite helpful in convincing an alcoholic to finally get the help that he or she needs. Once the nature of the concern is fully understood by the clinician, family members are often further consulted to aid in assessment. The research to date suggests that involving one's spouse is particularly helpful for men—more so than for women. It also helps the family member struggling with alcoholism when the family values and supports abstinence. Family therapy is often considered as one part of a larger, multidimensional treatment plan that involves individual therapy, psychoeducation, and psychopharmacology.

Patterson et al. (1998) suggest that family therapists assess for alcoholism and substance abuse early on, and when indicated, assess for "enabling behaviors" among other family members. It can be helpful, too, to assess the impact of the substance abuse on family beliefs and routines. It is also wise to remember that family members often vary significantly in how serious they see the substance use. Some may be quite concerned, while others may minimize the impact of the substance on the abuser or other family members.

It can also be helpful to remember that domestic violence is not uncommon in families in which one person abuses alcohol or drugs. Again, this can be asked about during the initial stage of assessment, and it may be helpful to have individual sessions with both spouses to facilitate understanding of the potential violence that may be complicating family treatment.

*Problems stemming from societal pathology.* In the section on problems of societal pathology, McRay, Yarhouse, and Butman (2016) discuss eating and sleep disorders as particularly salient examples of concerns connected in some ways to culture and systems. Minuchin, Rosman, and Baker (1978) published some early work on the families of girls with eating disorders, and more recent research appears to support some of the clinical observations about dysfunctional interactions that may contribute (as one factor among many) to later struggles with problem eating behavior.

In family therapy it is important to establish a working and empathic relationship with the individual and her family, in part because "the patterns surrounding eating or the avoidance of eating are difficult to change (as with any 'addictive' behavior) and may have become deeply rooted in family dynamics" (McRay, Yarhouse, & Butman, 2016, p. 434). Making meaningful, second-order changes to the system will require high levels of trust from all family members as family input will aid in maintenance of any gains made.

Family therapy is used less often with sleep disorders, but the main focus of family approaches tends to be psychoeducation about the various sleep disorders, such as the dyssomnias (e.g., primary insomnia, primary hypersomnia, narcolepsy, breathing-related sleep disorders, and circadian rhythm sleep disorders) and parasomnias (e.g., nightmare disorder, sleep terror disorders, and sleepwalking disorder). Family therapy can also be helpful in providing information about the five distinct stages of sleep and "sleep hygiene" or the use of specific habits that facilitate restful sleep (such as establishing a regular sleep and wake time, avoiding daytime naps, avoiding caffeine, and morning exercise).

***Problems of psychosis.*** Psychosis is the "ultimate psychological breakdown"; it reflects a "dramatic break with a person's sense of reality" (McRay, Yarhouse, & Butman, 2016, p. 330), and the most common problem of psychosis is schizophrenia, a long-term, chronic condition for most persons diagnosed with the disorder. Unfortunately, there have been a number of negative responses by the church and by the mental health community to the person suffering from schizophrenia. Many early theorists implicated the mother of schizophrenics in particular, suggesting that the nature and quality of the mother-child relationship contributed to psychosis (see Fromm-Reichmann's [1950] concept of the "schizophrenogenic" mother). We have personally known mothers who were blamed early on for their communication and response to loved ones suffering from schizophrenia, as if it was their interaction that caused the psychotic break. Thankfully, this view has been abandoned in favor of greater emphasis on biological vulnerabilities that may be inherited or acquired and stressors that may lead to a psychotic break (McRay, Yarhouse, & Butman, 2016). What remains is a greater appreciation for the role of expressed emotion in exacerbating symptoms and in relapse.

Treatment of schizophrenia took a dramatic turn for the better with the discovery of *conventional* antipsychotic or neuroleptic drugs and, more recently, *atypical* antipsychotic medications (e.g., Clozaril, Seroquel). These medications have led to remarkable symptom relief for many people who would have been institutionalized and forgotten only a few generations earlier.

Family psychoeducation can be useful in assisting clients to comply with prescribed medications. Family therapy, too, may help with generalizing self-help skills often learned in individual therapy. Therapy can also help the family engage the member suffering from schizophrenia, and vice versa, so that both the client and the family are better able to modulate strong emotions, hold realistic expectations, set attainable goals, and manage conflicts (Comer, 2003; Morrison, 2002; McRay, Yarhouse, & Butman, 2016).

*Problems of personality.* It is quite rare for individuals struggling with cluster A (e.g., paranoid, schizoid) or cluster B (e.g., borderline, antisocial) personality disorders to seek therapy of any kind. These individuals are much more likely to come to therapy in response to the concerns of others, such as family members or friends. Because of this, it is possible that these individuals may benefit from family-based approaches. Family therapy might focus more on translating concepts about personality disorders into language that is more accessible to family members and to establish principles for relating to one another that do not activate strong emotional responses among the individuals struggling with the personality disorder. A helpful resource for addressing "difficult people" is the book by Clinton McLemore, *Toxic Relationships and How to Change Them* (2003).

Individuals struggling with cluster C (e.g., avoidant, dependent) personality disorder are more likely to present for therapy of some kind. In each case, treatment is likely slow and difficult and, as with the cluster A and cluster B disorders, tends to be individually focused, complemented at times with group therapy with others who share similar features. Unfortunately, there is not much research conducted on family-based interventions for these conditions.

*Problems of sexuality.* There is an entire area of family therapy referred to as sex therapy that could warrant a chapter in a book on family therapy. There are very good resources available to the clinician who works with these concerns, both secular (e.g., Leiblum, 2007; Schnarch, 1991) and distinctively Christian (e.g., Penner & Penner, 1990; Rosenau, 2002; Yarhouse & Tan, 2014), as well as Christian readings on human sexuality in general that can be quite helpful as an adjunctive resource with a range of presenting concerns (e.g., McMinn, 2004).

Sex therapy represents an interesting balance of individual and systemic or relational concerns. It typically begins as a relationship/intimacy concern in which one partner—often at the urging of the other partner—seeks medical advice. This typically leads to an individual diagnosis (e.g., desire disorder, erectile dysfunction, orgasmic disorder) followed by case conceptualization that in contemporary approaches typically involves assignment of mutual responsibility to reduce the tendency to blame and to facilitate a collaborative focus in sex therapy. Sex therapy may begin with education for both partners about the condition, including theories for understanding contributing and maintaining factors. There may then be a shift in focus back to the individual with the diagnosis, depending to some extent on the diagnosis itself.

Consider, for example, a woman suffering from genito-pelvic pain/penetration disorder, a dysfunction in which there is pain during intercourse and in which, in some cases, the outer muscles of vagina contract when the couple attempts penile penetration. While both the woman and her husband may benefit from initial education about the possible causes and maintaining factors associated with genito-pelvic pain/penetration disorder, the focus will likely shift to important information obtained in her sex history (and likely his as well), and this may lead to exercises such as personal understanding of sexual anatomy and personal exploration of what is sexually meaningful and satisfying. This individual understanding is then translated into shared understanding with one's partner. Sex therapy at this stage typically involves improving communication in general, but especially in the area of sexuality, so that the couple can cultivate feedback-rich communication.

Other areas addressed in problems of sexuality include the paraphilic disorders and sexual addiction or compulsive sexual behavior. Sexual and gender identity concerns are addressed at length in chapter twenty, so we will briefly mention the paraphilic disorders and sexual addiction.

There does not tend to be as much literature on family-based interventions for the paraphilic disorders, although there does appear to be a benefit to involving spouses at some level when addressing addictive patterns of behavior, including Internet pornography and sexual acting out.

***Problems in childhood and adolescence.*** The individual mental health concerns addressed in problems of childhood and adolescence refer to concerns that are first diagnosed in childhood or adolescence. These include attention-deficit hyperactivity disorder, intellectual disabilities, learning disorders, autistic spectrum disorders, and elimination disorders.

Family therapy in the form of parent education and training is very common when addressing problems in childhood and adolescence. Of course, any of the previously discussed conditions, such as a mood disorder or anxiety disorder, may be present in a child or adolescent, and some of the same principles of parent management training would apply in those cases as well. Nichols and Davis (2017) note that parent management training focuses primarily on educating the parent about the condition in question (e.g., autism spectrum disorder) and targets the parents' ways of relating to the child or adolescent so that the interaction facilitates and does not undermine therapy goals. Most forms of parent management training also apply general social learning principles to improve parenting skills and shape the child's or adolescent's behavior. The parenting skills are often learned in session and then applied in the home.

For example, treatment for children and adolescents struggling with ADHD typically includes medication (e.g., Cylert, Dexedrin) but also behavior management training for parents (and teachers). The parent training component focuses on how parents might develop and implement a structured behavioral management program that sets clear goals, monitors progress, and provides consequences to reinforce goals and discourage targeted behaviors (McRay, Yarhouse, & Butman, 2011). Parent management training has also been used in the treatment of ADHD in adolescence, as has structural family therapy, and it has been used in the prevention of conduct problems among children (Nichols & Davis, 2017).

It should be noted, too, that one of the most successful approaches to problem adolescent behavior and juvenile delinquency is multisystemic therapy—an intensive, home-based, and community-based family therapy (Henggeler, Melton, & Smith, 1992). It is also being piloted with a number of other concerns in adolescence, such as medication compliance among teens with type 1 diabetes (e.g., Ellis et al., 2005).

*Problems in older adulthood.* The individual mental health concerns addressed in problems in older adulthood refer to a number of conditions that are more likely to be seen as people age, such as various cognitive impairments that include Alzheimer's disease, vascular dementia, delirium, and amnestic disorders. But it should also be noted that the other concerns, such as problems of mood and problems of sexuality, may also be present in older adulthood and mirror the disorders experienced by young and middle-aged adults.

Mental health professionals tend to prefer time-limited, structured interventions to help older adults (DeVries, 1996). This might include cognitive-behavioral therapy for mood and anxiety disorders; pharmacotherapy, supportive group therapy, and family therapy for substance use and alcoholism; and psychoeducation and pharmacotherapy to address sexual concerns (see McRay, Yarhouse, & Butman, 2016, chap. 13).

When addressing problems of cognitive functioning, behavioral therapy has especially strong empirical support, as has memory and cognitive retraining for slowing the deterioration in cognitive functioning. Support and assurance is typically provided to someone experiencing delirium.

One of the most important considerations with problems in older adulthood is the role of family caregivers and the use of family interventions to alleviate caregiver stress. There has been interest in the effects of chronic stress on the psychological well-being and coping effectiveness of family caregivers. There is a large literature documenting the high incidence of negative impact on caregiver well-being, and an emerging literature on the kinds of coping activities that are most helpful in buffering these negative effects (DeVries & Yarhouse, 1998).

Caring for a family member with a chronic psychopathology—such as ADHD, schizophrenia, or major depressive disorder—is very demanding. Often these chronic conditions, depending on the severity, result in limitations or impairment in social or occupational functioning or in the family member's ability to carry out activities of daily living.

Unlike other experiences of family crisis, family caregiving for a chronic, long-standing psychopathology is an ongoing, long-term commitment. Some conditions will be degenerative (e.g., Alzheimer's disease), while others may improve over time (e.g., bipolar disorder symptoms may not be as pronounced in middle or later life). Caregivers are often discouraged and worn down by the demands placed on them over time. Common symptoms of caregiver stress include depression, anxiety, and hostility or anger.

Role engulfment and loss of self can also be a concern among family caregivers. Some family members do report finding meaning and satisfaction in the caregiving role, while others feel they essentially disappear in the face of caregiving demands (Skaff & Pearlin, 1992). As DeVries and Yarhouse (1998) note, "The constriction of meaningful involvement in activities and social relationships resulting from expanding caregiving responsibilities can lead to the loss, shrinkage, or diminishment of identity" (p. 288). Younger family caregivers tend to report greater loss of self than older family caregivers (presumably due to the psychological sense of what they expected to be doing at this stage of life), and the frequency of problem behavior on the part of the person with the chronic condition can also be related to loss of self (DeVries & Yarhouse, 1998).

## CHRISTIAN CRITIQUE AND ENGAGEMENT

*Balancing individual and systemic concerns.* The Christian family therapist addressing individual psychopathology is faced with the question of how to best integrate information on individual concerns while thinking broadly about the family system. As Patterson et al. (1998) suggest, one way to stay open to family-based considerations is to be familiar with individual diagnostic categories and symptoms that reflect those categories so that one can determine if an individual does indeed meet criteria for a diagnosis. This is one reason we organized this chapter around the various problem clusters discussed in contemporary taxonomies. The Christian will want to be quite adept at identifying symptoms of individual psychopathology when working with families.

This will raise the question of competence to address a specific individual psychopathology. If the person should receive treatment for specific symptoms—say, panic attacks indicative of a panic disorder—does the clinician have the skills to recognize these symptoms and intervene in a way that will likely reduce symptom presentation? If not, should the family-based clinician make a referral while being available for the broader family concerns that may or may not exacerbate symptoms of anxiety? Ideally, the responsible Christian family therapist is competent to provide services related to a range of both individual and systemic concerns.

At the same time, the Christian will expand his or her clinical repertoire if he or she is able to recognize how systemic concerns may contribute to the etiology or maintenance of symptoms, even when those symptoms appear to be isolated to an individual identified patient.

We want to stress something very important in providing family therapy: Do not confuse the person with the diagnosis! Have you ever heard a mental health professional talk about the "borderline" he or she is working with? Or the "schizophrenic" they heard about on the hospital ward? It is all too common for professionals to talk about people by their labels. Is it any wonder people feel stigmatized by psychopathology? Or that people may avoid coming in to see a mental health professional?

Christian family therapists can be rightly suspicious of a medical model that reduces people to symptom clusters and provides them with corresponding labels. While it is understandable to use diagnostic labels to communicate with other professionals and to help people organize their understanding of their own condition, such labels run the risk of a reductionism that truncates the person and their identity and fails to take seriously the place of pain in our lives.

Labels also create distance. Family therapists can keep family members at arm's length by thinking about and talking to family members with reference to their label. We prefer that family therapists engage family members in real relationships that do not rely on a distance created by categories that lend themselves to us-and-them mindsets.

*Think about it:* What are some of the reasons for relying on diagnostic labels? What are the benefits and drawbacks of doing so? How can you step into a family's experience of pain rather than talk about it? What are some practical ways for family therapists to offer their active presence and respectful and attentive listening?

Beyond the question of competence is the issue of whether the Christian family therapist can balance both individual and systemic considerations. As McRay, Yarhouse, & Butman (2016) suggest, there is a need to recognize that individual psychopathologies have multiple causes and multiple maintaining factors. Christian family therapists will want to avoid the sin of "nothing-but-ism" (e.g., depression is caused by nothing but changes in brain chemistry). Just as the person focusing on individual psychopathology will want to expand their repertoire to reflect on systemic considerations, so too will the family therapist want to reflect on individually focused approaches to psychopathology while avoiding the reductionism that is often reflected therein.

***"Industry" concerns.*** If we were to point out a related but broader concern, it has to do with the mental health care "industry." It is the emergence and prominence of "managed care" and, as we suggested above, a tendency we see toward an overreliance on the medical model, which focuses exclusively on individual psychopathology and treatment. This leaves little room for family therapy and its role in addressing the interpersonal and environmental factors that lead to or exacerbate stress associated with psychopathology.

We are reminded of Mary Stewart Van Leeuwen's (1985) warning that the field of psychology not allow the marketplace to shape its understanding of what matters most: "When a discipline begins to let the demands of the marketplace shape most of its priorities, it shows a failure of nerve—it is taking an easy escape-route from hard questions about the basic nature and scope of its subject matter" (p. 243). We can see how Van Leeuwen's (1985) concern might be applied to the "industry" facets of contemporary mental

## INTEGRATIVE FOCUS: *Family Functioning*

The ways in which families come to terms with chronic mental illness is highly ideographic though they have nomothetic commonalities. That is, pain is highly subjective and personal, and Christian family therapists will want to keep this in mind in their work with families struggling with individual psychopathology.

At the same time, families struggling with pain do share some common experiences. We tend to locate experiences of individual psychopathology in the *Diagnostic and Statistical Manual*, and these symptoms can be discussed and addressed within the family context.

However, much of what we do as family therapists is to recognize the ideographic qualities of the pain of psychopathology. It is as though once we have a sense for the category of concern, we then set that aside for a time while we learn what the family's experience has been like. In other words, what has this category of experience been like in real life for this particular family?

*Think about it:* What examples have you seen of different families responding differently to a similar set of circumstances? What would you say accounts for some of those differences? In what ways is pain similar and in what ways is it highly subjective? What are the implications for the Christian family therapist?

health service delivery. It would be a shame to see family-based and systemically focused considerations lost to a marketplace that may value biological reductionism in the face of demands for symptom reduction. But the burden of proof is also on those who value systemic interventions. In the current climate they will need to demonstrate the value of such interventions in a competitive field of competing theories and interventions.

*Education and parent training.* We are encouraged to see the family therapy field embrace parent management training as an important aspect of therapy. Indeed, we see parents as critical proximal agents who spend far more time with family members than even the most enthusiastic and committed family therapist. For family therapy to be effective, we believe family therapists must work hard to establish trusting relationships with all family members, especially the parents, so that what is learned in family sessions can be applied more consistently at home.

From a distinctively Christian perspective, there seems to be a great opportunity for Christian family therapists to value parents in ways often overlooked in secular approaches where a common focus is individual self-actualization, sometimes at the expense of parental oversight and input.

Coming at parent training from a different perspective, it is also important that Christians value parent training because many parents are genuinely well-intentioned but simply lack the skills or the language at the present to intervene and engage their children in a way that effectively reflects their care and regard.

*Caregiving revisited.* In addition, we would like to elaborate on the family caregiver literature discussed above, which is often a consideration when providing family therapy. In other words, we work with a lot of conditions that may require a family caregiver to intervene directly. In terms of more explicit Christian engagement, the family therapist will want to be competent in the use of often-overlooked interventions, such as religious coping strategies, particularly among family caregivers. Various religious and spiritual resources can be utilized to support the caregiver. These include but are not limited to the caregiver's religious or spiritual beliefs and behaviors, such as prayer, corporate worship, participation in a faith-based support group, and forgiveness as well as key constructs such as sanctification.

Like other coping strategies, religious and spiritual strategies may be more or less helpful. It would not be hard to imagine that beliefs and values that emphasize self-sacrifice could keep a family member from asking for needed support or assistance (DeVries & Yarhouse, 1998).

Sometimes Christians struggle in the caregiving role because of the guilt and shame they may feel in response to their own negative emotions, such as anger or frustration. As a result, they may experience an increase in stress by denying or minimizing their own negative emotions that are above and beyond what they already experience in the caregiver role.

Furthermore, data suggest that most family caregivers of the frail elderly are female, either wives, daughters, or daughters-in-law (Stone, Cafferata, & Sangl, 1987). The Christian community might take a prophetic role in speaking to the gender issues represented in these findings and identify ways to rectify the disparities while simultaneously providing much-needed support and "permission" for self-care.

## INTEGRATIVE FOCUS: *Family Relationships*

Family relationships are increasingly recognized as important in the prevention and care of persons struggling with psychopathology. The family provides a natural means by which support can be sustained on a consistent and long-term basis.

The Christian family therapist can be particularly helpful in clarifying roles, expectations, and boundaries as well as reflecting on attitudes about and perceptions of those who need assistance. It can be hard to provide care to a loved one, but it can also be hard to be the loved one who needs care.

*Think about it:* Make a list of the kinds of concerns that might be especially conducive to family therapy. What do these concerns have in common? In what ways do you see improved family relationships as a key part of addressing the concerns you have listed?

## CONCLUSION

We have been discussing the dominant models in the mental health community that favor and reflect the medical model and individual psychopathology. While there is great value in understanding individual psychopathology, such an understanding may be balanced by an appreciation for broader, systemic considerations often found in family-based models.

## REFERENCES

Comer, R. J. (2003). *Abnormal psychology* (5th ed.). New York: Worth.

DeVries, H. M. (1996). Cognitive-behavioral intervention. In J. E. Birren (Ed.), *Encyclopedia of gerontology*. San Diego: Academic Press.

DeVries, H. M., & Yarhouse, M. A. (1998). Emotional and spiritual well-being in family caregivers. *Marriage and Family: A Christian Journal, 1*(3), 287-98.

Ellis, D. A., Frey, M. A., Naar-King, S., Templin, T., Cunningham, P. B., & Cakan, N. (2005). The effects of multisystemic therapy on diabetes stress among adolescents with chronically poorly controlled type 1 diabetes: Findings from a randomized, controlled trial. *Pediatrics, 116*(6), 826-32.

Fromm-Reichmann, F. (1950). *Principles of intensive psychotherapy*. Chicago: University of Chicago Press.

Henggeler, S. W., Melton, G. B., & Smith, L. A. (1992). Family preservation using multisystemic therapy: An effective alternative to incarcerating serious juvenile offenders. *Journal of Consulting and Clinical Psychology, 60*, 953-61.

Jones, S. L., & Butman, R. E. (2011). *Modern psychotherapies: A comprehensive Christian appraisal* (2nd ed.). Downers Grove, IL: InterVarsity Press.

Keyes, C. L. M., & Goodman, S. H. (Eds.). (2006). *Women and depression: A handbook of the social, behavioral, and medical science*. New York: Cambridge University Press.

Leiblum, S. R. (2007). *Principles and practice of sex therapy* (4th ed.). New York: Guilford Press.

McLemore, C. (2003). *Toxic relationships and how to change them: Health and holiness in everyday life*. San Francisco: Jossey-Bass.

McMinn, L. G. (2004). *Sexuality and holy longing: Embracing intimacy in a broken world*. San Francisco: Jossey-Bass.

McRay, B. W., Yarhouse, M. A., & Butman, R. E. (2016). *Modern psychopathologies: A comprehensive Christian appraisal* (2nd ed.). Downers Grove, IL: InterVarsity Press.

Minuchin, S., Rosman, B. L., & Baker, L. (1978). *Psychosomatic families: Anorexia nervosa in context*. Cambridge, MA: Harvard University Press.

Morrison, J. (2002). *Straight talk about your mental health*. New York: Guilford Press.

Nichols, M. P., & Davis, S. (2017). *Family therapy: Concepts and methods* (11th ed.). Boston, MA: Allyn & Bacon.

Patterson, J., Williams, L., Grauf-Grounds, C., & Chamow, L. (1998). *Essential skills in family therapy: From the first interview to termination*. New York: Guilford Press.

Penner, J. J., & Penner, C. L. (1990). *Counseling for sexual disorder.* Dallas: Word.

Rosenau, D. E. (2002). *A celebration of sex* (2nd ed.). Nashville: Thomas Nelson.

Schnarch, D. M. (1991). *Constructing the sexual crucible: An integration of sexual and marital therapy.* New York: W. W. Norton.

Skaff, M. M., & Pearlin, L. I. (1992). Caregiving: Role engulfment and the loss of self. *The Gerontologist, 32*(5), 656-64.

Stapert, K. (1994). Will pharmacological Calvinism protect me? *Perspectives,* June/July, 9-10.

Stone, R., Cafferata, G. L., & Sangl, J. (1987). Caregivers of the frail elderly: A national profile. *The Gerontologist, 27,* 616-31.

Van Leeuwen, M. S. (1985). *The person in psychology: A contemporary Christian appraisal.* Grand Rapids: Eerdmans.

Yarhouse, M. A., & Tan, E. S. N. (2014). *Sexuality and sex therapy: A comprehensive Christian appraisal.* Downers Grove, IL: IVP Academic.

# SUBSTANCE ABUSE

*Better to sleep with a sober cannibal*
*than a drunk Christian.*

**HERMAN MELVILLE,** *MOBY DICK*

*Drugs or overeating or alcohol or sex, it was all*
*just another way to find peace. To escape what we*
*know. Our education. Our bite of the apple.*

**CHUCK PALAHNIUK,** *CHOKE*

P HILLIP IS MY FRIEND.[1] We traveled, as boys becoming men, through junior high and high school; we shared in each other's growth and provoked our parents to age prematurely. When his parents went away for a weekend we drained his swimming pool to have a place to skateboard. It was really fun until Sunday evening when his parents came home! His family became my family, and my family his—in that common surrogate adoption that is a part of adolescent development. After high school our lives went different directions. I went away to college and grad school. Phillip enrolled in the "College of Alcohol" and then did graduate studies at "Cocaine University." Both of us spent the decade of our twenties in our respective schools. We both "completed our schooling" about the same time. I had formal education

---

[1]Due to the personal nature of many of the illustrations, we have chosen to write much of this chapter in the first person.

and the wisdom that comes from knowledge; Phillip gained a different kind of wisdom—one that emerges from the pain and failure of addiction. Sobriety requires self-examination, grace, commitment, struggle, and humble containment. As adults, our friendship was made new and we have spent the last fifteen years contemplating our lives, our families, our pasts, and our futures.

His story and that of the entire Hernandez family has been my compass point to understand family substance abuse. I attended the classes, read the textbooks, and was supervised in the treatment of families with addictions. But I cannot read academic journals or attend conferences without images of the generations of the Hernandez family whose lives were altered with the presence of alcohol and drugs.

They showed a pattern that is common to millions of homes—the generational presence of substance abuse, the disruption and alienation of relationship, and coping patterns of pain avoidance that are passed on to the next generation. Their story is fraught with pathos, grief, hope, and resilience. Their story reflects the severe complications in understanding the causes of and developing treatments for substance and behavioral addictions.

Peter and Mary Hernandez raised fourteen children: eight girls and six boys. They were a poor but dignified family. They were proud to be American citizens and proud of their cultural heritage from Mexico. Peter brought the craft of guitar construction from his family. Mary carried the tradition of cooking from Mexico. Their home had great music, great food, and a lot of beer. Their small, one-story, Orange County, California, home—with a groomed lawn and brightly trimmed paint—was a place of celebration and tragedy. They valued dignity, responsibility, and hard work. They believed in working hard, being present for one another, and serving in their country's military, and they especially believed you should never shame your family.

The family did not talk openly about fear, struggle, and failure. Advice and counsel were seldom offered because asking for them was not encouraged. An unspoken family motto could have been "We will be there in the good times; in the bad times, you're on your own." A second unarticulated message, "Don't mess up!" made the first theme all the more threatening. Those were lessons that were passed through the generations, especially the men. They were quick to lend a hand to help with each other's physical needs but slow to comprehend and respond to the emotional concerns. Pain could not be soothed within family through the comfort of conversation—instead, it was numbed by intoxication.

The genogram of the Hernandez family reveals the prevalence of alcohol and drug abuse extending through generations (see fig. 17.1). It reveals the suffering, secrets, healing, and estrangement. Ruptures remain between some members of the family—scars passed to the next generation, and potentially the next and the next and forever, until individuals choose to break the cycles for themselves and to offer hope for change to those who are also afflicted. Some in the family have discovered this. Phillip has, as have most of his sisters. However, most of the brothers and some nephews and nieces have not discovered that families can be a source of protection and assistance in the courageous struggle against pain.

Today, the family stands like a large, old, stately mansion. It's a sprawling relational estate numbering over one hundred people, including the first generation of children, their spouses, Peter and Mary's grandchildren, and now great-grandchildren. Sadly, the family structure shows evidence of disrepair and dilapidation to many sections of the roof and supporting walls. Many of the brothers continue to flee from the threat of health and well-being. They drink to soothe the pain from life and to calm their anger at themselves and their family for demanding that they be truthful. However, other portions of the Hernandez structure stand restored, or the restoration process is clearly under way. The beauty of grace extended to Phillip and many of his siblings and their spouses who have run the gauntlet of recovery and done the hard work of confession, honest expression, humble recognition, and courageous acceptance have caused their family home to reflect a warm glow. Mary's recipe for homemade tamales feeds the generation of descendants that she and Peter did not know. The relationships thrive in the support and encouragement through one another and languish in the despair and denial, softened by the continued abuse of drugs to soothe the pain of life. The Hernandez family story is the common family story telling the cycle of destruction and decay, grace and restoration. Its uniqueness is that alcohol and cocaine have functioned like the great magnifier—exposing the extremity of both debauchery and deliverance.

## HISTORICAL OVERVIEW

Families have always been at the center of the treatment of substance abuse and addictions. Possible reasons for this are that members have compassion for the suffering of others with whom they have love and loyalty attachments, so they are prompted to act and assist, and because families are harmed by the destructive effects that are associated or correlated with addictions. These include the consumption of family finances by the addictive behavior, underemployment and the loss of employment from the destabilization from the addiction, negative health effects, premature death, increase in violence, relational injury, and finally, the evidence of intergeneration transmission of the problem.

Prior to the formation of "talking treatments" such as Alcoholics Anonymous groups, the focuses of interventions were political and religious. For example, in the United States, the progressive movement between the years 1880 and 1920 was characterized by the majority of the population in almost every state viewing alcohol specifically, but also opium, as the primary cause of social unrest and family disintegration. Prohibition was the most noteworthy political outcome. But there were many other laws and regulations: the Smoking Opium Act, the Hague Treaty, and the Harrison Act are three other lesser-known political outcomes designed to protect men and women against themselves and ultimately to guard children from the effects of alcohol and drug abuse. The emphasis during the early twentieth century was on defining the substances—alcohol, opium, cocaine, and later, marijuana and other medical and designer drugs—as the evil, with the perspective that if you control the evil, you control the problem and protect the society.

During the middle period of the twentieth century, family-based treatments were still a rarity. Through the 1930s, 40s, and 50s alcohol remained a serious social problem, but narcotic use actually declined during this time (Musto, 1999). Possibly this is explained by the economic pressures of the Great Depression and the social focus of World War II. The 1950s were characterized by a gradual increase in opiate use—culminating in the Boggs-Daniels Acts, a series of federal laws that increased mandatory sentencing and even permitted juries to choose the death penalty for individuals selling heroin. Treatments for substance abuse for individuals or families remained relatively rare.

The popularity of the Alcoholics Anonymous (AA) model emerged as a major social force during this era. Alcoholics Anonymous has had a peculiar relationship with families in that harm to family is often the motivating force that gets people into AA participation. However, the family is never directly part of the AA recovery process. Instead they are separated and encouraged to seek help through Al-Anon or Alateen, which focus on teaching family members how they can become separated from the responsibility for and the effects of a family member's addiction.

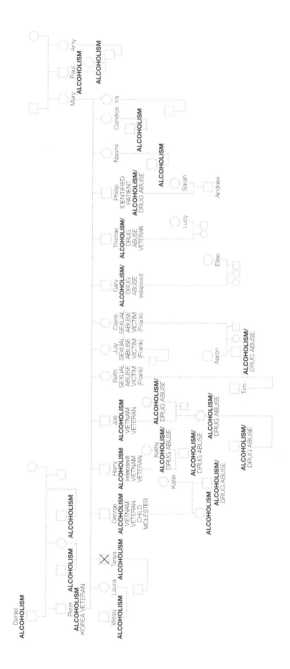

**Figure 17.1.** Hernandez family genogram

In the 1960s everything changed. The rapid increase of marijuana and other new illicit medicines—amphetamines, barbiturates, and lysergic acid diethylamide (LSD) as well as opiates and cocaine—among the youth culture created a national crisis. Attention turned to developing treatments for addictions as opposed to focusing primarily on the incarceration of offenders. Family-based approaches became extremely popular in the late 1960s through the 1980s. By the late 1970s Coleman and Davis (1978) reported that from over 2,000 agencies surveyed, 93 percent offered some form of family therapy to treat substance abuse and addictions. The evidence that family intervention is more effective in helping addicted family members maintain sobriety than individual treatment alone is a clear outcome of numerous meta-analytical reviews of research (Epstein & McCrady, 1998; O'Farrell & Fals-Stewart, 2000; Stanton & Shadish, 1997). The positive effect of family involvement in substance abuse treatment is an important component of a comprehensive treatment plan that usually includes detoxification, group therapy, individual therapy, drug testing, and AA or similar twelve-step programs.

During the 1990s the definition of addiction and its association with other pathologies was challenged. Historically, addictions have been associated with chemicals (e.g., alcohol, nicotine, heroin); DSM IV-R separates addictive disorders into substance abuse and substance dependence. The former is described as the continued use of a substance in spite of its continued negative effect on one's ability to function in work, school, or home; placing oneself at risk for harm while using the substance; experiencing legal or reprimanding consequences because of the substance use; or continued use of the substance in spite of harmful effects on relationships or social responsibilities. The latter, substance dependence, includes the characteristics of substance abuse stated above and also the continued use of the substance in greater amounts to obtain the desired effect (tolerance) and the experience of a negative physiological reaction when the substance is reduced or eliminated (withdrawal).

However, during this time there was an increase in the attention directed toward behavioral or "process" addictions (Juhnke & Hagedorn, 2006). A process addiction involves a repeated and habituated act that is conducted to bring pleasure but comes to dominate one's life and is continued in spite of negative consequences. Process addictions could include sex, gambling, religiosity, eating, work, shopping/spending, media use (television/computer/video games/Internet), hobbies, and exercise.

The debate as to whether process addictions are the same as substance addictions continues. The similarities and differences are noted in the professional literature. For the purposes in this chapter, we will be referring specifically to substance abuse and addictions, with the acknowledgement that many of the interventions might be applicable to families who are addressing process or behavioral addictions.

## FAMILY THERAPY TREATMENT MODELS

While the research data support the implementation of family therapy as either an ancillary or primary intervention for addictions, it is less clear which model is better and under which circumstances a given approach is best. Because no one model of family therapy conclusively works best in all situations, the common response to the discrepant outcome data is to assume either that (1) theories don't really matter; (2) some theories are better than others, and you should pick one and fervently study and advocate for it; or (3) one should try and master all of the approaches.

Juhnke and Hagedorn (2006) offer a useful and reasoned response to the quagmire of family addiction theory options. They advocate a progressive, sequential treatment plan of therapies that range from the models that emphasize brief, noninsightful, here-and-now interventions as the first forms of therapeutic intervention. Subsequently, if families do not achieve their treatment goals, then more long-term, historical, and insight-oriented approaches can be used. They advocate a seven-stage model of progressive interventions. The stages include (1) motivational interviewing; (2) solution-focused, MRI Brief Family Therapy; (3) cognitive-behavioral family therapy; (4) structural family therapy; (5) extended family systems therapy; (6) intergenerational family-of-origin therapy; and (7) psychodynamic/object relations family therapy.

These approaches are not presented as competing paradigms but are progressive structures selected because of their suitability with family characteristics and their place in the process of recovery. Families new to accepting and addressing addictive themes are most appropriate for the earlier stages. Families who have addressed recovery themes over time are likely to benefit from latter stages.

*Stage 1: Motivational interviewing.* The first stage counters the unproductive stereotype of the addictions counselor who uses harsh confrontational tactics to force the addicted family member to realize the error of his or her ways, repent of the destructive habits, and move toward a new commitment to sobriety and self-discipline. "In your face" tactics are good for television drama but are not realistic for family change. Instead, Juhnke and Hagedorn advocate a client-centered model that is drawn from Miller's (1983, 1985) finding that the environment created by the counselor contributes to the family's willingness to seek change. The aim of motivational interviewing is to prompt the family and the addicted member to confront himself or herself, taking ownership of treatment rather than developing resistance because of the counselor's externally imposed confrontation (Bell & Rollnick, 1996). The confrontation used in this approach is based on Prochaska and DiClemente's (1986) change model.

> The key to Miller's motivational interviewing concept is that counselors seek to understand the client's frame of reference through reflective listening. . . . counselors ask questions to learn how clients perceive their situation and then allow clients to make intrinsically based choices related to treatment. So, counselors listen to their client's presenting concerns, rather than preempt the treatment by confronting clients related to their "addiction." (Juhnke & Hagedorn, 2006, p. 233)

This form of family addiction intervention includes active listening to the concerns of all members with the counselor acting in a director/facilitator role, assuring that all members have been adequately heard and understood by the family. The counselor is free to point out discrepancies, inconsistencies, and issues beyond the family's knowledge, then encourage the family to pursue a treatment plan that is generated from within the group.

The Prochaska and DiClemente model helps the counselor lead the family through a progressive structure that can identify the treatment strategy most likely to be effective for the family. The six stages are pre-contemplation, contemplation, determination, action, maintenance, and relapse.

The *pre-contemplation stage* characterizes the family that has not had direct conversation regarding the nature of the addictive behaviors and their effect on the family as a whole. For example, a parent suspects marijuana use by an adolescent because of the odor from his laundry. The family—the parents and adolescent—attend the therapy session together and use the counselor as a mediator in helping the family understand itself and its needs.

The *contemplation stage* focuses on the addicted person's effort to rationalize, minimize, and deny the seriousness of the disorder or its effect on the family. The contemplative aspects are seen in the effort to reconcile internal views of self with additional information offered by the family that indicates the seriousness of the addiction problem.

The *determination stage* can be seen as the "aha" stage, where the effect of the addiction is acknowledged and accepted within the family system.

In the *action stage* the family's determination is implemented. It involves the family and individual members undergoing agreed-on treatments and altering previous patterns of action.

The *maintenance stage* is the management of the addiction—through ongoing treatment, lifestyle commitments, and supportive relationships.

The *relapse stage* within family addictions is a constant vigil, for recurrence of previously managed addictive behavior is a common reality. Discussion with the family about the recurrence of previously addressed addictions returns the family to one of the above stages, but the return is with greater knowledge and specific experiences not held in the initial processes.

The motivational interviewing form of family therapy is often an initial experience with the mental health profession, and it is an effective treatment for families who are capable of confronting, supporting, and regulating their behavior in a constructive manner.

***Stage 2: Solution-focused and MRI Brief Family Therapy.*** Solution-focused and MRI Brief Family Therapy are distinct approaches with a common heritage. The two share many common ideas and approaches and have emerged from the historical influence of Bateson, Erickson, Jackson, and Haley as well as that of social constructionism and postmodernism. The reader is encouraged to review chapters seven and nine to be familiar with the historical and theoretical underpinnings.

Family interventions developed through the solution and brief therapy paradigms show significant differences from the psychodynamic and disease models of etiology and therapy that have been the standard in addictions counseling. They are based on the assumption that substance abuse in the family must be maintained and supported by the system in order to exist. However, it is not caused by traceable events or knowable sources, nor does the substance play a stabilizing part in the family system. Adherents to these models advocate working with whole families or parts—any who are willing to bring change to the system, even when the substance abusers are resistant to therapeutic participation or to change.

It should be noted that MRI Family Therapy with substance abuse emerged from the second-generation of MRI research and practice—the Brief Therapy Center that began in 1965 under the leadership of Richard Fisch, John Weakland, and Paul Watzlawick. The center quickly took a leadership role in the development of brief therapy models. In 1989 the Family Recovery Project was launched, and it continues as an important intellectual epicenter for family addictions research and treatment (Brown & Lewis, 2000). The Family Recovery Project has continued to emphasize the systemic perspective with a pragmatic behavioral emphasis.

Similarly, Steve de Shazer, an originator of solution-focused therapy, trained at MRI and was significantly influenced by the brief, problem-oriented, present-focused approach. However, he broke with MRI because he believed that its model was too focused on defining the problem rather than discovering solutions. Shoham, Rohrbaugh, and Patterson (1995) distinguished the two by noting that the MRI model encouraged a different response to the problem and the solution-focused approach encouraged a different view of the situation— toward that of the solution rather than the problem.

The interventions within these approaches are short, usually less than ten weeks with the brief model, and shorter still with the solution-focused approach. It begins with an assessment that focuses on problem definition—why it is that the family has come to therapy. The counselor will seek greater specificity of the problem than substance use: one is seeking to define the problem in terms such as arguments, failure in school, intoxication in the home, failure to attend children's events because dad is out drinking with friends, or for adolescents, staying out past curfew hours or driving under the influence of alcohol. Specific precipitating events are sought as the motivation for initiating the counseling experience, as well as the sequence of behaviors that the family system exhibits subsequent to the targeted problem behavior. In addition, the counselor would seek to define the efforts to solve the problem and what has emerged as effective and what has not.

The second phase of treatment involves crafting an intervention that alters the pattern of interaction occurring within the family. All behavior occurs within a context of relational interaction. Oral communication is the most obvious form of relational behavior. But all sequential interplay between family members is the field of change. It is common for families to approach the intervention phase with a preconception that they have already tried everything and that there is nothing left to be done and no possible hope for change. The key element to employ is to understand the family interventions that have already been or that continue to be attempted by the family, yet without the desired outcomes, as paradoxical supports for the family addiction. Therefore, encouraging a person to stop drinking, or attend AA, or study with greater discipline are really behaviors that paradoxically support the addictive patterns within the family.

Alternatively, therapists would implement a radical departure from the status quo of family behavior. The counselor would help the family identify how actions of the family limit solutions that are within their realm. If nonaddictive families go on outings together, then this family should begin planning outings. If nonaddictive families speak directly to one another when there is a problem, then this family should begin to act in a similar manner. A counselor should seek to create the attitude of a scientist searching for a solution to a complex problem through intentional trial implementation and subsequent measure of effect. If after a designated amount of time the problem is not reduced, then an alternative method is employed. This may take the form of a series of changes in the way the family does business.

For example, imagine distraught parents of an adult son or daughter who drinks excessively while at home from college for the summer. The parents want their son to stop drinking. They have argued with him—done everything they could except demand that he find alternate housing. Arguments have occurred between the couple because of different beliefs about parenting. Yet the son continues to drink in spite of the problems that it is creating in his home. The parents report feeling powerless and disappointed in their son's decision making and his disrespect for their wishes. The son feels intruded and invaded. He is angry that they seek to control his life by inquiring about his drinking patterns. The son has no apparent desire to curtail his actions.

*Stage 3: Cognitive-behavioral family therapy.* The cognitive-behavioral family approach to addictions represents the major approaches to addictions interventions. The fusion of cognitive and behavior and family methods brings together three interrelated approaches to therapy. First, by maintaining the family-systems emphasis, the role of the system in the etiology, maintenance, and intervention of addictions and substance abuse is acknowledged.

Second, the approach guides the family to address the realm of individual and communally held thoughts, beliefs, and values that encourage and maintain addictions as an acceptable response and to alter and replace these thoughts, beliefs, and values with cognitive constructs that foster more effective responses. Finally, as a behavioral approach, interventions include the realm of subtle reinforcements.

Rotgers (1996) puts forth seven assumptions of behavioral theories and treatments. First of all, addictive behaviors are learned rather than determined by genetic or disease factors. Second, the same processes that prompted a problematic addictive behavior can be reversed and altered. Third, the context and the environment, such as the family, contribute to the addictive process. Therapy must include changes in the environment (i.e., family) as well as the addicted individual's response to it. Fourth, thoughts and feelings that operate to direct and motivate one to act can be changed through intentional learning. Fifth, one must act the new behavior in the context that it is to occur. Therefore, mature actions occurring within the real family system promote learning more than learning in a classroom or clinic environment. Sixth, a treatment plan must be developed that is unique to every individual and family system. Finally, the foundation for treatment is assessment.

The approach to cognitive-behavioral family therapy focuses on the assessment of antecedents to problematic behavior. For example, Margaret and Ivan are paying bills and balancing the checkbook together. The stress and tension between them is increased as they realize once again that each has spent money without the other's awareness, and they are forced to take money once again out of their savings. They deliver harsh words to one another to vent their frustration and to place blame on the other for their current financial condition. The words escalate into argument and Ivan leaves—changing his clothes into sweatpants and running shoes—and he goes off for a sixty-minute run. His energy to exercise exists on an addiction level—running at least an hour a day, longer when there is tension at home or work. His running is fueled by the desire to escape the conflict at home. Margaret is fueled by another motivation. She turns her frustration into addictive eating and consumes chocolates and pastries.

The task for the family is to identify the precursor—in this case the decisions around spending—and develop alternative behavioral patterns associated with spending and bill paying. Second, there is the cognitive task of examining the individual and communal thought processes or the beliefs held regarding financial decisions, the expectations of self and spouse regarding spending, the views of self that are triggered when these expectations are not met, and finally, the thought processes of self and spouse regarding how to appropriately cope with disappointments associated with failure to meet economic expectations.

*Stage 4: Structural family therapy.* A hallmark of substance abuse in families is the blurring of boundaries and the subsequent chaos that comes when family members assume responsibilities and tasks that belong to others (see chap. 5 for a more comprehensive description of the theory). Parents who protect their children from the natural consequences of their addictions, wives who make excuses to their husband's employer regarding his absence from work, parentified children who intervene between fighting adults in order to work out problems that they can't address themselves—these are the structures common to families who face addictions.

Structural family therapy challenges the family to realign around the marital, parental, sibling, and extended family subsystems by recognizing and respecting boundaries and rules. "Structural Family Counseling suggests that when the family's subsystems are healthy, happy, and working well, they in turn will mutually enhance the entire family system and lead to a decrease in the presenting addictive behaviors" (Juhnke & Hagedorn, 2006, pp. 258-59).

After joining the family and assessing to define the unique family structures, the specific treatment would involve the realignment of hierarchical power within the family and each subsystem. The counselor would likely start with the marital subsystem and focus on the relational skills, boundaries, and responsibilities needed for successful leadership of the family. If the addicted family member is one of the parents, the counselor would address the addictive behavior on that level first, before broadening to the other subsystems. Once stability in the marriage is achieved, the focus becomes the parental and sibling subsystems and how they might improperly collude in order to gain power over other parts of the family system and unknowingly provoke the addictive patterns.

*Stage 5: Multigenerational family systems therapy.* Murray Bowen (1976) considered the intergenerational tension between individual and family to emerge out of the paradox of being separate from others in the family and at the same time together with family in a healthy collaborative relationship (see chap. 3 for greater detail on this approach). He described the members of the family as pulled toward disengagement from others and feeling an opposite pull toward fusion. It is in this constant process of pulling and tugging that the inclination toward addictive behaviors emerges. The tension that is the result of enmeshment—others crossing boundaries and manipulating or controlling family members—is soothed and triangulated by the presence of a substance or a satisfying behavior. One is vulnerable to forming an addiction when the drug or the act functions both as a pleasure activity and as an intermediary between people—to calm or to soothe the tensions that exist in relationship. Another model for addiction formation is as a replacement for a family member with whom there is an effort to create emotional cutoff—I will reject or cut myself off from you and love "this thing" instead.

The essence of extended family systems therapy is to control the emotional intensity that would otherwise interfere with the family's ability to manage differences, solve problems, and attend to each other's needs. There are two means by which the addictions family counselor assists the family. The first task is to stabilize the relationships within the session so that a healthy and functional dialogue can occur between the members. This can occur if the counselor actively conducts the family's behavioral process. Counselors can offset the common triangulation process found in addiction-affected homes by demonstrating an alternative to implementing a third party to manipulate or retaliate against others in the family. This healthy triangulation occurs when the counselor disrupts the conversation occurring in session and guides the family toward a constructive conclusion. In this case the counselor acts as a triangulating entity, but rather than taking sides between warring factions within the family, the counselor provides stability in the system and prevents the conversation from escalating into emotional defensiveness.

An example can be seen in a counseling conversation with Mark, an adolescent who regularly smokes marijuana in the garage of the family home, and his parents, Gene and Robin, who are exasperated with Mark's disregard of their rules. Both parents work, and they expect Mark to watch his younger siblings after school. While the children are watching television, Mark is hanging with his friends smoking in the garage.

MARK: Hey look, I smoke marijuana. So, what! There are far bigger concerns that you should worry about.

**GENE (DAD):** The real problem here is you, and that you are totally disregarding the rules that we have set in our home . . .

**COUNSELOR:** *(interrupting Gene in mid-thought, but looking directly at Mark)* Mark, imagine that it's just me and you in this office. Tell me about your concerns that are far bigger than marijuana.

**MARK:** Well, if I were my parents, I would be more concerned with my dad's drinking than . . .

**COUNSELOR:** *(again, interrupting Mark in mid-thought as he tries to triangulate from the direct conversation by bringing in his father's drinking)* But you are not your parents, you're a sixteen-year-old kid who recognizes serious problems that have negative effects on you. I want to know the facts about what those issues are, and how they are affecting you.

**MARK:** When dad drinks, then mom . . .

**COUNSELOR:** Dad and mom are not here. Try, "When Dad drinks, then I . . . what?"

**MARK:** When Dad drinks, then I get . . . I don't know . . . it just becomes a mess . . .

**COUNSELOR:** Thank you. His stuff affects you in harmful ways. You are affected by the mess. Now let's talk for just a bit about how it affects you . . .

The same processes can be employed in listening and restricting Gene and Robin. The effort of the counselor is to direct the conversation away from heated exchanges of accusations and toward factual effects of the family's behavior on one another. Mark was almost there. His and his parents' difficulty in articulating the facts of the family dynamics is common with members early in the process, but grows with practice. The counselor's task with the family is to alter the "cast blame, then recruit an ally" pattern. Instead, the counselor is teaching the family to speak factually, experientially, and informatively about what is occurring in the family and how the dominos of one's behavior fall on another.

Once stability has been established around the exchange of information by establishing boundaries that block the violations of enmeshment or the escape of disengagement, the counselor can work with the family regarding the whole picture—that is, the patterns of intergenerational influence that have encouraged and prompted behavior and reactions for years. With the understanding of the pattern and the assumption of responsibility to act and communicate directly, the family is poised to make individual changes that heal the system, and systemic changes that heal the individuals.

***Stage 6: Intergenerational family-of-origin therapy.*** Juhnke and Hagedorn (2006) consider the contribution of James Framo an approach that mediates the intergenerational yet cognitive approach of Bowen in the previous stage and the insight-oriented object relations family therapy in stage seven. Framo's (1992) family intervention model permits for differentiation of adult family members from their family of origin, paradoxically through the reinstitution of relationship.

The previously described multigenerational model (stage 5) moved the immediate family system toward awareness of the multigenerational transmission of substance use and addictive patterns. But it does not encourage the direct involvement of the previous generation in direct communication about the experience of family during the formative childhood years. In stage 6, the family-of-origin members are encouraged to engage in factual recollections of important events and details of the family history—with each other. Juhnke and Hagedorn (2006) believe that this type of meeting can help adults differentiate from their family of origin by engaging in conversation with the members and comparing recollections of family experiences. They state that "these face-to-face adult meetings aid healthy persons in seeing their family-of-origin experiences, roles, and rules with the context of their adult vision" (p. 278).

For example, an adult who harbors resentment toward a parent for alcohol abuse and being such an embarrassment to him or her during adolescence might have the opportunity thirty years after the events to hear the parent and understand and place their recollection in context: "I know that I wasn't there for you. I was so depressed, discouraged and defeated with my own stuff—that I didn't go to your events, and I was often too drunk for you to have your friends over to the house." This element of recollection of events can serve to validate felt experience and clarify or correct assumptions about a parent's motive for acting through his or her addiction.

***Stage 7: Psychodynamic-object relations family therapy.*** The seventh and final stage focuses on the client's ability to understand how the internalized perceptions of self, family, and family of origin direct the manner in which family relationships are conducted and addictive behaviors pursued. The original understanding of substance abuse within the analytic tradition considered the addiction as "a regressive attempt to return to an infantile, pleasurable state" (Margolis & Zweben, 1998, p. 64). Reading Freud today, with a century of research and discovery, we can realize how generous Margolis and Zweben are in their assessment. Over a century ago Freud wrote that "insight has dawned on me that masturbation is the one major habit, the 'primary addiction,' and it is only as a substitute and replacement of it that the other addictions, to alcohol, morphine, tobacco and the like, come into existence" (Freud, 1950, p. 287). Remember that both Babe Ruth and Sigmund Freud, while being great home run hitters in their respective fields, also frequently struck out!

While the centrality of libidinal drives as the motive for all addictions has certainly passed (at least among most researchers in family-related addictions), there remain important contemporary ideas that address addictions in family contexts through the dynamic paradigm.

> Whereas early psychoanalytic theory centered around the drives, including libidinal and aggressive drives, oral wishes, and oral aggression, psychodynamic psychotherapists recently have focused more on developmental and structural deficits. The role of ego defenses, defense deficit, and affective experience have been connected to drug abuse and alcoholism. (Frances, Franklin, & Borg, 1994, p. 240)

One of the most important contributions made by original and current analytic and dynamic researchers is that substance abuse is a response to pain, particularly pain that occurs between people in close relationship, and to be more specific, pain between people in close relationship where intimacy and affection is expected. Such pain has an effect on the quality of relational attachments. Whereas life pain would normally be addressed, managed, and soothed within family relationships, the failure to accomplish "anxiety management" through core relationships prompts individuals to seek solace through alternative means such as substances or behaviors. These originate as acts of self-soothing and gradually become a dominating and controlling component in a person's life as they are more and more frequently relied on. The inability to connect with others to address life pain becomes a secondary effect of addictive substances or behaviors, thus producing another level of pain, from isolation, and additional fuel to drive the motivation for relief.

Cashdan (1988) describes a process of projection in which people in relation both induce and project destructive patterns of behavior. The inductive process states that a person needs others to confirm an internalized image about himself or herself; hence, the person acts in a way that prompts the other to act back so as to complete the circle and have the original image affirmed. Within addictive families this may look like the "I need you to be needy (induction) so I project judgmental attitudes, criticism, distance, and possessiveness in my relationship style; you need me to be needless (induction) so you project addictive characteristics such as dependence, inadequacy, failure, despair, and discouragement so that I can uphold and rescue you." This or a similar dynamic complement are frequently found in relationships where an addiction is present.

The task of family addictions counseling at this level is to form insight into how individual dynamic needs emerging from early object relations prompt family members to function in an intricate dance of undeclared interactions. To see it, understand it, discuss it, accept it, change it, and encourage growth through it is the focus of treatment.

*Conclusion to treatment modalities.* One of the most challenging tasks for any counselor, marriage and family therapist, or psychologist is to know what to and with whom to do it. The sequential family therapy addictions model is helpful in delineating the major approaches to family addictions counseling and providing a basic template for understanding the differences in the approaches to families addressing addictions. Regardless of the approaches there are fundamental skills required of the therapist in order to be effective. Common themes of therapeutic intervention are required regardless of the "psychomindedness" of the family.

## COMMON THEMES IN SUBSTANCE
## ABUSE FAMILY TREATMENTS

*Joining: trust-building and assessment.* Regardless of theory, all approaches require that the clinician join with the family—to construct a working relationship that permits the counselor to contribute to the current conditions to bring about change. In addition, one must establish trust and form a working hypothesis regarding the focus of the therapeutic experience. However, joining a family in the presence of substance abuse has a number of unique challenges. First of all, addictions and substance abuse are frequently not the presenting problem but a comorbid issue, and it is often viewed by the family, and particularly by addicted individual members, as not a problem at all. In fact, it can be regarded by some as a strength and essential coping tool. The family's denial system can construct normality around the addictions—much as a family of frogs is unaware of the gradually increased temperature of the water as they are slowly boiled in a pot on the stove. At other times, chemical or behavioral addictions are the presenting problem and the "us vs. him or her" battle lines have been in existence for years. Into this melee steps the therapist, who is hit with the family mistrust, resentment, and rage.

The task in joining with the family is to acquire an understanding of each person's need and perception of family functioning. McKay (1996) warns that addicted families frequently enter counseling with different agendas and dissimilar perceptions of the family problem. Patience in gathering family information and prudence in implementing interventions are essential in allowing for the family to reveal the complexity of its structure misaligned around the addiction.

Once addiction or substance abuse is established as a clinical issue, the second task emphasized by McKay (1996) in joining the family is to establish the behavioral ground rules that you will accept as a clinician for the family. These rules can include whether sobriety will be a requirement of treatment for all members of the family during the process of therapy, what will occur if members of the family do not attend appointments, how the topic of substance abuse will be addressed by the family subsystems (i.e., the married couple, or parents and adolescent abusers, etc.), and what ancillary treatments will be expected—hospital detoxification, AA, Al-Anon, Alateen—prior to and during treatment.

*Stabilization.* Stabilization refers to the family's capacity to create an environment that provides sufficient safety and security for all members. The safety component applies most directly to the substance abuser, assuring that the potentially harmful, destructive, or fatal aspects of continued substance use are controlled. Security applies most directly to those in the family who feel anxious about the dangerous behavior of their loved ones, such that they become inclined to disregard the boundaries necessary for healthy family functioning—creating a snowballing contribution by inciting adverse emotional reactions on the part of the abuser that are often soothed by increased substance use.

The counselor, as a leader of the treatment team of services for the family, assists each member in becoming involved in role-appropriate interventions. This would include detoxification treatment; group, supportive, twelve-step, or individual therapy for the addicted family member, such as Al-Anon and Alateen; and the recognition and respect of boundaries for the other family members. The stabilization of the family often includes the formation of behavioral contracts that define expected behavior over the short term of treatment, and what the result will be if the contract is violated by any of the family members. The counselor often is charged with reminding the family of the contract as they commonly test the strength of the boundary that is placed on them.

*Education and relapse prevention.* "This has all been well and good, but he still just hangs around the house all day. Why doesn't he go get a job?" So said the father of Peter, a young adult who had successfully accomplished one week of sobriety. His expectations were in danger of undermining the whole therapeutic process by not supporting and encouraging positive changes toward the desired outcome for the family in a reasonable time frame. Clearly it would not be in the son's best interest to get a job before sobriety is established. Most definitely having Peter establish himself as a self-supporting adult was everyone's intent. However, encouraging too much change in a short time would create the risk of producing more stress than Peter could manage, and the anxiety could pull him back into drug use.

While his father meant well with his suggestion, it was expressed from a position of wanting "normal" to return to his life and the life of his son and family. Walter, the father, like most family members, did not understand nor have experience with the process of recovery that families must endure. Therefore counselors often occupy the role of educator for the family. The therapist can provide information about the disease and the recovery process, help the family establish an agenda that is realistic to the problem severity, and serve as a guide or coach as the family interfaces with medical personnel and sometimes with the legal system as well.

One of the key areas of education is the topic of substance abuse relapse and relapse prevention. Relapse is often regarded as a one-sided argument. While the family can easily recognize the relapse behavior of an abuser, they do not as readily acknowledge the relapse of their own behavior in disregarding boundaries or failing to render support as was contracted.

Both relapse of the substance abuse and of the family pathology to which substance abuse is associated must be taught as serious violations of the family contract.

In the realm of education, it is important for families to recognize the points of vulnerability for one another and to discuss how the strain of life faced by individuals can be easily displaced onto vulnerable members of the family or translated into rationalizations for returning to substance use. For example, using the critical statement made by Walter toward his son regarding not getting a job, it would be expected that the family address the effect that the father's criticism has on not just Peter but everyone else. Furthermore, if Walter is critical toward Peter as well as other members of the family, he likely is more so at some times and less so at other times. Learning when those times are for Walter and for everyone else would contribute to the family's mature functioning. In essence, Walter and Peter and the family are becoming educated about their unique processes and where and when potential risks to family well-being exist.

Daley and Marlatt (1996) encourage the idea that relapse should not be viewed "only as the event of resumption of a pattern of substance abuse or dependency but also as a process in which indicators or warning signs appear prior to the individual's actual resumption of substance use" (p. 533). The idea emphasized here is that relapse prevention is a communal task in which everyone is vulnerable to returning to former patterns of behavior. Furthermore, it is crucial to educate the family regarding the difference between lapse and relapse. The former is a return to the designated behavior—a temporary fall from grace. The latter is a return to the addictive patterns and lifestyles that come with substance addictions. Whether a lapse into substance use or a lapse into family or relational behavior that is associated with substance use by other members of the family morphs into a true relapse depends on how the family has prepared for lapses in behavior. Counselors can educate families on the importance of forming contingency plans to address the possibility of threat to the system as well as the appropriate responses by all involved.

Regarding relapse, two ideas must be acknowledged. The first is that all relapses—both chemical and relational—are serious violations of how the family has agreed to function. Second, not all relapses (chemical and relational) are equal. Likeness in kind should not be mistaken for likeness in degree.

## CHRISTIAN PERSPECTIVES ON ADDICTION AND SUBSTANCE ABUSE

The Women's Temperance Movement, Alcoholics Anonymous, Teen Challenge and Rapha, and New Life Treatment Clinics are historical and current manifestations of the Christian faith involved in the social and mental health system's addressing addiction. These are examples of spiritual/religious forces manifesting themselves in the political, social, and medical realms to confront addictions. The place of the family has been prominent in every new social or clinical treatment. Protecting children within families from the destruction of chemical and behavioral addictions, and using the relational power in families to initiate change, has been an important mission in the role of spirituality in general, and in many cases Christianity in particular. Religious and spiritual perspectives have had a significant effect on substance abuse–related mental health intervention.

The treatment of substance abuse and family ministry has evolved in a way that tracks the larger society. As the treatment has emerged within the culture, those articulating an understanding of substance abuse themes have risen from the religious domain. And as the medical model for the treatment of addictions has created and applied chemical and experiential interventions, a significant representation of the interventions has been for religious-based contexts. Therefore, religious influences occupy a prominent role in the amelioration of substance abuse and the specific application of family intervention for addiction.

## A CHRISTIAN VIEW OF ADDICTION AND RECOVERY: UNDERSTANDING OUR SINFUL CONDITION IN LIGHT OF SHALOM

The first contribution that religion in general and Christianity in particular have made to the institution of substance treatment is a perspective on the nature of persons who encounter addictions. The place to begin is to consider how things are supposed to be. The word *shalom*, loosely translated "peace" in the common vernacular, means wholeness, fullness, or to flourish or be complete. To most, this idea connotes the absence of conflict—an "all is well with the world" homeostasis. Citing Wolterstorff (1983), Plantinga argues that shalom, as the starting place in understanding addiction recovery, "means *universal functioning, wholeness, and delight*—a rich state of affairs in which natural needs are satisfied and natural gifts fruitfully employed, a state of affairs that inspires joyful wonder as its Creator and Savior opens doors and welcomes creatures in whom he delights. Shalom, to put it simply, is the way things ought to be" (1997, p. 246).

In contrast to shalom, we can consider the way things are. Shalom is broken, interrupted, and made inaccessible. The condition of disruption in the experience of shalom is sin, an insidious moral, spiritual, and psychological cancer that has interrupted the peace between creation and creator. Biblically, sin is characterized as far more than acts of commission and omission. It is a contrary state of being at peace with God—it is an anti-shalom. "Sin does not build shalom, it vandalizes it. . . . Like a virus, sin attaches the life force and dynamics of its host . . . and converts them to new uses" (Plantinga, 1997, p. 249). Sin invites comparison to addiction, another persistent, parasitic, and exasperating human malady.

## INTEGRATIVE FOCUS: *Family Functioning*

*Control*—there's a word that can elicit conversation. Family members fight for control over just about everything from the television remote to the time that adolescents have to be home on Saturday night. The Scriptures speak frequently about the idea of control—for instance, to be controlled by the Spirit instead of being controlled by alcohol (Eph 5:18). Control is a central element in the creation of substance abuse and, subsequently, its intervention. The challenge of the family is in gaining corporate control over emotions, thoughts, and behaviors that are so painful that the system or members in the system opt toward an anesthetic substance rather than to face itself.

*Think about it:* Consider the ways that control is a dominating theme in your family. Don't complicate it yet by adding substance abuse. Just consider the efforts that everyone makes to maintain control over some or all domains. Now imagine (if you don't have direct experience with substance abuse in your family) or remember (if you do have direct family substance abuse issues) how the inclusion of chemical or behavioral addictions accelerates the demand for control.

Most of us are adequately trained in "Sunday School theology" to accept that we are all sinners. It is not difficult for most to acknowledge that we are not perfect—guilty of gaffes, blunders, or errors in judgment and action. We can relate to the classic "nonconfession" in American politics—"Mistakes have been made"—as a reflection of ourselves. In the general sense, we accept that we have sin. However, the biblical emphasis is that our sin is not a passive blemish but an active corrosion to which we are enslaved. Paul writes in Romans 7 of the controlling nature of sin, "But in fact it is no longer I that do it, but sin that dwells within me" (Rom 7:17). This same kind of enslavement describes the experience of addiction. Tragically, we can acknowledge that we are all sinners, yet there is a new dimension of discomfort to realize that we are all addicts.

Gerald May (1988) put it like this:

> I am not being flippant when I say that all of us suffer from addiction. Nor am I reducing the meaning of addiction. I mean in all truth that psychological, neurological, and spiritual dynamics of full-fledged addiction are actively at work within every human being. The same processes that are responsible for addiction to alcohol and narcotics are also responsible for addiction to ideas, work, relationships, power, moods, fantasies, and an endless variety of other things. We are all addicts in every sense of the word. (p. 3)

The Christian contribution to addiction and recovery is the acknowledgment that central to the human condition is a misdirected drive that pulls us away from peace with God, or shalom. Perhaps G. K. Chesterton summed up our human proclivity toward addiction by saying, "What is wrong with the world? Sir, I am!" The parallel between the Christian concept of sin and the social construct of addiction is most evident within the AA tradition. Step one of the twelve-step program is to admit we are powerless over alcohol—that our lives have become unmanageable. The powerlessness component of addiction parallels the theological perspective of being powerless over sin.

### INTEGRATIVE FOCUS: Family Relationships

The quote by May has serious implications for the Christian family. Few in the Christian world would argue against common depravity—that all of us are bent—and that this twisting of soul and spirit manifests itself in the form of misplaced values and misguided efforts to hide, conceal, and deny aspects of an ugly reality.

*Think about it:* Are we all addicts as May suggests, only differing in the nature of our "drug of choice"?

*The powerfulness of God and insufficiency of humanity.* The second essential contribution from the Christian faith to family addictions is the contrast of human inadequacy and the omnipotence of God. In the seminal work by May (1988), addiction is described as the basic descriptor of our insufficiency—we are addicted people, powerless to overcome that which we are. Plantinga (1995) returns to theological language, using addiction as a euphemism for sin. "Addiction is a dramatic portrait of some main dynamics of sin, a stage show of warped longings, split wills, encumbered liberties, and perverse attacks on one's own well-being—some of the same dramatic machinery that moves the general tragedy of sin forward" (Plantinga, 1995, p. 262). He goes on to cite McCormick (1989) as calling addiction a conversion unto death, drawing from Paul's writing of human powerlessness over sin found in Romans 7 and Galatians 5.

Plantinga (1995) observes that in both sin and addiction we are enslaved by our basic state, such that our very actions are an extension of that core condition.[2] Furthermore, "in light of our core condition, attempts to change specific behaviors are often ineffective. The problem is more fundamental than what is suggested by change in behavior" (Yarhouse, Butman, & McRay, 2005, p. 199). As we suggested above, a critical decision that can be made is to surrender oneself to God. "Addicts who succeed in recovery at some point surrender and take responsibility for the destruction that surrounds their addiction and for the hard work that constitutes their recovery. Those who are recovering addicts will be the first to say that recovery begins with heart-breaking surrender, because it is the surrender of one's ultimate concern and the present longing of one's heart (May, 1988)" (Yarhouse, Butman, & McRay, 2005, p. 200). Recovery begins by asking the question, to whom do I ultimately belong?

*The unique challenge of religion.* While we recognize that surrender is a critical part of recovery, we would like to add that one of the unique challenges we see in addressing substance abuse and addictive concerns in conservative Christians is that religion can sometimes exacerbate the pattern of addiction (Penner & Penner, 1990). Although the Penners are discussing sexual addiction in particular, the same can be said for patterns of substance abuse:

> Religion is often used by the addict as a co-addict to perpetuate his addictive
> pattern. In the addict's view, God is a part of the addictive system because it

---

[2]This section is adapted from Mark A. Yarhouse, Richard E. Butman, and Barrett W. McRay, *Modern Psychopathologies: A Comprehensive Christian Appraisal* (Downers Grove, IL: InterVarsity Press, 2005).

is God—along with his father, mother, and society—who carries the big stick and makes him feel guilt and shame. . . . When the addict first comes for help, God is not seen as an ally but as an adversary. Prayer is not seen as a resource but a source of guilt. The Scriptures are not seen as a message of solace and hope but rather as one more authority telling him he is worthless. The Holy Spirit is not experienced as a Comforter but as an accuser who keeps confirming from inside the addict that he does not measure up. Because the addict does not see his faith as an ally in the healing process, we often have to begin with restructuring and reframing his view of God, as well as his grasp of his disorder. (p. 289)

The unsuspecting family therapist can be discouraged when progress is not made despite attempts to draw on a common faith and assumptions. In these cases, it may be helpful to explore the substance abuser's view of God, particularly their emotional experience of God (or God image) as well as how their religious beliefs and values may end up being used in the context of their unique pattern of abuse.

While surrender to God is important, a shame-based "surrender" may not be surrender at all, and it may perpetuate the cycle of addictive patterns that lead to substance abuse.

*Family relationships.* We see family relationships as potentially playing an important role in recovery from addiction and substance abuse. There is evidence that the level of support available to an individual during treatment is a powerful predictor of positive outcome in treatment (Havassy, Hall, & Wasserman, 1991). So the family can be a critical resource for the extension of God's grace in the life of a family member struggling with addiction. The grace that is extended and experienced in close relationships helps address the self-inadequacy that often accompanies long-standing patterns of addiction. But motivation, too, can be powerful. This can occur when family members speak clearly to the loved one who is struggling about what they see happening to him or her and what family members are concerned may happen. Put differently, family members can help the person struggling with addiction to become aware of the negative consequences of their actions and how those actions affect those who care about them.

Building motivation through such a frank discussion is held in tension with respect and acceptance. Although one family member can be strongly disapproving of another member's behavior, it is important to still show respect for that person, which increases the likelihood that concerns will be heard. Family members express acceptance most clearly not by capitulating to the demands or manipulations of a loved one struggling with addiction, but through a sustained presence. What is critical about a sustained presence is that it will likely be tested, and it takes time for the interpersonal presence of grace and acceptance to compete with a rewarding addictive pattern. "Abandoning an addictive pattern is an act of courage many of us have not had to face, and it can seldom be done outside the context of sustained and supportive relationships" (Yarhouse, Butman, & McRay, 2005, p. 202). As Yarhouse, Butman, and McRay observe, the church also plays an important role in pursuing families struggling with addiction, as these families are inclined to withdraw and further isolate themselves from support.

In any case, however treatment is eventually pursued—inpatient, intensive outpatient, and so on—the family member struggling with addictive patterns of behavior will continue to need family support and encouragement in addition to professional help. What family members need most at this point is positive encouragement for change. This kind of support should be consistent and sustained. It is important to recognize times when the temptation to rely on external "support" such as alcohol or another substance of some kind can be overwhelming. Temptations to relapse will likely come in cycles or waves, depending on internal and external stress levels. It is often the case that a number of issues, such as relational issues, were put on the back burner during intensive treatment; it is important to help the family member meet the challenges of everyday living and to recognize and address the occasional desire to "escape" the mounting pressures of daily living (Yarhouse, Butman, & McRay, 2005).

## CONCLUSION

Substance abuse problems can tear a family apart. They are complex problems that require a great deal of creativity, engagement, sustained presence, and patience. An accurate understanding of substance abuse problems and the best hope for change will recognize the complexity of a number of overlapping influences. Family therapists can be in the trenches doing the hard work of supporting family members in their efforts to support change.

## REFERENCES

Bell, A., & Rollnick, S. (1996). Motivational interviewing in practice: A structured approach. In F. Rotgers, D. S. Keller, & J. Morgenstern (Eds.), *Treating substance abuse: Theory and technique.* New York: Guilford Press.

Bowen, M. (1976). Theory in the practice of psychotherapy. In P. J. Guerrin Jr. (Ed.), *Family therapy: Theory and practice.* New York: Gardner Press.

Brown, S., & Lewis, V. M. (2000). *The family recovery guide: A map for healthy growth.* New York: New Harbinger.

Cashdan, S. (1988). *Object relations.* New York: W. W. Norton.

Coleman, S. B., & Davis, D. I. (1978). Family therapy and drug abuse: A national survey. *Family Process, 17,* 21.

Daley, D. C., & Marlatt, G. A. (1996). Relapse prevention: Cognitive and behavioral interventions. In J. H. Lowinson, P. Ruiz, R. B. Millman, & J. G. Langrod (Eds.), *Substance abuse: A comprehensive textbook* (2nd ed.). New York: Wiley & Sons.

Epstein, E. E., & McCrady, B. S. (1998). Behavioral couples treatment of alcohol and drug use disorders: Current status and innovations. *Clinical Psychology Review, 18,* 689-711.

Framo, J. L. (1992). *Family-of-origin therapy: An intergenerational approach.* New York: Brunner/Mazel.

Frances, R., Franklin, J., & Borg, L. (1994). Psychodynamics. In M. Galanter & H. D. Kleber (Eds.), *Textbook of substance abuse treatment.* Washington, DC: The American Psychiatric Association.

Freud, S. (1950 [1887-1902]). Extracts from the Fliess papers. *The standard edition of the complete psychological works of Sigmund Freud* (Vol. 1, pp. 173-280). London: Hogarth.

Havassy, B. E., Hall, S. M., & Wasserman, D. A. (1991). Social support and relapse: Commonalities among alcoholics, opiate users, and cigarette smokers. *Addictive Behaviors, 16,* 235-46.

Juhnke, G. A., & Hagedorn, B. (2006). *Counseling addicted families: An integrated assessment and treatment model.* New York: Routledge.

Margolis, R. D., & Zweben, J. E. (1998). *Treating patients with alcohol and other drug problems: An integrated approach.* Washington, DC: American Psychological Association.

May, G. (1988). *Addiction and grace.* San Francisco: Harper & Row.

McCormick, P. (1989). *Sin as addiction.* New York: Paulist Press.

McKay, J. R. (1996). Family therapy techniques. In F. Rotgers, D. S. Kellerman, & J. Morgenstern (Eds.), *Treating substance abuse: Theory and technique* (pp. 143-73). New York: Guilford Press.

Miller, W. R. (1983). Motivational interviewing with problem drinkers. *Behavioural Psychotherapy, 11*, 147-72.

Miller, W. R. (1985). Motivation for treatment: A review with special emphasis on alcoholism. *Psychological Bulletin, 98*(1), 84-107.

Musto, D. F. (1999). *The American disease: Origins of narcotic control.* New York: Oxford University Press.

O'Farrell, T. J., & Fals-Stewart, W. (2000). Behavioral couples therapy for alcoholism and drug abuse. *Journal of Substance Abuse Treatment, 18*(1), 51-54.

Penner, J. J., & Penner, C. L. (1990). *Counseling for sexual disorders.* Dallas: Word.

Plantinga, C., Jr. (1995). *Not the way it's supposed to be: A breviary of sin.* Grand Rapids: Eerdmans.

Plantinga, C., Jr. (1997). Sin and addiction. In R. C. Roberts & M. R. Talbot (Eds.), *Limning the psyche: Explorations in Christian psychology.* Eugene, OR: Wipf & Stock.

Prochaska, J. O., & DiClemente, C. C. (1986). The transitional approach. In J. Norcross, *Handbook of eclectic psychotherapy* (pp. 163-200). New York: Brunner/Mazel.

Rotgers, F. (1996). Behavioral theory of substance abuse treatment: Bringing science to bear on practice. In F. Rotgers, D. S. Keller, & J. Morgenstern (Eds.), *Treating substance abuse: Theory and technique* (pp. 174-201). New York: Guilford Press.

Shoham, V., Rohrbaugh, M., & Patterson, J. (1995). Problem- and solution-focused couple therapies. The MRI and Milwaukee models. In N. S. Jacobson & A. S. Gurman (Eds.), *Clinical handbook of couple therapy* (pp. 142-63). New York: Guilford Press.

Stanton, M. D., & Shadish, W. (1997). Outcome, attrition, and family-couples treatment for drug abuse: A meta-analysis and review of the controlled, comparative studies. *Psychological Bulletin, 122*, 170-91.

Wolterstorff, N. (1983). *Until justice and peace embrace.* Grand Rapids: Eerdmans.

Yarhouse, M. A., Butman, R. E., & McRay, B. W. (2005). *Modern psychopathologies: A comprehensive Christian appraisal.* Downers Grove, IL: InterVarsity Press.

# GENDER, CULTURE, ECONOMIC CLASS, AND RACE

*The worst sin towards our fellow creatures is not
to hate, but to be indifferent to them.*

**GEORGE BERNARD SHAW,** *THE DEVIL'S DISCIPLE*

IN THE MOVIE *The Sting*, the cocky swindler Johnny Hooker, played by Robert Redford, peers across the golf course at gangster Doyle Lonnegan and says, "He's not as tough as he thinks." To which the senior con man Henry Gondorff, played by Paul Newman, says, with the wisdom of caution and experience, "Neither are we."

## INTRODUCTION: THE HUMILITY OF ETIC AND EMIC

Research and theory in group, class, racial, ethnic, and gender differences provide a consistent reminder of humility for the family therapist. Indeed, we are not "as tough as we think," if tough is a metaphor for being knowledgeable, skilled, and capable in working with the array of human differences influenced by historical experiences on groups characterized by nationality, race, gender, and so forth. The purpose for considering group differences is to challenge our presumptions regarding how marriages and families operate and what constitutes appropriate corrective interventions in our efforts to assist families in their goals.

This humble perspective is replicated in the New Testament where Paul is teaching the new multicultural church about how to conduct ministry and life together. His declaration that "There is no longer Jew or Greek, there is no longer slave or free, there is no longer male and female; for all of you are one in Christ Jesus" (Gal 3:28) does not pertain to the equality of experience. Rather, it is a statement of accommodation and acceptance of personhood above the obvious differences in culture, gender, and social position. It is as if Paul were saying to the Jewish Christians, "You are not as tough (read: special or important) as you think." Translated into the language of our day and applied to the circumstance of family counseling: "Though you may see yourself as a gifted counselor, capable of traversing cultural distinctions, be careful to respect your limits, biases, and presumptions."

Simultaneously, efforts in understanding group differences must not so undermine the mental health professional by creating the impression that counselors should work only with those of the same race, nationality, social economic status, religion, and gender. We recognize the counselor's ability to carefully and prudently apply the knowledge base of the marriage and family therapy profession to families of divergent backgrounds and traditions because of his or her capacity to listen to and understand their concerns; to sensibly project herself or himself into the family system so as to comprehend the issues of each member by utilizing creative, even artistic skills; and to sculpt experiences for the family that promote learning and encourage behavioral change within the system. That we are "one in Christ" does imply that there is sufficient commonality between us to bridge the obvious external barriers of race, culture, gender, or experiential differences.

This chapter will consider the roles of "different" and "same" in how families operate and how therapy with families is conducted. Two competing realities should pervade our understanding of families. Linguistic anthropologist Kenneth Pike (1954) created the terms *emic* and *etic* to distinguish two realms of knowledge and reality in understanding people groups. Pike believed that just as one could examine language through phonemic structures as well as phonetic structures, one also can understand cultural groups using different but mutually essential sources of knowledge. Pike's original use of these terms has gone through numerous alterations and revisions such that they have multiple meanings in current vernacular. However, the fundamental idea behind them was to represent coexisting and at times competing ways of understanding groups through an anthropological lens.

Cultural psychologist Hidetada Shimizu explains emic and etic through the dialogue between Winnie the Pooh and Christopher Robin. When Christopher Robin must tell Pooh that he is being sent away to school and will no longer be available to play in the Hundred Acre Wood, Pooh, of course, does not comprehend the meaning of Christopher's words. There is a cultural divide between school-age boy and nursery-room teddy bear. Pooh replies in song, with the lyric "I will be your friend forever . . . no matter where you go," and it refrains with the idea "forever and ever." There is a reality of "forever" explained by physics, philosophy, and theology. "Forever" is indeed a very big idea. This is *etic*. The meaning of *forever* is defined outside of Pooh, causing him to say more than he knows and understands.

There is another form of knowledge, a local or personal understanding of *forever* that doesn't extend beyond the locale of Pooh's Corner. Pooh's knowledge of "forever" is immediate. "The way Pooh *experiences* it would be emic, his own idea about what he projects to do with Christopher (stay with him 'forever'), which is part of our everyday discourse. Pooh's emic of 'forever' is right now, with no concept of variation or termination" (Shimizu, personal communication, April 5, 2007).

*Etic* and *emic* are both essential bodies of knowledge; marriage and family therapy that is multicultural must draw from each. Counseling that is exclusively *etic*—that is, that draws from an external body of knowledge (counseling research and theory, for example) cannot be sensitive to the internal language of individual families, especially when they are influenced by traditions, religious values, and family heritages that are outside the realm of empirical science. On the other hand, a counseling that is only *emic*, while sensitive and responsive to forming understanding to internal language and meaning, cannot assist a family toward a greater understanding of the events that are blocking their growth and progress. Understanding families and contributing to their growth demands a professional knowledge that draws both from etic and emic. Etic is the multiple overlays of knowledge from the profession, history, culture, law, education, work, and play—virtually all facets of life. Equally important in understanding and assisting families is an understanding of emic—the private knowledge and rules that guide family and individual existence.

Consider the story of Naomi and Pablo. They have been married for six years and have two young children of preschool age. Pablo is completing graduate school in theology and is a university campus minister employed by a parachurch organization. Naomi directs a local charitable organization. Naomi initiated the counseling relationship because she was feeling exhausted in her role of wife, mother, and employee. She felt discouraged with her options. She believed that her husband was incapable of changing and thought that her life was stuck with few options for alteration. At this point in the story it reads like an intake narrative common to many marriages—the stress of marriage, work, school, and children loading heavily on the wife and producing despair.

Now consider the context. Pablo is Peruvian. He is a legal resident working with international students who attend a large public university. English is his second language. His family of origin lives in Peru. He is estranged from them all. Alcohol has consumed his father and his brothers. He is the only one from his family that has escaped drugs, poverty, crime, and violence. During childhood he knew deprivation—materially, educationally, emotionally, and socially. His home was in the Lima slums. As a child he would go for days without seeing his parents—home neither offered nor provided even the most basic of life's essentials. The street was his house, school, and playground. He escaped this death trap through a relationship with a Christian pastor who befriended him, guided him, and taught him a way into a different life.

Naomi's life story was similar to Pablo's in that she also was a child of an intoxicated family system. Yet her story was one of North American privilege, in spite of the presence of substance abuse by her parents. Inside her home, alcohol soothed the pain of immature life for her parents and provoked chaos and instability between them and the children. Naomi met Pablo at an Inter-Varsity Christian Fellowship Urbana Conference. They dated by distance. Naomi spent summers in Peru doing short-term missions work. (You might say she had multiple mission projects associated with her work!)

To understand Naomi and Pablo through the paradigm of etic knowledge, one must consider the data regarding marriage challenges as they are affected by multiple variations in ethnicity, culture, language, gender roles, economic class, and family substance abuse. The literature contains volumes of information on how marriage is influenced by each of these components.

Yet if counseling intervention is derived solely from the professional literature concerning the presence of external characteristics of family structures, then one would be conducting therapy with Naomi and Pablo without ever knowing and understanding them as persons and as a dynamic organism. The emic knowledge would include the internal language of husband, wife, and couple. Each of them contains drive, ambition, and characteristics that transcend categories. As a couple, the fusion of their unique personalities creates a unique story that has created a unique challenge with a unique solution. In respecting differences, family counselors must artfully synthesize what they know from the profession (etic) and what they learn from the family (emic) and collaborate with the family as coactive collaborators toward creating change.

The existence of etic and emic realities motivates us to maintain a humble and respectful attitude toward the families we serve. Robert Brammer shares an illustrative story in his text on diversity in counseling (2004). He asks us to image that we are entering the Museum of Tolerance. We find two doors, the first is an ornate entry with the inscription "Non-prejudiced people enter here." The other door is a small, narrow side door with a handwritten sign, "Prejudiced people enter here." He writes, "Those who have the self-confidence and nerve to open the large door find it quite impenetrable. All patrons wishing to enter the building must crouch down and humbly enter through the smaller door" (p. 21). Indeed, an end effect of multicultural awareness ought to be a demonstration of respect for the unique significance of others, valuing them as God's beloved. In fact, one counselor who carries a life experience of an array of cultural, ethnic, and religious experience has come to call those with whom she works as her "dear ones."

There are three areas that will be addressed in this chapter that can inform the therapist, lay counselor, and pastor regarding family differences. These include gender, ethnicity, and economic privilege. Then we will consider an essential realm of etic knowledge, that of the influence of Christian theology and biblical values on categorical differences.

## GENDER ROLES AND FAMILY FUNCTIONING

Canales (2000) refers to gender as the first subculture within multicultural diversity. It is unique as a cultural variable because it traverses all families, transcending time, ethnicity, and geography. By gender we mean the manner in which the culture forms characteristics and behaviors that it deems fitting or proper. Simply stated, gender is the expectation for how men and women should be within the larger group culture. Gender is distinguished from sex in that sexuality is a genetic, physiological distinction between family members (i.e., males and females). There are very few role distinctions based solely on sexuality beyond procreation and maternity. (And thanks to the development of baby formula or the breast pump, even midnight feedings are gender behaviors determined by marital negotiation!) Gender role is the responsibility that a person carries within the family based on their function as mother, father, husband, wife, daughter, son, brother, or sister. This is "men's work" or "women's work" as designated by the culture and the family. Frequently, gender role is delineated by economics (i.e., Who brings home the bacon?) or domestically (i.e., Who will care for the children?). However, gender role contains many more subtle variations and tasks. A few of these include power and decision making, the use and restrictions of emotionality, the degree and nature of intimacy, and the management of conflicts within and external to the family system (O'Neil, Helms, Gable, David, & Wrightsman, 1986).

Tension from the misalignment of gender role can lead to individual or systemic conflict (O'Neil, 1990). The conflict is the result of family or society restricting an individual's intended life path because of gender (i.e., guiding a daughter's interest in medicine toward nursing school and away from medical school because nursing is more suited for her role as a wife and mother, or discouraging a husband to home school his children because he should "be the breadwinner"). Frequently, the tension with a marital dyad is the result of this conflict in role based on the immediate and extended family's expectation of gender role or the broader cultural values and restrictions of how men and women should live (Weigel, Bennett, & Ballard-Reisch, 2006).

Gender role has a unique manifestation with families who come from many religious traditions, as well as counselors who utilize Christian thought as a basis for counseling intervention. Gender role within the conservative Christian denominations is often bifurcated into complementarian and egalitarian views of marriage. The complementarian perspective is best represented by the Council on Biblical Manhood and Womanhood, an organization of evangelical scholars and clergy. "The Danvers Statement on Biblical Manhood and Womanhood" (1987; http://www.cbmw.org/Resources/Articles/The-Danvers-Statement) is an articulation of the core principles that represent the complementarian position. The premise is that male and female differences are extended to masculine and feminine differences as part of the created order. Roles within marriage were established just as roles were

constructed within the Trinity, and these roles are manifested through creation and the fall and are to include principles of male leadership/headship
within the home and church and female submission to male authority. The
family is defined hierarchically in the same way that Christian theology has
defined the relationship between the members of the Trinity—equal but
acting under submission. In the same way that the relationship between Christ
and the church is expressed, so too should the husband and wife act in leadership characterized by sacrificial service and respectful submission (Piper &
Grudem, 1991; Saucy & TenElshof, 2001).

The egalitarian position is best represented by Christians for Biblical Equality,
a nonprofit organization also made up of evangelical scholars and pastors.
Their position paper, "Men, Women and Biblical Equality" (1989; http://www
.cbeinternational.org), best represents this position. The egalitarian view considers marriage as an equal partnership in which men and women jointly administer authority over creation and over institutions such as marriage, family,
church, and society. The biblical basis for their position is found in passages
such as Galatians 3:28, in which Paul declares that the distinction between male
and female is removed "in Christ," and 1 Corinthians 7:1-5, in which Paul declares that both husbands and wives are to yield authority of their bodies to
their spouse (Mickelson, 1986; Pierce & Groothuis, 2005).

Marital counselors, therapists, psychologists, and pastors work with
couples from both ends of this debate—and from multiple gradations in between these two. Professional ethics codes mandate how therapists are to
respond to the range of marital roles determined by the unique values of the
family. We affirm the importance of marital therapists listening carefully to
the language of each person in the dyad, working to mature the voices within
the marriage toward gender-role designations that bring honor and respect
to each person, and to require accommodation, learning, and growth from
each. One Christian academic and activist in the gender-role debate stated
privately that when either side acts in the fullness and depth of their position,
the result is a God-honoring, biblical expression of love within marriage. We
believe that family counselors must respect both sides of this issue as serious
efforts to honor God and render mature love to husband or wife. Most definitely, counselors should and must provoke couples toward growth. But the
direction of the "provocations" needs to be consistent with the values exhibited by the couple.

Two examples from both sides of this debate would be appropriate. First, Mike and Carol are both forty-two. Both are committed Christians. Carol wants to pursue work outside the home. Mike is against the idea. He believes that she should be available to him and the children, who are in junior high and high school. Carol believes too that her primary responsibility is to her family, but she no longer feels sufficiently challenged in the home. Placing this scenario in a therapeutic context, the appropriate path would be to pursue with both Mike and Carol the meaning of servant leadership. How as the head of the home will Mike actively demonstrate his desire to see his wife grow and use the fullness of her gifts? If Mike exhibits belligerence, with an attitude of "I am the husband, and I should decide," then he would be acting outside the scriptural intent of considering others as more important than himself. When the principle of selfless service is integrated with leadership or headship, then the result appears very similar to the egalitarian perspective.

In the same way, egalitarian couples often find that equality in decision making is not efficient and does not support the unique strengths that individuals bring to relationships. They frequently create a hierarchy based on individual interests and skills. An example is Barb and Scott, ages thirty-two and thirty-three. They have no children and are two-income professionals who live in an urban high-rise. Early in their marriage they tried to make all major and minor economic decisions jointly. This was an important part of their marital identity—they valued the collaboration in decision making. However, they found it increasingly difficult to find the time where both were available to pay bills, balance the bank statements, and track their personal and retirement accounts. Eventually, Scott became assigned the permanent job of marital accountant. Barb checks in regularly, but Scott operates the books. He does so with regard to what they have decided as a couple and lets Barb know of decisions that he has made. Barb rarely seeks to override his choices as she sees him as more informed on the topic.

In both mature complementary and egalitarian structures, the value of both male and female is clear. Likewise, in immature marital systems where a lack of integrity, trust, and regard is common, the power structure doesn't appear to matter; there will be discord regardless of the marital pattern selected.

Issues pertaining to gender role extend beyond restricting freedoms and establishing roles within family. They include the tension that emerges from having role options. Every family system must tend to variations in gender;

that is, they must address the rights, responsibilities, and roles given to men and women within the system. These variations, particularly in Western cultures where people have more life choices due to economic advancement, are increasingly diverse. This expansion of diversity has increased options for both men and women but also can lead to an increase in life complications and stress. For example, a father who, in a previous era, might have been expected and encouraged to focus his attention on career advancement above family engagement now finds that he can and in many cases must be more involved in both. Likewise, the mother whose responsibilities may not have included as large of a percentage of economic responsibility now finds there is an expectation that she maintain a white collar salaried position and be available for in-school classroom parties and other parental responsibilities.

Thus, marriage and family counselors must be able to assist couples in negotiating the unique demands in creating a workable family structure that is consistent with the values, gifts, and interests of each person. Couples must face the role conflict that exists in a pluralistic society such that however they choose to structure their marriage and their family responsibility, there will be pressures from multiple sources that suggest they should be conducting themselves differently. The professional literature supports the position that when there is agreement as to expectations of marital/gender role, and when partners perceive a fairness in the allocation of power, control, and effort occurring in the marriage, then there is a high probability that marriage commitment will be high with both partners and there will be a greater likelihood of marital satisfaction (Blumstein & Schwartz, 1983; Steil, 2000; Weigel, Bennett, & Ballard-Reisch, 2006).

## RACE, ETHNICITY, AND FAMILY FUNCTIONING

Race, ethnicity, and culture are terms used, at times indiscriminately, to articulate distinctions between people and groups. All three of these terms defy simple definition and categorization. To many, the term *race* refers to characteristics within the population that identify group distinction through genetically transmitted physical characteristics. However, the classification of individuals into genetic-based categories is far more challenging. Atkinson, Morten, and Sue point out that "the concept of race resulting from common gene pools can be questioned. As Schaefer (1988, p. 12) points out, 'given frequent migration, exploration, and invasions, pure gene frequencies have not existed for some time, if they ever did'" (1993, p. 6).

It is more accurate to consider race as both a genetic and social entity. Selection and segregation of physical differences have been conducted with some features—skin color being the most common—and not other features, such as eye color or height. While these characteristics are genetic, the value or significance placed on the marker is a social creation. This genetic/social perspective of race is defined as "any people who are distinguished or consider themselves distinguished, in social relations with other peoples, by their physical characteristics" (Cox, 1948, p. 402).

Ethnicity refers to social/cultural groups that have developed over extended time, often centuries. Ethnic groups have formed commonality in language, family structure, diet, religion, and lifestyle. "Ethnicity, the concept of a group's 'personhood,' refers to a group's commonality of ancestry and history, through which people have evolved shared values and customs over centuries" (McGoldrick, Giordano, & Garcia-Preto, 2005, p. 2).

Culture is the most difficult of the three to define because it can refer to grand themes that cross racial and ethnic divisions (e.g., "civilized culture"). Likewise, it can refer to small subsets of peoples and the lifestyles that correspond with them. These cultures can be local to very specific neighborhoods and periods of time. Atkinson, Morten, and Sue (1993) found that Linton (1945) created the most succinct definition: "the configuration of learned behavior and results of behavior whose components and elements are shared and transmitted by the members of a particular society" (Atkinson, Morten, & Sue, 1993, p. 32).

Now that these three terms are defined, let's consider what they mean in light of the responsibility to render care to families. Differences in race, ethnicity, and culture require counselors to be more than just familiar, respectful, or even sensitive to the effects of these differences on the family existence of clients. It requires counselors to be experienced in the factors that have shaped the lives of families within their respective culture. For example, Sells et al. (2007) cite an example of a Honduran counselor who said that he does not begin to be effective with a family until he has had dinner with them in their home. In other words, this culture requires that trust be built through real relationships prior to the formation of professional relationships. The communal values supersede the importance of professional space.

Many authors refer to the importance of cultural, racial, and ethnic sensitivity (Brammer, 2004; McDowell et al., 2005; McGoldrick, Giordano, &

Garcia-Preto, 2005; Sue & Sue, 1999). Their use of sensitivity is not meant to be a passive but an active term in which we demonstrate efforts toward engaging others across culture, race, and ethnicity. It is easy to misconstrue the idea of sensitivity as similar to "good intentions" or "niceness." Someone who is well meaning is not the same as someone who is "well being." We are called by both profession and faith to bridge the gap between individuals. This calling is to work actively within the cultures of others, not merely have awareness or respectful assent. We are to be world counselors.

Toward this end, the American Counseling Association has put forth a set of competencies that should be characteristic of all counselors. These competencies rest on a number of core values:

> First, a culturally skilled counselor is one who is actively in the process of becoming aware of his or her own assumptions about human behavior, values, biases, preconceived notions, personal limitations, and so forth. . . .
>
> Second, a culturally skilled counselor is one who actively attempts to understand the worldview of his or her culturally different client without negative judgments. . . . Third, a culturally skilled counselor is one who is in the process of actively developing and practicing appropriate, relevant, and sensitive intervention strategies and skills in working with his or her culturally different clients. (Sue, Arredondo, & McDavis, 1992)

Counselors can involve themselves in many specific activities that create a bridge to understanding racial, ethnic, and cultural differences. The first and possibly the most difficult is to submerge oneself in an unfamiliar culture, develop the skills in language, and form a community of friendships outside one's culturally restricted environment and comfort zone. The most significant division between cultures and ethnicities is language. Intentional efforts to acquire the language of clients, who might experience components of shame and self-doubt for not being able to communicate in English with the same mental dexterity as in their native tongue, establish a clear and obvious sign of the counselor's regard for and value of another's culture.

Intentionally establish friendships with people who come from cultures other than your own. Once, a doctoral student was looking for a way to determine the degree to which racial prejudice was a characteristic of his subjects in his dissertation. Merely asking, Are you prejudiced? could not get to the real answer. Instead he asked his subjects, How many Christmas cards did you mail last year? And how many did you receive? How many of those cards were from friends or family of a different race or ethnicity than your own? We believe that when a counselor is immersed in the culture of another, when friendships are formed outside of his or her comfort zone, and when barriers of language, borders, and seas are crossed to spend time with valued friends whose way of life is different, such individuals are forming the life skills necessary for effective racial, cultural, and ethnic family therapy. A family therapist does not learn to be an effective transcultural agent, he or she lives to be one.

One of the most telling examples of the degree of cultural engagement one possesses is international travel. It has some limited value when a passport is stamped with visas from distant and diverse places. The real evidence is not that a person visits but that one goes back. The counselor who engages a culture, forms friendships with the citizens of another community, and builds intimate connections with people who live, think, and relate in ways at variance to one's own lifestyle is embracing the depth of multicultural understanding. This value of multiculturalism is not taught. It is embraced and embodied in the way the counselor values others and dedicates personal resources of time and attention.

## ECONOMICS, PRIVILEGE, AND FAMILY FUNCTIONING

*There are but two families in the world, Have-much and Have-little.*

Cervantes, *Don Quixote*

Few factors are as powerful in shaping the sculpture of family as are the economic factors. Almost every North American family has a Depression story (one that pertains to the Hoover/FDR era, not the mood disorder). Indeed, the role of poverty within our family systems often has a nostalgic tone—if the poverty is historical and the current economic status is above the subsistence level of existence. But if the poverty or deprivation is current it lacks the luster of "we survived difficult times." For these families, the difficulty is current and the question of survival still remains to be seen.

The most significant characteristic of poverty is the absence of options and resources. Economically poor families encounter greater stress due to the demands of life and have fewer options to alleviate that stress than do wealthy families. The role that economics plays in shaping a family is seldom understood in its depth and breadth.

Consider a typical week in the life of a working-class family of five. The Martin family consists of Mike, age thirty-three, and Marti, age twenty-nine. They have three children: Monica is nine and in third grade; Matthew is six and in first grade; Michele is three. Mike and Marti are high school graduates, with some community college training. Marti works as a receptionist in a physician's office. Mike works as a heating and air-conditioning technician. Their monthly income after taxes is about $2,400. They live in a suburb adjacent to a major urban setting. Their rent for a two-bedroom apartment is $1,200. After paying for insurance, childcare, food, and utilities they have nothing left for "extras."

While their story is common, consider the additional life choices that must be made in order to "get by." Both Mike and Marti must work—but in order to work they are forced to make many stress-producing lifestyle decisions. To save childcare expenses they drive thirty-five minutes each way to take Michele to Marti's sister during the day. Marti must leave by 6:30 to be able to arrive at work at 8:00. Mike picks up Michele after his work and gets home about 6:30 in the evening. Marti picks up the other two children from the YMCA childcare center. When they get home there are chores to accomplish, including completing homework and having dinner. The family does not have a meal together Monday through Friday as the older children need to eat before dad comes home with Michele. When one of the children becomes sick, it is a serious challenge: first, one must take a day off from work, at no pay, and second, they must pay $50 for their doctor's office copay and $20 for every prescription. They often don't take their children to the doctor—in hopes of not having the medical expense—but often lose in the long run because the child remains ill longer. When a car breaks down Mike can fix many things, but it means having to operate with one car until the weekend when he can repair it, and this adds additional hours onto each of their days. Weekends are spent completing household chores such as grocery shopping, laundry, and housecleaning. Sunday afternoon is their family playtime. If Mike and Marti experience conflicts, they do not have the monetary resources nor the time needed to adequately attend to them. Finding the time available to sit and work through details is a luxury not often afforded to them when there are lunches to pack and a leaky roof to fix.

Counselors, by the fact that they are employed in middle-class or upper middle-class occupations and have been educated to at least a master's level, are often removed from the direct experience of poverty. Therefore, counselors are prone to misunderstand the function of families facing economic deprivation. It is frequently the case that middle and upper middle-class salaried individuals are able to arrange their schedule to attend sessions. This is not the case for many hourly workers. For example, Frank and Maria participated in marital therapy. Maria worked for an airline; Frank was a union wage earner at a foundry. Frank's work was extremely stressful and demanding. There were threats of plant closings and threats of older, experienced, high-wage worker replacement (Frank was fifty-eight and had worked in this foundry for twenty-nine years). Frank had to cancel at least half of the sessions—usually with only hours' notification—because the foundry would call him and assign him to work in place of another colleague who was absent. Frank had to go. The counselor, becoming frustrated with the frequently missed sessions, believed that it was a sign that he was not really invested in the therapy process. The parallel process between work interfering with therapy and work exerting an excessive control and demand of Frank's life was not recognized.

## INTEGRATIVE FOCUS: Family Functioning

The function of a family is shaped by wealth. One wealthy parent reflected on the difference of his family of origin compared to his life with his wife and children. "My children know nothing of the hardship that I had. Oh, they know it, but they have no way to understand the feelings of wearing used shoes to school, or standing in the lunch line with the free meal ticket—and have all of your classmates know. I have tried to deny them some of the privileges that come with wealth, but I have found that it's not really possible. My kids are affected by wealth."

*Think about it:* How has your family's level of wealth had an effect on relational patterns?

Another frequent misunderstanding is to assume that family involvement represents intergenerational fusion. Lower socioeconomic status families must rely on family for support to greater degrees than do wealthier families. This reliance creates the impression of psychological dependence and excessive bonding. For example, a wife explained to a marital counselor the reason for their failure to complete a homework assignment. She said, "I know that the assignment was for us to go out on a date this week, but we were not able to do that because my mother had the flu." The counselor focused on the role that the mother played in preventing the dating assignment from occurring. To the counselor it was relatively easy to hire a babysitter. But this family was dependent on the informal economy of family. The infirmed mother was an essential part of the marriage and of the therapeutic process. In low-income families the ties and obligations to the extended family become more pronounced and explicit.

This image was impressed on us once while we were waiting for a shuttle at an airport. Beside us were two families. The first stood at the curb for only a few minutes. A mother, father, and two children had wheeled luggage that actually rolled. They stood at the curb with the father signaling the limo as it pulled up. A conversation with the children revealed that they were in Orlando to visit their grandparents and go to Disney World. Once their luggage was scooped into the trunk of the Lincoln, the family was in for a vacation of a lifetime.

The second family appeared to have fewer material goods than the first. Suitcases were older, reinforced by belts and ropes. The family revealed that they too were in Orlando to go to Disney World, and they were waiting for their aunt/sister to pick them up from the airport. When the van arrived, just as many people got out as were waiting to get in. Cousins hugged, aunts and uncle declared how big and grown up their children were becoming. They loaded everyone and everything into the van—and off they went to greet Mickey Mouse. The differences were startling. While there was likely no difference in affection between the first family and the second toward their extended family hosts, the former had the economic means to not "inconvenience" anyone. Can you imagine the conversation over the phone, "Oh, no need to come to get us. We'll just hire a limo. You don't need to fight with the airport traffic."

To the extended family with limited financial means, a limo would be a frivolous and needless luxury. The conversation would sound something like, "Of course we will come and get you. You may have to wait a bit until Don gets off work. We're excited to have you and look forward to seeing you then." Money altered the rules, roles, and responsibilities of the immediate and the extended family. Wealth regulates the distance between people, the degree of "self" reliance able to be exhibited.

For most people around the world, except in Western Europe, North America, Australia, and New Zealand, religion functions as a family adhesive. It defines the roles and describes the responsibilities that the generations will have toward each other. To many in the West, who conduct relationships with the highest regard for individual or secular space, there is little understanding for the murder of a person who chose to convert from their family religion to another faith. The space between husband and wife, brother and sister, parent and child, even grandparent and extended clan for most people in the world is a religious space.

*Think about it:* Would you describe the space between you and your family members as religious space or secular space?

## REGARD FOR DIFFERENCES WITHIN CHRISTIAN THEOLOGY AND TRADITION

*Differences applied: counseling family's gender, culture, economics, and race.* A powerful component of the Christian faith is its ability to thrive across cultures. Penn State scholar Phillip Jenkins has called Christianity "the only world religion" (Jenkins, 2002). It has permeated the boundaries of every culture. Even where it is illegal it is quietly practiced. The Christian message is one that provides instruction about who we are as individual creations of God and how we can live together in family and community—in grace, humility, justice, and truth. The Christian faith exists as an etic—as an external reality to which individuals and families are measured. Families everywhere, in Beijing, Montevideo, Mumbai, Dar-es-Salaam, Copenhagen, Des Moines, and all places in between apply the fundamental theology of the Christian tradition to life within their culture. Jenkins postulates that because of Christianity's unique presence within the world cultures, it will have a growing effect—particularly in the economically developing cultures of Asia, Africa, and Latin America.

Yet counselors committed to utilizing the principles and ideals put forth through the life of Jesus must attend to the Christian emic—that is, the unique cultural application of the Christian faith that exists within individual cultures. The counselor must be careful to utilize the Christian culture of the client as opposed to his or her own Christian culture as the primary lens through which the family is understood. For example, the influence of the Catholic tradition on family culture within Latin American families must be considered as a potential influence in all Latin American families, whether the family be Protestant, Catholic, secular, or religiously diverse. Internalized roles of Marianista and machismo, familismo and respecto have become integrated within both Protestant and Catholic families, and their effect becomes embedded in the language of the family. So the counselor who encourages the mother toward greater individualization or encourages the adolescent to share his or her feelings with others may be miscalculating the function of these interventions within the culture of the system.

Similarly, the use of honesty, confrontation, and directness that is an important value within many Western counseling traditions is often labeled "truthfulness," yet in many cultures what is defined as truthfulness is viewed as brash, arrogant, selfish, or manipulative. Subtleties in the broad cultural emic and the more focused Christian emic within cultures other than one's own require careful regard to how we interpret and how we intervene.

## INTEGRATIVE FOCUS: *Family Identity*

Do you remember Tevye in *Fiddler on the Roof*? He was faced with a series of identity crises involving his family as his daughters chose marriage partners. The first crisis was economic as he watched his oldest daughter fall in love with a poor tailor. The second crisis was ideological as he watched the next daughter fall in love with a Leninist. The third crisis was religious as he watched his next daughter fall in love with a Russian Orthodox Christian. In the first two situations, he accepted the crises and likened them to the challenge of maintaining balance while playing the fiddle standing on the roof. One plays with great care lest he fall off. The third he refused to accept. He could relinquish his dream of wealth and his dream of political peace, but not his faith.

*Think about it:* What have been the crises that your family has had to face that have been precarious threats to its survival? How has your family's identity sustained you or possibly failed to sustain you in such a crisis?

## CONCLUSION

We believe that the Christian faith and the profession of family therapy have an exciting symbiosis with multiculturalism. Just as the early church had to adjust to the presence of Parthians, Medes, Elamites, Mesopotamians, Asians, Romans, Judeans, and so on (Acts 2), so too the church involved in family ministry and individuals who seek to render care to families must engage the faith in the culture in order to be effective.

Social science of family theory and therapy has taught us much about methods to live—what are the essential experiences necessary for infants, children, adolescents, men, women, couples, and families to thrive together. But it cannot tell us what to live for, how to be in relationship with our creator, or how a meaningful existence can be created within the phenomenon of family. It is a method, but it has no meaning within itself. Likewise, the Christian faith has a world message about how life can become meaningful, but it cannot advise individual parents regarding choices of care for their child with special needs, or the middle-aged adult who is contemplating a career transition and must evaluate the effect of such a change on the others within the family, or the senior adult who must work with his or her adult children regarding end-of-life care.

The profession, faith, and culture each speak to these challenges. In addition, they are influenced by gender, economic, and ethnic variability. Christianity became relevant in the Roman world because it was multicultural. It went forth out of Judea. It demanded an etic from the culture; that is, it required that the culture adapt to it—as it altered the standard of regard for adults and children; men and women; slave and free; Jew, Greek, and barbarian. Simultaneously, it offered an emic, a sensitivity and accommodation to culture and individual need. The same message and skill set that permitted Paul to introduce Christianity to the Roman world informs and equips the Christian family counselor to attend to others utilizing the tools of our day within the cultures of our time.

## REFERENCES

Atkinson, D. R., Morten, G., & Sue, D. W. (1993). *Counseling American minorities: A cross-cultural perspective* (4th ed.). Madison, WI: W. C. Brown & Benchmark.

Blumstein, P., & Schwartz, P. (1983). *American couples: Money, work and sex.* New York: William Morrow.

Brammer, R. (2004). *Diversity in counseling*. Belmont, CA: Thomson Brooks/Cole.

Canales, G. (2000). Gender as subculture: The first division of multicultural diversity. In I. Cuellar & F. A. Pantiagua (Eds.), *Handbook of multicultural mental health*. San Diego: Academic Press.

Christians for Biblical Equality. (1989). *Men, women and biblical equality*. http://www.cbeinternational.org.

Council on Biblical Manhood and Womanhood. (1987). *The Danvers statement on biblical manhood and womanhood*. http://www.cbmw.org/Resources/Articles/The-Danvers-Statement.

Cox, O. C. (1948). *Caste, class and race*. New York: Doubleday.

Jenkins, P. (2002). *The next christendom: The rise of global Christianity*. New York: Oxford University Press.

Linton, R. (1945). *The cultural background of personality*. New York: Appleton-Century-Crofts.

McDowell, T., Fang, S., Griggs, J., Speirs, K., Perumbilly, S., & Kublay, A. E. (2005). International dialogue: Our experience in a family therapy program. *Journal of Systemic Therapies, 25*, 1-15.

McGoldrick, M., Giordano, J., & Garcia-Preto, N. (2005). Overview: Ethnicity and family therapy. In M. McGoldrick, J. Giordano, & N. Garcia-Preto (Eds.), *Ethnicity and family therapy*. New York: Guilford Press.

Mickelson, A. (1986). *Women, authority and the Bible*. Downers Grove, IL: InterVarsity Press.

O'Neil, J. M. (1990). Assessing men's gender role conflict. In D. Moore & F. Leafgren (Eds.), *Problem solving strategies and interventions for men in conflict* (pp. 23-28). Alexandria, VA: American Association for Counseling and Development.

O'Neil, J. M., Helms, B., Gable, R., David, L., & Wrightsman, L. (1986). Gender-role conflict scale: College men's fear of femininity. *Sex Roles, 14*, 335-50.

Pierce, R. W., & Groothuis, R. M. (2005). *Discovering biblical equality: Complementarity without hierarchy*. Downers Grove, IL: InterVarsity Press.

Pike, K. (1954). *Language in relation to a unified theory of the structure of human behavior* (2nd. ed.). The Hague: Mouton.

Piper, J., & Grudem, W. (1991). *Recovering biblical manhood and womanhood: A response to evangelical feminism*. Wheaton, IL: Crossway Books.

Saucy, R. L., & TenElshof, J. K. (2001). *Women and men in ministry: A complementary perspective*. Chicago: Moody Press.

Schaefer, R. T. (1988). *Racial and ethnic groups*. (3rd ed.). Glenview, IL: Scott, Foresman.

Sells, J. N., Giordano, G. F., Bokar, L., Klein, J. F., Panting, G., & Thumme, B. (2007). The effect of Honduran counseling practices on the North American counseling profession: The power of poverty. *Journal of Counseling and Development, 85,* 431-39.

Steil, J. M. (2000). Contemporary marriage: Still an unequal partnership. In C. Hendrick & S. S. Hendrick (Eds.), *Close relationships: A sourcebook* (pp. 125-36). Thousand Oaks, CA: Sage.

Sue, D. W., Arredondo, P., & McDavis, R. J. (1992). Multicultural counseling competencies and standards: A call to the profession. *Journal of Counseling and Development, 70,* 477-86.

Sue, D. W., & Sue, D. (1999). *Counseling the culturally different: Theory and practice.* New York: Wiley & Sons.

Weigel, D. J., Bennett, K. K., & Ballard-Reisch, D. S. (2006). Roles and influence in marriages: Both spouses' perceptions contribute to marital commitment. *The Family Journal, 35,* 74-92.

# COHABITING COUPLES AND FAMILIES

## Christian Counseling's New Reality

> *(Neal) and (Joanna) sitting in the tree*
> *K-i-s-s-i-n-g! (spell it out)*
> *First comes love.*
> *Then comes marriage.*
> *Then comes baby in the baby carriage,*
> *Sucking one's thumb,*
> *Wetting one's pants,*
> *Doing the hula, hula dance!*

**"THE KISSING SONG," AMERICAN FOLKLORE**

> *We don't see "typical American families" coming to our church. The ones that inquire are living together, having been married and divorced, sometimes two or three divorces. They have children from many previous relationships. They come with all kinds of "baggage." They come to church searching and hoping . . . Can you offer us anything to help those families?*

**CALIFORNIA MEGACHURCH PASTOR**

I NOW PRONOUNCE YOU HUSBAND AND WIFE. You may kiss your bride." That statement and directive used to mean something different than it does today for most people. It once was the defining moment when an individual changed their relational identity from a "me" to an "us." Many beginnings occurred with that declaration—usually a couple's initiated life together was marked by a shared home, shared economic resources, and a shared bed. The anniversary date meant much more than the day of the ceremony, the day of the public declaration. It marked the beginning day of life together. Currently, it is more common for couples to transition into family existence. Sexual unions are more likely to begin earlier in the relationship. Economic integration serves as a frequent motivation. Children arrive in near majority proportion before weddings occur. And with an interesting twist, pets—a puppy, a kitten, or a goldfish—often serve as the first formal bonds of commitment, before a pledge, a ring, or a vow.

We live and work in a new reality regarding marriage and family. There used to be a clear order to things as articulated in the childhood playground song. The "traditional path" to marriage and family followed a common route—introduction, dating, engagement, marriage, children, and after about fifty years, death surrounded by a family of adult children, their spouses, and grandchildren. However, beginning late in the twentieth century, couples walked down a different aisle toward marriage and family formation. Cherlin (2004) called it the deinstitutionalization of marriage to reflect an individualized order to mate selection and family structure. Within Christian circles it has been called the "decline of marriage" or the "attack on the family."

This new reality brings a challenge to counselors who think of marriage through a Christian ethic paradigm. Many see the marriage and family trends and think something like "we're off to hell in a hand basket." Doom, pessimism, and despair can be pervasive moods with the thought of being in a cultural decline. Christian counselors may find this to be a perplexing condition in which to work. Most Christian counselors hold to some form of marital sanctity; that is, the heterosexual union of husband and wife is a reflection of intimacy found in trinitarian theology. The phrase, "the two shall become one flesh" is not a metaphor for "we'll both get along . . ." Indeed, it is figurative language to reflect a deeper meaning and definition, which is that marriages thrive when we (a) consider the other as more important than ourselves; (b) see the object of our love as being a sacred and holy gift from God to nurture and receive nurture from for the length of one's natural life, except in unusual circumstances; (c) embrace a sexuality that emerges out of a and b with the subsequent emotion developing through our value and commitment toward the other; and finally (d) support social and political systems that make it easier for couples who embrace a, b, and c to become parents and so preserve these commitments for the next generation. Christian counselors carry a remedy, a model, a map for the formation of marital intimacy, and the healing of family wounds. In the minds of most, cohabitation is not on their map.

There exists another problem different from the marital decline articulated from America's pulpits. The culture is using a different map. The church and Christian counseling are verging on irrelevance to the majority of couples in the early stages of family formation. Cohabiting couples are not likely to seek Christian influence because they live outside of some of the church's moral boundaries. The Christian family perspective holds potential to be wonderfully and powerfully influential in today's culture even as couples disregard historic patterns of family formation and choose cohabitation as a predecessor or substitute for marriage. However, that influence is denied because couples don't access the Christian community to seek relational guidance out of the belief that they do not meet the "entrance qualifications." For many Christian counselors and pastors, it is challenging to embrace a cohabiting couple who does not first alter or repent from their continuing sexual relationship. As cohabitation continues to be the most common path toward marriage, pastors and Christian counselors must be prepared to involve their knowledge of marriage with the culture lest couples pursue alternative and less reliable sources of relational guidance (e.g., social media).

In this chapter, we will not focus our attention on the perceived "destruction" of marriage and the family other than presenting the data from the professional literature on cohabitation trends. While the direction that secular society and many in the Christian culture have taken regarding biblical sexuality is sad for its creation of greater challenges for couples, we believe that maintaining a winsome and engaging perspective toward marriage will serve the church and the public in the most effective manner. This chapter will focus on how the Christian counselor can address issues emerging from cohabiting relationships. We believe the tone "Well, if you would have never moved in together in the first place, your chances of success would be much higher . . ." serves little purpose for couples who are living together and seek assistance in making their relationships work better. We intend this chapter to serve as an aid to the pastor who we quote in the epigraph: yes, we can offer you strategies to help these families.

Even though the majority of couples now form their families outside of the sexual ethic put forth by the Christian tradition, we do not believe that these couples believe marriage is dead, outdated, or obsolete. The same couples who choose to forgo traditional marriage and family formation at the beginning of their relationship and family formation will also eventually marry—to each other or to someone else—at a rate of 84 percent, the highest among Western developed countries (Cherlin, 2009, pp. 16-17). So while people are choosing to enter sexual relationships and produce children without marriage and while popular tabloid magazine articles may declare marriage dead, the population also see themselves as married . . . eventually, and on different terms than their parents! Marriage is by no means obsolescent. And while the path taken by most people may not be the process likely to produce successful relationships, Christian counselors carry a unique opportunity to aid couples in gaining a foothold on a path that will lead to family achievement.

Monique and Mike's story represents the new "normal" in family formation. Monique, as a teenager, might have been the high schooler who lived across the street or around the corner in your neighborhood. In the middle of her high school years, her father filed for divorced, left her mother, and moved in with a coworker. After the divorce the new couple bought a house in the neighborhood so they could stay close to Monique and her siblings. Meanwhile, her mother had to sell the family home and find another that was smaller and more affordable. Monique and her brothers fought to make it in life independently through adolescence and early adulthood. She went to college with the determination to put herself through on her own—her mom couldn't afford to help. She was unwilling to permit her father to pay. Along the way Monique met Mike. He was *the one* for her. She knew it soon after they started dating. As they realized their love, Monique also realized she wasn't going to make it financially. College and life were too expensive for someone trying to make it on her own. After the apartment, tuition, books, lab fees, and car insurance, there was nothing left for food!

But there was Mike. They talked. They both knew they were going to marry—someday. Why not move into his apartment and share expenses? She could sell her car—they didn't need two. She moved in with Mike; it was a hard decision made easy by the press of her finances. While giving verbal assent to how glad she was to move in, the sparkle, the joy of life was gone. "This is not how I imagined my life to be . . ." With a raw sense of mixed emotion she said that her dad was very pleased with her decision. He told her "living with Mike was the best choice you could have made for your future marriage. This way you will learn before it's too late what it's really like. If I had lived with your mom first, I am sure we never would have married." Monique responded with tears. Her father was insensitive to the fact that when his marriage dissolved, Monique's family also dissolved. She wished her life were different but remained determined not to be her mother and not to marry anyone like her dad. After graduation from college Mike and Monique became engaged, and married a year later.

Now, some years after marriage, they do not have children, but they have a dog. Their pet is a symbol of commitment, something they share together, like a child without the inconvenience of a car seat. They made it. Three years into their marriage they are not the "poster couple" for why cohabitation is a bad idea. They report high satisfaction and optimism for the future. But she reports there is strain as the wound from her father has not healed. She remains bitter toward the man who dissolved her family and destroyed the memory of her childhood. Some of that bitterness is carried into the marriage because as a girl she believed that she would never have intercourse until after marriage. There is a constant wonder about how she might have lived differently if her father had not destroyed her mom's marriage and her family. She carries a mixture of emotion as she is committed to Mike but disappointed in herself—not with her decision to marry but with her choice to live with Mike beforehand. She thinks it was a decision forced on her by her father's affair and divorce from her mom. She has heard of the statistics—that cohabitation leads to a higher rate of divorce. She is determined to love Mike forever, but she also thinks, "That was what my mom said too."

Cohabitation is never one-sided. It is not just Monique relenting to Mike and delaying her expectation of marriage. Mike came from a mental place where he considered relationship options also. In conversing with Mike, it is easy to see a priority of immediacy—he valued being together. Because together is better than separate, he reasoned, "Why wouldn't we live together if we could?" At the time he knew a few things for certain. He knew he loved Monique. He knew he was happier and more content when they thought and acted as a team, and he knew that he wanted to figure out whether he would be comfortable making a life-long commitment to her. He did not know at that time if he was ready to be married. He would like to finish school, pay off his loans, and have a nest egg to buy a home. While he didn't believe he was ready to be married *now*, he thought marriage to Monique would probably be in his future. So living together had a whole bunch of positives and, from his perspective, no negatives. Two could live more cheaply than one. They could enjoy life together as they finished school. Finally, by living together they could really figure out if they were meant to be together. Mike told Monique, "What's not to like about this deal?"

Mike did not have a valued church background. He knew of Monique's faith, but he wasn't drawing from the same well. He technically was a Presbyterian—that was his grandparents' denomination, and when he was an infant, his mom baptized him in the church where his parents married. He didn't know the difference between a Presbyterian and any other Christian group. Church was not an interest to his parents, and it wasn't a priority to him. He knew it was important to Monique, and he was fine with that, but religious faith was never anything he spent much time thinking about. He understands her emotion about her hope for marriage. He thinks of it as he thinks of his childhood dream of playing football in the NFL: at some point you realize as an adult that your dreams of childhood take a different reality.

Mike and Monique were not social scientists who are immersed in behavioral outcome data. Their decision to live together before marriage was with the prevailing winds of culture. Without doubt, they wanted what is "best," meaning that which would provide each with immediate and long-term satisfaction, safety, hope, and well-being. Biological forces, social expectations, media trends, and personal needs propelled their decision. They don't realize it, but they are part of a large social movement that has redefined family in the twenty-first century. The social experiment of cohabitation as the primary initiation to family formation has provided social scientists with a vast laboratory of behavioral assessment. Was their decision the right or wrong process for successful marriage development and secure family formation? The literature suggests the answer is complicated.

## COHABITING, MARRIAGE, AND THE
## FAMILY: A LITERATURE REVIEW

Indeed, this social trend has redefined the way we have to think about marriage and the way we track human development processes extending through the human life cycle. Rhoades, Stanley, and Markman (2012) state that "family developmental theories often fail to include cohabitation as a stage or transition period, focusing only on premarriage, early marriage, parenting, and subsequent events" (p. 348). But it has become a game changer. Previously, our family-formation models were derived from the dating, courtship, engagement, marriage, sexual expression, infant, children, adolescents, empty nest, retirement, and elder years family model. "Throughout most of the recorded history of the Western world, a family consisting of a wife, a husband, and children was the main social institution that structured the lives, activities and relationships" (Thornton, Axinn, & Xie, 2007, p. 3).

Marriage, as we know it in its traditional context, has a social, governmental, and religious response to biological uniqueness of the human species. Rules that have come to define marriage have emerged within all societies so as to regulate the boundaries between clans, define property rights, facilitate human growth and development, and provide structures to protect against harsh elements, starvation, disease, and war. Toward this end,

> marriage is considered one of the fundamental characteristics that identifies our species as human. Along with large brains, language, culture, bipedal movement, and dexterous hands, the combinations of features defining the human solution to mating, childbearing, and childrearing is unique in the animal kingdom. Among these features are concealed ovulation, private sexual expression, sexual expression independent of ovulation, internal gestation, maternal nursing, prolonged dependency of the young, tremendous investment of parental time and resources in the rearing of children. The long-term bonding of women and men into family units and the investment of mothers and fathers in the bearing and rearing of children are important elements of human mating and reproduction. (Thornton, Axinn, & Xie, 2007, p. 4)

## COHABITATION FREQUENCY: WHO,
## WHAT, WHERE, WHEN?

The demographic data demonstrate a radical shift in family formation and family structures in the United States, Canada, and Europe occurring over the past fifty years. Axinn and Thornton (2000) identify this shift as one of the most important changes defining Western civilization to occur over the past several centuries. Writing for the Pew Research Center, Cohn, Passel, Wang, and Livingston (2011) offered evidence of the shift in family-related behaviors. In 1960, 72% of the adult population of the United States was married. In 2010, marital partners constituted just over 50% of the population. Forty percent of all births in 2010 were to unmarried mothers (Curtin, Ventura, & Martinez, 2014), compared to 5.3% in 1960 (Ventura & Bacharach, 2000). Cohn et al. (2011) also indicated that 39% of the overall American population believes marriage is becoming obsolete—and that percentage increases to 44% when looking at the marrying age group of 18-29 year olds. As recently as the 1980s, about 17% (1 in 6) of children were born outside of marriage (U.S. National Center for Health Statistics, 1982; Cherlin, 2004). By 2000, that number rose to 33% (U.S. National Center for Health Statistics, 2003). Cherlin (2004) states that "marriage is no longer the nearly universal setting for childbearing that it was a half century ago" (p. 894). Similar outcomes can be found in Western Europe and Canada, with the Nordic countries reporting rates over 60% (Kiernan, 2002).

The Centers for Disease Control's National Survey of Family Health (NSFH) (Daugherty & Copen, 2016) has produced meaningful information about the current status of many health-related family issues, cohabitation among them. Their data indicate that the percentage of people who were in a cohabiting relationship between the ages of 15 and 44 was 15% for women and 13.5% for men. This frequency has doubled since 1995, when the frequency was about 7%. Similarly, the NSFH reports that 52% of all males age 15-44 and 57% of all women age 15-44 had cohabited with their partner at some time in their life. In 1995 the frequency was about 40%. The NSFH reported that three-year outcome: thirty-two percent of cohabiting relationships will continue. About 40% of the relationships will have married sometime in the previous three years, and about 27% of the relationships would have ended. Of the couples who do not marry, Bumpass & Lu (2000) report that 54% of couples who cohabit have ended their relationship within five years.

From another data set a fascinating picture regarding family formation emerges. Betsy Cooper and a team of social science researchers examined the "rise of the unaffiliated"—that is, the group of generation Xers and millennials who espouse no religious affiliation. The data indicate that in the same years

of the rise of cohabitation—roughly 1990 to 2015—those young Americans
who identified with no religious commitment or affiliation rose from about
6% in 1990 to nearly 25% in 2015. The "Unaffiliated" is the single largest religious group in America.

These data points suggest a fascinating picture regarding the current state
and future trends of marriage. It's a simplistic response to see marriage as
being in decline. There is more to be considered. The cohabitation data do not
suggest that the age of marriage is past or becoming obsolete—make note that
40% of cohabiting couples are married within three years to the person they
are living with at the time of survey, and eventually nearly all of the remaining
60% of individuals who do not marry the person they are living with at the
time do marry somebody else. Marriage is by no means dead! Rather, the
cohabitation data indicate *how* couples make selection decisions regarding
marriage. Bumpass, Sweet, and Cherlin (1991) state that "sharp declines in
both first marriage rates and rates of remarriage have been largely offset by
increasing cohabitation. The increase in the proportion of unmarried young
people should not be interpreted as an increase in 'singlehood' as traditionally
regarded: young people are setting up housekeeping with partners of the opposite sex at almost as early an age as they did before marriage rates declined"
(p. 913). Couples are creating a path to marriage that is outside of traditional
church-affiliated passages.

Cohabitation has become the most frequently used decision-making path
for a majority of couples in the United States. Agree with the process, or not,
challenged by empirical data or not, it is how most couples decide to marry.
Cherlin (2009) reports that 90% of all Americans will marry at some time in
their lives. That is just about everybody! Since the 1950s, this statistic has
changed only about 5%. Couples have not rejected marriage per se but have
changed the way that they decide about marriage. Most couples are not deciding to enter marriage through a Christian sexual/marital/family ethic but
are deriving their decision-making process through an alternative worldview.
The majority of couples have rejected the principle of personally living with
sexual and individual boundaries until the consummation of a marriage commitment accentuated by sexual intimacy. Smock, Huang, Manning, and Bergstrom (2006) state, "Although most Americans marry at some point, *heterosexual cohabitation has dramatically transformed courtship, the marriage
process, and the life course of both adults and children*" (p. 3, italics added).

Furthermore, young adults (18-29) who are not in a romantic relationship overwhelming support cohabitation as the typical and desired path toward mate selection. While the majority believes that cohabitation is the best way to ensure a good marriage decision, Popenoe and Whitehead write, "the available data on the effects of cohabitation contradict this belief. There is no evidence that those who decide to cohabit before marriage will have a stronger marriage than those who don't live together, and some evidence to suggest that those who live together before marriage are more likely to break up after marriage" (1999, p. 16).

Numerous researchers have examined the motivations for cohabitation in American couples (Bumpass & Lu, 2000; Casper & Bianchi, 2002; Smock et al., 2006). Smock et al. found that couples entered or chose not to enter cohabiting relationships for divergent reasons. Being familiar with the motivation to cohabit may influence the focus and direction of counseling. The first motivation described was to experience greater affection and intimacy. Prager (2000) found that love was a significant factor for both men and women, though stronger for women. Couples cohabitated in order to spend more time together and to build the bonds of affection and intimacy. They believed the immediacy of shared living would increase the opportunity to nurture their love.

Sexual behavior was a second motivation for cohabitation. Men compared to women more frequently hold this motivation, but sexual motivation is by no means an exclusive male interest. Researchers have found that couples who choose to cohabitate are prompted in part by sexual experiences (Bouchard & Lachance-Grzela, 2016; Bouchard & Arseneault, 2005; Botwin, Buss, & Shackelford, 1997). It is important to add that this sexual motivation encompasses far more than mere orgasmic experiences but includes the emotional connectivity, attachment, and intimacy that come with sexual union.

Ridley, Peterman, and Avery (1978) described the third motivation as "testing." This is the most common motivation for cohabitation, cited by 51% of men and 56% of women. "This is a means of reducing risk and uncertainty. Cohabitation certainly provides ample opportunity for couples to learn about one another through sharing a residence" (Smock et al., 2006, p. 7). In the introductory case example, testing to see if Monique was compatible with Mike was the basis for her father's counsel and encouragement for Monique to cohabit.

Smock et al. (2006) and others describe the fourth motivation as closely affiliated to the previous idea of testing. It is the creation of interdependence.

Researchers suggest that cohabiting couples are seeking to form a type of re-lationship that reflects their internal image of ideal relationship. It is similar to Hargrave's "US" (2000). Interdependence includes the voluntarily loss of some individuality and personal freedoms in order to gain a more desired goal. Cohabitation is pursued to see if each is willing to consider the other as more important than self.

The fifth motivation is financial. Bumpass et al. (1991) found that for nearly a quarter of the couples surveyed, financial advantage was the primary reason for cohabitation, the second-highest endorsement behind "testing." These couples do not necessarily see cohabiting as the pathway to marriage but as a temporary living condition preferable to living alone. These financial motives create a type of cohabiting "entrapment." This is described by a plurality of researchers (Avellar & Smock, 2005; Casper & Bianchi, 2002; Fields, 2004). The entrapment is the lifestyle created by economic advantages that becomes integrated into a couple's way of being—they get used to it. Subsequently, if a couple considers ending the live-in relationship, it is not just the relationship that is ending but the economic advantages that have become normalized. There becomes an eco-nomic decline once the relationship is over. This is true for both men and women, but more accentuated for women (Avellar & Smock, 2005).

The final motivation addressed in the literature is to build a two-parent family. For some unmarried parents, cohabitation provides mutual access to children conceived in the relationship. Couples make a commitment to care for infants and children while not able to make the same level of commitment to their relational partner. As in marriage, couples usually do not enter co-habiting relationships just for "the sake of children." However, children do serve as a powerful contributing factor to cohabiting decisions (Manning, Smock, & Bergstrom-Lynch, 2009). This family motive may also be integrated with the economic motive. After a child is born there is a substantial economic burden placed more heavily on the woman (assuming she has custody and is the primary caregiver). The couple may combine households to make mutual availability for child care more accessible.

## DOES COHABITATION LEAD TO DIVORCE? YES, MAYBE, AND NO

Cohabitation is correlated with higher levels of divorce (Cunningham & Thornton, 2007; Van der Valk et al., 2008; Rhoades et al., 2012; Manning & Cohen,

2012). This oft-repeated finding has been confirmed in multiple studies and correlated with many other factors, including that cohabiting couples begin their relationships earlier, are less educated, and are in a lower socioeconomic status (SES) than couples who secure their relationship through marriage (Smock, 2000). Cohabiting couples have been found to experience lower relational satisfaction (Brown & Boothe, 1996). They report lower religiosity, lower confidence in the future of their relationship, higher levels of aggression, and lower positive communication than married couples (Jose, O'Leary, & Moyer, 2010). If looking at the data superficially, it is easy to create the argument that those who choose to cohabitate will experience greater life problems because of their cohabitation choice. Indeed, in some cases that may be the case, but the research creates a different, more complicated picture of the predictive effects of marital cohabitation. Rhoades, Stanley, and Markman (2012) summarize our knowledge of cohabitation:

> Overall, this literature suggests that when compared to marriage, cohabiting unions tend to be less committed, less satisfying, more conflictual, and more physically aggressive (Brown & Booth, 1996; Brown, Bulanda, & Lee, 2005; Brownridge, 2004; Forste & Tanfer, 1996; Nock, 1995; Stafford, Kline, & Rankin, 2004; Stanley, Whitton, & Markman, 2004; Treas & Giesen, 2000). At the same time, as cohabitation becomes more normative, it is less often followed by marriage (Lichter, Turner, & Sassler, 2010). That is, more and more individuals live with multiple partners rather than only the one they marry. As cohabitation becomes less of a stepping-stone to marriage, it becomes as important to understand how it compares to dating without cohabitation rather than only to marriage. (p. 349)

After years of research on divorce predictions out of cohabitation, a complicated image has emerged. There is a higher rate of divorce by people who cohabitate before marriage compared to people who enter marriage in a traditional manner. The divorce rate, which has been slowly declining, and the cohabitation rate, which has been dramatically growing, are connected. Fewer people are marrying; instead, they are cohabiting. When cohabiting couples break up, possibly three years after the onset of the relationship, they do not show up in the divorce statistics. Thus, the actual number of divorces is down in large part because the number of marriages is down also. And those who were inclined to initiate a cohabiting relationship instead of marriage because there were reasons that provided pause and concern would also be the couples more likely to divorce because of the presence of those problems. In other words, in decades past, couples who were at high risk of relational break up, characterized by high levels of conflict, infidelity, and/or lack of depth in emotional attachment, might still have married and subsequently divorced. They knew from the courtship that there were signs of poor outcomes, and they married anyway because their personal or community values did not support cohabitation. But it is more frequently the case that these conflicted couples chose instead to not enter marriage—thus, not entering the marriage databases. Instead, they confirm in those first few years that they can't live well together and break up—unless they don't.

It is probably inaccurate to declare that cohabiting relationships are a causal factor of divorce. They are a correlated factor, suggesting that there is a connection or relationship between cohabiting and subsequent divorce after marriage, but the causes are likely due to other issues. Identifying these "other issues" is an important focus in the marital literature. Predictions of relational outcomes of those who marry and of those who cohabit are central in the marriage literature. Every couple wants to know—in the presence of cold feet at a church wedding, or with the decision to move in with a boyfriend or girlfriend—the answer to the question, will it last? Kline et al. (2004) summarized the prevailing view about cohabiting predictions of marriage:

> The cohabitation literature is beset by controversy as to why negative marital outcomes arise for some couples who cohabit before marriage. The dominant perspective is that selection effects are operating such that the differences in the marital outcomes of those who cohabit before marriage and those who do not are due to preexisting characteristics of the individuals rather than the cohabitation experience itself. (p. 311)

Very important in the prediction of marital success after cohabitation is the status and commitment level of the relationship at the beginning of the cohabiting experience. Stanley, Rhoades, and Markman (2006) described the process of negative marital outcomes to be predicted by their "inertia" theory. The theory posits that couples who enter relationships with formal commitment to one another, such as formal engagement, have a greater likelihood of successful marriage. In other words, couples who cohabit for economic reasons, to provide stability for their children, to "test drive" the relationship before making a marital commitment have a lower probability of success than couples who marry without cohabiting or who cohabit after engagement.

*Listen to them.* They will bring to you their intention and goal for counseling. It is frequent that cohabiting couples seek the Christian counselor because the professional has a stellar reputation in the community and they are searching for therapeutic services to assist them in settling conflicts, attending to issues related to stepfamily integration, resolving tensions coming from family of origin, or a plurality of other concerns. The first task in caring for cohabiting couples is to listen as they express their needs and describe their goals for treatment. They have brought honor to you by making an appointment. Reciprocate the honor through careful understanding of their needs. Very clear problem identification will permit the Christian counselor to understand how clinical counseling competence might aid a couple in creating greater stability, intimacy, fidelity, commitment, and relational success.

*Respond to their expressed need, not the need you think they have.* Cohabiting couples rarely come to counseling with cohabitation as the focus of therapy. Seldom is the issue, "I want to get married, but he/she doesn't." Rather, couples enter therapy because they need help with life: patterns of communication, arguments, conflicts over boundaries, emotional accessibility, expectations toward respective families, and differences in parenting strategies. It is common for cohabitation and marriage to emerge as an ancillary treatment theme. Let it emerge from the couple. If the counselor creates marriage/cohabitation as the therapeutic issue before it is requested organically, the counselor likely will be seen as functioning from a preconceived agenda rather than attending to the needs of the couple. The ethicists would argue that clients carry the principle of autonomy, which includes the ability define the focus of treatment. It is common for the marital/cohabitation theme to emerge organically as a natural part of the therapeutic intervention.

*Encourage the formation of a telos.* A crucial theme addressed in chapter fourteen regarding successful couple counseling is the *telos*—that is, the long-term goal and objective for the relationship. It is common for couples to have a telos—"We hope to be married someday"—but no plan for success and no strategy to determine whether the couple is on track. Additionally, while marriage may be in their future plans, it does not describe the characteristics and the qualities of the relationship they desire. It is common to ask questions such as, When you were a child or early adolescent and dreamed of being married, being in relationship, or forming a family, what did you want? What did it look like from that vantage point of idyllic childhood? Once identified, the telos can be offered as the ultimate goal for counseling. It is the reality they really want, existing beyond the immediate problem, that draws them to therapy.

*Teach them as they seek to be taught.* The research on cohabiting couples suggests that there is a need and interest in learning how to be successful in relationship. If hesitation occurs that blocks a couple's ability to form commitments, then mentorship is called for as a remedy. Depending on the nature of the counseling relationship, relational coaching or mentorship may or may not fall within the bounds of the counseling. The purpose of such instruction is to mentor and model essential themes of relational and marital success. These themes include relational grace, patience, mercy, empathy, trust, faithfulness, integrity, perseverance, temperance, self-control, and many more.

## ALAN AND BRITTANY: A CASE STUDY

Alan and Brittany initiated counseling as a stressed couple. They were in their late twenties, with no children. They had been a couple for six years—meeting in community college where Alan was getting his degree in fire science and emergency medicine and Brittany was studying nursing. They moved into Brittany's apartment their last year of college. After graduation both got jobs, he with the fire department as an EMT and she at a hospital. Alan also joined the navy as a reservist. He was a medic assigned to a marine unit. Not long afterward they bought a house and were well on their way to a secure home. But there were problems. Alan's job was very stressful. The hours were long and, at times, the job was traumatic. He found himself ruminating on the trauma of his work. Exposure to car accidents, burn victims, and violence victims were taking their toll on his ability to sleep. In addition, Alan would be deployed twice over a six-year period for about eighteen months as a medic in a marine unit in Iraq. His unit was involved in frequent fires, and his work was extremely demanding. Back at home he found himself drinking often after work and on weekends. He never was intoxicated at work and never "out of control," but the alcohol consumption was consistent.

Simultaneously, Brittany was working twelve-hour shifts at the hospital on an infectious disease floor. She too would be coming home exhausted, only to find herself alone or in the "boyfriend caretaker" role. She found that Alan was not available for conversation, support, or fun. He was sullen, uninterested in sex, and at times nasty. She frequently found herself to be complaining, criticizing, and, though she loathed the word, the nagging "housewife type" (her words, not ours).

Pain and despair brought them to therapy. Marriage versus cohabitation was not discussed in the first session beyond the description of the history of their relationship. Because cohabitation was not an initial treatment theme, it was not defined as the problem to be addressed. The concerns they described were the stress, the drinking, the distancing, the demands, the nagging, the suspiciousness, and the anger. The pattern of relational conflict was tracked in the circular pattern of pain, defense, and injury/offense. The mutual injury from him to her and from her back to him was obvious. They ended the first session with a sense of relief for being understood and of shame for how they had treated one another.

The second session focused on their telos—what did they want, hope to receive, and dream for as a couple? It was quiet. It was here that the discussion of cohabitation and marriage became a natural part of treatment. They had not thought much about what they wanted—together. They each had dreams about a type of romantic fantasy marriage—"soulmate" language. They acknowledged that they each believed that the other was the "right person" but that they were not ready for the commitment to marriage. Commitment to one another was rather easy for them to imagine, but commitment to marriage, they realized, was very difficult. They were fearful, doubtful, and pessimistic of their ability to be married. Alan summed up their common position: "We don't know of anyone who is married who is happy! So for me, sure, I want to get married, but I look around and think that my life will likely be miserable and end in divorce just like most of my friends, my parents, and my parents' friends."

This conversation permitted the following reflection and question: "I am hearing that both of you know that you want to be with each other, and both of you carry fear that if you build security in your relationship—committing your life together and to your children—that you will be miserable and regret your decision. Is there an 'I want to make a commitment but I don't know how' aspect of your life?" Both of them agreed, which created space for the counselor to ask the most important question: "I hear that you have no model, no map, and few examples of how to create a successful family—starting with the two of you—and passing that model to your children and to your grandchildren. Great marriages run on grace, mercy, trust, fidelity, integrity, empathy, forgiveness—these are the components that, when combined, form a loving, intimate, joyful home. I am hearing that ultimately, learning how to give and receive these qualities—to love the other as more important than yourself—is really what you want from therapy. Am I close?" Hence was created a theoretical direction that provided an experience that they, up till then, did not know was possible.

## WHEN A CHRISTIAN COUNSELOR IS UNCOMFORTABLE WORKING WITH COHABITING COUPLES

It happens. Counselors experience internal conflict when the values of the client or couple are significantly different from the values of the counselor. With cohabiting couples, the tension experienced by many Christian counselors and pastors is the conflict when the couple seeking counsel is living outside of the counselor's moral boundaries of Christian marriage, which serves as the basis for their couples counseling theory and technique. This can create a challenge for the counselor as internal tension might emerge around whether the counselor is acting genuinely and congruently in working with the cohabiting couple. The tension emerges as, Do I stand for *truth*, my theology of marriage and fidelity, or do I stand for *mercy*, overlooking the life patterns of the couple as they seek help with their relationship?

We find that it is more common for the "truth" position to emerge within the evangelical pastoral counseling community as the expected path for the Christian counselor. Van Goethem (2005) demonstrates this as he writes to pastors and counselors who counsel unmarried couples:

Pastors have a responsibility to provide a thorough biblical education for their flocks including what the Bible has to say about marriage and sexual morality. Pastors must take the lead in outlining the proper understating of marriage conveying such to the leadership of the church and to the congregation. . . . Certainly the prevalence of and the casual attitude toward cohabitation argues for a clear and consistent approach to these couples by pastors. (p. 159)

Conversely, Christian counselors who carry a state license to practice counseling and/or those who abide by the ethics codes of professional organizations experience the professional expectation that mercy should trump truth through statements in the ethics code which impede "value-based" challenges to the counselor. The mental health profession has determined that it is an unethical practice to not treat or to refer clients to another counselor when the counselor experiences a value conflict with the client. This means that it would be unethical and inappropriate for the Christian couple's counselor to deny counseling services to a cohabiting couple just because the couple's counselor values marriage and works only with married couples.

## CHRISTIAN CRITIQUE AND ENGAGEMENT

There is a powerful scene in the movie classic *Fiddler on the Roof* when Tevye is saying farewell to his second daughter Hodel. They stand at railroad tracks early in the morning. She is leaving to be with her betrothed—sent in exile to Siberia. As the father releases his treasured daughter, there is a question and a promise:

> Tevye: And who, my child, will there be to perform a marriage there in the wilderness?

> Hodel: Papa, I promise you, we will be married under a canopy.

The dialogue reflects the primary tension that many within Christendom feel as we interact with the culture. Tevye's concern was not the wedding but the marriage. He wonders if there will be a rabbi in Siberia. Will my daughter's relationship be right before God? Hodel reframes the imagery, referring to the symbol of protection—the canopy. The *chuppah*, or canopy, was a like a tent but opened on all four sides. It is used in Jewish weddings and symbolizes the tent of Abraham, described in the Midrash, which also opened on all four sides. The tent was the source of protection, and guests were welcome from all directions. The daughter is reassuring the father as if she were saying, "Don't fear, Papa, we will remain under the protection of our faith." The grand theme of the film is that it is possible for the truth of Tevye's faith tradition to remain while context changes within social structures.

Now let's leave early twentieth-century Russia and return to twenty-first-century America. We are like Tevye—experiencing and possibly disagreeing with aspects of a severe shift in the cultural reality yet seeking to be relevant amid a changing culture. Relational cohabitation is a radical paradigm shift—toward which there has been little challenge. Influenced by a media model that misrepresents marital fidelity and by a Christian culture that has failed to teach couples how to excel in marriage fidelity and intimacy and to manage the complexities of challenging, difficult, and painful realities, we face a culture that does not regard the biblical model of family—even worse, it doesn't even understand what that model is.

We can see the church's response to this cultural shift. Primarily it has been negative—the term "break down" or "decline" of the American family is a popular phrase in references about the family by Christian leaders. Such a description is accurate. The data support the idea that couples enter the family less equipped to address the challenges of family life effectively. It is true that the family structures are formed with a greater disregard toward the "grace of family." Men and women enter relationships without the traditional structures that have provided meaning for centuries. The most obvious result is that those who begin families through cohabitation are not very likely to have regular contact with a supportive Christian community, not very likely to seek a Christian community when there is a challenge or threat to their relationship, and not very likely to use the church community to support them in the teaching of their children. This segment of the population devotes the crucial initial years of relationship creation and family formation with minimal to no church influence. The gospel of Jesus Christ is inert to these families. The marital paradigm shift represents the loss of an idea—that family would be understood through a Christian lens and would provide protection, like the symbolic canopy.

But the reality may be different than we thought. Thornton, Axinn, and Xie (2007) have written a comprehensive historical and sociological account of marriage and cohabitation in human history. Their findings are worth noting. Marriage as we know it and defined by both law and church approval—starting with a ceremony, followed by a sexual union, followed by childbirth—has been in existence only a few hundred years. Since around the time of the Reformation, marriage has been defined as we know it today by both law and church ordinance. The church has always determined a way to bring biblical truth to influence individual, couple, and family formation. The most important perspective that we have sought to emphasize in this chapter is that the priority of Christian counseling and pastoral ministry is not that couples "get married" but that couples experience a "good marriage." This teleological view permits counselors to have long-term engagement with couples as they mature in their relationship—looking toward maturity both in Christ and toward one another.

## OPTIMISM FOR WHAT GOD CAN DO INSTEAD OF
## PESSIMISM OVER WHAT THEY HAVE DONE

It is common to define the rise of cohabitation as evidence that we are living in a post-Christian age. Along with other changes in relational characteristics—such as cohabitation's high divorce rate, a humorous view of infidelity (except when you discover that it is your spouse who had the affair), and abortion on demand—cohabitation is seen as evidence that Christianity has lost its influence on the culture and is in danger of being removed to the sidelines. In response to this perspective, it is common for Christians to feel threatened and to take up a political cause to "save the American family." While we agree with the need for salvation in all its aspects, we have accepted a different lens to understand the current circumstance of the family—all the while maintaining our orthodox theological views. Charles Taylor published *A Secular Age* in 2007. His work is a commentary on culture, though it does not specifically address cohabitation or marriage. But his work has great implications in understanding marriage. To Taylor, secularism didn't just rise out in the past century as a reaction to and rejection of Christian thought. Rather, in the Middle Ages and the Reformation, Christianity created paths for secular thinking to emerge, and it has been a means of protecting faith rather than the scourge that kills the Christian way of life. Taylor sees in core tenets of Christian thought the freedom to follow conscience, exercise discipline, and define a knowable world as ideas that emanated from the Reformation. They built a foundation of civil society that could be defined by law, analyzed, debated, understood, and either accepted or rejected as one's conscience dictates.

By creating an open system of thought that encouraged secularized thinking, we "disenchanted" the universe and made all of creation, including ourselves, as knowable, definable entities. This also permitted a new faith to emerge, one that is spontaneous and driven by higher orders of intellect, affection, and love rather than by blind adherence to rules as was the case in the Middle Ages under Catholicism. To Taylor, the formation of a secular state and the secular mind has made Christianity stronger.

Now let's get back to marriage and cohabitation. A divorce rate in excess of 40 percent in a culture that is predominantly Christian suggests that marriage is only minimally affected by the faith that supposedly is present within the society. We prefer to think of cohabitation not as a secularization of marriage but rather as a return to a consistency between how one acts with what one believes. There is little reason for someone outside the faith to carry faith-like commitment to marriage, so no one should be surprised when a person who does not see marriage as creating "one flesh" doesn't wish to enter into a one-flesh union. Cohabitation is more like a "market correction" than a wholesale abandonment of faith. This means that co-habitation patterns as a form of consistency between belief and behavior. And the couple of faith is likewise able to demonstrate consistency. If there is a "one-flesh" belief and a "one-flesh" behavior both experienced by a couple and observable by the culture (and by family psychology researchers), then the differences between the Christian and secular worldviews and life commitments will become obvious.

## CONCLUSION

In the twenty-first century, most marriages begin with relational cohabitation. The majority of couples do not follow the church's teaching on sexual fidelity and restraint outside of marriage. Yet Christian counseling and pastoral min-istry is frequently used by the churched and the nonchurched for relational assistance. The church has a message, and counseling can provide a medium for strategic influence on early family formation. By utilizing empirically based best practices research and the biblical truth on which that research is based, Christian counseling can assist couples in the initial stage of family formation. But because these couples often have few lived experiences of re-lational integrity, relational commitment, and marital fidelity that are central to Christian marriage and articulated in the gospel message, counselors and pastors must accommodate the way that they counsel. Taking a long-term family development perspective, counselors can help couples in the twenty-first century develop relational skills that provide the highest probability for relational success.

## REFERENCES

Avellar, S., & Smock, P. J. (2005). The economic consequences of the dissolution of cohabiting unions. *Journal of Marriage and Family, 67*(2), 315-27.

Axinn, W. G., & Thornton, A. (2000). The transformation in the meaning of mar-riage. In L. Waite (Ed.), *The ties that bind: Perspectives on marriage and co-habitation* (pp. 147-65). New York: Aldine de Gruyter.

Botwin, M. D., Buss, D. M., & Shackelford, T. K. (1997). Personality and mate preferences: Five factors in mate selection and marital satisfaction. *Journal of personality, 65*(1), 107-36.

Bouchard, G., & Arseneault, J. E. (2005). Length of union as a moderator of the relationship between personality and dyadic adjustment. *Personality and Individual Differences, 39*(8), 1407-17.

Bouchard, G., & Lachance-Grzela, M. (2016). Nontraditional families, family attitudes, and relationship outcomes in emerging adulthood. *Canadian Journal of Behavioural Science / Revue canadienne des sciences du comportement, 48,* 238-45.

Brown, S. L., & Booth, A. (1996). Cohabitation versus marriage: A comparison of relationship quality. *Journal of Marriage and the Family, 58,* 668-78.

Brown, S. L., Bulanda, J. R., & Lee, G. R. (2005). The significance of nonmarital cohabitation: Marital status and mental health benefits among middle-aged and older adults. *The Journals of Gerontology Series B: Psychological Sciences and Social Sciences, 60*(1), S21-S29.

Brownridge, D. A. (2004). Understanding women's heightened risk of violence in common-law unions revisiting the selection and relationship hypotheses. *Violence Against Women, 10*(6), 626-51.

Bumpass, L., & Lu, H. H. (2000). Trends in cohabitation and implications for children's family contexts in the United States. *Population Studies, 54*(1), 29-41.

Bumpass, L. L., Sweet, J. A., & Cherlin, A. J. (1991). The role of cohabitation in declining rates of marriage. *Journal of Marriage and the Family,* 913-27.

Casper, L. M., & Bianchi, S. M. (2002). *Continuity and change in the American family.* Thousand Oaks, CA: Sage Publications.

Cherlin, A. (2009). *Marriage, divorce, remarriage.* Boston: Harvard University Press.

Cherlin, A. J. (2004). The deinstitutionalization of American marriage. *Journal of Marriage and Family, 66*(4), 848-61.

Cohn, D., Passel, J. S., Wang, W., & Livingston, G. (2011). *Barely half of US adults are married–A record low.* Pew Research Center.

Cunningham, M., & Thornton, A. (2007). Direct and indirect influences of parents' marital instability on children's attitudes toward cohabitation in young adulthood. *Journal of Divorce & Remarriage, 46*(3), 125-43.

Curtin, S. C., Ventura, S. J., & Martinez, G. M. (2014). *Recent declines in nonmarital childbearing in the United States.* US Department of Health and Human Services, Centers for Disease Control and Prevention, National Center for Health Statistics.

Daugherty, J., & Copen, C. (2016). Trends in attitudes about marriage, child-bearing, and sexual behavior: United States, 2002, 2006-2010, and 2011-2013. *National Health Statistics Reports, 92*, 111.

Fields, J. (2004). America's families and living arrangements: 2003. *Current population reports* (pp. 20-553). Washington, DC: U.S. Census Bureau.

Forste, R., & Tanfer, K. (1996). Sexual exclusivity among dating, cohabiting, and married women. *Journal of Marriage and the Family, 58*, 33-47.

Hargrave, T. D. (2000). *The essential humility of marriage: Honoring the third identity in couple therapy.* Phoenix, AZ: Zeig, Tucker & Theisen.

Jose, A., O'Leary, D., & Moyer, A. K. (2010). Does premarital cohabitation predict subsequent marital stability and marital quality? A meta⊠analysis. *Journal of Marriage and Family, 72*(1), 105-16.

Kiernan, K. (2002). The state of European unions: An analysis of partnership formation and dissolution. In M. Macuraand & G. Beets (Eds.), *Dynamics of fertility and partnership in Europe: Insights and lessons from comparative research* (Vol. 1, pp. 57-76). New York, Geneva: United Nations.

Kline, G. H., Stanley, S. M., Markman, H. J., Olmos-Gallo, P. A., St Peters, M., Whitton, S. W., & Prado, L. M. (2004). Timing is everything: Pre-engagement cohabitation and increased risk for poor marital outcomes. *Journal of Family Psychology, 18*(2), 311.

Lichter, D. T., Turner, R. N., & Sassler, S. (2010). National estimates of the rise in serial cohabitation. *Social Science Research, 39*(5), 754-65.

Manning, W. D., & Cohen, J. A. (2012). Premarital cohabitation and marital dissolution: An examination of recent marriages. *Journal of Marriage and Family, 74*(2), 377-87.

Manning, W. D., Smock, P. J., & Bergstrom-Lynch, C. (2009). Cohabitation and parenthood: Lessons from focus groups and in-depth interviews. In E. Peters & C. Kamp (Eds.), *Marriage and family: Perspectives and complexities* (pp. 115-42). New York: Columbia University Press.

Nock, S. L. (1995). A comparison of marriages and cohabiting relationships. *Journal of Family Issues, 16*(1), 53-76.

Popenoe, D., & Whitehead, B. D. (1999). *The state of our unions: The social health of marriage in America 1999.* National Marriage Project, New Brunswick, NJ: Rutgers.

Prager, K. J. (2000). Intimacy in personal relationships. In C. Hendrick & S.S. Hendrick (Eds.), *Close relationships: A sourcebook* (pp. 228-45). Thousand Oaks, CA: Sage.

Rhoades, G. K., Stanley, S. M., & Markman, H. J. (2012). The impact of the transition to cohabitation on relationship functioning: Cross-sectional and longitudinal findings. *Journal of Family Psychology, 26*(3), 348.

Ridley, C. A., Peterman, D. J., & Avery, A. W. (1978). Cohabitation: Does it make for a better marriage? *Family Coordinator, 27*(2), 129-36.

Smock, P. J. (2000). Cohabitation in the United States: An appraisal of research themes, findings, and implications. *Annual Review of Sociology, 26*, 1-20.

Smock, P. J., Huang, P., Manning, W. D., & Bergstrom, C. A. (2006). Heterosexual cohabitation in the United States: Motives for living together among young men and women. Ann Arbor, 1001, 48106.

Stafford, L., Kline, S. L., & Rankin, C. T. (2004). Married individuals, cohabiters, and cohabiters who marry: A longitudinal study of relational and individual well-being. *Journal of Social and Personal Relationships, 21*(2), 231-48.

Stanley, S. M., Rhoades, G. K., & Markman, H. J. (2006). Sliding versus deciding: Inertia and the premarital cohabitation effect. *Family Relations, 55*(4), 499-509.

Stanley, S. M., Whitton, S. W., & Markman, H. J. (2004). Maybe I do: Interpersonal commitment and premarital or non-marital cohabitation. *Journal of Family Issues, 25*(4), 496-519.

Taylor, C. (2007). *A secular age*. Cambridge, MA: Harvard University Press.

Thornton, A., Axinn, W. G., Xie, Y. (2007). *Marriage and cohabitation*. Chicago: University of Chicago Press.

Treas, J., & Giesen, D. (2000). Sexual infidelity among married and cohabiting Americans. *Journal of Marriage and Family, 62*(1), 48-60.

Van der Valk, I., Spruijt, E., de Goede, M., Larsen, H., & Meeus, W. (2008). Family traditionalism and family structure: Attitudes and intergenerational transmission of parents and adolescents. *European Psychologist, 13*(2), 83-95.

Van Goethem, J. (2005). *Living together: A guide to counseling unmarried couples*. Grand Rapids: Kregel Academic.

Ventura, S. J., & Bacharach, A. (2000, revised). "Nonmarital Childbearing in the United States, 1940–99." *National Vital Statistics Reports, 48*(16), 1-40.

# LGBT+ COUPLES
# AND FAMILIES

*Integrity simply means not violating one's own identity.*

ERICH FROMM

*It is always the same: once you are liberated,*
*you are forced to ask who you are.*

JEAN BAUDRILLARD

Iɴ Jᴜɴᴇ ᴏꜰ 2015 the United States Supreme Court rendered a 5-4 decision on *Obergefell v. Hodges* that gay and lesbian persons have a constitutional right to marry. Many people celebrated that decision as a landmark case in establishing equal rights to gay persons, while those who are more socially conservative expressed concern about what these changes mean for the institution of marriage and for the broader society.

In the first edition of *Family Therapies* we discussed sexual identity primarily in terms of conflicts that may arise in a family in which a person comes out—it could either be an adolescent who announces a lesbian, gay, bisexual, or transgender (LGBT+) identity or a spouse who after years of marriage discloses his or her same-sex sexuality.

In this edition we recognize that those issues will still be important considerations for family therapists. At the same time, we anticipate cultural shifts in response to the Supreme Court ruling and simply more exposure to gay marriages and requests to serve LGBT+ persons in family therapy contexts. We believe in the not-so-distant future, "gay marriage" will not be the language in the United States but rather "marriage" will be the terminology, and it will simply be the case that some marriage therapy will occur with gay couples. Likewise, family therapy will be provided to gay couples who have a family either by adoption, a previous relationship, or through artificial insemination, and family therapists are already today and will to a growing extent be called on to provide services to an increasingly diverse array of family presentations.

## LGBT+ PERSONS AND THE FAMILY

It may be helpful to provide a brief overview of the research on sexual identity and LGBT+ persons and families. We do so by discussing prevalence estimates as well as various concerns that might lead LGBT+ persons and families to seek family therapy.

Recent research suggests that when asked about their sexual identity, about 1.6% of U.S. adults identify as gay or lesbian and 0.7% identify as bisexual (Ward, Dahlhamer, Galinsky, & Joestl, 2014). A much smaller percentage identifies as transgender (ranging from 1 in 215 to 1 in 300; Conron, Scott, Stowell, & Landers, 2012; Gates, 2011), which is an umbrella term for many ways in which a person might identify or express or live out a gender identity differently than those for whom their biological sex (as male or female) and gender identity align (Yarhouse, 2015).

As we turn our attention to couples and families, it is helpful to note the limitations in terminology. Some people prefer to designate same-sex couples to be broader and inclusive of both gay male and lesbian couples. Others might use LGB or LGBT or LGBT+ to designate the many ways in which people may adopt sexual and gender identity labels. In this chapter, we tend to describe gay male couples and lesbian couples and at times will refer to LGBT+ couples and/or families, recognizing that the vast majority of research reflects the experiences of gay male and lesbian couples, with relatively less research available on the experiences of bisexual men and women or transgender individuals (Goldberg, 2010).

The literature on LGBT+ couples and families can be organized in terms of couples, children of LGBT+ parents, parents with LGBT+ youth, and mixed-orientation couples. What do we know about each of these possible presentations?

*LGBT+ couples.* With the recent United States Supreme Court ruling we anticipate the research on LGBT+ couples will expand considerably. It has been estimated that in countries in which gay marriage has been legalized, about 20% of LGBT+ persons choose to marry. However, a Gallup poll conducted one year after the Supreme Court ruling found that 10.1% of LGBT+ Americans were married to a same-sex partner and 10.1% were cohabiting with a same-sex partner (Gallup, 2016).

It has been argued that LGBT+ relationships do not last as long as heterosexual ones because of higher frequencies of sex outside of the current relationship, indicating lower levels of commitment. For example, the National Lesbian Family Study (NLFS) conducted by Gartrell and colleagues (Gartrell et al., 2011) found that forty out of seventy-three lesbian-mother relationships dissolved by the time their child was seventeen years old. Other research (Goldberg & Garcia, 2015) has shown that relationship dissolution of lesbian or gay couples is about as frequent as it is for heterosexual couples. Both studies have relatively small sample sizes, and each gives its own reasoning for why the number is not higher or lower, depending on the point of view.

In terms of LGBT+ couples, most gay couples present for services asking for assistance with the same kinds of concerns requested by heterosexual couples. These include difficulties with communication, finances, parenting and shared responsibilities, and sexual intimacy (Green & Mitchell, 2008). Unique challenges are often associated with experiences of discrimination and varying degrees of family and social support, which can vary considerably for individual partners in a relationship and for a couples as a whole.

Discrimination and societal views have historically affected how same-sex couples met, what was modeled in terms of dating and relationship exploration, and expectations for the relationship. While this has historically meant limited opportunities to socialize and meet one another, recent cultural support for LGBT+ persons has expanded opportunities as evidenced in internet dating, social networks, and religious faith communities that provide avenues for meeting, dating, and socializing that was previously limited (Giammattei & Green, 2012).

*Children of LGBT+ parents.* As we consider family services to children of LGBT+ persons, it may be noted that LGBT+ parents form families in many ways. Some coupes pursue adoption; others consider artificial insemination. Still others are LGBT+ stepfamilies, by which we mean "one or both of the partners brought children to the lesbian or gay relationship from a previous heterosexual coupling" (Lynch & McMahon-Klosterman, 2012, p. 233). Each of these pathways to family will present different and unique considerations that we discuss later in this chapter.

It is difficult to get accurate estimates of how many children are raised by LGBT+ parents as well as what the experience is like for them. The political interests on both sides of the larger culture wars have made it difficult to get a very clear picture of what it is like for children raised by LGBT+ parents.[1] Proponents on both sides appear interested in proving a point or obtaining certain evidence, which may affect their ability to objectively disseminate findings. The Witherspoon Institute published a book titled *No Differences? How Children in Same-Sex Households Fare: Studies from Social Sciences* (Samuel, 2014) that aims to provide evidence that children who are raised by gay parents have significant differences from those raised by heterosexual parents. This book was a direct challenge to the APA's 2005 document stating there were no studies of children of LGBT+ individuals that showed any negative effect.

Marks (2012) argues that previous research that shows no difference is centered on small convenience samples and should be called into question. Regnerus's (2012) study that indicated significant differences on twenty-five out of forty outcome measures for a large group of children is also highlighted. Regnerus reported that children of same-sex parents scored suboptimally on measures of receiving welfare, needing therapy, STIs, sexual victimization, and lower educational attainment, to name a few. Altogether, the text paints a picture that "in a cross-section of children raised by parents in same-sex relationships, life outcomes tend to resemble those of children raised by single and divorced parents" (Londregan, 2014, p. 14).

On the other hand, those from the mainstream LGBT+ community have multiple problems with the research presented by the Witherspoon Institute. For example, Cheng and Powell (2015) reexamined Regnerus's (2012) study based on the belief it reflected poor methodology. They stated that there was not a valid or reliable measure of family type, which may conflate some of the findings. Additionally, they indicated that Regnerus may have overestimated

---

[1] This section is adapted from Mark A. Yarhouse, Justin Sides, and Cassandra Page, "The Complexities of Multicultural Competence with LGBT+ Populations," in Craig Frisby and William O'Donohue (eds.), *Cultural Competence in Applied Psychology: Theory, Science, Practice, and Evaluation.*

the number of children with gay or lesbian parents, as his definition of an LGBT+ family was somewhat confusing. After reanalyzing the data, they believe that, had all the respondents been properly categorized, there would be no significant difference between those raised by same-sex parents and those raised by heterosexual parents.

Other research conducted by those in the mainstream LGBT+ community consistently find that children of same-sex parents have outcomes similar to those raised by heterosexual parents. Some suggest that these children are better off because they must create new identities, examine what they believe, and think critically due to their different situation (Sasnett, 2015). Others suggest that the psychological well-being of children with same-gender parents is better than those of heterosexual parents (Fedewa, Black, & Ahn, 2015).

There is essentially no consensus among researchers who represent such different interests, and it may be that each side is serving its own bias. Because of this, there are many things that we do not know. We do not know if having same-sex parents will increase the likelihood of an individual exploring same-sex sexuality or identifying as lesbian, gay, or bisexual (and on one "side" of the cultural debate the very question is itself not a concern). We also do not know whether or not having same-sex parents has a universal effect on the psychological well-being of children or their development. Additionally, we do not know any mediating factors that may be influencing findings. In sum, what is uncertain is this: If there are differences, are they a direct result of the parents themselves or of other factors in the environment, such as societal views and relational strains with extended family? These are ample avenues to pursue in future research.

Despite the disagreements and the questions surrounding the research, there are a few things that we do know. We know that there will be an increase in LGBT+ families and that there are different views which may affect how the families operate and how they experience themselves. We also know that LGBT+ parents oftentimes face more discrimination and more obstacles in parenting, specifically when adopting (Farr & Patterson, 2013). Furthermore, we know that there is no consensus on LGBT+ families and their effect on children and society as a whole.

*Parents and LGBT+ youth*. Parents often view news that their child has come out as LGBT+ as a crisis for the family, a response that has been seen among families in general (e.g., Strommen, 1993) and among Christian parents specifically (e.g., Maslowe & Yarhouse, 2015; Yarhouse, Houp, Sadusky & Zaporozhets, 2016). As Savin-Williams (1989, p. 3) observed, many parents "consider their children to be extensions of themselves," and negative implications of being gay can sometimes be the first thing to come to a parent's mind. Parents also often have dreams for their children's future based on an assumed heterosexual identity. These dreams may include traditional marriage and grandchildren, which may feel at risk or lost when a child comes out.

It has been suggested that negative responses from parents may be based on applying past negative connotations of homosexuality onto their teen (Strommen, 1993) or may be a reflection of a worldview response that reflects a perceived incompatibility with Christian faith and sexual or religious identity (Maslowe & Yarhouse, 2015). It will be interesting to see whether this changes with increased social acceptance of civil rights issues related to homosexuality, but at this time many parents may have such negative connotations, which may be further complicated by guilt and shame on the part of parents who often fear they may have caused their adolescent's homosexuality (Ritter & Terndrup, 2002).

Common negative emotional responses reported by parents include shock, confusion, and value conflict (Maslowe & Yarhouse, 2015). Often parents' religious faith communities have shaped their understanding of homosexuality as a sin and immoral, and the realization that their long-held beliefs now apply to their own child is difficult for many parents. Parents who deeply love and care for their child may find great difficulty in navigating a relationship postdisclosure.

The parent-child relationship is the best predictor of a child's well-being over time: "Both risk and protective factors can be found within the family, and family relationships can generate stress as well as provide instrumental and emotional support that promotes mental health" (Elizur & Ziv 2001, p. 129). Parental responses that are supportive and accepting toward gay children have been shown to be important. These supportive responses include maintaining the relationship, participating in open communication, and showing emotional support (Elizur & Ziv, 2001). Negative parental reactions that rise to the level of rejecting behaviors—such as verbal, physical, or emotional abuse; blaming; and isolation from family members—can have a lasting adverse psychological impact on gay youth (Ryan, Huebner, Diaz, & Sanchez, 2009; Szymanski & Gupta, 2009). Emotional and psychological consequences can include risk for increased mental illness, suicidality, and decreased self-esteem (Ryan et al., 2009).

When conflicts in the family arise that center on sexual or gender identity, we see several frequently asked questions, such as What causes a homosexual orientation? and Can a homosexual orientation change? If we were to summarize the literature of causation, we would have to say that the origins of homosexuality are not clearly understood. The most often-cited psychological causes are related to psychodynamic theory, which has tended to implicate parent-child relationships. Critics argue that there is little or mixed empirical support for the dynamic theory. However, proponents of a psychodynamic viewpoint to studies implicating early childhood development, including factors such as disordered family relationships (e.g., loss of a parent because of death or divorce), early homosexual experiences, and childhood sexual abuse (for a review of this literature, see Jones & Yarhouse, 2000).

Much more attention has been given in recent years to the biological hypothesis—that is, that there may be genetic or prenatal hormonal influences on later sexual orientation. Research on genetic differences includes twin studies (e.g., Bailey & Pillard, 1991) and chromosomal markers that may be associated with a homosexual orientation (e.g., Hamer, Hu, Magnuson, Hu, & Pattatucci, 1993; Hu, Pattatucci, Patterson, Li, Fulker et al., 1995).

In any case, both psychological and biological theories of the etiology of homosexuality have some empirical support. No research to date provides ample support for any one theory to the exclusion of another. It may be more accurate and more helpful to pursue an "interactionist hypothesis" (Byne & Parsons, 1993; Jones & Yarhouse, 2000) where various psychological, environmental, and biological antecedents contribute to differing degrees that vary from person to person (in addition to decisions made by the person at key points in his or her life). In any case, perhaps future research will provide greater clarity than what is available at present, although there is no compelling reason to believe that any one theory will sufficiently explain such a diverse and complex phenomenon.

A similar story can be told about the causes of gender dysphoria, which refers to the distress some people report when their biological sex and gender identity do not align. The most popular theory of causation today is called the "brain-sex" theory, which considers the implications of different times that sex differentiation occurs in the developing fetus. Since we know that sex

differentiation of the genitals occurs earlier in fetal development and sex differentiation of the brain occurs later in fetal development, is it possible that
the genitals differentiate in one direction while the brain could differentiate
in the other direction in rare instances? The research to support this theory is
mixed, and other theories implicating environment are also under consideration, such as insufficient adult role models, parental psychiatric issues, and
parental preference for a child of the other sex (see Yarhouse, 2015, pp. 67-80).

The question, Can a homosexual orientation change? is also a challenging
one to answer. On the one hand, is it possible that there is greater fluidity in
sexual attractions or orientation for some people than others? That appears
to be the case, and some research of sexual minority females, in particular,
suggests that this natural fluidity can lead to changes in self-report of attractions, fantasy, and behavior over time (Diamond, 2006). On the other hand,
is it possible to change sexual orientation apart from any natural fluidity?
The most sophisticated study on sexual orientation change (Jones & Yarhouse, 2007) followed participants in Exodus ministries over three to four
years and reported the following categories: Success: Conversion (15% of the
sample); Success: Chastity (23%); Continuing (29%); Nonresponse (15%);
Failure: Confused (4%); and Failure: Gay Identity (8%). "Failure" was from
a ministry perspective in which the ministry was assisting the person in
leaving homosexuality and moving toward chastity and is not intended to
suggest anything about the persons who made different decisions about
their own attractions and behavior. The major improvement in this study
over previous research was the prospective, longitudinal design of the study.
However, even those who reported success also reported same-sex attraction
from time to time, and it is probably accurate to say that while there was an
average shift along a continuum of attraction for people, those averages suggested that there was more of a shift for some than for others, and many
people reported no such shift. Indeed, most probably did not experience as
much change as they had hoped for.

Taken together, there is much more consensus that sexual behavior can be
changed, and there is some evidence that attractions can also change, though
it appears to occur less frequently. Some changes may be a reflection of
natural fluidity.

In family therapy, the questions of causation and change usually center
on the follow-up questions from parents, Am I the cause? and Can you do

something to fix this? Our response is that we do not see the parents as the cause of their son or daughter's sexual orientation or gender identity, nor do we see family therapy as a context for sexual orientation to change. We focus more on helping parents express love to their child, as the parent-child relationship is the most important predictor of their child's well-being over time. Teens and emerging adults often feel loved conditionally when their parents place a premium on change of orientation, and parents would do well to put their energy behind embodied love and support for their child as he or she is navigating important sexual or gender identity questions at this time.

*Mixed-orientation couples.* Mixed-orientation couples are couples in which one partner experiences same-sex attraction and may or may not identify as gay, while the other spouse is heterosexual (Buxton, 2001, 2006). It has been estimated that between one and two million individuals in the United States have been in or are in a mixed-orientation marriage, based on the latest census and conservative estimates that take into account the percentage of the population that is estimated to be gay and the average percentage of those who marry (Buxton, 2001, 2006). National health statistics showed that for individuals aged fifteen to forty-four, 0.4% of currently married men and 2.1% of currently married women identify as bisexual (Chandra, Mosher, Copen, & Sionean, 2011). A Gallup poll (2016) published a year after the Supreme Court ruling in favor of gay marriage found that 13.6% of LGBT+ Americans were married to a partner of the opposite sex and that another 5% were cohabiting with a partner of the opposite sex.

Studies have shown that individuals in mixed-orientation marriages enter into such relationships for a variety of reasons: a lack of awareness or denial of orientation at time of marriage, social pressure/social acceptance, family expectations or a desire to leave home, desire for children, desire for a family life, genuine love or affection, sex, companionship, pregnancy, disillusionment with the LGBT+ lifestyle, and/or seeking a solution to same-sex attraction (Buxton, 2006; Latham & White, 1978; Yarhouse, Pawlowski, & Tan, 2003). Others have suggested that religious socialization is a primary reason (Hernandez & Wilson, 2007). At some point in the relationship, it is likely that the heterosexual partner will learn of their spouse's sexual orientation. That experience may precipitate a crisis and is often the focus of care and crisis management in family therapy, which we discuss later in this chapter.

## COMMON PRESENTING CONCERNS

We discussed above the many ways in which LGBT+ persons and families may enter into family therapy. We take a look now at common presenting concerns for LGBT+ couples, work with parents whose kids have come out, services to children of LGBT+ parents, and mixed-orientation couples.

*LGBT+ couples.* The literature on working with LGBT+ couples is likely to expand significantly in the coming years. Much of it to date distinguishes gay male and lesbian couples, although we recognize many other couple formations that would include bisexual and transgender persons; however, there is much less literature available on their experiences.

Gay male and lesbian couples tend to "operate on the same principles" as heterosexual couples in many respects (Gottman et al., 2003, p. 24). Gay couples tend to report greater autonomy than heterosexual couples as well as "fewer barriers to leaving" (p. 24), although this may change to the extent that gay couples enter into marriage.

When gay male couples come in for therapy, they often do so around common couple concerns, such as finances, communication, and sexual intimacy. Tunnell (2012) discusses common therapeutic tasks for couples in general and then connects those tasks to services provided to gay male couples. The three tasks are (1) creating a boundary around a couple, (2) dealing with differences and conflict, and (3) regulating closeness and distance.

This historical lack of role models for gay males has been cited by many authors as a limitation that affects how gay males see themselves and their relationships. The fact that gay marriage is legal in the United States does not mean most gay males (or lesbians) will enter into marriage, but marital therapy with gay male couples will likely entail identifying how the couple has created a sense of "us" or cohesion. What boundaries exist between them as a couple and those around them? Again, this is true for all couples, but given the lack of role models for gay males, it may be especially helpful to highlight the impact of the lack of modeling on them as a couple as well as the societal messages about gay male sexuality and sexual behavior that may prevent them from seeing the potential in their relationship.

As family therapists consider differences and conflict among gay couples, they can normalize this as a common adjustment all couples face following the initial honeymoon phase (Tunnell, 2012). What may be a more unique challenge for gay males is staying emotionally engaged long enough to hear one another out, to air differences, and to identify helpful styles of communi-cation that lead to conflict resolution. Gay males tend to escalate rather than shut down: "When fighting becomes too intense in heterosexual couples, the man eventually shuts down; whereas in male couples, the men continue to fight as though it would be shameful to back down to another man" (p. 27). In previous research (e.g., Gottman et al., 2003) validation was important for gay males (compared to lesbian couples, who placed greater value on affection).

Interestingly, in Gottman's research on gay couples, it was reported that healthy gay (and lesbian) couples tended to be more emotionally expressive, with higher levels of physiological activation, which contrasts sharply with re-search on healthy heterosexual couples, for whom "high levels of physiological arousal were found to be associated with lower relationship satisfaction and higher risk for relationship dissolution" (Gottman et al., 2003, p. 39). Gottman sees this as potentially reflecting "emotional engagement," "mental effort," and a "positive state of involvement rather than detachment" (pp. 39-40).

Family therapists can also help gay male couples regulate emotional closeness. This is related to emotional engagement, but it also addresses the tendency for men to be more autonomous, separate, and emotionally self-reliant (Tunnell, 2012). Attachment-based therapy has been recommended for work with gay males and would entail engaging clients in "an in vivo 'corrective emotional experience' where warded-off feelings are felt in the body and ex-pressed in the presence of a caring and encouraging attachment figure" (p. 30).

Lesbian couples are also considered similar to heterosexual couples in many regards. Differences have been noted in terms of autonomy and egali-tarian roles as well as more frequent relationship dissolution, but, again, this may change among those who enter into marriage, and some preliminary research seems to support that (Gottman et al., 2003).

With lesbian couples, there is more discussion of the experience of emo-tional closeness as something more unique to women than what is found among gay males and among heterosexual couples. Some authors express concern that lesbian couples may be pathologized or held to a heterosexual norm if red flags are raised with respect to what is at times referred to as en-meshment (e.g., Connolly, 2012), but it is at least important to be aware of a tendency toward emotional closeness in ways that may or may not be part of the presenting concern or otherwise play a role in difficulties being brought to therapy.

Part of what has been identified in the research literature that connects to emotional closeness is the desire for emotional expression through affection rather than validation, which gay male couples tend to prefer (Gottman et al., 2003). In addition to emotional closeness, family therapists can be aware of how gender roles have been modeled for women and how they play out in lesbian relationships:

> Women in particular value connection, are encouraged to do so, and often define themselves in terms of the relationships in their lives. . . . Thus when lesbian couples experience conflicts or difficulties in a relationship, individual needs frequently become secondary to the relationship needs. (Connolly, 2012, p. 46)

The gender roles discussed above are related to emotional closeness and socialization and may also be helpful to discuss in therapy.

Although there are many approaches to working with lesbian couples, therapists often draw on feminist theory to inform clinical practice. This entails not only respect for women's experiences and a collaborative posture in therapy but also becomes a means of "validating, strengthening, and promoting resilience in lesbian couple treatment" (Connolly, 2012, p. 48).

**Children of LGBT+ parents.** It can be helpful to keep in mind the areas of stress and vulnerability for children of LGBT+ parents and/or for LGBT+ stepfamilies. There simply has not been a social structure for support for these increasingly visible families. The literature on providing services to children of LGBT+ parents suggests that assumptions about what a "normal" family looks like can be difficult for children who experience their own family as "different" or "less than" what is considered the norm (Kuvalanka, 2012).

LGBT+ parents may also need assistance working through the events that led up to the formation of their family. These could include adoption, surrogacy, donor insemination, or a heterosexual relationship (Kuvalanka, 2012). These pathways to family may be important to assess and be aware of in providing services.

Parents may also seek assistance in disclosing their LGBT+ identity to their own children. In most cases, this appears to be more common when a parent adopts an LGBT+ identity following the birth or adoption of their child and the child was exposed to their parent as heterosexual (Kuvalanka, 2012). This would be in contrast to *de novo* (or from the beginning) families, in which an LGBT+ identity was established by the parents prior to birth or adoption.

For LGBT+ adoptive parents, family therapists can be aware of three specific challenges that may arise. The first is simply making sense of one's adoption story:

> Marcos, a young Colombian child, adopted at age 5, spent the first full year with his adoptive family making the same statements during dinner each night: "You came to get me in Colombia and I was with Maria and now she is in Colombia and we're here and you're my mami and she isn't, right? Why did you come and get me?" Before a response could be given, Marcos would continue with his statements. "Is Maria still my mami? Are we going back to Colombia, or are we staying here? Does Maria know where I am? Will I always stay here with you?" A child's ability to make sense of his or her adoption story and discover language to create his or her own narrative facilitates attachment as well as identity formation. Practitioners can best support this goal by providing concrete strategies for parents that include recalling the child's adoption story during such family rituals as those engaged in during dinner and at bedtime; looking at life books, photographs, and other memorabilia related to adoption; and, finally, demonstrating increased comfort with the child's memories of parents, caregivers, and experiences that predate the adoptive parents' arrival in their child's life. (Kuvalanka, 2012, p. 224)

In addition to making sense of one's adoption story, there is also the challenge of peer group response in childhood. Family therapists can work with parents to help their child respond to hurtful words from peers about their family. This would include coaching on how a child in third grade, for example, responds when a peer asks, Where is your real mom? or Why do you have two dads? (Gianino & Novelle, 2012, p. 223).

In adolescence, this would shift to forming one's own identity while also having a family identity. Decisions to disclose family structure to other adolescents can present unique challenges, and family therapy may provide a setting for processing that. Frequently asked questions may include "Who is safe (or not safe) to tell? How do I choose? Can I trust they will keep it a secret? What will I do if they freak out? Do I have to tell—can't my friends just figure it out? It is not me—I'm not gay, so why do I need to tell anyone at all?" (Kuvalanka, 2012, p. 226).

So the role that secrets play in some families may be important. These secrets may be about identity and may be based on parental fear or concern that greater openness may lead to negative evaluation or stigma or other consequences, such as when parents wish to protect their children from being teased, harassed, or bullied by their peers because of their parents' LGBT+ identity (Kuvalanka, 2012).

Assessing the relationship the family has to their own families-of-origin will be important, as there may be resources and support available; conversely, a family therapist may find that there are cut-offs and strained relationships that isolate this family, or that stigma and shame is a part of what the family faces. It is the frequent experience of many LGBT+ couples that they cannot rely on their families-of-origin for support regarding relational issues, and this separation requires them to create a communal family with others outside of their biological relationships. The family therapist plays a crucial role in helping systems heal the divide that has occurred—sometimes related to the same-sex partnership and other times related to a common life crisis such as illness, job loss, natural disaster, and trauma.

Family therapists may also play an important supportive role in the local school. Whether this is elementary school, middle school, or high school, there may be a role to play in discussing or advocating for safety in some school settings (particularly in response to verbal harassment but potentially much worse) as well as helping families make decisions among school systems, if that is a consideration (Kuvalanka, 2012).

*Parents and LGBT+ youth.* The model of family response to LGBT+ identity discussed by Strommen (1993) suggests several stages that can begin with the suspicion that the young person may be struggling with sexual identity questions. This has been characterized as an early, unacknowledged sense among some family members that the young person may be sexually attracted to the same sex. It is also possible, of course, for other family members to be taken completely unaware, adding to the intensity of their emotional response when faced with a disclosure.

This unacknowledged sense may be tied to adolescent self-report of feeling different from their peers in childhood (Yarhouse & Tan, 2004). They may have played more with the opposite sex or shared more interests and activities with members of the opposite sex, engaging in cross-sex-typed play, as when a boy plays more with dolls or prefers to dress up like a princess, or when a girl plays more with trucks and prefers to dress up like the king or prince. However, some adolescents who have same-sex feelings do not report gender-atypical play and dress, so the disclosure or discovery that an adolescent is identifying as gay may be a genuine shock to his or her parents. (Of course, some heterosexuals report engaging in cross-sex-typed play during childhood, so this is not a consistent indicator—just a more consistent and robust association.)

When we discuss parents who may suspect a young person is dealing with sexual or gender identity, concerns may be more likely in cases of gender dysphoria. Most cases of gender dysphoria reflect what is referred to as "early onset," by which we mean experienced at a young age (perhaps as young as two to four years of age) and is less of a surprise to parents (Yarhouse et al., in press; Yarhouse, 2015). Although gender dysphoria is a rare phenomenon, increased exposure to the topic in media and entertainment has more parents thinking about the possibility and having some idea of what it could mean for an adolescent to identity as transgender.

The next stage reflects the impact on other family members of the disclosure or discovery of same-sex feelings, behavior, or identity. Often young people disclose to their parents last, after they have already disclosed to friends and siblings. In studies of Christian young adults, for example, disclosure to a youth pastor often occurred first or just after disclosure to a friend, but in almost every case it occurred prior to disclosure to one's parents (e.g., Yarhouse, Brooke, Pisano, & Tan, 2005; cf., Yarhouse, Stratton, Dean, & Brooke, 2007). So by the time most parents learn of their adolescent's sexual identity concerns, their teen has likely already been discussing their experiences with others. What makes this challenging is that it's often the first time the parents are taking in information that is emotionally charged, yet the adolescent has been processing the concerns for some time. This actually may facilitate the teen taking a more "settled" position on their identity when they are talking to their parents. A settled position may be met with acceptance by some parents, but others will be quite distressed, in part because they have not been participants in what they see as an important time in which their son or daughter has been navigating sexual identity questions. Feelings of confusion, grief, and anticipatory loss may be communicated as anger or personal disappointment, which can make building bridges even more complicated.

We mentioned above that gender identity concerns are different than sexual identity concerns insofar as gender dysphoria in most cases is "early onset." It is possible for gender dysphoria to present as "late onset" and be very much a surprise to parents and lead to requests for family therapy. In these cases, there is often a pressure from the teen to pursue specific resolutions or adopt a cross-gender identity or make a social transition of some kind, while parents are often left in a place of great skepticism toward the gender dysphoria diagnosis itself.

In any case, this stage of disclosure and its impact on family members is often followed by a time in which family members try to help. What form that help takes may vary considerably from family to family and can range from outright acceptance to the expectation that the teen enter professional or ministry counseling to assist them with change of orientation or healing. Other family members may talk of it as a "phase" or may otherwise try to keep the issue hidden from others to reduce family stigma. This last point appears to be especially salient in conservative religious circles and in some ethnic minority groups. In any case, early efforts to help often reflect a desire to "fix" the situation or the adolescent, and this can be very upsetting to the teen.

A free-floating sense of anxiety and loss and some anticipatory grief has also been reported by parents (Maslowe & Yarhouse, 2015). A free-floating sense of anxiety and loss (or just negative affect) can be present and may come out "sideways" in relationships. Parents may also grieve the loss of how they thought things would unfold for their son or daughter and for themselves in the next ten years or more. That could include a picture of grandchildren, family gatherings, and so on (Strommen, 1993).

Gender identity concerns in childhood tend to resolve by the time a child reaches late adolescence or emerging adulthood. When they do not resolve, then gender dysphoria does not tend to go away and the person is faced with decisions about how to manage the dysphoria, and these management strategies can vary considerably from person to person. Oftentimes, family therapy is suggested to help improve communication and support as the later adolescent or emerging adult is facing really difficult decisions about interventions—some of which are medical interventions—that can be partially reversible or irreversible.

There frequently comes a time when families face the reality of their loved one's same-sex sexuality or enduring gender dysphoria. There is clearly an underdeveloped "theodicy of sexual identity" or "theodicy of gender identity" in the church today—a lack of appreciation for what it means to find meaning in perceived loss when one's experiences and constraints seem to be in sharp contrast to cultural assumptions about sexual self-actualization or simple resolutions of gender identity conflicts. This can lead to a reappraisal of what options are worth exploring, and adolescents and parents may differ as to what they see as options at this point. Family therapists can help family members improve the quality of their interactions as they discuss assumptions, expectations, and wishes as well as practical considerations for relating to one another within the family and to those outside of the family.

Although a more extensive Christian critique will be offered later in this chapter, it should be noted that families coming out of a conservative religious perspective seem especially interested in the possibility of healing and/or change of orientation. Often an adolescent is also concerned about same-sex feelings in light of his or her own beliefs and values. While this is often referred to as "internalized homophobia" in gay literature and resources (Ritter & Terndrup, 2002), it may also reflect a competing and alternative way of thinking about one's same-sex feelings so that they are not the central dimension of a person's identity (Yarhouse & Burkett, 2003; Yarhouse & Tan, 2004; Yarhouse, Stratton, Dean, & Brooke, 2007).

Be that as it may, we want to highlight that the family therapy aspect that is often most salient is to recognize the desire to "fix" a family member rather than sit with a family member and offer support in the context of existing family relationships. While there may be value in exploring a range of options provided everyone is interested in doing so, the focus of family therapy would be on improving communication and mutual understanding and respect so that support—in whatever form it takes—can be offered and received.

*Mixed-orientation couples.* As we turn our attention to common presenting concerns among mixed-orientation couples, the primary concern is the crisis that frequently follows awareness of one's spouse being gay. In most cases, the heterosexual spouse is unaware that they married someone who is attracted to the same sex. This becomes known over the course of time through disclosure by the LGBT+ spouse or by discovery. There are four broad stages of relationship change postawareness of the mixed-orientation status in a marriage: awareness, emotional response, acceptance of reality, and negotiating a future (Yarhouse & Kays, 2010; cf., Buxton, 2004; Hernandez & Wilson, 2007).

The first stage, *awareness*, refers to the disclosure or discovery itself. This experience varies considerably. Did the spouse who experiences same-sex attraction bring this to their husband or wife as a kind of ongoing struggle? Or is awareness a result of the discovery of a same-sex relationship? In other words, there are many ways to enter the stage of awareness, and the entry points become much of what a family therapist responds to and often sets a course for therapy.

The second stage is *emotional response*, which is frequently disbelief, shock, anger, and confusion. A spouse's emotional response is connected to awareness, obviously, but it also can eventually shift to greater compassion and empathy depending on the circumstances and relationship.

The next stage is *acceptance of reality*. This is essentially coming to terms with the reality of one spouse's same-sex sexuality. It may also entail coming to terms with any same-sex behavior or relationship as well as the practical implications of those experiences or relationships. Both spouses move away from denial or minimization of the impact of awareness and come to terms with decisions that both will be making about the future of their relationship.

The final stage is *negotiating a future*. This involves making a decision independently and together about where each person and the marriage goes from here. Many considerations are brought to the table, including commitments spouses have made to each other and to their children, the love and friendship or companionship that they have enjoyed, and issues related to sexuality and sexual intimacy.

We recommend an approach to family therapy referred to as the PARE model (Yarhouse & Kays, 2010). There are four steps: (1) provide sexual identity therapy, (2) address "interpersonal trauma," (3) foster reliance, and (4) enhance sexual intimacy.

To offer a summary of this approach, Sexual Identity Therapy (SIT) is a client-centered, identity-focused approach to navigating sexual identity conflicts among sexual minorities (Throckmorton & Yarhouse, 2006; Yarhouse, 2008). It follows a theoretical model and empirical research on sexual identity development (Yarhouse, 2001) and empirical research (Yarhouse & Tan, 2004) on the experiences of Christians who identity as gay and those who dis-identify with a gay identity. In terms of core elements, SIT focuses on (a) a three-tier distinction between same-sex attraction, a homosexual orientation, and a gay identity; (b) differences in weight given to aspects of identity; (c) attributional search for sexual identity; and (d) facilitating personal congruence.

The primary work in SIT will be with the spouse who has come out, but both this spouse and his or her heterosexual spouse can benefit from the psychoeducation component found in explaining the three-tier distinction, weighted aspects of identity, and attributional search for sexual identity. There is something to be gained in using descriptive language and coming to an understanding that decisions can be made about achieving congruence.

The main focus of the next stage of the framework is responding to the potential "interpersonal trauma" of discovering that one's partner is attracted to the same sex. It has been suggested that disclosure or discovery of same-sex attraction or behavior in a marriage relationship can feel to the non–sex minority spouse like a betrayal of trust, particularly if there has been same-sex behavior (e.g., Yarhouse & Seymore, 2006). Even in cases in which there has been no same-sex behavior but only attraction, it can feel confusing to the non–sexual minority spouse who may wonder if there has been deception or a misrepresentation of their spouse's identity and experience.

Although mixed-orientation couples have not been studied per se, other couples researchers have looked at stages couples go through following major relationship offenses, such as affairs, deception, and violation of trust. This is the original of the phrase "interpersonal trauma," a phrase used to designate relationship offenses, such as betrayals and affairs (Gordon, Baucom, Snyder, Atkins, & Christensen, 2006).

It can be helpful to work through a three-stage approach to the potential "interpersonal trauma" associated with disclosure or discovery of same-sex attraction or behavior in a mixed-orientation relationship. The three stages are (1) impact, (2) a search for meaning, and (3) recovery (Gordon & Baucom, 2003).

A conversation around impact would spend some time on how the spouse first came to discover his or her partner's same-sex sexuality and/or behavior. It could look like this:

THERAPIST: How did you first come to learn about your husband's same-sex sexuality?

WIFE: I actually saw a text message on his phone one day. It was pretty careless of him to leave it out, but I looked. I just thought there was something wrong, something "off" about his time away from home. I don't know. But there was this text from a man I guess he was seeing.

THERAPIST: What happened next?

WIFE: He was in the other room. I went right up to him and put the phone in his face and said, "What's this?" He stammered a little.

I think he was in shock. I know I was, but I was also angry and hurt and confused.

THERAPIST: You think he was in shock and that you were in shock.

WIFE: Yes. I was really stunned. I knew that there was some distance in our marriage. We had drifted, but I guess I thought every couple drifts. Do you know what I mean? I wondered about an affair, about whether he would ever cheat, but I had no idea that he would be with a man. That blew my mind.

Discussion of the impact will cover several sessions. At some point the spouse is beginning to explore what the discovery means in terms of an overarching story that makes sense. This is called a search for meaning. A therapist could explore a search for meaning in many ways, but here is one example:

THERAPIST: How do you make sense of all of this today? The affair? Your husband's same-sex sexuality?

WIFE: I don't know. I'm trying to work it out in my mind. I pray about it. My husband told me before we were married that he had been approached by a man when he was an older child, and that the man had invited him to watch pornography and had done some things. So I knew there was a history of abuse. But there hadn't been any sexual behavior on my husband's part—at least, that I knew of—after that or during our marriage. So it's confusing to me. I'm trying to get a handle on what it means.

THERAPIST: So part of getting a handle on it has been reflecting on the abuse your husband reported going through many years ago. That that was part of his history, part of his story. But that still leaves you with questions.

WIFE: Yes. I feel bad for him when I think of him as a boy and when I think of that early exposure to pornography and to sexual behavior. I feel bad for him. I do. But I don't know how to connect that to where we are today. I feel like that was then, but we have a marriage here to figure out. We have children to raise. We have a life to live.

THERAPIST: You also mentioned you pray about it.

WIFE: Every day. I ask God why it happened. What is this all about? What do you want me to do? All of it. It's been the hardest thing I've ever faced.

Finally, recovery in this context refers to coming to a place where the spouse can make a decision about the future of the marriage. A search for meaning can take a person in many directions. Some spouses wish to release their partner, who they see as gay and who they believe would be happier in a same-sex relationship. Other spouses see their partner wanting to stay in the marriage for a variety of reasons. They, too, may wish to stay in the marriage. They may together come to view the same-sex attractions as part of the spouse's life and a challenge that they face but not as something that needs to be central to either identity or behavior. They may decide to stay together. But staying together or ending the marriage is often connected to a search for meaning. A spouse who is recovering from discovery of same-sex sexuality and/or behavior is at some point in a better emotional state to make decisions about that future trajectory.

For those couples that decide to stay together, what are some practical steps clinicians can take to foster resilience? Although the research is not as well-developed as we might like, we do see some themes emerging from the studies that have been conducted thus far (for an extended discussion of these themes, see Yarhouse & Kays, 2010). These themes are associated with communication, cohesion/commitment, and flexibility/role negotiation.

It is important to communicate early on that the couple is developing something unique together. In other words, they are not comparing their sexual intimacy to that of others or to past experiences; rather, they are pouring into their own relationship and creating something that they can both enjoy. This is very similar to what we communicate in general sex therapy with a heterosexual couple, but it is important to convey, as couples in mixed-orientation relationships may have worries that lead them to make comparisons that will ultimately detract from their experience. This can include a discussion of "ghosts" in the bedroom or thoughts of former partners or the insecurities that can come when the non–sexual minority spouse worries about that being on the mind of the sexual minority spouse.

## CHRISTIAN CRITIQUE AND ENGAGEMENT

*Recognize tensions in role integration.* Individuals who pursue licensure to practice as family therapists or in another mental health profession agree to be regulated by the applicable law and regulations in the state they are licensed. There is a sense of professional accountability to serve the public. When we discuss Christians entering into this public place of trust—this fiduciary space—we refer to this as role integration. Role integration refers to serving the public good and doing so self-consciously as a Christian (Yarhouse & Hathaway, 2016). Challenges involving role integration arise when Christians consider working with a range of presenting concerns that may represent value conflicts for the clinician. How does a Christian enter into a regulated profession, agree to abide by the regulations, and answer to the regulators for their practice activities while at the same time work with people who may make choices or have experiences that differ considerably from their own?

For example, do Christians provide services to heterosexual couples who are cohabiting? Do they work with people of other religious faith traditions or no faith tradition? Given the topic of this chapter, do Christians provide couples therapy to a gay couple? What about family therapy to a gay couple that is raising adopted children? Do Christians provide therapy to a person navigating gender identity questions and who is seriously considering hormonal treatment and/or surgical interventions?

On the other hand, what does it mean to refuse to offer such services? If it is ultimately about having a cultural witness, is it more of a witness to refuse services on the grounds that there is a potential value conflict, or is it more of a witness to serve the public good with competence and integrity?

Some Christians may assume they can carefully select a client population to maintain a caseload of preferred family cases that represent no value conflicts or no risk-management concerns and that in many ways reflect their clinical preferences. However, family therapists simply cannot predict how individual clients and families will present over the course of time, and in an increasingly diverse and pluralistic culture, we see it as important that Christian family therapists are prepared to serve a wide-ranging client population (Yarhouse & Hathaway, 2016).

We are likewise ambivalent about conscience clause legislations, particularly as they in recent years have reflected perceived conflicts with LGBT+ issues. Completely separate from the recent focus on LGBT+ issues, we recognize that there is a long list of potential points of conflict for family therapists that span from histories of abortion; religious/spiritual beliefs that vary from their own; infidelity; separation; divorce and remarriage; criminal conduct, including child molestation; and so on—experiences that may not be in keeping with a family therapist's own values or may in other ways reflect a point of conflict or tension. Family therapists who are not prepared to navigate such conflicts would likely be stilted in their ability to practice in almost any setting, even in their own private practice (Yarhouse & Hathaway, 2016). These are larger issues for family therapists and for training programs as well as for what it means to provide resources that serve a diverse and pluralistic culture.

*Recognize competing frameworks.* In addition to questions about Christians who provide family therapy and serve the public, it may be helpful to critique and engage the broader landscape of discussion surrounding sexual and gender identity concerns. It may be helpful to distinguish three different frameworks people often rely on to understand sexual and gender identity concerns. These frameworks function as lenses through which people view the topics. These three contrasting frameworks are (1) the integrity framework, (2) the disability framework, and (3) the diversity framework.

The first framework is the *integrity* framework. This framework or lens through which people see these topics views sex and gender and, therefore, sexual and gender identity conflicts in terms of what one evangelical theologian refers to as "the sacred integrity of maleness or femaleness stamped on one's body" (Gagnon, 2007, p. 3). Homosexuality is viewed as problematic because sexual intimacy between members of the same sex is viewed as a violation of the "sacred integrity" that was intended to come together in an appropriate context of monogamous union between one man and one woman. Likewise, cross-gender identification is a concern in large part because it is viewed through this lens as challenging the integrity of male/female distinctions. From this perspective, same-sex sexual behavior is sin in part because it does not "merge or join two persons into an integrated sexual whole"; the "essential maleness" and "essential femaleness" is not brought together as intended from creation. When extended to the discussion of transsexuality and cross-gender identification, the theological concerns rest in the "denial of the integrity of one's own sex and an overt attempt at marring the sacred image of maleness or femaleness formed by God" (p. 3).

Most theologically conservative Christians will resonate with this framework. To them, the integrity framework most clearly reflects the biblical witness about sex and gender and becomes the primary lens through which they view same-sex sexuality and gender dysphoria. Same-sex sexual intimacy becomes a "line" if you will (although identifying a line when discussing sexual intimacy can also be difficult and a point of considerable discussion). While it may be even more challenging to identify a "line" in thought, behavior, and manner that reflects cross-gender identification, there becomes a point at which the integrity framework is concerned that cross-gender identification moves against the integrity of one's biological sex, an immutable and essential aspect of one's personhood.

It should be noted that many people, some Christians included, do not view gender dysphoria or transsexuality or every experience of cross-gender identification as an extension of homosexuality in precisely this same way. They may be uncomfortable with cross-gender identification or have reservations about the more invasive procedures (e.g., sex reassignment surgery), and they may not have another way to conceptualize the phenomenon. However, from a theological perspective and in terms of a traditional Christian sexual ethic, they do not reach the conclusion that the experience of gender dysphoria or attempts to mitigate the dysphoria belongs to the same class of behaviors that are deemed immoral. For example, the media went abuzz when television evangelist Pat Robertson said

> I think there are men who are in a woman's body. . . . It's very rare. But it's true—or women that are in men's bodies—and that they want a sex change. That is a very permanent thing, believe me, when you have certain body parts amputated and when you have shot up with various kinds of hormones. It's a radical procedure. I don't think there's any sin associated with that. I don't condemn somebody for doing that. (Sieczkowski, 2013)

A second way to think about sexual identity and gender identity is to consider the variations that occur in nature. These are nonmoral realities that reflect a concern about proper function. This can be referred to as a *disability* framework (Yarhouse, 2015). For some Christians who are drawn more to this framework, sexual identity concerns and gender dysphoria are viewed as a result of living in a fallen world in which the phenomena—like so many concerns—is a nonmoral reality. Whether we consider research from Nature or Nurture for the origins of sexual identity or gender identity concerns, the causal pathways and existing structures are not viewed by proponents of the disability framework as functioning in the way originally intended. If the various aspects of sex and gender are not aligning, then that nonmoral reality reflects one more dimension of human experience that is "not the way it's supposed to be" (Plantinga, 1996).

Those who are drawn more to this framework seek to learn as much as can be learned from two key sources. The first source is special revelation, and we are thinking here of meaningful themes regarding sex and gender from Scripture. The second key source is general revelation. Here we are thinking of research on etiology, prevention, and intervention as well as the lived reality of persons navigating sexual identity concerns and gender identity conflicts. The care provided would be through a lens of compassion and empathy. The question then arises, how should we respond to a condition with reference to the created order, the reality of the fall, and the hope of restoration?

Christians may recognize that the disability framework may be of some limited use, but they will likely have reservations depending on the primacy of the integrity framework. Christians recognize that we live in a fallen world and that every aspect of the created world is touched in some way by the fall, so they can see how same-sex sexuality and gender dysphoria could be such manifestations. They may recognize the utility of the disability framework insofar as the person has not chosen to experience same-sex attractions or gender dysphoria, and the disability framework evokes in the Christian a greater sense of compassion and empathy.

The third way to think about sexual identity and gender identity is to see them as something to be celebrated, honored, or revered. The sociocultural context in which we live in the West has rapidly moved in this direction. This as a *diversity* framework. The diversity framework highlights LGBT+ issues as reflecting identities and a culture to be celebrated as expressions of diversity. Current models that celebrate an LGBT+ identity and community reflect this framework. The mainstream of the field of family therapy and related mental health disciplines has clearly embraced the diversity framework with reference to LGBT+ issues as a point of multicultural competence. Although gender dysphoria remains in the *DSM-5* as a diagnosable disorder, many changes in that nosology suggest differences in gender identity are moving away from being viewed as a disorder and that perhaps it remains in the diagnostic nomenclature for the purposes of receiving insurance coverage.

Some Christians are understandably wary of the diversity framework. Christians often see among those who reflect the diversity framework a small but vocal group that calls for the deconstruction of norms related to marriage, heterosexuality, sex, and gender.

It would be wise for Christians in the field of family therapy to at least recognize that these different frameworks are in play in our cultural discussions surrounding sex and gender. That is a first step—just being able to clearly identify the assumptions behind each framework and how they contribute to the larger cultural discourse. If you adhere to the integrity framework but are talking to someone whose reference point is the diversity framework, you will quickly speak past one another.

Family members, too, will often speak past one another. Imagine a father or mother voicing concerns from an integrity framework while their teenage son is speaking from a diversity framework. Perhaps a sibling is drawing on a disability framework. It can be very difficult to get much headway when working from such different points of reference. We encourage family therapists to develop an awareness of these different lenses to facilitate a kind of perspective-taking, to help identify lenses and to help recognize the appeal of these different lenses to family members who are drawn to them.

Consider a family dinner table conversation about "Cousin Mike" who shared last week on a family Facebook page that he was transgender, changing from Mike to Mikka, and hopes that the family can love and support the transition to a woman.

MOM: I remember Mike—or Mikka now—playing with both of you kids. From an early age it seemed that he didn't fit in with boys and wanted to be with the girls. When you kids were small it was cute, but in adolescence I started to see how he couldn't be in either world.

DAD: I feel sorry for Mike Sr. and Jenny (parents). They have tried so hard to help him understand who he is as a child of God and a member of their family. I don't understand how all this gets confused in people's minds. I love that kid, always have from the time I held him as an infant, but this isn't the answer. It can't be.

TERRY: *(Twenty-one-year-old daughter)* I have always seen him as trapped—like he wanted to be someone he couldn't be. I'm proud of her.

DAD: Her? Is that what we are going to say now? Let's not get into that. I'm not calling a man a woman. And "trapped"? What does that even mean?

MOM: I think it's been difficult for everyone.

TOM: *(Twenty-three-year-old son)* To me he will always just be my cousin, Mike or Mikka, it doesn't matter. I hope for him to be happy—if he is happy as a woman, then I am happy too.

**DAD:**    I think we all want him to be happy. But I can't imagine that he will be happy as a woman. I don't think it's what God wants for him. I don't think people get "trapped" or whatever we are calling it. God doesn't "trap" people, and God doesn't make mistakes. When you walk out a path that isn't God's best for you, there are going to be consequences.

**TERRY:**  But aren't there consequences in not being happy? I mean, we are talking about Mike or Mikka, I'm sorry. She was always kind of distant and sad in some ways. Until now. Honestly, now it seems like this change has made a big difference. If we can't be who we are, what are we supposed to do?

These can be difficult discussions that are made more difficult when people speak past one another. Recognizing the different lenses is at least a place to begin. It may also be beneficial to consider what each lens brings to the discussion and whether an integrated lens could be of use in family therapy. Any one lens—to the exclusion of the best the others have to offer—may seem insufficient in finding a way forward in family therapy. In any case, integrating these lenses is beyond the scope of this chapter and is discussed in great detail elsewhere (Yarhouse, 2015).

## INTEGRATION CONSIDERATIONS FOR SEXUAL AND RELIGIOUS IDENTITY CONFLICTS

*Sexual identity concerns in family therapy.* We would like to close this chapter with a more focused discussion of sexual and religious identity conflicts that Christian families often face. We have seen in the integration literature more of a discussion of how to navigate those concerns from a cognitive-behavioral and narrative family therapy perspective (Yarhouse, 2008). From a cognitive-behavioral perspective, it can helpful to conduct an assessment of what is going on in the family, whether this is a presenting concern for a couple or with an adolescent. This would involve a sexual identity interview in which family members can describe the concerns that are bringing them in for counseling, how long these have been concerns, and how different family members have responded to the concerns so far. This interview also provides the counselor with information about any mental health difficulties facing the identified client or other family members, diagnosis and treatment history, and current treatment, if indicated (Yarhouse & Tan, 2005).

Assessment can also look at the milestone events in sexual identity development, from initial feelings of confusion by having same-sex feelings in a culture that is predominantly heterosexual, feeling different from others for gender-related reasons (such as stereotypic play preferences), attributions about sexual attractions, disclosure to others, and private and public identification and involvement in same-sex relationships. Such an interview can be conducted with the person who experiences same-sex attraction, and an adapted interview can be conducted with the spouse in the case of marital therapy or with parents in the case of adolescent sexual identity questions.

From an integrated cognitive-behavioral and narrative perspective, this approach builds on the psychoeducational approach mentioned above in which the therapist shares information in the following areas:

1. Causes of sexual orientation, attraction

2. The three-tier distinction between sexual attraction, orientation, and a gay identity

3. Developmental milestone events in the development of a gay identity

4. Metaphors for understanding identity (discovery and integration)

5. Dominant narrative tied to the presenting concern

6. Professional approaches available

7. Paraprofessional and nonprofessional ministry approaches

8. Possible benefits and risks of various approaches

We mentioned above some of what might be discussed with a family about the causes of same-sex attraction and a homosexual orientation as well as some of the professional and paraprofessional approaches that might be available. Several of the other content areas are tied more explicitly to a narrative family therapy approach. In what ways might a narrative approach be helpful?

*A gay script.* Many gay-affirmative narrative approaches identify organized religion as developing a problem story for persons who have same-sex feelings, and argue that a counternarrative is to integrate experiences of same-sex attraction into a gay identity (Yarhouse, 2005). But from a Christian perspective, the problem story is actually informed by the assumption that same-sex attraction indicates who the adolescent "really is." The perspective offered by the gay community is that same-sex attraction signals a naturally occurring (that is, "intended by God") distinction between homosexuality, heterosexuality, and, in some cases, bisexuality. This perspective has become the canonical discourse or "gay script" suggesting that same-sex feelings signal who the adolescent "really is" as a person and that the attractions are at the core of who the adolescent is as a person. If a teen reads from this script, he or she learns that same-sex behavior is simply an extension of that core so that it is morally blameless. The script goes on to say that the person has every right to actualize their potential, and this translates into self-actualization of their sexual identity.

## INTEGRATIVE FOCUS: *Family Functioning*

With sexual identity concerns, as with most family concerns, family functioning is often impaired, and this is precisely what brings the family in to see a therapist. Improving family functioning or reducing the immediate symptoms of family dysfunction often involves allowing for the space that has been created by the sexual identity conflict. Much of what reflects problems in family functioning may be the result of unacknowledged feelings about the sexual identity concerns, as family members may find it hard to share how they feel, including fears, worries, confusion, loss, and grief, even if it is anticipatory loss and grief for what they thought life would be like for their family. Improving family functioning entails enhancing communication and problem solving as well as the expression of these worries. It can be particularly helpful to translate expressions of "anger" into the "softer" feelings that often reside beneath anger: confusion, worry, disappointment, fear, and so on. Some of these feelings may be directed at other family members, but more often than not they are directed to God as family members do not know how to make sense of the sexual identity concerns and wonder what answers—if any—God can provide. This is also an opportunity to explore negative emotions toward God and questions family members have about their faith and how to best understand sexual identity in light of their religious beliefs and values.

*Think about it:* What would you say are the common negative emotions people have toward God? What are some of the potential benefits and drawbacks to identifying and processing these emotions? What are some ways in which religious identity might be impacted by sexual identity and vice versa?

*A shame script.* Other scripts may also be in play. One of the most common scripts from a conservative Christian perspective has been that of shame and/ or abomination. A young person can be told that "gays are ruining this country" or "gays are ruining marriage" and quickly pick up that it is not safe to share with others from one's faith community that they experience same-sex attraction or are sorting out questions related to sexual identity. The shame script communicates that there is something fundamentally flawed about the person and that the person is morally culpable for that flaw. It can lead people to self-rejection and to keep others at "arm's length" for fear that others would reject them, too, if they knew about their same-sex sexuality.

It is also difficult to imagine a future story based on a present story of shame or abomination. How can a person flourish living into a story line like that?

Also, a shame script can be applied to an entire family so that when a young person comes out, it can be difficult for parents to find resources. They may blame themselves for their son or daughter's same-sex sexuality, and they may choose to isolate themselves from social support, which further reinforces the shame.

In order to explore alternatives to both a gay script and a shame script, the Christian family therapist can help create a safe place to explore the potential conflict with these dominant narratives. This might begin by mapping how the dominant narratives have been constructed and how the person has coped with messages from the gay community and from their local faith community. The therapist can highlight attributions and meaning-making that supports the dominant narratives and begin to consider exceptions to the dominant narratives. This can be thought of as *mapping* sexual identity. This would entail mapping both the influence of sexual identity concerns on the person as well as mapping the person's influence on his or her sexual identity concerns. It is the mapping of sexual identity and the identification of exceptions to the ca-nonical discourse that can contribute to an emerging counternarrative.

If one dominant narrative is understood as the "gay" script and a second dominant narrative is understood as a "shame" or "abomination" script, the emerging counternarrative is what we might refer to as an "edited" script. The family therapist can highlight identity-congruent reconnecting activities by highlighting attributions and meaning-making that support the edited script. The family therapist can then also identify strengths and resources that support that edited script.

The family therapist can also take a narrative approach by *audiencing* the progress made in therapy. These are specific displays of support as the family comes to a greater understanding of ways to reassure and encourage one another as well as ways in which gains are made in consolidating the new, emerging counternarrative.

**Case example.** The Hadden family can illustrate the cultural discourse that encourages the identification of same-sex feelings as signaling a "gay" identity. The therapist is meeting with the parents and with the teenage son, Lambert, all of whom identify as Christian. The point in the exchange is not to keep Lambert from a gay identity but to begin to deconstruct the meaning of "gay" and to begin a discussion about different messages from different sources about what same-sex sexuality means to a person.

MOTHER: Lambert, we are concerned for you because we think you are too young to talk about yourself as "gay." It goes against what your father and I believe and how we raised you.

LAMBERT: Mom, I feel what I feel. I didn't choose to have these feelings.

FATHER: But Lambert, we also want you to think about what you do about your feelings. You are a Christian, and that should mean something to you.

THERAPIST: I think the idea of meaning is important, and perhaps it is something we can unpack further. Let me say at this point that many families find it helpful to make a distinction between feelings of sexual attraction, a sexual orientation, and a gay identity. I wonder how much of what is becoming difficult in your discussion is because we have jumped from feelings of sexual attraction to a gay identity and what your parents hear when they hear the word "gay."

LAMBERT: I guess I've always assumed that my feelings mean I'm gay or at least bi. I don't know. I've never really given it much thought. It just is what it is.

MOTHER: I think we all get that message a lot these days. It's everywhere. On TV, movies, the Internet—it's no surprise we are upset about it. All I can think about are those parades and half-naked men frolicking around. I don't know. It just upset me.

FATHER: I just don't want him to take in all of these messages, and I'm not sure what to do about it.

**THERAPIST:** So we can discuss a couple of things here. One, Lambert, is the reality of your same-sex sexuality. I don't hear anyone questioning that. But the other is how you make sense of your experiences, what those experiences of attraction and labels mean to you. Lambert, you seem open to discussing the difference between attractions, orientation, and identity, and we can come back to that. You may find that helpful. Some people do. But I also hear your parents expressing concerns about the messages about same-sex sexuality that they have come across and that they think you have come across.

**LAMBERT:** Yeah, that's fine. We can come back to those differences. That could be helpful. But I'm a little concerned about what my parents are saying about messages. I'm not sure I get what they are concerned about. I'm not marching in parades.

**THERAPIST:** I know you're not. I heard them identifying possible messages about being gay from TV, the Internet, and other places. Mom and Dad, you mentioned media, like TV and the Internet. Let's talk about the messages you believe come from those sources. What stories are being told about same-sex sexuality from those sources? And then after we do that, I think it might be helpful to explore messages from other sources, especially your religious faith tradition. You all shared that the church you grew up in has shaped you in some ways. It may be helpful to hear about the messages Lambert may have heard growing up in the church.

This brief exchange points to some of what might happen in sexual identity therapy from a narrative perspective. The clinician might introduce the three-tier distinction to the family and begin to consider with the family the problem narrative and explore alternative discourses to "thicken the plot" of the family story. A discussion can also take place about the different stories being told about same-sex sexuality. From some sources, that story is one of celebrating a sense of identity and culture. This reflects the diversity lens mentioned earlier in this chapter. From other sources, such as their local church, they may have been exposed to a story of abomination or shame, which would be very difficult for Lambert to ever consider living into. There is no way to picture a future story where you can thrive. Identifying the stories from the media and entertainment helps the parents discuss their worries. Discussing the stories from their religious faith community may help Lambert give voice to his own fears and frustrations with the messages he has heard growing up. These may be reflections of the integrity lens we introduced earlier. In any case, identifying these problem stories could eventually lead to greater mutual understanding and empathy for one another as well as lead to a discussion of potential counternarratives that would be worth exploring together.

A place to begin in family therapy is to track and monitor attributions about what same-sex attractions signal about the partner who has them. Does the person who has same-sex feelings see them as defining who they are as a person? In a mixed-orientation marriage, for example, there is a difference between saying to oneself, "I am a lesbian trying to make this marriage work" and "I am a woman who is married and who also experiences attraction to the same sex" (Rosenau & Yarhouse, 2002). The former statement identifies the person with her attractions and makes the marriage secondary to her sexual feelings and identity. The latter statement focuses on the person's marriage and her gender and suggests that her same-sex feelings can be understood in the context of her commitments, beliefs, and values about marriage. The family therapist can help the spouse who experiences same-sex attraction to think about aspects of her identity—what is at the center of that identity and what is at the periphery.

A narrative approach might also consider competing metaphors for understanding sexual identity. From this perspective the dominant metaphor in the gay community is that of *discovery* (Yarhouse, 2008). In the case of marriage therapy, one person might find himself experiencing attraction toward the same sex. Much as we just discussed with the gay "script," this experience is taken to reflect the discovery of who he "really is" as a person. But an alternative metaphor is that of *integration*. The understanding is that the person experiences same-sex attraction and now makes choices about whether or not to integrate those experiences of attraction into a gay or lesbian identity—to talk about and relate to others as a different kind of person by virtue of attraction to the same sex.

A narrative understanding of sexual identity might incorporate a discussion of competing scripts and alternative metaphors for making sense of experiences of same-sex attraction. Ultimately, after identifying dominant stories that have contributed to the conflict a person experiences, it can be helpful for family therapists to work with the family on counternarratives that tell a different story about one's identity and/or worth.

The integrative Christian family therapist will quickly learn how important family relationships are when addressing sexual identity concerns. What is perhaps most challenging is creating a therapeutic space in which multiple stakeholders can have and express their beliefs and values about sexuality, its expression, and issues pertaining to identity. It can be helpful to focus on the *process* since the therapist and the family are well aware that sexual identity has become the *content* of the family discussion. Family therapists can assist the family in how they talk about the sexual identity questions or concerns.

Creating a therapeutic space for the various stakeholders is facilitated in part by assisting family members in expressing their feelings without being "bullied" or "pushed around" by their emotional conflicts. To switch metaphors, what we mean by this is that emotions can quickly jump into the driver's seat of the family car and take the family for a ride. We are not against the emotions or the expression of family emotions, but from a Bowenian perspective, we do not want them driving the family car; we want them in the car and we want to direct them through a process that allows family members to reflect on what they think and feel and to share that with one another.

As we have suggested, Bowenian family therapy may be particularly helpful in assisting individual family members to differentiate between thinking and feeling and in recognizing boundaries between family members. Structural and dynamic approaches can be helpful here, too. Family relationships are very important for the well-being of young people sorting out sexual identity issues, and it is important that the integrative Christian family therapist facilitate supportive relationships while allowing for genuine differences in beliefs and values to be shared.

*Think about it:* What challenges do you anticipate would come with "allowing for genuine differences in beliefs and values to be shared"? In what ways are sexual identity conflicts similar to other family conflicts? In what ways are they different?

## CONCLUSION

The Christian who provides family therapy today is serving an increasingly diverse culture. The diversity represented by LGBT+ persons, couples, and

families may be particularly challenging. This chapter explored various ways
in which LGBT+ persons might present for family services, including couples
therapy, family therapy to address a family member who has come out as
LGBT+, providing services to children of LGBT+ parents, and the unique
experiences and needs of mixed-orientation couples.

These broad clinical presentations also challenge the Christian to reflect on
what it means to enter into fiduciary space of public trust in the provision of
mental health services. We do not anticipate consensus on how Christians
ought to answer each difficult question that arises, but we do encourage discussion and reflection on what it may look like to provide family therapy
services to increasingly diverse family presentations.

We also see unique contributions in Christian thinking on sexual identity
and clinical services for those who experience a conflict between their sexual
or gender identity and their identity as a Christian.

## REFERENCES

Bailey, J. M., & Pillard, R. (1991). A genetic study of male sexual orientation. *Archives of General Psychiatry, 48*, 1089-96.

Buxton, A. P. (2001). Writing your own script: How bisexual men and heterosexual
wives maintain their marriages after disclosure. *Journal of Bisexuality, 2*, 155-89.

Buxton, A. P. (2004). Works in progress: How mixed orientation couples maintain
their marriages after the wives come out. *Journal of Bisexuality, 4*(1/2), 76-82

Buxton, A. P. (2006). Counseling heterosexual spouses of bisexual men and
women and bisexual-heterosexual couples. *Journal of Bisexuality, 6*(1/2), 105-135

Byne, W., & Parsons, B. (1993). Human sexual orientation. *Archives of General
Psychiatry, 50*, 228-39.

Chandra, A., Mosher, W., Copen, C., & Sionean, C. (2011). Sexual behavior, sexual
attraction, and sexual identity in the United States. *National Health Statistics
Report, 36*, 1-49.

Cheng, S. & Powell, B. (2015). Measurement, methods and divergent patterns:
Reassessing the effects of same-sex parents. *Social Science Research, 52*, 615-626.

Connolly, C. M. (2012). Lesbian couple therapy. In J. J. Bigner & J. L. Wetchler
(Eds.), *Handbook of LGBT-affirmative couple and family therapy* (pp. 43-56).
New York: Routledge.

Conron, K. J., Scott, G., Stowell, G. S., & Landers, S. J. (2012). Transgender health
in Massachusetts: Results from a household probability sample of adults.
*American Journal of Public Health, 102*(1), 118-22.

Diamond, L. M. (2006). What we got wrong about sexual identity development: Unexpected findings from a longitudinal study of young women. In A. M. Omoto & H. S. Kurtzman (Eds.), *Sexual orientation and mental health: Examining identity and development in lesbian, gay and bisexual people.* Washington, DC: American Psychological Association.

Elizur, Y., & Ziv, M. (2001). Family support and acceptance, gay male identity formation, and psychological adjustment: A path model. *Family process, 40*(2), 125-144.

Farr, R. H. & Patterson, C. J. (2013). Lesbian and gay adoptive parents and their children. In A. E. Goldberg & K. R. Allen (Eds.), *LGBT-parent families: Innovations in research and implications for practice* (39-55). New York: Springer Science and Business Media.

Fedewa, A. L., Black, W. W., & Ahn, S. (2015). Children and adolescents with same-gender parents: A meta-analytic approach in assessing outcomes. *Journal of GLBT Family Studies, 11*, 1-34.

Gagnon, R. A. J. (2007). Transsexuality and Ordination, August, 2007. http://www.robgagnon.net/articles/TranssexualityOrdination.pdf.

Gallup poll (2016, July). Same-sex marriages up one year after Supreme Court. Available at: http://www.gallup.com/poll/193055/sex-marriages-one-year-supreme-court-verdict.aspx. July 22, 2016.

Gartrell, N. K., Bos, H. M., & Goldberg, N. G. (2011). Adolescents of the US national longitudinal lesbian family study: sexual orientation, sexual behavior, and sexual risk exposure. *Archives of Sexual Behavior, 40*(6), 1199-1209.

Gates, G. J. (2011). How many people are gay, bisexual, and transgender? The Williams Institute, 1-8. Available at: http://williamsinstitute.law.ucla.edu/wp-content/uploads/Gates-How-Many-People-LGBT-Apr-2011.pdf.

Giammattei, S. V., & Green, R. J. (2012). LGBTQ couple and family therapy: History and future directions. *Handbook of LGBT-affirmative couple and family therapy*, 1-22.

Gianino, M., & Novelle, M. (2012). Considerations for assessment with lesbian and gay adoptive parents and their children. In J. J. Bigner & J. L. Wetchler (Eds.), *Handbook of LGBT-affirmative couple and family therapy* (pp. 215-31). New York: Routledge.

Goldberg, A. E. (2010). *Lesbian and gay parents and their children: Research on the family life cycle.* Washington, DC: American Psychological Association.

Goldberg, A. E. & Garcia, R. (2015). Predictors of relationship dissolution in lesbian, gay, and heterosexual adoptive parents. *Journal of Family Psychology, 29*(3), 394-404.

Gordon, K. G., & Baucom, D. H. (2003). Forgiveness and marriage: Preliminary support for a measure based on a model of recovery from a marital betrayal. *The American Journal of Family Therapy, 31,* 179-99.

Gordon, K. C., Baucom, D. H., Snyder, D. K., Atkins, D. C., & Christensen, A. (2006). Treating affair couples: Clinical considerations and initial findings. *Journal of Cognitive Psychotherapy: An International Quarterly, 20,* 375-92.

Gottman, J. M., Levenson, R. W., Gross, J., Frederickson, B. L., McCoy, K., Rosenthal, L., Ruef, A., & Yoshimoto, D. (2003). Correlates of gay and lesbian couples' relationship satisfaction and relationship dissolution. *Journal of Homosexuality, 45*(1), 23-43.

Green, R. J., & Mitchell, V. (2008). Gay and lesbian couples in therapy: Minority stress, relational ambiguity, and families of choice. *Clinical handbook of couple therapy, 4,* 662-80.

Hamer, D., Hu, S., Magnuson, V., Hu, N., & Pattatucci, A. (1993). A linkage between DNA markers on the X chromosome and male sexual orientation. *Science, 261,* 321-27.

Hernandez, B. C., & Wilson, C. M. (2007). Another kind of ambiguous loss: Seventh-day Adventist women in mixed-orientation marriages. *Family Relations, 56,* 185-95.

Hu, S., Pattatucci, A., Patterson, C., Li, L., Fulker, D., Cherny, S., Kruglyak, L., & Hamer, D. (1995). Linkage between sexual orientation and chromosome Xq28 in males but not in females. *Nature Genetics, 11,* 248-56.

Jones, S. L., & Yarhouse, M. A. (2000). *Homosexuality: The use of scientific research in the church's moral debate.* Downers Grove, IL: InterVarsity Press.

Jones, S. L., & Yarhouse, M. A. (2007). *Ex-gays? A longitudinal study of religiously mediated change in sexual orientation.* Downers Grove, IL: InterVarsity Press.

Kuvalanka, K. (2012). The kids may be all right, but some might still end up in your office. In J. J. Bigner & J. L. Wetchler (Eds.), *Handbook of LGBT-affirmative couple and family therapy* (pp. 167-82). New York: Routledge.

Latham, J. D., & White, G. D. (1978). Coping with homosexual expression within heterosexual marriages: Five case studies. *Journal of Sex and Marital Therapy, 4,* 198-212.

Londregan, J. (2014). Introduction. In A. Samuel (Ed.), *No differences? How children in same-sex households fare: Studies from social science* (pp. 1-17). Witherspoon Institute.

Lynch, J., & McMahon-Klosterman, K. (2012). The gay and lesbian stepfamily. In J. J. Bigner & J. L. Wetchler (Eds.), *Handbook of LGBT-affirmative couple and family therapy* (pp. 233-48). New York: Routledge.

Marks, L. (2012). Same-sex parenting and children's outcomes: A closer examination of the American Psychological Association's brief on lesbian and gay parenting. In A. Samuel (Ed.), *No differences? How children in same-sex house-holds fare: Studies from social science* (pp. 28-86). Witherspoon Institute.

Maslowe, K. E., & Yarhouse, M. A. (2015). Christian parental reactions when a LGB child comes out. *American Journal of Family Therapy, 43*(4), 1-12.

Plantinga, C. (1996). *Not the way it's supposed to be: A breviary of sin.* Grand Rapids: Eerdmans.

Regnerus, M. (2012). How different are the adult children of parents who have same-sex relationships? Findings from the New Family Structures Study. *Social Science Research, 41,* 752-70.

Ritter, K. Y., & Terndrup, A. I. (2002). *Handbook of affirmative psychotherapy with lesbians and gay men.* New York: Guilford Press.

Rosenau, D. E., & Yarhouse, M. A. (2002). Homosexuality: Expanding alternatives and choices. In D. E. Rosenau, *A celebration of sex* (2nd ed., pp. 367-77). Nashville: Thomas Nelson.

Ryan, C., Huebner, D., Diaz, R. M., & Sanchez, J. (2009). Family rejection as a predictor of negative health outcomes in white and Latino lesbian, gay, and bisexual young adults. *Pediatrics, 123*(1), 346-52.

Samuel, A. (2014). *No differences? How children in same-sex households fare: Studies from social science.* Witherspoon Institute.

Sasnett, S. (2015). Are the kids all right? A qualitative study of adults with gay and lesbian parents. *Journal of Contemporary Ethnography, 44*(2), 196-222.

Savin-Williams, R. C. (1989). Coming out to parents and self-esteem among gay and lesbian youths. *Journal of Homosexuality, 18*(1-2), 1-35.

Sieczkowski, C. (2013, July 29). Pat Robertson on transgender community: "I don't think there's any sin associated with that." *Huffington Post.* Retrieved from www.huffingtonpost.com/2013/07/29/pat-robertson-transgender_n_3672244.html.

Strommen, E. F. (1993). "You're a what?" Family reactions to the disclosure of homosexuality. In L. D. Garnets & D. C. Kimmel (Eds.), *Psychological perspectives on lesbian and gay male experiences* (pp. 248-66). New York: Columbia University Press.

Szymanski, D. M., & Gupta, A. (2009). Examining the relationship between multiple internalized oppressions and African American lesbian, gay, bisexual, and questioning persons' self-esteem and psychological distress. *Journal of Counseling Psychology, 56*(1), 110.

Tasker, F., & Malley, M. (2012). Working with LGBT parents. In J. J. Bigner & J. L. Wetchler (Eds.), *Handbook of LGBT-affirmative couple and family therapy* (pp. 149-65). New York: Routledge.

Throckmorton, W., & Yarhouse, M. A. (2006). The sexual identity therapy framework. Available at: www.sitframework.com.

Tunnell, G. (2012). Gay male couple therapy. In J. J. Bigner & J. L. Wetchler (Eds.), *Handbook of LGBT-affirmative couple and family therapy* (pp. 25-42). New York: Routledge.

Ward, B. W., Dahlhamer, J. M., Galinsky, A. M., & Joestl, S. S. (2014). Sexual orientation and health among US adults: National Health Interview Survey, 2013. *National Health Statistics Reports, 15*, 1-10.

Yarhouse, M. A. (2001). Sexual identity development: The influence of valuative frameworks on identity synthesis. *Psychotherapy, 38*(3), 331-41.

Yarhouse, M. A. (2005). Same-sex attraction, homosexual orientation, and gay identity: A three-tier distinction for counseling and pastoral care. *Journal of Pastoral Care and Counseling, 59*(3), 201-12.

Yarhouse, M. A. (2008). Normative sexual identity therapy. *American Journal of Family Therapy, 36*, 1-15.

Yarhouse, M. A. (2015). *Understanding gender dysphoria: Navigating transgender issues in a changing culture.* Downers Grove, IL: IVP Academic.

Yarhouse, M. A., Brooke, H., Pisano, P., & Tan, E. S. N. (2005). Project inner compass: Young adults experiencing sexual identity confusion. *Journal of Psychology and Christianity, 24*(4), 352-60.

Yarhouse, M. A., & Burkett, L. A. (2003). *Sexual identity: A guide to living in the time between the times.* Lanham, MD: University Press of America.

Yarhouse, M. A., & Hathaway, W. L. (2016). Ethics and values in training of students and provision of clinical services to LGBT persons. *Journal of Psychology and Christianity, 35*(4), 357-67.

Yarhouse, M. A., Houp, D., Sadusky, J., & Zaporozhets, O. (in press). Christian parents' experiences of transgender youth during the coming out process. In Sheyma Vaughn (Ed.), *Transgender youth: Perceptions, media influences, and social challenges.* New York: Nova Science Publishers.

Yarhouse, M. A., & Kays, J. L., (2010). The P.A.R.E. Model: A framework for working with mixed orientation couples. *Journal of Psychology and Christianity, 29*(1), 77-81.

Yarhouse, M. A., Pawlowski, L. M., & Tan, E. S. N. (2003). Intact marriages in which one partner dis-identifies with experiences of same-sex attraction. *American Journal of Family Therapy, 31*, 369-88.

Yarhouse, M. A., & Seymore, R. L. (2006). Intact marriages in which one partner dis-identifies with experiences of same-sex attraction: A follow-up study. *American Journal of Family Therapy, 34*, 1-11.

Yarhouse, M. A., Stratton, S., Dean, J., & Brooke, H. (2007). Sexual minorities: Christian students and their sexual experiences. Poster presented at the American Psychological Association's Annual Conference, August 18, 2007.

Yarhouse, M. A., & Tan, E. S. N. (2004). *Sexual identity synthesis: Attributions, meaning-making, and the search for congruence.* Lanham, MD: University Press of America.

Yarhouse, M. A., & Tan, E. S. N. (2005). Addressing religious conflicts in adolescents who experience sexual identity confusion. *Professional Psychology: Research and Practice, 36*(5), 530-36.

# CASTING A VISION

# CONCLUSION

## Casting a Vision for
## Christian Family Therapy

*When eight strong fellows are out to row,*
*With a slip of a lad to guide them,*
*I warrant they'll make the light ship go,*
*Though the coach on the launch may chide them.*

**RUDOLPH CHAMBERS LEHMANN, "AT PUTNEY"**

WITH THIS BOOK WE SEE OURSELVES in the role of the coxswain, the member of an eight-person rowing team that sits in the stern to steer the boat, call out the rhythmic cadence, and encourage the rowers to strain toward the prize. The muscular crew of family theorists, researchers, and clinicians established a robust array of literature regarding the care of families. It is our intent to offer coordination and a direction to the process of therapy—in particular, therapy conducted through the lens of the Christian tradition. We do so with respect toward those in the profession and the church who have preceded us, and with a commitment to influence the emerging generation of professionals who render care to couples and families.

Put differently, we have offered our perspective on family theory and intervention in hopes that it would blend with many other views regarding the theory and practice of family therapy. Our views include a dimension not frequently voiced by those who have formed theory—usually in the great institutions of learning, primarily in the United States. The integration of Christianity as the organizing principle around which theory and practice emerge is distinct from the secular viewpoints that govern the profession. We have been the beneficiaries of their insight, knowledge, creativity, research, and skill. We hope that this work will have influence—first to the Christian family therapist, both emerging and practicing, and second to professionals not familiar with the traditions and values of Christian thought—toward shaping the practice of family therapy to consider ways in which it might be understood within distinct religious traditions.

In the opening section of this book we introduced the reader to some of the qualities and characteristics we see as important to a Christian view of the family. We located this discussion within the four acts of the biblical drama: creation, fall, redemption, and glorification. We then developed the foundational dimensions for Christian critique and engagement: family identity, functioning, and relationships. We argued that these three dimensions are an extension of considerations first developed within discussions of how human beings image God.

We then discussed how the broader field of family therapy emerged and developed over time. We wanted to orient the reader to two essential understandings that inform this book: a Christian worldview and the assumptions and history behind family theory as it has developed primarily in the context of a secular worldview. The task of integration is to bring these two perspectives into a meaningful, purposeful dialogue.

In part two of this book we offered a critical evaluation of primarily first-generation family theories and discussed some of the second-generation approaches to the family. Critical evaluation of family theories cannot substitute for Christian reflection on the family and the formats therapists might use with families (Roberts, 1993). But we see tremendous value in helping Christian family therapists reflect on, evaluate, and engage the existing models of family therapy so that they come to an understanding of the assumptions that lie behind the theories of family dysfunction, family functioning, and the road map (of therapy) that is intended to get a family from a place of dysfunction to a place of proper functioning. The closing chapter of part two offered a theoretical map for a proposed integrative Christian family therapy organized around the three themes introduced in chapter one of the book: family functioning, family relationships, and family identity. We see these as central considerations for the

Christian, and each is touched on to some extent by the major first-generation models of family therapy. The second-generation models mentioned briefly in chapter twelve are attempts to bring together themes and interests shared by more than one first-generation model. Rather than follow that lead, we believe the Christian family therapist can recognize the value of key concepts in the early models while organizing those themes around the three central concepts of identity, functioning, and relationship.

Part three of this book addressed specific concerns that often face family therapists. Although not exhaustive, we offered a fairly comprehensive overview of some of the key areas that can be quite challenging in family therapy. In the second edition of this book, we added a chapter on cohabitation and we significantly revised the chapter on sexual identity to address LGBT+ couples and families. In these chapters we wanted to extend the work of integration by thinking about these topics from a distinctively Christian perspective. We did this and also discussed to varying degrees how the Christian might think about the issues of identity, functioning, and relationship when reflecting on specific presenting concerns. We also saw these chapters as opportunities to expose the reader to what the broader field is often thinking about with respect to these topics and what is being suggested for family intervention.

In this closing reflection we hope to place this discussion of integrative Christian family therapy in a changing, diverse global context. We anticipate changes in family therapy intervention and ministry in the years to come, and we believe these changes will have a local effect on the structures of families and on the way the Christian therapist, counselor, and pastoral counselor "rows the boat."

## THE CHANGING FAMILY AND COUNSELING INTERVENTION AND MINISTRY

If you initiate a conversation about the changing family during the waxing years of the twenty-first century within the culture of the Christian tradition, the anticipated content will be the disregard of sexual mores that were characteristic of a previous era in North American society, the jettison of marital commitments by many couples and choice of noncontractual cohabitation arrangements instead, the debate of same-sex unions and same sex-marriage, and current demands on the family. While all of these are important cultural presses that must be vigilantly challenged, we believe there is an important point missed in the discussion. Focusing on the decline of family in secular culture puts the Christian in a place with a negative lens through which he or she sees the world. We would like to expand this discussion and the lenses through which we view global changes by considering other developments within the Christian community that will influence family counseling and family ministry through the twenty-first century.

In response to this trend we hold an optimistic view of the family rooted in the biblical (not traditional) context of family. Most who have an awareness of the biblical text recall the narrative of Daniel and his colleagues Hananiah, Mishael, and Azariah, who all entered the Babylonian king's service as governmental apprentices. They objected to the order to eat food from the king's table, desiring to uphold Judaic dietary rules. Their holding to their principles and opting for a diet of vegetables and water resulted in the king finding none equal to them as they entered into his service. We see this story as having parallels to the cultural circumstances of our time. Western culture does not embrace the biblical ethic of marriage or sexuality. Nor should it unless individuals within the society also embrace the message of redemption and reconciliation to which individuals and families are called within the Christian faith. However, we believe families who adhere to faith in God through the restorative acts of Jesus and the reviving presence of the Holy Spirit, as articulated in Holy Scriptures, have the highest probability of meaningful, significant, and joy-filled existence. Pain and suffering have a purpose and function, success and pleasure are respected as a gift to fully embrace and partake.

We want to draw the reader's attention to two broad roles for the Christian family therapist today. Although there are many potential roles, one consists of being a family therapist for the Christian community. In that sense Christian family therapists may have their own questions to answer, their own research agendas to follow (see Plantinga, 1984). After all, if Christian family therapists are not cognizant of the needs of the Christian community, how can we expect others to take a lead in addressing these needs?

At the same time, Christian family therapists will have another role that involves engaging our increasingly diverse culture both at academic and applied levels by being a part of the broader community of family therapists who serve and minister to a range of families. Christian family therapists have an opportunity to be salt and light, providing ministry and service in our offices.

We do this in part as we work competently and with integrity and because it is good work to do and is pleasing to God, as we believe God ultimately delights in the restoration of the created order in whatever small ways that occur. We believe God takes delight in family relationships that are improved and renewed and demonstrate a kind of love and mutuality valued within Christianity. We believe God takes delight in families that are functioning better than they did previously as a result of a therapist working with them to repair destructive patterns of interaction. We believe that God delights in families that reflect well on their own identity and create a place for family members to locate themselves in his world.

His *world*—this brings us to the challenges facing the future of family therapy as it expands into a broader, more diverse global context. In the years ahead the Christian family therapist who practices locally will be impacted by a shrinking world that reflects great cultural diversity and many family forms.

## CARING FOR THE FAMILY IN CHINESE, SPANISH, ENGLISH, BENGALI, HINDI/URDU, ARABIC

The original family intervention theories are often stretched to inapplicability because of the variations in family context. Terms such as "hierarchy" and "boundaries" become blurred when the identified patient is a sixteen-year-old male whose mother works a twelve-hour day and whose father was deported back to Guatemala, or a twenty-eight-year-old woman who has three children to different fathers, all of whom have shared custody rights and have children from other relationships. Or the grandparents who are caring for three children ages five, eleven, and fourteen while both parents serve criminal sentences for drug distribution. While we are saddened that families no longer share evening meals, we regularly find families who do not share the same zip code. This social change alters the rules for family engagement and parental authority. Who decides whether an all-night party is good for a thirteen-year-old to attend? The father who works fifteen hours a day, the stepmom who actually raises the youth but is not the legal guardian, the mother who has joint custody every other week, or the stepdad who is convinced that "she is getting away with too much!" Clarity of roles and responsibility becomes obscured by the variations of relationship. The dynamic church and the competent Christian family therapist are engaged in thinking and then living the vibrancy of the living gospel in families of our culture.

The emphasis of Christian family therapy and counseling-related ministry has been toward family divergence prevention—that is, creating a culture that expects and values monogamy and sexual abstinence until marriage and supports divorce only in situations of infidelity or in physical abuse. While this priority is one that we support, it does not assist the Christian family therapist or family pastor in reconciling issues within a current family where the father-mother-offspring structure has been altered. These families are not "illegitimate" or "dysfunctional" because of their structure. These structures are far more complicated to understand and develop effective family intervention, so it is easier to label them as dysfunctional and wash our hands of any responsibility for their success. While the family therapist—Christian or secular—may do this, the parent cannot. The problematic structure is what it is, and assistance in nurturing and developing adults and children into psychological, social, relational, and spiritual maturity remains. The use of negative terms such as "illegitimate" serves no good purpose except to demean and to establish a false image of the "good family" (which as we see in Scripture are few and far between) and the "bad family." What makes a family "good" is what God is capable of doing in and through them, and in many respects what God is doing or capable of doing is beyond us and not for us to evaluate. Chesterton (1994) noted that all families carry the characteristics of dysfunction:

> I cannot conceive why they (couples) are not all divorced. I have known many happy marriages, but never a compatible one. The whole aim of marriage is to fight through and survive the instant when incompatibility becomes unquestionable. For a man and a woman, as such, are incompatible. (p. 46)

In truth, the challenge for twenty-first-century marriage and family counselors who espouse a Christian worldview is to adapt the truth of Scripture to the social environment of the day. It is required of us to have a missionary mentality, just as Hudson Taylor adapted the gospel message to nineteenth-century Chinese peasants, and Margaret Nicholl Laird attended to the needs of the Banda people of the Central African Republic region of Ubangi-Shari, and Cameron Townsend realized that the Bible has limited use to Guatemalan mountain people who spoke Cakchiquel. Family therapy within the Christian context must be equally creative in its capacity to adapt its method of facilitating the reparative constructs found in Scripture to a society that does not possess the cultural knowledge as it might have in decades past.

We thoroughly uphold the biblical model of monogamous heterosexual marriage as the basis for family existence. Marriage boundaries offer children the highest probability of successful acquisition of life skills during childhood and adolescence; they offer the clearest image of roles and responsibilities of extended and multigenerational family; and they provide a clear moral obligation for adult children to care for aging parents. But we agree with Clapp (1993) in his assertion that the "traditional" family was never really traditional, if traditional meant the majority of families throughout the major portion of recorded history. And if the church is going to have an impact on the culture regarding a rich understanding and application of relational skills, it must engage culture and the families representative of that culture in their present condition, without the antecedent of conformity to a social system that is not yet theirs. If the Christian family therapist's clinical template is limited (or constrained) to only what they believe to be true of "good" homes, then they will bring less creativity and redemptive presence to their work with families in the twenty-first century.

Garland (1999) offers four recommendations to churches who seek to have influence on the secular family through family ministry. Her recommendations include the following:

Any teaching about what is ideal should be firmly grounded in grace and love and inclusion for all those who might otherwise inadvertently be drawn out of the circle of concern. . . . Rather than seeing ourselves as sieves controlling what comes into the boat called the church, it seems better to see ourselves as nets cast out to gather in all kinds.

The church's teachings constitute one of several shapers of family life, including economic, social and cultural realities. Thus teachings and programs should be sensitive to the intended and unintended interactions with other forces in family life.

Different Christian traditions have defined the relationship between family and church differently, based on their theological premises and cultural traditions.

Although the influence of the church on family life has evolved over time, there have been watershed points when this change outpaced other social and cultural changes—the Reformation, the Christianization of indigenous peoples, even today's parachurch movements. In short, the church can be a powerful force for dramatic social change. (p. 297)

Garland's call takes seriously the importance of supporting structures that promote biblical family existence. We appreciate her ideas because they are grounded in thoughtfulness. By this we mean they reflect the complications of social realities faced by families and require churches to accommodate their ministry to match the needs of families as they are nurtured into Christian maturity.

As we come to the close of this book, we ask you to reflect on Garland's call. Looking at her first point, in what ways does the Christian family therapist extend grace to families under his or her care? How is that communicated in terms of one's clinical presence? Does the image of casting a net capture what is possible in Christian ministry? What are some practical strategies that could be used to extend ministry to those in greatest need?

Her second recommendation challenges the local church and the Christian family therapist and pastor to creatively engage the culture in the provision of ministry. It is unlikely that the church can "program" to make changes in existing families; but the church can creatively engage the culture and meet families where they are, as when churches provide daycare and afterschool programs and support to families.

Garland's third point is to recognize that there may not be one model for relating the family and the local church. Rather than argue for one exclusive model, we might instead focus on a range of models that may address the deepest needs within a local community, knowing that this model may not work in other communities.

Finally, the church can be an agent of social change, but it often does so through changes in the very people that make up the church. It is not that policy and legislation do not matter; they do, but social change can be sparked by changed lives—by the reality of redemption being lived out in love by real people who relate to one another out of mutual regard.

As Christian family therapists pursue their vocation to minister to the needs of families in their many forms, we encourage you to consider family functioning, relationships, and identity. We encourage the critical reflection on and engagement with the existing theories of family therapy, especially given their philosophical and theoretical assumptions about healthy family functioning, family dysfunction, and ways to intervene. We also see emerging areas of concern within our society and ways in which Christian family therapists can play an important role in providing services in especially difficult areas. These issues and concerns will only expand further into a global community with needs that are quite difficult to anticipate. We hope that a Christian integrative model brings the kinds of resources needed to a wider audience interested in the concerns facing families in the years to come.

## CONCLUSION

Early on in our discussion we introduced you to the location of a gravesite, N-IV-16. Do you remember? The locator stands for "North of the Cross, row 4, 16 graves in from the aisle." We do not mean to suggest that family therapists should give their lives to the cause of family therapy. Rather, we believe that families, in order to be healthy, must embrace a quality of self-sacrifice. Bonhoeffer's (1937) call to discipleship provides a powerful parallel: "When Christ calls a man, he bids him come and die." If the Christian family must understand the qualities of selflessness articulated in Scripture and Christian theology, then those involved with guiding, teaching, prompting, and encouraging families toward wholeness must embrace the message as well. If Christian marriage is distinct because of a respect for the covenant—understood as God's sacrificial promise to his human creation—then those professionals who advocate for therapeutic processes that reflect the Christian tradition must also embrace these ideals as the core from which their theory and practice of family therapy emanates.

## REFERENCES

Bonhoeffer, D. (1937). *The cost of discipleship* (R. H. Fuller, Trans.). London: SCM Press.

Chesterton, G. K. (1994). *What's wrong with the world.* San Francisco: Ignatius Press.

Clapp, R. (1993). *Families at the crossroads: Beyond traditional and modern options.* Downers Grove, IL: InterVarsity Press.

Garland, D. (1999). *Family ministry: A comprehensive guide.* Downers Grove, IL: InterVarsity Press.

Plantinga, A. (1984). Advice to Christian philosophers. *Faith and Philosophy: Journal of the Society of Christian Philosophers, 1*(1), 1-15.

Roberts, R. C. (1993). *Taking the Word to heart: Self and others in an age of therapies.* Grand Rapids: Eerdmans.

# AUTHOR INDEX

# SUBJECT INDEX

# ABOUT THE AUTHORS

**Mark A. Yarhouse** (PsyD, Wheaton College) is the Hughes Endowed Chair and professor of psychology at Regent University where he directs the Institute for the Study of Sexual Identity and is a core faculty member in the doctoral program in clinical psychology. A licensed clinical psychologist, he practices privately in the Virginia Beach area, providing individual, couples, famil,y and group counseling. Yarhouse has published over eighty peer-reviewed journal articles and book chapters and is author or coauthor of several books, including *Understanding Gender Dysphoria*, *Modern Psychopathologies*, *Understanding Sexual Identity* , *Sexuality and Sex Therapy*, and *Homosexuality and the Christian*. He serves on the editorial board of the *Journal of Psychology and Theology* and *Christian Counseling Today*, and has served as an ad hoc reviewer with *Journal of Homosexuality*.

James N. Sells (PhD, University of Southern California) is professor of counseling and director of the PhD program in counselor education and supervision at Regent University in Virginia Beach, Virginia, where he has taught since 2005. He has served on the faculties of Northern Illinois University and West Texas AM University, and he is also a licensed psychologist. He is the coauthor of *Counseling Couples in Conflict* and *Family Therapies*. Sell's research, private practice, and teaching seminars have focused on marital conflict, reconciliation, and forgiveness. Additionally, he has published work in clinical supervision, individual and group psychotherapy, and international applications of the counseling profession. His research has been published in the *Journal of Counseling Psychology*, *Journal of Counseling and Development*, *Journal of Marital and Family Therapy*, *The Family Journal*, *Journal of Family Therapy*, and *Journal of College Student Development*.

## ALSO BY MARK A. YARHOUSE AND JAMES N. SELLS

Counseling Couples in Conflict

Family Therapies